An Empire on Display

An Empire on Display

*English, Indian, and Australian Exhibitions
from the Crystal Palace to the Great War*

PETER H. HOFFENBERG

University of California Press

BERKELEY   LOS ANGELES   LONDON

University of California Press
Berkeley and Los Angeles, California

University of California Press, Ltd.
London, England

© 2001 by the Regents of the University of California

Library of Congress Cataloging-in-Publication Data
Hoffenberg, Peter H., 1960 –
   An empire on display : English, Indian, and Australian exhibitions
from the Crystal Palace to the Great War / Peter H. Hoffenberg.
      p.   cm.
   Includes bibliographical references and index.
   ISBN 978-0-520-21891-8 (cloth : alk. paper)
   1. Exhibitions—Great Britain—History.   2. Exhibitions—India—
History.   3. Exhibitions—Australia—History.   I. Title.

T395.5.G7 H64   2001
907'.4—dc21
                                               00-059003
                                                    CIP

Manufactured in the United States of America

10   09   08
10   9   8   7   6   5   4   3   2

To my family, near and far

Who can describe that astounding spectacle? Lost in a sense of what it is, who can think what it is like? Philosopher and poet alike are agitated, and silent; gaze whithersoever they may, all is marvellous and affecting; stirring new thoughts and emotions, and awakening oldest memories and associations.

Samuel Warren, *The Lily and the Bee:*
an apologue of the Crystal Palace, 1851

Contents

Illustrations

Preface

"This is the age of exhibitions," proclaimed London's *Illustrated Weekly News* in its inaugural issue, published shortly before the 1862 International Exhibition at South Kensington and at the time of preliminary expositions in the British colonies of New South Wales and Victoria.[1] Exhibition mania was ignited by England's Crystal Palace, or Great Exhibition, and soon spread throughout Europe, North America, and the British Empire. Eleven years later, those enthusiastic English editors boasted that

> we have exhibitions of nearly all possible and impossible things under the sun—exhibitions of pigs, of paintings, of performing fleas, of parrots, . . . of steam engines, and of babies. We have national and international gatherings, local, vocal, and rural shows. The list seems all but complete; yet, as there is nothing more fertile than the imagination of exhibiting mankind, fresh addenda continue to drop in every day.[2]

What drove men and women to exhibit "nearly all possible and impossible things" and what were the consequences of such displays for visitors and their societies? The social and political forces, institutions, and persons shaping the display and observation of objects and people at the popular exhibitions are described and analyzed in the following pages.

This historical study is intended to provide fresh addenda to answer those questions about "the imagination of exhibiting mankind" at major exhibitions in England, Australia, and India between the Great Exhibition in 1851 and the Festival of Empire sixty years later, on the eve of the First World War. Mine is a dialogue with the past, as well as with others studying and interested in the vast cosmos of exhibitions. In particular, I argue for the importance of English and colonial exhibitions after the Crystal Palace show, an epic event still dominating our understanding of the exhibition phenomenon, the permanent effects of what others have considered ephemeral events, and the interactive and participatory nature of the exhibition experience. Finally, organizing and visiting "national and international gatherings" revealed tension and irony as much as certainty and power; they were filled with both dissent and celebration.

Exhibitions were part of the self-conscious reworking of fluid national and imperial identities during the Victorian and Edwardian eras; after all, the London editors' "age of exhibitions" was also the age of empires and nation-states, subjects and citizens. What were the connections between those national and imperial institutions, sets of ideas, social visions, and cultural practices, fashioned in the dynamic contact between and among elites and commoners at the exhibitions? The answers suggest that exhibitions can be understood not only as discrete events but also as part of wider historical contexts and dynamic trajectories. Exhibitions shaped cultural and social order within borders but also across them, in the large transnational system of the British Empire. In doing so, they required the participation of citizens and subjects, workers and consumers—the "real actors" at the exhibitions, in the words of John Forbes Watson, a prominent English exhibition commissioner.[3]

Exhibitions organizers and displays were at the core of a participatory system, constructing a tripartite imperial world of "England," "India," or subject colonies, and "Australia," or settler societies. Each provided distinctive and complementary exhibits of machinery, commercial goods, workers, ethnography, and public history. Australia stood for other white-settler communities, such as Canada and Southern Africa; India was the dominant image of subject colonies, which included the West Indies and much of sub-Saharan Africa by the time of Rudyard Kipling's Empire at the turn of the twentieth century. Exhibitions were intended to promote external commonwealth and internal nationalism, differing forms of cooperative federation, rather than competition among and within those communities.

Whereas Australia was recognized at the exhibitions for its "progress" under the direction of white settlers, India was celebrated at the same shows because of its restored past. Visitors to Australian exhibits observed photographs of rising cities, samples of gold, and manufactured goods. As they continued rambling through the exhibition halls, they turned to the Raj's artisans weaving tapestries and dramatic models of India's ancient monuments. Australia was settled and colonized by the British; India was ruled by the Indian Government and Anglo-Indians. The Australians generally chose the ways in which they would represent themselves at the exhibitions, thereby confronting tensions between national and imperial identities. On the other hand, the Raj's exhibition objects were most often, but not always, determined by British and Anglo-Indian officials.

This imperial picture did not erase those significant differences between settler and subject colonies, but institutionalized them, providing explanations and uses for imperial diversity in economic, social, and cultural terms. Exhibitions presented the opportunities to organize and participate in these distinctions, sometimes as alternatives to competitive political economy and sometimes as ideal market societies. Commissioners, visitors, and exhibitors attempted to create and reconcile distinctions among those ideal-type societies at the same time that they confronted crises in nineteenth-century capitalism and political authority. This was the dress rehearsal for twentieth-century federation, or the British Commonwealth, as well as their economic complements, nonfree trade preferences. Exhibitions provided the economic, cultural, and social foundation for those later political developments. They were at the center of the interactive cultural system circulating men and women, ideas, and material between and within the Empire's political units, thereby producing the lasting and sometimes paradoxical ideas and culture of both the Commonwealth and colonial nationalism.

What role did such shows play in the history of the British Empire and colonial nationalism in Australia and India? If, as J. R. Seeley suggested in 1883, England conquered the world in a "fit of absence of mind," then the English and their allies overseas certainly took conscious steps to integrate those communities into their political culture and mythology.[4] Exhibitions were central parts of this cultural process. If, on the other hand, England conquered the world with intention and forethought, as others have suggested, then exhibitions popularized and gave explicit, accessible meanings to that political effort. Exhibitions were at the heart of imperial and national social and commercial enterprises during the Victorian and Edwardian eras. They were spectacles of tangible fantasy, in which participants forged nations and the Empire, both imaginary and material. Imperial, colonial, and national inventories were linked at the exhibitions by official tests and jury reports, consumption, tourism, and historical pageants. The power to organize, study, and compare this diversity strengthened the authority of commissioners and their states, often revealing tensions between and within the Empire's political communities.

This project contributes to the current discussions about the relationship between knowledge and power in light of British imperialism and nineteenth-century culture, science, and art in England, Australia, and India. In doing so, it takes up the challenging work of Edward Said, Bernard S.

Cohn, and John MacKenzie. For the past twenty years, Said has provoked a renewed study of the ideological sources of European expansion and the cultural interplay of core and periphery.[5] His analysis of the ways in which knowledge and images shaped the imperial enterprise invites us to think about the exhibitions in new ways, often transcending strict disciplinary boundaries, asking about how they reflected and contributed to the dynamic discourses of empire and nation.

Cohn's work extends the anthropological vision to the historical sociology of knowledge within the colonial context of British India.[6] He and his students study the Raj's cultural projects, such as museums, ceremonies, and photographs, which paralleled Indian exhibitions, and the ways in which the Raj was represented in England and India itself. At the same time, MacKenzie and his colleagues have pursued "the new socio-cultural approach to the study of imperialism," arguing that imperialism was more than a set of economic, political, and military institutions and phenomena.[7] Participants in this relatively new school explore the ways in which imperialism interacted with education, entertainment, propaganda, hunting, and masculinity, suggesting the roots and forms of what has been traditionally termed "popular imperialism."[8]

Exciting new scholarship on the institutions and activities in colonial and metropolitan civil societies continues to probe the ways in which imperialism shaped and was shaped by cultural images, forms, ideas, and experts.[9] The envelope continues to be pushed as we ask a series of new questions and continue to ask the old ones, but in new ways, about how the imperial and national world was organized to give it meaning. For example, might knowledge produced and consumed at the exhibitions have destabilized and subverted, as well as strengthened, imperial rule, contributing to both imperialism and colonial nationalism? This detailed study of the ways in which exhibitions were organized and unfolded helps answer this and other historical queries: Who were the imperialists, and in what ways did imperial ideas shape popular culture? Where and how did imperial and national visions publicly clash? What were the interplays between social power and racial differentiation in Australia and India? What are the continuities and disjunctures between "Old" and "New" Imperialism and, later, between the eras of New Imperialism and postcolonialism?

This book builds upon these reformulations of the historical questions of imperialism and nationalism, analyzing the dynamic meeting of cores and peripheries, elites and commoners, consumers and producers at the series of popular exhibitions in England, Australia, and India during the Victorian and Edwardian eras. Those shows were of various types: local, intercolonial, and international. Exhibitions were self-consciously constructed to reveal the political cultures of these communities; they were moments in which tensions, uncertainties, and dissent, as much as consensus and hegemony, were played out and shaped. The organizers mapped out the world in terms of ceremonies, participation, and material culture, but they could only produce such maps with the participation of visitors, the public. Here were living inventories of imperial and national political communities, many of which persist well after the formal end of political colonialism.

My debt to the growing body of scholarly studies on the relationships between exhibitions, cultural production, national identity, and imperial power will be apparent to readers.[10] That scholarship now invites readers to consider the geo-political breadth and cultural depth of the exhibition movement as it has developed around the world since 1851. Earlier studies chronicled the major exhibitions, sometimes placing them in their political contexts; more recent works pose important questions about the ways by which such shows represented consumerism, modernity, and authority in contexts as varied as nineteenth-century Toronto and twentieth-century Seville.[11] Contemporary scholars commonly address the fundamental problems of representation faced by organizers at the exhibitions. We have moved from issues of consensus to those of contest; questions of hybridity, audience participation, and shifting identities inform current exhibition studies.[12]

The debate with earlier and current students of the expositions is shaped by these common interests and the shared understanding that exhibitions were meaningful events for participants struggling with the social, political, and economic dilemmas and opportunities of their era. It is undertaken with respect for those authors and their ideas. My understanding of the ways in which exhibitions were organized and how they functioned was also assisted by the galaxy of social, cultural, and literary theories discussed with colleagues. The latter included North American, South Asian, Australian, and British historians and anthropologists, who shared their views in speech and print. These are just some of the many shoulders upon which I stand, fully aware that my historical vision owes much to their efforts across the disciplines.

Scholars analyzing the long-term and controversial relationship between the state and cultural life in Britain have provided additional helpful insights as they chart debates over issues such as government support for the arts and sciences.[13] This book on imperial and colonial exhibitions extends such concerns with the construction and implementation of official cultural policy to other political and geographical spheres, most notably

Australia and British India. Exhibition commissioners were among the first generation of cultural bureaucrats; they applied administrative skills and scientific knowledge to the questions of public culture and national education. As professionals, or a "clerisy," their expertise produced that strange beast known as "culture." Their heirs continue to shape official cultural policy in seemingly postcolonial Australia and India. The twentieth-century nation-state and, in some cases, the transnational corporation and media have assumed the cultural role created by their Victorian-era imperial and colonial predecessors and experts.

I have found the "reader response" approach to be particularly helpful in studying and representing exhibitions and their participants; a modified version of its methodology guided my efforts.[14] The exhibitions are described and analyzed as social "texts" that were authored, or inscribed, by official and private commissioners and, in turn, "read," or consumed, by visitors. These are dynamic and fluid texts; their analysis requires an appreciation of experience as well as of language. Although their official authors intended only one reading, my study suggests that there were many, some of which competed with one another. The organizers' and the sponsoring elite's and state's cultural influence could not be hegemonic, and thus reading became a source of instability as well as stability, contest as much as control. Over time, these texts, or events, merged to create a mimicking, self-referential "exhibition" tradition, with its own sense of memory and history. That sense of an exhibition past might even be used to justify current and future shows.[15]

These were truly texts: events and experiences, opening social visions as much as enframing them. The shared moments of such active reading formed and reformed the nation and empire as "interpretive communities" at the exhibitions. Experiencing exhibitions as commissioners, visitors, and other participants did reveals not only the instability of the relationship between England and its colonial subjects, but also the internal social tensions between elites and commoners within those social and political groups, or "communities." The exhibition experience was more than a reflection or index of society; it altered society and, in some cases, was society itself. The effects of the exhibition experience were not unidirectional, not completely controlled by an a priori determinism, but shaped by the nearly limitless fantasy of public participation.

These shows were venues of socially constructed, mediated, and consumed knowledge. Unlike the private act of reading, participation at the exhibitions was a public and mass-oriented textual experience. In the words of one nineteenth-century Australian visitor and showman, exhibitions "amuse the public and draw strangers from all parts of the world; they provide incident for the thoughtless and food for the thoughtful."[16] These imperial and national rituals were educative and integrative, creating larger interpretive communities of citizens, nation, and empire as visitors experienced "moments" of interplay—the Australian's "incidents"—with structures created by the commissioners. The latter acted as the authors. Their guidebooks, classification systems, and organization of physical space provided the grammar for this reading process. Those were the Australian's "food."

The interpretation of any text requires proceeding through a series of guided or directed interactions in which "open spaces" provide opportunities for imaginative constructions. There were many of the latter at the exhibitions, where the visitor/reader was surrounded with sensual provocations. "I must tell you what I saw," wrote a visitor to Melbourne's Intercolonial Exhibition in 1867, "for I cannot well remember all or half of what I heard."[17] Rudyard Kipling discovered a similar sensation in 1878. His father was busy organizing "the Indian Section of Arts and Manufactures," so the future author wandered unguided among "kiosques and pavilions, . . . this great wheel of colour and smells and sights."[18] Here were worlds of ritualized and participatory fantasy. Poetry mingled with art. Enchantment reigned: labor in a mine was transformed into a comfortable truck ride; colonial conquest became mosques and minarets.[19]

Visitors were part of that extensive social drama, observing and, in turn, being observed. "Central to the reading of every literary work," or, in this case, social text, "is the interaction between its structure and its recipient."[20] This project describes and interprets the various interactions between the structure and both its producers (commissioners and exhibitors) and consumers (visitors), as well as among the latter. These interactions were dynamic, ironic, contested, and, at times, policed at the exhibitions. Visitors tasted new foods and beverages from the colonies, purchased paintings and sculptures in a variety of Art Union schemes, and heard music, some of which they did not like. A prominent South Australian visiting the 1884 International Health Exhibition at South Kensington found the Chinese village "most interesting, . . . [including] tea houses with *excellent* tea & execrable [*sic*] music by the National Bands." Not one to embrace subtlety, he concluded that "the Chinese songs are the oddest most uncouth things you can imagine."[21] Soapstone wares, clay figures and toys, grains, merchants, and commissioners completed the Chinese Court.[22]

Part of the magic of exhibitions was their seeming inability to be described or contained in one image or one volume. The challenge to do so and the immediate emotional consequences of that vastness were captured by one popular English author at the time of the Great Exhibition: "Who can describe that astounding spectacle? Lost in a sense of what it is, who can think what it is like? Philosopher and poet alike are agitated, and silent; gaze whithersoever they may, all is marvellous and affecting; stirring new thoughts and emotions, and awakening oldest memories and associations."[23] The Great Exhibition's comprehensiveness seemed to defy language and taxonomy. After touring the Crystal Palace, one chronicler concluded that "nothing was too stupendous, too rare, or too costly for its acquisition; nothing too minute or apparently too insignificant for its consideration." He had observed "every possible" invention and machine, as well as "the philosopher and the savage, . . . the accomplished artist and the rude boor."[24]

Did the shows challenge the very representational skills of the Victorians and Edwardians with such stirring and awakening? Perhaps this was part of their mystification and power. On the other hand, each mystification contains its own demystification. Critics were very capable of finding systematic ways to contain and attack the exhibitions, official commissioners, and the sponsoring English and colonial states. The exhibitions celebrated nation and empire; they also revealed tensions inherent in those communities for critics. That variety of interpretations and experiences at exhibitions reveals the fluidity of national, imperial, and colonial identities during the 1851–1914 era of High, or New Imperialism. Identities were both shaped by and reflected in the organization of and attendance at the shows. The exhibitions highlight the complex symbolic construction and reception of such social ideas and categories. The project thus also points to changes in the political relationships within the British Empire and the general South Asian and Australasian regions, as well as the altered contexts in which the governing elites and the states' cultural experts articulated their political and social visions at home and in the colonies.

My approach is also comparative and interdisciplinary: I call upon a variety of primary and secondary materials. The former were collected from North American, Australian, and English archives and libraries, and include the public and private papers of exhibition officials and exhibitors; contemporary periodicals and newspapers; the memoirs, correspondence, and diaries of visitors; exhibition handbooks and catalogues; and, among other sources, the annual reports and letterbooks of the many participating state institutions and voluntary societies. Among those were chambers of commerce, museums, societies of art, labor organizations, and government departments of trade from London to Melbourne, and from Sydney to Calcutta. Exhibitions were part of this very public world. Nineteenth-century photographic albums also provide a sense of the architectural space, physical dimensions, and layout at the exhibitions.

Research was made both easier and more problematic by the self-conscious attempts of exhibition organizers to create their own historical record of the events. For example, the Executive Commissioner for Queensland at the 1886 Colonial and Indian Exhibition prepared a ground plan with enlarged photographs of the colony's court; solicited reports to accompany natural history, ethnographic, mineralogical, and pastoral objects; and provided a visitor's book for comments. The commissioner concluded in his official report to the colonial legislature that these materials "will be of great value for future reference in the public library" in Brisbane.[25] I found his words prophetic.

The structure of the book includes an introductory thematic section and several case studies. The former discusses the roles of exhibitions in the construction of imperial and local knowledge, the creation of a new class of cultural experts and bureaucrats, and the expansion of the state's cultural authority. This includes analysis of influential Australian, English, and Indian exhibition commissioners and their various projects. Such officials could be found in London and Calcutta, as well as Melbourne and Dublin. They were charged with "the preparation, collection and despatch of exhibits, and . . . methods for their display."[26] Among the commissioners' specific projects were attempts to classify and control material culture, publish reports, introduce new or improved colonial economic products, such as Australian wines and Indian cotton, attract emigrants and capital, and promote a particular vision of social order.

This analysis provides the political and social background for the exhibitions, as well as the larger cultural context in which "science and art" experts struggled to assert their professional identity and authority. What was the relationship between these grand events and the New Imperialism unfolding around the world? New forms of technology, local political threats, and changing views on mass entertainment shaped the ideas and projects of these officials as they built empires and nations at the shows. In a very practical sense, museum and art school administrators, trustees of national art collections, government officers, and private showmen were responsible for the production, circulation, and reception of exhibition displays. Commissioners evaluated exhibits in their capacity as jurors and organized an extensive imperial superhighway by which the exhibits were exchanged, reproduced, and studied at both the imperial core and the colonial periphery. These experts managed the growing political economy of knowledge and material culture as a new "clerisy," linking organizations such as the Agricultural and Horticultural Society of Western India (Bombay), the Australian Museum (Sydney), and the Science and Art Department (London) in both national and imperial networks. They did not do so without controversy.

The succeeding chapters discuss these issues within the framework of specific themes: commerce, industrialism, ethnography, art, and modes of visitor participation. The operation of machinery-in-motion displays was just one way in which visitors actively embraced the shows. This part of the project focuses on the attempts to create public culture in England and the colonies with traditional Indian arts and crafts, state ceremonies, machines and labor, anthropological displays, travel, and the policing of mass entertainment itself. The exhibitions suggested the market and factory as representative and explicative metaphors for the normative relationship of federation among the Empire's various classes, races, and nations. Commissioners invited the "world" to their shows and then policed that crowd to construct imperial and national communities.

Those sections also develop my general views on the interactive arena of such exhibitions and the ways in which they were used by the imperial and colonial states and elites to address both local and Empire-wide social tensions. Exhibitors and commissioners put on display people, objects, and machines in order to promote trade and create the picture or language of both imperial federation and colonial nationalism. Art, industrial, and international exhibitions in India and Australia during the second half of the century were intended to reconcile tensions, but often created and revealed conflicts between imperial and national economic and cultural policies. The rise of colonial nationalism and the opportunities to form national identities at the exhibitions also made public various internal social questions.

Physical exhibits and the modes by which visitors participated revealed the tensions between the visible and invisible components of these reconstructed national and imperial cultures. Exhibitions created and offered selective visions and histories. Traditionalist South Asian artisans and Indian princes, as well as Australian bush figures and miners, were part of these pictures, but modern workers, nationalists, and women were often absent. The imperial economic vision included the artisanal labor and products of Indian potters and female weavers, but excluded the common work of unskilled males. The exhibitions expressed and created a cultural and social order in which were privileged South Asian handlooms, small-scale Australian mining technologies, and the self-regulating, factorylike "machines-in-motion," which did not require modern workers.

This argument implies that we can view imperialism and nationalism as cultural practices and social systems. Organizing and visiting exhibitions in England, Australia, and India created the ordered grid of meaning and symbols in terms of which new forms of public interaction and identities were imagined and observed, and in which they took place. The exposition experience provided the language of, access to, and legitimacy for, this new participatory framework of national and imperial beliefs, values, and behavior.[27] "Australia" was represented by its exhibition commissioners and their displays at the shows at the same time that "Australians" were inventing themselves.

Exhibitions in England and the colonies offered millions of visitors the opportunity to view the seemingly authentic and experience the sense of historical continuity required amid fears of social disintegration and class division at home and in the colonies. The invention and representation of such traditions at the exhibitions were part of what Eric Hobsbawm has termed the European-wide modern project of "responses to novel situations which take the form of reference to old situations."[28] Where the latter could not be found, as in the case of the authentic Indian artisan, they were invented and put on display. Such was the seemingly limitless fertility of exhibiting mankind between 1851 and 1914.

Acknowledgments

Nineteenth-century exhibitions were vast and limitless by design. Those "magical gardens" persistently challenged their organizers' and visitors' vision, stamina, appetites, and imagination. Even if not all were "marvellous and affecting," they never failed to stir thoughts and awake memories. Such has been the case with this project as well, since its rather innocuous origins in a family trip to England and Scotland, a postcard, and a graduate research paper. The communiqué, sent to me from Australia, included the image of the Sydney International Exhibition's official medal; the latter discussed the various ways Indian art was represented at exhibitions in England and Europe. My interests in Australia and Indian art continue to this day, happily united in this book, and the subjects of future book projects. But that union, as was the case with those who visited fairs in Sydney, Melbourne, Bombay, Calcutta, and London, was not a solitary task. I have also not traveled and consumed alone.

I am indebted to the staffs of more than a score of British, Australian, and North American museums and libraries, who generously processed my book and copying orders and patiently awaited my fumbling with foreign currencies. Among the legions of helpful librarians, archivists, and copyists who opened the exhibition halls for me were those working in and around London at the British Library's Manuscript, Newspaper, and Oriental and India Office collections; the National Art Library; Imperial College Archives; Royal Institute of British Architects Library; Trades Union Congress Archives; Guildhall Library; and Foreign and Commonwealth Office Library. Outside of London, help arrived in the hands of staff members at the Public Records Office, Kew, the Pitt-Rivers Museum, Indian Institute, and Rhodes House Library at Oxford University, the Manuscript Collection at the Cambridge University Library, and the Kipling Collection at the University of Sussex Library. My gratitude to the National Trust and Earl Baldwin for permission to read and cite from the extensive treasure of Kipling family correspondence, newspaper clippings, and illustrations.

While "down under" in the antipodes, I was the beneficiary of liberal assistance from employees of the State Library of Victoria, Melbourne University Archives, Royal Historical Society of Victoria, National Museum of Victoria Library, and Victoria Public Record Office in and around Melbourne; the State Library of New South Wales, Macleay Museum, Archives Office of New South Wales, and Power House Museum in the general Sydney region; the State Library of South Australia and the Record Office of South Australia in Adelaide; the Noel Butlin Archives Centre at the Australian National University and the Australian National Library in the A.C.T.; and the State Library of Queensland and Queensland Records Office in Brisbane and its environs. I owe them doubly: they not only assisted with my labors but made my tenure in Australia a truly memorable one. I only hope that I can repay their generosities when they visit these shores or I return to the antipodes.

Closer to home, the research and interlibrary loan staffs at the University of Hawaii, Manoa, and various University of California and California State University campuses provided essential assistance to compensate for sources overlooked in Australia and Britain. As can be discerned from the notes and bibliography, I owe much of this project's structure and contents to the patience and persistence of these staff members. They complied with good spirit and speed to many often confusing requests.

Various scholars and colleagues also provided guidance, citations, and theoretical insights during the many years devoted to this study. This list of "conspirators" includes Thomas Laqueur, David Lloyd, and Thomas Metcalf (who sent the initiating postcard), my trinity of dissertation advisors at the University of California, Berkeley, who provoked, directed, and encouraged me during my graduate career; Christopher Pinney, School of Asian and African Studies, University of London, who took an early interest in my work and shared ideas and sources about India, photography, and anthropology; Tom Griffiths, Monash University and State Library of Victoria, Peter Bridges, scholar and gentleman, and other Aussies, who welcomed this Yank into their backyard and opened unforeseen windows of study and archival sources about Australian history; Marc Rothenberg, editor of the Joseph Henry Papers, Smithsonian Institution, who kindly offered the opportunity to discuss the contours of the U.S.–Australian relationship during the nineteenth century (the subject of a future study) and to coauthor an article with him; and my intimate fellow travelers, including Professors

Charles Geshekter, Joseph Conlin, Patrick Miller, John McBratney, Douglas Haynes, and Maura O'Connor, who exchanged tall tales about university life, archival expeditions, dissertation writing, and publication. Their examples always inspired and held out promise for my own career. To all of them and those I have unfortunately neglected only in writing, not in memory, go praise for admirable insights and turns of phrase, but no blame for errors and misdirections.

Substantial financial assistance for travel, overseas housing and living, and general research expenses was provided by a variety of sources. My deep gratitude to the Fulbright-Hays Training Grants for Dissertations Program and the Institute of International Studies and Graduate School at the University of California at Berkeley, for their confidence in my project and their generosity. This project could not have been completed without the extended ventures into archival and library collections in Britain and Australia made possible by such support.

Exhibition visitors were most commonly accompanied by their immediate family and other relatives during their moments of education and entertainment at the shows in England, Australia, and India. My visits and journey would also not have been possible without the continuous assistance of my family and close friends. The latter gazed with wonderment, disbelief, and nearly miraculous patience as I chose to read exhibition memoirs and catalogues rather than return phone calls or venture forth to contemporary substitutes for the spectacles of those earlier generations; their friendship and companionship never wavered. Thank you, Eric, Perry, Saundi (before and during our marriage), and too many others to list.

This book is dedicated to my family near and far—daughters, wife, father, mother, and older brother—and to their unyielding belief that my efforts were (and are) worthwhile. They taught me that scholarship offers its own rewards and opportunities to see the truth about and beyond oneself, the present, and the future with the lenses of the past. This project was truly born on a family trip to England and Scotland more than two decades ago, and I can only hope the final text does not disappoint them. It is filled with the spirit of that trip and of the three nearest and dearest to me: Saundi, Elena, and Libby.

1 Exhibitions and the New Imperialism

"All London is astir . . . and some part of all the world," noted John Ruskin in his diary for May 1, 1851.[1] Although the metropolis was in a frenzy over the official opening of the Great Exhibition at Hyde Park's unprecedented Crystal Palace, the famous art critic remained at home, ignoring the public birth of the international exhibition movement. Ruskin began writing the second volume of his *Stones of Venice* while sitting in his "quiet room, hearing the birds sing." Outside of that room, the city's noisy streets overflowed with goods and people. Among those striding to and fro or in carriages were foreigners, colonials (Indian princes and Australian politicians), provincials, and an array of London's own aristocrats, dandies, merchants, and workers. Thomas Babington Macaulay wrote enthusiastically that "the sight among the green boughs was delightful . . . the boats; the flags; the music; the guns;—everything was exhilarating."[2]

Cities as varied as London, Manchester, Glasgow, and Dublin in the British Isles, as well as Calcutta, Toronto, Auckland, and Melbourne across the wider British Empire welcomed millions of visitors to their own "delightful" and "exhilarating" exhibitions during the next sixty years.[3] Such events made "exhibitions . . . a fashion of the hour," in the words of the Scotsman Patrick Geddes in 1886, as he described "at least seven or eight special exhibitions" organized that year alone. Those included Queen Victoria's pride and joy, the Colonial and Indian Exhibition, which drew over five million visitors to South Kensington.[4] British and colonial proponents crafted that exhibition "fashion" by holding one major show nearly every year or two between the Great Exhibition of 1851 and the outbreak of war in 1914.[5]

The numbers and variety of visitors remain an impressive mark of English, Australian, and Indian exhibitions. Over six million visited the 1862

1

London International, and annual International Exhibitions held at South Kensington during the early 1870s drew nearly one million each year.[6] Such enthusiasm did not die. One generation later, Australian officials reported that "about 2,500,000 persons" visited the Greater Britain Exhibition at Earl's Court in 1899.[7] Colonial shows were also magnets for local, intercolonial, and overseas visitors. Over 20,000 visited the Indian art and industry exhibitions organized by Governor Richard Temple in the Punjab and Central Provinces during the 1860s, and 235,000 visitors "poured through the rooms" at the Jeypore Art and Industrial Exhibition during its opening weeks in early 1883.[8] The Calcutta International Exhibition's doors opened in December of that year, and over one million visitors had been admitted by the time those doors closed four months later.[9]

In the case of Australia, the 1875 Melbourne Intercolonial's Executive Committee invited exhibitors and visitors from "all the British, French, and Dutch possessions in Australasia and the neighbouring islands."[10] Over 74,000 ticket-holders visited the exhibition during its first three weeks, nearly doubling the attendance of the 1872–73 Victorian Exhibition.[11] Many of the visitors to such colonial shows took advantage of reduced railway fares as well as organized school and company excursions. Journalists reported that at least "two special trains" brought workmen to the Jeypore exhibition in 1883.[12] Visitors observed and participated in a vast cosmos of exhibits and ceremonies. In one well-documented case, the New South Wales commissioners at the 1880–81 Melbourne International Exhibition organized a special court for their galaxy of wines, tin, gold, copper, coal, diamonds, local vegetation and flowers, photographs, and "a splendid collection of telegraphic apparatus."[13] People as well as goods were put on display within the grand exhibition halls; they participated in these spectacles of fantasy by consuming food and drinks, purchasing souvenirs, and acting in pageants.

Imperial exhibitions in London, colonial and imperial displays at European and North American exhibitions, and the series of popular events in major colonial urban centers displayed ideas, images, and practices of both imperialism and nationalism. Those spectacles were at the heart of the "New" Imperialism dominating world affairs in the generations preceding the Great War. Exhibitions represented the idealized relationships between groups within the nation and empire, in the sense of Benedict Anderson's articulation of the modern political unit as "an imagined political community";[14] that is, one that is "imagined as both inherently limited and sovereign."[15] The exhibits of material culture and the visitors' experiences represented the imagined relationships between groups across the British

Empire's borders and those within specific polities, such as India and England.

My project draws upon Anderson's volume, but suggests that the exhibitions provided for a simultaneous and shared envisioning and for physical participation in addition to the collective psychological and cultural processes of imagining the nation and empire. Anderson emphasizes the importance of common reading experiences, such as mass consumption of novels and newspapers. The exhibitions were also read, but as a public, mass-oriented, collective experience, not one in which the simultaneity was only imagined because immediate sharing was prevented by distance. Simultaneity was observed and visually validated at the shows, often by direct contact. Participation at the exhibitions implied an identity as a "citizen" of this community, defining limitations and sovereignty but not precluding tensions between and within groups. One might even suggest that participation in the exhibitions did not only generate public opinion, a topic on the minds of most politicians at the time, but, in fact, created what we might call the Victorian public itself. The expositions organized by government officials, such as those of the Science and Art Department in England, and the Revenue and Agriculture Department in India, were part of the more general late Victorian and Edwardian attempt to create social order by means of large-scale cultural events and institutions. Advocates contended that the spectacles, displays, and performances would not only mediate imperial and colonial identities, but also resolve tensions between social classes within a polity. Australian and Indian officials expressed similar views as they used exhibitions to establish public art, trade, and history collections and a sense of national culture in the wake of mineral rushes in Australia during the early 1850s and the Sepoy Mutiny, which rocked the Raj in 1857–58.

The integrative process of social order remained a controversial political issue in England and the colonies during the nineteenth and early twentieth centuries as governments experimented with various forms of home rule, federation, and shared governance, such as dyarchy. The exhibitions were one of many attempts to resolve that crisis of representation and change, to mediate political and social tensions by suggesting cultural bonds and shared fantasies. Imperial commissioners represented some groups in this sociocultural formation at the exhibitions, while others had the authority to represent themselves. This established, mirrored, and in some cases challenged the hierarchies and oppositions within and between English, Australian, and Indian societies.

Confidence in the power and influence of exhibitions was expressed across the British Empire. Sir Arthur Hodgson, a prominent Queensland official, told his audience at London's Colonial Institute in 1878 that "the modern systems of Exhibition [were] more than a gigantic advertisement."[16] These shows, including the just-concluded Paris Universal Exposition, "give an impulse to trade, create keen competition and by a mutual interchange of compliments and civilities bring the whole world into harmonious & peaceful contact with each other." The New South Wales commissioners for the Colonial and Indian Exhibition were even more confident about the advantages of participating in exhibitions. The 1886 show would be "the best opportunity ever afforded, in the greatest market of the world" for the colony to display its raw materials and secure new trade.[17] Furthermore, the exhibition court could provide an advertisement for "the Europeanization" of the colony; that is, evidence of its progress and attractiveness as a new home for emigrants. With such goals in mind, the commissioners solicited for exhibition woods, building stones, wines, minerals, railway maps, furniture, and working mining and agricultural machinery.

Enthusiasm for exhibitions was also articulated across the Indian Ocean from the Australian colonies. An influential Indian government official bursting with the Raj's hubris suggested that the observation of European art and ornamental exhibits by South Asian visitors at Indian exhibitions would "inform their [South Asian] minds with fresh ideas of the Beautiful, while the machinery and implements might give them an impression of powers and forces unknown before, and so fill them with reflections regarding the useful."[18] The shows would "excite the wonderment of the Native multitudes" to the potential wealth amid their "picturesque" setting.[19] European and English visitors would gain "a far more accurate knowledge than they would otherwise have possessed" regarding Indian products and resources, and that new knowledge might stimulate overseas trade with British India.

Anglo-Indian and South Asian science and art experts joined ambitious local exhibition committees. As official commissioners, they publicized their own scientific essays and art projects, introduced European consumer items, struggled to establish national Indian markets and trade networks, and encouraged visitors to compare their animal husbandry and tools with those from other parts of the Raj.[20] The Anglo-Indian press was as enthusiastic about the effect of those local endeavors. "Distant provinces have been made acquainted with each other's products," boasted the *Calcutta Review* after the Madras Industrial Exhibition in 1855. They "have had an opportunity of observing their own dependencies. In no country is this likely to be fraught with good as in India, as there is no country in which there is so little intercourse between places far apart." The many "valuable reports prepared by the jurors in the different classes" of exhibits offered the opportunity to compare goods from various countries, as well as from among India's many regions.[21]

In this way, the exhibitions offered the intellectual, economic, and cultural sinews, or "intercourse," to tie together the vast leviathan of British India by testing and promoting new technologies, agricultural methods, and crops for internal economic development and overseas trade. Exhibitions could thus serve national, as well as imperial, purposes, and the Indian National Congress took advantage of that "intercourse" to represent its vision of India. Congress officials appropriated the exhibitionary mode, sponsoring various shows around the turn of the twentieth century. There was "a political significance . . . in these displays," one contemporary matter-of-factly concluded.[22] Here were competing local and national South Asian objectives, as well as broader imperial British and Anglo-Indian ones. The same could be said about local, national, and imperial objectives at Australian exhibitions as well.

THE GHOST OF 1851

The confidence in exhibitions as panaceas reflects the nearly religious aura surrounding the Great Exhibition of 1851. This study recognizes the impact of that show in material and imaginative terms, while at the same time addressing the importance of popular post-1851 shows in England and the colonies. We can perceive an exhibition tradition in which organizers and visitors recalled the ghost of 1851 for inspiration and criticism, but did so as their reproduction of the Great Exhibition contributed to a new and different event in the present. Until recently, scholarship on exhibitions tended to ignore or downplay the series of exhibitions held in London between 1862 and 1914, as well as the proliferation of shows hosted by colonial cities, such as Sydney and Calcutta.[23]

Some English historians, in particular, remain obsessed with the Great Exhibition of 1851. At times, they echo "the old gentleman" in Thomas Hardy's 1893 short story, "The Fiddler of the Reels," whose opinion about the event was nothing short of adamant: "Talking of Exhibitions, World's Fairs, and what not, . . . I would not go round the corner to see a dozen of them nowadays. The only exhibition that ever made, or ever will make, any impression upon my imagination was the first of the series, the parent of them all, and now a thing of old times—the Great Exhibition of 1851, in Hyde Park."[24] Those fictional words could have been the nonfictional ones of Lord Broughton, who was certain that the Crystal Palace "produced an effect such as I never witnessed before, and never shall again."[25] No historian denies the impact of the Great Exhibition as a spectacular, perhaps unprecedented, event, but at the same time, many are like Hardy's character and Lord Broughton: they do not consider its successors in "the series" of exhibitions, the post-1851 children of the Crystal Palace "parent."

Such silence is understandable up to a certain point, since there were over six million admissions to Paxton's controversial Crystal Palace, and "exhibition" became a popular noun and adjective as a result of the event. The Great Exhibition cast a wide shadow over Victorian Britain and scholarship about that era. It provided, at least in popular memory as voiced by Hardy's rural characters, a dividing line between the past and the present. In the words of the prominent social historian Asa Briggs, the year and event "formed in many ways an extraordinary chronological frontier or transit-line, . . . a sudden bringing of ancient and modern into absolute contact" in both personal and community lives.[26]

Visitors to the 1851 show brought to later ones their experiences and thus their expectations about the ideal "exhibition." A natural comparison with the "Great" Exhibition resulted. Its role as a watershed became even more apparent as the event receded into history and memory. The Great Exhibition seemed one of the key events of the century as Victorians and Edwardians considered their age. Sixty years after the event, Frederic Harrison remembered spending "hours" at the Crystal Palace, his memoirs distinguishing between the superiority of British manufactures and science and the inferiority of "Victorian" art.[27] The memory of that art's ugliness at the exhibition helped Harrison define himself during the Edwardian era as a "Georgian" rather than an "Early Victorian."

It is impossible to ignore the burden of the 1851 exhibition, which both haunted and provoked the organizers of post–Crystal Palace exhibitions. Official and unofficial records highlight this sense of history and tradition. Years after 1851, exhibition commissioners in England and the colonies struggled to realize the expectations stimulated by the Hyde Park publicists. They confronted the long shadows of that "exceptional event," in the words of those organizing the subsequent international exhibition in London.[28] Commissioners attempted both to exploit the memory of the Crystal Palace and to differentiate the 1862 show at South Kensington by arranging exhibits according "to classes, and not countries," adding music and painting, and encouraging objects which demonstrated "the progress of Industry and Art" since 1851. Commentators could not avoid comparisons with the Great Exhibition, even in the face of such significant changes. One contemporary was convinced that the new show was disappointing because it paled beside the glow of the novel and mythical Crystal Palace.[29] The public was uncomfortable because its experiences at the show were "mirrored in our recollections of the first Exhibition."

George Frederick Pardon, author and editor of exhibition guidebooks for the general public, hailed the mythic impacts of the Crystal Palace at the time of the 1862 London show. He proclaimed in the opening pages of his popular guide to the International Exhibition that "the Exhibition of 1851 did for this nation what foreign travel does for the individual Briton."[30] His memory suggested that the first show made the English less insular, more generous to foreigners, and more appealing in the eyes of those foreigners. Pardon concluded that a comparison between the current and previous exhibitions would demonstrate the progress of some communities and show "the backward how to mend their pace."

On the other hand, visitors, commissioners, and exhibitors could take advantage of time to reflect on errors and omissions made in 1851. Those not blinded by devotion to the Great Exhibition struggled to avoid its mistakes at the Paris Universal Exposition four years later and at subsequent exhibitions as a thread of reference developed that knit together an exhibition tradition. As one Bombay newspaper editor reminded his readers, "The Exposition of 1855 will at least have over the Exhibition of 1851 the immense advantage of experience."[31] Others noted that the series of exhibitions after the Crystal Palace provided opportunities to measure and represent the "progress" realized or imagined since the previous show.[32] That progress included ways to organize the exhibition displays and experience. Exhibitions were used as historical references, measurements, and stocktakings undertaken at points along a continuum starting in 1851 and continuing well into the twentieth century.

Anglo-Indian exhibition commissioners were also burdened and inspired by the memory of the Great Exhibition. Officials at the Madras Exhibition in 1855 followed the Crystal Palace precedent for classifying and organizing the exhibits. They created a jury of experts for each class of objects and published an official catalogue with the jurors' reports.[33] The local political agent's opening address for the Jeypore Exhibition nearly thirty years later alluded to "the International Exhibition of 1851, which . . . provided instructive amusement to thousands." This memory justified his optimism regarding the Indian event's capacity to mirror the Crystal Palace by stimulating, encouraging, and instructing the local "working classes," as well as the Raj's other subjects.[34]

COLONIAL EXHIBITS AFTER THE CRYSTAL PALACE

The Crystal Palace was, however, only one exhibition in an extensive history of shows. As the editors of an English trade journal boldly asserted two decades later: "National and international Exhibitions have become a prominent feature of the age we live in, and there are always hundreds ready to enter the arena of competition."[35] The memory or quasi-sacredness of the Great Exhibition tends to diminish the significance of those English and colonial exhibitions that followed. Many of the latter were equally if not more popular and, it might be argued, more influential in developing imperial and national cultural systems and social identities. Colonial and English officials embraced these post-1851 exhibitions to refashion the ideas and practices of Britain and the Empire, develop the culture and commerce of the New Imperialism, and forge colonial nationalisms.

Colonial displays were more comprehensive and visitors became increasingly more active at exhibitions in England, Australia, and India after 1851. The variety of, and connections between, British and colonial exhibits impressed visitors. One American commissioner at the London International eleven years later noted the significant increase in economic displays since the colonial courts at the Crystal Palace. His official government report praised the quality and quantity of "imperial" carpets, minerals, flax and hemp, and, among other commercial items, tapestry and lace manufactures from Ireland, India, Canada, and Australasia.[36] The colonial exhibits were more impressive because both imperial and colonial organizers made greater efforts to include the colonies after 1851. The International Exhibition's executive commissioners, for example, offered more gallery space to exhibitors from the Australasian colonies and East India than they had in 1851, and their colleagues in the colonies spent more time and money collecting and preparing exhibits.

The later London show also opened up the exhibition experience to include a wider variety of exhibits and activities, most of which could be taken advantage of by colonial organizers and visitors. Commissioners in 1862 included educational and fine arts exhibits not encouraged eleven years before, including "a retrospective collection of paintings and sculpture," and offered refreshments for consumption and curios for purchase.[37] The beverages included wines and spirits from the colonies in contrast to the temperance-induced items at the Crystal Palace. Sir Henry Cole, acting executive commissioner in 1851, feared that the sale of "wines, spirits, beers, or intoxicating drinks" would "allow the building to assume the character of an hotel, tavern."[38] Tea, ginger beer, coffee, chocolate, lemonade, and seltzer were sold in their place. By the time of the Colonial and Indian Exhibition in 1886, visitors sampled wines and spirits in various courts and purchased bottles in a room directed by the Royal Commission.[39] A few years before, the "clanging of glasses and draining of nobblers" was heard throughout the day at the intercolonial show in Sydney.[40]

Whereas not all of the Australian colonies had the time, funds, or inclination to participate at the Crystal Palace, each one sent exhibits for the 1862 show; the British Colonies covered over 13,000 square feet of exhibition space at South Kensington.[41] The same was true for European exhibitions as well. A London newspaper praised "the manner in which our Australian colonies have exerted themselves to obtain an adequate representation of their industry" at the 1855 Paris Universal Exposition in contrast to their disappointing presence at the Great Exhibition four years before.[42] The colony of Victoria was particularly aggressive at these overseas shows. Its commissioners forwarded exhibits to nearly every significant exhibition in England, France, Ireland, and North America after 1851. The colony occupied over 5,660 square feet of exhibition space (compared to the 2,500 used by the older colony of New South Wales) in 1862, and its governor appointed an official Board to organize displays for the Dublin International Exhibition three years later.[43] Australian displays expanded during the century and occupied over 110,000 square feet by the time of the Franco-British Exhibition in 1908.

Although praised for their displays at the Crystal Palace, Indian commissioners also actively lobbied for additional space at subsequent shows. Limited to 24,000 feet in 1851, the Raj's officers filled over 65,000 square feet in the Colonial and Indian Exhibition halls and an additional 40,000 in the separate Indian Palace in 1886.[44] Those exhibits included a reconstructed gateway, a courtyard filled with working artisans, and a Durbar Tent draped with shawls.[45] Similar palaces and bazaars were constructed for the Indian displays at the series of Paris Universal Expositions held during the last quarter of the nineteenth century.

Colonial courts were often situated in close proximity to British exhibits to symbolize imperial unity and power to colonial subjects and foreign (particularly French) visitors. The "Agent for South Australian Exhibits" at the Calcutta International Exhibition suggested that commissioners group together "all the countries flying the British flag . . . for the sake of the . . . significance the native princes will attach to it."[46] English officials, including Joseph Chamberlain and Foreign Office bureaucrats, recommended an "Imperial Court" for the 1900 Paris Universal Exposition to demonstrate that the Empire was "employing millions of capital and . . . workmen."[47] If a united court could not be engineered, then perhaps an imperial silk or coal court might be arranged.

The suggestion of a united imperial court was made in the face of rising colonial nationalism. Others might argue that it had already arrived by the time of the Paris show![48] Many Australian exhibition officers and politicians proposed their own pavilions to meet common expenditures and to demonstrate national identity and local wealth. This was not a new idea. It had been recommended by Sir Redmond Barry from Melbourne as early as 1866 in preparation for the following year's Paris Exposition.[49] The potential "greater weight and dignity" of a joint Australian court did not move either the reluctant British commissioners or Barry's colleagues from New South Wales and Queensland, so the various Australasian colonies exhibited in their own distinct areas. By the turn of the century, colonial commissioners could draw upon more political consensus and the changing sentiment on both sides of the imperial line.

Federation was in the air, and Australia's exhibition organizers were not bashful about exploiting it in 1900. They found a more immediate exhibition precedent in the recommendations of Queensland's executive commissioner for the 1893 Chicago Columbian Exposition. He had suggested that a united Australian building would reduce costs and represent to visitors "the spirit of [Australian] Federation."[50] Tensions thus developed between assertive colonial officials determined to represent national and local interests and their imperial counterparts, fearing German, French, and American economic competition and colonial independence. Herbert Jeckyll voiced the imperial point of view before the Paris show by admitting that French authorities would look enthusiastically upon the omission of a united imperial section, "in which we could show an overwhelming superiority to all other Powers including themselves."[51]

COLONIAL EXHIBITIONS AFTER 1851

Britain, Europe, and North America were not alone in hosting shows. Over fifty major exhibitions filled the colonial horizon after the Great Exhibition. The editors of London's *Art Journal* were prescient when they suggested in the glowing wake of the Dublin Industrial Exhibition in 1853 that "all things considered, the experiment is such as to encourage rather than to discourage attempts in the several provincial cities of the empire."[52] Australian and South Asian cities were among the most active in this far-flung exhibition culture, hosting a series of agricultural, art, industrial, intercolonial, and international shows to display their social and cultural progress and invite commerce. The success of those and other colonial expositions provoked the proponent of "a Grand International Exhibition in Manchester" to conclude in 1882 that "these Colonial Exhibitions are doing a vast amount of good, both in developing the native resources of the several colonies, and in bringing to the notice of the colonists the newest inventions and productions" from Europe, North America, and Britain.[53]

Exhibition advocates throughout the British Empire agreed with those bold claims, and an exhibition rivalry soon developed among host cities. Vocal supporters of the Bombay International Exhibition noted in 1868 that Leeds "is inviting everyone to its Art Exhibition which the Prince of Wales is to open."[54] Appealing to intra-imperial competition, they concluded in their argument for a local show that "surely we are handsomer to look on, and sweeter to smell than Leeds!" Such shows were often scheduled as a preliminary to overseas international exhibitions and resulted from the sponsorship of local governments and agricultural societies.[55] After inspection by visitors and jurors, commissioners determined which objects would be forwarded as official representations of the colony to major French, British, and North American exhibitions. For example, Sir Redmond Barry, Trustee of the Melbourne Public Library, Museum, and Art Gallery, reviewed commercial, ethnographic, and artistic exhibits at the Victorian Exhibition of 1861. He selected many for display during the following year at the London International Exhibition.[56]

The success of those earlier, smaller-scale exhibitions prompted Australian, South Asian, and Anglo-Indian politicians, merchants, and exhibition commissioners to organize their own international shows. These were ambitious efforts to increase trade and international status, celebrate imperial attachments and, not always inconsistently, negotiate local or national identities.[57] Major colonial cities, including Calcutta (1883–84) and Adelaide (1887), hosted such shows. Sydney initiated the series of colonial international exhibitions in 1879, welcoming over one million visitors during eight months to celebrate Australian "progress." This surprisingly vast crowd attended after late planning and only limited overseas advertising by officials from New South Wales at the preceding Paris Universal Exposition.[58]

Sydney's rival, Melbourne, hosted its own International Exhibition one year later and subsequently entertained two million visitors at its Australian Centennial Exhibition in 1888. That number compared favorably with Melbourne's own population of less than 500,000 at the time.[59] The Centennial show was intended to "commemorate" the industrial, economic, and social development of Australasia since the first convict settlement in 1788. Its *Official Record* left no doubt about this progress: "At the close of 1887 a comparatively small portion of the Australian continent still remained un-explored, but its extent was daily being narrowed by the encroachments of pastoral and mining pioneers."[60] To complete the celebration and mark "Australia's" (not only Victoria's and Melbourne's) entry into the international community of nations, the commissioners invited exhibitors from Great Britain, India, Canada, South Africa, Ceylon, North America, Europe, and East Asia.

WERE EXHIBITIONS EPHEMERAL EVENTS?

Did colonial exhibitions leave lasting legacies in Australia and India? Did such seemingly ephemeral events affect the host society in Britain as well, long after official closings? Historical studies of expositions often empha-size the ephemeral character of the exhibition experience and the exhibits themselves, mirroring the comments of some contemporaries. Rudyard Kipling recalled the fleeting moments during which he enjoyed "the full freedom of . . . spacious and friendly" Paris during the Universal Exposi-tion of 1878.[61] But the Anglo-Indian author's memories of the ceremonies and exhibits were so pleasant he returned to Paris for the 1889 Universal Exposition, suggesting a longer lasting personal attachment to the exhibi-tion experience.[62]

My research demonstrates that exhibitions produced not only momen-tary results, but also long-term legacies at the personal and collective lev-els. While it is true that certain parts of the shows were ephemeral and of-ten intended to be so, it was also the case that the exhibitions permanently affected the ways in which material culture was organized and studied, as well as social and political relationships. Furthermore, individual and social memories were often anchored in the exhibition experience, participation at the shows shaping a strong sense of the past. Exhibition reports and cat-alogues remained authoritative points of reference, and public art, indus-trial, and economic collections in English and colonial cities developed from exhibition displays. The production and organization of knowledge at the exhibitions by commissioners sometimes challenged imperial control of science, art, and public history, providing cultural authority for national-ists and the postcolonial states in Australia and India.

Public museums were among the "results and summaries" of the great exhibitions, providing access to both the displays and the scientific arrangement of the material world illustrated by the spectacles.[63] Thomas Hendley, a high-ranking Indian government official in Jeypore, concluded in 1914 that at least twelve local exhibitions resulted in permanent museum collections of art objects, scientific displays, and commercial goods in British India.[64] This was notably the case in Calcutta, where the International Exhibition provided the core collection for a revived public museum.[65] Many collections destined for permanent housing in such museums enjoyed an extended life, traveling from show to show as the "nucleus" of mobile exhibition courts. The exhibition secretary for the colony of Victoria echoed his colonial, foreign, and English colleagues by suggesting that the Australian displays at Philadelphia in 1876 should be used in the courts at the 1878 Paris Universal Exposition before donation to the proposed Colonial Museum in London. This would save time and diminish the colony's expenses by "at least one half."[66]

The exhibition displays not only resurfaced at future shows and resulted in permanent displays for museums and libraries, but also affected the ways in which material culture was organized and studied. The commissioners created a taxonomy and order for science and art objects transplanted from the exhibitions. In Madras, officers of the Government Central Museum and its provincial satellites followed the Crystal Palace commissioners' classification schema to organize their local, imperial, and international collections.[67] The curator noted that the Great Exhibition's taxonomy was comprehensive and thus could include "every article that may be received" for the arts, manufactures, geological, and raw materials sections.[68]

Exhibition officials and exhibitors also published, in the words of one American commissioner, a "vast amount of industrial literature."[69] Those texts were generally divided by nation and type of exhibit for easy reference, usually mirroring the organization of the displays at the exhibitions. Others were read as modern encyclopedias.[70] Either way, these publications challenged the Victorians' capacities and imagination, revealing their struggle to enframe the known world. In the case of the 1867 Universal Exposition in Paris, English and colonial commissioners published six volumes describing and analyzing their exhibits. American officials praised those efforts, claiming that "these printed results make the exposition a permanent one. The teachings survive the demolition of the buildings." The three hundred separate volumes spread "into the remote corners of the earth, interesting and instructing artisans and others who could not leave their homes to see with their own eyes."[71] By the early 1880s, readers at the library of the Royal Asiatic Society of Bengal could review exhibition catalogues from Bombay, Dublin, Edinburgh, London, Manchester, and Sydney.[72]

DISCONTENT AND IRONY AT THE EXHIBITIONS

Exhibition collections and publications represented imperial and national intellectual and social order but, in doing so, also revealed the tensions and ironies inherent in those systems. Celebrations of imperial commercial wealth, for example, were also opportunities for colonies to display their own economic treasures and imply the advantages of independent, not dependent, trade. British and colonial shows provoked and focused voices of dissent during Victorian and Edwardian eras, whether those visions were colored by national, social, or racial lenses. Critics noted how those apparently grand celebrations of national and imperial triumph revealed contradictions, weaknesses, and inequalities in Victorian society and political economy, in the state, and in imperial governance. These were moments of triumph as well as criticism, venues for exhibitionists and anti-exhibitionists.

Among those critics were prominent public figures, such as Thomas Carlyle, editors of republican, working-class, and socialist publications, such as the *Bee-Hive* and the *Friend of the People,* and, surprisingly, editors of various elite periodicals. The latter included the *Leisure Hour.* Carlyle, for example, wrote to Ralph Waldo Emerson that the Great Exhibition was "a universal Children's Ball."[73] Its ocean of visitors? Merely "a sanhedrin of windy fools from all countries of the Globe," which he concluded "were surely never gathered in one city before." The Victorian man-of-letters described the summer of 1851 as one dominated by "the Wind-dustry involving everything in one inane tornado."

Although an advocate of the exhibitions for economic and intellectual purposes, even Charles Babbage found various reasons to complain about the commissioners and the role of government at the international exhibitions in 1851 and 1862. In one case, the prominent scientist argued that the government or, more accurately, English "statesmen" did not appreciate the importance of voluntary societies, and thus the state did not engage them as much as it should when organizing the Great Exhibition.[74] He was not referring to the Royal Society of Arts, which provided much of the staff for that and future shows, but to other groups, generally comprised of scientists and businessmen. Babbage contributed to the chorus of criticism and analysis brought to bear on the form of exhibitions themselves, the ways in which they were managed by official commissions and the composition of those commissions, what was displayed, and how workers were treated. Conservatives and Socialists argued against the exhibitions in an attempt to find alternatives to the political economy celebrated by those spectacles. Radicals attacked London's commissioners as part of the elite "Science and Art clique" at the heart of the State.[75]

Exhibitions provided contemporaries with a seemingly clear revelation of their society and culture, but as it unfolded, that revelation crystallized both consensus and dissent. The exhibitions were contests, then, for the hearts and minds of the visitors, subjects, and citizens, rather than only festivals of hegemony and rational recreation. Some critics even attempted to appropriate the exhibitions for their own alternative visions of the host nations and the British Empire. In turn, the shows are historical moments in which we can view the sinews holding together the British Empire as well as English, Australian, and Indian societies.

As with all visions and symbolic constructions of public culture, the display of objects and persons hid and mystified as much, if not more, than it revealed. While making some identities visible, the exhibition commissioners and government officials reduced others to the realm of invisibility. In general, the representation of traditionalist colonial life or culture and the ideology of the Commonwealth extricated productive processes, commodities, and lifestyles from their original social relations and those influencing their further local development, whether in the colonies or England. Inherent inequalities and persistent political tensions were shed in such presentations. Government officials, exhibition commissioners, and other contemporaries praised modern workers for building the dramatic and monumental exposition halls, but such laborers were absent from the exhibits themselves once the events opened.[76] Millions of workers and their families in India, Australia, and England visited the exhibitions, where they observed products and machines as representations of abstract work, rather than images of their own labor processes.

Exhibits generally represented the value of traditional labor forms and social groups, such as the craftsmanship of the visiting Indian artisan, and the uses of modern technology in motion, but rarely the more common forms in both England and the colonies of unskilled manual work. Sympathetic commentators reminded readers that workers and their labor were erased. Prizes, for example, went to the official exhibitors of commercial products, and not to the laboring producers. The *Working Man* was more blunt about this injustice at the time of the London International in 1862. Who was rewarded? "Those who, with the help of Mammon, have known how to purchase and to seduce the starving inventor, the houseless labourer, the ragged Working Man."[77] The artist and laborer would never know fame and fortune because of the award-winning exhibit, but continue his struggles in anonymous poverty. In this case, the exhibition revealed class divisions rather than the intended mid-Victorian social unity.

The imperial and national portraits painted at the exhibitions contained their own hierarchies. Sometimes exhibition officials worked within the wider social structures outside of the event; at other times, they challenged them. Jules Joubert, executive commissioner for the Calcutta International Exhibition, confronted strong opposition in his attempt to invite South Asian women in *purdah* to leave their isolated private sphere for a public walk through the exposition grounds. "In order, if possible, to break through the impenetrable barrier of the zenana," Joubert wrote in his memoirs, "the Sunday afternoon was set aside for the admission of 'females.'"[78] Not surprisingly, debates about the Zenana Days in 1884 filled local newspapers for several weeks, elevating Joubert's presence and increasing the previously disappointing number of admissions, but also revealing political and social tensions.

Joubert's Australian contemporaries regularly organized ethnological models of and collected curios and weapons from the indigenous Aboriginal communities. On the other hand, they only invited "converted" Mission Station Aboriginals to several exhibitions during the last quarter of the nineteenth century. Those indigenous Australians generally lived a significant distance from Melbourne, Sydney, and Adelaide, the host cities. Rather, government officials commonly represented Aboriginals at the exhibitions by forwarding for display photographs of "Aboriginal Natives" and "native products," such as arrowroot.[79] However, there were exceptions, such as the 1879 Sydney International Exhibition, at which visitors "had an opportunity of seeing . . . specimens of the aboriginal people of the great Australian continent, who on request being made on their behalf, were admitted free of charge to the Garden Palace."[80] Once inside, they were not always treated as the natural history exhibits they were intended to be, but sometimes as fellow visitors and Australians. In the case of the 1887 Adelaide Jubilee International Exhibition, the formerly invisible Aborigines were invited to visit and remained in the host city for several days. Organizers required them to wear European clothes, sing both English and indigenous songs, and demonstrate their "primitive" and "savage" rites, such as boomerang throwing and the *corroboree*.[81]

Those South Asian and Australian cases suggest the radical moment when the generally invisible or passive objects of vision and public culture could momentarily return the colonizers' gaze and participate in such prac-

tices and communities as more than an exhibit. Although exhibition officials differentiated those who saw and those who were seen, they did so
with ambiguity. Michel Foucault has suggested that the status of always being seen as an object or subject maintains the hierarchy and discipline of
the social order.[82] Subjection, though, could be active in the case of the exhibitions, at which colonial and class subjects actively participated and observed, creating a sense of community among visitors and exhibitors, a
duality to the process of vision. Colonial peoples were both objects of observation and observers themselves. The imperial "gaze" was interactive at
these exhibitions.

At the exhibition's center, the "specimens," including South Asian
women and Australian Aboriginals, returned that imperial and social gaze;
they were both observers and observed. The colonial object's vision was returned upon the imperial subject; subordinate and passive identities threatened to become for the moment active and equal, if not dominant. Social
and cultural divisions were either bridged or reconstructed with such interactions. Colonial visitors were more than "freaks" and oddities at the
exhibitions; their participation provided a momentary role in the reinvention of their identities as artisans, settlers, "Australians," and "Indians"—
that is, national and imperial citizens. Visitors were "subjects," as well as
"objects"; their roles included those of consumers, producers, and citizens,
in addition to passive displays.

VISION AT THE EXHIBITIONS:
EMPIRE AND NATION AS POPULAR PICTURES

Such visitors were part of the quest to privilege vision and the ethnographic
mode of picturing the world. "The Great Exhibition itself," remarked one
newspaper columnist in 1851, "is a representation to the eye, is a part of
the same progress" of vision as the illustrated press and photography.[83]
"Like sun painting [early photography] it [the Great Exhibition] speaks all
tongues," as it literally speaks to the eye. The ways in which exhibitions
were organized suggested seeing as a privileged, but not the only, form of
social contact and the organization of knowledge.[84] Observation was not
necessarily the universal language, a de facto imposition of authority, but
that does not mean that commissioners did not attempt to make it so at the
exhibitions. They intended vision to create its own sense of hierarchy, enabling social intercourse and the shared consumption of culture among the
various constituent parts of the diverse Victorian and Edwardian British

Empire. This was part of the process by which vision was diffused, shaped, and finally established as a dynamic of social control and integration within and between polities. Empire and nation could be envisioned, illustrated, and imagined according to common ethnographic terms and visual modes at the exhibitions.

The envisioning of the material and social worlds at the exhibitions made public and visible much that was generally private and invisible. The exhibitions revealed, for example, peoples, goods, and machines usually hidden behind walls of various types and, in doing so, made visible and comprehensible various commercial and social links. These illustrated the growing ideologies of Britain's New Imperialism and colonial nationalism in living pictures. Exhibitions created images of empire and nation which, in the words of one English scientist, "annihilated" time and space, or previously assumed chronological and geographical distances, while simultaneously creating other distinctions.[85] Here were illustrations of self-contained and functioning social and economic systems, images representing the racial ideas, hierarchy, and oppositions of empire and nation in aesthetic terms. Exhibitions offered the empire and nation as total, participatory pictures.

Among the exhibits and ornamental projects offering that portrait of the Empire were Messrs. Doulton and Co.'s "Impasto" panels of England, India, and Australia at the 1886 Colonial and Indian Exhibition (Figure 1). According to a contemporary account, Doulton's subjects were: 1. "typical of India's native art, and represents an Indian potter working at his wheel, while a native woman is decorating the ware"; 2. "typical of Great Britain, as represented in her manufacturing industries; the figures are those of an engineer and blacksmith"; and, 3. "the remaining lunette represents Australia, as typified by a gold miner and a farmer."[86] The various exhibition classifications of art, race and industry (that is, *culture* and the ideas of both social identity and the wider imperial and national communities) discussed in this project are clearly illustrated in the three "Impasto" images created for the show at South Kensington.

The colored clay panels were idealized essences of those three communities, representing in two dimensions what was happening in three in the exposition courts. Commissioners situated the trinity of panels to ensure that they greeted visitors entering the turnstiles in the main entrance hall. They were located in a central spot, near the model of the Prince of Wales on horseback (the original statue was in Bombay) and photographs revealing the "progress" of the Australian colonies.[87] Critics praised the terracotta work for its resemblance to traditional stained glass work, the purity of its jointing, the reduced labor required, and the integration of the images with the general wall and architectural space.

Doulton's contribution was only one in its long-term relationship with the exhibition movement.[88] The company's wares filled courts at English, Indian, European, and other overseas shows, garnering a series of prizes during the nineteenth century.[89] Seemingly apolitical, these panels were self-conscious emblems for the language and consequent roles of industrialism, labor, and race in defining the cultural hierarchy and connections of the British Empire. This included reestablishing distinctions between white-settler colonies and the Indian Empire. Here was a grammar to memorialize the colonial exhibits and visitors—both the latter's activities at the exhibition itself and their essentialized roles in the imperial community. Doulton's panels provided a reworking of the ethnographic or imperial "scientific moral" of the participatory exhibition experience and an accessible aesthetic text, which drew its social and cultural vision from the spectacle.

The panels, collection of material objects, and visitors themselves provided pictures of the imperial and national communities. This was the age of "the world picture," which, "when understood essentially," according to Martin Heidegger's provocative study, "does not mean a picture of the world but the world conceived and grasped as picture."[90] At the exhibitions, this accessible and participatory picture included Australian miners and commissioners, South Asian artisans and princes, and both colonial and English tourists, as well as art, technology, and economic products from England and the colonies. The visitors' presence was often dynamic, not static; the panels illustrated what could directly be observed in action in the exhibition courts and provided an aesthetic representation and interconnection for the three-dimensional exhibits, or "picture." The imperial world was conceived and grasped as a picture that included nationalist and social shapes and shades.

The Doulton frescoes suggested such imperial and national readings on the diffusion of art, industrialism, and thus culture. Here were the various values and types of labor, people, and materials within the modern or "Second" British Empire integrated by culture (rather than politics) as a participatory practice that could be represented in the traditionalist language of visual art. The panels were also an emblem for a multicultural Commonwealth with apparently clear gender, class, and racial distinctions, but in which such social groups might still be linked by collective production, vision, and consumption at the exhibitions. These were living pictures, both sources and representations of identity.

IMPERIAL AND NATIONAL IDENTITIES AT THE EXHIBITIONS

Among other scholars, Eric Hobsbawm has recently considered the many grounds for asserting "nationhood," or a sense of the "nation," since the French Revolution.[91] The exhibition experience offers an addition to his list of historical, racial, ethnic, linguistic, electoral, and geographical criteria for national and imperial identity. One might go even further and argue that the British Commonwealth's cultural, economic, and social roots lie in the series of such explicitly imperial exhibitions in London, the popular expositions hosted by major Indian and Australian cities, and in the colonial contributions to Britain's displays at overseas exhibitions in Europe and North America. Those events produced, integrated, and diffused Hobsbawm's various sociocultural and political criteria.

Representations of imperial, national, and colonial identities, power, and production were common between the Great Exhibition of 1851 and the Festival of Empire Exhibition in 1911. Their zenith occurred as part of the exhibition movement in the 1880s and thus provides a new perspective on the debate about the foundations, structures, and functions of "the ideology of The New Imperialism" and imperial federation during that era.[92] The exhibits presented a vivid and accessible picture of federation and how its meanings as an idea and a practice penetrated everyday life in so many ways in England, Australia, and India at the time. Exhibitions offered political, social, and economic federation right before the eyes of their participants. Contemporaries reflected that such spectacles assumed active roles in the creation of the British Empire and its new form of imperial federation; the same would be said generations later with the creation of the Commonwealth of Nations. An enthusiastic observer of the Colonial and Indian Exhibition concluded in 1886 that

> above and beyond the intrinsic value of this splendid Imperial Exhibition as a means of national education, its Royal originator [Prince of Wales] may justly claim that it will probably have the effect of binding Great Britain, India, and our Colonies more closely together, thus conducing in no small measure towards that great Confederation [Imperial Federation] which has been earnestly advocated by the Earl of Rosebery and other far-seeing statesmen, and which bids fair to be consummated with the consent of both the great Parties in the State.[93]

Exhibitions helped create the ideas and forms of "Great Britain, India, and our Colonies," as well as binding together these polities. Such shows were also object lessons for the authority of the cultural experts organizing the events and the state itself in both Britain and the colonies. Participatory cultural practices, such as consumption, tourism, pageants, and machines-in-motion, were alternatives to modern political society and ones to which "both the great Parties" might consent. They created the enduring racial and economic categories of civil society and the underlying social links between the Commonwealth's politically diverse national units.

The construction at the exhibitions of new symbolisms and forms of social interaction, such as the market, provided a public language for social order and mediated the perceived distance of cultural and spacial dislocation for Australian settlers and Anglo-Indians. Exhibitions were about the past as well as the present and future. Historical displays anchored overseas communities in time and place. The shows were moments of contested reconciliation in which the racial similarity and distinction of such relatively timeless new groups could be read in cultural and aesthetic terms. Political, economic, and social hierarchies were actively reinterpreted. That social totality was among the objectives of exhibition commissioners and their qualified success points to the complex, multivocal, and interactive nature of the exhibition experience. Visitors were expected to become not only "British" or "Australian," in contrast to French "assimilationism" at the Paris Universal Expositions, but members of more universal classes. These included producers and consumers linked in an imperial market which preserved and institutionalized racial and national distinctions. Participation at the exhibitions implied a shared way to organize, observe, and consume the material world in light of political economy and the growing state, not only in terms of political national identity.

The exhibitions exposed generally hidden production processes and industrial operations, linking them with the resulting artistic and consumer items. The shows integrated these activities and represented a seemingly self-sufficient economic community, or commercial commonwealth. Exhibition halls provided a transparent and participatory moment in which the public and private spheres of production and consumption merged as a seemingly shared cooperative project, an economic federation.[94] Elites and commissioners also used the shows to transform the exhibited objects into national and imperial relics at this new nexus of the public and private, thereby representing their vision of contemporary society and its history. That social order and its origins could be envisioned across time and space at these shows.

This imperial cultural policy included an attempt to replace the coercive state with the moral and cultural one, representing the ideal of a voluntary and participatory Commonwealth. Sir John Seeley and his generation of imperial intellectuals provided the philosophical framing for that idea of

Empire and its successor, the British Commonwealth.[95] This was, in a sense, imperialism as the national culture or civil religion in England and, less successfully, in India and Australia. "Like every act or event which occurs in the life of men and nations," wrote the author of a popular account of the 1851 show, "the Exhibition is the index or reflex of an opinion, or idea."[96] The idea of cultural federation was implicit in the exhibition experience and the series of such shows across the British Empire gave it continuity, accessibility, and a language, providing both an index and reflex for ideas of imperial federation and commonwealth. The exhibitions represented the idea of association, which conflated concerns about national culture, social integration, the free-trade market, and imperial federation within colonies and between the latter and Britain.

FEDERATION, COMPETITION, AND THE MARKET

Australian, Indian, and English exhibitions suggested a self-sufficient, imperial, economic community with interlocking roles for racial and national groups and without other nations and empires. At times, the exhibitions celebrated national, or colonial economic ambitions as much, if not more, than imperial ones. The ideology was ostensibly one of Free Trade, whereas the structure represented an imperial economic federation, or Zollverein. Exhibits moved increasingly along the path of Joseph Chamberlain's vision for "forward" imperial economic order. This idealized, self-contained empire of raw materials, capital, artisans, manufactured products, and consumers contrasted sharply with the reality of British trade with, and investments in, the United States, Latin America, and Imperial Russia, and with the growing Australian and Indian interest in independent and direct trade with North American and European nations. Economic displays created a picture of the imperial market in which differing and often conflicting racial and social groups participated as producers and consumers. The market idea paralleled that of imperial federation, offering similarities and a reconciliation of distinctions. This provided a metaphor or an idealized normative representation of the empire and the relationship among its racial and political units.

The market and its functioning at the exhibitions symbolized a cluster of ideas and practices to explain and describe imperial relations, or federation.[97] Exhibitions were more than a revised index or reflection of this market idea; they constituted the market. Australians and Indians were both consumers and producers, but their particular niche within the imperial socioeconomic system was represented at the exhibitions by differences among colonial visitors, workers, and objects. The culture of the market—that is, the practice and language of consumption and production—provided a seemingly neutral and natural representation of these oppositions. Exhibitions created, illuminated, and revealed the public politics and social meanings of economic goods as artifacts and signs. They represented the various economic roles of the Empire's racial or national types. Here was the empire as market and the market as empire.

Thomas Richards has suggestively argued in his work on "commodity culture" that the Great Exhibition offered the spectacle of commodities and the emergence of a new capitalist form of representation.[98] The Crystal Palace housed consumers and consumerism, or, in his words, "a functioning microcosm of mid-Victorian capitalism," centered by the distinctive ways in which the commodity was represented. Commissioners undertook that representational project at the exhibitions for economic, cultural, and political reasons, applying the principles of political economy and the practice of imperial cultural policy to questions of production, commerce, and consumption. The development of commerce as a particular form of social relations paralleled the ideas of nation-building as the construction of a social market and contemporaneous views about federation, whether of the Empire itself, or within particular units, such as Canada and Australia. Consumers were, after all, citizens and subjects, and vice versa, and consumerism was both an ideology for and mode of participation in the nation and empire. If the Crystal Palace made the commodity the focal point, as Richards argues, it and its successors also offered the visitors' relationship to imperial commodities as a metaphor for political and social relations.[99] This metaphor was fluid and mutable, adjusting to ideas about the market's benefits and deficiencies.

The staging of exhibitions linked the ideal types of empire, or nation, and the market as participatory practices. Expositions provided information and evaluation in the forms of written materials and direct consumption. Jurors offered expert judgments, which could then be tested right on the spot by the visitors themselves. Men and women both observed and participated in the demonstrations of economic goods. As with the promise of political economy and federation, different social groups were brought into direct contact at these shows and defined by that market relationship. Babbage claimed at the time of the Great Exhibition that direct observation of craftsmen and contact between consumers and producers (as individuals, classes, and nations) "removed the veil of mystery" about commercial transactions.[100] Here could be the ideal political economy and a working example of the market's authority and power to improve taste, create value, "civilize," and establish social order.

Sir Henry Cole shared Babbage's views about the commercial roles and meanings of exhibitions. Cole suggested in his capacity as executive commissioner for the British Section at the 1855 Paris Universal Exposition that such shows would allow producers and consumers to compare the goods and various economic strengths of the participating countries.[101] "Every nation has something peculiar to itself which is useful to another, and it is the increased ease of interchange which international exhibitions chiefly promote." In contrast to the "mysteries" of the private guilds, exhibitions showed the advantages of the open, public, free market and drew "a direct connexion between the two parties" involved in commercial transactions. Governments and businessmen could then see how "fruitless" it would be to ignore the "natural tendencies" of their own country and produce goods that were "natural" for other nations to produce. The shows' illustration of a neo-Ricardian sense of comparative advantage might then erode support for the French tariff and promote a seemingly neutral system of free trade between European powers. The English and French governments signed such a free trade accord in 1860, only five years after the exposition.

The comparison of economic exhibits, or "tendencies," revealed and appeared to make natural the national, cultural, and racial characters of the producers and represented those in the economic language of the market. Cole recognized that England could send "iron and coal" to the Paris Exposition and thus European consumers, and that, in return, the French authorities would offer "wines, silks, and all kinds of articles connected with the luxuries of civilized life."[102] Exhibitions might offer an inventory upon which to base such commercial decisions. A deputation to the Paris Exposition from Bradford agreed that the show provided economic information but complained that the French producers only exhibited luxury items and goods prepared specifically for the event, rather than those intended for the mass market, as found in the British courts.[103] One could not determine the future contributions of such foreign goods to the mass consumption of the middle and working classes, geared towards what one contemporary termed "cheap and common articles."[104] Rather, the show's display of economic diversity distorted or, at least, misled, without providing Cole's promises of complete information.

Exhibitions thus revealed and naturalized, or, it might be argued, created cultural oppositions between utilitarian Britain and luxury-oriented France, the former providing for the middle- and working-class consumers, the latter for wealthier social groups.[105] Similar social and national distinctions were drawn at the shows between Australia and India. The Indian courts at the Colonial and Indian Exhibition offered silks, jewels, wood carvings, and teas. Visitors passed from there to the Australasian sections, in which one was "met with no Oriental, but a sturdy British element," offering "science," landscape painting, manufactures, minerals, wood and wool.[106] The distinction was made visible in the contrast between village artisans representing India and the Australian grazer and miner in Doulton's panels at South Kensington. As France needed England, and vice versa, for economic prosperity and trade, so did Australia and India need each other. They performed complementary roles within the vast, interconnected, and organic market of economic federation.

The South Kensington exhibitors drew upon the precedent established at earlier shows, including London's International Exhibition in 1862. That year, Alexander Hunter, director of the Madras School of Art and Industry, reviewed exhibits from Lahore and the Punjab, finding most of them like those from France: "costly and ornamental articles of luxury."[107] These were best suited "to the requirements of the wealthy, or the pomp and display of Native durbars." Indian displays suggested that the arts were exercised to gratify the taste of the few rather than supply the demands of mass society in India.[108] They represented the increasingly common picture of Indian society and culture dominated by the picturesque feudal myths of the Punjab and its Indian princes, village-communities, and artisans.[109] This was not necessarily a false picture, but one intentionally shaped and policed by imperial and local elites uncertain about the alternative India of middle-class South Asians and commercial cities.

India's economic exhibits contrasted with those of the Australian colonies. Those distinctions created and underscored cultural, historical, and racialist views; they also might have reduced the wider and longer-term economic advantages offered by the exhibitions. Hunter thought so and concluded that India's commissioners should exhibit items "suited to the requirements of the middle and lower classes . . . [and] likely to be in demand to any extent amongst the European population."[110] This offered a different, but potentially more lucrative, image of India by appealing to more consumers than the fancy silk and cotton goods. Hunter proposed the useful in place of the exotic, the common rather than the aristocratic.

Comissioners also increasingly reflected and promoted complementary, rather than competitive, relationships among imperial exhibitors and exhibits. Babbage was adamant about the importance of the principle of "competition" at the Great Exhibition, and was greatly disappointed when the prices necessary for seemingly disinterested comparison were not provided at the show or in the new Crystal Palace, Sydenham.[111] He attacked the policy of Lyon Playfair and other influential English commissioners, who promoted comparison by a system of juries and awards, rather than prices in 1851. Playfair's scheme was more in keeping with visions of federation. The commissioner's tour of Leeds, Birmingham, and other manufacturing districts revealed that potential exhibitors were less reluctant to participate in the Great Exhibition upon hearing of the opportunity to win an award.[112] For nearly all, the promise of expert reviews and prizes removed the "apprehension" about (and also much of the competition at) the show.

By the time of the 1862 London International, Playfair, as both scientist and commissioner, argued that jurors and awards should substitute for prices, creating in place of economic competition a "bond of union" among exhibitors and the public, whether they were imperial or "international."[113] Francis Cunliffe-Owen and the Royal Commissioners appropriated this argument to promote imperial "harmony and goodwill" at the Colonial and Indian Exhibition over twenty years later.[114] They sponsored a series of official reports and offered exhibitors a commemorative medal and diploma in an attempt to prevent the "invidious comparisons" produced at previous shows by the jury system and competitive classifications. By the mid-1880s, Cunliffe-Owen was expressing not only optimism about imperial federation, but also doubts about the free market system of prices and competition.

Colonial commissioners were called upon to prepare the classification system most appropriate and suitable to their own exhibits at the 1886 show. In this way, categories represented the seemingly unique characteristics, culture, and history of each colony, but in doing so offered overarching imperial rule as the sole source of uniformity. Previous classificatory systems had enabled jurors and visitors to measure the "progress" of each colony according to standard scientific criteria and stages. Confidence in the political and economic values of those universal standards was waning, being replaced at the exhibitions by new, perhaps more relative, cultural ones, whose value was their relationship to one another, not an absolute condition. Displays representing such cultural differences and their advantages proliferated at the revised nexus of race and economics.

CONCLUSION: EXHIBITIONS, PARTICIPATION, AND HISTORIANS

The interpretations of and reactions to exhibitions were shaped by political conditions in England, Australia, and India. Politics affected visitors and exhibitors. These events were thus important elements in the general nine-teenth-century programs of nation- and empire-building and of socialization, or social control. They were significant not only because of their scale and popularity, but also because of their integrative, participatory, and long-term nature.[115] Exhibitions were not mere mirrors of the political and social order but agents of change, creating by participation and not coercion a sense of natural order, consensus, and hierarchy. The exhibitions' effectiveness in mobilizing political bias towards national and imperial objectives, and as socializing activities resulted from this more subtle and complex relationship between their elite organizers and general visitors.

That interplay of participation, propaganda, advertising, and spectacle presents a less hegemonic and unilateral interaction. It suggested Edward A. Ross's initial articulation of "social control" in 1901, rather than more recent interpretations of that term, most notably during the 1970s.[116] Ross argued for the integration of various types and modes of socialization, influence, and control, including beliefs, public opinion, art, education, custom, and law. To some degree, this study also suggests a return to the older German sociological vocabulary in which the term *social masses* (for example, exhibition visitors) was used in an activist sense, rather than with the American meaning of masses acted upon.[117]

Exhibitions also offer historians the contested ground where the official and unofficial ideas of "Englishness" and colonial national identities converged, were actively created, interpreted, consumed, and mediated.[118] This was the space in which public opinion was shaped—the heart of civil society. Similar processes occurred with the formation of and visits to natural history, national, and universal survey museums, among other nineteenth-century public cultural collections.[119] Those, however, did not offer the sense of participation, movement, and direct consumption enjoyed by visitors to events such as the London International Exhibition in 1871, where machines for "printing, composing, and distributing type" at the London *Times* were exhibited in full working order.[120] Visitors could purchase and read copies of the special exhibition supplement printed before their eyes at South Kensington, before or after turning those steam type-composing machines and making their own tiles.

Exhibitions offered living pictures of the nation and empire as natural and universal markets. In this case, the market was both an idea and practice. Although some students of popular culture and politics perceive the imposition of a coherent elite ideology at the exhibitions, my study suggests that the success of nationalism and imperialism as ideologies in the face of indifference and, on occasion, direct political opposition required a more subtle and participatory process for its permeation and acceptance. Exhibitions were hybrids of high and low, elite and popular, national and imperial. Rather than products of an "arbitrary, rationalistic and willed" ideology and social practice, national citizens and imperial subjects participated and were represented at such shows as "historically organic," natural, and local, to borrow from Antonio Gramsci and Cultural Studies scholars.[121]

The shared observation, purchase, and operation of exhibits created and reconstructed both imagined and envisioned communities. One Melbourne firm exhibited its "powerful medal stamping machine" at the 1874 Sydney Metropolitan Exhibition and sold observing visitors a variety of its pewter and brass products manufactured at the event. An observer noted the "vast amount" of interest shown in this "whole process" of minting.[122] Such direct physical consumption and contact allowed visitors to prove, test, or demonstrate the products and the identities they represented, whether those were social, national, or imperial. Empire (and the nation), for example, became feasible; participation in ceremonies, the purchase of souvenirs, and the consuming of commercial goods made imperialism (and nationalism) part of an accessible and comprehensive popular culture, part of a fantasy which was not escapist, but explanatory. Echoing the words of Richard Hoggart, this was an imperial (and national) culture which became increasingly "homely and personal and local."[123]

The visitors' voluntary and nonpassive participation at these events was in contrast to passive ethnographic displays of colonial types. Rather than being represented by such models or by others, many visitors represented themselves and their nation, colony, or race. This made participation at the exhibitions an important part of the reworking of imperial, national, and colonial identities during the second half of the nineteenth century. Visitors were agents in the construction of this national and imperial public sphere and offer a suggestive example of how the idea and modes of participation created rather than destroyed social order. This was part of a new strategy of socialization, one that encouraged rather than discouraged mass entertainment, and of colonial rule, which complemented, although it most certainly did not replace, the violence of military and economic domination. As the Times noted in 1876, it was time "to sheathe the sword which our forefathers made so good use of, and found the way to power" and to replace (or complement) it with new strategies of governing by "the intercourse of the European and the Asian . . . to sustain . . . to teach . . . to govern."[124] The sword undoubtedly remained part of the governing strategy in India and was often unsheathed and bloodied, but it existed alongside the exhibition as part of imperial rule and "intercourse."

People and social groups were not only collected like objects and passively represented under the glass of exposition buildings. Official and private visitors actively participated in the social "intercourse" at those exhibitions. They became part of the imperial and national pictures along with economic products and works of art, but they actively created those pictures. This reminds us that social categories were made up at the shows, and those who filled them were not always passive in the process of creating and filling them. The exhibitions situated South Asian women, Australian and Indian science and art experts, colonial workers, and Australian Aboriginals in the public spheres of imperial culture and the colonial nation.

Visitors exercised agency by participating in a variety of ways. They were not passive observers of the exhibits, since vision itself implied an active relationship between object and subject. Visitors were both on display and displaying themselves; being gazed upon and returning the gaze. Men, women, and children also turned the cranks on machines, consumed and inspected new colonial products such as Indian cigars and Australian fruits, and purchased souvenirs and curios, which they then took home to memorialize the event. A visitor from Trinidad to India's Economic Court at the Colonial and Indian Exhibition purchased "fine carpets, and fancy work, jewels and brass-ware" and observed coffee, tea, and cigars prepared for sale.[125]

Exhibitions did not merely reinforce or unidirectionally manipulate previously formed ideas about nationalism, class, race, empire, and society. The structure of such events provoked an active reworking of this information and its accompanying behavior and bias. The popularity of and participation at those events implies that the general public cannot be labeled only "indifferent" to national and imperial issues. We can consider the process of organizing and visiting expositions, including writing official catalogues, judging displays, acting in historical pageants, operating "machines-in-motion," and purchasing consumer products as nation- and empire-building actions complementary to the more commonly cited ones. Among the latter are reading novels and children's literature, screening films, voting, staging mass demonstrations, and attending sporting events.[126]

Exhibitions in England, Australia, and India during the 1851–1914 period expressed and shaped the developing ideas, practices, and meanings of empire and nation. In turn, participation at such events as commissioners, exhibitors, and visitors created social identities as citizens of these communities. As signs for and products of such events, Doulton's panels provided more than an image of vast wealth in raw materials and labor or the Victorian vision of human progress from Macaulay's Tasmanian to his Londoner. They were also part of and the early sign for a ritualized and integrated community, founded upon a particular participatory practice of culture. Such imperial pictures encoded racial, aesthetic, and economic oppositions and hierarchies, but also suggested the empire and nation as reconciliating pictures.

This master narrative managed in aesthetic terms difference and similarity, duality and unity. Issues of race and ethnicity were recast as "imperial connections" in an accessible language at the exhibitions in England, Australia, and India. James Anthony Froude popularized this articulation of a community linked by organic bonds of art, sentiment, and culture in the 1880s.[127] Ironically, Froude was drawing upon the politically anti-imperial writings of Goldwin Smith and his social and cultural definition of imperialism as "the connexion of blood, sympathy and ideas."[128] Smith claimed in his lectures on the British Empire delivered in the early 1860s that such "connexions" would not be affected by the formal political separation of the colonies and England. Participation at the expositions provided the experience, language, and material culture necessary to imagine and envision such seemingly nonpolitical and persistent national and imperial "connexions." This was the case not just from the mid-Victorian Crystal Palace of 1851 to the Festival of Empire celebration in 1911 but beyond as well. Those events created the underlying cultural, social, and economic practices of the modern British Commonwealth of Nations during the era of "New" Imperialism, suggesting the postcolonial persistence of older colonial practices and ideas; here were social and cultural continuities accompanying political discontinuities.

2 The Exhibition Wallahs

Commissioners and the Production of Imperial Knowledge

Exhibitions were part of perceiving and organizing the participating societies as immense administrative and informational challenges during the Victorian and Edwardian eras. This was true of nation-states and their colonies, such as Britain and India, as well as transnational units, including the British Empire itself.[1] As science and art experts, the commissioners responsible for those expositions were at the center of that project. They used the shows to link the Empire's national communities, along with the various classes and regions within those polities, into networks of knowledge. That knowledge was intended to secure social order both within and across political borders.

Cultural experts and the events themselves created, institutionalized, and diffused imperial knowledge in the forms of material culture and ideas in England, India, and Australia. They circulated and linked people, ideas, and cultural capital throughout the empire. In doing so at the popular expositions, they were able to legitimate the ideas and practices of empire and their own status at home and abroad. Commissioners traveling in India after the popular Calcutta International Exhibition were recognized in local bazaars as "The Exhibition Wallahs," while others in Britain and the colonies earned professional and royal honors for their exhibition activities.[2]

Science and art experts responsible for exhibition activities also constructed the intellectual and social bridges linking public and private cultural organizations and institutions in Britain and the colonies. In this way, commissioners contributed to what one scholar has termed "a delicate network" connecting voluntary societies and administrative bodies throughout the British Empire.[3] This was also the case within a single polity, such as Australia, where their actions contributed to the idea and sinews of the nation-state and its civil society. Commissioners developed such imperial and national cultural policies via personal contact, conferences, displays, and exchanges of literature and objects at the exhibitions. For example, visitors to the annual shows of the Ballarat (Victoria) Agricultural and Pastoral Society exhibitions in the 1870s could observe, sample, and purchase cereals, grasses, and machines collected by commissioners from "the leading agriculturalists and Agricultural Societies of the various countries" in the British Empire.[4]

The exhibitions not only circulated objects and information, but also created and sustained communities of experts, many of whom were both imperial and national. Australian experts were linked with other Australians, but also with their complements overseas in Britain and India. Contact at the shows and the constant exchanges of displays between the exhibitions provided the shared experiences necessary for this sense of communal identity and continuity, generated at the nexus of political, social, and cultural boundaries. The forging of intellectual and social connections among anthropologists and other experts at exhibitions was, in the words of George W. Stocking, Jr., "the institutionalized interaction of the community of scholars."[5] This regularized interaction began with the Great Exhibition in 1851 and complemented the array of learned societies and congresses in London and other capital cities. Exhibitions quickly evolved into a floating institutional foundation for imperial and national art and science experts.

Charles Babbage, the outspoken Victorian man-of-science, noted a similar development in his controversial critique of the Crystal Palace show.[6] He praised "associations for [the] occasional discussion of men pursuing the same or similar studies," contending that they had connected art with science and had contributed to manufactures. Those "associations" performed some of the Great Exhibition's functions on a more permanent (but less popular) and sustained basis. The Crystal Palace show and its many successors offered opportunities for less politically and geographically limited intellectual contact. The State of Maine's commissioner in 1851 recognized that his official position "gave him [as well as other commissioners] access to some desirable sources of information, which he could not otherwise have commanded."[7] These included meetings with other commissioners, museum officials, Prince Albert, engineers, and users of new labor-saving technologies as part of a general "intercourse . . . with intelligent gentleman from different nations."

Aside from the continued direct contact with French, German, and American authorities, most of the exhibition commissioners' efforts were intended to promote a network of imperial scholars and cultural bureaucrats. Australians were anxious to turn the intellectual, scientific and commercial "intercourse" in that imperial direction for possibly national advantages, particularly at English exhibitions. One of Victoria's commissioners chose to forward scientific samples with "peculiarities" to the 1862 London International Exhibition, noting as justification to the chief secretary that the unusual colonial minerals and woods "may open up or facilitate Scientific inquiries of the highest importance to the Country" during and after the show.[8] The result? Kew Gardens officials solicited the exhibits and found Victoria's woods "unrivalled."[9]

The prominent architectural critic James Fergusson observed in 1857 that "every Government of Europe . . . and not only the great metropolitan cities, but even the capitals of the great European empires possess collections" of art, natural history, and technology.[10] Exhibition commissioners linked such collections and cities, making the institutions, experts, and forms of knowledge not only more mobile, but potentially polycentric and interactive rather than stationary. Most art and science institutions were, as Babbage noted at the time of the Great Exhibition, "located for convenience in some capital or large city," whether that was London or Sydney, but the cultural system overseen by exhibition commissioners gave them fluidity, connecting them with complementary associations in the provinces, other colonies, and Great Britain.[11]

Imperial cultural policy and the exhibitions not only encouraged the formation and study of such metropolitan and colonial collections, but, in so doing, defined "culture" (science and art) as a social practice and an enduring imperial link. "Culture" suggested the ways of doing what was known as art and science, as well as the representation of those practices in the forms of ideas and objects.[12] Imperial rule and the construction of nations called upon a participatory cultural process, which included active roles for colonial and national subjects. A new class of cultural experts arose during the period of colonial expansion and the exhibitions to establish the informational systems and circulate the materials by which producers and consumers of such culture became citizens of the British Empire and its colonial nations. These experts shaped and supervised that participatory culture. In one sense, commissioners authored the categories of knowledge, forms of social identity, visual images, and commodities by which the ideologies of imperialism and nationalism were articulated. The contributions of exhibition commissioners to the larger cultural project of the British

Empire and its constituent political units remind us of the strong interconnections between professional expertise, public service, practical commercial enterprises, and civic identity during the nineteenth century.[13]

Exhibition commissioners were among the architects and supervisors of the network in which scientific, commercial, and artistic objects were also exchanged, reproduced, and studied. This was the case at botanic gardens, libraries, museums, and art schools, as well as expositions, and commissioners linked those institutions. Museum curators and trustees in England, Australia, and India, for example, often served as exhibition commissioners. Their contributions to the creation and institutionalization of knowledge about the colonies provide important evidence when studying the ways in which England and imperial elites came to know and thus control, as has been argued by some, the colonial periphery. The activities of imperial and colonial exhibition experts point to the interactive and dynamic process by which such knowledge was produced; apparent representations of imperial power also established the foundation for local, colonial authorities. Increasingly, the participation of exhibition commissioners from the colonial periphery made imperial culture a more collaborative and less hegemonic practice. The exhibitions created early nationalist intellectual communities and public cultures, as well as the cultural sinews of the British Empire. The ways in which English, Australian, South Asian, and Anglo-Indian commissioners created and diffused knowledge asserted both imperialism and colonial nationalism at and after the shows.

EXHIBITION COMMISSIONERS: MEASURES AND MEN

Commissioners assumed a variety of responsibilities at exhibitions in their capacities as official organizers, judges, and exhibitors. They participated sometimes as agents of their government and sometimes as private citizens or representatives of voluntary societies. Sir Redmond Barry, executive commissioner for the colony of Victoria during the 1860s and 1870s, noted that commissioners were responsible for inducing persons to contribute objects; making the necessary preparations for their classification and effective display; obtaining judgment on their merits and evaluating them in official essays; and repacking them for return, exchange, or a future exposition.[14] The Australian commissioner fulfilled such obligations at exhibitions in Melbourne, Sydney, Paris, London, Philadelphia, and Dublin during those years. Barry and his colleagues often displayed their own personal materials as well as those associated with their governments.

Commissioners oversaw the exhibition process as professional managers in a manner similar to that found among their commercial and industrial contemporaries. Jules Joubert organized exhibitions in India, Australia, and New Zealand, recommending that they be managed on a "business basis."[15] He advocated restricting salaries, selling advertising space in the catalogues, and limiting the size of committees. Large commissions might be "very well in their place, but they are a costly luxury if too much latitude is allowed to them" by the host government. Joubert's remaining commissioners were busy at the shows. As a business, exhibitions required the organizational techniques and expertise found in other large-scale Victorian-era collective projects, such as manufacturing or the state. In one case, the executive commissioner for New South Wales at the 1887 Adelaide Jubilee Exhibition received and dispatched over 1,230 telegrams and 4,620 letters in less than eight months.[16]

Exhibition bureaucrats managed enterprises producing knowledge and culture, or the spectacle of exhibitions, and not a specific commercial or industrial product. On the other hand, they did so in an environment surprisingly similar to that of the noisy and chaotic nineteenth-century factory. John Lockwood Kipling, director of the Mayo School of Art in Lahore, organized "a large collection" for the Calcutta International and wrote that he and his three South Asian assistants worked amid a "howling chaos of packing cases, bales, Bengalee baboos, bamboo scaffolding, Chinese carpenters, [and] perspiring Britons."[17] Not always anchored in their offices or the noisy exhibition halls, commissioners often traveled to provincial areas in England and the colonies to encourage local exhibitors and struggle with businessmen suspicious of international shows. Sir Henry Cole and Lyon Playfair toured English manufacturing regions to solicit exhibits and financial support for the 1851 Great Exhibition.[18] Twenty-five years later, Charles Moore visited the Upper Hunter River Agricultural and Horticultural Association to select objects for the 1875 Melbourne Intercolonial and 1876 Philadelphia Centennial Exhibitions.[19]

Personal memoirs, official reports, newspaper accounts, correspondence, and public speeches describe the labors of these cultural bureaucrats, but they are not the subjects of any analytical studies. We have contemporary descriptions, but no scholarly interpretations. The literature on nineteenth-century cultural policy and the rise of professional groups generally considers the work of "Wallahs" in seemingly more daring arenas of public expertise, such as health, engineering, science, industry, and finance, rather than the apparently undramatic efforts of "The Exhibition Wallahs." This is not to say that exhibition commissioners were invisible in public life. Many were active members of various voluntary and learned societies, such as the Royal Society of Arts and its colonial complements, but they participated as science, art, and commercial professionals, not as exhibition commissioners per se. Government botanists in Australia, such as Ferdinand von Mueller and Moore, represented their professions at local Royal Society meetings, but in the name of their science or government, not as agents of the exhibitions.[20] Commissioners never formed their own professional organization, unlike nineteenth-century engineers, architects, and anthropologists. Neither did they construct their own "intellectual aristocracy," with its structure of family ties and seemingly inherited offices.[21]

On the other hand, the exhibition commissioners organized knowledge and collections, or, in other terms, the ways of doing science, art, and public culture. They helped create the ideas of "culture" and "society," which were useful to other members of the growing professional classes and political elites. Commissioners framed and transformed the common paradigms of knowledge in the nineteenth century with exhibition displays and literature, often suggesting the shifts from ethnological, comparative, and philological taxonomies to increasingly developmental and functionalist ones. These included powerful distinctions, analogies, connections, and associations between and among the British Empire's objects and subjects. This system of knowledge provided the language, metaphors, and meaning, or the "fundamental codes of culture," for the new group of professional experts, as well as for British imperialism and colonial nationalism in India and Australia.[22]

Many of the commissioners constructed these codes by applying their shared background in medical training to the organization of artistic and commercial exhibition displays. This was not only the case with influential English commissioners, such as Playfair, but also with their prominent Anglo-Indian colleagues, including Sir George Birdwood and Sir George Watt. Medical and biological taxonomies shaped their exhibition displays and accompanying art handbooks and economic dictionaries. The same might be said about the powerful ideas expressed in Orientalist literature, art, and philosophy. Orientalist assumptions linked many of the commissioners around the Empire, and those affinities were institutionalized not only by participating on exhibition committees, but also by attending the many Orientalist Congresses held in major European cities during the last quarter of the nineteenth century.

Finally, it is interesting to note that certain key cultural texts, including Owen Jones's *Grammar of Ornament* (1856 and 1865), influenced the way Sir Redmond Barry in Australia, Birdwood in Bombay, and other commissioners comprehended their region's indigenous, or traditional art, and represented it at the imperial and colonial exhibitions.[23] Exhibition categories and displays acted as templates for comprehending the material world in the nineteenth century, but they did so in association with other, often very broad, cultural and intellectual developments. Those associations not only help us place exhibition commissioners in their historical contexts, but also remind us that their labors at the shows were most influential when they were linked to wider systems of thought and action, rather than operating as isolated islands unto themselves.

SOUTH KENSINGTON, SIR HENRY COLE, AND THE IMPERIAL COMMISSIONERS

The story of the exhibition commissioners begins in London at South Kensington. Prominent officers of the Science and Art Department orchestrated the imperial cultural network radiating out from that point. Cole, Playfair, Sir Francis Philip Cunliffe-Owen, and C. Purdon Clarke, among others, promoted the collection and exhibition of colonial articles, organized museums and expositions in England, and oversaw official British Sections at overseas shows from South Kensington.[24] As commissioners, they also repeatedly referred to the 1851 experience as a guide for exhibition committees and classifications. Cole and his colleagues were among the first generation of professionals to manage British public collections and develop the models for their administrative structures. Moving freely within the circle of London's learned societies and elites, these officials advocated a strong role for government in the creation of national culture. They were assisted by the Prince Consort and, after his unexpected death in 1861, by the Prince of Wales.[25]

Cole's training as assistant keeper of public records and various projects with the Royal Society of Arts provided precedents for his work at international exhibitions and South Kensington. The future exhibition commissioner oversaw the examination, preservation, and selection for publication during the early 1830s of "about six thousand documents," many of which had been "heaped together in two great sheds or bins" on the site of the new National Gallery.[26] Cole later proposed a variety of schemes to develop national art and science collections in London during the 1840s, including an annual exhibition of the works of living ("Modern") artists and the use of funds from the sale of their pictures and admissions for a centralized National Gallery.[27] He also recommended the relocation of the Hampton Court Palace's art collections to a more central and accessible site, where they could be observed and studied by "all classes."[28]

Cole brought to the Department of Practical Art (later renamed the Department of Science and Art) and the South Kensington Museum this administrative experience, understanding of how to organize knowledge and material culture, and respect for the value of national and imperial relics. He ensured that official cultural policy radiated from South Kensington, doing so in a manner which assimilated Benthamite ideas about the classification and utility of material culture in the effort to civilize and moralize. Working with Prince Albert and the commissioners of the Great Exhibition, Cole was positioned at the heart of the interventionist state, overseeing the newly ambitious programs of the metropolitan government from the department's museum.[29]

The Royal Commission and Cole extended the lifetime and impact of the Great Exhibition and its successors by distributing the surplus from the 1851 show. They also offered advice to British and colonial exhibition commissioners and provided funds for gardens, research, and public collections.[30] In doing so, they were generally following the guidelines articulated by Albert to create a public cultural center at Kensington Gore "for the dissemination of a knowledge of science and art among all classes."[31] Cole expanded this objective by including the English provinces and colonies in many of the projects of the Science and Art Department of the Council on Education.[32] W. E. Forster wrote to the secretary of the treasury in 1873 to praise the museum keeper: "It has been mainly due to the zeal, energy and ability of Mr. Cole that so large an amount of success and of public favour has attended the efforts of the Science and Art Department."[33] It is hardly surprising that others found Cole's zeal to be a form of ruthlessness or personal aggrandizement.[34]

Regardless of the assessment of Cole's character, the department's officers and staff were notably active during his tenure. South Kensington employees purchased and exhibited a wide variety of art and industrial works, many of which were circulated to regional and colonial museums, galleries, and expositions.[35] These loans were intended to assist in "laying a foundation for local Museums, and improving the Public taste."[36] Such activities were not limited by Britain's borders. South Kensington officials participated in the cultural interaction between the imperial core and colonial periphery by organizing lectures and art schools in Australia and India, and by providing examinations, curricula, and various models to instruct their students in painting, drawing, and sculpture.[37] Prominent Anglo-Indian art school administrators and instructors, such as Lockwood Kipling in Bombay and, later, Lahore, received their early training at South Kensington.[38]

Cole and his assistants turned to the exhibitions for other direct links with the colonies. South Kensington financed a series of handbooks on colonial material culture written by exhibition commissioners and jurors.[39] For example, Birdwood authored "a popular handbook" for the opening of the Indian Section at the Museum in 1880, drawing upon guidebooks and displays prepared for earlier exhibitions held in London, Paris, and the Punjab.[40] The India Office expert offered analyses of metal work, arms, furniture, and pottery which had traveled the paths of those expositions before finally resting within the cases at South Kensington. Such a volume and other complementary "official" guidebooks provided commentary for exhibits purchased or acquired by exchange for permanent display by the officers of the museum.

The energetic Cole also found time to sponsor the identification and cataloguing of "ancient" Indian monuments for South Kensington and various Indian museums, thereby shaping the sense of India's past in Britain, Europe, and South Asia.[41] As South Kensington's director, Cole "paid special attention to the representation in the Museum, of Indian Architecture and decorative carving," including casts of Buddhist, Hindu, and Muslim art.[42] Under his guidance, Indian objects became historical relics, although Cole emphasized the process of copying by casting rather than the removal of original works of art and architecture. Cole's relics were not to be confused with Elgin's Marbles! Cole's obsessive administrative zeal and self-promotion aside, he was not a plunderer of the East.

Cole used such experiences and the authority of his position at the state's cultural center to prepare guidelines for the organization of exhibitions in London and Paris between 1851 and his retirement in the early 1870s.[43] These were the foundation texts for nineteenth-century British exhibition activities. Cunliffe-Owen succeeded Cole after assisting him at most of those exhibitions and directing the foreign sections for the London International in 1862. He also applied his generally recognized administrative skills as executive commissioner for the South Kensington shows during the mid-1880s, including the popular International Health and Colonial and Indian Exhibitions, and in his capacity as England's executive commissioner at overseas exhibitions. Those responsibilities took him to Paris, Vienna, and Philadelphia.[44]

Cole and Cunliffe-Owen officially solicited colonial exhibits for English and European shows in their dual capacities as directors of the South Kensington Museum and imperial executive commissioners. They turned to Australia for unique animals of "great interest," such as wombats and black swans, and to India for raw materials, among which were silks and dyes.[45]

Struggling to convince potential exhibitors in India and England to participate, Cole argued before the Crystal Palace Exhibition of 1851 that "a more
extensive knowledge among European manufactures of the Raw Products
of the Indian soil could hardly fail to increase its commerce, . . . [for] it is
indeed remarkable how little the various products of India are known."[46]
The executive commissioner counseled Prince Albert that expanding the
classes for colonial specimens to include art-manufactures (e.g., ivory and
carpets) would increase trade between England and India and improve public taste in Britain.

Official correspondence and the events themselves brought the experts
at South Kensington into direct contact with their colonial colleagues. That
link promoted the creation and exchange of knowledge within the empire
among commissioners and the general public. The British Guiana Committee for the 1855 Paris Universal Exposition confirmed the value of those
connections. Correspondence between the secretary of state for the colonies,
the Science and Art Department, the Royal Society of Arts (London), and
the local Royal Agricultural and Commercial Society produced the official
exposition committee and its displays.[47] British Guiana exhibited and offered for exchange various woods, oils, "fibrous substances," and "saccha-
rine products & articles of food" after consultation with the imperial commissioners in London.

The English commissioners also oversaw the purchase of exhibits for
permanent display in official museums and galleries. These projects transformed the seemingly ephemeral exhibitions into permanent parts of the
cultural landscape in South Kensington, Manchester, and Dublin. Various
South Kensington collections, including sculpture and animal products,
resulted from purchases with Parliamentary funds from the 1851 and
1862 London shows and the 1867 Paris Exposition Universal.[48] Committees of cultural experts and exhibition commissioners—Cole, Fergusson,
and Richard Redgrave among them—selected and then oversaw the study,
classification, and display of these objects.[49] Cole was particularly active in
this process and told members of Parliament in 1867 that he intended South
Kensington "to show the best state of art applied to manufactures at the
present."[50] He later selected European, Chinese, Japanese, and Indian art objects from the Paris show, which he argued would improve English products and "educate the eye and the hand of the artizan." Anxious to develop
collections of "Oriental" art for display at the metropolitan museum and
for instruction at various provincial schools of art, Cole approved extensive
purchases of Indian artware. Among those were lacquered wooden boxes,

jade, ivory and marble carvings, a marble pillar from a tomb at Ahmadabad, and terra-cotta painted statuettes. Indian princes and Queen Victoria also donated artware exhibits and "a very attractive and beautiful collection of Indian arms" after the 1851 and 1862 shows.[51]

Cole was among those most enthusiastic about transforming exhibitions into permanent museum collections. He advised the committee debating the future of the Crystal Palace and its contents that "when you have once got hold of public opinion," as it had with the Great Exhibition, "it is as well to keep it and make the best use of it that you can."[52] In this case, Cole argued that the "best use" was to build a large museum for merchants, artisans, and consumers from the Palace's exhibits; the latter was the "nucleus of a trade collection," since it offered products of manufactures from around the world. Using the Vienna Museum as a successful precedent, Cole testified that such public collections offered novelties and staples from England, Europe, and the colonies for visitors to inspect, handle, and examine. The "great public benefit" of education and cultural development could be turned to commercial gain as well.

The acquisition of exhibition displays to either create or augment permanent collections was even more important for the colonial committees. The ability to obtain displays from European shows and from overseas exhibitors at their colonial expositions helped limit the "tyranny of distance" and sense of cultural isolation which restricted Australian and, to a lesser degree, Indian public collections.[53] One English newspaper noted at the time of the 1862 London Exhibition that the colonial commissioners were busy exchanging their exhibits for various English and European ones after the show and that the colony of Victoria was "especially likely to do well" with those transactions. "From this source . . . their commissioners are likely to take back the nucleus of a very valuable museum."[54] Over twenty years later, local officials purchased exhibition items from the Calcutta International Exhibition in 1883–84 and housed them in the host city's central museum.[55] Public funds were used for their purchase and reorganization.

The acquisition of exhibition displays for permanent collections was among the top priorities of museum curators, trustees, and scientists serving on Australian exhibition committees. Reports from the major libraries, museums, and art galleries in colonial cities hosting exhibitions reveal the magnitude of such acquisitions and reflect the persistent impact they had on local cultural policy.[56] Following the South Kensington pattern, objects in central colonial museums were subsequently copied for or circulated among provincial institutions. As was the case in England, this cultural process generally enhanced the reputation and authority of the centers and their experts, most notably the colonial exhibition commissioners in Melbourne, Sydney, and Calcutta.

AUSTRALIAN EXHIBITION COMMISSIONERS

Australian executive commissioners were among the most active and influential public figures in their colonies. Emigrants from England, Scotland, or Europe dominated the committees during the second half of the nineteenth century. This small group included judges, pastoralists, manufacturers, scientists, and elected government officers, almost all of whom also held prominent appointed or administrative positions in colonial voluntary societies. They promoted the development of colonial culture by patronizing local science and art organizations and serving as trustees and officers for museums, libraries, and art galleries.

Leading commissioners were the most eminent figures in the colonies. Sir Samuel Davenport, South Australia's executive commissioner at exhibitions in the 1870s and 1880s, was considered "the most popular man" in the colony by one noteworthy contemporary.[57] The author of a handbook for emigrants recognized Barry as "the great patron" of the arts and "a public benefactor" in Melbourne during the 1860s and 1870s, concluding that he "may be called the Maecenas of Victoria."[58] Several years later, Barry was introduced at the Philadelphia Centennial Exhibition as judge, university chancellor, "member of a good family in Ireland, and a gentleman of high intelligence, and [having] wide acquaintance with Art, Science and Literature."[59] The title "judge" hardly did justice to Barry's position as the chief justice of Victoria.

Those executive commissioners oversaw committees for local and overseas exhibitions, calling upon the expertise and experience of a relatively limited number of settlers. Many of the same names appeared year after year in exhibition catalogues and governmental records as commissioners. Representative among those were Edward Combes, John G. Knight, and Joseph Bosisto. Combes was active in New South Wales as an engineer, pastoralist, politician, and painter. He served as a juror and commissioner for the colony at expositions across the globe, from Paris to Philadelphia, and, closer to home, in Melbourne and Adelaide. Exhibition experience and painting talents led the executive commissioners to select Combes as the director of the Art Section at Sydney's International Exhibition in 1879.[60] Neighboring Victoria was home to Knight, who applied his administrative and architectural skills to the oversight, transportation, and display of exhibits. As exhibition secretary for Victoria, he worked as Barry's official assistant in Europe, England, and various Australian colonies. Knight earned the praise and gratitude of one prominent colonist for traversing Victoria to provide information about and solicit exhibits for the 1862 London International Exhibition.[61]

Born in Hammersmith, Bosisto took his skills as a chemist and businessman to Australia in 1874, where he was best known for promoting the production and sale of eucalyptus oils. He found an effective venue for that project at the exhibitions, forwarding scientific and commercial samples to a series of Australian and overseas shows. Building from his position as local expert and exhibitor, he represented the colony of Victoria in London, Melbourne, Paris, Philadelphia, and New Orleans.[62] Bosisto served as the colony's executive commissioner for the Colonial and Indian Exhibition, noting the show's promising economic advantages for Australian trade. He was later selected as a Trustee for the Melbourne Exhibition Building and remained active in the Chamber of Manufacturers and Pharmaceutical Society of Australasia.

Colonial botanists were among the most active local science and art experts on exhibition committees. Charles Moore in Sydney and Ferdinand von Mueller across the border in Melbourne participated in Australian and overseas expositions by providing local flora for ornamentation and study, authoring authoritative essays about such displays and local timber, and soliciting examples of overseas and intercolonial vegetation for their embryonic but growing public gardens and museums. Officials chose samples which not only represented the uniqueness of their colony, but might also induce exchanges and both scientific and commercial interest. Von Mueller's botanical samples at the Sydney International earned a "First Degree of Merit" for their scientific value and "instructive character," particularly for local pastoralists.[63] His lengthy essay for the 1861 Victorian Exhibition included discussion of the colony's vegetation and called for the introduction of economic products, such as tea and rice.[64]

Prominent producers of colonial trade items were also asked to join exhibition commissions. The New South Wales colonial secretary appointed William Macarthur, the colony's most influential pastoralist, as its official executive commissioner at several exhibitions in the 1850s and 1860s. Macarthur was expected "generally to direct & superintend" all preparations for the colonial courts.[65] In that capacity, the "bunyip" aristocrat conducted "all correspondence with the authorities in London and Paris" and collected timber, vegetable, and wine exhibits, including some from his Camden Park estates. Macarthur also prepared catalogues in English and

French to introduce colonial products (including his own) to overseas scientists and merchants.[66]

Official "colonial agents" in London were expected to assist with the building of exhibition courts, organizing of displays, and completing of exchanges and purchases. Commonly known as "Agents-General," these representatives were "an informal, but essential nexus" during the course of routine commerce and between the Australians and overseas governments.[67] They also helped link producers and consumers at the exhibitions. Sir Arthur Blyth, the South Australian Agent-General, assisted Davenport during the 1886 Colonial and Indian Exhibition and admitted in a letter that "*I never worked harder* than I now do."[68] Blyth spent at least two days each week at South Kensington, where he read and responded to correspondence, hosted visitors to South Australia's court, and oversaw financial arrangements for the display. Queensland and New South Wales had called upon their Agents-General in London to act as official representatives at the International Fisheries Exhibition in South Kensington three years earlier, rather than incurring the "unnecessary expense" of appointing an additional official.[69]

Under the direction of Australia's executive commissioners, exhibition committee members and government officials searched exhibition courts in Europe and the United States for art reproductions, library volumes, and handbooks on organizing public collections. This was part of the effort to reproduce and adapt overseas cultural practices and institutions, including ways to organize museums, artistic models, and the popular mechanic's institutes. Those were adapted from England and the continent, as well as North America, for transplantation with modification in the new cultural soil of Australia.[70] Barry was at the forefront of borrowing from overseas cultures to form public taste in the colonies. He urged his associates visiting London and Paris to purchase, copy, and return to Australia with "the most admirable illustrations of high, ancient and modern classical art" to mold public character.[71] This was his vision of nineteenth-century secular "rational recreation." The trustee emphasized the traditional periodization of art, including the Classical and Renaissance eras, but also advised against settling for the notion that "anything is good enough for a colony." Inferior works would create "apathy or dissatisfaction"; they would misguide the mental, artistic, and cultural development of the colony.

Rather, Barry and the public would only be satisfied with "the best selection of the choicest objects of the approved schools, executed in the most perfect manner." Since the colony did not have unlimited funds to acquire those works, it was most efficient to coordinate exchanges or take plaster casts and photographs, rather than purchase the originals. Barry charged Victoria's Agent-General in London with the collection of materials at the 1862 London International for Melbourne's young public library, museum, and art gallery. Among the English exhibits he desired were those items necessary to "form not merely a miscellaneous collection of casts and busts, but to bring together a comprehensive and well balanced series of groups to illustrate national characteristics, and exhibit the history of the growth of refinement and intellectual excellence in the arts."[72] The Victorian commissioner advised the creation of "a set of Specimens of timber indigenous to the Colony" and displays of other natural resources to offer in exchange for the overseas art works and literature. While in the British Isles for the show, Barry secured "*very extensive* contributions" to the Melbourne Public Library, Museum, and Art Gallery and provided catalogues of those institutions and the Victorian exhibition courts to "every newspaper in Ireland."[73]

EXHIBITION COMMISSIONERS FOR THE RAJ

Barry's efforts were often mirrored by those of his colleagues representing British India at the expositions. The Indian government canvassed for exhibition commissioners among officials at the India Office in London and within the Raj's vast network of public works and cultural institutions. Those included museums, botanic gardens, libraries, and art schools. The same politicians, scientists, and art experts appear year after year on committee rosters, paralleling the dominance of the small group on Australia's commissions. On the other hand, the Indian government encouraged the participation on exhibition committees of indigenous elites, such as South Asian princes and businessmen, unlike their Australian colleagues, who only invited Aboriginals to participate at the shows as exhibits, or performers, but never as commissioners.

British India's commissioners organized and oversaw some of the largest and most ambitious displays during the nineteenth century. Paul Greenhalgh notes that India "was the most carefully displayed [imperial] possession at the Great Exhibition and continued to be so" throughout the century.[74] Impressive displays one generation later at the 1878 Paris Universal Exposition were produced by a representative collection of commissioners. Among the latter were members of the Indian Civil Service, the India Office Reporter, the governor of Bombay, Lord Lytton (Viceroy and governor-general in India), officers from the South Kensington Museum, and Indian princes.[75] Cunliffe-Owen applauded "the very complete exposition of the resources, products and manufactures of the Indian Empire" at South Kensington eight years later, noting that it was the result of the "persevering work of a large body of private and official, native and European gentlemen in all parts of India."[76] This "body" included Indian princes, private collectors, Art School administrators, and local government officers in India. Prominent officers in the Department of Revenue and Agriculture, such as E. C. Buck and Sir George Watt, and influential businessmen, including Thomas Wardle, the silk magnate, bridge the Victorian and Edwardian regimes by joining Indian exhibition committees between the 1880s and the Franco-British Exhibition in 1908.[77]

Among the most authoritative exhibition commissioners for British India were the official "Reporters on the Products of India" at the India Office. Hyde Clarke, influential treasurer for the Royal Society of Arts in London, suggested that the Reporter be "some man of authority practically conversant with the subject [of trade], and in whom the public would have confidence."[78] Reporters collected and distributed information about the Raj by organizing exhibits and accompanying literature, supervising exchanges with other institutions and governments, delivering public lectures, and overseeing museum collections. These activities brought them into direct contact with their colonial and metropolitan colleagues.

John Forbes Watson and John Forbes Royle held the office of Reporter during the mid- and late-nineteenth century and were active in collecting, describing, and distributing India's material culture.[79] They were also keen advocates of exhibitions, whether it was Royle recommending provincial shows throughout India, or Watson voicing support for India's participation in overseas exhibitions in England and Europe.[80] Royle argued that South Asians visiting local exhibitions could compare, judge, test, and emulate labor practices and goods, receive prizes as inducements to improve arts and agriculture, and break down regional barriers which had prevented improvements in one district from being known and applied in another.

Watson served as director of the Indian Department at the 1862 London International Exhibition and in that capacity compiled India's official exhibition catalogue. That volume included "a correct guide," statistical tables, and illustrations to accompany the South Asian exhibits he solicited and arranged.[81] Watson provided information about the source, exhibitor, and use of the displays, suggesting "that, in a commercial point of view, the value to India and to this country [England] of the present Exhibition will be considerable." Several years later, he forwarded similar "Raw Products and Manufactures" to the New Zealand International Exhibition from his offices in London.[82] These formed a permanent display at the local museum after the show. Exhibition activities also took Watson to Europe, where he coordinated the Indian Department at the Vienna International in 1873 as chief commissioner and director.[83] Watson's efforts at the India Office and exhibitions complemented the labors of other experts at the cultural nexus of Britain and its Raj.

IMPERIAL CONNECTIONS AND EXCHANGES

London's exhibitions provided opportunities for direct interaction among representatives of the imperial core and colonial periphery. In turn, those interactions helped challenge the core-periphery distinctions and borders. Among the participants were Watson and his Australian colleagues, notably Redmond Barry. While in England, Barry was particularly active in this effort and oversaw the distribution of Victoria's natural history and mineral samples after the 1862 London International. The commissioner received a variety of requests from major and minor libraries and museums, but he was adamant about only exchanging his colonial displays with prominent institutions and receiving original or well-crafted reproductions of European and English exhibits in return. Barry ensured the most effective overseas advertisement for his colony at Kew Gardens and the British Museum and, in return, the long-term representations of English culture and taste in Melbourne.[84] The commissioner's New South Wales colleagues were not much less discriminating, as they dispersed exhibits to noteworthy museums and individuals in Britain and Europe, rather than only assuming a subordinate position.[85]

Colonial commissioners visiting the London shows also developed professional links among themselves. Australian and Indian officials commonly created and sustained connections on the personal and institutional levels. E. P. Ramsay, New South Wales museum administrator and one of the colony's visiting commissioners, took advantage of the 1883 International Fisheries Exhibition to develop scientific and social links with his Indian colleague, Deputy Surgeon-General Francis Day. The Australian Museum officer purchased over 750 "specimens of fish from India and the Indian Ocean" and forwarded them for permanent display in Sydney.[86] The Ramsay-Day transaction was part of a growing, direct, intercolonial network involving the representatives of Indian and Australian museums at exhibitions without the direct oversight of English authorities. Annual exchanges and purchases continued. One year later, the Agricultural and Horticultural Society of India gave seeds to the New South Wales commissioners at the Calcutta International Exhibition. This gift initiated direct botanical exchanges with various Australian agricultural societies and Sydney's Botanical Garden.[87]

These exchanges remind us that colonial officials and commissioners were not always in subordinate and dependent positions at the exhibitions. English scientists and institutions cultivated exchanges with visiting commissioners, but the latter generally returned with objects for their own study and display at the periphery, and were quite capable of exchanges among themselves. Australians struggling to create national institutions and a sense of culture thus benefited greatly from these relationships. In some cases, British exhibits were donated outright to colonial institutions. For example, the English art forwarded to the Australian international exhibitions in the 1880s by Queen Victoria, the Royal Society, and the Department of Science and Art remained in local public galleries after the shows.[88] Such a political economy of material culture was a two-way link, requiring the active participation of both imperial and colonial experts and commissioners.

Commissioners from New South Wales, Queensland and Victoria exploited their colonies' unique natural history and ethnography to secure such exchanges, donations, and purchases. They displayed kangaroos, eucalyptus oils, and Aboriginal implements and then traded them for seemingly exotic objects of European artware, machines, and manufactured goods. Such was the case after the Melbourne International Exhibition of 1880. The superintendent of the host city's Industrial and Technological Museum offered "several specimens of Victorian gold," copies of Brough Smyth's ethnographic treatise, *Aborigines of Australia*, "native plants," and von Mueller's botanical publications in exchange for mosaics, tiles, terra-cotta ware, and models of stoves exhibited in the Imperial German court.[89]

Those exchanges and other contacts contributed to the public authority of local and imperial experts, science, and art figures in Calcutta and Melbourne, not only in London. Participation helped position experts within colonial society, and to position their colonies' role within the wider imperial cultural system. In this way, the colonial subjects, or apparent subalterns, participated in the construction, circulation, and evaluation of knowledge as recognized experts. Australian and Indian exhibition collections and publications underscored colonial contributions to the creation of imperial knowledge and culture. Furthermore, colonial commissioners created their own local knowledge while preparing exhibition displays by soliciting professional papers and statistical tables from local experts to represent the colonies.

Barry turned to Melbourne's science and art professionals for essays about their colony's natural history, geology, botany, and social statistics at the time of the London International in 1862.[90] The result? Smyth, von Mueller, and Frederick McCoy, among others, provided "the most interesting particulars connected with the physical, Scientific, and Social History and condition of this Country" in their own "authentic and authoritative" terms. J. G. Knight prepared for the Melbourne and Paris shows a few years later by soliciting "some account of the resources of the several Provinces" to accompany the exhibits. He noted that the request generated "a greater mass of general statistical information with regard to the Australian colonies" than had been previously published.[91] While it was true that exhibitions provided the ways for England to know its colonies, it was also the case that the shows enabled the colonies to know themselves, to develop their national identity out of the construction, applications, and uniqueness of this local knowledge in contact with imperial knowledge. Here were the opportunities for such experts and savants to take stock publicly of their expertise and colony.

Knight's and other exhibition publications offered overseas and empire-wide audiences for their author's views and, in doing so, revealed the tensions within the increasingly complex organization of seemingly imperial knowledge. While exhibitions appeared to present "imperial" or "European" knowledge and collections, they were also part of local science and art culture in the colonies. The ways in which they were exhibited and diffused reflected not only imperial hegemony, but also the complex interplay of material culture and ideas, sometimes produced overseas, often consumed at home in the colonies. The exhibitions could be turned, in von Mueller's view, to clear Australian or, more specifically, Victorian advantages. The Baron included local information when describing Australian scientific collections and provided a commentary with Aboriginal and settler names and applications for exposition and museum timber displays. These labels not only made the samples more accessible to the general public, but also provided a local context for this scientific knowledge. His report on the popularity of eucalyptus oil samples at the London International Exhibition in 1862 urged that a small laboratory be built on the Botanic Gardens grounds to take colonial and civic economic advantage of such interest.[92]

LOCAL KNOWLEDGE, LOCAL POWER

Colonial members of the rising imperial science and art community gained prestige after performing overseas exhibition duties. Their authority as experts was enhanced by judging displays and authoring handbooks. Local commissioners now stood poised to challenge English dominance at and beyond the expositions with colonial intellectual and cultural power. This was true at home in the colonies and overseas, whether in Europe or Britain. White Australians, but not Aboriginals, were members of the local cultural bureaucracy exercising that new authority. In India, unlike Australia, the development of official imperial cultural policy and participation in local and overseas exhibitions encouraged the training and employment of experts from the subject population. The majority of the Raj's commissioners were Anglo-Indians and Indian government officials, but a significant number of Indian princes and other South Asians participated at the expositions.

Perhaps the most influential exhibition official from the Raj's subject population was Trilokya Nath Mukharji, from Calcutta, whose contributions to the shows were recognized by various Anglo-Indian and British officials. Cunliffe-Owen's official memorandum for the Colonial and Indian Exhibition cited the assistance of "Babu Trilokya Nath Mukharji" in ensuring "the proper representation of the vast resources" of the Raj.[93] The South Asian earned praise for his part in "the very complete exposition of the resources, products and manufactures of the Indian Empire," including answering enquiries from merchants about India's commercial exhibits and lecturing around the host country. The executive commissioner concluded that Mukharji was "a most attractive lecturer and in this way did great practical good."

Mukharji was one of many South Asians employed in the Raj's vast system of libraries, art schools, museums, literary societies, and other public cultural projects.[94] He undertook exhibition duties in his official capacity as exhibition assistant for the government of India's Department of Revenue and Agriculture. The department was initially organized in 1871 and then broken up and reconstructed between 1879 and 1881.[95] It was funded as part of the general scheme to organize knowledge about the country, continuing the century-old practice in British India of scientific surveys and statistical compilations.[96] The department's original charge was to "collect, collate, and disseminate information as to the condition of India in its agricultural aspects."[97]

That general objective included the study of famine, application of the scientific approach to economic questions, and development of new materials for export. Officials were responding to the demand for efficient management of agricultural and commercial projects and the quest for markets. These efforts required new forms of knowledge and expertise. Sir Richard Temple wrote that "the supervision now wanted was specifically different, namely, a scientific attention, which could not properly be afforded by a department concerned in other branches, fiscal or commercial."[98] This approach required a new class of experts and professionals, not "purely scientific men," but also managers and bureaucrats who could cast a national vision over the development of India, organize knowledge about art and science, and link the Raj with England and other parts of the British Empire. According to one of the department's secretaries, these cultural experts and their public projects introduced "science and order as part of the national system into the wilderness of facts and figures."[99] Part of the Raj now retooled to include a scientific education for South Asians, which would complement and compete with the existing literary one.[100]

A separate branch of the department was responsible for exhibitions and museums during the years between 1871 and 1905.[101] Edward C. Buck and George Watt, two influential secretaries for the department, used exhibitions to develop an economic and cultural network representing a particular vision of "India."[102] This intellectual grid reworked common perceptions of Indian culture during the later nineteenth century and assimilated the South Asian periphery and its products or "wealth" into the imperial cultural system at events such as the Calcutta International and Colonial and Indian Exhibitions. Buck and Watt brought scientific and organizational skills to the department. The former entered the Bengal Civil Service in 1862 after taking his degree at Cambridge. He oversaw the network of local committees comprised of curators, governors, surveyors, art-school administrators, and Indian princes in his capacity as executive commissioner for India at the Colonial and Indian Exhibition in 1886.[103] While in London, Buck organized exhibits and lectures on silk worms, weaving, and reeling to promote Indian silk production and trade.[104] The commissioner centered his project in the India Silk Culture Court at South Kensington, where he encouraged the participation of various English and Anglo-Indian experts, such as Watt and Thomas Wardle, and the incorporation of earlier studies on silk, including those by John Forbes Royle.

Whereas Buck called upon his bureaucratic skills to organize the department and its various projects, Watt applied a scientific expertise developed from studies in medicine and botany. Similar training provided a template for Birdwood's contemporaneous studies of the Raj's economic products and traditional artware. The new taxonomies for India, whether represented by exhibition courts or Watt's *Dictionary of the Economic Products of India*, resulted from the convergence of these discourses, or disciplines, under the direction of the imperial state and individual initiative.[105] The Raj recognized the power of this modern rational authority, although it challenged the traditionalist authority of two "gentleman" rulers: the Indian prince and the older Indian Civil Service officer.

The professionals Buck and Watt turned to for collecting, organizing, labeling, and evaluating India's wares were members of the department's "scientific cadre" of "first class experts." They were trained to investigate botanical, ethnographic, artistic, meteorological, and other matters in the subcontinent. The Anglo-Indian and South Asian staff collected "vital economic and agricultural facts and statistics" and oversaw a variety of public projects. Those included the Archaeological Survey of India, the Geological Department and Survey, the Inspector of Mines, and the Indian Museum, as well as exhibition displays. The work of those experts at India's displays at the 1886 Colonial and Indian Exhibition "made it easier to obtain an idea of the produce of each Province or Native State," according to the English executive commissioner.[106]

The East India Company had used local South Asian guards, copyists and instrument repairers for surveys as early as the 1830s.[107] Building on that precedent, the Revenue and Agriculture Department employed South Asians to collect, analyze, organize, and publicize material displays as part of official scientific and commercial projects. These exhibits included the art works and raw products sent to English and European shows and those materials permanently housed in the series of public Indian museums. B. A. Gupte, head clerk at the Bombay School of Art, was a member of this indigenous "cadre." He collected and organized various displays for Indian and overseas exhibitions during the 1880s with Lockwood Kipling.[108] The executive commissioner at South Kensington concluded that Gupte's "intimate acquaintance with all the exhibits, and the intelligent and ready aid which he afforded on all occasions proved of the highest use . . . the additional experience which he must have gained by his visit to Europe cannot fail to have rendered him a very valuable man if any suitable permanent post can be found for him."[109] South Asians, including the assistant curator at the Lahore Central Museum, also assisted Kipling with "a large collection" of art objects at the Calcutta International Exhibition.[110] Such local experts and assistants were important links in the creation and diffusion of imperial cultural policy and the construction of knowledge about India at home and abroad.

THE CASE OF T. N. MUKHARJI

The most notable of those South Asian cultural experts and officials was Mukharji, the highest-ranking South Asian in the Department of Revenue and Agriculture, where he was assistant for exhibitions and assistant curator in the Art and Economics Section of the Indian Museum, Calcutta. The latter position put Mukharji in charge of the collection that had formerly been the Bengal Economic Museum.[111] He rose to the government rank of class II assistant/clerk. Mukharji worked directly with Buck and Watt at the Department of Revenue and Agriculture, where he was initially responsible for the collection of raw products. Expertise in that area secured his position as juror for raw produce at the Jeypore Exhibition in 1883. According to one visiting journalist, Mukharji's suggestions concerning vegetable products and manufactured articles could, "if carefully carried out, be productive of much profit to the public, and the rulers who contributed."[112] Advice on growing exhibited grains and seeds during years of scarcity was particularly appreciated.

Mukharji was also responsible for writing various official exhibition publications intended to accompany India's displays. Those catalogues introduced and described artware and commercial objects exhibited at local and overseas shows, including the popular international exhibitions held in Amsterdam (1883) and Glasgow (1888).[113] Readers ascertained information about the common and local names of the products, as well as their location, uses, and prices. The Anglo-Indian press also took notice of Mukharji's publications. Editors at Calcutta's influential *Statesman and Friend of India* praised the descriptive catalogue prepared for the Amsterdam Exhibition, noting the inclusion of scientific and vernacular names, the work's thoroughness, and the margin notes providing information about the uses of each product described. The South Asian expert had "produced a neat volume . . . sure to become a standard of reference in [the] future."[114] Watt was also impressed. He later recommended that Mukharji author "a special pamphlet" on Bengal mats, matting, and matting-sedges.[115] This was only one among his many government monographs on artware and commercial products.

As noted, South Asians were often hired by Schools of Art and the Indian government to assist with the collection, organization, and evaluation of exhibition displays. Such activity, though, generally occurred within India itself. Mukharji, on the other hand, traveled overseas as an official expert and representative of the Indian government and its public institutions. He assisted with the accounts and disposal of government exhibits at these overseas exhibitions, and answered visitors' queries about Indian artware and commercial goods. Mukharji was particularly active at the Colonial and Indian Exhibition, where he introduced Indian arts and economic products, participated in several debates about India at the Royal Society of Arts, and delivered public lectures on the Raj's resources.[116] Although anxious for "a European expert" to oversee the exhibits, the Indian Exhibition Commission relied heavily on Mukharji during the show, as evidenced by Cunliffe-Owen's praise for his "especial service" in 1886.[117]

Mukharji was among the colonial experts who took advantage of the exhibitions' publishing opportunities to enhance their prestige and role in the local and imperial communities. In the case of India, Mukharji prepared a collection of "Indian Raw Produce" for the Calcutta International, and it was considered of such high quality that the vice president of the Exhibition Committee requested "a short description of the articles" for the visitors.[118] This expanded to a more general work on "the products of India as a whole," in which Mukharji reworked the indexes and classifications of earlier Indian exhibition commissioners. By revising the work of Lockwood Kipling, Birdwood, and Watson, he produced a more comprehensive and accessible work than their previous publications on the subject. That nearly encyclopedic survey of India adapted the projects of those experts in their "particular branches," reduced "geographical, historical and other matters," and placed him in an influential position to represent India's resources.

In a written parallel to the exhibitions themselves, Mukharji also proposed "a sort of Index to the manufactures and raw materials of the great continent of India."[119] Visitors could refer to the index for a description of what they observed in the courts. Mukharji's "tentative survey" of artware included descriptive notes from exhibition catalogues; reactions from jurors at Melbourne, Venice, Paris, Indian, and London shows; location, size, chief characteristics, and uses. He noted those art processes which were in decline and others which offered financial returns. The Calcutta expert was forthright at the time of the Amsterdam show, writing that "the object . . . is to interest European visitors at the Exhibition in the old Indian arts."[120] An aesthetic and commercial rebirth might result from the attention the government officer drew to the artware's "beauty of . . . design, the excellent selection and arrangement of colors, the minuteness of patterns and the high 'finish' displayed in . . . execution." Mukharji then described the more ostensibly commercial and economic displays, such as oils, minerals, and woods in the second part of the catalogue.

Mukharji followed the precedent of Watson at the India Office and provided one for Buck's displays at the Colonial and Indian Exhibition by dividing India's art-manufactures and raw products according to the region of origin, rather than by class or type. Such an intellectual system merged aesthetic and commercial interests, providing a sense of India's diversity and shared heritage. More practically, it offered a model for Watt's later dictionaries of Indian products and art. The Anglo-Indian officer adopted many of Mukharji's analytical interpretations. Watt was not alone in acknowledging the South Asian's contributions to the various exhibition "Index collections" and surveys during the early 1880s. Mukharji's commentary and catalogues became part of the accepted canon on traditional Indian art, influential pages in the thick text of materials intended to revive those crafts. Analyses provided for the Glasgow and Amsterdam shows became common reference points for future writings by European and Anglo-Indian art experts.[121]

CONCLUSION: IMPERIAL KNOWLEDGE, LOCAL POWER?

Mukharji's activities at the exhibitions contributed to the development of Indian national institutions and public culture. By participating in these shows as commissioners, experts and exhibitors, Mukharji and the Indian princes became active agents in the invention of Indian art and in its systematic classification, promotion, and public presentation. These analyses formalized the study of that art, encouraging comparisons across regions and types, restoration, and sales. To some degree, Mukharji's exhibition projects nationalized Indian art, remapping the political landscape both materially and symbolically so that visitors could easily conclude that there was "Indian" art, and not only crafts from the "Punjab" or "Bombay," and that it was produced, sold, and evaluated by South Asians.

Mukharji's exhibition projects and status as an art expert also offered, at least in the eyes of N. N. Ghose, his editor, an argument for South Asian participation in India's public service. "The travelled Hindu," wrote Ghose in his preface to Mukharji's travel memoirs, "becomes a source of instruction to his countrymen and a centre of influence among them."[122] Mukharji had fashioned himself and, at times, been fashioned by others as an imperial expert, subaltern, and nationalist. He had become a model for nationalist progress.[123] Thus, it was nearly inevitable, in the politically charged atmosphere of late Victorian British India, that his memoirs and professional activities placed him in the ongoing debate about the employment of South Asians in the Raj's bureaucracy.[124]

The South Asian officer's participation at the overseas exhibitions and travels in England and Europe as an "expert" on Indian economic and cultural products gave him direct and personal familiarity with, and placed him astride, the two worlds of empire and colony, metropole and periphery. Even within India, he might bridge the worlds of the city and the countryside. That personal bridging allowed Mukharji to be more than a source of instruction and influence among the Raj's subjects, as Ghose hinted. Intimate and direct knowledge of the English was unattainable in India, where, Mukharji contended, South Asians saw "very little of the English people. . . . Neither do we know them nor do they know us."[125] Now, wrote Ghose, Mukharji could act as an intermediary between the English Raj and its indigenous subjects upon his return. The exhibition commissioner's "familiarity, acquired at first hand and not through the reading of novels and newspapers, with Western habits of thought and life, puts him in complete sympathy with the dominant race and qualifies him to be an interpreter of the Government to the people."[126] As a result of his travels, Mukharji had become the mirror image of the Old India Hand: he was now the Old English Hand as a South Asian source of knowledge and authority about the distant mother country and its people.

Mukharji intended to use his overseas experiences to help fashion a modernized Indian nation, founded upon economic development and the rational order represented by the exhibitions. South Asian readers of his travel memoirs could overcome the "vanity, undue reverence for the past, and reluctance to alter the present" obstructing the march of that nationalist vision.[127] The exhibition officer was bold, proclaiming that his writings and displays would create a common understanding among Indians of different creeds and races, provoking them to use science and technology for local improvements. Might the ideas of the "Indian native" be turned upside down and used to strengthen rather than weaken the Raj's "subjects?" As Ghose perceived, these memoirs could excite controversy with "observations on matters social, religious, and political" in India and abroad.[128] They might excite the same changes that Mukharji intended his commercial and art exhibits and catalogues to realize.

Thus, Mukharji's career raises questions about the much-discussed relationship between knowledge and power within the British Empire and its discrete political units. What were the roles of indigenous experts, or creators of knowledge, in the colonial context? Over twenty years ago Edward Said asked us to reconsider the ways in which Europe and the West in general had come to "know" the Orient, or "the Other."[129] Applying doses of Max Weber, Jacques Derrida, and Michel Foucault, the Columbia University scholar probed the textual and political construction of knowledge and the consequent representation and control of the colonial subject. His Orientalism stimulated a reconsideration of subject and object in fields as varied as History, Art, Anthropology, Sociology, Political Science, and Comparative Literature.[130] Not surprisingly, Said's work provoked considerable debate and controversy.[131]

Students of British India—including, in particular, Bernard S. Cohn—have worked on a similar project to suggest the development of a sociology of knowledge about India anchored by powerful imperial images and tropes, cultural forms and practices. Among these were anthropological tableaux, exhibitions, ceremonial durbars, law, clothing, and the village-community system.[132] Cohn uses the concept of "culture" to describe and analyze what he terms "the sense of a system of meanings which are embodied in symbols and which communicate, shape, and maintain knowledge of the world."[133] Thus, he and his students highlight the key cultural technologies and their effects in the British Orientalist discourse, or system of knowledge, since the early days of the Royal Asiatic Society in the 1780s. Their studies run through the construction of museums and libraries in the major cities of the Victorian Raj. Whereas Said draws upon literary criticism to better understand the construction of Orientalist knowledge, Cohn turns to the traditions of anthropology and sociology.

Such scholarship has reworked our former understanding of the cognitive relationships between the imperial center and its colonial periphery. Cohn, Said, and their students provide a vital foundation to better understand the relationships between power and knowledge in the colonial context. In most cases, their work suggests a hegemonic and unilateral model. In general, the active European or English expert, scientist, and government officer has been credited with creating knowledge and validating objects without the significant participation of colonial intermediaries or collaborators—that is, without an appreciation of the cultural subalterns or their roles in the political economy of imperial knowledge. It is a selective "India" which results from this process of naturalization, and the only authority necessary is that of the imperial agent.[134] We have come to better understand the power of cultural categories and their uses, but perhaps downplayed the dynamic process by which such imperial knowledge was formed and consumed. We have not asked whether that knowledge, in the end, could challenge and perhaps subvert, or at least destabilize, colonial authority, since among its producers were the colonial subjects themselves.

On the other hand, the activities of Australian and South Asian—that is, colonial—exhibition commissioners suggest that the construction of imperial knowledge was a more participatory, multilateral, interactive, and mediated process, which might have contributed to the questioning and undermining of Britain's dominant intellectual role, if not English political rule itself. The knowledge celebrated at the exhibitions resulted from a hybrid of English, Anglo-Indian, and South Asian producers and consumers of science and art in the case of the Raj, and the exhibition activities of self-consciously "Australian," or settler, experts in the antipodes. This was local, colonial, and national knowledge as much as it was imperial.

The organization and representation of knowledge about India, for example, was part of a vast political economy of culture which required the participation of South Asian producers and consumers of ideas, objects, and structures. These men and women were part of a larger policy and circulatory network, which mediated the introduction, diffusion, and representation of Victorian culture and the cultural production of the British Empire. As Cohn argues, Anglo-Indians and English experts transformed objects into artifacts.[135] They did so with the assistance of South Asians and, in many later cases, for an audience comprised of the Raj's subjects. South Asians contributed to the production and consumption of material culture's meaning and value at the exhibitions.

Few, if any, scholars would today question the presence of what the South Asian historian of science Deepak Kumar calls "a close link" between science and imperialism in British India.[136] Expansion, consolidation, profit, and scientific study were partners dancing to the mutually pleasing tunes played by the Raj as piper. This was most notably the case in those areas of scientific knowledge which could be turned towards economic gain, such as geological surveys and botanic gardens. Roy Macleod's work points to similar connections between science and imperial power in the Australasian colonies.[137] Some scholars would extend links between science and imperialism to include parallel connections between art and the imperial experience.[138] This line of argument does not necessarily end with the Saidesque conclusion that totalizing knowledge resulted in total control. While it is true that inventions and experiments were often driven in the interest of commerce—one thinks here about teak and teas harvested in government gardens and mineralogists pointing out coal fields—it was also the case that the representation and performance of science could bring colonial rule into question, just as the development of art schools could provoke nationalist or local reactions to what were deemed overseas and imperial aesthetics and subjects.

In this case, I am calling upon the suggestive work of Gyan Prakash, most notably the cultural analysis of colonial science in British India. Prakash has argued that the performance and spectacle of science at nineteenth-century Indian exhibitions and museums revealed the Empire's power to identify, name, value, and compare elements of the material world but, at the same time, subverted the necessary hierarchy and distance between the colonial subject that is studied and the colonial subject who can study.[139] South Asians consumed exhibition and museum displays; therefore, they became knowing subjects, not only subjects to be known. The performance of imperial knowledge could provoke nationalist response, particularly when it included colonial actors as well as audiences. The allegedly ignorant and unteachable South Asians become, in Prakash's provocative analysis, teachable and knowledgeable.

What about the complementary step, in which some South Asians organized and represented that knowledge about India? In the case of the Royal Asiatic Society of Bengal, local South Asians delivered scholarly papers and sat on the series of governing committees.[140] Indigenous science and art experts, such as Mukharji, organized exhibition and museum displays and wrote their accompanying official guidebooks. By the turn of the century, the Indian National Congress had appropriated the exhibition form in a series of annual nationalist shows. Exhibitions in Calcutta (1901) and Madras (1903) transformed the formerly imperial spectacle into celebrations of *swadeshi*, or economic self-sufficiency, and artistic self-determination.[141] What happens when the subaltern in these and other cases becomes not only the consumer of knowledge but also its producer and organizer; that is, a cultural professional, or expert, a museum curator, or exhibition commissioner? Might this not only be disruptive, but potentially destructive of the colonizer's political enterprise in India? How might South Asians have turned discussions and agendas about exhibiting history, art, science, relics, and material culture itself to their own political advantages by the final years of the nineteenth century?

Anglo-Indian and English officials depended upon the labor of such subalterns for collecting, describing, naming, and comparing the Raj's world of goods. They were agents in the production of knowledge in a parallel to Prakash's South Asian agents in the consumption of that knowledge. Exhibition committees in India and England were composed of imperial representatives, Anglo-Indians, and South Asian "wallahs." For example, the Central Committee for India at the Great Exhibition received exhibits from a series of "native noblemen and gentlemen," and the Bombay Committee collecting and forwarding materials for the 1871 London International Exhibition included prominent local figures, such as Sir Jamsetjee Jeejeebhoy and Dr. Bhau Daji.[142] Buck praised Indian clerks, princes, and Maharajas who "rendered conspicuous assistance in the equipment of the Indian Courts" at the Colonial and Indian Exhibition.[143]

Colonial expertise and knowledge developed from the constant cultural interaction between England and the colonies in the forms of correspondence, publications, congresses, and exhibitions. Colonial exhibition commissioners often oversaw the collection and forwarding of materials exchanged with other institutions and governments, as well as the writing of official guidebooks, doing so as "assistants," or lower-ranking employees in India, but as executive commissioners and Agents-General in Australia. These duties as exhibition officers balanced, or mediated, the relations of status and access, or power and control, between the center and periphery, often creating alternative and potentially competing centers in the colonies and nearly equal partners among some colonists. Their efforts questioned the assumed rigidity of that core-periphery distinction.

There are no formulas to accurately measure the relative degree of imperial influence and colonial autonomy in the construction of knowledge. Intellectual development within the colonial setting and exhibition contexts combined the labor of English, South Asian, and Australian experts; seemingly imperial knowledge evolved from the constant contact among English and colonial producers and consumers. This process could not be under the complete, hegemonic control of imperial figures, or even their representatives in the colonies. Knowledge might produce local power to compete with imperial authority. Colonial commissioners and the science and art professionals they turned to for collecting and evaluating material culture contributed to the anticolonial language, imagery, and knowledge of their respective nationalist movements.

The Raj's art and science policies created South Asian professionals, and the learned societies formed by these experts were part of the movement for national self-determination between the 1870s and independence.[144] Cultural policy provided the language for imperial rule, but also for resistance. Indian (and Australian) professors, artists, museum curators, exhibition officials, and scientists helped construct the grammar of the imagined postcolonial nation by using the language of Victorian imperial knowledge and its popular expression at international and local exhibitions. The practice of art and science contributed to the sense of nationality. This language also contained a socioeconomic component, suggesting the class-based nature or social foundation of national visions. After all, Mukharji and Barry envisioned urban, commercial, propertied futures for their colonies. Mukharji wrote that participation in international exhibitions would awaken South Asians "from the dull apathy" of economic stagnation.[145] The president of the Congress's exhibition committee boasted in 1911 that "the great value of Exhibitions" was their display of industrial resources, creation of markets, and promotion of employment—rather sound Liberal ideals, and ones shared by Mukharji.[146] In the cases of Australia and India, miners and peasants were to become some combination of workers, citizens, and consumers. Commissioners intended exhibitions to resolve social concerns within England and her colonies, as well as tensions between and among those polities.

Colonial participants in the vast imperial cultural system were often forced to choose between the two worlds of nation and empire and were, in both the neutral and political definitions of the term, "collaborators." [147] They offered a seemingly "non-European foundation" for the British imperial system in India, if we choose to identify Mukharji and his colleagues in racial terms, or to look at Barry and his associates as early Australian nationalists. We might choose historical and social terms as alternatives, or complementary components of this hybrid subaltern identity. As such, their participation in the culture of empire resulted in a modernist, national enterprise, an escape from the imprisoning "vanity" of the past.

Museum and exhibition displays in the British colonies represented not only India and South Asians, or Australia and Australians, to the English and other foreigners, but also represented colonial society, culture, and history to the colonial subjects themselves. These materials and experiences influenced the self-images held by South Asians and Australians as they imagined their own postcolonial political communities.[148] Mukharji's art and commercial displays and official writings about them contributed to the way in which Britain came to "know" India, but also to the process by which South Asians came to "know" themselves and, in doing so, offer an alternative political community to the Raj. The endeavors of imperial science and art provided the language, material objects, and authority necessary for the culture of colonial nationalism, or, more specifically, for one compelling and competing definition of India. After all, more than one India could be imagined from the knowledge generated and displayed at the exhibitions.

Writing during the self-conscious days of the Edwardian Empire, C. F. G. Masterman, Radical journalist and M.P., noted a particular irony in the relationship between the acquisition of knowledge and the exercise of imperial power: "The conquering race cannot understand the conquered. No conquering race ever has understood the conquered: except when, understanding, its Imperial rule has begun to decline." [149] This is an important reminder for our studies of the creation and application of colonial knowledge, since we have grown accustomed to associating with effective rule the nineteenth-century European drive to categorize, map, and classify. Referring to the colonial relationship central to most of his readers, Masterman concluded in 1909: "If the English in India . . . commence to understand India, the episode of English rule in India would be nearing its close." Subaltern experts, such as T. N. Mukharji, might very well have played a surprisingly pivotal and ironic role in that final act, as they were seemingly celebrating Victoria's empire and the imperial knowledge necessary to understand India at the exhibitions. The processional of such knowledge might have also been the rather un-Saidesque recessional of England's political power.

3 Commissioners and the State
Power and Controversy at the Exhibitions

Exhibition commissioners were leading actors in the epic nineteenth-century drama of creating imperial and national public cultures. Such cultures included specific administrative structures, languages, traditions, and forms of knowledge at their political centers; it is reasonable to conclude that the commissioners were active in the construction of those rather stationary cultural building blocks. It is also the case, though, that exhibition officials managed the vast world of goods and people at their shows in England, Australia, and India, producing an accessible and participatory political economy of culture which was often mobile. They created, evaluated, and circulated not only knowledge in its many forms, but also social categories and taste. The imperial and local commissioners did so as members of a new cultural aristocracy, revealing both the power of the state and its strong critics. Those cultural experts were part of the general trend in the nineteenth century towards more interventionist and active administrative states. Governments increasingly created and organized both national and imperial public cultures. That pattern evolved in Britain and its colonies as well as on the Continent.[1]

The state called upon those experts for science and art reforms, national education, and the management of public galleries, libraries, and museums. Exhibition organizers were among the first experts in Britain and its Empire to apply modern scientific, economic, and management techniques to the production of culture; that is, cultural activities, ideas and objects. Commissioners undertook such projects as cultural bureaucrats, using the exhibitions in their battle to achieve authority, acceptance, and prestige as a new public "clerisy," or class of seemingly disinterested public servants.[2] Exhibitions were public venues for the experts' authority. From that position, they organized ideas and objects associated with the states' political econ-

omy of public culture. Thus, the exhibitions validated the cultural authority of both the experts as a new class and the state itself. Close connections
with the state proved to be both beneficial and detrimental to the commissioners, who wielded authority in its name; in doing so, however, they also
found themselves vulnerable when public criticism turned against the state
in England and the colonies. They were both lionized and found guilty by
their association with the state.

Supported by government funds and the state's authority, commissioners brought their artistic, organizational, and social agendas to nineteenth-
century exhibitions. Official and private writings reveal that commissioners often defined themselves as connoisseurs, or critics, whose purpose was
to create and direct public taste.[3] Exhibition experts attempted to do so by
establishing accessible collections of material culture and providing opinions to guide the visitors' reading of those objects. Exhibition projects undertaken by these officials suggest that the British imperial state as a cultural
project paralleled similar developments in other modern European societies,
including France and Germany. Here is a mirror to what historians perceive in the centralized nineteenth-century French state and its system of
museums, universal expositions, and art inspectors.[4] Those parallels point
to active, interventionist British and colonial states and to what the Victorians considered the state's "moral" role in forming taste, public collections, and scientific links.[5]

Commissioners and their staffs brought out objects and bodies from private and enclosed spaces, such as homes and factories, reconstructing and
reclassifying them with new meanings and value for shared public observation and consumption at the exhibition halls.[6] They were thus part of the
more general nineteenth-century reorganization of public space and the
bodies and commodities that occupied that space.[7] Participation in that cultural formation enabled experts to organize the empire and its constituent
parts into accessible objects and categories and, in the process, to validate
their sources of authority and the roles of various social groups within that
system. The production of categories and taste was not only an administrative and informational act, since both the action itself and the resulting
displays offered new languages of power and authority for the experts and
the state to which they were attached.[8] Exhibition commissioners were part
of a new cultural elite, or aristocracy, whose authority lay in naming and organizing, not in physically producing, material culture.[9]

Exhibitions transformed into comprehensible and consumable objects
the geographical and political concepts of empire and nation. The power to
collect, label, and organize objects and people—and thus create identities

and inventories—provided the underlying authority for these imperial experts and their spectacles. The ways in which commissioners displayed objects created and made public the imperial and national relations connecting otherwise separate and local items. The ability to make such connections accessible to the general public revealed the power of the commissioners and the imperial state. After visiting the 1886 Colonial and Indian Exhibition, a contributor to the *Westminster Review* concluded that the Raj's displays demonstrated the British and Indian governments as a united "power acting the part of a regenerator, guiding the myriad hands in paths of reproductive industry, making the most of natural gifts, and supplementing them by all the appliances of modern science."[10] Exposition officers and their staffs prepared and oversaw the explosion of surveys, maps, encyclopedias, and other public representations of imperial knowledge, which made sense of that regenerative role. The ability to organize "microcosms of the British Empire" at exhibitions underscored their power as experts, whether as Anglo-Indians, Englishmen, Australians, or South Asians.[11]

Commissioners did not always exercise their cultural and social power without controversy. Debates over pricing and selling exhibition displays highlighted tensions within the ideology of this new professional group, whose members were at times uncertain about their relationship to the market or political economy. While the exhibitions validated the cultural authority of both the experts as a new class and the state itself, the events also made both vulnerable to critics from various parties, such as socialists and conservatives, both the Chartists and Thomas Carlyle. Exhibition officers and executive committees were attacked as part of the governing elite, a "Science and Art clique," or, in the words of one English M.P., "the Kensington Party."[12] They were found guilty of misusing public funds and abusing their authority at the center of political power. The radical voice was more blunt about that "clique." One *Bee-Hive* banner headline declared the 1862 International Exhibition a "FAILURE," in good part because of the commissioners' "jobbery and robbery," which lined their elite pockets at the expense of the nation."[13] In Australia, a local opponent of the 1866–67 Melbourne Intercolonial Exhibition "trusted that a few gentlemen [exhibition advocates and commissioners] would not be allowed to play ducks and drakes with the public money for their own glorification and amusement."[14]

Commissioners in England and the colonies shared social and political problems with one another and with their counterparts across the seas in France. Among those were tensions between imperial and colonial, metropolitan and provincial objectives, focused and persistent opposition to the use of public monies for scientific and cultural projects, the push and pull of party politics, and uncertainty as to which works and ideas should form the basis of national public displays.[15] Exhibitions, then, were moments of often contested public cultural production and consumption in which the state and its new cultural elite were revealed, making both accessible to critics and supporters. There were many vocal public voices of dissent, as well as of praise. This was not surprising, since, after all, commissioners uncovered bodies, relics, commodities, factory production, and art, bringing them out from their hidden privacy for display, evaluation, and consumption. This was, most certainly, an exercise in power, but also a contested revelation, or demystification, of themselves, the state, and political economy.

THE CULTURAL PROFESSIONALS

The ways in which the commissioners shaped the meanings, sales, and display of objects at the exhibitions represented arguments about new sources of cultural authority in nineteenth-century Britain and its colonies. George Cornewall Lewis, Poor Law commissioner, editor of the *Edinburgh Review,* and under-secretary at the Home Office, wrote in 1849 that such cultural specialists provided authority in a new era dominated by "public opinion."[16] Lewis claimed that "the judgement of persons of exercised taste and observation" was necessary to direct this new public culture. Commissioners acting as cultural experts personified what the editors of the *Quarterly Review* termed in 1857 "that larger conformation which is most ordinarily acquired by long and early contact with public affairs, but which is also often gained by extended intercourse with the world, or by the discharge of responsible duties."[17] This was the ideology of the disinterested country gentleman—the ideal type of the universal class—which the new cultural professionals appropriated and which found ready support in the majority of public responses to exhibitions. Here was a new form of cultural, rather than political, virtual representation for nineteenth-century civil society.

The interconnected ideas of a disinterested professional class and the apolitical pursuit of empire were institutionalized by groups such as the Royal Colonial Institute in London. Its officers wrote in their *Objects and Constitution* that "no Paper shall be read, nor any discussion be permitted to take place, tending to give to the Institute a party character."[18] Organized by a self-defined group of "noblemen and gentlemen" in 1869, the institute's growing membership was committed to preserving the British Empire from "a school of politicians" by providing a location for its study and discussion.[19] The reading room, library, and museum offered a place "to undertake scientific, literary, and statistical investigations in connection with the

British Empire" and promote the "interchange of experiences." Complementing the Great Exhibition commissioners who welcomed "all sects, ages, and conditions of Mankind" in 1851, the institute's leaders intended to promote "loyalty" and appealed to the sentiment of "British citizenship."[20]

The idea of the Empire as a state-directed social and cultural community without modern interests and politics was also articulated by John Seeley. The professor and imperial historian expressed this view in a variety of published works and public addresses.[21] Those include the introduction to a series of essays written for the 1886 Colonial and Indian Exhibition, in which he underscored in cultural terms "that vital, sensitive network that covers the ocean."[22] The imperial links revealed the ties of blood, language, tradition, and economics. Seeley imagined further links with the exhibitions, driven by the shared popularity of his *Expansion of England* and the shows. Not a bashful author, Seeley wrote his publisher requesting "thirty or forty thousand copies" of that book to accompany his essay for the Colonial and Indian show at South Kensington and publication of a cheaper edition for the 1900 Paris Universal Exposition.[23] The efforts of imperial politicians and publicists, such as Seeley, to escape accusations of "party" and "interest" and to assume the mantles of "nation" and "empire" at the exhibitions paralleled the assumption of the gentleman's cloak by the new cultural bureaucrats and commissioners who were creating public culture at those shows. Cultural professionals did not necessarily seek a new group identity and ideology founded upon examinations or a specific association, as had other nineteenth-century professions; rather, they sought to assume the stance of a new aristocracy and create national and imperial material cultures.[24] This was the foundation and authority for the new professional ideal.[25]

Exhibition specialists were essential for the functioning of the Victorian political economy of culture, as critics such as John Ruskin perceived it.[26] Exhibitions, museums, and galleries allowed the state to collect cultural objects in the name of the empire and nation, but such a system had to be managed. In Ruskin's words, these managers were "to accumulate so much art as to be able to give the whole nation a supply of it, according to its need, and yet to regulate its distribution so that there shall be no glut of it, nor contempt." As the state's representatives, exhibition commissioners acted as public "stewards"; they managed that system by evaluating, purchasing, exchanging, and reproducing objects at the shows. The stewardship did not end there, since commissioners also organized permanent collections of the exhibits at metropolitan museums and art galleries before circulating some works among provincial art schools and museums.

Administration and evaluation were particularly needed during an era in which so many art works were being removed from their unique place of original production and mechanically reproduced. Others, as Walter Benjamin later suggested, were designed for such reproducibility.[27] As early as 1828, Sir Francis Palgrave's review of the public call for a Museum of Antiquities in London suggested the problems in recontextualizing art works for permanent exhibition. He submitted "that it will be a sacred duty on the part of the Curators of the museum, to refuse any statue or specimen, detached or removed from any structure sufficiently stable to ensure the reasonable protection of its contents. There are few spectacles more rueful than the historical relic torn from the time-honored walls to which it belongs, and turned into a show."[28] To make matters worse, some "curators" combined relics of different regions, styles, and eras; such behavior revealed, to Palgrave's frustration, "the destructive eagerness of the child."

Photography, casting, lithography, electrolyte plating, and other new reproductive technologies created a seemingly limitless volume of moveable material culture. The result? Conceptions of authenticity and artistry— that is, "value" and "labor"—were created, contested, transformed, and sometimes revived. Exhibition commissioners produced the criteria and the organizational structure necessary amidst this flood of materials to validate both the original and the reproduced art works. They made sense out of new contexts, providing objects with value. The exhibitions were not only popular and effective venues for demonstrating those criteria, but also for the ways in which commissioners might turn new technologies to their advantage. Innovations in reproductive processes resulted from joint imperial projects in England, Australia, and India and often received their first general public review at the exhibitions. Indian and Irish art reproductions at expositions demonstrated the cultural experts' authority to evaluate and recreate in this world of new technologies and objects.[29]

New sources of expertise and authority developed during this explosion of visual and physical information. John Stuart Mill observed that in a world of "bookseller's advertisements, and the ill-considered and hasty criticisms of newspapers and small periodicals," it was the role of responsible men of letters to distinguish what was worth reading and consuming.[30] Mill's cultural bureaucrats and experts would create "a collective guild" to review, judge, and oversee the distribution of written materials. The exhibition commissioners positioned themselves as that guild of experts in the world of mass production; they mediated the relationship between material culture's reproductions and originals. This included conventions and treaties about art works and the casting, circulation, and collection of "national antiquities" and colonial relics.[31] These cultural experts determined the authenticity and negotiated the value of such exposition displays, commonly using the authority of the shows' official catalogues and their own government positions to do so.

Experts were also responsible for overseeing the transfer of private treasures to new public galleries. In Palgrave's terms, the cultural professionals replaced the "housemaids" and wealthy private proprietors as the guardians of art and, in doing so, established the texts of national and imperial public culture.[32] Specialists sought to construct accessible public cultures which also authorized their role founded upon, according to one contemporary, "the quality of mind" independent in a scientific, and not literary, way.[33] This echoed Samuel Taylor Coleridge's pleas for a new clerisy, or intellectual establishment, which would create the national and imperial cultural values and practices necessary to link the past and present and avoid social disintegration, class conflict, and unbridled economic individualism.[34] This caste would transcend the utilitarian, commercial interests of early political economy to endow the state and nation with cultural values and continuity.

Coleridge's cultural priests mediated the relationships between the private and public practices of culture. They were a "repository of experience" in cultural goods, services, and ideas. The poet and critic wrote in 1830 that

> The objects and final intention of the whole order being these, to preserve the stores, to guard the treasures, of past civilization, and thus to bind the present with the past; to perfect and add to the same, and thus to connect the present with the future; but especially to diffuse through the whole community, and to every native entitled to its laws and rights, that quantity and quality of knowledge which was indispensable both for the understanding of those rights and for the performance of the duties.[35]

Exhibitions validated this public role for members of the cultural clerisy and the imperial state to which they were linked as the "improver" of civilization. Commissioners throughout the Empire proposed, as members of Coleridge's universal class, integrative and comprehensive cultural collections. Those included works of art, scientific samples, ethnographic relics, and economic products from England, Europe, the colonies, and other regions.

Cultural experts formed an imperial clerisy with their exhibition commissions and juries. They not only fashioned themselves as Coleridge's new artistic and cultural clerisy, but also clothed themselves in gowns similar to those of mine and factory inspectors. Karl Marx considered this ideal type of expert in his discussion in *Das Kapital* of the "periodically appointed commissions of inquiry into economic conditions."[36] Parliamentary commissions required, but rarely received, the services of "men as competent, as free from partisanship and respect of persons" as were the era's heroic factory inspectors, medical reporters, and housing investigators. The Home Office began appointing such scientific experts to investigate mining disasters as early as 1835. Michael Faraday and Charles Babbage, among other experts, made significant contributions to Parliamentary inquests and committees, but not without controversy.[37] The exhibitions provided an additional experience to validate a public role for such experts and their states as "improvers" of civilization.

Imperial policy and exhibitions helped create the myth of such "independent-minded" experts in fields as varied as fine arts, ethnography, natural history and machinery, and as all-encompassing as culture itself. This was true in England, Australia, and India. Sir Henry Cole called them "Eminent men of science" and invited them to classify and judge the exhibits at the Crystal Palace in 1851, for which he served as executive commissioner.[38] The special commissioner for jurors at the 1866–67 Melbourne Intercolonial Exhibition promised readers of the juries' reports that "no interference whatever should be permitted, either with the language of the Reports or the nature of the Awards. The decisions herein recorded are given on the sole authority of the Jurors."[39] Contemporaries reflected that such specialists and their projects contrasted with both the business, or retail, mind in the world of commerce and the political, or party, mind found in legislative bodies comprising local, self-assertive interests. "Thorough impartiality, combined with an efficient technical knowledge," in contrast to the partiality of party politics and the deception of commercial advertising, were considered "vital considerations" for committees of exhibition jurors.[40] Those jurors represented nation and empire, rather than "interests," at least in the minds and words of their advocates.

TEACHING VISITORS TO SEE AT THE EXHIBITIONS

The manipulation of vision was one project in which seeming "impartiality" and "technical knowledge" converged among the exhibition experts. Commissioners shaped the ways in which visitors gazed at exhibits and the visual organization of those exhibits, thereby influencing how the material world was classified, observed, and interpreted—or, in general, naturalized and consumed. The exhibition officials' visual language and taxonomy for the Empire's material world shaped its reading by millions of visitors.[41] This would be the case even if collections were only observed, but not physically engaged by visitors. Others argued at the time that vision itself was an active process. The act of seeing was a metaphor for federation; it suggested a shared, integrative activity for the imperial and national reorganization of society. "To be taught to see," proclaimed Ruskin to his audience at the Cambridge School of Art in the late 1870s, "is to gain word and thought at once, and both true."[42]

The exhibition experience was to a significant degree about teaching vision and the ways to manipulate the process and products of sight. Commissioners established hierarchies of seeing and being seen at these events.[43] The shows demonstrated new forms of vision, including photography, and suggested the empire and nation as ways to visually organize unprecedented variety and quantity. Exhibition classifications paralleled the camera's capacity to organize and authenticate the particular and discrete within a general schema; this process merged the universal and the particular, providing imperial and local or national meanings to the exhibits observed. The world became a series of images expressed in an aesthetic grammar for observation and consumption at the shows. This mirrored the way in which the material world was viewed with the new art of photography.[44] Those connections did not escape contemporaries. Impressed by the scope and scale of the Great Exhibition, one visiting American commissioner claimed that "it is, indeed, the World Daguerreotyped. What a spectacle!"[45]

Exhibition commissioners in 1851 and afterwards visually transformed the unfamiliar, abstract, and distant. "India" and "Australia" retained their fantastic character, but officials also made them comprehensible and tangible by enframing them with what William Whewell, scientist and commissioner, termed a "scientific moral."[46] Such views were common throughout the Empire. A local Hindu proponent of the Bombay Central Museum in the early 1860s suggested the new institution would serve the same purpose as the British Museum: "a book with broad pages and large print, which is seen at least; and by their mere inspection teaches somewhat, even if it be not read."[47] Supporters were confident about the social effects and cultural authority of properly organized and represented collections as texts and spectacles. "Curiosities would be doubly enhanced in their interest by being combined with others and arranged in classes in its shelves, and put up for comparison and illustration. It is by observation and comparison that the work of practical education is advanced; and a good Museum here will be a good School of Art and of Natural History, at which all classes of the people may peacefully and profitably pursue their studies."[48] It was among the imperial and colonial cultural experts' roles to instruct the public on what and how to observe or "read" such industrial, scientific, and artistic objects at museums and exhibitions. They organized the "observation and comparison"—that is, the production and consumption—of material culture. This shared experience of reading thus created its own interpretive communities—empire and nation—with both similarity and distinction, equality and hierarchy, among the subjects and objects of such vision. Exhibition commissioners "combined" and "arranged" the material world.

A similar emphasis on direct and active vision marked the Australian cultural landscape. Trustees of the Melbourne Exhibition Building were keen to offer their galleries as "a national educator, to teach by the eye, to bring under the notice of the rising generation the natural resources of the colony."[49] Among the most influential Australian exhibition commissioners was Eliezer Montefiore, noted art expert and patron. He was best known for his public lectures on art criticism and visual appreciation, as well as for collecting pictures for public galleries in New South Wales and Victoria. He served as an exhibition commissioner at home and overseas for both colonies and, along with Barry, as a trustee for the Melbourne Public Library, Museum, and National Gallery.[50] The exhibitions were part of his wider campaign to develop general artistic taste in the colonies. National and Agricultural Society expositions offered venues where that public taste could be cultivated and shaped. In doing so, though, Montefiore had to reconcile the often competing interests of artists, commissioners, and the general public, encountering a series of "difficulties" requiring "concessions" on all fronts.[51] One way to reduce this "clash" was to expand the art works acceptable for exhibition to the shows, using that wider spectrum to encourage educated, active, and correct vision.

Direct observation at the exhibitions suggested the aura of authenticity, allowed visitors and jurors to judge the quality of objects, and created relationships among the displays and visitors. This public exercise of private vision, essential for the participatory objectives of the exhibition experience, required its own science and experts. Montefiore was such an expert, as was Sir Charles Eastlake in England. Eastlake held commanding positions on the Fine Arts Commission and Royal Academy; he also organized the National Gallery collection in the mid-1860s. At least one M.P. was pleased that the government and trustees had put the gallery's arrangement "into the hands of the ablest man in England."[52] The politician was confident that Eastlake's selections, classifications, and displays would provide the country with an institution of instruction and taste, rather than "a kind of strange old curiosity shop in which curious odds and ends were collected and arranged without any definite object."

Eastlake's exhibition career began with the Crystal Palace in 1851. He served on that first Royal Exhibition Commission and later organized the Fine Arts courts at several shows in England and Europe. Among his publications was the influential essay on vision entitled "How To Observe," intended for visitors to public art collections, such as those at the new National Gallery and the 1857 Manchester Fine Arts Exhibition.[53] Eastlake shared Ruskin's views about vision. The latter had argued in 1859 that "not only is there but one way of *doing* things rightly, but there is only one way of *seeing* them, and this is, seeing the whole of them."[54] Eastlake and other exhibition commissioners provided Ruskin's lessons in comprehensive and integrative vision at the shows. In particular, the royal commissioner intended to "assist the intelligent observation of works of art" by suggesting how one should admire art and why one should do so. Vision was the essential link between the observer, the work of art, and the artist; sight created the necessary "associations" between and among those elements.

Vision provided an aesthetic link, but also synthesized empire and nation; it integrated imperial subjects and national citizens in a shared, simultaneous experience at the shows. The process of seeing the world as a picture was as important as the image itself as the product of that activity. That was easy in theory, but difficult in practice, if for no other reasons than the vast cosmos of objects and people to see at the exhibitions and the potential to see and interpret exhibits in different ways. The commissioners provided one answer to that dilemma of riches by authoring descriptive and illustrated volumes to guide the visitors' vision and make sense of the spectacles. The author of one such guidebook in 1851 thought that his might "relieve some . . . persons from the bewilderment which appears to follow the Oriental dream of splendour to which the [Great] Exhibition at present gives rise."[55] The same could be said about the Crystal Palace's many successors. Reading such catalogues and guidebooks before entering later "crystal mazes" prevented the visitor from "running about in quest of some undefined object" and thus undermining the influence of the commissioners' classifications or ordering of the material world. "Running about" subverted the efforts to guide vision; it turned vision into a chaotic and individualistic association, rather than an orderly and collective one.

Exhibition commissioners echoed not only Eastlake and Ruskin, but also Harriet Martineau, who wrote in 1838 that "the powers of observation must be trained, and habits of method in arranging the materials presented to the eye must be acquired before the student possesses the requisite for understanding what he contemplates."[56] The author and political economist was offering a method for ethnographic observation and analysis; she articulated a science of vision in the relationship between observer and observed, traveler and subject. In a similar way, the writing and reading of exhibition literature, such as guidebooks, integrated the many discrete objects and provided an overarching idea or scientific moral while training the visitors to see. Catalogues and handbooks balanced the totality of the event or collection and the meanings of specific objects. They encouraged Martineau's "habits" of seeing, arranging, and comprehending the physical world as an organic picture. Art museum officials had provided visitors with catalogues during the early Victorian era. Those included titles, names of artists, and short descriptions of the art works. Exhibition commissioners then drew upon that practice to domesticate vision at their own shows, exploiting its power to create and legitimate the world as a picture.

Exhibition officials and the events themselves created and illustrated imperial connections of peoples and products in an era of foreign competition and internal turmoil. An exhibit in "this masterly visualization" represented a class of product, its geographical, ethnographic, and national origin, and its place in the broad sweep of national and imperial culture.[57] This was a total and "living" picture of the ideal empire and nation. Expositions revealed the various forms and meanings of visual representation. They remind us of Martin Heidegger's bold and important claim about the ability to picture the world in an accessible form and the social meaning of such a product.[58] Empire and nation were comprehensible, observed, and sometimes participatory pictures at the shows. By calling upon the authority of vision, exhibition officials expressed the idea of empire as a picture as well as a picture of empire. Exhibition organizers constructed a particular vision of the world or empire and its various social and material parts as a picture. In a similar vein, Timothy Mitchell suggests that French commissioners "enframed" their subjects, such as "Egypt" and "the Egyptians," at the Paris Universal Expositions. They simultaneously created the Orient as a picture and a picture of the Orient.[59]

British and colonial commissioners also participated in that modern quest to privilege vision. Applying various technologies which played off of the myth and power of the eye, those officials both constructed exhibitions as visual texts and edited the way in which they were read. Ruskin lectured his Cambridge audience in 1879 that teaching "sight" is the most important lesson, as it is the function of all art education "to enable the student to see the natural objects clearly and truly."[60] Commissioners taught the public that lesson at the exhibitions. Consensus on the nature of knowledge and its visual production, consumption, and representation underlay the Victorian era's imperial cultural policy. That privileging of sight remained among its stronger undercurrents. Direct and shared vision was the essential form of communication at the Festival of Empire in 1911 as it had been at the Crystal Palace in 1851, although it faced new challenges from the growing medium of film, changes in the aesthetic of painting, and a new understanding of perspective on the eve of the Great War.

CONTEXT AND VALUE AT THE EXHIBITIONS

The display, exchange, testing, and evaluation of objects at the exhibitions formed a political economy of material culture in which officials created new values for those imperial and national objects. Exhibits were provided with meaning from the ways in which the commissioners displayed and described them.[61] The official arrangement of these worlds of goods in the courts and publications created "physical visible statements," in anthropological terms, suggesting the cultural, social, and political value of the exhibits. An exhibit's location and juxtaposition with other items influenced the meaning derived by visitors. Recontextualizing commercial, ethnographic, and art displays within exhibition halls also provided them with an imperial or national "aura" to replace that found at their point of origin and production. A sense of ritual or labor value was replaced by their economic and exchange roles as commodities in the imperial and national networks.[62] Objects also became signs of the racial character and social roles within that imperial system of the various national social groups or types which produced, exhibited, and consumed them. Jurors evaluated objects after experiments and tests, in relation to what could be exchanged for them and according to novelty or authenticity. Aboriginal weapons from the Australian colonies, for example, gained value as contrasts to settler manufactures and fine arts, representations of the colonial commissioners' power to preserve the "authentic" past for display, and as goods to be exchanged for other exhibition displays. They were a form of currency in the market of material culture.

Art works were often appreciated according to a specific aesthetic canon and, in the case of Sir George Birdwood's analysis, the social nature of their artisanal craftsmanship. The Indian commissioner measured the quality and authenticity of the Raj's arts and crafts by the degree to which they represented what he termed "the Hindu Pantheon," or utopian religious and cultural tradition of the South Asian village community.[63] The inclusion of artisans and their traditionalist machinery, such as the looms at Indian Silk Courts, attempted to recreate at the exhibition site itself both the original "aura" of artwares and authentic "India." That organization of traditionalist art courts echoed Ruskin's admonition that one must be "familiar with the conditions of Labour and natures of material involved in the work" of art.[64] Decorative art objects, in particular, were "fitted for a fixed place, such as a temple front or wall-covering for a suite of apartments." This was not a "Portable Art," which suggested an "ignoble art." The art experts and exhibition commissioners struggled to ensure that their mode of display replicated and reconstructed as close as possible Ruskin's original "fixed place," creating value for the "noble" art object and cultural authority for themselves and the state.

Official jury reports emphasized a variety of market criteria for evaluating commercial exhibits, including the strength of woods and terracotta ware, or the taste, common price, fullness of body, and stability of wines and teas.[65] Colonial raw materials derived value from their contributions to the empire's productive wealth and from the sheer amount exhibited. Queensland's commissioners to the 1862 London International boasted that they displayed "400 lbs. of cleaned Sea Island cotton" in contrast to smaller displays from other colonies.[66] Obelisks and pyramids were often used to represent the value of Australian mineral extractions and the promises of future wealth. Visitors to the Garden Palace at the time of the 1879 Sydney International Exhibition were greeted by "The Mineral Trophy," a towering obelisk representing and thus comparing the various Australasian colonies' output in ores. Sections of the trophy matched the vertical sections of coal seams worked in the host colony of New South Wales (Figure 2).[67] The author of a popular handbook for visitors to the Adelaide Exhibition a few years later reviewed the various symbols of colonial production and noted that "the pyramid seems a favourite shape with the majority of exhibitors, and at every turn one sees so many of them that recollections of the land of Egypt, the Pharaohs, and the great pyramids loom up with the strange significance."[68]

The South Australian author was unsure whether these exhibits were intended to copy "Eastern originals," but they certainly revealed the common pattern of "new" settler colonies turning to European and classical models to represent their own history and contemporary society, linking both with a recognizable past. By establishing those standardized forms to represent their mineral productivity, Australia's commissioners provided a visual grammar for visitors and jurors to compare and determine relative and absolute wealth (value) at the exhibitions. Those were expressed in historical and aesthetic terms. Placed alongside the working Australian mining machines, such symbols represented the yield of minerals, such as gold, coal, and tin, and suggested both historical continuity with the wealth of earlier imperial civilizations and optimism in the colonies' future. Two visitors to Melbourne's Intercolonial Exhibition in 1866 remarked in a letter to their relative that the show's mineral pyramid represented the quantity of gold from the colony's mines which could do "a great amount of good" in the civilizing process.[69] They queried, "How many bibles would it print? How many missionaries would it support? How many ships would it build? How many poor would it clothe & feed?" The wealth could be applied to "spread comfort and happiness in many sorrowing hearts," as well as fill the pockets of manufacturers.

THE DEBATE ABOUT PRICING AND SELLING EXHIBITS

Commissioners and jurors could not always agree on the criteria for classifying exhibits or for determining the value of such displays.[70] Some officials and observers called for the application of price tags in an effort to provide a direct market value for visitors and to facilitate sales. Cole included prices for the art works displayed at South Kensington's exhibitions, as well as those later listed and described in official catalogues. He testified to Parliament in his capacity as museum keeper and executive exhibition commissioner that "we always publish the price of everything we buy at South Kensington."[71] Cole's assistant keeper at the Museum complex proposed a series of "Peoples Catalogues" listing the prices of objects at London's International Exhibitions in the 1870s.[72] Perhaps those officials recalled the urban folktale about the son who declines his father's invitation to visit the British Museum because there was no admission price. "It's all free my son," encouraged the father. "Bosh! let's go where it costs something to get in," replied his son, suggesting that an admission price represented value.[73]

Australian commissioners followed suit. They allowed exhibitors to affix prices at most colonial exhibitions, including the Melbourne Intercolonial. This policy earned the praise of at least one local journalist, who claimed that prices allowed visitors to compare domestic and overseas goods to the colony's advantage. The exhibition would prove that "a very superior article could be produced at a price to the consumer equal to that paid for imported goods."[74] Colonial politicians expected that such a reaction would justify Victoria's controversial protectionist tariffs in the face of free trade advocates at home and abroad. A generation later, local Melbourne shopkeepers complained that the fixing of prices on exhibits and their subsequent sale within the halls of the city's Centennial Exhibition was "unfair competition."[75] The debate continued well into the twentieth century.

Disagreement continued, in part, because the listing of prices encouraged on-site sales in England and the colonies. Those transactions were one of the means by which economic communities were brought into contact at these shows, mirroring the promise of political economy, although at the same time threatening local merchants. Charles Babbage, the noted scientist and active exhibitor, enthusiastically claimed that prices, direct observation of the production process, and contact between producers and consumers at the Great Exhibition "removed the veil of mystery" about commercial transactions.[76] Without middlemen at the show, prices linked those groups and demonstrated the market's power. The advocate of political economy added that listing prices verified the authenticity of displays, prevented dishonest exchanges, and allayed fears about false advertising.[77] Prices and sales enabled the Great Exhibition to function as a pure, trustworthy market. After all, to a proud mid-Victorian, such as Babbage, the market not only improved taste and created wealth, but it also civilized and established social order.

But, alas, the executive commissioners at the Crystal Palace failed to realize Babbage's earthly paradise. It was within their grasp, but they forbade the attachment of prices, what the scientist considered "the most important quality by which men judge of commodities."[78] The absence of price was "injurious both to art and to artists: it . . . removes from the field of competition the best judges of real merit" and eliminated the method by which the public could "form any just estimate of . . . commercial value."[79] The evaluation of that merit and value now depended on nonmarket influences, such as aesthetic taste, utility, mere popularity, or the commissioner's official catalogues and essays.

This debate about pricing and selling objects at the exhibitions was part of the wider controversy over the nature of the cultural expert's authority and the power of the marketplace to determine value. As a professional class, did the commissioners truly draw upon the disinterested mind of a new cultural aristocracy, or the retail mind of the businessman? Merchandise was enthroned by the authority of the state, attributions by experts, and the power of the visitors' imagination at the exhibitions, but were these sufficient sources of value in a capitalist society, particularly one in which people were being drawn to new department stores and other forms of mass consumerism? The sense of wonder, fantasy, and optimism at the exhibitions was made more permanent with the growth of those large department stores and their vast overseas collections.[80]

Exhibitions and stores offered for sale similar colonial objects and influenced each other's style of display and advertising. Sir Henry Trueman Wood, secretary of the Society of Arts and of various Royal Exhibition

Commissions, admitted at the time of the 1886 Colonial and Indian Exhibition that "an exhibition is, of course, an enormous advertising agency and to say this is not in the faintest degree to disparage the exhibition system. Traders and customers are brought together in a perfectly legitimate and useful manner."[81] Fascinated by the Paris Universal Exposition, the *Art-Journal's* editors proclaimed "an international exhibition is an immense showroom," organized according to the same principles as "every shop window in the world."[82] Visitors enjoyed the advantages of classification and the facility for comparison of "selected articles" arranged in a manner "to show off the qualities to great advantage." Exhibitions and department stores made the fantastic both observable and tangible; fantasy itself became a consumable commodity at what Benjamin called "sites of pilgrimages to the commodity fetish."[83]

Ruskin noted in 1860 that the consumer purchased what he "wished for" as much, if not more, than what he "needed."[84] Thus, economic wealth and even national and imperial regeneration would be possible by manipulating such "visions, idealisms, hopes, and affections" at the exhibitions. The regulation of the purse was thus a regulation of the heart and imagination, rather than Babbage's regulation of the mind and reason, an appeal to irrational, as much as, or perhaps more than, to rational appetites. One influential twentieth-century expert advised exhibitors to organize their displays in order to "minister to the appetites" of the visitors.[85] He suggested the latter would be impressed by playful "light and movement, . . . activity and development."

Agents-General and other colonial commissioners took these comparisons and suggestions even further. They often transplanted exhibition displays of raw materials and manufactured products to major department stores. Those displays retained the organizational and ornamentation schemes applied at the expositions; department store arrangements mirrored commercial rooms found at the larger exhibitions. Displays of commodities and other forms of material culture shared the exhibitionary mode as more than inventories. Queensland's exhibition commissioners and Agents-General recognized such similarities and noted which forms of representation were particularly attractive to visitors at expositions, department stores, and agricultural fairs in the United Kingdom around the turn of the twentieth century. Lessons learned at the Greater Britain Exhibition in 1899, for example, were subsequently applied to Queensland's displays at Selfridge's in London.[86]

Commissioners and exhibitors created a common mode for advertising commodities. They established shared forms of visual organization, tax-onomies, and loci. Recent studies of Indian popular and visual culture invite us to consider the relative success of such representational modes in England and Australia in light of the challenges they faced in South Asia.[87] This was, after all, not always a passive form of spectacle, or mere observation, since visitors were also consumers, purchasing, tasting, and manipulating those commodities within a specific political context. These could also be spaces of debate among and between the groups competing for power in civil soci-ety—within Australia and India, as well as between England and its colonies. Questions about value, sales, and prices were part of that dialogue at the exhibitions.

Some commissioners disagreed with collapsing the distinctions between exhibitions and department stores, publicly opposing the sale of items within the exhibition halls. They preferred to preserve the "purity" of cul-ture or art and perceived the system of pricing as a threat to the value they provided by testing, demonstrating uses, and otherwise applying their ex-pertise. Sales might suggest the presence of the "retail mind," rather than that of the disinterested professional, violating the separate sphere of culture with the utilitarian concerns of "interest" and commerce. Commissioners sometimes feared attacks from nervous local merchants and charges of run-ning an advertising bazaar, or, as one editor claimed in 1870, "nothing bet-ter than indefinite extensions of Oxford Street."[88] Critics claimed that the exhibits were determined by the interests of advertising, and not by those of science and art. The shows had become "Regent Street with a halo of Royal commissions thrown around it."[89] The debate about including prices and selling exhibits revealed those deeper anxieties about political economy and rational economic behavior during the era of their apparent triumph. These tensions were not resolved for all observers and participants at the exhibitions.

Commercial transactions at the 1887 Adelaide Jubilee International Ex-hibition revealed the difficulties in reaching consensus on the issues of prices and sales. Commissioners advised exhibitors that attractive and artistic dis-plays would prove both popular and profitable; they would capture visitors and consumers. Marbles, frames, columns, and trophies for products such as wines, wheats, and ores would make the exhibits "effective as well as representative" and promote their consumption.[90] "So much really in the eye of the public is governed by appearances and effect more than value & worth," wrote the executive secretary to one exhibitor intending to sell his wares at the show. "After all, the verdict will rest with the *people*"—that is, the visiting consumers. The Finance Committee attempted to control transactions by requiring licenses and rental fees for the sale of items such as pencils, fruits, and oils in the exhibition stalls.[91] Sales were "extensively carried out" inside the main Adelaide exhibition building. Among the most popular sales items were "Eastern goods," including Japanese earthenware, various "Indian" crafts, and vanilla and coco d'mer from the Seychelles. The manager of the profitable Japanese Village provided the host commission with a percentage of receipts as his fee.[92]

Business appeared to favor all parties, but there were complaints. Alexander Dobbie, an influential local manufacturer, wrote to the executive commissioner that exhibitors were selling items manufactured outside of the building.[93] His letter represents the fears of many local merchants in England, Australia, and India that expositions would threaten their businesses. Dobbie expressed the perceived threat to the exhibitions' promises to make direct the relationship between producer and consumer, reveal production processes, and introduce into the colonies only new products. Dobbie argued that sales should be limited to those items "manufactured in the Exhibition," whose quality could be verified by observation, and to other goods, which were "of such a novel character as not to interfere with the ordinary trades people." Those suggestions mirrored the "Sales and Delivery" regulations established by the executive commissioners at the 1883–84 Calcutta International Exhibition. Stall holders were required to pay a weekly fee to preserve their sales privileges, and they could only sell "duplicates" of exhibits or items "made in the Exhibition and shown by Manufacturers."[94]

India's commissioners at London exhibitions after 1851 avoided such problems by constructing separate annexes for the sale of their displays. "All kinds of Indian manufactures [shawls, pottery, wood carving, etc.] tempting to purchasers of taste" were sold in a bazaar adjoining the entrance to South Kensington in 1871.[95] At the Colonial and Indian Exhibition fifteen years later, "considerable space was set apart" for private exhibitors displaying under the direction of sales agents rather than government officers.[96] Commissioners noted that "a good many" Indian and English firms took advantage of this opportunity to increase business both during and after the exhibition in the restricted commercial space. Over four hundred visitors purchased Indian artware after the Franco-British Exhibition closed in 1908. "Hand-worked embroideries and lacquered ware" from Kashmir proved to be the most popular displays and, like the other exhibits, were sold at about one-half of their original price.[97]

EXHIBITION PUBLICATIONS

Commissioners also pursued commerce and knowledge by participating in the explosion of official and private exhibition publications. Not surprisingly, the Great Exhibition's official guidebook and its photographic illustrations provided the most influential precedent for English and colonial commissioners. One journal noted at the time that "this great book, gleaming in blue and gold, and swelling to three portly volumes, . . . equally with the Exhibition itself, may lay claim to a degree of novelty in its conception and production which must long clothe it with a peculiar attraction." [98] It was only one of "the almost countless number of publications . . . on this apparently inexhaustible subject" available before, during, and after the event.[99] Among its nearly equally "countless" successors after the early 1850s were catalogues, guidebooks, jurors' reports, illustrated children's books, and formal economic and scientific studies published for later exhibitions. Some provided the "dry details of goods exhibited and lists of exhibitors," while others described the advantages of living and investing in the colonies for foreign visitors.[100]

"The gigantic scale of the International Exhibition of 1862," began one popular guide, "renders it almost, if not utterly impossible for any individual, however laborious, to acquire a thorough and comprehensive insight into its collective details." [101] Commissioners provided that "insight" and described both the "general impression" and "salient points" of such public collections. The array of "confusing, curious and beautiful" objects also challenged the ways in which the material world was commonly measured. "Many of the objects are so huge," continued the 1862 guidebook, "that they tend to deceive us in regard to the true height, width, and extent" of the building and the displays themselves.[102] Vision required the visible hand of the commissioners not only to ensure that it was a shared experience and social process, but that it did not subvert the authenticity, absolute and relative sizes, and value of exhibition displays. The reading of these guides represented the idea that consumption of cultural objects required the expense of disciplined and policed visual labor, not only individualistic visual pleasure, on the part of the visitors.

Exhibition publications were written for a variety of other reasons and more specific audiences as well. Official reports allowed the authors to enhance their authority, introduce and highlight selected exhibition displays among the vast cosmos of objects, attract tourists and capital, and create new aesthetic canons. Victoria's commissioners were optimistic that French, German, and Italian translations of their official catalogue would encourage new emigrants and investors.[103] In London, Birdwood's Indian Art handbooks provided historical background for exhibits and stimulated a new appreciation of such crafts among scholars, artists, and general visitors. Those volumes included the popular handbook published for the 1878 Paris exposition.[104] Well received by the press at the time of the French show, Birdwood's study was praised as "very interesting and instructive . . . a compendious, concise, and minutely accurate historical account."[105] The London reviewer concluded that "we never met with a catalogue so well worth keeping and studying for years after the [Paris] Exhibition."

Birdwood introduced his interpretations of "ancient" settlements, trade routes, and religious values in addition to describing the origins, materials, and uses of the many exhibits. The latter had been collected by Anglo-Indian government officers, Indian princes, English curators, and "leading importers." Woven carpets and decorated woodwork were among the exhibition objects which promised future commercial relations and revealed the "timeless" aesthetic traditions of the region. Rather than divide exhibits by their region, as was done in some Indian exhibition courts, Birdwood offered interregional comparisons of art types, such as pottery and metalwork, thereby suggesting a sense of "Indian," or national aesthetic unity, a thread which would be picked up by later, self-consciously "nationalist" politicians and artists at the exhibitions sponsored by the Indian National Congress. Birdwood's volume also provided the model for those published later by various Indian government officials, who created an alternative national vision for India, painted with the Raj's palette, rather than the colors of the I.N.C. Those later volumes included George Watt's official catalogue for the Delhi Indian Art Exhibition and Durbar in 1903.[106]

Exhibition publications were also weapons in the very public battle for cultural and intellectual authority, establishing the credibility of English and colonial professionals and resources at home and abroad. Imperial experts, such as Birdwood, publicized and made more permanent their controversial views by means of "official" essays and handbooks, while in the case of New South Wales, the official collection of essays for the 1867 Paris Universal seemingly proved that the "Colony numbers several gentlemen who are prominent in letters and sciences."[107] It was hoped that their contributions to that catalogue revealed the colony's intellectual "progress." Exhibitions might also reveal the tensions inherent in such colonial progress. For example, intellectual development included open debate among those holding differing opinions on scientific and artistic questions. Publications at the time of the 1855 Madras Exhibition articulated disagreements among commissioners from the Anglo-Indian scientific community. One critic felt "compelled by a sense of justice, to speak in terms of unmitigated censure" about official Jury Reports for that exposition, pointing to "the most glaring, and, if they were not at the same time mischievous, some of the most laughable, mistakes" about South Asian geological and fossil formations.[108]

Might progress also create in its wake a sense of nostalgia for a pure past, most particularly in the realm of arts and crafts? The editors of the official catalogue for the Jeypore Exhibition in 1883 thought so, as had Birdwood several years before. They included illustrations and commentary on local artware "to secure, for the benefit of the public, and of the Indian workman, copies of the beautiful art treasures which still exist in the country, but are being rapidly dispersed throughout the world, with the certainty that such masterpieces will never be produced again."[109] The plates and commentaries highlighted works worthy of imitation and those which should be avoided, because of "mischief" resulting from "the contact between Oriental and European art." The catalogue was part of the Raj-wide project of excavating and promoting a seemingly pure, traditionalist, and thus authentic Indian art.

Other authors expanded their intended audience to include general readers in addition to those experts interested in more specific commercial and artistic issues. A. J. R. Trendell produced for the Colonial and Indian Exhibition "a popular series of Colonial handbooks, of a wider scope, and of a more general and instructive character" than the commonly published specialized reports.[110] Trendell, a local barrister, also edited volumes for previous South Kensington exhibitions during the early 1880s. His books for those and the Colonial and Indian show included an introduction to each section "written by the first experts of the day" and were intended to be the highest and most useful popular authority on the subject "for the benefit of the masses" of the British public. Rather than only a list of items in the exhibition courts, these handbooks could, in the case of the 1886 show, entertain as well as inform, while offering the Agents-General and "other competent Colonial Authorities" the opportunity to solicit emigrants and investors.[111] Trendell's popular essays and guidebooks paralleled the official publications of Queensland's commission. Its leading members requested funds from the colonial secretary in Brisbane for "essays, written in popular style and capable of being readily understood by the masses" at the Colonial and Indian show.[112] Maps and photographs illustrated the essays in this official attempt to not only solicit middle- and working-class emigrants and investors, but also transform the popular perception of Australia and introduce the relatively new colony of Queensland.

The powerful medium of exhibition essays, guides, and catalogues extended the advantages of the events to a wider and longer-term audience. "The life of the Exhibition is limited to a few months at the most," noted a journalist preparing a guide for the general public at the time of the 1878 Paris Universal.[113] "We propose, however, to supply a more permanent record of the most worthy features of the Exhibitions." Exhibition publications were brought to the longer-term attention of a community larger than the number of visitors and other commissioners by this empire-wide circuit of knowledge and material culture. Volumes were distributed and exchanged among British and colonial learned societies, mechanics' institutes, museums, and public libraries as more permanent records. Visitors to the Bombay Chamber of Commerce's library were offered nearly twenty official exhibition catalogues and jurors' reports in the late 1880s. This collection included volumes from English, Australian, Indian, and European shows.[114] In the case of Australia, a "set of publications in connection with the . . . Fisheries Exhibition" and copies of the official handbooks from the Colonial and Indian Exhibition were forwarded by South Australia's Agent-General for Adelaide's Public Library and the use of its many readers after the series of South Kensington shows in the mid-1880s.[115]

The information created by and for the exhibitions was also distributed in various other ways to additional audiences in other parts of the world. Official publications provided information for "popular" encyclopedias of practical information in England. Across the Atlantic in America, George Dodd wrote a "useful" dictionary during the late 1860s and turned to "trustworthy sources," including the jury reports from French, British, and North American exhibitions to provide information on "those numerous matters which come generally within the range of manufactures and the productive arts."[116] By the turn of the century, Francis Edwards, a London bookseller, included in its "Australasia and the South Pacific" collection the catalogues and jury reports from most of the region's major exhibitions, including those held in Melbourne, Sydney, and Christchurch.[117] The post-exhibition reading of handbooks, guides, and other publications assisted the diffusion of the shows' influence and the commissioners' authority as experts. As these texts spread, so did the exhibition experience and the structures of knowledge it represented.

EXHIBITION COMMISSIONERS AND THE STATE

Most of the exhibition publications represented official governmental displays and policies. This reminds us that exhibition commissioners generally embraced and represented the state. They sought and, more often than not, received financial contributions from English, Australian, and Indian governments.[118] Debates over funding were not uncommon, but outright denial was. Public funds were used to pay salaries, purchase and transport exhibits, build exhibition halls, and publish reports. By 1910, the English government had allocated over £650,000 in direct financial expenditure to twenty-five of the most popular exhibitions since 1851.[119] The colonial shows were poor cousins in relation to the monies expended for Royal Commissions at the Paris Universal, Philadelphia Centennial, and Chicago Columbian Exhibitions. In addition to grants from the public treasuries for their exhibition collections, English commissioners, such as Cole and Birdwood in London, participated in the shows as part of their regular employment and thus were compensated in the form of their government salaries.

Cornewall Lewis noted that such official support was a necessity for cultural experts and their projects. "Scientific and literary endowments," as well as employment at public museums, libraries, botanic gardens, and academies, were the "best provision" for those specialists unsupported by the naked market economy.[120] Lewis continued with a justification for public expenditure on such noncommercial ventures. That funding was "intended to afford to the cultivators of sound knowledge and learning facilities which they could not derive, in an equal degree, either from their own means or from private patronage." Exhibition commissioners used public funds to regulate the political economy of culture from their positions as state "cultivators," or government bureaucrats. Even Cole, formerly a strong advocate—at least in public—of the laissez-faire approach, eventually called for such a union, or, in his terms, "dovetailing" of public and private interests forged by "the Government."[121]

From the earliest exhibitions in the 1850s, colonial governments and commissioners dovetailed more efficiently than their complements in England. This was for a variety of reasons, revealing different ways in which commissioners were connected to their respective states and the various roles that those states played in colonial politics and culture. In general, there were fewer bureaucratic and internal governmental divisions in British India and Australia than in England; that condition enabled colonial commissioners and government officers to focus their efforts and funds. Colonial states also readily admitted the necessity of their direct financial and administrative participation in public culture, such as exhibitions, museums, and art galleries. This was the result of social, political, and economic circumstances.

In part, colonial governments were responding to the lack of local aristocratic patrons, rarely a problem in England. Australian pastoralists and

Indian princes struggled to, but could never fully, wear the mantle of England's "gentleman" patrons.[122] On the other hand, since many local Australian politicians were active in philosophical and scientific societies and colonial governors served as their patrons, it is not surprising that offers for legislative assistance were often forthcoming. This was nearly always the case during the collection of "national" exhibits for overseas shows or the sponsorship of local and intercolonial exhibitions and museums. Furthermore, the pattern of colonial state intervention in questions of public policy, such as railways and land management, was well established during the early years of official colonization in New South Wales and Victoria.[123] Exhibition organizers drew upon this local tradition, consented to by even the most "conservative" pastoralists and politicians. That consensus informed the colony's exhibition and other cultural activities, privileging formal government funding and coordination, rather than the actions of voluntary societies and temporary semigovernmental bodies. Colonial exhibitions would not have been possible without that official funding and other public contributions, such as in-kind services provided by government printers.[124]

Private patrons and local voluntary societies rarely had the funds themselves to host ambitious intercolonial and international exhibitions, or even to participate in promising overseas shows. Commissioners and exhibitors required and received direct government grants. Public money in Australia, for example, financed the collection by government officers of timber, mineral, and ethnological exhibits and the publication of official handbooks. Indian organizers were also in pursuit of public monies for their shows and looked enviously at the wealth of British and European exhibitors and commissions. The editors of the *Calcutta Review* noted in the mid-1860s that English "cattle shows and other agricultural exhibitions" were generally undertaken by private societies, whereas the Bengal Agricultural Exhibition was "an enterprise originated by the [Indian] Government, and its expense defrayed out of the revenues of the country."[125]

Participation at the 1880–81 Melbourne International Exhibition underscored the necessity for the Indian government to take a direct financial and organizational role. British private merchants and exhibitors assumed much of the responsibility after their exhibition official arranged the courts; "on the Government of India, however, the whole of an Exhibition, from purchasing the exhibits in India to finally disposing of them, falls. Private trade, if left to itself, would do nothing."[126] The government embraced this Melbourne opportunity and spent Rs. 37,000 for general exhibits and offered the Indian Tea Syndicate an additional Rs. 10,000 for its displays. Several years later, government officials promised £20,000 for the Colonial and Indian Exhibition's guarantee fund.[127] The Indian government also provided the services of its employees, such as engineers and architects attached to the Public Works Department.[128]

Local governments in India supplemented the exposition grants from their central government. Significant amounts of local money were provided for selected exhibitions. The Bengal government contributed Rs. 50,000 for the collection and display of articles at the Calcutta International Exhibition in 1883–84, and the Bombay authorities provided over Rs. 89,000 for exhibition activities during the 1858–1871 period.[129] The Bombay government funded the purchase, transportation, and insurance costs for exhibits and compensated the local Agri-Horticultural Society for its expenses. Government funds contributed to exhibitions in Paris, London, Agra, Akola, and Nagpore. Local authorities also donated public land for Indian shows.[130]

Those colonial governments' generosity and focus contrasted with popular perceptions of the English government's role in the funding and organizing of exhibitions. Uncertainty about what to expect from the government diminished the effectiveness of English exhibits and limited the powerful union of public and private interests which drove the Australian and Indian displays and shows. This was particularly the case for English participation at overseas expositions. The chairman of the British Art Committee at the St. Louis International Exposition in 1904 complained about confusing directives from the government. The Foreign Office, Board of Trade, and royal commissioners intervened in European and North American exhibitions, but did so in often contradictory ways. The chairman testified that the "primary cause of the difficulties" was that Britain, unlike other powerful countries, such as Germany and France, did not have a "permanent and special department" for organizing displays at either English or overseas exhibitions.[131]

The confusion and controversy at the St. Louis show and the strong commitments of the French, German, and American governments to the earlier Columbian Exposition in Chicago provoked the establishment of a Parliamentary Committee to review the status and responsibilities of the British government at international exhibitions. Committee members faced the explosion of exhibitions at the turn of the century and the stunning realization that Britain's economic competitors in Europe and North America, as well as the newly independent-minded colonies, were turning these events to their own commercial advantage. Solutions for current exhibition dilemmas required consideration of previous exhibition actions at home and abroad.

Direct governmental oversight, direction and funding of exhibition activities in Australia and India had been more focused and thus more effective than in England. India and Australia had already developed administrative departments specifically for exhibitions; England did not do so until the turn of the twentieth century. The organization of exhibits and exhibitors generally came under the umbrella of an ad hoc Royal Commission during the first fifty years of official British exhibition participation. Officers of the Science and Art Department and the Royal Society of Arts oversaw the commission's activities, but there was only limited direct government participation.[132] On the other hand, there were many personal links among these bodies, since Cole, Wood, and Cunliffe-Owen held positions in the government, private societies, and exhibition commissions. One scholar notes that "a core group from the Society of Arts . . . moved *en masse* to the [1851] Royal Commission and became its executive branch."[133] By the time of the International Health Exhibition in the mid-1880s, the Royal Society was regularly loaning jurors, offering prizes, and distributing information for exhibition commissions. The society's reading room and library for the Health show provided colonial and foreign books about education, public health, and work-related injuries.[134]

Walter H. Harris, a former sheriff of London and a royal commissioner for the Chicago Columbian Exposition in 1893, corresponded with the Foreign Office to suggest the creation of a permanent, centralized, and governmental exhibition committee.[135] This paralleled the single official committee assisting German and French exhibitors. Harris drew upon his experiences at North American, European, and Australasian exhibitions to propose large-scale, direct government subsidies for British Sections at future shows and oversight of exhibits and funds by a "Commissioner-General." The latter could "take up his residence in the city of the Exhibition," where he would have "full power to act in concert with other foreign Commissioner-Generals" and the host executives to ensure a strong showing by the British exhibitors. This would prevent a repetition of the failures at Chicago, where, Harris concluded, the British "were signally outstripped by Germany."

The Board of Trade created its Exhibitions Branch and Committee ten years later to study expositions and oversee official British exhibits at shows in North America, Europe, and the colonies. This was a response to complaints from British exhibitors and in the face of significant contributions by centralized foreign commissions. Established by Lloyd-George, President of the Board of Trade at the time, the committee convened in 1906 to study "the nature and extent of the benefit accruing to British Arts,

Industries and Trade" from formal and official participation in the international exhibitions. Members and witnesses confronted hostility or no interest on the part of many British manufactures to exhibit and questioned
whether government financial and administrative support might stimulate
additional private-sector involvement.[136] This was an era of economic warfare; thus, the committee concluded that British producers could not afford
not to exhibit. The report's authors also noted that "participation and representation of the nation's industries cannot fail to be ultimately of material advantage to the commercial development" of Britain itself. The union
of private and public funds and expertise would ensure "effective and complete" industrial and artistic displays at international exhibitions and a de-
fensive stand against aggressive foreign economic adversaries.

Assistance for exhibitions had been arriving from the state in various
forms, some of them rather indirect. Among these were subsidized transportation rates and reduced customs charges. The New South Wales government, for example, supported the 1870 Sydney Metropolitan Exhibition by providing grants to the local Agricultural Society for the collection
of exhibits and their subsequent transmission to the 1871 London International Exhibition, and offering free use of the public telegraph lines and
railways.[137] Local authorities established special trains for provincial and
intercolonial visitors and lowered customs barriers for exhibits originating
outside of the colony. In England, Her Majesty's Board of Customs regarded
the 1862 London International Exhibition "as a bonded warehouse," and,
under certain conditions, permitted the free import into the exhibition of
objects liable to duty.[138] This policy repeated the earlier admission without
payment of duty of foreign and colonial exhibits bound for the Crystal
Palace.[139] Additionally, strong patent and trademark legislation protected
from piracy any new machines or innovations exhibited during the show,
thereby reassuring some fearful exhibitors.

Such extensive governmental support for exhibitions calls into question
one of the sacred cows of "1851." Organizers and general supporters claimed
that exhibitions were possible without government assistance and much of
the Crystal Palace's mystique resulted from the popular impression that it
was a product of only private initiative, learned societies and voluntary cooperation. Ironically, Cole, an employee of the English government, was
among the most vocal sources of this mystification. He intended to establish "Annual International Exhibitions of Industry . . . relying not on state
aid, but on the voluntary support of an educated people."[140] Private guarantors, the participation of commercial and scientific societies—including
the Royal Society of Arts and Chambers of Commerce—and grants from

the Royal Commission of the Great Exhibition were very helpful, but the English, Australian, and Indian governments provided significant and essential direct financial support to exhibition commissions, as well as the indirect assistance noted above.

Governmental participation "imparted an official character" to exhibitions.[141] It enhanced and magnified the event's image in contrast to that of the private shows managed by showmen, such as Imre Kiralfy in England and Jules Joubert in New Zealand, Australia, and India. Those entertainment entrepreneurs could never completely escape suspicions of personal greed, speculation, secretiveness, and unreliability. Australia's Agent-General sued the Franco-British exhibition authorities, including Kiralfy, because of lighting, space, and advertising inadequacies. One Australian commissioner wrote home that "Mr. Kiralfy is profuse of promises, but very niggardly of performance."[142] Such criticisms aside, Kiralfy and his exhibition company annually turned Earl's Court into a popular wonderland of fantasy and consumption during the 1890s; he personally assisted with a variety of international exhibitions as well.[143]

Although his exhibitions were also generally popular, shadows of doubt continued to surround Joubert as well, most notably in Calcutta. He was accused of organizing its International Exhibition for "no end to gain save his own aggrandisement" and of ill-treating South Asian visitors.[144] The local press called for the government to organize the next exhibition, since "there is nothing an Australian speculator . . . can do well, that the state, through its own officials, cannot do better."[145] At least the exhibition accounts would be public in that case. In a more private vein, Lockwood Kipling wondered in a letter to his wife "why Joubert should be in it [the Exhibition] to take the money only—a wonder which still remains."[146]

The inclusion of private guarantors for exhibition projects, on the other hand, reaffirmed the participatory nature of such events, linked showmen and commissioners with the host community's elites, and suggested a further merging of public and private interests. Promoters and guarantors for Australian exhibitions included prominent politicians, colonial secretaries, major merchants and businessmen, pastoral companies, foreign commissioners, and exhibitors.[147] In the case of the Colonial and Indian Exhibition, English and imperial contributions exceeded £199,000 before the official opening; this was an amount, according to the Royal Society of Arts, which was "far in excess of that of any" previous exhibition at South Kensington.[148] Funds from colonial governments and private parties, such as publishers, the Union Bank of Australia, and the Peninsular and Oriental Steam Navigation Company, provided "the financial basis" for the Royal Commission to carry out its organizational plans without the fear of bankruptcy and loss at the end of the exhibition.[149]

The Council of the Royal Society of Arts and the royal commissioners for the Great Exhibition solicited private contributions for the 1862 London International's guarantee fund. Their experience provides insight into the construction of "private" support for such public events. The circular requesting financial support received mixed responses. Railway companies, Sir Charles Dilke, Joseph Paxton, and various members of the South Kensington science and art clique, such as Cole, were among the contributors. In contrast, the rejections stand out for their echoing of common complaints against the 1862 and other Kensington Gore projects. One respondent suggested that the International Exhibition was unnecessary. The Crystal Palace at its new home in Sydenham fulfilled the country's need to publicly display "those improvements and discoveries in the several branches of Manufactures and of Science since 1851" (one of the stated purposes of the 1862 Exhibition). An Epsom gentleman apologized that "the feelings of the people of this locality are not in favour of the project" (repeating common provincial-metropolitan tensions concerning the funding of events in London). In the end, the campaign was generally successful with a lengthy list of common guarantees of £1,000 per person.[150]

CRITIQUING THE COMMISSIONERS:
THE ESTABLISHMENT UNDER ATTACK

The commissioners' associations with the state and host governments were not always seen favorably by contemporaries. In England, links with "the establishment," or William Cobbett's "Beast" and "THING," could provoke attack from an array of critics, most notably those suspicious of the growing state, the persistent influence of the aristocracy, and the power of an appointed "Science and Art Clique."[151] Reformers and radicals agreed that the exhibition commissioners represented what was wrong with English society and governance, rather than what was right. Babbage, for example, analyzed exhibitions in light of such shortcomings, as well as triumphs. The prominent scientist provided his most systematic analysis of exhibitions and, in particular, the Great Exhibition in *The Exposition of 1851; or, Views of the Industry, the Science and the Government of England.* Two editions were published during 1851, and the volume was the subject of a lengthy essay in the *North British Review.*[152] Babbage's was not an insignificant voice. He had already achieved considerable fame by the time of the show as the author of *The Economy of Manufactures* and as the inventor of the Calculating Engine, or Differential Machine, an embryonic computer.[153]

Babbage's critique of the Great Exhibition was an attempt to shine a critical light upon larger problems. He proposed using the Crystal Palace "for taking a more correct view of the industry, the science, the institutions, and the government of this country," all of which were revealed in "this Diorama of the Peaceful Arts," as he termed the exhibition.[154] For example, the failure to properly integrate learned "associations" and practical scientific exhibits at the Crystal Palace was evidence of governmental disregard for science and scientists, illustrating "the position of science in this country," where its practitioners were not recognized as a profession or a class.[155] By 1862, this train of thought had curved to include what he considered disdain for his own scientific exhibit, the "Difference Engine." He noted with irony that it had been "placed . . . in a *small hole* in a *dark corner,* where it could, with some difficulty, be seen by six people at the same time."[156] In contrast, "a trophy of children's toys, whose merits, it is true, the Commissioners were somewhat more competent to appreciate," filled a prominent position in the exhibition hall.

What was at stake here, besides the pride of Charles Babbage? His anger found three targets: the continuation of patronage within English society, which enabled some exhibitors to claim prominent places for their displays and left others in the "dark" corners; the continued lack of interest in practical science among the governing elite and its representatives, the commissioners; and, in a slightly different twist, the commissioners' inability or reluctance by the time of the second "great" exhibition to treat exhibitions as money-making, commercial enterprises. Working-class and other radical commentators argued that the London International Exhibition turned a profit, albeit a corrupt one enjoyed only by the commissioners, speculators, and "moneyed-interest."[157] In contrast, Babbage saw the missed opportunity to turn such a profit. "Favouritism" and ignorance created an excessively rigid economy at the International Exhibition, preventing the calculating machines and other potential money-generating exhibits from producing both public gratification and profit.

Two years after the show, Babbage suggested in his autobiographical *Passages from the Life of a Philosopher* that all of the working calculating machines could have been placed in one room, to which admission would have been charged.[158] The experience might have included lectures, observation of mechanical drawings, and the sale of "illustrations of machinery used for computing and printing Tables." In one final slight upon the commission, Babbage concluded that if its "dignity" did not permit its members to make money from this court, then they could have announced that the proceeds of the tickets would be forwarded to "the distressed population of the Manchester district." There would then have been, in his view, even more "crowds of visitors" to see the calculating machines in action. He wrote this with full knowledge that the commissioners had proven reluctant to contribute to the relief effort in 1862 in a marked contrast to the charity of many other public figures.

Critics of the exhibition commissioners could also be found on the opposite side of the economic playing field from Babbage, that is, among Victorian radicals or, more specifically, within the republican, socialist, artisanal, and working-class press. The editors of such journals and newspapers often found economic or class-based targets among the commissioners and private organizers. Criticism and analysis were brought to bear on the ways in which commissioners managed the exhibitions and the composition of those commissions. In this way, the Victorian Left attacked not only the new cultural experts as an elite, but also the state which sponsored and apparently benefited from their actions, interpreting the commissioners through class-colored lenses. This critique brought the passion of their anti-aristocratic visions of "Englishness" to bear on what appeared to be celebrations of orthodox, Victorian-era national and imperial identities, societies, and states.

As early as February 1850 and well over one year before the Crystal Palace officially opened, the *Mechanics' Magazine* was expressing discontent about the composition and behavior of the Executive Committee charged with overseeing the event.[159] A "low state of moral feeling" was found amidst its members, many of whom were, in the words of the editors, "obscure individuals" from the Royal Society of Arts. Not men with eminent and confidence-inspiring names, they were "people distinguished for nothing whatever in the world." They were self-serving; they put themselves forward to "reap the benefits of the fraud practised on the Crown." In this case, the journal was not attacking the exhibition itself but, in a sense, reworking the old theme of the "King's Evil Advisors."

Prince Albert, the good "Patriot King," was surrounded by impostors or, perhaps even worse, the nominees of impostors. The Prince Consort gave his name to the commission, but he could hardly be expected to watch over the affairs with hourly diligence. As a result, the event was in the hands of a "pack of characterless nobodies," such as Cole, Matthew Digby Wyatt, and Francis Fuller, examples of a new breed of cultural bureaucrats, who represented their own elite "interest," rather than that of the nation. The Crown was in danger of being "sullied" by its alliance with such "trickery and imposture" in the form of a commissioner's conspiracy. The commissioners were perceived as their own party and not disinterested public servants.

The magazine's attitude toward such bureaucrats and experts, as well as their home, the Royal Society, hardly improved by the time of the London International twelve years later. The editors' criticism revealed uncertainties about the new forms and practitioners of intellectual and cultural authority during the mid-Victorian era.[160] Could these men and their voluntary societies be trusted as a learned elite in the transition away from traditional authorities on scientific, artistic, and economic questions? In political terms, would they represent the nation or only the aristocratic and corrupt Establishment? The *Mechanics' Magazine*'s review of the Royal Society's annual exhibition before the South Kensington show provided answers to both questions. The editors criticized the society's elitist stance and apparent lack of interest in applied models. The show did not fulfill the purpose of an exhibition; that is, it did not provide "records of the nation's progress."[161] Here was only "a quiet little collection got together somehow, to amuse the secretary and tickle the vanity of a few investors." National shows required exhibition space and displays, which only the government could provide. In this way, the inadequacies of the society's exhibition were further proof of the need for public organization and funding of the upcoming London International and its separation from the Royal Society.[162]

Over ten years after the *Mechanics' Magazine* first questioned the scruples and competence of the Great Exhibition's Executive Committee, the *Bee-Hive* found a similar target in the London International Exhibition's executive commission. Its leading editorial writer, "Scourge," critiqued the "jobbery" and "mismanagement" of the event, focusing on the ways in which the aristocratic and commercial classes benefited from the exhibition in 1862 at the expense of the workers and the nation.[163] The "monster booth of Kensington," as the writer nicknamed the show, revealed not only speculation and "a vile, trading, huckstering spirit," or the drive of mid-Victorian capitalism, but also its ally within the state, "the 'art and science' clique." What was this cabal? The powerful combination of bureaucrats, officers, and experts from the Department of Science and Art, the Royal Society of Arts, the *Times*, and the circle around Prince Albert most responsible for organizing and publicizing the exhibition. The *Mechanics' Magazine*'s shadowy figures had now moved from outside to within the state, where they were highly visible. They organized from that privileged position an event with more visitors and more open days than the Crystal Palace, but one with less profit and a series of "discouraging" financial statements.[164] The exhibition as a form of entertainment and education was not at fault, but the "clique" was.

"Scourge" continued that this "clique" had organized the event for its own financial and political gain. Its members had allowed contractors to ignore overtime pay for workers building the exhibition structure. At the same time, those commissioners had refused to contribute to the nationwide relief fund for Lancashire, as Babbage and much of the public knew.[165] Readers were reminded that even the Music Hall owners had donated to that fund. This was one more sign that the commissioners and their exhibition did not represent the interests of the nation and people, but the interests of an elite state, the establishment, "or parochial authorities of South Kensington." Rich politicians and aristocrats got fat off of the show, filling their "well-lined pockets" with various schemes and "dodges," while starving working-class families got thinner. The leading editorial about the show's closing concluded, "Shame and disgrace upon these Commissioners that they so mismanaged their business, as to be unable to sacrifice even one day's receipts in the cause of charity!" for Lancashire's unemployed or for the widows and orphans created during the construction of South Kensington. Mismanagement and speculation tampered with "the rights and wages of . . . workmen" before, during, and after the show.

CONCLUSION: EXHIBITIONS, COMMISSIONERS, AND THE LEGACY OF DISCONTENT

Criticism of exhibition commissioners and the state from radical groups continued during the later nineteenth century. *Reynold's Newspaper* considered the Colonial and Indian Exhibition in 1886 "a wretched spectacle" intended to celebrate the union of capital and Crown at the expense of the English worker and colonial subjects.[166] Perhaps the show might reveal what "the people can do," suggested the editors, "in spite of bad government." In that case, the exhibition would be more successful than previous ones, which promised peace but were followed by years of war, or held out the promise of public art collections but were turned into "frequent junketings." Those included "the establishment of the Sheepshanks collection in an aboriginal hut" after the 1862 London International. The journal's republican sentiments also found fuel in the Prince of Wales' attempts to turn the exhibition into a celebration of Queen Victoria and the authority of the Crown over the far-flung British Empire. Ironically, the exhibits suggested "the lesson . . . of what free peoples can do apart from governmental machinery," or at least in the case of the Empire, far away from the English state.

The radical press continued its assault after the turn of the century. Commissioners and events were criticized for celebrating the connections between Empire, Crown, and state, and for exploiting the English worker. The *Clarion*, for example, attacked the Festival of Empire Exhibition in 1911 as part of the Coronation's "circus, . . . a great debauch of pageantry." [167] This was the biggest dose of "monarchical flummery that even this nation has had to endure." Among those exploited were "the Coronation slaves," or the adolescent seamstresses hired to produce the fancy tailored products for the various ceremonies that year. Attendance at the series of events also cost the workers wages and the loss of free meals at school for their children, whose normal routine was overturned by the celebrations.

Expositions, like museums, mechanics' institutes, political economy, and the state itself, appeared to be self-regulating "bee-hives" of Victorian equipoise, seemingly without but, in fact, permeated with conflict, class, party, and interest. Such experiences, however, offered for some a moment of reconciliation and mediation as a parallel to the ideal integrative, participatory, nineteenth-century state and the various disciplinary institutions discussed by influential scholars of the Victorian era.[168] Exhibitions invited participants to share an imagined and envisioned nation and empire, intended, according to one observer in 1862, "to bring painters from their studios, bookish men from their books, philosophers from their abysses of inner consciousness, gardeners from their artful-natural parterres, and foreigners from all quarters of the globe." [169] Such varied interests and social groups could physically mingle, consume, and observe at the exhibition, suggesting a participatory or active cultural formation. Participation in the exhibitions also helped affirm the public roles and authority of the commissioners as new experts, strengthening the state's cultural power in England, Australia, and India during the era of New Imperialism.

On the other hand, the events also provided opportunities for dissenting views to be expressed and, perhaps as important, focused. The exhibitions suggested an equipoise but in doing so revealed the fissures and tensions within that order, making the state and its commissioners open to criticism from various positions on the political spectrum. Here were historical moments that revealed the sinews holding together society in England and its colonies, as well as the ways in which that revelation crystallized dissent. Exhibitions were contests, then, for the hearts and minds of the Victorians and Edwardians, rather than only festivals of uncontested nationhood and rational recreation.[170] Some critics even attempted to appropriate the exhibitions for their own alternative visions of England, Australia, India, and the Empire. The historian Victor Kiernan once remarked that "nations, like individuals, are only aware of themselves in any critical sense at times of intense experience."[171] He referred to wars and revolutions, but we might extend his argument to include the intensity of organizing and visiting the exhibitions between the Crystal Palace in 1851 and the Festival of Empire sixty years later.

4 Consumers, Producers, and Markets

The Political Economy of Imperial Federation

Imperial economic displays inspired such awe and wonder at the exhibitions that visitors often found them difficult, if not beyond their capacity, to describe. They were truly "marvellous and affecting." After touring the British and colonial courts at the 1878 Paris Exposition, the secretary of the Royal Colonial Institute told his London audience that "it was impossible for anyone to find himself within the boundary of that vast arena without being deeply impressed. A feeling of wonder, and well nigh of awe, must have struck the most casual observer, at the vivid grouping of the almost countless mass of objects of beauty and utility, and the myriad articles of human skill spread out in every direction, in such rich and abundant profusion."[1] Eight years later, one British M.P. was so overtaken by seemingly "countless" objects of imperial wealth at the Colonial and Indian Exhibition that he rose in Commons to call for immediate Imperial Federation, proposing a conference of English and colonial leaders "so that advantage will be taken" of the show in foreign affairs, commerce, and defense.[2] Public praise for commercial exhibits during the Victorian and Edwardian periods also provoked calls for more practical projects, such as the building of imperial trade museums, which England's continental competitors enjoyed in Berlin, Vienna, and Paris.[3]

Australian and Indian commissioners, exhibitors, and businessmen shared this enthusiasm for commercial displays. They hoped that improvements in trade and production would result from touring the commercial collections and studying both the discrete exhibits and the overarching imperial treasure chest. Colonial participants were optimistic about the local and national, as much as, if not more than, the imperial economic advantages to be gained by exhibiting. Participation in the apparent political economy of the Empire at the shows might be the first step in creating their own Australian and Indian national political economies with overseas connections. Celebrations of imperial wealth revealed potential conflicts between British and colonial economies, agents of the former attempting to secure imperial control, and participants of the latter arguing for increased commercial independence. Exhibition displays revealed both paths.

South Australia's *Journal of Industry* encouraged local merchants and manufacturers to display their wares at the 1911 Festival of Empire Exhibition in London. Its editors promised that the event "will be exclusively a British Empire Exhibition" to illustrate imperial economic wealth and self-sufficiency.[4] Readers were informed that "the main idea of the organisers is to show that every product needed in any part of the Empire may be produced in some other part, and that we are not necessarily dependent on foreign countries for our supplies." The Crystal Palace show would demonstrate the apparent strength of the economic links between England and the Australasian colonies, suggesting economic interdependence, or perhaps, more radically, economic independence for the Australians. Such Edwardian musings echoed those of the previous Australian generation. John G. Knight, secretary for Victoria at several English and Australian exhibitions, concluded in 1866: "The great aim of an Exhibition is to give the fullest possible notoriety to new manufactures and processes, and bring the manufacturer and inventor more closely in contact with the merchant, speculator, and capitalist."[5] This "most practical method of advertising" promised "to enlarge the basis of trade" for Australians.

Commercial exhibits from the Raj revealed similar center-periphery economic benefits and tensions. Exhibitors sought to resolve the commercial ambitions of both local and imperial parties. E. C. Buck, secretary to India's Revenue and Agriculture Department, was among the strongest Anglo-Indian advocates of using exhibitions to advertise the Raj's current and potential goods. Shows would demonstrate that "much that the cheap labor, the clever workmanship and the fertile climate of India could supply to the outer world still lies undeveloped."[6] Exhibits were intended to encourage internal "improvements" and reveal India as both a producer of such goods and a new market for English and European products. T. N. Mukharji, one of Buck's most active assistants, agreed. He displayed "the admirable manufactures" of British India at the 1883 Amsterdam Exhibition in an effort to strengthen existing trade connections and create new markets.[7] The chief exhibition officer's efforts complemented the projects of the Bombay Chamber of Commerce. Amsterdam offered a market with "gradually increasing export trade from Bombay," so members organized a subcommittee to collect and forward "the most suitable articles connected with . . . trade."[8] Increased trade in "articles" such as wool, cotton, and grain promised national and local, as well as imperial, benefits.

Exhibitions offered more than inventories of imperial and national wealth. They also suggested idealized markets, or a direct relationship between producers and consumers, according to strong advocates, such as Knight, Sir Henry Cole, and, when in a favorable mood, Charles Babbage. These spectacles did not just represent the idea of political economy or mirror its process; they were political economies themselves. Commissioners, politicians, tradesmen, and advertisers attempted to carve out an imperial economic system according to nearly sacred free trade principles in the face of declining confidence in those principles, growing foreign competition, and increasing cries for independent colonial trade policies. "Great Britain is now hard pressed by foreign nations in competition and trade," wrote one exhibition expert in 1894 as a preface to his proposals for government financing and organization of commercial courts.[9] Centralized funding, planning, and managerial oversight of exhibition courts would provide "a good . . . advertisement" for English and imperial products. He promised that those efforts "would not exceed the cost of one small vessel of war" during this era of economic (and potential naval) conflict.

British commissioners attempted to paint an economic picture without nonimperial intermediaries and with the imperial state, or England, as the middleman for metropolitan and colonial economic regeneration. This was in contrast to Babbage's bold claim for an international free trade market at the Crystal Palace in 1851, where "The Exposition is calculated to promote and increase the free interchange of raw materials and manufactured commodities between all the nations of the earth."[10] Rather, the sense of "free trade" commerce and social relations informing the organizers and visitors at later shows assumed a clearly imperial character. This was free trade among and between imperial units, reflecting the growing disenchantment with the pure free market and concern about England's economic standing in the wider world. Colonial displays as early as the 1862 London International Exhibition were read by one contemporary as the sign of a working, restricted, free trade empire, in which commercial ties offered a foreshadowing of future imperial political federation.[11]

There could be no doubt about the imperial nature of Britain's political economy one generation later at the Colonial and Indian Exhibition, where only England and its possessions were represented. There was no hint of international "Free Trade" at South Kensington; 1851's non-British participants, such as France and the United States, were noteworthy because of their absence. Messrs. Doulton's panel adorning the courts suggested this self-contained imperial network of goods, minerals, and manufactures (see Figure 1). The products of Australian miners and pastoralists, Indian artisans, and British engineers linked together a self-sufficient, internally differentiated, imperial economic system. Their activities highlighted the Empire's association of differing racial groups in a commercial commonwealth in the face of hostile internal and external threats. The *Imperial Federation Journal's* editors boasted that South Kensington's displays in 1886 revealed the "new resolution to stand back to back for the Empire against the world." [12]

Australian raw materials and wine, as well as Indian artware and teas, were among the economic success stories of this increasingly imperial and decreasingly free trade system at the exhibitions. Commissioners and other exhibitors sold samples during and after the shows, encouraging additional production back home and reminding visitors of the Empire's capacity to generate economic progress. Yet the transnational enthusiasm for commercial exhibits was not shared by all parties. Colonial nationalists in India and Australia complained about England's economic dominance and wanted to turn the commercial exhibits towards local economic advantage, such as direct trade with Europe and North America. Other critics expressed more fundamental and systematic economic concerns. Antimarket public moralists, social conservatives, socialists, radicals, and trade unionists attacked the spectacles of imperial and national wealth or, more specifically, the market nature of that wealth. They voiced discontent with political economy and suggested alternatives to its market-oriented relations. Those critics occupied various positions on the political and social spectrum, from Thomas Carlyle on the Victorian Right to George Julian Harney, positioned far away on the Victorian Left. Correspondence and editorials provide colorful evidence of their shared opposition to the celebration of the nineteenth-century market society at the exhibitions.

ECONOMIC COURTS AND COMMISSIONERS

What economic goods did commissioners, politicians, and businessmen choose to exhibit? Or, as was more often the case, what were they able to exhibit? Displays of Canadian timber, Indian art, Victorian wool, and South Australian copper were signs of "the nascent power" of the empire. Those commercial exhibits resulted from both imperial solicitations and colonial initiatives. Economic goods represented what the Scotsman Patrick Geddes in the late 1880s termed the "production of wealth"; wool, tobacco, wines, minerals, and manufactured goods, such as soap and leather, were colonial and imperial signs of "the progress of well-being."[13] Those exhibits not only displayed "modern progress," continued Geddes, but also promoted the commercial and social links necessary to create demand, thereby encouraging further "improvements" and strengthening existing economic connections. Here was a vast world of economic goods from England, Australia, and India to observe, purchase, and consume; these were active commodities promoting dynamic consumers and consumerism, "a sort of Imperial Federation" in the face of international economic "progress and rivalry."[14]

Local officials at the Madras Exhibition in 1855, for example, organized displays to show "how great and varied be the capabilities of India to minister to the wants of the Western world."[15] Visitors viewed and acquired "useful" as well as "ornamental" regional articles of trade; those included shawls, metalwork, minerals, and drugs. One official highlighted "wool and hair, cotton, iron, steel and timber" among the Punjab's contributions.[16] Thirty years later, Queen Victoria expressed "special interest" in the Economic Court at the Colonial and Indian Exhibition and an official visitor from Trinidad noted that "surely in no better manner could one become familiar with known products or investigate new ones than by paying a visit" to South Kensington.[17]

Commissioners understood that such collections not only reflected current production and trade patterns, but might also stimulate economic growth and change. Here was a way to create demand for English and colonial economic goods. Advocates embraced exhibitions as engines of renewed trade and economic development during the "great" depression and persistent competition of the late nineteenth century.[18] Members of the Victorian Royal Commission for the 1862 London International advised their local collectors that displays "should be more particularly illustrative of objects which are the sources of present wealth and prosperity, or of indigenous products which there is a reasonable presumption may hereafter prove to be of economic value or of commercial importance."[19] Sir Redmond Barry recommended in a circular to prospective exhibitors that all forwarded exhibits should reflect "utility, beauty, perfection . . . cheapness, a universal adaptation to all markets, or a special fitness to meet a particular want."[20] The Madras Central Committee for the Great Exhibition in 1851 had been equally confident that their art, botanical, and mineral displays would introduce to consumers items "little known" in England, but which might form a new commercial link, "if a demand could be created" at the Crystal Palace.[21]

John Forbes Royle was an early advocate of using exhibitions to test, compare, and sell economic products from the colonies and thereby create new, and enhance existing, imperial trade links.[22] These commodities included both items unique to India and those which various other colonial communities could contribute. In the first case, South Asian producers held an inherent advantage and could appeal to the "novelty" of their oils and medical substances, among other exhibits. Indian producers of goods made elsewhere, such as paper and flax, were also encouraged to take advantage of overseas shows, including the Paris Exposition in 1855. Potential customers would not only review displays for purchase, but would provide comments to improve production back in India.[23]

The Board of Trade in London asked Royle to prepare a report on the "Indian and Colonial Products, Useful as Food and for Manufactures" exhibited at the Paris Exposition.[24] The India Office expert reviewed coal, cotton, wheat, silk, gums, oils, and woods, recommending that both the scientific and local names should be used to emphasize specific applications and comparisons. He reminded his readers that "the troubled state of Europe"—including the recent Crimean War—provided an open door for such colonial exports. India, New Zealand, and the West Indies could create an imperial fiber network of jute and hemp, freeing England from its dependence on unstable Russian and other Baltic region suppliers.

Royle argued that contributing Indian items for comparison with similar products from foreign exhibitors could provoke improvements in local production. Overseas exhibition awards and sales might even promote the expansion of "some crops which would themselves be profitable." Similar results could be reproduced at local Indian exhibitions in towns such as Nagpore and Agra, where Royle and other Anglo-Indian officials struggled to introduce European consumer items.[25] Such ambitious objectives were not always realized. Nagpore officials were left with mountains of unsold, "unredeemable" European goods after the close of their exhibition in 1865.[26]

British and Anglo-Indian exhibitors displayed samples of South Asian raw materials in the exhibition courts adjacent to the machines which processed them. These exhibits were intended to remind visitors of the ways that the Raj's goods were transformed daily in English factories. Organizers of the working cotton machinery and spinning mules at the London International in 1862 made those imperial economic connections explicit. In one case, exhibitors posted adjacent to the "self-acting cotton-spinning mule" in motion a sign on which was written "Surat" to identify the South Asian source of the raw material.[27] The display of cotton consumer products nearby completed this effort to inform visitors about an imperial commercial network particularly pressing during the American Civil War and cotton famine of the early 1860s. The economic goods and the associated production process served to represent the empire as a commercial commonwealth, or market-based federation in which Indian cotton could replace American cotton in England's factories.

Australian wool paralleled Indian cotton. Barry recognized his colony's vast wool-based wealth and, as Victoria's visiting executive commissioner, advocated the integration of natural products, machinery, and finished consumer items in one wool "Process" court at the International Exhibition.[28] Exhibits of the stages of wool production illustrated Victoria's role in the imperial commercial network. Barry solicited "about 300 lbs" of the finest wool available in the colony and urged that the bales be exhibited alongside their manufactured consumer products. Visitors could observe "the various stages of preparation until it [wool] finally appears in the most perfect form of manufactured excellence," thereby comprehending the "uses to which Australian wool is capable of being brought to by the resources of Manufacturing Art."

AUSTRALIAN RAW MATERIALS AND PRODUCTS

The variety and success of Barry's economic collections held out the promise of future commercial gain for other exhibitors and their displays. Grains, minerals, timber, and wines from Victoria and New South Wales, for example, competed for attention with similar goods from other colonies and countries. Such exhibits were particularly well received at early exhibitions in London and Paris, where they encouraged expanded trade. Edward D. S. Ogilvie toured the Australian galleries at the 1855 Paris Universal Exposition, noting that "the [gold] nuggets of course create a great sensation, and are all day surrounded by admiring crowds."[29] The colonial pastoralist added that visitors also observed "numerous woods which have been worked up into articles of furniture," muslin, "a sample of Moreton Bay cotton," and a collection of New South Wales wines. That colony's executive commissioner boasted to Ogilvie that the wines "have passed their examination with great eclat, taking high rank among their French and German rivals, and causing much speculative discussion here in connexion with the vine disease, which is so seriously affecting the production of wine in Europe." Seven years later, William Westgarth suggested that Victoria "owes much for the successful marshalling of her industrial triumphs upon the great international scene of trial and victory" at the 1862 London International Exhibition.[30]

Visitors often observed Australian trade articles in glass cases and wooden boxes, arranged as both trophies and as a commercial inventory. Such was the case with the popular Queensland Annexe at the South Kensington shows in the early 1870s (Figure 3). The colony's well-organized exhibits provided opportunities for new or expanded commerce in the displayed goods. For example, the many offers to purchase Queensland's brooches and gems at the 1871 International Exhibition prompted Richard Daintree, the colony's Agent-General, to take direct action. He solicited more local manufactures and rough agates for display at future overseas exhibitions.[31] Daintree appealed to quality and novelty in the case of those gems, but other Australians turned to the size of their exhibits to attract visitors and consumers. This was often the case because wool, woods, minerals, and grains might also be found in other exhibition courts, such as those for Canada and South Africa. Indian artware and teas were unique to the Raj, but Australasia's significant displays were rather common. Judges might then be impressed by size and quantity. Jury awards for white soft wheat, Burra Burra copper, and merino wool also helped legitimize colonial goods in the English market.

Visitor consumption of Australian goods at the shows proved to be an effective vehicle for their commercial introduction and placement in wider markets. Consumers directly compared Australian fruits and meats with their competitors at special Colonial Markets, such as the one at the Colonial and Indian Exhibition (Figure 4). Tourists, local produce sellers, and visiting London families sampled Australasian pears, apples, and mutton in this display of imperial self-sufficiency, settler "progress," and the benefits of British rule. Refrigerated, or "cold air" chambers on steamers guaranteed colorful and tasty products, thereby allowing visitors to enjoy fruits which only "a few weeks since were denizens of an Antipodean orchard."[32] This was a welcome change from the earlier reliance on nonrefrigerated transportation and wax models, both of which had prevented visitors from tasting and purchasing colonial produce, and officials from judging their potential market value.

At more than one overseas exhibition before the 1880s, commissioners and Agents-General opened crates to find spoiled fruits, vegetables, and beverages, which could not be exhibited or sold. In contrast to the fresh goods at South Kensington, "fossil like remains of Grapes" and an "undistinguishable and quite worthless ... consolidated mass" of fermented fruits greeted a South Australian commissioner as he opened a case shipped from Adelaide.[33] By the turn of the century, one Victorian "grower of fruit" forwarded more than thirty cases each week to London for display, sampling, and sale in the colony's court at the Greater Britain Exhibition.[34] The Visitors' Book in Victoria's Court contained more than three thousand names, including "the leading Distributors and Merchants of Colonial Produce from London and the provinces," many of whom were anxious to sample and purchase those fresh Australian fruits.[35]

Australian pastoralists were also aggressive about displaying and selling their goods at exhibitions. The prominent Australian Agricultural Company charged its local general superintendents with organizing wool and coal exhibits as early as the Great Exhibition in 1851. Employees in New South Wales packed "samples of coals from the two seams at present worked" in cedar cases and forwarded them to the Crystal Palace.[36] The cases were also intended to illustrate to visitors, jurors, and potential customers the quality of colonial timber and woodworking; they were subsequently used for the company's wool specimens. That wool had been forwarded after the shearing season as "a product of New South Wales given without any artificial treatment."

Eleven years later, the Agricultural Company's Board of Directors responded to the calls by Barry and other exhibition commissioners for current economic goods and potential trade items. The directors solicited for display at the London International Exhibition "any products that will . . . help to show the value of the Company's possessions in the Colony."[37] They were particularly anxious that the company's manager in New South Wales provide "a prime sample of Coal," and were pleased with the inclusion of information about the fossil and geological formations in which the energy source was found.[38] The company's exhibit "was just suited to the purposes of an International Exhibition—the right mean between Science and Industry."[39] Local officers also forwarded "genuine samples" of wool and coal in bulk form ready for direct sale and use in the English and French markets.[40] These were attempts to stimulate capital investment for untapped coal fields, increase local and imperial trade, and create new markets for the company's products in Europe. Australian pastoralists were also using the expositions to advertise the expansion and diversification of their economic power within colonial society at the historical moment in which their previous dominance was being challenged.

THE CASE OF AUSTRALIAN WINES

Pastoralists sent wine samples to complement their wool and coal exhibits. Bottles of the local vintages were intended for both jurors and consumers. Such Australian vintages were relatively unknown outside of England and their home colonies until the 1860s, but mid-century visitors to the antipodes were impressed by the settlers' early viticulture. One noted after touring New South Wales that "the brandy is not very good, but the wine is better than the bad Spanish and Portugese wines imported from England."[41] He applauded the efforts of colonial governments and agricultural societies to improve local vintages, concluding that "the vine will be, no doubt, cultivated greatly by and by." Favorable jury reports, consumption at exhibition bars, and the phylloxera outbreaks in Europe stimulated cultivation and export during the later nineteenth century. Ogilvie had noted such favorable developments at the Paris Exposition as early as 1855.[42]

Local growers and agricultural societies turned to the English government and overseas learned societies to promote the entrance of Australian wines into the British and European markets. One wine grower from Irrawang in New South Wales earned the Silver Medal from the Royal Society and corresponded with its officers about the promotion of Australian wines.[43] He recommended the active participation of the English government in securing the capital, ships, land, and other resources necessary "to render New South Wales an abundant wine-growing country." The cultivation of the soil would result in further trade for both England and the colonies. Viticulture would also provide "the only durable source of [the] country's wealth . . . and the influence and institutions of civilised life," in contrast to the ephemeral and chaotic results of the gold and silver rushes of the 1850s. The Royal Society called for a "combination of Australian and English capitalists" to develop the colonial wine industry at later London and Paris international exhibitions.[44]

Also in New South Wales, the Macarthurs and members of the Australasian Botanic and Horticultural and Hunter River Agricultural Societies forwarded wines to exhibitions in London, Sydney, and Paris.[45] The midcentury efforts of those producers and exhibitors resulted in only limited overseas commercial success, but convinced local observers that "all our wine may be made good, and next, that we have a profitable market for it."[46] Colonial commissioners preparing samples for the shows reminded jurors "estimating the qualities of our Australian wines . . . that they are the product of a new Country."[47] In an expression of settler optimism, they claimed that the climate, continued experimentation by the government and growers, increase in local demand, and cheap labor promised improvements in colonial viticulture.

Australian wine producers faced other problems as well. Samples were often ruined during the long overseas voyages and, once delivered, faced general English and European disregard for colonial products. Furthermore, the consumption and purchase of alcoholic beverages on exhibition grounds did not become a popular element of the fairs until later, overcoming the temperance-influenced refreshments at the Crystal Palace and its immediate successors. Exhibitions after the 1850s offered visitors an array of wine bars and cellars; commissioners invited men and women to sample and purchase Australian wines, and to compare them with better-known European vintages. Jurors tasted Australian wines at the 1862 London International and found similarities with popular European imports.[48] Experts concluded, though, that the colonial "yield is yet very small and quite insufficient for the home supply."[49] The Cape Colony and Europe offered more and better vintages for the English market.[50] On the other hand, several colonial exhibitors, including the Macarthurs, earned medals for their samples. This led the official wine reporter to note after the exhibition that "the wines generally of all the Australian colonies exhibited on this occasion are of much promise."[51]

Colonial exhibitors continued to feature wines, often as part of government-sponsored or private competitions to award "improvements" in Australian viticulture. William Macleay took advantage of those incentives and pursued "an opportunity for introducing" his wines in the food and beverage saloons at the Sydney International Exhibition in 1879.[52] Domestic demand and local duties helped spur colonial production and the changes necessary for competition in the overseas markets. Exhibition commissioners also publicly praised the medicinal value of the vine's fruit.[53] Among those was Rev. J. I. Bleasdale, who promoted the display of Australian wines at various local and international exhibitions, and recommended, for example, their use in hospitals, infirmaries, and lunatic asylums. He publicly suggested substituting those wines for beer and spirits.[54]

Australian wine producers used local shows as testing grounds for their "best" vintages.[55] Those intended for later export to England and Europe were sampled and compared by visitors and competitors. The annual exhibitions of the Royal Agricultural Society of South Australia included such samples among their more popular exhibits to show "the great improvements . . . in the quality of wines manufacture."[56] Nearly three hundred bottles for experts to taste and the general public to purchase were provided by commissioners at Melbourne's Intercolonial Exhibition in 1875. The wine bar and sales court contrasts with early exhibitions at which visitors "saw the bottles . . . read the labels, and had to take for granted that the taste of the experts as to quality was correct."[57]

Joubert served as a wine juror for various exhibitions; the ambitious Sydney International was among them.[58] That show provided an opportunity to compare Australasian with popular French, Spanish, and Italian vintages. Joubert and his fellow jurors were "judging side by side the wines of all countries" for the first time in the Southern Hemisphere. Favorable results were published after over fifty meetings and testings at the exhibition. That final report was notably optimistic about Australian wine becoming one of the "most hopeful sources of our national prosperity" because of the local climate and improvements in cultivation and bottling since earlier exhibitions.

European and English breakthroughs for the Australasian wines were finally made at the 1867 Paris Universal Exposition and the series of International Exhibitions held at South Kensington during the early 1870s. One wine juror reported to the Royal Commission after the French show that English consumers must "awaken to the knowledge of new sources of good, cheap, wholesome, and natural wines." [59] He concluded that the Australian wines offered a "priceless desiderata to a country like England, whose taste has been for more than a century systematically vitiated" by European imports. Jurors in Paris expressed surprise at the quality of such wines when directly compared to the more commonly known European vintages; the official reports were quite favorable, noting improvements since the 1862 exhibition. By the end of the 1880s, one Queensland politician could boast that "the wines of Australia are now a successful and permanent industry, and the trade is rapidly expanding. They were in great request at the [1878] Paris Exhibition, where they were deservedly awarded a gold medal." [60]

This confidence provoked the establishment of an Australian "self-supporting wine depot" in London to challenge the European dominance of the English market.[61] The professional staff oversaw the placement of Australian wines in the London, British, and European commercial regions and provided information about those markets to vineyard managers in the colonies. South Australia's Vinegrower's Association was among those contributing to the Depot, and its members' investment was rewarded when officials were able to sell over sixty thousand gallons of South Australian wine during 1897.[62] Such success prompted its officers to suggest an expansion of the Depot's charge to include the introduction at English agricultural fairs and stores of Australian fruit, wool, and lamb.

INDIAN RAW MATERIALS AND PRODUCTS

The quest for new and stronger markets also encouraged the participation of Indian commissioners, merchants, and manufacturers at the Crystal Palace and subsequent overseas exhibitions. The "possibilities and potentialities" of British, Australian, European, and North American consumers provoked the Indian government and private parties to forward extensive commercial displays.[63] Mukharji, one of the Indian government's representatives at the Amsterdam Exhibition in 1883, participated in this long-term use of exhibitions to organize knowledge about India according to economic and market objectives. His official guidebooks for India at the Calcutta and Amsterdam International Exhibitions were constructed with such mercantile interests in mind.[64] The Revenue and Agriculture Department official described artware, minerals, and oils as articles for potential trade as part of his call for "the admirable manufactures of India to be introduced into the western markets by European merchants." Among such merchants were those visiting the exhibitions.[65]

Mukharji's introduction to the official Indian art catalogue for the Glasgow Exhibition in 1888 reminded readers that displays at the Colonial and Indian show two years before had created the taste and demand for Indian artware. Traditional Indian art was appreciated not only for its aesthetic or cultural value, but as a trade item whose promotion would provide local employment and revenue. Historical and aesthetic analyses included comments about the availability and uses of those goods. This ambitious program of economic development required government investment at the local level and the purchase by exhibition visitors, jurors, and their countrymen and women. Mukharji attempted to create and appeal to a larger market rather than one directed only to a luxury trade, as had often been the case at previous shows. Could he marry the high patronage of royalty to the mass demand of the marketplace for the benefit of "native merchants and manufacturers"?[66]

Mukharji and his colleagues also exhibited as part of the century-long struggle to overcome general impressions about the "impurity" of Indian goods, such as wheat and cotton.[67] Royle had discussed what he termed that "imperfect culture" of cotton cultivation in India as early as 1840.[68] Nearly fifty years later, one English editor still complained that when his country imported "a vast quantity of Indian wheat, not less, indeed, than one million tons, annually, with it we import no fewer than one hundred and fifty thousand tons of dirt."[69] Exhibition courts, juries, and experiments provided the direct observation and comparison with other nation's products necessary to convert consumers skeptical about Indian commercial goods and overcome detrimental conclusions about Indian labor and environment influenced by Victorian racialist ideas. Overseas exhibits were part of broader cotton improvement programs undertaken by the East India Company in the 1840s and twenty-five years later by the Government of India.[70]

Royle was among the first "improvers" to use expositions for that purpose; he also expended considerable time investigating the effects of climate, soil, and packing techniques on the quality and quantity of Indian exports.[71] Exhibitions provided a public evaluation of those efforts and stimulated further advances with jurors' reports and visitors' comments. Overseas reviews would require local producers to improve the "cleanness" and general "preparation" of commercial items. The authority and prestige of exhibition awards, whether earned or only competed for, might provoke displays "carefully harvested, or well cleaned and prepared for market."[72]

The 1862 London International Exhibition offered the ideal venue to display the improved "culture" of Indian cotton, not only because of direct contact with consumers at the show, but also because it was held at the time of the American Civil War and its accompanying Federal blockade of the Confederate cotton exporters. This opened a large window of trade opportunity.[73] Local Indian committees forwarded numerous samples of both cotton bales and finished cotton products. British India's executive commissioner organized an extensive collection in the Northeast Transept at South Kensington to show the "culture, character and extent of supply"; the Cotton Supply Association also forwarded dyed cottons in reaction to charges of impurities.

Commissioners, merchants, and private visitors commented on the quality of the samples, including their packing, and noted reduction in the "adulteration" after a formal government commission had investigated the problem in India.[74] The deputy superintendent for the colonies concluded that the Indian cotton exhibits were superior to those of the Egyptian producers and "cleaner and better" than the Raj's displays at the 1851 and 1855 exhibitions.[75] The *Times* was equally enthusiastic about the improved quality of South Asian cotton products. Its review of "the Indian Court" concluded that "the district" producing "such fibre ought to take more than an average rank as a great cotton-producing country."[76] Visitors were advised to take notice of the "large number of samples of dyed and printed fabrics" in cases adjoining other South Asian displays.

Mukharji energetically participated in this project of Victorian "improvement" while attending a conference on silk production at the later Colonial and Indian Exhibition.[77] The commissioner rose, "as a native of India," to thank Thomas Wardle for his efforts to revive the Bengal silk trade. He continued, arguing that there were three obstacles to the success of such a revival: the deterioration in the quality of the silk, which could be resolved by more careful cultivation; the "faulty reeling," which could be remedied by introducing the production process described by Wardle; and, finally, the high price, which resulted from the "exorbitant" charges for land. The South Asian expert expressed a commitment to inducing "the native reelers to improve their methods," upon his return to India so that Indian silk would be brought up to "the desired European standard." It was up to the Government of India to address the question of property prices!

This general response to the attacks on the quality of Indian labor and commercial goods has a twentieth-century parallel in the efforts of the Indian National Congress and Gandhi to promote home-spun materials and to advertise the purity of such *swadeshi* in party films and local "national" exhibitions.[78] Those included the Ahmedabad Industrial Exhibition in 1902, organized by the Exhibition Committee of the Indian National Congress, at which commissioners and exhibitors demonstrated the advantages of home-spun cloth and economic self-sufficiency at the same time they critiqued "British" art and technology.[79] Mukharji and the modernizers looked to the West for reeling technologies, while Gandhi and his traditionalists turned to India's past. Mukharji's embrace of European forms of technology and labor—the imperial culture of production and consumption—points to persistent ambivalence and tensions within Indian national culture about modern machinery and the market, as well as the potentially subversive or, at least, destabilizing uses of Western applied science, machines, and exhibitions by nationalists.[80]

BREWING INDIA'S TEA MARKETS

Indian cotton producers continued to forward exhibition displays to overseas shows, but faced significant competition from other sources throughout the century. It is difficult to determine the specific economic gains from their exhibits. In contrast, the ambitious and popular exhibition projects of India's tea merchants resulted in noticeable and measurable success, opening new and expanding existing markets.[81] Exhibitions offered an opportunity for India's tea companies to supply directly (without imperial or British middlemen) markets which had been, like Melbourne and to a lesser degree London, monopolized by what one contemporary termed "Heathen Chinese" teas.[82] Additionally, overseas exhibition displays removed London as the exclusive point of entry for Indian Teas in the world market. New ports were created in Europe, North America, and the Australian colonies between the Great Exhibition in 1851 and the turn of the century.[83] By then, Indian tea manufacturers were known as one of the few South Asian "trading communities" not reluctant to finance exhibition displays, and their success at those shows prompted other merchants to embrace exhibitions for commercial advantages.[84]

Tea manufacturers and sales companies turned to exhibitions in the 1850s and were among the earliest Indian producers to use such shows for economic gain. In 1851, the Assam Tea Company dispatched special boats to bring down to Calcutta over twenty "small boxes" of tea packages.[85] These were "found in good order" and shipped for exhibition in London, where the company was awarded the Bronze Medal for its "assorted teas." Its efforts earned further praise in a public lecture delivered before the Royal Society of Arts after the Great Exhibition.[86] Other tea companies and botanic gardens followed this precedent; they forwarded samples for testing and sale at shows in India and abroad. The Madras Literary Society noted that Himalayan teas were "in much request . . . and realizing good prices" at the local Industrial Exhibition in 1855.[87]

The Indian Tea Districts Association, or "Tea Syndicate," drew upon these earlier exhibits, embracing the exhibitions during the last quarter of the nineteenth century and well into the early twentieth.[88] Merchants, bankers, and tea-growers organized the group in the late 1870s to promote joint English and Anglo-Indian interests. Those included expanding trade with Britain and confronting the apparent monopoly of Chinese tea producers in key markets, such as Australia and North America. The association's members and staff collected information on production and overseas trade, lobbied for supportive legislation in India and England, and mounted an extensive, worldwide advertising campaign to promote "Indian" teas. The association exhibited and sold teas at nearly all of the major exhibitions between the Sydney International in 1879 and the Franco-British in 1908. Open chests of tea, a growing tea plant, and a variety of maps, photographs, and diagrams entertained visitors at the later show. Visitors included H.R.H. the Princess of Wales, who had just returned from a tour of the Raj and its tea growing districts. Officials also distributed over ten thousand copies of "A Few Facts about Indian Tea and How to Brew It," the pamphlet written specifically for the exposition.[89]

Thomas Carritt, agent for the syndicate, argued that Indian and overseas exhibitions provided the most effective advertising to expand existing markets and to open new ones. He organized displays at the Amsterdam and Calcutta International Exhibitions in the early 1880s to prove his point. Exhibits included extensive tea samples in boxes and cases, working models of the tea manufacturing and packaging technology, and gardens in which visitors could sit and consume the product. Carritt contacted Australian commissioners at the Calcutta show and lobbied for trade with their colonies. This objective was apparently realized, as exports to Australasia zoomed during the mid-1880s after the exhibition.[90]

Carritt applied considerable time and energy to those international exhibitions and general sales in Belgium, Holland, and Germany. Yet the Tea Association's managers were most interested in increasing trade with England. In order to do so, they turned their attention to the series of South Kensington shows during the 1880s. Carritt traveled to London to sort samples, organize tea gardens, and display large models of tea plantation machinery. One exhibition court also included a map of India with the tea districts highlighted, statistical tables presenting the number of acres under cultivation, and photographs of the Assam landscape and natural scenery. Commissioners included tea plants in the garden area and contracted with English firms, such as Messrs. Hornimans, to "represent public taste" and to aggressively compete with Chinese teas in this market.

Tea planters shared the concern of the cotton industry about the public impression of "impurities" in Indian exports. In response to those accusations, C. Purdon Clarke's Tea Garden and Indian Village at South Kensington highlighted the quality of the Raj's products. The association's exhibit invited consumers and "competent judges" to consider the total process of tea manufacturing and consumption. Displays revealed the seeming advantages of estates managed by "skilled Englishmen" overseeing local workers operating machinery. The combination's exhibited products were intended to contrast with the "adulterated" Chinese ones and to counteract similar charges against Indian goods. Picking and packing by the Raj's machines, such as the "Sirocco Tea Drying Machine" and "Jackson's Tea Roller," addressed common concerns about South Asian labor practices. They suggested the "pure" quality of the Indian machine-produced teas, considered "clean" in opposition to Chinese teas produced by "hand—which is distinctly dirty." Hornimans advertised the resulting Indian teas as "strong, pure, delicious."[91]

The International Health Exhibition in 1884 entertained over four million visitors and thus offered to the association's secretary an opportunity to stimulate "the popular knowledge of, and demand for, the teas of India." He hired an assistant for Carritt to organize the direct sale of tea samples to merchants and tourists. The syndicate's samples proved so popular with exhibition visitors that its employees constructed "a miniature tea garden" in which those passing through could sample and observe at a more leisurely pace. The garden offered "the cultivation and manufacture of tea in all its usages."[92] Costumed employees provided a variety of Indian and Ceylon teas and coffees in what one imbibing journalist termed "welcome oases."[93]

He enthusiastically and favorably contrasted the garden to the hot refreshment rooms found elsewhere at South Kensington, reminding visitors that it offered "the truly Eastern luxury of a punkah."

Over a hundred and fifty thousand cups of tea at 3 p. per cup were sold during the Health Exhibition. These sales provided an attractive return for the subsidies provided by the association's members. The tea exhibits also earned six medals, among which was one for the working machinery.[94] Editors of a popular guidebook concluded that "what was required is exactly what this Exhibition has made possible, concerted action on the part of the principal tea planters in India, so that now, if Indian teas be what they are pronounced by competent judges to be, they will obtain due welcome from the British public."[95] That success prompted the association to prepare a more ambitious Tea Court for the 1886 Colonial and Indian Exhibition. Messrs. H. S. King and Co., agents for the Royal Commission, were hired to oversee the Indian Tea Exhibit and the association's own subcommittee arranged for the collection and selection of the tea samples.[96] Exhibits were in glass vessels according to the district from which the tea originated. Organizers of the court included the maps, diagrams, and photographs used at the Health Exhibition, but enhanced the imperial character of the exhibit with models of workers and "arms and Trophies of the Chase."

Several influential Anglo-Indians traveled to London for the event and oversaw the display and sales of teas from Assam, Cachar, and Kangra Valley. Growers forwarded samples of various types of teas, including those new to the English market.[97] Some were sold in packets for resale by merchants or consumption in the visitors' homes, whereas others were available as infused tea by the cupful "at moderate prices." By the end of the exhibition, over 24,000 lbs. of tea had been sold in packets and an additional 300,000 cups consumed at the Tea Court in South Kensington. The official catalogue concluded that the Court offered "the largest assortment of samples that has ever been collected together."[98]

The association continued its "concerted" efforts to improve trade by displaying and selling tea at exhibitions in Melbourne, Glasgow, Paris, Chicago, and Antwerp during the following decade. Officers visited major urban areas, where they provided tea samples at "certain shows, Church Fairs, and Bazaars," and complemented demonstrations with press campaigns to advertise the advantages of machinery-produced Indian tea over hand-rolled Chinese tea leaves. The Tea Association's London group also established its own American and Foreign Tea Committee to create more permanent advertising and trade opportunities. Its members worked with the Calcutta Steam Company and other groups in the association to finance the

Indian Palace at the 1889 Paris Universal Exposition.[99] Free passage was given to twelve "Native Attendants" who spoke French; they served tea at the exhibition. The association established an Indian restaurant in the capital after the show to regularize the sale and consumption of Indian teas and develop "favourable auspices" for long-term trade.

NEW TEA MARKETS IN AUSTRALIA AND NORTH AMERICA

The Assam Tea Company expressed interest in opening a market in Australia during the early 1850s. A former employee on a tour of the colonies reported the potential for large-scale sales of "inferior qualities" of tea and of "a better class if the price be not too high."[100] The company's director supported such a venture. He dispatched tea samples to "a respectable agent" in Adelaide and suggested larger quantities for consumers "in the bush." The Tea Association's formal, "concerted" efforts to introduce Indian teas into Australia began with the 1879 Sydney International Exhibition and included the establishment of direct commercial links with local merchants in major cities.

Among the most prominent and influential of those businessmen was James Inglis, a former tea planter in India and commissioner for the Indian government at the early Australian international exhibitions.[101] Inglis worked with both the association and the Indian government's Department of Revenue and Agriculture to exhibit, sell, and exchange teas and other South Asian exhibits at the Sydney, Melbourne, and Calcutta shows.[102] He served as India's resident commissioner and later promoted "commercial relations with the outside world" at Colonial Institute and chambers of commerce meetings.[103] Inglis corresponded with Anglo-Indian officials at various times during the late 1870s and 1880s in an effort to organize lecture tours to introduce Indian products in Australia, exchange museum samples among the various public institutions in both colonies, and establish strong tea markets in Sydney and Melbourne.[104] He acted as the "agent" for the Tea Association during these years and received official governmental authorization from the Department of Revenue and Agriculture to represent the syndicate at the various Australian exhibitions. Keen on integrating producers and consumers, as well as educating the general public, Inglis created the popular logo of an Australian bushman making his Billy Tea from Indian leaves and gave lantern lecture tours in Australia.

The combined efforts of the association, Inglis, and the Government of India resulted in the rapid ascent of its members' tea exports into Australia.[105] That trade was fueled by all parties: Australians and Anglo-Indians, consumers, producers, and middlemen. The superintendent of the Government Central Museum in Madras suggested there was a mass market in Australia after displaying his region's teas at the Melbourne Exhibition in 1880–81. They were recognized at that show for their "greater strength and stronger aroma" in contrast to Chinese imports.[106] Exhibition tea kiosks, pamphlets, public speeches, and the continued sales of samples at James Inglis and Company, Ltd., in Sydney and Brisbane stimulated Indian and Ceylonese tea shipments to Australia, appealing to, or even creating, this mass market. South Asian tea surpassed Chinese imports by the early 1890s, and the association then applied its antipodean methods in North America at the 1893 Chicago Columbian Exhibition.

Eager to enter the promising American market, the Indian government and the association started organizing for the Chicago show in 1890 and forwarded shipments two years later.[107] The Calcutta Special Committee sent a "staff of Indian servants" in red and gold uniforms to the American exhibition to sell and serve samples at the Tea House. Students at the Calcutta School of Art provided decorated tin boxes for the tea samples, and the Indian government financed the forwarding of other artware to provide a total "Orientalist," or seemingly authentic, context for the observation, purchase, and consumption of the teas. Samples were given to various American institutions and the Imperial Institute after the event.[108]

The Chicago effort was among the largest organized by the association in North America. Over 150 packets from Calcutta and 300 more from London provided over 31,000 lbs. of tea for display, tasting, and purchase. Working under the supervision of the much-traveled Richard Blechynden, the association's "Special Agent," the court's employees dispensed nearly 3,000 lbs. in the Tea House alone. Commercial agents sold an additional 25,000 lbs. to merchants and other customers before the end of the year. Applying lessons learned in Europe, Blechynden and his "staff of native servants" opened the "Palais Indian Tea House, Limited" and other commercial ventures in Chicago. Aside from sales to existing merchants, most of these activities closed by the beginning of 1894, and the remaining tea was forwarded to the British Section at the Antwerp International Exhibition.[109]

AUSTRALIAN-INDIAN TRADE CONNECTIONS

Tea sales at major exhibitions revealed the vast potential for direct trade among various imperial units, particularly Australia and India, without the intervention of English middlemen or the British state. The president of the Melbourne Chamber of Commerce addressed this promising new regional trade in teas and other goods in his annual report after the Melbourne International Exhibition.[110] He was not alone. Intent upon promoting commercial relations with the Australian colonies, India's commissioners forwarded samples of cotton, hides, medical plants, and woods to the earlier Sydney International Exhibition. In return, they pursued, among other items, Australian manufactured goods and "Livestock, Horses, principally" for the Indian Army.[111]

Jules Joubert shared this new enthusiasm for Australian-Indian trade, particularly the potential market in India for Australian manufactured products and raw materials. He wrote that Allahabad was "a great emporium of trade, as well as a great manufacturing city," particularly of carpets, and described Bombay as an inviting "great mercantile center."[112] He was particularly active in organizing the trade network among New South Wales, South Australia, and India in the 1870s and 1880s and argued that colonial exhibitions might play an important role in forging and maintaining such commercial links. While in Sydney, for example, he encouraged South Asian displays at the series of Metropolitan Exhibitions organized by the local Royal Agricultural Society.[113] Joubert also urged Australian participation in the Calcutta International Exhibition as a strategy to enter such markets and returned to South Australia from his first official trip to the host city with "seventy-seven large packages filled to the brim with purchases" of potential trade goods.[114]

Joubert successfully solicited Australian exhibits and obtained the cooperation of "mercantile and manufacturing firms in England and on the Continent" in his capacity as executive commissioner for the Calcutta International.[115] Supporters in that city claimed Joubert's efforts were "likely to have a very important effect in developing and promoting the commercial prosperity of India" and that since he "is an experienced man in such undertakings, . . . no doubt exists as to his ability to bring the undertaking in India to a successful issue."[116] Joubert found a receptive audience in Melbourne, where the local Chamber of Commerce distributed notices inviting Australian exhibitors to Calcutta and nominated several of its members to serve on the colony's exhibition commission.[117] The chairman of the South Australian Chamber of Commerce also responded to Joubert's call for participation at the Calcutta show, but only after the colonial government promised financial support and official recognition for the exhibitors.[118]

The Anglo-Indian community embraced the Australian exhibits at the Calcutta International as "the basis of a future important trade between

Australia and India."[119] One local reviewer of the Australian courts and catalogues concluded that wines and preserved meats offered the most promising colonial exports, since the Australians could ship their goods in refrigerated chambers, thereby increasing efficiency and quality while simultaneously reducing cost.[120] The exchange of labor and produce between the two imperial communities could be "productive of unmixed good" for both, suggesting the promises of both Australian federation and a "more extensive and powerful federation" between India and Australia. The foundation of such a federation was the promise of direct trade suggested by the exhibition.

This call for increased Australian-Indian trade without intermediaries or the customary reshipping from Colombo was embraced by a variety of government officials and businessmen on both sides of the Indian Ocean. P. G. King, general superintendent for the Peel River Land and Mineral Company in New South Wales, corresponded with the Indian Department of Revenue and Agriculture concerning the direct supply of Australian horses for the Indian Army.[121] After contacting local Australian government officials, King forwarded information about colonial horses from an official catalogue for the 1888 Melbourne Centennial Exhibition and requested information about the sizes, uses, and colors preferred by the Raj's troops. In this case, the exhibitions promoted an attempt to regularize and expand an existing trade connection. The same could be said about the attempts to sell Australian woods at the exhibitions for the construction of Indian railway sleepers. Exhibition displays noted the hardness of New South Wales woods and their imperviousness to the white ant.[122]

H. J. Scott, official agent for South Australia at the Calcutta International Exhibition, visited "all works & manufactures in South Australia which [were] likely to lead to trade with India" before that show opened and urged them to forward commercial exhibits.[123] Scott collected minerals, wines, wheat, marble mantle pieces, and biscuits for the mass South Asian and more limited Anglo-Indian consumer markets. The agent applied strong pressure on flax and food-preserving firms to forward samples and suggested that a working model of the Stump Jumping Plow would be "of great import" for the colony's reputation and trade. With much less fanfare, officers of the Royal Agricultural Society of South Australia organized exhibits, reports, and visitors at the show.[124] These officials subsequently oversaw exchanges among museums and the expansion of trade links on both sides of the Indian Ocean.

THE QUESTION OF INDEPENDENT COLONIAL TRADE

Colonial correspondence, exchanges, and displays raised the question of independent trading without the imperial middle man. What were the national meanings, for example, of the New South Wales exhibit in London which included bales of merino wool alongside the technology used in European cities to transform the raw material into a manufactured consumer good? Such Australian commercial displays were emblems for the British Empire's economic links and wealth, but also signs of the colonial reliance on England and Europe as middlemen for overseas trade. "We observe, with regret," sighed an Australian commissioner in Paris for the 1867 Exposition, "that almost the entire quantity comes to the French manufacturer, not direct from the producing countries [the Australian colonies], but indirectly through England and Belgium, and this to an amount of nearly one hundred millions of francs in value."[125] The author of the official report only queried, but did not answer, whether the lack of direct trade resulted from "a want of spirit of enterprise in our merchants" or, as was hinted, "the rules and regulations of our [imperial] administration."

The American market appeared limitless to some colonial producers. Most New South Wales wool merchants found the high tariffs a strong reason for not leaping at the invitation to participate at shows such as the 1876 Philadelphia Centennial Exhibition, but other pastoral and wine companies forwarded samples with the optimism that the American exhibitions would pressure the American government into lowering duties. Sydney's major manufacturers were less optimistic and turned down the Philadelphia opportunity as a wasted effort. On the other hand, perhaps feeling a kindred protectionist spirit across the Pacific and dreaming of new consumers, Victoria forwarded samples and received both praise and awards for its manufactured goods.[126] Nearly ten years later, the colony's commissioners shipped woods, oils, and Ballarat tweeds for display and sale at the New Orleans World's Industrial and Cotton Exposition in an attempt to take further advantage of the North American market.[127] Economic collections, such as Victoria's at Philadelphia and New Orleans, suggested the possibilities of independent, as well as imperial-oriented, Australian and Indian trade policies. Those exhibits attracted merchants and consumers in Europe, North America, and other colonies. One Melbourne journalist recommended that colonial trade "naturally follow" those market forces, rather than imperial edicts, thereby questioning the allegedly sacred imperial trade connection with Britain.[128]

Australian manufacturers and traders also took advantage of local exhibitions to promote direct trade with Germany, France, Italy, and the United States. Merchants from those countries forwarded extensive exhibits for review. With those efforts in mind, the local executive commissioner for the 1879 Sydney International Exhibition remarked that "it is certain that the extraordinary interest displayed by the public examining the Industrial & Art sections of the German Court will lead to a more accurate knowledge of German Manufactures by the large and daily increasing body of consumers in this Colony and it is hoped that the commercial relations already existing with Germany may be strengthened and increased and made more profitable to both countries." [129] The commissioner expressed similar sentiments about the French and Japanese exhibits, reminding his audience that they also held out the promises of lucrative direct trade with these countries in the future. One year later, the Melbourne Chamber of Commerce presented the Italian commissioner with a proposal for "direct trade relations" and his German counterpart with plans for "direct steam communication." [130] In the midst of a trade depression, the chamber's officers suggested that Victoria could take advantage of the Melbourne International Exhibition to open trade with Naples, Milan, Venice, and Rome. The consul from Venice was particularly interested in "the different kinds of corn" which could be shipped from Victoria.[131] No direct trading schemes resulted at the time, but the show initiated long-term discussion about foreign trade and steamship routes between France, India, and Australia.[132]

At the same time, though, there was significant unease in England about the role of German and other European exhibitors at the Australian international exhibitions in the 1880s.[133] Were the cultural contact and apparent invasion of European commerce preludes to German imperial expansion in the South Pacific and the creation of direct Australian trade with Britain's continental rivals? One Australian tried to address such concerns by noting that "it is most natural and probable that the great bulk of the European goods should come in British ships to Australia." This did not ease anxiety about growing connections between Germany and Australia. In fact, Australian behavior stoked the coals of that imperial uneasiness. The former president of the Victorian Chamber of Manufactures made a special effort to tour the German art and economic displays at the 1888 Melbourne Centennial Exhibition. He was so impressed that he subsequently visited Germany to study its art and industrial schools. Other colonial officials corresponded with prominent Germans about machinery and overseas trade.[134]

By the 1890s, Australian officials were also requesting their own exhibition buildings or at least a collective display to promote direct trade and represent internal federation at overseas shows. Interested in opening markets for Australian goods in North America and reducing exhibition costs, the Sydney Chamber of Manufactures lobbied the colony's premier for one Australian Court at the 1893 Chicago Columbian Exposition, rather than the separate colonial courts constructed for preceding shows.[135] Advocates also articulated a nationalist purpose: "An 'Australian' Court would identify the group of Colonies which it represented in the minds of visitors far better than by having one to each Colony as heretofore." Seven years later, Australian commissioners at the Paris Universal Exposition were concerned about the "subordinate" position in which their exhibitors might be placed in a British Building.

The Australians confronted English colleagues appealing to visions of imperial grandeur. Imperial commissioners worried that arranging exhibits by types or in separate colonial buildings would make "an imposing display impossible on the part of any other country" than France.[136] Australian commissioners responded that Great Britain's industrial and political position could be best represented by distinctive colonial sections. This would enable the colonies to represent their own wealth, challenge the orchestrated French world display, and suggest direct and independent colonial trade. English officials were noticeably uneasy about the divided display of imperial wealth. They feared the potential for direct trade between the colonies and other countries that colonial or regional exhibits implied.

Sensing growing nationalism in exposition activities, the Foreign Office and Royal Commission for the Paris show refused to allow colonial exhibitors and commissioners to accept French honors.[137] The president of the Western Australia section at the show wrote the Royal Commission at the Foreign Office that India, Ceylon, Canada, and his colony had accepted the invitation to advertise their economic products with the intention of promoting commercial relations with the host country. The colonial commissioner concluded that Western Australia's "object was to attract population & capital & to extend the market for our timber and other commodities." The establishment of "a business & friendly connection between France & ourselves" and the increased knowledge about French commercial regulations justified the colonial commission's expenses and efforts. He hoped that the earning of various medals, including several Grand Prize and Gold awards, would stimulate trade between France and the colony. Reconciliation between British and colonial commissioners was apparently achieved at the Franco-British Exhibition eight years later. Canada, Australia, and India exhibited in their own palaces, but these were integrated into a coherent imperial message: Britain and London were the centers of a powerful, racially diverse Empire shortly before the Great War.[138]

By that time, though, the exhibition experience had publicly revealed the Australian inclination to pursue social and cultural models, as well as economic connections, beyond the Mother Country of Great Britain. Commercial exhibits, in particular, might be read as signs of that rising colonial nationalism, as well as of imperial economic interdependence. No major diplomatic crises or governmental divisions resulted from such Australian-German interactions, for example, or from Australian displays at European exhibitions. Direct trade with overseas nations was slow to develop. But, on the other hand, contemporaries understood that the exhibits and contact provided an assertion of colonial economic strength at a time of suggested independent political and cultural policies. Economic exhibits illustrated the vastness, but also the tensions and uncertainties, of the imperial market during the late-Victorian and Edwardian eras. In doing so, they reflected, and at times challenged, the economic roles assigned to the Commonwealth's national or racial groups.

Fifty years before the Paris Exposition, imperial economic displays, such as those of Australian coal, iron, leather, wood, and wool at the Great Exhibition, had imparted "a new impression of . . . colonial strength" and revealed "a wonderful world of production."[139] Such exhibits represented imperial wealth, self-sufficiency, and interdependence, but those were not the only possible meanings to contemporaries. While the exhibition picture of an economic division of production and consumption—or commercial federation—created during the era of New Imperialism reflected and shaped imperial participation, it also suggested hints of colonial economic resentment and independence. In the case of the 1866–67 Melbourne Intercolonial Exhibition, local protectionist policies confronted an invasion of British manufactured goods. Critics claimed the show was "a grim joke" to colonial commerce since "specimens of colonial industry and colonial wealth were placed in the background, or thrown aside as useless lumber" to avoid competing with English commercial exhibits.[140] Economic exhibits in Melbourne and elsewhere suggested that the self-contained commercial system faced both internal and external challenges, many of which ironically resulted from participation at these allegedly imperial exhibitions.

Australian and Indian commercial exhibits revealed the future assertion of national trade and development policies in the face of calls for imperial preference. In India, the Bengal Chamber of Commerce advocated participation at North American and Australian exhibitions to create direct trade in local teas and remove London as the exclusive overseas point of entry for that important commodity.[141] Australians began to be equally independent-minded about direct and expanded trade. "We do not trade with England from any patriotic motive," concluded one writer from Melbourne in 1869, "but simply because she can supply our wants more cheaply than any other country."[142] His concluding words reflected and provoked independent Australian commercial measures undertaken at local and overseas exhibitions between 1851 and 1914: "Whenever our interests are better served by dealing with others, we do not hesitate to pass her [England] by."

POLITICAL ECONOMY UNDER ATTACK

Many Australians and Indians were eager to take economic advantage of the exhibitions to promote independent and direct commercial connections. They were not attacking the idea or practice of political economy itself, but the dominant role that England seemed to be playing in a seemingly free trade system. They were interested in using the exhibitions to promote national or regional market connections, rather than an imperially dominated economic order. Other critics were less limited in their discontent. They aimed their critiques at the nature of political economy and the ways in which the exhibitions represented the relatively new ideas about the market as a metaphor for society. This was most particularly the case in England among contributors to the radical press and public moralists wary of political economy. Among the most vocal were Thomas Carlyle and the *Friend of the People,* the mid-Victorian republican-socialist newspaper.

Carlyle was among those cultural critics suspicious of market-oriented competition as a source of authority, taste, and order. Such public moralists critiqued the exhibitions as representations of modern political economy.[143] Critics had no doubts that this was a brave new world, a social and cultural equipoise vastly different in style and scope from previous times. Carlyle was among those drawing upon and contributing to this tradition of cultural criticism in the face of the exhibitions' undeniable popularity. After all, over eleven million visitors toured the shows in 1851 and 1862. We can perceive in Carlyle's response to the Great Exhibition a sense of his general disdain for modern, urban society, with its noise and massive numbers of people running to and fro. Although contained within exhibition halls, the shows appeared to represent the seemingly limitless chaos and social disintegration of the new, more democratic age of the market. Carlyle wrote just before the Crystal Palace show closed that "palaver, noise, nonsense and confusion, in all its forms, has been the order of the day."[144]

Carlyle's letters to various correspondents, including his brother, Alexander, and Ralph Waldo Emerson, the influential American man of letters, reveal his antipathy for the Great Exhibition, and do so in no uncertain terms. He wrote Emerson that the event had depressed trade—an irony, since it was intended to promote commerce—and put him in a "pathetic grandfatherly feeling" about this "universal Children's Ball, which the British Nation in these extraordinary circumstance is giving itself!"[145] Out of prescience or a keen taking of the nation's pulse, Carlyle understood that the Crystal Palace would be the beginning of a movement, rather than its finale. Carlyle's advice? If the event produced noise, then he recommended silence. "Silence above all, silence is very behoveful!" If not silence, then flight, and he traveled northward to Lancashire and Scotland to escape the exhibition-dominated city and its "sanhedrin of windy fools." He hoped that the Crystal Palace would be dismantled and taken "quite away again" by the time of his return to London.[146]

Writing to his brother, Alexander, on the eve of the show's official closing, Carlyle repeated his deep antipathy for the Great Exhibition.[147] After apologizing for not writing in quite some time, the Victorian sage then launched into a direct attack upon the Crystal Palace, which marked what he termed "such a year of nonsense here as was seldom seen ever in London." This letter develops a theme somewhat buried in Carlyle's earlier responses to the exhibition. After repeating his standard charges of foolishness and noise, he elaborates upon the economic harm of the show. Not only can he not find any good "to be got out of this big Glass Soapbubble, and all the gauderies spread out in it," but he pontificates against the event's alleged damages to labor and trade. "England, I think, must have *lost* some 25 per cent of its year's labour by the job (the London shopkeepers are nearly bankrupt by the want of business)." Was this something more than an exaggeration of the oft-heard complaint that exhibitions were unfair competition for local tradesmen, creating, as it were, a protected bazaar within the host city? Perhaps it was.

The "nonsensical talk, thought and speculation" at the Crystal Palace in 1851 were not, in Carlyle's vision, an aberration, but a revelation of this dismal new order. Exhibitions were his dreaded "cash nexus" writ large and predominant. His suggestion that lost labor and financial debt would never be recovered was a critique of the alternative society and economy represented by the Great Exhibition projected over a long horizon of time. Did England lose 25 percent of its labor because of the event? Not likely. Yet the boldness of Carlyle's statement was intended to suggest the dramatic sea change in England signified by the exhibition. Carlyle's response to the closure of the Great Exhibition was consistent with his earlier critiques. He found in the "blessed tranquility" and stillness of London's streets the most appropriate antidote to the noisy Crystal Palace and the most meaningful sign that the show "has dissolved itself, all gone or going to the four winds." [148] Carlyle had attacked the Great Exhibition for being what its advocates wanted it to be: an ideal market and celebration of political economy. Cole and Babbage embraced the spectacle of commodities, consumers, and producers. Their Heaven on Earth was Carlyle's Hell.

Carlyle's anger was echoed far away on the political spectrum of Victorian England by the radical press in 1851. The critic's disregard for the Great Exhibition found an unexpected ally in the Left's suspicion of the event and of exhibitions themselves. In one confrontational example, the *Friend of the People*'s editors asked before the opening of the Crystal Palace, "What have exhibitions done for the people?" [149] The answer for the republican-socialists: not much, at least for the people, or laborers of England, but plenty for its aristocrats and swindlers. George Julian Harney's newspaper later attacked the Palace's "essentially aristocratic" opening ceremony, preferring to see the exhibition "opened not in the presence of the richest, but of the worthiest of the nation, selected by popular election, to represent not a class, but *all*." [150] Hyde Park could have been England's *Champ de Mars*. But exploitation and capital were the words of the day, rather than enjoyment and labor. The reverse could only come about, concluded the editorial writer, when the supremacy of labor and the sovereignty of a republican nation replaced the national and social vision on display at the Crystal Palace: "flunkeyism . . . the rule of masters, and the royalty of a degenerate monarchy."

The *Friend of the People* also assaulted the Great Exhibition's apparent equipoise of competitive political economy among nations. The paper carried a series of open letters urging that the event be turned in a more internationalist and socialist direction, exhibiting "those principles which would unite all nations in one common bond of brotherhood, each contributing to the welfare of all." [151] Rather than a celebration of free trade, the exhibition should become a celebration of socialism. These critics disagreed with the elite commissioners on the message of the event, but agreed with them that the exhibition could serve an educational purpose. It might even be a stage for presenting nonviolent reforms, such as the People's Charter, as an alternative equipoise. In that vein, George Holyoake and other radicals published a further open letter to Robert Owen asking him to "deliver a series of lectures" as part of the commissioners' efforts to translate and distribute "lectures on political and social subjects" during the show's season.[152]

The year 1851 might be as memorable in "the progress and development of civilization" and radicalism as 1517 (Luther's posting of his theses, "proclaiming the ascendancy of reason"); 1649 (the execution of Charles, outlawing of monarchy, and "triumph of popular will"); 1776 (the Declaration of Independence from "the Old" World); and 1793 ("the birth of those European Revolutions").

Owen responded favorably, suggesting that "the opportunity to disseminate important truths to nations in a short period has never before occurred under such favourable auspices."[153] The Crystal Palace provided a large-scale popular moment to transform English society in the aftermath of the political defeat of the Chartist Movement. In this way, the Great Exhibition complemented the Charter for Harney, suggesting the union of direct political action with educational and cultural practices, representing labor as a class and idea at the shows, as well as its expression in the forms of protests and strikes. At the same time, Harney and his colleagues were reluctant to turn the event into an opportunity for open revolt in the face of so many soldiers and police in London. The exhibition was not the revolutionary moment.[154]

Radicals continued to attack exhibitions for celebrating political economy and imperial wealth. The Colonial and Indian show at South Kensington in 1886 was "just a piece of commercial advertisement," for the *Commonweal*, the official journal of the Socialist League. Its editors toured South Kensington and found evidence of economic destruction in India and the ironic "glory of the British arms gained in various successful battles against barbarians and savages."[155] This reflected William Morris's hatred for the militarism, destructiveness, and economic exploitation of British imperialism and—in this case—its public celebration at the exhibition.[156] His *Commonweal* editorial dripped with satire. It reminded readers that they could visit the show and see "the mercy of Colonists towards native populations" with the "strong magnifying glass" on display, or "the daily rations of an Indigo ryot and of his master under one glass case, with a certificate of the amount of nourishment in each, furnished by Professor Huxley." These and other exhibits realized the organizers' purpose: "The exposition of the Honour, Glory, and Usefulness of the British Empire." We cannot travel much further from the simultaneous celebrations of the market as both symbol for and practice of imperial wealth, national fantasy, and political economy at the exhibitions.

5   *Terrae Nullius?*
Australia and India at
Overseas Exhibitions

"We are glad to find that the Australians are alive to the importance of exhibiting specimens of their wares," remarked the *Athenaeum*'s editors on the eve of the Paris Universal Exposition in 1855.[1] "In some places [including Melbourne and Sandhurst], the matter is being taken up with considerable spirit," in marked contrast to the apparent lack of colonial interest in the Great Exhibition four years earlier. At that time, one popular guidebook had unfavorably compared the growing economic and political importance of the Australasian possessions with their courts in the Crystal Palace, which "had nothing very new or very showy."[2] Delays and controversies limited the timely arrival of Australian exhibits in 1851, so that the first edition of the exhibition's official catalogue included only "about twenty exhibitors" from New South Wales and half of that number from South Australia.[3] The Australians were ready for Paris by 1855, though, and organized comprehensive and attractive courts.[4] One visitor suggested that Victoria's exhibits reflected "the desire of the colonists to make a suitable appearance on that stirring occasion."[5]

India's officials shared the exhibitionary "spirit," but it was not a new one for them. They had captured public attention with "curious, abundant, and valuable" Crystal Palace displays four years earlier and drew upon that success while aggressively organizing the Raj's displays for Paris.[6] The 1851 experience proved useful. India's commissioners repeated successful art exhibits and corrected the less successful raw produce ones by the opening of the Universal Exposition.[7] Among others, the governor of Bombay was optimistic that overseas exhibitions "opened the eyes of Europeans" to local South Asian natural products and artware not known, or incorrectly understood, outside of India.[8] Thus, colonial commissioners from both sides of the Indian Ocean enthusiastically embraced the shows as opportunities to present their societies to the world. The images of Australia and India at over-seas exhibitions offered visitors the dichotomy between future and past, settler and subject, raw materials and artisanal crafts. These were lands of the imagination, in which visitors could survey landscapes and peoples, and dream along with the colonists. Such fantasies were made seductively vis-ible and tangible at the exhibitions.

Exhibits created a sense of place for the colonies both within the Empire and in popular notions of Australian and Anglo-Indian history. While do-ing so, the exhibition experience flattened time and space, highlighting con-trasts between British India and the antipodean possessions. Commission-ers exhibited those sharp, yet reconcilable distinctions. Popular guidebooks for the 1862 London International Exhibition distinguished between "East India" and the "Australasian Colonies"; authors noted the different exhibits one could expect to see in the respective colonial courts.[9] One official visitor to the Paris Universal Exposition sixteen years later explicitly differenti-ated the displays of Australian economic wealth (wool, wines, fruits, wheat, copper, and timber) from those of Indian art wealth (jewelry, pottery, silks, precious stones, and metalware).[10]

Commissioners and exhibitors at South Kensington's Colonial and Indian Exhibition in 1886 drew upon this tradition, but developed the distinctions even further. They represented Australia and India in a self-contained imperial world without the participation of non-British societies, whether they were settler nations, such as the United States, or "Oriental-ist" ones, including China and the Ottoman Empire. The Australian courts at South Kensington offered evidence of "progress": photographs, manu-factured goods, and lithographic urban street plans. The Indian collection "charmed and fascinated the eye of every visitor" with its traditional artis-tic "triumphs of human art and skill."[11] Doulton's impasto panels con-trasted Australia and India for the show's five million visitors in the gram-mar of different clothing, labor, and products (see Figure 1).

Oppositional, yet integrated, exhibits echoed distinctions articulated by Victorians between subject and white-settler colonies. Goldwin Smith and John Seeley were among those most vocal about the imperial differences.[12] Exhibition displays suggested a taxonomy of colonial possessions in which "Australia" and "India" represented the ideal types found in their writings. John Ruskin also constructed such a grammar of distinction when he con-trasted Britain's Scottish and South Asian subjects in his art lectures on "The Two Paths" at the time of the Indian Mutiny.[13] The art critic reflected upon the divergent national character, culture, and thus loyalty of the two races. This opposition between "the races of the jungle and of the moor" was a persistent element in British imperial discourse, whether or not the source in question linked a people's character and race with their art.[14] In the case of the Doulton panels, the comparison had become one between the jungle and the Australian bush, or outback; artistic and labor differences mattered.

The ordering of goods and representatives by exhibition commissioners provided evidence that the imperial elites and their networks could create and balance the apparently natural diversity between, and commonalities shared by, different colonies. Officials and exhibitors took advantage of such images in an effort to make their displays at overseas exhibitions attractive, popular, and profitable. This was notably the case with the ambitious efforts to induce immigrants and investors to Australia and to advertise and sell traditional Indian artware. Comparisons were drawn by visitors and jurors between Australian and Indian machinery and ethnographic exhibits. The racial opposition between the two colonies was also expressed in historical terms. India was a "traditional" society, and Australia a "new" country. Commissioners resurrected the past of the former and invented a history for the latter.

Late-Victorian elites faced potentially devastating new crises at home and abroad, both within Britain's borders and across the Empire. They reconstructed cultural and social forms to express and resolve Ruskin's paradox of "two nations . . . in direct opposition," which show "the effects on moral sentiment of art without nature [India], and of nature without art [Scotland, or the Australasian settler colonies]."[15] Doulton's panels reworked such themes in the somewhat less heated days one generation after the Mutiny. By then, not only access to technology but also the typology of the latter as well as natural resources, work, and race determined the culture and society of the imperial unit and its role in the Empire. Each group performed a particular function and type of premodern labor in this vision of an imperial world. Doulton's craftsmen and colonial exhibition commissioners adapted Ruskin's strategy of representing racial differences in aesthetic, economic, and cultural terms. The Scottish (Australian) culture offered natural landscape painting and rugged labor, whereas its Indian counterpart produced colorfully ornamented artware that "never represents a natural fact" and traditionalist artisanal work.[16] Such were the Australian and Indian fantasies at overseas exhibitions.

COLONIAL COMMODITIES AND AUSTRALIAN "PROGRESS"?

The economic and political advantages of exhibiting abroad at those shows were apparent to many Australian officials. As early as the mid-1850s, Sir

William Thomas Denison, governor of Tasmania, advised members of the Australian Agricultural and Horticultural Society to participate in French expositions by forwarding local products and studying overseas displays.[17] In doing so, colonial producers might overcome "slovenly" agricultural practices and improve their "miserable" stock animals and wines. Denison concluded to his audience, which included several local exhibition commissioners, that commercial advantages could be gained by applying the lessons in the relationship between science, economy, and machinery represented at the upcoming Paris Universal Exposition.

Once the decision to participate had been made in cities such as Sydney and Melbourne, local organizers still faced a final daunting question: What should they exhibit? To some degree, Australians responded by forwarding what English commissioners requested. Officers from South Kensington and the Royal Society were keenly interested in Australian flora and fauna—that is, unique natural history exhibits for the scientifically curious, which might also have some commercial uses. They turned to Australia for those unusual animals, such as wombats and black swans, and local economic products, including wool, with the same great interest that they sought silks and dyes from India.[18] Australian officials also took it upon themselves to exhibit raw materials for which they were pursuing overseas markets in Britain, North America, and Europe. Those "genuine" colonial products included wool, coal, woods, grain, and beef.

South Australia, for example, forwarded to the 1851 Great Exhibition at the last moment a collection which, though great in variety, "almost exclusively," according to Samuel Davenport, the colony's executive secretary, "belong[s] to the class of 'Raw Materials'."[19] The twenty-five packages shipped from Adelaide in late November, 1850, contained samples of copper, malachite, wheat, oats, dried native plants, soap, and olive oil. Copper and fibrous malachite from the famous Burra Burra mines had already captured British attention; they were expected and eagerly anticipated in London. Those samples were praised by one visitor as "the finest sort"; the keeper of mining records at the Museum of Practical Geology found them "very remarkable."[20] Smaller specimens of gold in those ores showed more promise than performance, but their "discovery" and display were greeted with public enthusiasm abroad.

One Australian at a later London International Exhibition admired the industrial and cultural objects displayed by other nations, but admitted in Davenport's earlier spirit that "the resources of a new country are chiefly in the form of raw materials."[21] Those "materials" need not only represent current wealth, but also future economic and social opportunities. They suggested both what Australia lacked and what it promised during the mid-Victorian years. Daniel Cooper, executive commissioner for New South Wales at the 1862 London International Exhibition, organized displays to show visitors that colonists in such new countries had "within ourselves everything in the shape of raw produce that can be desired by a nation and if we only had labour & skill & a home market we could manufacture anything we might desire on the spot." [22] Cooper was aware that New South Wales and other Australian colonies faced English and European "ignorance" and "sneering," but he wrote home that the "fine style" of the court and the manufactured exhibits revealed to visitors that there was more to New South Wales than "grass to feed sheep & cattle." Coal, cotton, and furniture samples offered the promise of a wealthy future. He confidently concluded that "a few different opinions will now be held of the Colonies & they will be far more esteemed."

Such esteem resulted from what was exhibited and what was held back. Even exhibition enthusiasts in Melbourne recommended "all parties interesting themselves [in the Great Exhibition] not to attempt too much; to avoid the fatal error of too high an ambition," particularly for "the youngest of British colonies." [23] In this case, youth was not only measured by the calendar of days, but also the calendar of economic development. Even sixteen years later, Victoria's commissioners were concerned that their manufactured goods might appear "out of place and unnoticed" among the many European displays at the Universal Exposition in Paris. [24] They sent minerals, wool, timber, and cereals not only because those were the treasures of new settler societies, as Cooper and the South Australians realized, but also because Australian pianos and furniture would be "useless" and out of place amid Europe's own products. They would not attract purchasers. Space limitations also influenced display decisions. In this case, though, the Australians wanted to present an economically viable picture of those items "valuable commercially as exports," urging the collection and forwarding of items "specially prepared" for the European market and visitor.

The resulting Australian exhibits were similar in type and organization to those displayed in other British settler-colony courts. Those included Natal's at the 1862 London International and Paris Universal Exposition five years later, as well as "Prosperous go-ahead Canada's" at the Colonial and Indian Exhibition in 1886. [25] Such courts suggested a particular type of settler history, economic vision, and social structure in the nineteenth-century taxonomy of nations. Natal's natural history and ethnographic objects provided ornamentation for maps, economic samples, and art works at South Kensington in 1862. [26] The "Equipment of a Pioneer Colonist" display included an ox-drawn wagon and iron tools. Those exhibits and the wool, coal, and timber samples offered a suggestive contrast to the collection of indigenous spears, rings, and drinking bowls. The official surveyor general's maps underscored the rugged pioneer country, seemingly transformed into a fertile land of pastoral, farming, and plantation wealth. Early oil paintings of the natural environment and printed proceedings of learned societies offered "culture" to balance the more utilitarian objects.

Settler relics and the representation of South Africa's particular landscape, flora, and fauna suggested the grammar of white colonial nationalism similar to that being constructed in Australasia at the same time. The combination of raw materials, Aboriginal "curios," working mining machines, and historical artifacts filled the New South Wales and Victoria courts at the London International. For example, Victoria's commissioners displayed a "working battery of 12 stampers for crushing quartz and amalgamating gold" alongside timbers, newspapers, boomerangs, and the "pack saddle, as made for the Burke and Wills exploring expedition," which ended in the tragic death of both explorers.[27] Here were various "striking illustrations of Melbourne progress" in contrast to the world upon which the settlers had stumbled or, in some cases, to which they had been transported. Not surprisingly, settler pride filled Australians touring exhibition courts in Britain and Europe.

Colonial machinery played an important role in highlighting that settler "progress" and its accompanying pride. Working mining machines linked the Australian colonies to the modern world of mechanical production and distinguished them from the "primitive" world of hand labor, whether that be practiced by their own indigenous Australians or the Raj's common subjects. Australian technological exhibits offered visions of the future, rather than of the past, inviting visitors to imagine the seemingly limitless wealth of local agricultural and mineral resources. This is not to suggest that colonial machinery could rival the large-scale technology of American and European exhibitors, but that, on the other hand, Australian technology was generally small-scale and relatively simple. It was attractive in part because of those characteristics and because it was created to address specific local predicaments. Thus, those machines were advertisements for colonial ingenuity without threatening independence. The Australasian colonies captured visitors with their innovative devices, such as the Jump-Stump Plow from South Australia and Thomas L. Mitchell's boomerang propeller from New South Wales, and did so without challenging British manufactures.[28]

Mining machines provided the popular rhythm to accompany other symbols of Australia's economic progress at the overseas exhibitions. Commissioners from Victoria and Queensland, among other Australasian colonies, organized mineral crushing and washing machines to display wealth and progress, as well as attract emigrants and investors. Such colonial machinery turned out to be among the most popular exhibits at English and European exhibitions between the Great Exhibition and the Festival of Empire sixty years later. Barry and his colleagues from Victoria organized a "battery of stamps" to process their colony's ore displays at the 1862 International Exhibition, and one commissioner wrote home that "the space immediately adjacent is always crowded," often with members of the English working class.[29] The colonists were also pleased with the technology's reception by visiting scientists. Barry hoped that the interest shown in the display "among Scientific Gentleman" might result in further technological improvement on his young colony's gold fields.

Visitors remained fascinated by working mining machinery during the later Victorian era. The *Times* reported that crowds surrounded the Queensland mining displays "every day" at the Colonial and Indian Exhibition in 1886.[30] What did those visitors observe and enjoy? The display included a working quartz-crushing battery, manufactured for the government's commissioners by a Brisbane company and operated by visiting colonials.[31] It processed twenty tons of gold ore sent from the Phoenix Gold Mining Company's fields in Gympie before the eager eyes of potential investors and emigrants (Figure 5). South Kensington's visitors could observe the extraction of gold and its melting into a bar by this machinery in the South Promenade and then turn their gaze upon large nuggets and quartz samples in the Queensland Court's glass cases.[32] The Queensland "Gold Digger" daily washed for alluvial gold by hand in front of the visitors, reminding the public that mining machinery did not completely replace human labor in the colony's gold fields.[33] As a final touch, pyramids or "trophies" representing the total value of the colony's mineral production decorated the court. Those exhibits offered a socioeconomic vision of the present and future which integrated the European, English, and colonial experiences.

Objects signifying such "progress" contrasted not only with Australian Aboriginal weapons and tools, but also with the "ornamental" displays organized by India's commissioners. This was the case at the Crystal Palace and Universal Exposition in the 1850s, as it would be throughout the century's exhibitions at home and abroad. A South Asian treasure-chest of luxury goods and handicrafts, jeweled crowns, and thrones greeted visitors to the Great Exhibition (Figure 6).[34] Here was "fair India, whose bright sunny land / Has sent to the Palace, with no sparing hand, / The richest of fabrics, and jewels most rare."[35] Amid this Orientalist spectacle, the famous

Koh-i-Nor diamond "appeared to be the chief object of attention."[36] The richly carpeted East Indian court at the Paris Universal four years later recalled those displays. It was described by one London journalist as a "panorama of treasures."[37]

South Asian artware, arms, tapestries, and inlaid tables contrasted with Australasia's utilitarian and scientific objects. Those included exhibits from New South Wales "illustrating the natural resources of the country; rich as it is in mineral wealth, and in all else connected with a bounteous soil. The useful, accordingly, has in this collection predominance over the ornamental."[38] The "useful" included models of dry docks, iron ore, wines, and wool samples. These contrasting Australian and Indian displays revealed different expectations on the part of the overseas visitors, diverse roles within the larger imperial community, and differing images of each colony's past, present, and future. Australians, South Asians, and Anglo-Indians had a surprising amount of influence in those matters at the exhibitions.

THE IMAGE OF AUSTRALIA

Australia's exhibition commissioners faced the challenging task of improving the generally unfavorable collective self-image and equally unflattering images about their communities in overseas economic reports, popular literature, and dioramas.[39] This was the case in England, Europe, and North America. The public interpreted Australian exhibits in light of commonly held preconceptions about the colonies' pre-industrial economy, frontier violence, and large Irish Catholic population. Needless to say, these were not conducive to favorable receptions. Those images gained currency due to Australia's distance from England and Europe, and their apparent consistency across colonial borders. The chaos of silver and gold rushes in 1850 and 1851 did nothing to improve upon those impressions. Rather, contemporaries such as Thomas De Quincey lumped together the Australian colonies with California and other wildly meteoric mineral-rush societies.[40] A daunting "thick text" evolved during the nineteenth century to shape the ways Australians perceived themselves and were perceived by others.

Colonial officials did what they could to address or circumvent those perceptions. They attempted to enhance their public image by differentiating their products from those of other colonies. Commissioners and exhibitors emphasized the unique qualities of such exhibits and offered them as signs of settler progress in the antipodes. This was not easily achieved in the cases of important items, such as wool, wheat, and cotton, which many of the other British colonies and various other nations could also exhibit at the shows and offer to European and English consumers and manufacturers. While reviewing the wool exhibits, Richard Owen, the influential naturalist, listed China, Tibet, Iceland, Scandinavia, the United States, the Cape of Good Hope, and the various Australasian colonies as just a few of the many sources for wool.[41] Australian wool held its own with its "very valuable examples," most particularly from New South Wales, but still faced considerable competition.[42] It proved difficult for Australian commissioners to follow the advice of the colonial showman R. E. N. Twopeny and take advantage of "the love of the fashionable and the love of the new."[43] What was truly "fashionable" and "new" in their colonies' exhibits? Not much, except for natural history and ethnographic exhibits.

Facing such disadvantages, Victoria's commissioners forwarded to the 1862 London International Exhibition those local exhibits best able to represent the growing sense of Australian national identity and "the progress of colonisation."[44] These might promote trade, investment, and emigration. Under Barry's guidance, the colony's committee collected and forwarded "a complete collection of the indigenous timber" of the colony and wax models of local flowers, plants, fruits, and vegetables.[45] Officials also solicited the best stock and wool samples from various local agricultural societies. Intending to create "a physical atlas" of the colony, they advised potential exhibitors and financial contributors that "it is highly desirable to bring prominently before those who will congregate in London, the results of the intellectual and scientific as well as the animal and manufacturing industry of the people of Victoria."

Barry confronted foreign ignorance, antipathy, and general indifference towards the antipodes in his attempts to represent such colonial "progress" at overseas exhibitions. He was repeatedly frustrated as executive commissioner for Victoria by metropolitan unfamiliarity with the political geography of the Australian colonies. On more than one occasion, museum and exhibition displays were forwarded to him with the wrong "national" or colonial address on the label. The city of "Melbourne" was placed in at least three different colonies. To Barry's amazement, this was done by officers of the South Kensington Museum and the Royal United Service Institution.[46] Angered at this ignorance or indifference—particularly since by the early 1870s the colony had exhibited as "Victoria" at three English exhibitions and several more in Europe—Barry offered maps (including one published in London!) and statistics to address this "indifference to the geographical situation of Melbourne." In response to one misaddressed shipment, the Victoria commissioner wrote "it appears to me of no slight moment that the geographic position of these important dependencies of the Crown should be understood and recognised in England." Viewed as imperial disrespect, such behavior only strengthened the sense of distance and national identity within the colony.

Images of Australia representing the general type of utilitarian, crude, and culturally undeveloped white-settler colony persisted during the nineteenth century. These affected both the creation and reception of the displays presented by its exhibition commissioners. On the other hand, this picture of the settler colonies also provided a language for early colonial national identity centered upon the experience of distant migration and settlement. William Westgarth, who regularly traveled between the Australian colonies and England, noted in 1863 that "an impression is prevalent in the mother country that her [Australian] colonies are for the most part people from the humbler walks of her crowded society."[47] In a written complement to Doulton's impasto panel of the Australian "types," Westgarth described a colonial society filled with "the mechanic, the field-labourer, the able workman in all departments of bone and muscle," but not those with "brains and mental cultivation."

While it is true that Barry struggled to redress this image of the Australian colonies, he was also fully capable of exploiting it at exhibitions. Victoria's commissioner took advantage of overseas fascination with Australia's unique flora and fauna (eucalyptus, kangaroos, and wombats) and commercial objects (gold, wool, and timber) to secure purchases and exchanges. At the same time, he recognized the importance of remaking the popular image of Australia created by novelists and journalists, among others. Victoria's exhibits were intended to convey the additional message of settler identity and national "progress": economic prosperity, cultural taste, and social order. Barry and Victoria's other commissioners urged local officials to collect "pictures and drawings" as well as the expected natural history and economic samples for display at the 1862 London International.[48]

In keeping with his own request, Barry forwarded copies of "The Biographical Charts of Painters of the Italian School" to the later London and Vienna International Exhibitions.[49] That display included engravings executed by the Department of Lands and Surveys and bound by the Government Printer, both in Melbourne. Barry intended the exhibit to demonstrate "the excellence of the workmanship" developing in the colony in contrast to or, at least, in coexistence with the popular image of "wild" (frontier and mining) Australia. The Victoria official warned the commissioners and Agent-General about "careless handling" of the display, because copies had been prepared for Queen Victoria, the South Kensington Museum, and the Empress of Austria. Barry hoped these parties would return the favor after the exhibitions by forwarding art works and publications for the Melbourne Museum, Public Library, and Art Gallery. European paintings, sculpture, and volumes could then be expected to develop aesthetic taste and national culture in the colonies—thereby further eroding the local and overseas impression of a frontier and strictly utilitarian society.

New South Wales commissioners were also anxious "to show . . . progress in intelligence, letters, in science and in art as well as in material wealth."[50] They displayed paintings, etchings, and sculptures to accompany commercial and scientific exhibits and to compete with neighboring Victoria's colonial art exhibits. T. A. Murray, the colony's executive commissioner at the 1867 Paris Universal Exposition, solicited "some of the best paintings" crafted by colonists for display. He aggressively requested the works of Adelaide E. S. Ironside, an Australian-born artist who had achieved prominence as one of Ruskin's students in England and contributed paintings to previous exhibitions in London and Dublin.[51] Not knowing Ironside personally, Murray turned to Rev. John Lang to lobby the artist. A prominent politician, Lang had previously introduced a motion in the colonial Legislative Assembly to honor the painter.

"I am desirous of showing that young Australia has within her some love of letters, science and the fine arts," Murray wrote Lang from Sydney in 1866, "and that her growing youth have some aspirations beyond those immediately connected with our staple commodities, in business and beef and mutton and tallow and wool."[52] Lang agreed that it was necessary to provide "an illustration of the rising genius of our country," but he warned the commissioner that commercial wealth should not be ignored at the colony's Parisian court. He forwarded Murray's original request to Ironside and appealed to her patriotism for New South Wales and her professional pride. Lang suggested she could look forward to premiums offered by the commission, "service" to the colony, and "future fame both at home & abroad" from participation at the Universal Exposition.[53]

Shows in Paris and other overseas cities allowed Australia's commissioners to illustrate the "progress" of the colonies and thus their suitability for new capital, emigrants, and self-government. Exhibition courts provided the opportunity for colonials to represent themselves rather than be represented by English officials. Many chose to advertise their commercial resources, available land, and culture. Richard Daintree, Queensland's Agent-General, was among the colonial commissioners who turned to exhibitions for "making the colony, and its resources, more thoroughly known by the general public" in England, North America, and Europe.[54] In an effort to solicit emigrants and capital, the Agent-General exhibited photographs, aboriginal weapons, minerals, and agricultural products at the Vienna, Philadelphia, and London international exhibitions in the early 1870s (see Figure 3).

Daintree and other colonial commissioners organized their courts by using photography and classification schemes borrowed from metropolitan museums and galleries. Those represented the diffusion of imperial culture and its defining orientation of knowledge, not just the objects of material culture, but also their public representation in an imperial, or English mode, rather than a distinctively colonial mode. "After all," as one British Museum official wrote to Barry after the 1862 London International, "the true interest of a Colony is to exhibit its products to the best advantage. It is from their being thus appreciated that the reputation and the demand for them will be increased."[55] The form of exhibition providing "the best advantage" was determined by science and art experts at the imperial center in the years before the establishment of rival colonial cultural establishments and their integration into national economic and political structures. The value of colonial materials was thus determined, in part, by recognition, study, and display ("reading") at "the center," which was, in this case, the British Museum, South Kensington exhibitions, and their officers.

Colonial commissioners could, though, take advantage of metropolitan technologies and experts to better position their own exhibits. Australians applied modern map-making and photographic apparati to create and copy exhibition objects, articulate a sense of permanence to the shows, and demonstrate local, or colonial progress. Maps and photographs provided colonial officials with relatively inexpensive, durable, and "realistic" exhibition displays to make known their "distant" and "new" lands. Australian officials appreciated maps as sources of useful information and as "interesting" works of art and science in their own right as early as the Great Exhibition and Paris Universal Exposition in the 1850s. T. L. Mitchell, the influential surveyor-general for New South Wales, was at the forefront of exhibiting colonial maps at such overseas exhibitions.[56] Twenty years later, Daintree used colored photographs to present the geological and farming contexts in which Queensland's ores and agricultural exhibits were originally found. Samples of gold, for example, were exhibited under views of the alluvial regions where they had been recently excavated.[57]

J. G. Knight was among the strongest advocates for exhibiting Australian photographs as illustrations of colonial life and as works of art themselves at exhibitions in the 1860s and 1870s. Photography was a sign of intellectual progress in this inversion of the colony as photographic subject. As secretary for the 1866 Melbourne Intercolonial Exhibition, Knight solicited images of public and private buildings "in the most picturesque and attractive manner" after the success of similar photographs at the 1862 London International Exhibition.[58] The six hundred photographs shown at South Kensington had earned praise for their artistic excellence and the novelty of the Australian landscapes they portrayed. Most were given to the South Kensington Museum and the Free Library of Liverpool after the exhibition.

Riding the wave of such overseas interest, Knight encouraged photographic contributions to the colony's court at the upcoming Paris Universal Exposition. He advised potential exhibitors that photographs provided the "readiest and cheapest" way to illustrate Victoria's resources. Original colonial photographs offered to visitors "a perfect idea of the conditions under which the towns of Victoria were springing into existence, and the country being reclaimed from the wilderness of nature." The Australian commissioner invited colonial contributors to focus on "principal business places and residences in the city and suburbs" for judges and visitors, some of whom might be future emigrants and investors. Overseas men and women observed and verified (because of the confidence in early photography's veracity) the tangible images and results of colonial economic, social, and scientific development and, at the same time, appreciated the modern form in which they were publicly represented. These objects were both illustrations of, and signs for, colonial progress.

THE COMPETITION FOR EMIGRANTS

Australia's photographic exhibits were part of its direct competition with the Cape Colony, Natal, Canada, and the United States for British and European emigrants. The scramble to offer the Australian colonies as a new home for such settlers was implicit in their exhibition courts and often explicit in commissioners' reports. Those "new" societies shared a vision of settler capitalism and nationalism, defined against Europe, England, the *indigene*, and "the Orient" at the shows. They offered comparable opportunities and fears as new overseas homes. Exhibits and accompanying promotional literature were intended to solicit citizens from among the millions of visitors; they highlighted the promise of a new life on new shores. Australians had little difficulty in answering why Australia and not England, but why Australia and not Canada or the United States was a tougher query. Even within the Australian continent, colonies battled with one another for the new settlers and overseas capital. Why settle in New South Wales rather than Queensland?

Emigrants might be seduced by exhibits and literature. Victoria's commissioners enthusiastically wrote home about the crowds surrounding their gold-washing displays at the London International Exhibition in 1862. They hoped that such demonstrations and the free pamphlets about the colony would "influence a considerable increase of emigration."[59] South Australia's Agent-General prepared a special volume for the South Kensington shows in the mid-1880s to inform potential emigrants about how to get to Australia and what climate, educational "advantages," and savings bank results one could expect in that new home.[60] The exhibited applications of modern science and technology to a seemingly limitless agricultural and mineral foundation attracted potential emigrants and investors. Printing presses, agricultural machinery, and photographs of public buildings contrasted with Aboriginal displays, popular images of the gold rush and the bush frontier, as well as with crowded cities and unemployment in Britain and Europe. Commissioners offered an environment with all of the cultural, social, and political advantages and none of the economic disadvantages of the Old World.

Other British colonies might be able to do the same or, at the least, make the same claims. Canada was among those. If distinction marked the Australian–South Asian comparison, then close similarity marked the Australian-Canadian one. Officials from South Australia and New South Wales, for example, well understood the competition for the "proper" class of emigrants, as well as for trade and capital, as early as the Great Exhibition in 1851. The strong and attractive Canadian exhibits were perceived as competing beacons to attract and guide settlers that otherwise might disembark on Australian shores. It did not help the Australians that those North American exhibits received nearly universal praise.[61] One London magazine concluded that Canada was "the most advanced in the arts" and displayed "the largest and most valuable collection," among which were furniture, woods, minerals, and fire-engines.[62] "Canada is strong and complete in almost every department," echoed a second visitor to the Crystal Palace, "and gives the most satisfactory evidence of high civilization, united with natural advantages, rarely surpassed."[63] Models of bridges, manufactured goods, grains, and other displays suggested an attractive new homeland for emigrants and their skills. Australia's 1851 commissioners thus began their century-long competition with Canada at the Crystal Palace at a disadvantage.

That race for settlers was alive and well as late as the Franco-British Exhibition in 1908, although the Australians were gaining some ground by then. Queensland's commissioners at the show recognized that "Canada as usual has spent a large sum of money" to appeal to emigrants.[64] In response, the Australians distributed over 40,000 postcards and 23,000 leaflets advertising Queensland's attractiveness as a future home. One of the colony's commissioners wrote home that he "undertook to show six Australian products to every one exhibited by Canada" and was able to explain the colony's "advantages . . . in the way of climate." His message was spread by a school essay contest on Queensland's exhibits.

Australian exhibits and literature illustrated "the life and processes in connection" with the colonies' industries that emigrants could expect upon their arrival.[65] Drawing upon his experiences with exhibitions in France and the antipodes, one Australian showman argued that if the commissioners first attracted with visual displays, such as models and photographs, they then could teach with lectures, pamphlets, and magic lantern shows. A "strong popular element" of bush scenes, "wax, life size, Australian types," and local foods and wines would provide "a hook for every fish," or potential settler visiting the exhibition courts. "Would it [Australia] not then become to him a living thing, speaking in distinct and unmistakable tones of a far-off land, where the conditions of life are easy . . . and where many industries are prosecuted with success?" Those promises of economic successes were matched by suggestions of social order and public history. Wary of their frontier image, Australian commissioners struggled to ensure impressions of a tame social life in the antipodes. One might even find continuities with British and European societies. Queensland's executive commissioner reminded visitors to the 1878 Paris Universal Exposition that "the laws of the colony are based upon those of Great Britain, but are framed and administered so as to apply to the conditions of a new country."[66]

The collection of Australian settler resources and Aboriginal relics for display at overseas exhibitions demonstrated the quest for a sense of public history modeled on Europe's and North America's that would appeal to the cultural needs of current settlers and future emigrants. Australian commissioners for the Parisian shows solicited a variety of Aboriginal weapons, tools, manufactures, and "an account of the modes of using each" from local exhibitors.[67] Opossum cloaks, barks used for tonic or to "stupify fish," walking sticks, and feather fans forwarded from Victoria to Paris in 1867 were such historical signs. They reminded the author of Victoria's official catalogue that "the native is fast dying out from the colonised area," as he was in other settler regions, as well, but that his relics highlight "the progress of colonisation."[68] Modern guns, wool samples, and mineral trophies underscored the productivity and apparent triumph of European settlers, according to the catalogue's introduction.

The sense of nineteenth-century "Englishness" or national identity often relied on the dialectic between "modern" England and "traditionalist" Scotland and Ireland.[69] Australian colonists displaced onto the Aboriginal such an opposition in these overseas exhibition displays. Aboriginal weapons and fishing implements were intended to show the original state of man, as did, to a lesser degree, those relics being unearthed at concurrent archaeological digs in England and Europe.[70] The exhibitions offered the contrast between "man in his 'stone age,' as exemplified by the aborigines of Australia, in juxtaposition with man in the golden age of his present civilization," as could be found "in the great capitals of the old world."[71] The Australian settler negotiated and occupied the historical space between those two stages; he was both the link and the agent of that linkage.

The novelty of Australian society and land was suggested by countless displays of characteristic local animal, human, and plant life. Ethnographic specimens, for example, highlighted the complementary sense of difference between the settler and the *indigene*, but also the placement of Australia in the common framework of naturalized Darwinian development. "Rude" implements and crude products, including those observed at Pitt-Rivers' ethnographic collections in the South Kensington and Oxford Museums, commonly represented the origin of advanced types during the second half of the nineteenth century.[72] The Aboriginal displays at the exhibitions were early parallels, prototypes, or models of what evolved later: the canoe prefigured the iron-clad, and the spear and fishing line suggested other modern (or, "English" and "European" white-settler) ways to control the environment and animal life.

Other colonial exhibits provided a reflecting mirror for the metropole's domestic cultural policy, as well as a standard by which to measure the colony's "progress" and "Englishness." Similarities between Australian and British exhibits provided potential emigrants with the sense that their "new" home was a comprehensible and less hostile frontier. Twopeny's potential emigrant would notice that "home is reproduced" in Australia, "where English habits and customs prevail."[73] Educational exhibits suggested such similarities. In the case of the 1871 London International Exhibition, imperial and colonial commissioners requested objects to illustrate "the educational works and appliances, as well as the teaching."[74] Queensland's secretary and general inspector for the Education Office responded from the colony that such displays would only attract the attention of those interested in the overseas applications of English models and thus offer nothing truly new to visitors. Brisbane's representative noted that Queensland's educational work and its methods of school management did "not differ in any material respect" from those practiced in England by certified teachers. They would not be interesting to those looking for what was novel or unique in the colony; the process of cultural transplantation had been too successful. The colonial official concluded, "Our appliances, when not imported, are simply adaptations of the best models found in the old country."[75] On the other hand, their display might reassure potential emigrants wary of "new" cultural conditions.

Exhibition commissioners from New South Wales also eased emigrants' anxieties about Australia's novelty by highlighting their colony's "urbanized" population. The colony's official catalogue in 1862 compared the demographic composition of England with that in the colony and suggested that newcomers could expect a "large proportion inhabiting the metropolis [Sydney]" and the consequent "complete division of labour, organization of industry, and the mental activity produced by the aggregation."[76] These were similar conditions to those found in the urbanized Old World. The colony's promise was reflected in the significant numbers between the ages of fifteen and forty-five. New South Wales was truly a "new" and "young" nation, but also, in contrast to popular images, an urban one. It offered "a home of comfort and plenty to the surplus population of the old world" and, in doing so, guaranteed a transplanted British "birthright."

Emigration agents in London and North America were among the special commissioners organizing such exhibits to attract new settlers at overseas exhibitions. Their efforts were notably successful during the Philadelphia Centennial Exhibition in 1876. Among the immediate and direct results of the "extensive display of Australian products and manufactures" was the emigration of "between six and seven hundred persons" from North America for Sydney.[77] The passengers from New York, Pennsylvania, New England, and Canada were generally "persons of respectability," who had paid eight pounds for the passage, and "whose attention was directed to this colony [New South Wales] mainly by the admirable show made" at the Exhibition.[78]

Authors of the *Official Catalogue* for New South Wales at the Philadelphia show were optimistic about what those migrants could expect upon arrival in Australia. They proclaimed that the resources of the colony "may be enjoyed among a people whose whole social life is so like Home that it is scarcely possible for the emigrant to feel like 'a stranger in a strange land.' The language, customs, habits, laws, literature, education, religion, are all thoroughly English."[79] Here was a new home for the "sober, healthy, and industrious," in which "life and property" were secure. Not all were sought, but only those found "desirable," such as men and women who could afford to pay for their passage, who realized cultural and ethnic requirements, or who fulfilled particular economic needs, such as that for wine-growers.[80]

MID-CENTURY COLONIAL ETHNOGRAPHIC EXHIBITS

Australian and Indian commissioners included ethnographic models and curios to accompany commercial, art, and machinery displays in their overseas exhibition courts. Visitors to the Colonial and Indian Exhibition walked amid "figures of the various races of India, clad in their regimentals" and "a life-like representation of native life in Australia."[81] Models of Sepoy troops implied local participation in colonial rule to the exhibition visitors and thus post-Mutiny loyalty. English officials also took advantage of such displays to construct imperial "Museums of Mankind" at the shows, representing the vastness and diversity of the Empire's races and cultures. In one case, commissioners for the 1874 London International ambitiously proposed "a great National Museum of the Empire upon which the sun never sets."[82] From London, they solicited "Life-size and other Figures representing the Aboriginal Inhabitants in their Ordinary and Gala Costumes" from colonial commissioners to "illustrate the Ethnology and Geography of the different portions of the British Dominions."

These exhibits were both decorative and educational. They drew upon the tradition of ethnological shows in London and other British metropolises since the early nineteenth century. By the 1850s, Londoners regularly visited and viewed a wide variety of popular ethnographic shows and dioramas of "noble savages."[83] John Conolly wrote in 1855 that there is "scarcely a year in which, among the miscellaneous attractions of a London season we do not find some exhibition illustrative of the varieties of mankind."[84] The ethnographer argued that, rather than instructing audiences about science and art, many of these shows were commercial novelties intended to promote sales. Others apparently distorted science for the public by emphasizing the subjects' "marvellous character." As a substitute for travel, however, these "attractions" worked well. Models and living subjects introduced "Aztecs," "little Africans," and peoples from the regions of North America and both South and East Asia.

The exhibitions played an important role in centralizing and institutionalizing the ethnographic mode of display. Commissioners solicited models as ornamentation for courts and as exhibits themselves. They were judged for their aesthetic quality and the realism of their representation. Two models of American Indians "in aboriginal costumes" stood at one side of the

Crystal Palace's American Court, and one visitor found them realistic "enough to frighten any European."[85] Montanari's models of Mexican peasants, "savage Indians," and Osceola, the Seminole chief from Florida, earned praise and medals as both artistic and scientific exhibits at the Great Exhibition in 1851 and four years later at the Paris Universal Exhibitions.[86] Cole also promoted the display of ethnographic dioramas at the exhibitions and South Kensington. By the early 1870s, models of Indian weavers and potters provided context for his many displays of South Asian artware at the museum.[87] These had been forwarded by local Indian committees for display at various international exhibitions.

The Ethnological Court at the Crystal Palace, Sydenham, provided a mid-century model for an imperial Museum of Mankind. R. G. Latham's models of African peoples entertained and educated thousands of visitors before they burned in the large fire at the Crystal Palace during the 1860s. The Palace officers and Latham organized these models geographically and, as a precedent for later exhibition displays, provided examples of the trees, plants, and animals found in the "natural" habitat of the particular social group. The Old World of "Europe, Asia, and Africa" filled one side of the section and faced across the aisle "the New World" of America.[88] Although recognized as somewhat "inaccurate," the models were praised as "the only materials generally accessible to the public in London" by which on a permanent basis the "popular mind" could familiarize itself with racial variety and the new science of ethnography. The editors of the *Anthropological Review* considered the models' destruction by fire "amongst the most important anthropological events" of the mid-1860s.[89] Representatives of the scientific community recommended that the replacement models include, as did the ethnographic dioramas and figures at the exhibitions, "all necessary accessories of costume and furniture" and that they maintain "the expression of living subjects" as much as possible.

The Crystal Palace's organizers at the Science and Art Department, including Owen Jones, offered complete scientific pictures in cases where the visitors' imagination was previously forced to extrapolate from relics, bones, weapons, and fragments. Here was visual evidence of the empire's subject races and its experts' ability to study and represent them. Organizers compared the ethnological models to those of "extinct animals" displayed in their appropriate geological strata on the Palace grounds. Latham and B. Waterhouse Hawkins turned to these models to justify to the general public the prominent positions and authority of geology, zoology, and ethnology within the scientific community. Lessons about public taste and display strategies learned at the Great Exhibition revealed that "the simple use of the organs of sight, and little more than the natural instinct of a child" could produce knowledge from common things scientifically organized.[90] These "things" included peoples, as well as economic and artistic objects.

COLONIAL ETHNOGRAPHIC EXHIBITS
AFTER THE GREAT EXHIBITION

Similar guidelines and objectives informed the projects of ethnographic exhibitors at the major exhibitions after 1851.[91] Taxidermists and model builders, such as Rowland Ward in Britain and Herr Saupe in South Australia, featured the total environment of animals, flora, and dwellings. They attempted to represent active human models in a natural context. Commentators noted that dioramas at the Colonial and Indian Exhibition provided "a good general idea of the state of native life." [92] Ward designed a variety of displays, including the popular jungle scene in the Indian court at the South Kensington show in 1886. His displays combined the "scientific and picturesque" to make the standard "museum arrangement" more attractive.[93] Ward also offered the South Australian commissioners "naturalistic scenes and specimens of, in picturesque grouping, (1) the aboriginal ethnology, (2) the (fauna) animals and birds, (3) the general flora, of the region, by typical examples." Painted panoramas provided the horizons and landscapes. Such dioramas at the exhibitions in the 1880s featured Aboriginals hunting, fishing, and in family groups, such as Ward proposed.

The Victorian and South Australian courts at the Colonial and Indian Exhibition included such displays. According to one contemporary account, the model from Victoria shows "the various wild animals indigenous to the Colony, as well as the character of the vegetation, and the aboriginal inhabitants in their primitive condition of life." [94] The newspaper also described "the well-executed group of natives and animals indigenous to South Australia" and the integration of hunting, cooking, and family life as "wonderfully effective." The displays "give a good notion of the aboriginal life of the South Australians." [95] Although the models conflated animals and tools from various regions and thus represented an Aboriginal archetype, or portrait, they were noted for their increased realism and scientific accuracy in light of earlier exhibition displays.

If the Colonial and Indian dioramas were subject to debate, at least their nearly total inclusivity, including land animals, seals, and Aboriginals, was beyond questioning. They emphasized Aboriginal integration with the unique Australian flora and fauna. Artists followed Sir Redmond Barry's earlier proposal of taking casts from living Aboriginals, rather than death masks, which were not considered always to provide the proper physiognomy of the individual and thus would not be representative. The Victorian commissioner had contacted local artists and protectors of Aborigines during the 1860s to acquire "casts in plaster taken of the heads of some of the Aboriginal natives" for the London and Paris exhibitions.[96] He proposed displaying these with baskets, weapons, and natural history samples labeled "in the original language, as correctly as possible."

In the case of the indigenous Australians, ethnographic models, relics, and weapons served to represent what was allegedly a disappearing, or "stone age," race. The exhibition displays provided one of the few public representations of the Australian Aboriginal amid the general late-nineteenth-century "silence" about the early European-Australian frontier.[97] Aboriginal weapons and bones also decorated exposition courts and proved attractive to English and European exhibition commissioners seeking permanent museum displays. Enlarged photographs of Aboriginals dominated the back wall at the Queensland Annexe in South Kensington during the early 1870s (see Figure 3) and the colony's commissioner at the 1878 Paris Universal Exposition noted that their weapons were "sent as matters of curiosity only."[98] Skulls, weapons, and products were not only attractive ornaments; they were also useful currency for Australian commissioners seeking samples for their own institutions of "modern" and "stone age" European objects. Barry organized the exchange of such Aboriginal "curios" for overseas art and manufactured products.

Those ethnographic models were presented as natural history exhibits as much as anthropological texts; their manufacture by noted museum taxidermists, such as Ward, provided a sense of scientific reality and authority to the preservationist project, but, in doing so, mirrored similar representations of "wild" animals. But, after all, those displays represented existing social groups, although generally classified with archaeological and natural history exhibits. The New South Wales commissioners at the Calcutta International Exhibition in 1883 collected and displayed photographs of local Aboriginals, samples of their weapons and tools, including boomerangs and shields, and a glass menagerie of an Aboriginal camp and kangaroo chase. These were classified with other "Ethnology, Archaeology, and Natural History" exhibits, such as stuffed animals, fishing lines, and implements from various South Pacific indigenous communities, rather than, for example, "modern" weapons and tools.[99]

India's commissioners and exhibitors also displayed ethnographic models with curios at overseas shows. Whereas Australian officials struggled to represent communities facing extinction, if not already extinct, as in the

Tasmanian case, their South Asian and Anglo-Indian counterparts exhibited signs of revived and seemingly active social groups.[100] Visitors to the Indian Courts at South Kensington in 1886 were greeted by what seemed to be a full army of Sepoy soldiers and the government's Ethnological Court accompanied these military models with ones of the various "tribes" and "castes" found in the Raj.[101] One popular guidebook noted that "few things more vividly impress the beholder of the immensity of the area embraced by the Indian Empire than the wide variety of races which these native examples exhibit."[102] Plaster-of-paris and clay "ethnological figures" were among the exhibition displays sold by public auction or exchanged for other objects after the events. The government of India sent "figures of typical native races" cast and clothed at the Calcutta School of Art to several European, English, and South Asian institutions after the close of the Colonial and Indian Exhibition. Among the recipients were the Berlin and Nagpore Museums.[103]

The Raj's ethnological exhibits strengthened the already strong and self-consciously "Orientalist" imperial courts. Indian and other "Eastern" architectural details, such as carved screens, monumental gateways, and tents, were incorporated into the Indian Departments as early as 1851 and provided the background for ethnographic models, artware, and economic displays (see Figure 6). The "total" exhibition courts induced visitors to imagine and envision a timeless India of fantasy and tradition. The Canadian commissioner to the 1855 Paris Universal Exposition was particularly struck by the Indian court, and he painted a literary picture of its attractive dynamism and totality in his official report. "First there is an Indian village, or more properly speaking a bazaar in the country, consisting of an enclosure in the form of a parallelogram, made of bamboos, covered with thatch; in the court, herding together, are women, children, men, horses, cattle and elephants, on the roof of the house are troops of monkeys basking in the sun, or gamboling in a fantastic manner."[104] He noted how the "bazaar" and its models transported the visitor "into the midst of the scenery in that strange land of Civilization" and caused minds to wander within "the Tales of the Thousand and one nights, and the enchanted shores and palaces of fairy land." Some of those ethnographic figures had been prepared to represent India's many castes, religious groups, and artisans for South Asian and Anglo-Indian visitors to the 1854 Bombay Metropolitan Exhibition. At that time, they were praised for their scientific accuracy and for being "beautifully made. . . . It is not alone in the faultless and exquisite formation of the figures, and the natural coloring, in which the *Soortees* excel: the expression was most life-like. The Mahommedan can be distinguished from the Hindoo not only by his beard and garments; but by the general contour of his features."[105]

Later Indian exhibition courts and pavilions were also ornamented with similar models representing various castes, professions, and regions. These projects became more and more ambitious. Purdon Clarke expanded on Digby Wyatt's architectural contributions to the Crystal Palace and Paris Universal Exposition in the 1850s by designing and building more elaborate Indian Pavilions for the series of later Parisian shows in the 1870s and 1880s.[106] Clarke utilized architectural sketches and photographs taken during a tour of India for the South Kensington Museum.[107] Back in India, Bombay's commissioners forwarded a large collection of clay figures representative of both castes and economic groups to the Calcutta International Exhibition. They were available for purchase after the exhibition closed, and the official catalogue provided prices for the model figures of aboriginal and domestic servant family groups.[108] The final touch of Orientalist spectacle was the display of live animals at French and English shows near the turn of the century.[109]

INDIA'S PAST: HISTORICAL LANDSCAPES
AND EXHIBITION DISPLAYS

South Asian ethnographic displays were part of the wider program of coming to terms with the subcontinent's past at and beyond the exhibitions. British India's commissioners at the overseas shows transformed objects into artifacts, providing historical contexts for artware and economic goods.[110] Ethnographic displays contributed to that contextualization. Exhibitions also created a historical foundation and continuity for the Raj and its seemingly transitory Anglo-Indian community. The latter appeared to comprise, as one Australian noted in the late 1870s, "mere sojourners in the land," in contrast to the more permanent settlers in Australasia.[111] "Whether rich or poor," remarked an Anglo-Indian in 1862, "the Europeans [in India] are regarded as birds of passage."[112] Exhibition commissioners addressed these problems of spatial, chronological, and social disruption by filling their overseas courts with relics from the East India Company and India's village-communities. These exhibits not only constructed a public history from the Raj, but also naturalized the presence of a creole Anglo-India in contrast to an alternative Eurasian one.

In England, Imre Kiralfy solicited and displayed over five hundred "Relics and Memorials of the Late Honourable East India Company" at his Empire of India Exhibition in 1895.[113] Visitors to Earl's Court that year observed manuscripts, seals, medals, trophies, battle engravings, petitions, and portraits of influential Anglo-Indians. Some of the relics were part of Lord Clive's "intensely interesting collection."[114] Many of the exhibits were copies or photographs of the original objects, but that did not detract from the comprehensiveness of this cabinet of curiosities or its valuable contribution to collective memory. Similar "historic" pictures, portraits, and statues from the history of British India decorated the Indian Court at the Festival of Empire Exhibition sixteen years later.[115] Visitors walked among prominent statues of Sir William Jones and the Duke of Wellington, as well as traditional crafts and Orientalist texts. There was, admittedly, "no attempt to decorate the Court as if it were an Indian building"; it appeared rather as a museum of the Raj. Those displays provided a sense of history for British imperial presence and rule; they naturalized Anglo-India.

Commissioners continued to display a variety of South Asian relics, as well, including casts of ancient monuments, manuscripts, weapons, and artware. In this way they claimed India's history. The Raj's commissioners appealed to the authority of the past, a traditionalist approach in contrast to their Australian colleagues, who made bold claims about the lack of such a past in the antipodes. Apparently, the Australian colonies were without those tangible historical connections. On the other hand, exhibiting India's monuments was part of the imperial historical project at the shows. Sir Henry Cole actively selected, catalogued, and took casts of "ancient" Indian monuments from the imperial center of South Kensington.[116] Casts from the various South Asian traditions, including Islam, Buddhism, and Tamil, would not only save "the original parts of ruined buildings," according to Cole, but also provide a sign of India's and England's post-Mutiny political links. The "beauty, novelty and suggestiveness of Indian architecture" reflected the fact "that India and the United Kingdom are under the same Sovereign," sharing history and authority.

Cole highlighted the urgency of his project by suggesting that "modern art is daily becoming more and more corrupted and all originality and identity being lost." South Kensington's imperial mission was the preservation and study of this original art and the representation of India's past. Art objects, such as statues and building ornamentation, were transformed into artifacts. Casts collected for exhibitions and the South Kensington Museum would preserve the authentic art which was "worthy of serious consideration" and, in doing so, do much more. Cole corresponded with Indian government officials and the secretary of state for India to promote the display of such casts in South Asian and overseas museums and exhibitions. He intended to organize the exchange of national relics.[117] Science and Art

Department officers forwarded copies of European and royal plates and regalia to local Indian museums; in return, Cole brought casts back to South Kensington.[118]

Historical ruins and relics fired the Victorian imagination. One mid-century Anglo-Indian called them "the fragments of wreck."[119] Seemingly "new" lands, such as Australia and America, could not provide such associations with the past; older ones, notably India and Greece, were filled with them. Many of India's "fragments" were recontextualized in the exhibition courts, where they symbolized former and current empires as reminders of the Raj's authority over the Indian past and present. For example, Alfred Lyall donated several inlaid columns from the Marble Palace in the Fort of Agra to the Colonial and Indian Exhibition in 1886. It was rumored at the time that they had been found on the ground within the palace "after the fall of the Moghal Empire, at the hand of the victorious Hindu besiegers."[120] Their excavation and display thus signified the Raj's assumption of that historical pattern.

Among other notable ruins displayed at the exhibitions was the Eastern Gateway of the Sanchi Tope. It captivated English and Anglo-Indian officials alike as "one of the most remarkable" examples of "Buddhist architecture—the oldest type of Indian art known."[121] Unlike the other Sanchi gateways, the Eastern one did not suffer "much damage from weather and other disastrous effects," but was a well-preserved "fragment" from the past. The parent cast of the Tope was "a gigantic work, employing above a hundred persons in the jungle of Central India." These workers were supplied by bullocks and servants traveling over "trackless districts."[122] According to government reports, it took over sixty carts to convey the necessary materials and the 737 square feet of the carved gateway required over one hundred separate casts. Modern reproductive and photographic techniques enabled it to be studied and copied in England, where the full-size cast dominated the Picture Galleries at the 1871 London International Exhibition.[123]

The cast dwarfed visitors and other exhibits (Figure 7). One official reporter considered the cast of the gate among "the most remarkable . . . marvels" of Indian architectural art and noted how its sculptural high relief and surface ornament revealed "how good Indian work often is."[124] It also attracted the eyes of many envious foreign commissioners seeking to organize exchanges of their exhibition displays for additional reproductions. Cole and his associates in India intended to make six copies of the Tope: three for South Kensington and one each for the French, Prussian, and Indian governments.[125] The South Kensington official wrote Lord Mayo that there was "great talk in Europe" about the monument and the castings, and that "the sight of these things will be more impressive of the greatness of India than hundreds of volumes of writing."[126]

Exhibition commissioners displayed models of other ancient Indian monuments and created new ones for the shows. Those creations included the "Gwalior Gateway" welcoming visitors to the Indian Bazaar at the Colonial and Indian Exhibition (Figure 8). Not found anywhere in India, this exhibit was originally built for the Calcutta International Exhibition in the early 1880s by one thousand "Gwalior stone carvers" in just four months under the guidance of local government and art school officials.[127] The Gateway was not a copy of a conventional entrance, as was suggested by some of the accompanying written references, but an attempt to illustrate "the carving of many periods," thereby collapsing time. It drew attention to "a once flourishing industry . . . and a quantity of beautiful ornament" preserved by both the Indian artisan and the government of India.[128]

The Gateway was not an isolated case of creative traditionalism at South Kensington. It was placed near "five cathedral arches" intended to represent the Kantanagar Temple. The *Official Guide* for the Colonial and Indian Exhibition admitted that the series of arches "was dictated by the necessities of the Exhibition, and does not resemble anything" found in the Temple itself.[129] On the other hand, as was the case with the Gwalior Gateway, the arches provided "a fair idea" of the type of labor and ornamentation in India. These relics were signs for and of the traditionalists' authentic and original India, representing the Raj's capacity to essentialize India's history and society, revive older art forms and processes, and integrate the work of various regions and times. One of the organizers claimed that the forms at Gwalior were "not dead but merely in abeyance and would revive with patronage." Revival under the Raj's patronage contrasted with the advice of some prominent Victorian art critics, including Owen Jones, to avoid merely reproducing old art forms.[130]

As patrons of the past, Anglo-Indian art experts and exhibition commissioners often presented such architectural relics as illustrations of religious life, which, if strengthened, might prevent the modern social transformations increasingly blamed for both the Mutiny and the Indian National Congress.[131] Traditional Indian stone carving, such as that illustrated by the Gwalior Gateway project, represented to some art critics the "pious" labor and conservation efforts of the Jain community.[132] Joint projects with Indian princes also suggested the reconstruction of "the village community" and personal rule in the subcontinent in the face of Nationalist proposals for self-rule and the expansion of the market economy.[133] Traditionalist art and politics went hand in hand. As Birdwood argued, the princes' patronage of art objects revived their central political and cultural role at the local level.[134]

MANUFACTURING THE INDIAN PAST

Exhibitions were important components in the invention and representation of a traditionalist India, with its particular cultural topography of public architecture and political authority. Portraits of "the Greatest of the Moghul Emperors," casts of ancient monuments, collections of ethnographic types, and the display of working artisans created the sense of that Indian national past at the shows.[135] These displays mirrored the increasingly common impressions of officials, such as Temple, that Northern India was the essence of the Raj, for it was a land of "temples, spires, and palaces," in which the past stared at the present in a series of picturesque moments.[136] The social and political contexts were the seemingly stable princely states and their local village-communities, in which the imagination was excited by timeless "antique remains" and natural beauty, rather than the much-feared "anarchy" of a new Mutiny, additional Liberal reforms, and India's cities. Authority in the North was personal, not bureaucratic, as it seemed to be in the cities.

Princes were encouraged to participate in this project by forwarding artware and relics from their regions to the exhibitions. Banni Singh, for example, employed skilled artisans and painters at his Ulwar palace and exhibited illuminated volumes at the Simla Art Exhibition in 1879.[137] One notable volume was estimated to be worth Rs. 50,000. It included an embossed leather cover and gilt binding executed by his artists. The Maharajah of Ulwar also published general volumes with illustrations of "the most beautiful and interesting" art works in his private collections.[138] This paralleled official exhibition catalogues and the government-sponsored *Journal of Indian Art and Industry*, published between 1886 and 1917. The Raj thus claimed its local allies in the attempt to be the natural successor to past regimes, regenerator of Indian Art, and preserver of the traditionalist historical and social vision.

English authorities in India established an Archaeological Survey as part of that effort to identify, preserve, and regenerate India's architectural treasures and "ancient" monuments.[139] Indigenous experts participated in this project by contributing to local volumes, such as *The Antiquities of Orissa*. That volume included photographs and prompted casts of "some of the more important sculptures of ancient India."[140] Government archaeology officials worked with and encouraged exhibition officers, claiming that they were saving such treasures from the encroaching environment, local neglect, and, in some cases, deliberate plundering and vandalism by South Asians. "The art is purely traditionary," wrote one advocate of these efforts, "but, like all traditionary art, is in danger of being starved." [141] The government of India would provide sustenance to prevent that starvation.

Major J. B. Keith was in charge of the Archaeological Survey's division for Oudh, the Central India Agency, and the Central Provinces. He also superintended the construction of the Gwalior Gateway for exhibition in Calcutta and London. [142] Keith recommended the establishment of a "Museum for Archaeological fragments, as well as a place of registry for decayed workmen." He forwarded a "representative stone carving" to the Calcutta International Exhibition to solicit public support for this preservationist work in the face of commonly perceived challenges. Keith wrote that "the greed of a Mahomedan contractor . . . for dressed stone" resulted in "rich medieval pillars [being] ground down into road material, whilst temple friezes and bas reliefs were converted into targets for rifle practice." [143] Although these cases were most likely the exceptions, rather than the rule, indigenous neglect was a common self-justifying refrain among preservationists.

These efforts were part of the imperial mission to rescue, preserve, study, and exhibit the Indian past because, it was argued, the Indians themselves ignored it, and the wild South Asian environment reclaimed and hid relics. "At Ajunta, Kannari, and Karlie," wrote a reviewer of James Fergusson's work on Indian architecture and "cave" art in the 1850s, "the caves are for the most part in deep, rocky ravines, from whose sides hang the spreading boughs of the sacred tree of the Hindus, and whose bottoms are filled with the densest jungle, the resort of tigers, leopards, and other beasts of prey. The entrances are concealed by enormous masses of fallen rock, . . . [and] . . . their sole tenant is now some crazy fanatic." [144] The apparently heroic rescue and restoration from jungles, tigers, and "crazy" fanatics of sacred texts and monuments in India provided materials for British India's public history in contrast to the Australians' contemporaneous "silence" about their continent's past. [145] Architectural monuments served the historiographical purposes of coins, languages, and tools in an effort to reconstruct general Indian history and find earlier "intercourse" between East and West. This would provide an historical precedent or continuity for the "Paramount Government" of the new mughals: the Imperial Raj and its Anglo-Indians. "India has a great aesthetic beauty, which archaeologists have set out in skilful and convincing fashion," concluded one Edwardian on the eve of the Great War.[146] Among the active "archaeologists" were the exhibition commissioners constructing Indian courts at overseas shows.

Preservation projects required the participation of Indian artisans and princes, who joined English and Anglo-Indian officials. Casts and photographs resulting from these partnerships were displayed at international exhibitions and afterwards either exchanged for foreign art objects or retained for permanent museum collections. Cole was hardly alone in seeking "to obtain a complete representation of Indian architecture," as commissioners and government officials around the Empire advocated the comprehensive displays of Indian relics at exhibitions.[147] They did so for imperial and national reasons. The South Kensington official advised Lord Mayo that the international exhibitions would "afford a very favourable opportunity of making the world acquainted with the casts of Indian architecture."[148] Casts of monuments such as the Sanchi Tope provided visitors with the "outward & visible signs of India" and inspired professional and educational interest in the country and its architecture. The executive commissioner also suggested that copies of the casts could be exchanged for other exhibition items desired for study and display by museum officers in England and India. The casts were a form of currency, noted for historical and exchange value.

Casts of ancient monuments and ornamental doorways complemented traditionalist Indian machinery displays. South Asian pottery wheels, for example, seemed as much at home adjacent to hand-crafted arches as they seemed out of place exhibited in close proximity to working Australian mining machinery. To the surprise of many visitors, some Indian technology resolved overseas, or transnational, technological dilemmas. That was the case with cotton-cleaning and "coin-sorting" machines displayed at the Great Exhibition.[149] More generally, though, Indian machines addressed specific colonial problems. Technology made such problems and their resolutions comprehensible to overseas visitors. The many "simple appliances" forwarded by local Indian committees to the Great Exhibition also revealed how "the natural productions of the country, whether animal, mineral, or vegetable, were converted into marketable commodities, many of which proved important staples of export and of coasting trade."[150] This was particularly true of the handmade artware and coarser cloths produced by handlooms, popular at the exhibitions and within South Asian regional markets.[151]

The Raj's commissioners implicitly claimed that the technological solution to many of their local concerns did not require the importing of large-scale machinery, as observed in the English and European exposition courts, but the restoration of local labor practices, notably those considered pure and historical. The culture of industrialism at the shows suggested the Empire's power to reconcile modern economic development and traditionalist social order. This might be done by exhibiting what Cole termed the "certain processes of manufactures performed by natives," as well as by the dynamos and steam engines.[152] The executive commissioner's assistants for the Paris Exposition in 1867 recognized that India would "probably be unable to show much in the way of machinery." This was not all bad, though, since limited mechanical displays suggested the return to political order, social stability, and gradual economic development after the Mutiny. The Raj might rule in the name of local tradition as well as British progress.

India's exhibition courts included the tools and implements used by local artisans to produce "the most delicate and exquisite works of art and industry."[153] One Anglo-Indian recalling India's contributions to the Great Exhibition suggested that the same implements were still in use and on display at the Calcutta Agricultural Exhibition almost fifteen years later. In contrast to improved English, European, and Australian "machines-in-motion," the Indian samples offered "no signs of the least improvement" since the Crystal Palace. They represented a sense of timeless labor. One reading of those displays would relegate the Indian productive sector to primitive status and offer an unfavorable contrast with the working engines forwarded by European and North American exhibitors. An alternative reading would suggest the picturesque craftsmanship of such crude tools and the Empire's capacity to preserve such a tradition. Amid fears of rebellion and change, here were signs of order and continuity. One India Office expert concluded in a public lecture after the Great Exhibition that "it has been owing in a great measure to the village system of the Hindoos, that we are to ascribe the permanence of the arts in India."[154]

EXHIBITING INDIAN ARTWARE

Traditional arts and crafts were among the most popular Indian exhibits at overseas shows. They represented popular notions of "permanence" in Indian society and culture; most certainly, Cole held such beliefs. Commissioners organized the production, display, and sale of baskets, metalwork, and pottery to promote an image of the Indian village community, suggest the value of artisanal labor, and collect revenue. Tourists and merchants were encouraged to purchase those displays before and after the shows. Those sales caught the attention of contemporaries. The editors of the *Prim-*

rose Record, a conservative journal, highlighted the "rapid sale" of Indian arts and crafts at the Colonial and Indian Exhibition in 1886, noting the direct relationship between the English purchasers and the Indian artisans.[155] Visitors continued to observe and purchase India's exotic art exhibits (which contrasted with Australia's utilitarian displays) at the Franco-British and Festival of Empire shows on the eve of the First World War.[156]

The practice of exhibiting seemingly traditional and, therefore, timeless arts and crafts began with the Crystal Palace in 1851. Rather than displaying the fine arts, such as painting and sculpture, India's commissioners offered inlaid and laquered woodwork, carpets, jewelry, and pottery. These emphasized a princely India and were considered "fancy manufactures" not intended for mass and popular consumption. Other exhibits, including silver trays and cigar cases, were offered in the attempt to stimulate overseas demand, but still represented artisanal art forms.[157] British India's commissioners took extensive measures to ensure that the courts and bazaars in which artware was exhibited were also attractive, although this did not always guarantee successful sales.[158]

Almost forty years later, John Forbes Watson wrote George Birdwood from Paris that "very large numbers of people pass thru the [Indian] Pavilion and so far we have had our share of patronage."[159] That patronage of India's wares depended, in part, on their apparent uniqueness and authenticity. The Official Catalogue for the Indian Pavilion guaranteed that its merchants sold "articles of genuine Indian manufacture," and the various exhibition committees financed the transportation, housing, and craftsmanship of "native" artisans in keeping with that promise.[160] Visitors were also attracted by the novelty of Indian art. This was particularly the case at the Australian international exhibitions, where the editor of one local guidebook observed that the exhibits in the Indian Court at the 1880–81 Melbourne International Exhibition were "quite new to the colony."[161] Australians purchased seemingly authentic and, what was more important to them, previously unavailable "Eastern" items as souvenirs for themselves, relatives, and friends.

Ambitious projects were undertaken to suggest the sense of "Orientalism," or authenticity, and use it to promote consumption and trade. Kiralfy and Birdwood worked together to recreate Indian village bazaars with artisans at the series of exhibitions during the 1880s and 1890s in London and various European cities.[162] Kiralfy reconstructed a Bombay street scene, Benares temple, and Lahore shop fronts for his Empire of India Exhibition in 1895. His sources for those Orientalist structures and fantasies included Clarke's photographs and sketchbooks, Birdwood's various volumes on India, and woodwork from condemned houses in Poona.[163] Clarke wrote Birdwood that the Empire Exhibition and the "Indian City" at the Antwerp International Exhibition held the previous year offered visitors "a grand affair." Among his reasons was the number of South Asian weavers and metalworkers brought to the shows to craft sale items in front of visitors at this reconstructed and imaginary point of artistic origin.[164]

Visitors also observed weavers and potters working alongside the recreated Indian Durbar Hall and Palace at the Colonial and Indian Exhibition (Figure 9). Again, as was the case with the Gwalior Gateway, the Hall and Palace were not copies of existing buildings, but intended to "represent . . . typical" structures "in feudal India."[165] One contemporary described the accompanying bazaar for his readers in 1886: "On the left side of the Imperial Court are four small shops similar to those found in the average Indian villages. These have been arranged so as to display the surplus stock of the exhibits which are shown in the Index Collection. They have been constructed of bamboo and thatched with Indian straw, according to the system commonly seen."[166] Those displays provided the traditionalist framing for artisanal labor and sales. Here was either the magical Punjab filled with village-communities and princely leaders, considered by many to be the true "India," or a traditionalist space within the modern cities of Bengal. Either way, India's commissioners constructed the Hall and bazaar as seemingly authentic contexts in which they could display and sell carpets, silks, and other artware.

The direct gaze of the visitors could thus, it was argued, verify the quantity, quality, and authenticity of the artistic products crafted and purchased at the shows. Production at the exhibition site provided a further reconstructed "aura" to replace that found in the locale of the object's origin and lost in this era of mechanical reproduction and mobility.[167] Exhibition commissioners recreated that unique "pre-historical" site at the shows by annihilating historical time and geographical distance. Birdwood ensured that only qualified Indian artisans worked within those bazaars and even challenged the authenticity of items sold in competition with the Raj's artware. The Indian Office expert accused "Greeks & Levantines" of increasing prices and selling "Birmingham & German rubbish at several hundred per cent profit" at the expositions.[168] Goods sent to the Alexandra Palace in London after the 1873 Vienna International Exhibition were inspected by British officials and stamped "to ensure their genuineness" before display and sale to prevent the introduction of "inferior workmanship, manufactured expressly for the English market."[169] The opportunity for direct contact and observation offered an alternative to the unpopular distortion of professional advertising, allowed the visitor to verify the authenticity of the product, and provided Anglo-Indian elites and Indian Office officials with an opportunity to craft the traditionalist image of India.

Social identity and integration were suggested not only by what was produced and exhibited, but also by what was purchased and consumed. The reproduction of exhibits for purchase and as free souvenirs extended the memory of India's image for the visitors. Commissioners did not intend contact with Indian art and artisans as an ephemeral experience, but rather as a permanent one. The memory of the exhibition and the souvenirs purchased at the show might form cultural and political links between the English people and their Indian subjects. The museum curator H. H. Cole suggested in 1874 that the display of Indian art at the South Kensington Museum and exhibitions would "familiarise the people of England with the productions of India" and thus deepen "our sympathy with them."[170] The rediscovery, preservation, cataloguing, observation, and consumption of genuine art objects would result in "the creation of a true knowledge of these millions of people," which was necessary for responsible and effective rule.

The *Primrose* editors reached a similar, but more poetic, conclusion during the Colonial and Indian Exhibition in 1886: "As the Briton gazes in his home on the bit of crockery or silverware that some Indian craftsman turned out, his heart will go out to that humble artisan, and the two people will consequently become locked in one another's arms after the manner of lovers."[171] Nineteenth-century exhibitions did not create the practice of copying and collecting relics, but, as the journal's editors suggested, these events democratized and commercialized that process.[172] Commissioners removed objects from their original, often private context, and displayed them in public. Visitors observed those materials, purchased them as souvenirs, and although they returned to a new, relocalized, private space in their homes, they did so with new political meanings and, perhaps, romantic attachments. Art provided this sympathetic link because it could make a claim for universal values.[173] The Canadian commissioner at the 1855 Paris Universal Exposition remarked that visitors would not be disappointed in the Indian art exhibits, which represented skill, brightness of color, and an "originality of design" appealing to the more general pursuit of contemplation and nature.[174] The purchase of such art works represented an investment or direct participation in Empire, and the craftsmanship revealed the traditionalist urge found in England's discovery of its own and India's folk cultures. Indian arts and crafts were not singular and strangely peculiar as were many of the Empire's natural history exhibits of exotic flora and fauna. Neither were they direct economic competitors in the marketplace. Thus, India's traditional art was not a metaphor for internal imperial differences, colonial rebellions, nationalist movements, or commercial threats. Art works were signs of cultural affinities and historical links among the imperial units. The crafts suggested an India with a past and the Indian artist working within that tradition. These exhibits offered imperial connections which were different than, but complementary with, those between English exhibition visitors and the "new" settler societies of Australia.

THE POLITICS OF THE PAST

This thirst to study and know India's past mirrored a general Victorian preoccupation with acquiring historical and ethnographic knowledge about the colonial possessions and "Merrie Olde Englande" itself. Men and women across the Empire restored artisanal labor and preserved ancient monuments; others turned away from the indigenous past to preserve the "historic sites, ancient buildings, monuments, and cemeteries" of European and British settlers.[175] Australian and Indian exhibition officers at overseas shows were successful, in part, because their efforts complemented influential British domestic preservationist projects. Among those were the labors of Pugin and his neo-Gothic journal, the *Ecclesiologist*, and of Sir Benjamin Stone, the prominent late-Victorian photographer.[176] The latter's images capturing rural workers and Lichfield Cathedral offered notable complements to the photographic studies of South Asian ethnography, architecture, and landscape shown at exhibitions by Samuel Bourne and his colleagues during the same years.[177] In a more official vein, the series of Ancient Monument Protection Acts provided governmental funds and expertise for English architectural preservation, complementing India's official Archaeological Survey.[178]

Panoramic and detailed images of ancient monuments were particularly popular at exhibitions, including those organized by Photographic Societies and art school administrators.[179] Architectural relics, traditional arts and crafts, and folk rituals were additional emblems of a premodern mythic past, constructed by imperial cultural experts and captured by photography and artisanal reproduction. Commissioners represented this shared past with Indian gateways and reconstructions of "Old Edinburgh" and "Old London" street scenes. The "quaint and picturesque thoroughfare" representing London before the Great Fire of 1666 for the International Health Exhibition at South Kensington in 1884 embodied this impulse.[180] It was intended to offer an aesthetic contrast with contemporary structures by highlighting eaves, gables, tapestries, and other ornamentation; it also reminded observers of the distinctions between "the insanitary dwellings of those days, and the more wholesome ones of the present time." The domestic past was not always a source of nostalgic longing.

Preservationist exhibits restored the ideas of the authentic art and labor of the premodern community shared by East and West and the authority of traditional political leaders, but with varying success. Images offering the past-in-the-present for the Celtic Fringe and India found more receptive audiences than the illusions of the English past. On the other hand, English visitors dissatisfied with modern politics and the market found at least momentary relief in the traditionalist displays. The purchase of souvenirs, including Indian and Irish artware, prolonged both that vision and its contrast with the present. Photographs, casts, costumed models, and art works provided modes to create and diffuse relics for the new generation of artisans and consumers in Britain and India.

We can ask further about the connections between overseas preservationist projects and, for example, the Council of the Society for Promoting Industrial Villages, which was active in England during the 1880s.[181] What were the institutional and ideological links among the various British and colonial commissions to preserve ancient monuments?[182] On a more personal level, what drove Cole to cast ancient Indian monuments and organize the Tillingbourne Association "for the improvement of agricultural labourers?"[183] Exhibitions offered the venues for Cole and his colleagues to construct these national and imperial pasts and to represent them with Indian, Scottish, and Irish peasant jewelry, ornamental crafts, model villages, and natives in costume.[184]

The commissioners of the London International Exhibitions held at South Kensington in the early 1870s were particularly interested in such art forms. They solicited articles of peasant jewelry from the various participating nations. Irish and Indian Schools of Art were among those responding to such requests.[185] Their administrators (many of whom were also local exhibition commissioners) forwarded displays of traditional art crafted by their students and instructors to overseas exhibitions. The official announcement for the 1872 show noted the importance of "the Delhi Jewellery of the Upper Provinces." One year later, officials of the Calcutta, Madras, Bombay, and Jeypore Schools of Art forwarded pottery, bas-reliefs, and other traditional artware to South Kensington.[186]

Peasant industries offered a return to the allegedly essential, authentic, and harmonious village-community at home and abroad in India. Such conservatism anchored this generation's perception of the Indian past and

often shaped its vision of Englishness. Temple, who served the Indian government for forty years in Calcutta, Bombay, and the Central Provinces
succinctly articulated the paralleling: "The son of an English Country
gentleman, I took out to the East the traditions of rural life in England, and
religiously brought them back with me."[187] This was possible because of
Temple's mirroring of rural England and village India; gentlemanly personal rule commanded authority in both contexts. That political and social
vision was represented by religious festivals, artisanal crafts, and ancient
monuments. Visitors to the Colonial and Indian Exhibition could observe
the traditionalist dualism of that imperial connection in the adjacent
placements of the "Old London" Street and Gwalior Gateway at South
Kensington.[188]

Echoing Sir Henry Maine, the Raj's exhibition commissioners suggested
that an appreciation of Indian art, history, and society could also teach the
English not a little about themselves and their national past. This self-
consciously constructed traditional India offered, as Maine told his Cambridge audience in 1875, "the materials of knowledge by which the Past,
and to some extent the Present, of the West may be interpreted."[189] His
studies of "Indian or Oriental" law, social structure, and political society
were, Maine argued, "a far more trustworthy clue to the former condition
of the greatest part of the world than is the modern social organisation of
Western Europe, as we see it before our eyes."[190] The exhibition of Indian
art and Anglo-Indian relics would then place before visitors' eyes the objects representing that historical analogy and the Empire's role in such cultural processes. These historicist parallels also anchored the Anglo-Indian
community with the authority of the past as it negotiated its identity and
power between local indigenous and overseas imperial cultures.

Traditionalist exhibition projects represented "proprietary curiosity" in
the past, as one scholar has termed the general late-Victorian interest in India's history.[191] At the same time, they represented more than that. Preserving traditional social and cultural forms was part of the reworked systems of colonial authority and rule. Cole and the members of various Royal
Commissions urged, for political as well as scientific reasons, the public
preservation of Indian relics. The promotion of Indian artware was part of
this general political strategy, not only an aesthetic statement. Cole suggested that the casts of the Sanchi Tope, among other ancient memorials,
would "awaken a new public interest" in Indian art, archaeology, and architecture, and thus in Indian affairs in general. They would help preserve
"the numerous varied and unrivalled works of art still remaining in that
country, which furnish the best memorials of its history for the last two

thousand years." [192] The "memorials" and their history provided authority from the past for the Raj, its Anglo-Indian community, and the Indian princes.

However, there was an inherent tension here. Artifacts do, after all, have political meanings and uses, some of which might even be contradictory. While creating a Eurocentric and modern sense of imperial historical structure and knowledge, the application of English cultural classifications and technologies also created the material culture necessary for the public memory of colonial nationalism. Exhibitions did "awaken" public interest, but did so for different groups with sometimes differing objectives. Imperial commissioners mystified the "golden" precolonial ages at the overseas exhibitions and, in doing so, provided nationalist language and relics for Australians and South Asians to challenge imperial authority and its control of the past. The "best memorials" of an imperial past and present might very well turn out to be the "best" building blocks of a postimperial future.

6 Machines-in-Motion
*Technology, Labor, and
the Ironies of Industrialism*

Visiting France in 1878, Alexander Dobbie commenced his tour of the Paris Universal Exposition in the Machinery Department, where he walked amid the popular agricultural, paper-making, and pumping "machines-in-motion."[1] The South Australian engineer and machinist also noted that Thomas Edison's exhibits were "intensely interesting" and "always honoured with admiring crowds." Dobbie was not a disinterested visitor.[2] He collected information about machinery in Paris for possible applications back home in Australia and exhibited his own machines at local exhibitions, earning the First Degree of Merit at the Sydney International one year after his tour of the Universal Exposition.[3] Neither was Dobbie a lone Australian pilgrim on this technological quest. The New South Wales executive commissioner in Paris wrote his government's officials in Sydney that the colony's proposed exhibition would also "directly instruct our Artisans and Colonists generally, by giving them an opportunity of studying labor saving machinery, instruments, and apparatus, brought from all parts of the world for their inspection."[4]

Machines attracted Australians visiting English exhibitions as well. George Russell, manager of the Clyde Company in Victoria, was generally overawed by the Great Exhibition in 1851, but found "the machinery department, with models of new invented machines . . . particularly interesting."[5] Over thirty years later, Sir Arthur Blyth described "the great excitement here in London" with the "Annexe and Machinery in motion" court at South Kensington's International Health Exhibition.[6] Queensland's officials expressed interest in importing the fiber-treating machines they observed in operation at the subsequent Colonial and Indian Exhibition.[7] Those Australians were hardly alone in finding machines attractive at the exhibitions. Visitors from around the world observed and operated "machines-in-motion," including ones for milling, cutting, and carding woolen and worsted products, printing the *Times*, crafting pottery, brewing beer, and extracting gold.[8]

Working "steam-engines" appeared to be everywhere at the exhibitions in the 1860s, and over twenty years later the courts with machines "seemed to attract . . . people more than anywhere else" at the Colonial and Indian Exhibition.[9] Visitors came to expect such machines-in-motion displays and public testing of new technologies. Russell had carefully noted those in "motion" during his tour of the Crystal Palace in late May 1851.[10] By the turn of the twentieth century, Queensland's Agent-General wrote to his colonial secretary from Scotland that "it is not enough . . . to bring home [to England] exhibits and show them only in Museum style—they must be enlivened in some form."[11] He added that displays should include "something moving or working," as had been the case with popular exhibits at the recent Glasgow International Exhibition.

Machines at the exhibitions illustrated and made tangible what the scholar David Landes has termed transformations in "the getting and working" of raw materials, metals, and chemicals.[12] That connection was drawn across time and space at the shows. After visiting the machinery displays at the Crystal Palace, the Regius Professor of Mechanics at the University of Glasgow suggested that the term "manufacture" no longer implied the product of human manipulation, but now the articles made by machinery from raw materials found around the world.[13] Exhibitions celebrated not only mechanical devices and inanimate power, but also the new industrial and scientific organization of society. In keeping with that spirit, popular technological displays produced consumer goods and curios on the spot. Those suggested present and future fantasies of mass production in an industrial world with national and imperial connections.

English, Australian, and Anglo-Indian exhibition commissioners and other elites used the forum of major expositions to introduce new machinery and inanimate power sources, the ideal of the rational and self-regulating factory as a metaphor for society, and the general ideology of industrialism.[14] In doing so, officials and exhibitors mystified the social process of industrialism by hiding common workers and their forms of often hand-powered labor and offering instead an industrial system of various alternative forms of technology and work. Those included both traditional artisanal and modern heavy-capital production. Drills, presses, and other "self-acting" machines captivated exhibition audiences and offered a society without human work, masses of unskilled laborers, and trade union strikes. Imperial and colonial exhibition officials turned to the shows to naturalize that vision of an industrial social order. Machinery displays replaced and made invisible modern unskilled labor, but operated alongside visible traditional labor, such as South Asian and female craftsmanship.

Doulton's panels at the 1886 Colonial and Indian Exhibition illustrated the Empire and its various societies, divided into differentiated, yet linked, worlds of labor and machinery (see Figure 1). "England," "Australia," and "India," represented three ideal types of productive culture, including different, but interdependent, technology and work. Exhibitions suggested a social model for positioning the type of work and the worker according to racial, cultural, and thus apparently natural characteristics. Demonstrations of new machines at these shows and the permanent display of both those modern and contrasting traditional technologies at museums after the exhibitions diffused this imperial ideology of industrialism and played a significant role in the wider movement of technical education in England and the colonies.[15] Jules Joubert and government officials in South Australia were among those confident that the annual exhibitions hosted by agricultural societies in Sydney and "the country" could be used to introduce new machinery during the 1870s. Complementary museums would become permanent vehicles for the assimilation into local economies of such new technologies.[16]

Technological exhibits contained a type of political meaning or value, embodying forms of power and ideas of authority which took off in two very different trajectories. Such tension was not precluded or suppressed at the shows. The imperial and national industrial order made public at the exhibitions revealed the duality of technological innovation associated with the scholarship of Lewis Mumford.[17] He contrasted centralized and autocratic forms of industry with those that were decentralized and democratic. Machines that visitors operated seemed more democratic, man-centered, and diffused; larger technology that they could not operate themselves was more authoritarian, system-centered, and centralized. The various meanings of the exhibition displays, buildings, and artifacts reflected this dualism and, in the promotion of small-scale and flexible technology, suggested alternatives to heavily industrialized production. Many of those choices continue to influence postcolonial national culture in India and Australia, where both elite and rank-and-file debate industrialization's past, present, and future.[18]

On the other hand, large-scale, heavy-capital public works were one important aspect of the imperial experience; their authority was grounded in awe and spectacle. The exhibition displays of surging locomotives, colossal engines, and Henry Adams's "Dynamo" represented this part of the dualism inherent in Victorian industrialism.[19] Those exhibits performed the spectacle of technology, creating energy and power which challenged their own capacity to be measured and controlled. Here was the cosmos of force, the symbols of "infinity."[20] The popularity of the alternative industrial vision of accessible and participatory man-centered machines at the exhibitions reminds us that there were and are other centers of economic dynamism than those of the colossal public works illustrated by exhibition dynamos and built by ambitious imperialists. Highlighting this duality and the various tensions and ironies in machinery displays strengthens our understanding of how exhibitions and museums helped diffuse industrial innovations in England and the colonies after 1851 without the extensive adverse reaction of the early Victorian era.[21]

Effective diffusion of machines and industrialism required accessibility and immediacy—not only imposition and grandeur. Those alternative characteristics were found in the participatory experiences visitors had with smaller-scale machines-in-motion, such as the printing presses, pumps, and tile-making machines at the 1871 London International Exhibition.[22] Men and women visiting South Kensington that year could also turn the wheels of steam type-composing machines and evaluate the fruits of their labor. Similar experiences with accessible technology were shared by visitors at Indian and Australian exhibitions. They observed and tested agricultural engines, drills, and plows with, admittedly, varying degrees of effectiveness and sales.[23]

Machines were among the most popular exhibits at shows in the Australian colonies, as they were in England, where their displays often led to purchases and applications. This is not to suggest, though, that the exhibitionary mode fueled enthusiasm in all political and socioeconomic contexts. In contrast to Joubert's optimism in Australia, for example, Anglo-Indian officials were doubtful that English and other overseas machinery could be sold for local use after their shows in cities such as Nagpore and Bombay. Exhibition committees complained about the central government's waste of funds in bringing overseas machines to the festivals and its alleged guarantees of selling them; the sales would only be realized, according to one influential commissioner, if the local Resident forced the region's landlords and manufacturers to purchase the machines.[24] The machines-in-motion displays and attempts to diffuse the new industrialism point to both the effectiveness and limits of exhibitions in the colonies.

Exhibitions demonstrated the power of new machinery and its sponsors, including experts and the state itself, but at the same time revealed the various ironies of both the technology and its accompanying ideology of industrialism. Celebrations of self-acting machines without the participation of laborers included the intentional participation of the very workers and their families that the technology was displacing. Machines-in-motion whistled and whirred peacefully within structures built by struggling and often striking laborers. Exhibitions introduced industrialism as a new ideology and form of social practice with roots in the past. Seemingly modern machines were clothed in traditional gowns, avoiding the challenges of a new industrial aesthetic, which would not triumph until well after the turn of the twentieth century. And, in perhaps the most telling irony, exhibitions to honor peace included the display of machines of war.

Exhibitions were not only industrial spectacles, but living examples of the industrial process and its resulting new social order. Participation provided the meanings, language, and symbols in terms of which new forms of social interaction were imagined and took place, but not without irony and contest. The structure of the exposition experience for both organizers and visitors provided access to and legitimacy for this new framework of industrial beliefs and behavior. Exhibition literature and machines-in-motion displays made connections for the visitors between new technology, the organization of production in the factory, and the social organization of both nation and empire. As with all visions and symbolic constructions of public culture, the display of machines in Australia, England, and India hid and mystified as much—if not more—than it revealed, and provoked discontent as well as celebration.

MACHINES-IN-MOTION:
EXHIBITION COURTS AND DEMONSTRATIONS

Technological displays had been included in various pre-1851 exhibitions, including those organized by the British Association for the Advancement of Science, the Royal Society of Arts, and provincial mechanics' institutes.[25] Charles Babbage was enthusiastic at mid-century about machine-makers "who flocked to the annual meetings of the British Association . . . to interchange their ideas," while the *Manchester Guardian* applauded an early exhibition offering visitors "the products of the British loom, British machinery, and of the first and most perfect of all machines, the human hand."[26] Those were "educated by the intelligence, and guided by the idea of England's skilled artisans and artists." As early as 1763, the Royal Society of Arts offered trials of new agricultural implements, such as continental scythes, which were subsequently displayed as museum pieces in its Machine Room in London's Strand.[27] The Society continued this tradition by including machines and models at its many *conversaziones* in the 1880s.[28]

Separate rooms at such local events presented machines, instruments, diagrams, and models, but unlike the machinery halls and annexes at the later international exhibitions, these displays were generally static. They could not be observed in operation on a constant basis. Early organizers celebrated scientific innovation, philosophy, and labor to a greater degree than later commissioners, who underscored the power of the self-acting machine's and technology's roles in imperial expansion and national development. Machines tended to be isolated from other examples of material culture at those earlier exhibitions, whereas they were integrated with other exhibits at later shows, suggesting a more comprehensive and organic picture of modern industrial culture and society.

Working pumps, presses, drills, and engines filled the galleries at exhibitions in England and the colonies starting in 1851. Those machinery exhibits presented a total, dynamic, and open vision which prefigured the modern industrial society; they offered images of the factory as a new and attainable ideal. English exhibition commissioners, such as Thomas H. Huxley, the prominent scientist and defender of Charles Darwin, and Sir Henry Cole, superintendent of the South Kensington Museum, were among the most vocal advocates for including machinery-in-motion courts. Both emphasized this point during their testimonies in 1867 before the Parliamentary Committee called to consider the Paris Universal Exposition of that year.[29]

Among the committee's charges was the determination of which exhibits should be purchased for future display at English exhibitions and museums. Witnesses listed a variety of European and "Oriental" manufactures and artworks for cases at the British and South Kensington Museums. Huxley also argued that the public should have access "to all the best aids to science that can be obtained," including "mining models, or things applicable in the processes of the arts."[30] Cole continued that not only the general public, but "the operative classes," in particular, would benefit from viewing such new technologies in operation. They would thus "have the means of understanding what are the great instruments upon which our well-being depends," or at least what it appeared to depend upon in Victorian England.[31]

Elites and voluntary societies throughout Britain and the Empire agreed with the educational value of such demonstrations and collections. Many sent official deputations to observe and study machinery courts. Organized visitors from Halifax and Bradford, for example, were asked by their sponsors to pay particularly close attention to French and other European examples of cotton- and cloth-making machines at the 1855 Paris Universal Exposition and to note "any improvement in the manner" of working wool and cotton.[32] Australians mirrored such activities. Over twenty years later, the South Australian Chamber of Commerce and the colony's official commissioners suggested sending "artisan reporters" or "one or more intelligent artisans" to the Sydney International Exhibition for a report on agricultural and manufacturing machinery exhibits.[33] One of the subcommittees voted funds to the chief engineer to select and finance the group and called upon "the Manufacturers as a body" to assist this "national" project to study English and North American labor-saving machines.

Exhibition demonstrations and post-show trials introduced new inventions to industrialized urban populations and those living in rural and relatively unmechanized areas during the last half of the nineteenth century. Commissioners drew upon successful competitions at exhibitions, agricultural shows, and county fairs when introducing new technologies and techniques. In England, the Royal Agricultural Society and the Smithfield Club Shows provided precedents with their cattle and machinery competitions. Battles among the "Barons of Beef" and harvesters displayed the drive for efficiency and ingenuity within the context of a changing rural society.[34] Those agricultural shows also revealed the social and cultural tensions of new machinery. Rural elites grounded in land ownership and family wealth faced the challenge of new experts, such as engineers and scientists offering more powerful machines and larger cattle. One group appealed to traditionalist sources of authority, while the other turned to new ones, such as science. They faced the challenge of introducing those new ideas and technologies without the much-feared social anarchy that a sharp break from the past might provoke. Exhibitions often provided a traditionalist and ceremonial event in which innovations might be introduced and diffused without emphasizing discontinuity, offering, perhaps, improvement without instability.

As we now recognize, the nineteenth-century diffusion of new technologies was not as rapid and comprehensive as originally suggested by some contemporaries and scholars. Revisionist studies of the Industrial Revolution have challenged us to rethink both terms of that bold title.[35] On the other hand, research suggests that exhibitions in Australia, India, and England introduced and disseminated certain significant machines in a relatively fast, widespread, and permanent manner. Among those was Cyrus McCormick's reaper, which dominated the American room devoted to agricultural implements at the Great Exhibition. As long as two months after the Crystal Palace opened, one observer still remarked that "this machine continues to excite considerable interest among agriculturalists and their machinists; and it is seldom that two or three farmers, and often farm labourers, are not to be found examining the details of its construction, and speculating upon its success in effecting the desired object." [36] William Drew, commissioner for the State of Maine, noted that the famous "Reaping machine" was tried on various fields "near London" and, after satisfying the juries, "is entitled to the greatest Premium of the Fair." [37]

Success in 1851 was repeated at later exhibitions in England and Europe. [38] The speed and efficiency of reapers and plows were on display both during the 1862 London International at South Kensington and then again afterwards during a series of field trials in Yorkshire. [39] One report concluded that "the superior quality of steam cultivation was . . . sufficiently well shown" at the local agricultural society's tests. To contemporaries, the English countryside was crowded with such machinery by the end of the 1860s, and various trade museums in Europe and the colonies offered models for display and study. [40] The chairman of the Jury on Agricultural Machines at the 1862 show wrote several years later that "there is now no large arable district in the country where the reaping machine is not employed, nor any extensive district of pasture land where the mower is not at work." [41] Much of the reaping in the fields of northern England was done by such machines—testament, in part, to the influential role of "machines-in-motion" displays and tests at exhibitions in the mechanization of British agriculture. [42]

EXHIBITION CATEGORIES AND
ORDERING THE INDUSTRIAL WORLD

Machinery exhibits also illustrated distinctions in the way material culture was defined and organized during the nineteenth century. Courts and classifications created a grammar for the industrial order which reflected and shaped the Victorian era's fundamental opposition between the Industrial and Fine Arts. [43] As George Wilson, professor of technology and director of the Industrial Museum of Scotland, told his audience in 1855, "The Fine Arts, are, in a certain sense, superfluous Arts. The Savage does not know them." [44] On the other hand, his address at the University of Edinburgh suggested that both savage and civilized man require and apply some form of industry. "All societies have roots, stems and leaves, but only the advanced is with the flowers and fruits." Wilson used the recent exhibitions in London and Paris to demonstrate these points to his students and in his writings. His lectures echoed Lyon Playfair's conclusions that the display of "industrial products" marked the stages of civilization at the Great Exhibition in 1851.[45] A tour of the Crystal Palace confirmed that "civilized states differ from barbarous nations in their manner of employing natural forces as aids to production." Classifications at the shows naturalized those distinctions and the criteria of machinery to measure man and society.

The taxonomic schemas devised by commissioners enframed the material world, creating special categories for machinery and technological processes. Those intellectual systems in the exhibition halls and accompanying catalogues invited and facilitated the comparison of products and technology within a country as well as by class of exhibit, revealing both internal social as well as external political or, perhaps later, racial differentiations. The various "systematic" and "scientific" arrangements presented new technologies according to their national origin, source of energy, and type of product manufactured or raw material processed.[46] Agricultural implements were often displayed and tested in their own group area. In other cases, "process courts" revealed the imperial links between colonial sources of wool, cotton, and minerals and their final overseas British manufactured and consumer products. Machines-in-motion displays adjacent to bulk displays of colonial timbers, ores, and grains bridged such classes and conflated time, space, and the practices of production.

The Royal Commission for 1851 created space in the Crystal Palace for national courts and subsequently subdivided those displays for judging and for their description in the official catalogue. Additionally, "Four Divisions" were set aside for machinery-in-motion, the largest reserved for "Flax, Silk, Lace, and Hemp Machinery, Lathes and Engineering Machinery and Tools, Mills, Etc."[47] Three different "salons," in the words of one American commissioner, offered "Agricultural Implements, of English invention and manufacture," including a "Scotch Seed Planter" and a machine for making hollow bricks.[48] He later reviewed "American" machines-in-motion, such as an electric telegraph and the Yankee Cotton Gin.[49] Visitors could thus observe some machines adjacent to nontechnological objects and others in special Machinery Courts. Fairbairn's new crane and a patent hydraulic press used to raise bridge tubes were among the "colossal" exhibits captivating eager visitors in one special machinery area of the Crystal Palace.[50]

Subsequent commissions offered variations on this theme, although not without controversy. The placement of machinery remained a point of contention. "Pictures cannot be arranged with steam-engines, or locomotives with Lyons silks, or porcelain with smelting," commented one observer as commissioners prepared classifications and courts for the upcoming 1862 London International Exhibition.[51] He concluded that all machinery should be "in one spot," to facilitate comparison and attract visitors. Manufactures and raw materials would then be exhibited elsewhere. Visitors to the 1862 exhibition subsequently compared various cotton gins in one court and agricultural reapers and harvesters in another part of the building.[52]

Some machines-in-motion required special arrangements, such as steam, which could only be provided in one spot; this necessity concentrated, rather than diffused, the comparative geographical schema at the exhibitions. In other cases, comparable technologies were spread out in separate national courts. Such was the case at the London International Exhibitions in the early 1870s, where commissioners offered German, Austrian, English, Chinese, French, Japanese, and Indian ceramic displays and technology for observation and comparison.[53] One "Popular Guide" to the South Kensington show in 1871 invited visitors to contrast the steam-driven potter's wheels in the English section with the "simple mode" of hand power illustrated by the Indian crafts.[54] This comparison might lead the curious to ponder machines and the type of work as representations of national culture and racial character, as they followed a path of industrial "progress" through the courts.[55]

Commissioners in the Australian colonies applied similar organizational schemes at their international exhibitions, but also provided the spatial privileging of labor-saving machines and colonial processes. The Canadian Commissioner's official report from the Sydney Intercolonial in 1877 informed readers that "a visitor on entering the grounds is struck in the first place by the variety and abundance of the exhibits in agricultural implements and machinery, including reaping and threshing machines, mowing machines, horse rakes, ploughs, . . . wool presses, and windmills and other apparatus for raising water of every description, and a bewildering variety of ingenious labour-saving machines."[56] Not surprisingly, "many of these were shown at work." North American agricultural technology dominated the machinery sections at the show, but there was also notable interest in mining machinery. Visitors to Melbourne's Centennial Exhibition eleven years later compared the gold production and manufactures of the participating colonies and overseas nations and considered the self-contained courts of particular Australasian communities.[57]

Working machines provided "an adequate idea of the progress" realized by the Australasian colonies drawing upon the "natural" foundation of their minerals and soil.[58] The stoves, ploughs, pumps, screw steamer, and mining equipment at the 1875 Melbourne Intercolonial Exhibition served "to illustrate those various branches of manufactures which are upon a firm footing in the Colonies." Australian exhibitors invited visitors to continue on this path of industrial progress by observing and testing the products of working machines, including tin, gold, and wheat. Local officials boasted by the time of the Centennial Exhibition in 1888 that their machinery courts "are furnished with ocular demonstration that even in the simple matter of dress shirts and collars, hand labour seems to be almost entirely superseded."[59]

Exhibition categories and displays offered a division of the world into centers and peripheries according to the vocabulary of industrialism. Visitors could then reflect on the diffusion, or "progress," out from Europe of new machinery and on its colonial applications or, in the rare case, local generation. The vastness of the collections provoked awe and the comparison of the levels of technological productivity and distribution among the participating nations and their colonies, creating distinctions which remain common today with those using machines to measure man and society. Machines were one measure of man for Victorians and Edwardians, a yardstick by which to determine the progress for each exhibiting nation.[60] The technology displays offered an evolutionary lesson. Visitors at one exhibition could literally walk a trail of social and technological development from the "stone celts of the pile works seen in the Museum of Antiquities" to the arms and instruments of Homer's time; and, in turn, the "cannons, boilers, [and machines for] steam spinning."[61] The history of machines told the history of man.

EXHIBITIONS AND FACTORIES: REVEALING INDUSTRIALISM

Nineteenth-century museums and department stores hid from public view modern manufacturing processes. They physically separated those operations from their resulting consumer goods, hiding that particular technological sense of history and progress. Objects were decontextualized or, more accurately, recontextualized, by those modes of representation and commerce. In contrast, exhibitions integrated production and consumption, making both public and visible, revealing a seemingly self-sufficient economic community at the shows and an accessible sense of industrial history. Iron and glass machinery halls and annexes provided a transparent and participatory moment in which the public and private spheres merged.[62]

Industry, the industrial process, and the domestic uses of industrial products no longer remained hidden, as noted by the author of a popular handbook for producers and consumers of pottery at the 1871 London International Exhibition. The show revealed "objects of use and ornament in every house and family" and "the opportunity presented itself to examine the processes of manufacture" usually hidden by factory walls.[63] The author, an American civil engineer, described and discussed the formerly private uses in England, Europe, and the colonies of these objects, treatment of materials, and technological innovations. His handbook highlighted distinctions between modern and traditional objects and labor, recommending some for adoption and relegating others to the dustbin of the past.

English and colonial governments encouraged manufacturers and industrialists to participate in this earthly revelation by providing various forms of security. Legislative measures protecting patents and inventions prompted inventors and factory owners to display their products and processes by reducing fears of piracy. Measures such as the "Patents, Designs and Trade Marks Act" of 1883 were among the first exhibition actions of government officials in England, Australia, and India.[64] Local commissioners, including those from the Board of Trade in England, were further empowered to certify and provide legal protection for official exhibits from Great Britain, the colonies, and foreign nations.[65]

The factory walls had been torn asunder to find apparent harmony and wealth, not the "satanic-mills" of Romantic and Victorian literature.[66] The machinery departments were "bee-hives" of activity and order, seemingly without the influence of "party" and class; machines-in-motion courts were idealized factories within an idealized industrial society. One American commissioner remarked that the machinery rooms at the Great Exhibition were "as noisy as any other factories; but everything in them is exceedingly neat and orderly."[67] These model factories offered "all sorts of manufacturing," including a curvilinear saw which threatened to make obsolete the manual labor of his home state's "enterprising carpenters."

Commissioners arranged for on-site motive power in the forms of steam, electricity, and water to operate the exhibited technology and the machines necessary to build and keep comfortable the seemingly self-sufficient and self-contained exposition halls. The official visitor from Maine thought that "it was a capital idea" to create and provide steam power from the center of the Crystal Palace for the various sections of the exhibition. This contribution meant that "all new matters of machinery could be put to the test, and exhibited in actual operation." Observed as a group, the various machine courts and halls created "a young Birmingham and Manchester, under a glass roof."[68]

Australian exhibition officials followed that precedent. Organizers of the

Melbourne Centennial show provided a 1500-horsepower steam engine and two Brush dynamos for their galleries in 1888.[69] That was, in the words of one local official, "electrical lighting upon the most extensive scale that has ever been attempted" in Australia.[70] Those and other on-site energy sources suggested an enclosed, integrated, active, and self-sufficient system, such as the ideas of the modern factory and imperial federation. Turnstiles, clocks, barriers, and guides organized and managed the flow of visitors through the machinery courts as they did industrial workers in factories and workshops.[71] Printing machines borrowed from the local railways produced tickets at the Melbourne Intercolonial in 1866–67 and simultaneously numbered them consecutively for visitors.[72]

Rows of machines-in-motion at the Great Exhibition and subsequent shows replicated the idea and image of the new factories as a collection of "self-acting machines." Those displays echoed the factory archetypes advocated by Andrew Ure and Charles Babbage in their works on manufacturing and political economy.[73] Commissioners seemingly applied Babbage's "mechanical principles" when organizing the exhibitions' industrial space; they also offered Ure's "perfection of automatic industry" in the machines-in-motion courts. The engraved frontispiece to Ure's study on the *Philosophy of Manufactures* showed the power loom factory of Thomas Robinson, Esq. in Stockport; it was mirrored years later by machinery courts at the exhibitions.[74] In those cases, a few "skilled artisans" operated parallel rows of machinery. The machinery-in-motion factories and exhibition courts offered idealized visions of a self-regulating industrial system with limited human agency and labor. Here were the powerful continuities and similarities in the representation of the new industrialism—that is, the ways that mid-Victorians imagined the factory as a metaphor for society.

Ure argued that "self-acting machines" left the attendant with "nearly nothing at all to do," thereby replacing human labor as a source of value with the machine's work. With no calling for his physical skill, the attendant now exercised "vigilance and dexterity."[75] This vision of the modern factory was a paradigm for society; it constituted a new social form and practice requiring obedience, regimentation, hierarchy, and interdependence seemingly without individual agency or class "interest." It thus represented not only a powerful metaphor for national equipoise, or the idealized relations between and among England's classes, but also for colonial federation as considered at the time in Canada and Australia, and the imperial commonwealth between England and its possessions. These suggested utopian relations between and among the British Empire's political and social units in light of the relationship between man and machine.

INVISIBLE WORKERS AND
THE MODERN PRODUCTION PROCESS

References to Ure and Babbage remind us that the commissioners offered a selective representation of work and workers at the exhibition building sites and among the multitude of exhibits. Officials and exhibitors created a picture in which traditional labor could be observed and its products consumed, but which also made more common laborers invisible as workers, although not as consumers. The exhibits articulated a hierarchy among modes of production, in which self-acting machines and traditional artisanship were privileged. Elites used the exhibitions to offer images of an industrial society and its division of labor without the strong trade unions and strikes facing them in England and the colonies. Not all workers were invisible, but those that were present labored in harmony with one another, employers, and machines. This was an image in sharp contrast to the building and exhibition sites themselves.

There was an implicit and, one might venture to say, tragic, irony about labor in most contemporary exhibition commentaries. These included common images of labor and workers, as well as the ways that factory space was constructed at the shows and in the accompanying literature. The workingman was made invisible, erased as a laborer, but, after all, as one observer of the Crystal Palace noted, "Enchanted palaces that grow up in a night are confined to fairy-land."[76] In "this material world of ours," on the other hand, "the labours of the bricklayer and the carpenter are notoriously never-ending," including in the erection of Joseph Paxton's exposition structure and its successor, the South Kensington complex. The anonymous pamphleteer noted that St. Peter's required "300 years to build" and St. Paul's "35 to complete." Common workers were necessary for the erection of such buildings, even if they were erased from the chronicles. A closer look at the Crystal Palace would have revealed three hundred thousand hand-blown glass panes encasing the whir of self-acting machines.[77]

The process of erecting the exhibition buildings presented to visitors and other contemporaries new machinery in union with traditional work. Snapshots of such labor were captured by photographers in the colonies and Britain. The progress of Sydney's Garden Palace in 1879 was marked by one photograph each week from the same spot.[78] No workers were present in these images as the exhibition building appeared to grow magically from blank space. Sir Charles Wentworth Dilke prepared a similar album to chronicle the 1862 London International Exhibition Building. He organized photographs of managers, workers, horse-drawn carts, and steam engines as they combined to unpack carts, construct ribbed ceilings, and, in general, erect the magical exhibition palace. The steam engine was most certainly part of his photographic vision, and he captured it moving building materials and larger exhibits.[79] Dilke's images "showing the progress of building" the exhibition hall emphasized the role of such machinery in the construction process and a sense of harmony between man and machine. Status at the site was represented by both the type of work and the style of clothes worn by the subjects. Laborers sported cloth caps in Dilke's photographs, while officials were adorned with the equally common middle-class stovepipe black headwear. Regardless of class, all of the men were dwarfed by the domes, girders, scaffolding, and steam engines at South Kensington.

Not all was peaceful at those building sites. Strikes and accidents were common during the construction of most exhibition buildings during the nineteenth century. The Crystal Palace was no exception. The *Friend of the People* chronicled industrial actions by painters and glazers as the Crystal Palace went up in late 1850 and early 1851.[80] Although such strikes were covered by the press, it is not surprising that they are generally absent from exhibition photographic albums and "official" histories and catalogues. The catalogue for the Sydney International Exhibition offers an exception, describing a strike and its defeat by the commissioners and contractor.[81] The latter had moved quickly that year to crush the industrial action by four hundred skilled carpenters at the exhibition building project.[82] Perhaps it was the success of this reaction to organized labor's challenge which prompted its inclusion in the official commemoration and history of the event. Successful strikes at other exhibition sites were excluded from their public records. Those labor actions were generally forgotten amid the euphoria of, and then nostalgia for, the exhibitions. The photographic monuments, official speeches, and machinery-in-motion displays created powerful myths about both the building of these structures and contemporary work as part of the new industrial order and its ideology in England and throughout the Empire.

Railways carried some displays, and a handful of steam engines assisted with moving larger exhibits, but the majority of labor at the exhibition sites remained man- or animal-powered. Most shipping crates and exhibition objects were moved and erected by workmen at the buildings, such as those receiving "packing cases . . . and two enormously bulky packages . . . from

Prussia" at South Kensington's exhibition halls in 1862 (Figure 10).[83] One of the latter contained a reproduced wood hut. Workmen at the exhibition site moved and placed over seventy-nine thousand articles and packages.[84] The size of the packing-cases and the pace of their arrival increased as the deadline for accepting exhibits neared. The scene was no different in the antipodes. Workmen received, moved, and unpacked thousands of crates in "a scene of bustle and activity" at the Melbourne Exhibition Building a few weeks before its official opening in 1880.[85] Crude pulleys, horses, carts, and brute human strength continued to move and organize most exhibition displays, including the preparation of machinery departments, which, ironically, made that type of labor invisible, or appear obsolete.

Exhibition commissioners used a limited number of steam cranes at the major exhibition building sites in London and Paris during the 1860s. Although this transformation of the production process was slow, it greatly impressed Cole.[86] He noted that cranes such as those used at the exhibition sites made the movement and arrangement of "many crates" more efficient and replaced the "multiplication of human hands." The use of cranes also created the exhibitions in a manner seemingly reminiscent of the ways "the old Egyptians" collected and moved goods. Cole was suggesting a further nineteenth-century comparison between empires and their respective historical monuments: in this case, the pyramids of Ancient Egypt and the exhibition halls of modern Britain and France. Cole contrasted the "modern" cranes at the Paris Universal in 1867 with their apparent absence from previous exhibitions, reworking, once again, the memory and historical value of the Great Exhibition of 1851. Paris offered illuminating progress in the use of applied and "mechanical" knowledge when compared to the Crystal Palace.

The construction and organization of the later exhibitions suggested the modern industrial system in which scientific management mystified and hid unskilled labor by representing it with the artisanal labor of the craftsmen and the contributions of technology. The latter appeared to produce without human agency. John Young, a prominent contractor in New South Wales, understood both the efficiency and volatility of this situation. He founded the Master Builders' Association of New South Wales to control the workforce and the production process; he was among the first contractors to use electrical arc lights at exhibition work sites to extend the work day in Australia.[87] Reports reached London that this innovation allowed the erection of Sydney's Garden Palace to be carried on by night as the official opening day approached.[88] The local Peel River Land and Mineral Company manager wrote his Board of Directors in London that Young was mak-

ing, "marvellous strides" in the construction process.[89] He was particularly
enthusiastic about eight hundred men working at night with the electric
light, although he was not convinced that this promising innovation was
"a success yet."[90]

The application of electricity and machinery speeded up the already
rapid rate of work at exhibition sites. Such a pace conspired with public
opinion and competition among contractors. The result? Fatal accidents on
more than one occasion as exhibition buildings rose in England and Australia. The London International Exhibition offered such a moment of conflicting visions and interpretations in 1862. The press praised the rapid rise
of South Kensington's exhibition building and its twin domes. London's
Morning Chronicle, for example, recorded the apparently "perfect labyrinth
[of] columns and girders," noting that the famous "domes are advancing
with great strides."[91] A less enthusiastic voice was heard from "One Employed on the Works." His letter to the editors reminded readers that this
"hurried way" of construction had its costs. Among those were weekly accidents. "Poor fellows . . . have lost their lives or been injured for life in carrying out the great national building."[92] Workers had fallen to their deaths
in the frantic race to complete the twin towers before the official opening
of the exhibition. An assistant smith was also killed by a hammer blow
while driving rivets in one of the girders on that building site.[93]

In Sydney, even Young's innovative arclights "cast very black shadows,
not a few accidents resulting therefrom."[94] On the other hand, the application of new technology enabled the contractor to present to the New South
Wales public in 1879 a more pleasant vision of such work than at his earlier exhibition projects. Journalists and photographic albums chronicled the
"modern" construction in opposition to that at earlier sites. Night work at
Alfred Park in preparation for the Sydney Metropolitan Exhibition in 1870
had provided the image of a "satanic mill." Torches—not gas or electrical
lights—illuminated with shadows and mystery the erection of this early
iron building on the grounds of the local Royal Agricultural Society. A reporter noted that "the scene at night has been of a most fantastic character," including "dark figures working in perilous places" amid the din of
hammers and "the glare of numerous . . . fire-balls."[95] Working by torch-
light might have appeared safer and slower in retrospect, but nostalgia
tended to erase accidents at those sites from personal and collective memory. Labor was less mechanized and frantic, but not necessarily much safer.

Machinery displays erased the common worker from public view, elevated self-acting technology, and, ironically, encouraged the expression of
anti-industrial and pro-labor sentiments among vocal critics. For example,

a one-penny broadsheet published at the time of the Great Exhibition attacked "the Glasshouse of Mammon" [the Crystal Palace] and called for an alternative celebration of Labor, "from whom all wealth proceeds."[96] Working-class and radical publications were particularly outspoken about the exhibitions' celebration of capital and technology, rather than of labor. One of the lead editorials in the *Working Man* at the time of the 1862 London International shouted that the Royal Commissioners "talk of giving medals and rewards to the exhibitors, whose produce will transcend the others in beauty, utility, economy, etc.—*to the exhibitors*—that is to say, to those who, with the help of Mammon, have known how to purchase and to seduce the starving inventor, the houseless labourer, the ragged Working Man, to sell him the child of their genius or of their industry."[97] Contributors underscored the application of human power, the workers' "industry," at the exhibition sites themselves, and the persistence of hand power in nineteenth-century workshops. They noted the slow growth of mechanization, and thus the apparent contrast between the Temples of Industry found at the expositions and the material conditions of the economy, most notably those of the working class.

Not often considered friends of the English working class, the editors of *Leisure Hour* agreed, claiming in the 1860s that exhibitions kept "the real worker, who had performed the miracle of art or ingenuity . . . entirely in the background."[98] Writing at the time of the 1865 Dublin International Exhibition, they suggested that at "the grand national displays, in which peoples contended with peoples, . . . employers, exhibition commissioners and other officials assumed credit for the workers' productions."[99] The major international exhibitions, concluded the editors, represented "unlimited capital leagued with the most consummate art" under the supporting wing of governments and states. The worker was in the "background." The irony of this situation did not escape contemporaries. After all, the exhibitions attracted many working-class visitors. Those attending the London International in 1862 "instinctively . . . felt that it was their hive, and like bees they swarmed to it."[100]

Subsidized by local employers, many workers and their families crowded the railways taking them to the metropolis. They often visited the South Kensington galleries in 1862 for one day and returned home that evening. Working-class visitors—John Forbes Watson's "real" exhibition actors—came "to see and to ponder on what has been *wrought* and *done*" at the London International Exhibition, but generally viewed what had been wrought and done by machines and workers from the colonies. English workers observed *what* was produced, but only saw machines and overseas artisans producing at the exhibition. This was also an ironic picture, since it contrasted with the continued prevalence of hand-powered and unskilled labor in Britain and the colonies.[101] More than half the demand for power in manufacturing in England was supplied by people and animals ("muscle power"), as well as by increasingly efficient windmills and water wheels, as late as the 1860s, although visitors would not have known that from the economic order on display.[102]

What was the solution to the invisibility of England's workers? How could workers be placed in the foreground at the exhibitions? The *Leisure Hour* proposed specialized "industrial exhibitions," such as that held at the Agricultural Hall in Islington during the mid-1860s. Those shows demonstrated "the unassisted production of the working man," rather than the exhibits of "prosperous tradesmen and manufacturers who work with the hands and brains of others."[103] Similar Workmens' and Working Men's Industrial Exhibitions were held in manufacturing centers outside of London as well. Birmingham, Manchester, Glasgow, and Preston, among other industrial cities, hosted shows celebrating working-class "ingenuity, industry and correct natural taste."[104] Organizers exhibited the work of "amateurs, or the working classes," rather than that of wealthy collectors or "the manufacturing, advertising element."

The value of labor, or the laborer, was confirmed at these exhibitions by affixing the name of the worker to the display, rather than that of the middleman or collector, the *Working Man*'s "exhibitors," as was common practice at the national and international shows. This tradition was continued later in the century by the London Trades Council, which sponsored National Workmens Exhibitions as alternatives to the major expositions. The council appropriated the form of those spectacles, but changed their meaning, participants, and displays. Labor shows revealed "the great advantages of excellence of production in all industries instead of the manufacture of slop-work" at the international exhibitions, which was "a fraud upon the public and deeply injurious to the best interests of labor."[105]

THE AESTHETICS AND IMAGES OF IMPERIAL LABOR

Modern forms of labor, as well as the workers themselves, were absent from popular exhibition displays. Government officials, exhibition commissioners, and other contemporaries praised workers for building the dramatic and monumental exposition halls, but such laborers were absent from the exhibits themselves once the events opened. Millions of workers and their families visited the exhibitions, and they observed products and machines as representations of abstract work, rather than images of their own labor processes. Indian bazaars, machines-in-motion, and ornamental art works, such as Doulton's panels at the 1886 Colonial and Indian Exhibition, reduced labor to an abstraction or represented it by traditional and artisanal forms of work and production (see Figure 1).

Doulton's fusion of modern pottery techniques and formal terra-cotta painting in the panels reflected the nineteenth-century imperial combination of traditionalist forms and modernizing practices. That synthesis was part of the pursuit to articulate an imperial aesthetic to represent imperial labor. Such art forms suggested social reconciliation and cultural federation, a union of past and present, East and West. Modern management and technologies were applied to the preservation and promotion of Indian, Irish, and other "traditional" artware, as well as to the application of Indian or "Oriental" ornamentation to British crafts.[106] Exhibition displays resulting from this policy included a "Hindu Saracenic Buffet," one of the popular art works at the Colonial and Indian Exhibition (Figure 11). The "Buffet" caught the attention of judges and the press, as it integrated South Asian traditionalist ornamentation—"oriental motifs"—and English artisanal labor and organization.[107]

The Australian, English, and Indian exhibitions offered various images of hand and pre-industrial work in an imperial division of labor. Skilled craftsmen produced Indian artware in recreated bazaars as well as various ornaments for the exhibition buildings and souvenirs for visitors in on-site workshops. Women's Labor courts displayed homecrafts and art works, also produced by hand. An American commissioner at the Great Exhibition praised "a large and beautiful carpet presented to the Queen [Victoria]" and exhibited in a special gallery.[108] He concluded that such a "specimen of ladies' handiwork" showed that in some cases "labor-saving machines have not the advantage over human hands in the cheapness of production." In a later example, the First Australian Exhibition of Women's Work in 1907 offered to its visitors sixteen thousand fine arts, needlework, and nursing displays.[109] The success of this event was repeated at a similar exhibition during the early 1920s. Both shows drew upon the Women's Courts popular at various international exhibitions held in Australia during the 1880s and the pervasive displays of female and non-European traditionalist labor and products.[110]

India's commissioners found it relatively easy to collect such traditionalist products and manufactures for the Colonial and Indian Exhibition, but one official thought that "something more was wanted to give the British public an idea of the manner in which the native artisans performed their daily work in India in former times." [111] He turned to various Indian princes and even the superintendent of the Agra jail to find and transport such craftsmen. Henry S. King and Co. undertook their maintenance while in England and financed the return trip to India. Visitors at the show observed an unprecedented number of colonial subjects: "Hindus, Muhammedans, Buddhists, Red Indians from British Guiana, Cypriotes, Malays, Kafirs and Bushmen from the Cape, and inhabitants of Perak and Hong Kong." [112] Those native artisans and craftsmen—totaling over forty-five from South Asia alone—were in addition to, and worked among, the many ethno-graphic figures and "numerous models of dwellings," representing their society and lifestyles. They were one of the exhibition's "special features." [113] Sir Francis Philip Cunliffe-Owen, the show's executive commissioner, wrote afterwards that the "body of native artizans" provided "undoubtedly the most attractive feature of the whole Exhibition." [114]

The Raj's artisans created and sold their artware in South Kensington's Indian court and bazaar. Carpet weavers in the Palace courtyard and near by pottery-makers presented a traditionalist view of the labor process (Fig-ure 12). In some important respects, they returned the value of labor to human production in contrast to the "machines-in-motion." [115] The pro-motion of this pre-industrial artisanal craftsmanship and of the bazaar and village-community as its natural contexts, or "aura," not only appealed to traditionalist impulses at home in England, but also played an important part in the post-Mutiny governing strategies of Indian administrators.[116] Many of the latter were responsible for representing the Raj at interna-tional exhibitions. Their displays suggested that the small-scale aspect of industrialism and its accompanying hand labor played significant roles in imperial rule, social stability, and British India's self-image. These and com-plementary traditionalist processes and products were celebrated while unskilled workers and animals erected the structures, moved crates, and unloaded boxes. An image from the 1889 Paris Exposition captures the si-multaneous dual worlds of labor: traditionally clad workmen struggle to roll tubes and crates, while the Eiffel Tower, modernist monument to in-dustry, iron, and machinery rises in the background.[117]

TECHNOLOGY AT COLONIAL EXHIBITIONS

New machines generally traveled out from the center to the periphery, where local exhibitions in Australia and India provided a forum for their introduction. Displays at Australian shows included both colonial and over-seas machinery. Such exhibits promoted labor-saving technology in a land facing both a limited population and a strong trade union movement. Most of the machines were powered by steam, although the new power source's replacement of the human hand took many more years than the impression created at these courts. Steam-powered sheep-shearing demonstrations at the Adelaide International were, in the words of one official, "a never-failing attraction to all classes of visitors," in good part because of their novelty.[118] The New South Wales executive commissioner at the show considered them "one of the most important exhibits ever shown in the Australasian colonies"; they offered the idealized picture of future, but seemingly attainable, mass mechanized production with reduced human agency and without workplace conflict.

Machines were also popular at nineteenth-century Indian exhibitions. Commissioners at the Nagpore Exhibition in 1865, for example, constructed two special sheds with galvanized iron roofs for the display and operation of English and European technology.[119] Among the machines-in-motion were cotton gins, steam engines, and pumps. Of particular notice were the new technologies for iron-processing and threshing. These machines covered more exhibition space than was devoted to the display of poultry, horses, minerals, and forest items. Colonial commissioners and machinery experts advocated demonstrations at these shows to instruct visitors. One Anglo-Indian studying machines at the Akola Exposition in 1868 was disappointed upon seeing country ploughs lying side by side.[120] Rather than "a ploughing match" to demonstrate the advantages of the imported British machinery over local tools, the exhibitors prepared an inert display which "might as well have been in their shops at Ipswich." This was "a very quaint" display, but one "wholly uninstructive," leaving visitors puzzled about the exhibitors' claims of efficiency and utility.

Overseas businessmen embraced machinery demonstrations at the colonial shows as opportunities to create new markets. This was the case with visiting government officials as well. Canada's commissioner at the Sydney Intercolonial in 1877 displayed working agricultural machinery among other goods in his effort to establish "a regular trade" with the Australian colonies, as his home colony enjoyed with the United States.[121] He suggested a commercial exchange of local wines, wools, and wheat for the Canadian technology and, while visiting Melbourne, Brisbane, and various provincial towns, exhibited machines previously demonstrated to Australia's commissioners at the Philadelphia Centennial Exhibition.

The repeated displays and demonstrations of overseas mechanized reapers, strippers, and binders at Australian shows resulted in a sharp increase in their local application after the mid-1880s.[122] In one notable case,

European technology displayed at the 1880–81 Melbourne International Exhibition helped revolutionize the production and structure of Victoria's grain-milling industry. Those new applications were fueled by the similarity in "hard" wheats found in Victoria and Hungary, where the specialized roller machinery originated.[123] Ganz and Co., a firm of milling engineers from Budapest, organized an impressive display at the exhibition and sold its technology almost immediately. Business was so good in the colony after the show that the company replaced its local agent with an official branch office in Melbourne.

Australian demonstrations of North American machinery remained popular during the late nineteenth century. Country visitors to the Sydney Metropolitan Exhibition in 1872 surrounded "mowing, reaping, winnowing" and other working machines, and six years later Canadian reapers, California Diamond Drills, and Yankee Harvesters attracted "large crowds" at the local Agricultural Society's Intercolonial Exhibition.[124] The "intense interest manifested" in such agricultural, mining, and manufacturing machines provoked Australian commissioners to build special annexes for their display and demonstration. Officers of Queensland's National Agricultural and Industrial Association (N.A.I.A.) proposed building a "temporary shed—iron, forty feet square without walls" for the popular Diamond Rock Drill at their Annual Exhibition in 1877.[125] Executive Committees in Sydney, Melbourne, and Adelaide during the 1880s pursued more ambitious plans for their international exhibitions. They prepared large, self-contained Machinery Halls similar to those at European, and English shows, where, in the case of Adelaide's Jubilee Exhibition in 1887, exhibitors were provided with steam, pulleys, water, and direct rail connection with the harbor.[126]

Enthusiasm for North American machines-in-motion did not guarantee their application, but reflected the general Australian consensus to follow multiple industrial paths, rather than only the English road. The governor of Tasmania and president of the amalgamated Australian Agricultural and Horticultural Societies called upon members to "follow the example of the English and Americans" as early as the mid-1850s. He publicly encouraged the importing and application of foreign machines, including those considered "labor-saving."[127] Australian elites also encouraged local technological innovations by offering special prizes for new machinery at various shows sponsored by colonial governments and agricultural societies.[128] The Agricultural Society of New South Wales created special "non-agricultural" categories for machinery at its local shows, and the 1866–67 Melbourne Intercolonial Exhibition offered its visitors a variety of solicited "agricultural and horticultural machines and implements, and cooperage" designed and built by Victoria's engineers.[129]

Machine demonstrations were also popular at provincial and international exhibitions in India during the second half of the century. In two early cases, commissioners and exhibitors filled separated rooms and annexes at the Madras (1855) and Calcutta (1864) exhibitions with working technological displays.[130] Among these were European and English machines for cleaning fibers, crushing and grinding ores, and printing large volumes of published materials. Experts also demonstrated agricultural machines in special outside areas. Exhibitors at the Calcutta show "paraded [machines] before a vast concourse of Bengali Natives" and subsequently undertook "several experiments with steamploughs."[131] Businessmen thirsting for local clients rarely missed these opportunities for introducing technological wares.

Sir Richard Temple and J. Forbes Royle were among the most enthusiastic proponents of displaying overseas machinery at Indian exhibitions, but their expectations of immediate purchase and application were far lower than the lofty ambitions of their Australian colleagues.[132] Modern machines contrasted with their indigenous counterparts, as they had at European shows; this marked their novelty and "progress." Their public exhibition also revealed that, although they were impressive and in demand, the temporary exhibits and the spectacle of display would be insufficient to guarantee diffusion and application. This did not result from a lack of effort on the part of commissioners, but from deeper issues dividing Indian and English societies and economies, some of which were embedded in the imperial relationships of the Raj. That was the case in Nagpore in the mid-1860s.

The secretary to the chief commissioner at Nagpore's exhibition in 1865 reported that cotton gins, threshers, and steam engines provoked interest among large numbers of South Asian visitors.[133] The "Machinery and Implements" department attracted local interest because of the speed of the machines and their products, as well as the contrast offered to "indigenous agricultural machinery from many districts," which was "curious and interesting, rather than useful." The chairman of the Machinery Subcommittee argued that observation and application of European and English technology might place "the native workman upon a fairer stage in competition" with overseas workers. Machinery demonstrations highlighted contrasts with local labor practices, emphasizing the fundamental distinction of industrialism between hand and mechanical power, both within India and between India and England.

Local curiosity and "astonishment" were not always the first steps towards immediate application. Frustrated commissioners suggested the purchase and display of European and English machines by the Nagpore School of Design to provide a long-term exposure for the Raj's subjects. That policy would preserve the impression of technological power and "practices" in the minds of visitors. The secretary concluded in his official report that "natives cannot understand a new thing, unless it be held up before their eyes with something of continuous performance. The first time they may wonder; the second time they may understand; the third time they may observe with a view to practice." [134] Temple agreed with those views, arguing that the practical gains of the new technology would only be apparent with extended, nearly permanent, display in museums and shows. [135] This seemed particularly true with the majority of visitors arriving "from rural districts where the sound, and hardly the name of the Steam Engine, had never been heard," and where the most common form of technology was an "old fashioned, though not ill designed creaking wooden sugar cane mill." [136] Such conclusions were informed by both racial and social predispositions.

South Asian suspicions of overseas technology and disparate environmental, soil, and climatic conditions often prevented the rapid dispersion from the exhibitions of English and European machinery. Contemporaries also continued to blame local reluctance to apply such technology on racial and cultural factors. The *Times* recorded "a large number of spectators" at the public demonstration of "a steam plough and cultivator" during the Calcutta International, but its correspondent concluded that "it may be doubted, however, . . . whether it, as well as other agricultural machines in the Exhibition is not too expensive and too complicated to meet Indian requirements." [137] Machinery displays once again revealed the limitations of imperial spectacle in India. This response to machines-in-motion was in sharp contrast to similar displays in Australia, where American and Canadian drills, reapers, and plows were embraced as visitors flocked to demonstrations and perceived common forms of economic and social development among settler societies. Crowds surrounded working machines in Bombay, Calcutta, and Nagpore, but commissioners turned to museum curators and design-school administrators to preserve and strengthen interest in the new machinery, to make ephemeral displays more permanent.

NATURALIZING MODERN MACHINERY IN INDIA

The picture of an imperial cultural hierarchy founded upon ideas of race and industrialism both shaped and, in part, was shaped by the ways in which the machinery collections were organized and technology represented at Australian and Indian exhibitions. Access to machinery and its subsequent use and diffusion became a measurement of a particular society's solidity, stability, and integration—not just its "progress." Scholars of imperialism and technology often focus on the construction and introduction of large-scale technologies, such as canals and railways, and ignore or downplay small-scale technologies in imperial strategies of economic integration and social order.[138] This perspective reflects the nineteenth-century obsession with and optimism about the capacity of applied science and technology to "improve" society.[139]

One confident Victorian empire-builder proclaimed that "the great public works" in India exerted a powerful impulse of "improvement."[140] He concluded that such projects during the late 1850s "are carried on with European capital; they demand European skill and superintendence; and their results cannot fail to extend the interest of Europeans in the interior of the country. We believe that in no part of the world is there such a field for the advantageous employment of skill and capital as on the public works of India." While such projects and the accompanying sentiments were essential for imperial confidence, military control, and economic linkages, they often produced an overwhelming sense of awe and disruption. Their introduction was not without anxiety on the part of both imperial administrators and colonial subjects. Exhibitions addressed such concerns. The shows assisted the diffusion and naturalization processes by displaying machines in a more acceptable, less disruptive manner. Commissioners offered decontextualized or, it might be argued, recontextualized aesthetic and participatory representations of technology at exhibitions and museums.

This was necessary because the application of large-scale machinery in India often sharply contrasted with the robust and tranquil vision of imperial industrialization. Such machines and industrial public projects might challenge social order, perhaps undermining, rather than strengthening, imperial authority. No one doubted the transformative powers of machinery, but contemporaries disagreed about its effects on Indian society and thus British rule. In one noteworthy example from the time of the Sepoy Mutiny, Harriet Martineau discussed the ways in which canals and railways affected local religious practices. She feared that "the accommodation of the rail will lessen the merit of pilgrimages" in India, with unsettling consequences.[141]

Rudyard Kipling's father, a prominent artist and museum curator in Bombay and Lahore, participated in this public discussion. He noted that the Raj's large-scale public works and machines were "imposing" and had "the prestige of authority," but were always considered a foreign construction.[142] They contrasted with indigenous architecture, art, and technology. While it was true that they often provoked awe, it was also the case, as the elder Kipling pointed out, that many South Asians regarded such British projects as "ugly." The challenge to local machines and production processes represented by those foreign developments might very well result in the defense of so-called Indian atavisms, or traditions. Uncertainties and disappointments were the possible results of relying on the "Colossal" and authoritarian representation of imperial industrialism. Recognizing the power of such technology to influence but also alienate, the Raj's subjects, Anglo-Indian officials attempted to ennoble and naturalize with spectacle and art the introduction of railways, canals, and other public works.[143]

This is not to say that large-scale overseas machinery was ignored at the Indian exhibitions. To the contrary, visiting land owners and Indian princes were curious about those novel technological exhibits. Demonstrations of European and English machinery captured the attention of such visitors at the Bengal Agricultural Exhibition in 1864 and thirty years later at the Calcutta International as well.[144] Jules Joubert, executive commissioner for the Calcutta show, noted among Indian visitors a "craze for out of the way modes of locomotion."[145] One of the Indian princes observed a traction road engine manufactured in England and was "so struck" by it that it was purchased and subsequently used as a steam carriage in his palace grounds. In this case, the European machinery brought "prestige" to the colonial exhibition for visitors, owners, and operators, but not the intended imperial economic application.

South Asian exhibition visitors observed and, at times, participated in the British Empire's technological development. This was also part of the nineteenth-century imperial vision. The study and diffusion of small-scale technologies to promote progress without social disruption and the assertion of new and threatening socioeconomic classes were made public at the exhibitions. Whereas heavy capital items created a shadow of social disintegration, demonstrations of this alternative and accessible technology offered social synthesis and a different national vision. Varying reactions to imperial machines and industrialism on display at the exhibitions also provided the psychological and cultural bases, as well as the language, for different visions of Indian nationalism.

One embraced large-scale industrial projects to overcome a sense of colonial weakness, providing a Eurocentric shape for the imagined Indian nation. The competing image offered accessible, small-scale, and traditionalist forms of technology and production. Both visions informed the series of Industrial and Agricultural Exhibitions organized by the Indian National Congress between 1901 and the outbreak of the Great War in 1914.[146] Here were exhibits of *swadeshi* and railways coinciding with Congress sessions in Madras, Bombay, Benares, Lahore, and other major centers. The South Asian president of the committee organizing the Lahore exhibition noted that the "great value of Exhibitions is that they show the industrial resources of the countries which display their goods," encouraging new industries and improving the quality of existing ones.[147] Exhibitions promoted industrialism and its social vision, whether articulated by the Raj or the Indian National Congress.

MAKING TECHNOLOGICAL EXHIBITS PERMANENT

Exhibitions were an attractive and popular way to introduce new machines for nationalists and imperialists, but not always the most effective mode for their long-term diffusion. Machines-in-motion courts and demonstrations drew crowds in England, Australia, and India, but more permanent measures were necessary for the development of industrialism and industrial society. Museums, technical and design schools, and government-supported ceremonies naturalized new machinery and the ideas of industrialism introduced at the exhibitions. Those public ceremonies and collections were an important part of what one contemporary called "the Progress of Mechanical Invention," or the establishment of an industrial public culture.[148] Exhibitions benefited from and contributed to the growing network of museums, agricultural societies, technical and art schools, and mechanics' institutes assimilating new machinery in Britain and the colonies.

Local visitors to the 1865 Nagpore Exhibition of Arts, Manufactures, and Produce, for example, appeared awed at the collection of European and English cotton gins and steam engines. Similar reactions of "wonder" greeted "an improved telephone" at the 1883 Jeypore Exhibition.[149] Anglo-India officials argued, however, that it would be necessary to repeat public demonstrations and retain models at government model farms, public museums, and schools to make the lasting impression necessary for the general application of new and foreign technologies. "If there was merely one Exhibition never repeated," asserted the exhibition secretary after the Nagpore show, "it would be like a flash of light, beaming around for a moment, but leaving all as dark as before."[150]

Alexander Hunter, superintendent of the School of Art and Industry in Madras, urged the Indian government to purchase steam machinery displayed at the local exhibition and incorporate such specimens in the instruction at industrial and art schools. He wrote in 1863 that "a great deal may be done in India both in the way of constructing and repairing complicated machinery, and the natives can be taught to make turning lathes, fan blast, and even steam engines."[151] Turning to the official catalogues of the Madras Exhibition for reference and descriptions, Hunter advised the acquisition of both European and "native" technologies, tools, and machines for the proposed School of Industrial Arts in Lahore. The suggested items included materials for the local production of horn, ivory, and sandalwood artware products.[152] His own educational institution in Madras offered in 1862 a series of lessons in practical mechanics which taught the fundamental applications of geometry to motive powers, and introduced both simple and complex machines. Among those were pumps, water wheels, and steam engines.[153] The school was a model for a more permanent and pervasive method of diffusing industrialism and industrial culture.

Success at the Great Exhibition eleven years before had rewarded and validated Hunter's technical education efforts in Madras. The seemingly ubiquitous Prof. Royle noted in a lecture after the show that the School of Art's pottery revealed great "improvement" and garnered a Prize Medal.[154] Hunter and his students earned similar accolades from experts and visitors at the Vienna International Exhibition in 1873. In addition to receiving the "Medal of Good Taste" for exhibits in the Pottery and Porcelain section, the Indian collection also "excited the admiration of the skilled jurors and raised a feeling of regret" that further awards could not be provided.[155] Those exhibits and awards resulted from Hunter's long-term projects to apply European science and small-scale technology to local art production. This included the field of pottery and put Hunter in company with many other local Anglo-Indian officials.[156]

Hunter considered the chemical qualities of South Asian clays and oversaw controlled experiments to devise the most efficient materials and processes. These projects expressed the pre–Sepoy Mutiny confidence in "modern" social and cultural practices, rather than the later embrace of traditionalist artisanal work and tools. The application of scientific knowledge and machinery to such production processes was spreading in India as a result, in part, of local and overseas exhibitions. By the turn of the century, museums and schools in nearly all of the major Indian cities could boast of technological collections acquired from exhibitions for use in ambitious technical education projects.[157] In one revealing example, officials at the Indian Museum in Calcutta collected machines for permanent display and study after the city's International Exhibition in the early 1880s.[158] They followed the precedent established in Bombay, where local museum officers had steadily developed a machinery collection since the initial display of technology prepared for and then returned from the 1855 Paris Universal Exposition.[159]

Public institutions in provincial India also purchased European and British machines exhibited at local exhibitions. Their officers attempted to adapt machinery fitted for the use of the Raj's laboring subjects according to what were deemed "traditional" patterns of work. The success of the Industrial Exhibition in Poonah in 1888 resulted in the formation of the Reay Industrial Museum and the Industrial Association of Western India, both of which were dedicated to introducing technical education and new overseas technology to the region.[160] The application of technology would, it was argued, reduce the price of Indian wares and thus increase their sales and revenue. The permanent collection of exhibition machinery might diffuse imperial industrialism and knowledge but also balance the Empire's inherent duality between large- and small-scale technologies. Such displays suggested the future integration of machinery with the assistance of trained indigenous experts.

Technological exhibition displays were also purchased and exchanged by the administrators of various Australian institutions. Prof. Frederick Mc-Coy provided an early local precedent by organizing "many excellent models of European mining machines" at the National Museum in Melbourne in the 1850s.[161] Later, Sir Redmond Barry advocated the collection of working machines by the School of Mines in Ballarat in order to study and apply changes in electricity, steam power, and engineering.[162] Most of these had been demonstrated at Australian and overseas exhibitions. Those collections were colonial reflections of John Forbes Watson's confidence in the power of trade museums to introduce new machinery and to educate the general public about its uses. Such institutions were common in the capital cities and centers of commerce of the British Empire's major European competitors. Writing during the series of International Exhibitions at South Kensington in the early 1870s, Watson, the India Office Reporter on products, concluded, "If Trade Museums and Technical Museums existed they would not only act in furtherance of trade and manufactures, but would allow of the introduction of a splendid system of commercial and technical education."[163]

Only a few local museums and the Crystal Palace, Sydenham, offered such institutions in Great Britain. On the other hand, Watson's colonial complements created a series of such public collections in their cities, urging the acquisition and permanent display of working machines and technological models from exhibitions. One "important and substantial result" of the Sydney International Exhibition was the establishment of a Techno-logical Museum, formed from gifts and purchases arranged at the show.[164] Members of Adelaide's Chamber of Manufactures shared such interests in the late 1870s and recommended the purchase of exhibition machines-in-motion to form "a standing museum of South Australian industries, open to public inspection."[165]

Working machines were object lessons in power, production, and social organization. They were also essential to attract and entertain visitors to exhibitions and museums who might be overwhelmed and bored by a mass of inert objects. Watson was frustrated by such visitors who, in his words, cared "little about manufacturing or commercial specimens, [and] not much about machinery unless in motion."[166] The commissioner admitted that experimental trials with machinery at such shows could be an important agent for spreading industrial education, yet he regretted the emphasis on temporary spectacle. Watson finally resigned himself to presenting ma-chinery as entertainment, but at the same time urged the permanent dis-play of technological exhibits at museums in major manufacturing centers, including Leeds and Bradford. He recommended that those institutions dis-play the exhibition machines relevant to their local industries and do so ac-cording to the "systematic arrangement" of such articles at the shows.

THE AESTHETICS OF TECHNOLOGY:
MAKING THE NEW OLD AND THE UGLY BEAUTIFUL

Exhibition demonstrations and museum collections of working machinery were not the only strategies employed to introduce and naturalize new technology and the industrial vision. English, Australian and Indian offi-cials also enveloped those power sources with signs of beauty and tradition. They created an imperial style of display for new machines, an industrial aesthetic which drew visitors for whom technological utility, complexity, and movement were not always enough. After all, many exhibition visitors were "wearied with the extent and variety of things exhibited: with the endless lumps of coal, the colossal cakes of soap, the thousands of labelled bottles, the colossal engines, and the curious models."[167] Thus, machines were no longer placed on columns as if they were monuments in rows, but were decorated. Exhibitors painted them bright colors and surrounded them with ornamentation and architectural framing. This mode of display provided an important link with the world of art and earlier craftsmanship; it also made them accessible to the public.[168] Accessibility encouraged their introduction into society and enhanced the prestige of both exhibition organizers and the owners and exhibitors of the machines.

Whereas the colossal aura might be sufficient for technology such as the Dynamo to make an impression on exhibition visitors, other machines required a more artistic presentation, including ornamented frames, banners, and ribbons. This was even the case with McCormick's prize-winning reaper. European judges appreciated the efficiency, but often criticized the form, of that machine. McCormick responded to the criticism by building a model farmer's home as part of the display at Paris in 1867 and by forwarding a silver-plated binder and mower to the Universal Exposition eleven years later. His staff also prepared a particularly ornate reaper for the 1862 London International. This model included varnish, gold stripes, and woodwork of grained ash. R. H. Thurston, an American engineer and juror at several exhibitions in the 1870s, noted that such mechanical displays were "perfect gems, wrought and polished with true artistic taste."[169]

There was a pervasive drive in England and the colonies to clothe machinery displays in more traditionalist gowns as part of this industrial aesthetic. Commissioners and exhibitors draped machinery displays with historical decorations to provide continuity with the past and a sense of the monumental. Traditionalist art forms reduced anxieties about the novelty of industrialism's social and cultural practices. Machinery displays were often ornamented with neo-Gothic and naturalistic decorative materials to provide this reassuring aura of tradition. Reconstructed Indian monuments, ornamental ironwork, medieval banners within iron and glass buildings, and brightly painted machines were part of the process to create an imperial industrial culture and its own history. They expressed what Walter Benjamin termed "the inclination noticeable again and again in the nineteenth century to ennoble technical necessities by artistic aims."[170]

The machinery-in-motion exhibits and the buildings which housed them were part of this larger cultural project at home in England and abroad in the colonies. "Scarlet tapestry . . . coats-of-arms, banners, [and] crystal chandeliers in gilded frame work" decorated the Crystal Palace's light blue iron network.[171] Eleven years later, Captain Fowke grouped banners "exhibiting every variety of strange device and recording many a curious and forgotten page of History" around displays of the most current steam technology at the London International Exhibition.[172] Paralleling Haussmann's urban projects in France, the mid-Victorian exhibition commissioners used artistic ornamentation for the new machines and exhibition hall architecture to suggest continuity with the past.

This aesthetic conservatism mirrored the uncertainty and frustration with glass and iron buildings, as well as with large-scale machinery. Industrialism presented a new and different sense of beauty which did not take hold as its own aesthetic form until after the turn of the twentieth century. The exhibitions illustrated the contests over how to develop that new style and taste. Exhibition buildings and machinery displays, particularly after the Crystal Palace Exhibition, were presented in a more traditionalist mode, reflecting tensions and ambiguities about applying visible engineering skills and iron to constructed spaces. Perhaps, in some ways, the Crystal Palace was the beginning and the culmination of this industrial boldness, its bold iron and glass framework destined to be clothed in more traditionalist garb, making the industrial sinews invisible to most observers.

After 1851, visitors might be able to observe modern iron ribbing and framing from the inside of exhibition halls; unlike at the Great Exhibition, it was now generally invisible to those on the outside. Brickwork and other ornamentation covered the iron. Reactions to industrial and aesthetic innovation help explain the use of more traditional architectural and ornamental styles for the later permanent exhibition buildings and machinery halls. The "Italian Renaissance" style and materials of Melbourne's Exhibition Building, for example, were heavily influenced by the architect's observation of Romanesque brickwork during his travels in northern Italy and the Australian settlers' quest for historical and cultural roots abroad.[173] Girders were hoisted over sixty feet above the ground to support the mass of brickwork rather than incorporating iron in the dome and walls, suggesting to one English observer that the "great and rapid progress" of the colony was opposed to the assumed teaching of the "nineteenth century—the iron age."[174]

The machines supplying power at the shows were often attractive exhibits in their own right, demonstrating both traditionalist art and modern energy. Cole participated in this aesthetic project by designing an ornamental terra-cotta structure to house the boilers providing steam to the British machinery at the 1867 Paris Universal Exposition.[175] The executive commissioner discussed the South Asian sources of that structure at a meeting of the Royal Society of Arts in London one year before the show opened.[176] He claimed that the overall design was "somewhat in the form of a Mohammedan temple," discussed in a popular book on Indian architecture and monuments, and the chimneys represented the reworking of a mosque. That ornamentation suggested continuity with a pre-industrial past and the ways in which Indian art was displayed at the exhibitions. Integrating modern technique and traditional design, Cole oversaw the use of terra-cotta, rather than Indian stone, in the construction of this "ingenious" and "attractive" structure.[177] In a more practical sense, Cole's project created an open architectural framing in which visitors could directly observe and study the working boilers. The merging of Eastern design and Western function revealed the imperial vision of aesthetic industrialism, as would the "Hindu Saracenic Buffet" at the later Colonial and Indian Exhibition (see Figure 11).

Modern rotary presses, steam engines, and other colossal machines operated within recreated palaces and Parthenons. Here was the ironic, yet soothing, covering of modern technology with neoclassical and neo-Gothic clothing. The prominent American architectural critic, Montgomery Schuyler, reviewed the long colonnades and arcades of exhibition Machinery Halls and was reminded of the monumental architecture from Karnac, Thebes, Rome, and Athens.[178] A "decorative envelope" from the past eased the introduction of modern technology and its cultural system inside. At the 1893 Chicago Columbian Exposition, for example, British machines appeared to rest within a solarium-type structure, thereby mystifying technology within the symbols of the American pastoral. The addition of foliage and raw materials in geometric shapes encouraged a naturalistic and harmonious representation of technology.[179]

THE TERRIBLE INDUSTRIAL BEAUTY OF WAR?

The quest for a sense of beauty in industry resulted in a further, more "terrible" irony at the English and colonial exhibitions: armament displays from Sam Colt pistols to naval vessels were celebrated for their attractiveness.[180] A contributor to the *Sixpenny Magazine* noted the contrast between the sense of peace in 1851 and the militaristic "state of public feeling" represented at the subsequent 1862 London International Exhibition. "Ten short years have passed, and the most attractive court in all this Exhibition will be devoted to Class 11, comprising military engineering, ordnance, and accoutrements."[181] He was not alone. Others toured South Kensington and shared similar sentiments: "When we have gone all though the Exhibition, observing the finish and ingenuity of its labours of peace, we are not a little struck at finding greater finish, greater ingenuity, and more meaning grace in its works of war."[182] Among such "works" were ships, or "ironsides"; the "chiefest handiworkers in the world" no longer built cathedrals, but ships of war. A "terrible beauty" had been born since the Crystal Palace.[183]

Enfield and Colt weapons, models of ships and fortifications, and military maps represented the aura of organized industrial power and the "Art of War" in 1862.[184] Conspicuous trophies for the Birmingham and Armstrong gun factories marked the military court as they did its complement at other shows. These signified the union of manufacturing and war for the "progress" of industry, nation, and empire, further examples of the tendency to use traditionalist ornamentation and architectural forms to represent the new cultural and social system of expansionary industrialism. The Birmingham Small Arms Company trophy celebrated the "extended use of machinery" in its factories during the 1860s; streamers, columns of rifles, and coats-of-arms wedded the monumental grammar of the past to the industrial power of the present.[185]

A variety of weapons greeted visitors to the colonial exhibitions as well. Armstrong Guns "guarded" one of the main courts at the 1866–67 Melbourne Intercolonial, and "the military court" at the Calcutta International in 1883 displayed model hospitals and various shells.[186] "Modern" Australian and Anglo-Indian weapons provided contrasting symbols of power to adjacent exhibits of indigenous spears, shields, and daggers at these shows. In an interesting variation, one visitor to the courts at the 1886 Colonial and Indian Exhibition commented on the seeming invisibility of these "engines of war." [187] The defense of the colonies appeared to rest with "the mother country," since "weapons of war, excepting those of savages, exhibited as curiosities, are conspicuous by their absence." Rather, the colonies revealed their engineering interests and industrial applications in the forms of mining, agricultural, and railway machines-in-motion.

India's officials suggested that economic progress and the intellectual ordering of the subcontinent could complement the violence of the Indian Army and thus preserve social order without turning only to the sword and rifle. Of course the Army was present and active on the ground in the subcontinent, but it was not in the Raj's political interests to emphasize that picture of the Indian Empire at the exhibitions. In the case of the Australian colonies, overseas settlement had included long-term frontier conflict and conquest, but such violence was either relegated to the past or not considered true warfare. Visions of a "new" society growing in an empty land did not include battlefields, an erasure consistent with the collective "silence" about settler-Aborigine confrontations.[188] Furthermore, colonial legislatures were reluctant to fund military enterprises for defense against invasion, and thus it was in their political and economic interests to recall the Great Exhibition's pledge for peace, progress—and imperial protection!

Here was a frightening marriage at the heart of the exhibition experience: the mystification of the relationships between military power, industrialism, national consolidation, and imperial expansion. Machines of power and control were recontextualized and clothed by art in seemingly peaceful modes of beautiful self-action and monumentality. The Whitworth and Armstrong gun exhibits caused one visitor to conclude that "Cellini never wrought more painfully at his metal-work than the gun founder has done at *his*."[189] Public objects of war assumed a natural, historically inevitable, and artistic existence as they appeared to function without human agency and human victims. The state and the private sector were explicitly united in this quest at the 1862 London International Exhibition. Such a partnership was celebrated in the form of the tall and commanding trophy of guns and coils from the Royal Gun Factories at Woolwich. Visitors viewed a center shaft of guns and streamers, rising like an obelisk or pyramid until crowned by a banner with the Queen's initials and the motto of the Board of Ordnance (Figure 13). Flagstaves and geometrically arranged weapons completed this monument, which was enclosed by a handrail of wrought iron, stained with a "rich brown coating," as were the guns themselves.[190]

The military exhibits did not escape the notice of John Bright, a frequent visitor to exhibitions. The influential Quaker, Free-Trader, and M.P. from the North crossed paths at the shows with Joseph Whitworth, the prominent engineer, inventor, and, in those cases, exhibitor during the 1850s and 1860s.[191] Among his innovations on displays were "his machine for measuring the millionth part of an inch" and "improvements in rifle and cannon." Bright remarked at several points in his diary how ironic it was that such genius resulted in more efficient weapons of war and their popular display at exhibitions, which had been intended to promote Peace and Free Trade. The politician concluded at the time of the 1855 Paris Universal Exposition: "Melancholy to think that the greatest ingenuity of the country is now employed on instruments of destruction!"

One of Bright's contemporaries visited the London International Exhibition seven years later and noted that "this reproachful ghost" of militarism was found at every turn of the show in the forms of marine architecture and military engineering.[192] The guns offered attractive objects, resulting from the organized union of skill and machinery, science and art. Here one reluctantly found the convergence of taste, beauty, and strength missing from the other machines-in-motion. Were such "dreadful engines" an inevitable part of the Victorian condition or "forced on" the nineteenth-century? In a sense, the visitor's query was merely a rhetorical exercise; warfare's pervasive representation at the exhibition made it so. "Seriously, there is no avoiding warlike works; and alas for the fact!" responded the chronicler to his own question. The irony was almost too obvious and painful: "No wonder the ghost of 1851 is so restless. Peace, so loudly invoked to the first Exhibition, scarcely expected to see *this* as a result of it in the second."

Punch echoed those sentiments, publishing a cartoon of "Peace. . . . Design for a colossal statue which ought to have been placed in the [1862] International Exhibition" (Figure 14).[193] That statue would have been out of place at South Kensington, mocked by events since the Great Exhibition. Its classical female figure sat astride and subdued the cannon, representing the powerful myth of 1851, but not the bloody Crimean War and Sepoy Mutiny of the intervening decade nor the revelation at South Kensington of the structures, ideology, and practice of industrialism. That cultural and social system both produced and was produced by the modern nation-state and its popular emblems, the "great" exhibitions. Such shows and their machinery displays in England, Australia, and India reminded "men how enormous were the powers for their use and benefit," as well as for their destruction.[194]

Figure 1. "Messrs. Doulton & Co.'s Impasto Panels" at South Kensington's Colonial and Indian Exhibition in 1886. The subjects are (top to bottom) "typical" Indian, Australian, and British figures at work. Source: *Builder* 51 (1886), p. 268A.

Figure 2.   The Mineral Trophy in front of the Garden Palace at Sydney's
International Exhibition in 1879. The mounted obelisk, which dwarfed visitors,
represented the Australasian colonies' coal and gold output in absolute,
comparative, and monetary terms. Source: *Illustrated Sydney News*, October 4,
1879, p. 5. Mitchell Library, State Library of New South Wales, Sydney.

Figure 3.   Queensland's Annexe at the London International Exhibitions, 1871–
74. Richard Daintree, the colony's Agent-General, organized the collection to
promote interest in the colony's raw materials, natural history, and potential trade
goods. Photographs illustrated the context for items displayed in the customary
museum-type cabinets in this colonial taxonomy. Source: *Australasian Sketcher*,
April 15, 1873, p. 8. Reproduced by permission of the National Library of
Australia, Canberra.

Figure 4.   Australian fruit stalls in the Colonial Market at the Colonial and
Indian Exhibition. Visitors and merchants sampled, compared, and purchased
fresh apples and pears from antipodean orchards and other produce from around
the Empire, including mutton from New Zealand and pineapples from the West
Indies. Source: *Graphic*, June 5, 1886, pp. 602, 609.

Figure 5. Quartz-crushing mill, Colonial and Indian Exhibition. The mill processed more than twenty tons of gold ore from Gympie, Queensland, in view of visitors. On hand are the officials and workers responsible for this popular "machine-in-motion," posed before a map of the colony highlighting its many mineral districts. Source: *Colonial and Indian Exhibition, London 1886 — Ground Plan and Views of the Queensland and New Guinea Courts*, Negative Number 40893. Collection: John Oxley Library, Brisbane.

Figure 6.   The East Indian Pavilion and Throne Room at the Great Exhibition, 1851. The Orientalist grandeur of England's mid-century Raj was evident in the jewels, silks, and other luxury items that surrounded the hand-crafted ivory throne, suggesting "Eastern" opulence and power inside the "Western" Crystal Palace. Source: V & A Picture Library, Victoria and Albert Museum, London, Number H. 220.

Figure 7.   Cast of "the great gateway" from the Buddhist Tope at Sanchi in Central India, the most imposing exhibit in the Picture Galleries at the International Exhibition in London, 1871. Considered one of the finest specimens of ancient religious carving, it provoked the interest of artists, government officials, and most of South Kensington's visitors. Source: *Graphic*, May 6, 1871, p. 423.

Figure 8.   The Gwalior Gateway at the entrance to the Colonial and Indian
Exhibition's Indian courtyard. Gwalior stone carvers produced the gateway in the
space of "barely four months," using seventy-five tons of carved stone. The
project enjoyed the joint patronage of the Maharaja of Scindia and several
prominent Indian government officials in their attempt to revive traditional stone
carving in the region. Source: *Builder* 51 (1886), p. 10A.

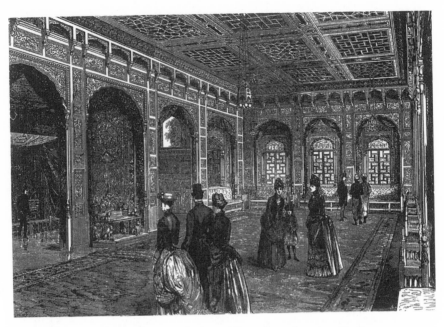

Figure 9. The Indian Palace's "Durbar Hall" at the Colonial and Indian Exhibition. The exhibit continued the tradition of total Orientalist architectural spaces initiated at the Great Exhibition. South Kensington shows during the 1870s and 1880s offered several of these fantastic escapes to "the East," including tea gardens and bazaars. Source: *Illustrated London News*, June 17, 1886, p. 89.

Figure 10.   Receiving goods at the International Exhibition Building, South Kensington, 1862. Exhibition materials were moved by animal and human power. These "enormously bulky packages . . . from Prussia" at the 1862 London International Exhibition contained a variety of exhibits, including a wooden hut. They were part of the nearly constant flow of packing cases as the official opening day drew near. Source: *Illustrated London News*, March 15, 1862, p. 271.

A HINDU SARACENIC BUFFET
DESIGNED·BY E ·WIMBRIDGE·ARCHT

Figure 11. "Hindu Saracenic Buffet," representing the merging of Western labor and "Oriental" motifs. Designed by an English architect using traditionalist Indian ornamentation and constructed by English craftsmen, it was displayed at the Colonial and Indian Exhibition. The "Buffet" was one of many attempts to create a popular, integrative, imperial aesthetic during the later Victorian and Edwardian eras. Source: *Building News* 50 (1886), p. 855.

Figure 12.   South Asian carpet weavers laboring in full view of visitors and
judges during the Colonial and Indian Exhibition. These workers occupied a
central space in the Indian Palace courtyard and provided the legitimating aura
of "authentic" Orientalist labor to the wares sold at the nearby bazaar. Artisans
were housed away from the exhibition; they returned to India after the show.
Source: *Illustrated London News,* June 17, 1886, p. 88.

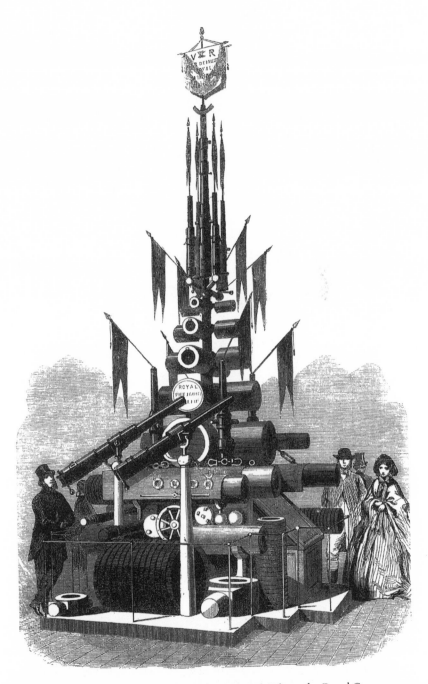

Figure 13. Trophy of "Armstrong Guns and Coils" from the Royal Gun Factories, Woolwich, built for London's International Exhibition. It celebrated not only Britain's industrial might, but also its readiness for war, at a moment of seeming peace in 1862. Armaments and other military displays were common at the exhibitions. Source: *Illustrated London News,* June 14, 1862, p. 618.

Figure 14.   The angel of "Peace" sitting astride one of the many exhibited cannons, presented as "a colossal statue" that should have been at London's International Exhibition, but was not. The editors of *Punch* could not resist reminding their readers of the ironic juxtaposition of so many military displays with artistic and commercial ones at exhibitions intended to promote "Peace and Progress." Visitors to the exhibition were surrounded by military exhibits. Source: *Punch* 42 (May 3, 1862), p. 177. Reproduced by permission of Punch, Ltd.

THE HAPPY FAMILY IN HYDE PARK.

Figure 15. *Punch's* "Happy Family in Hyde Park," illustrating how the transparent walls of the Crystal Palace not only captured the vast human taxonomy, putting men and women on display, but also served as a reflexive mirror. Acting as an official exhibition guide, Prince Albert points for a group of visitors on the outside to an identical group celebrating inside as visitors or as exhibits themselves. The world of man was both inside and outside Paxton's vast palace. Source: *Punch* 21 (1851), p. 38. Reproduced by permission of Punch, Ltd.

Figure 16. The "Courtyard of the Indian Palace" at the Colonial and Indian Exhibition in 1886. Exhibition commissioners and other advocates boasted that "East and West" could meet in such venues. Parts of South Kensington were redesigned as Indian bazaars where visitors and exhibitors could commingle, observe, and consume. The architectural ornamentation and social composition provided an authentic "aura" for these contact zones. Source: *Illustrated London News*, July 17, 1886, p. 85.

Figure 17. Londoners and others going to and fro during the International Exhibition of 1862. Exhibitions invited contemporaries to reimagine their host cities as chaotic, energetic, and workable social environments. At times, the frenzy of the exhibition halls mirrored the frenzy of the host city's streets, but with a sense that both were viable and that things would not fall apart into social disintegration, as some critics had feared. Source: *Leisure Hour* 12 (1862), p. 793.

Figure 18. "The Main Hall" of Melbourne's Intercolonial Exhibition in 1875 — the merging of old and new. Modern dress, museum cases, and building materials were clothed in the traditions of flags and banners; some of them represented modern nation-states, and others hailed more medieval associations. Such ornamentation contributed a festive air of pageantry to the shows and also tied them to broader traditions. Source: *Illustrated Sydney News*, October 16, 1875, p. 13. Mitchell Library, State Library of New South Wales, Sydney.

7 Imperial and National Taxonomies

Entertaining and Policing
Exhibition Visitors

Exhibition commissioners entertained, educated, and policed an unprecedented galaxy of visitors from seemingly all corners of the globe and social classes. "I should think that there must have been near three hundred thousand people in Hyde Park at once," Thomas Babington Macaulay wrote enthusiastically in 1851, overcoming his initial skepticism about the Great Exhibition.[1] The author of a popular illustrated book published for the show turned to verse to describe those visitors: "The People, who came from all parts, / Of the earth, just to see this collection of arts; / To London they hurried, all bustle and fuss, / Arriving in thousands, by cab, rail, and bus."[2] Here was humanity itself, a challenge to the Victorians' sense of the world's size, diversity, and movement. New strategies of intellectual and social order were required for both control and comprehension.[3]

Macaulay observed the social mass in 1851 and was "not a little curious to know whether the resort of foreigners be really such as to give anything like a new character to the streets of London."[4] Exhibition officials were also curious, but faced the challenge of shaping the "character" of that "bustle and fuss" so that it had imperial and national meanings and order. They did so by organizing the visitors into social taxonomies and painting collective portraits of those "who came from all parts" of the world. Visitors filled the exhibition halls, offering "a living picture" of the Empire, nation-states, and the world. *Punch* noted the reflexivity of that organized picture in its cartoon entitled "The Happy Family in Hyde Park" (Figure 15).[5] Prince Albert and a variety of international and British visitors viewed others—but, in reality, themselves—at play and work through the Crystal Palace's transparent walls; in a sense, those walls mirrored visitors and participants, linking those inside with those outside.[6]

Charles Babbage promised in 1851 that the Great Exhibition provided for "all enlightened observers of human nature" the opportunity for taking "a more correct view" of industry, peoples, and institutions.[7] Writing with great expectations on the eve of the show, the scientist noted that the official invitation to attend, if "universally accepted, will bring from every quarter a multitude of people greater than has yet assembled in any western city: these welcome visitors will enjoy more time and opportunity for observation than has ever been afforded on any previous occasion."[8] Those visitors were also part of the spectacle alongside artware, raw materials, and manufactured goods, sometimes as active subjects observing one another and sometimes as passive objects, being observed. The commissioners took it upon themselves to construct Babbage's "correct view" by managing the mass numbers and variety of visitors, thereby constructing informal, active, imperial and national censuses at the exhibitions. Here were visions of the imperial community. Its various national, social, and material parts arranged for visual, and policed for physical, order.

Babbage's advice before the show was echoed in William Whewell's inaugural lecture on "The Results of the Great Exhibition," delivered after the Crystal Palace closed. Whewell, secretary of the British Association and Master of Trinity College, Cambridge, considered the Crystal Palace a "cabinet in which were contained a vast multitude of compositions—not of words, but of things."[9] He suggested that the organizers provided a "scientific moral" in the way that they classified and ordered the many objects on display.[10] The same could be said about human displays and visitors. Divisions by area, type of labor, art and technology, costume, and other criteria not only domesticated an apparently undifferentiated mass, but also suggested a momentary social integration. The Great Exhibition's classification schemes naturalized differences and similarities among peoples, as well as products, collapsing some distinctions and creating new ones.

Whewell's "things" included "nations," or people, which could be compared after commissioners annihilated space and time. Nations and races, resemblances and differences, were invented, coordinated, and legitimized in a reconceptualized vision of the modern functionalist society. Social identities were formed by labeling, integrating, and at times opposing visitors. This was true of the English, imperial, and colonial societies on display and inventing themselves at the exhibitions. What Harold Perkin defined as "a viable class society" expressed in social terms during the mid-Victorian era was increasingly constituted as a viable multiracial society in cultural terms by the last quarter of the century at the exhibitions.[11] This reflected the ascent of race and imperialism in the myths and language of national identity, as well as the decline in Liberal optimism about the capacity of the market and its accompanying categories of "class" to forge social order.

Visitors were as numerous and varied as the exhibition displays themselves. Celebrities moved among commoners, Europeans rubbed against non-Europeans. The list of those who daily "brushed against" one Australian exhibition official included "Royalties, Statesmen, men of letters, men and women of mark in every department of life." [12] "But for the student of human nature," he concluded, "there was just as much interest to be got out of the middle-class and the great unwashed" visiting the show. The Colonial and Indian Exhibition in 1886 brought together colonists from "the ends of the world," who also appeared "from every clime, and including . . . every shade of colour, and of every grade of civilization." [13] Among those at South Kensington were artisans and princes from Ceylon and India, as well as politicians and miners from Australia. Colonial visitors reflected the expansion of formal empire and its political borders since 1851; many represented "communities which had no [imperial] existence when the first Exhibition was opened." In retrospect, the Crystal Palace marked an historical beginning for the exhibition movement and a defining moment in national identity and history. The Colonial and Indian Exhibition redefined English shows and both that national identity and its accompanying sense of the past.

The variety of visitors and participants mirrored consensus about Britain's diverse imperial demography. "Not a single one of our colonies," concluded a contributor to the *Edinburgh Review* in 1851, "is inhabited by a homogeneous population. In none, is the British race the sole one; in scarcely any, is it the most numerous." [14] Some of these dependencies were "taken from savage tribes" and others conquered from other European nations. At the time of the Colonial and Indian Exhibition thirty-five years later, one of the *Review*'s rival journals noted "this enormous population consists of numerous races and tribes, including every imaginable shade of colour." [15] The Royal Anthropological Society's conference at South Kensington on the many races of the empire held during the exhibition validated this view. As living examples of their studies wove tapestries and sold cigars, English and colonial experts discussed the ethnographic variety of the imperial possessions and promoted the governmental applications of their "science of man." [16] Francis Galton noted in his opening remarks that the exhibition provided an "unprecedented" opportunity "of meeting men from all parts of the Empire who are familiarly acquainted with its native races, and of inspecting collections of high ethnological interest." The exhibits would enable the Empire's anthropologists to "learn the condition of the native races at the present moment" and to "gather opinions concerning the value of the influence of the white man upon them."[17]

Australian and Indian commissioners also invited the world of urban artisans, provincial farmers, overseas dignitaries, and neighboring colonial officials to their local and international exhibitions. John Mills Hughes took his family to watch the "grand procession" at the openings of the Melbourne Exhibitions in the 1880s and observed "a great number of visitors . . . from all countries."[18] There were marching "governors, sailors, soldiers, friendly societies, etc." Visitors' books for the major Australian international exhibitions during the last quarter of the nineteenth century reveal ticket-holders from the colonies' metropolises and provincial towns, as well as from India, England, France, Germany, and North America.[19] Local exhibition organizers greeted those visitors with universalist decorations; allegorical frescoes and arches were adorned with lists of the world's prominent cities and countries. Upon entering the Melbourne Exhibition Building, visitors looked upwards to view figures representing Europe, Asia, Africa, and America in the corners of the transept and naves.[20] Such ornamentation provided an idealized presence to represent those who were absent as well as complement those who were in attendance from those regions. In this way, exhibition commissioners, architects, and designers linked participating visitors and their allegorical representations.[21]

In the case of the Indian exhibitions, contemporaries noted the bazaar-like mixing of Anglo-Indians, Indian princes, artisans, and foreign visitors. "The natives of India are fond of ostentatious displays," remarked one observer at the 1864 Bengal Agricultural Exhibition.[22] Among the Raj's subjects in attendance were "a large number of the native nobility and gentry" from Calcutta and its provinces. However, it might have appeared to others that the Anglo-Indians, including the lieutenant-governor, were enjoying the spectacle as much, if not more, than were the princes and other South Asian elites. The same might have been said of the English press. The *Times* boasted that over forty princes would attend the opening ceremony for the Calcutta International Exhibition nearly twenty years later. Its readers were kept informed by a list of the names and addresses of "Native Chiefs in Calcutta" during the show.[23] Indian government officers repeatedly proclaimed the seemingly "natural" regional and ethnic diversity of such princes and the Raj itself; exhibitions, like railways, promised the idea, if not the practice, of social integration, association, and reconciliation amidst that variety.

The creation and ordering of difference at the shows was part of a more general strategy of imperial rule in nineteenth-century British India. In this way, the exhibitions complemented science, censuses, literature, and other means of defining, comprehending, and ordering colonial society.[24] Commissioners juxtaposed and ordered peoples, as well as objects, for instruction at colonial and English exhibitions. Organizers created a social and anthropological "taxonomy" according to the grammar and agenda of imperial cultural policy and nationalist aspirations.[25] George Augustus Sala, a frequent visitor to and commentator on the major expositions of the era, remarked that exhibition courts were occupied by different nationalities, and that the "chief benefit" derived was "in the instruction . . . from this juxtaposition of . . . the various countries."[26] The social and intellectual process of organizing humanity and its products was the underlying "moral" and cultural message of the events. Ordering the visiting "mass" made it accessible, observable, and comprehensible. But the process of creating the inventory was as powerful as the inventory itself.[27] The ability to draw the multitude to the exhibitions and classify it illustrated the power of the commissioners and the states they represented.

The attempts to tame this "bustle and fuss" and create a social taxonomy out of the chaos provided precedent for the later construction of the political British Commonwealth of Nations. Like their twentieth-century public policy successors, English, Australian, and Indian exhibition commissioners were faced with the challenge of defining cultural difference and policing social intercourse after inviting the world to attend their shows. Looking back, we can perceive how the responses to temporary visits from imperial subjects in the nineteenth century helped shape later responses to the permanent migration of the twentieth century; exhibitions were an important part of the long-term history of contact, or the "bustle and fuss" of modern society. There was a significant continuity to the cultural organization of the imperial and national social mass, an overarching history to the construction and policing of social taxonomies out of peoples and material culture, whether during the era of New Imperialism, or the later postcolonial period.

PAINTING IMPERIAL AND NATIONAL PORTRAITS

A visitor to the 1877 Sydney Metropolitan Exhibition found in its galleries "many objects of interest, but which it was scarcely possible to inspect" because of the large numbers of people moving in all directions.[28] The size and variety of that mass was not new in the late 1870s. One American commissioner to the Crystal Palace over twenty-five years before observed a crowd of more than sixty thousand visitors and declared, "Now look at the

People! Mixed in moving masses amongst all these objects of utility or curiosity are men and women of every nation, language, and custome [sic],
from Sunny Ind to Central America; . . . everywhere below, around, and
above us, are human beings, of both sexes, and all ages, nations, languages,
and costumes."[29]

Sir Henry Cole was also impressed by the racial and national diversity of
exhibition visitors in 1851. The Science and Art Department official found
in the variety of visitors to the Great Exhibition a sign of the "cosmopoli-
tan . . . character" of the English nation itself. He observed exhibitors, commissioners, and tourists from Europe, North America, and the colonies,
concluding,

> What more natural than that the first Exhibition of the Works of In-
> dustry of *all* Nations should take place among a people which beyond
> every other in the world is composed of *all* nations? If we were to ex-
> amine the various races which have been concerned in the production
> of this very audience, we should find the blood of Saxons, Celts, Ger-
> mans, Dutchmen, Frenchmen, Hindoos, and probably even Negroes,
> flowing among it.[30]

The exhibition provided a sign of, and mechanism for, the integration of
such cultures into the mid-Victorian national identity of "Englishness."
Visitors constituted an historically imperial England. They were not only
a reflection, or index, of that social mix; they were that mix itself. The
Crystal Palace's variety of exhibits and visitors expressed a particular cos-
mopolitan vision of English national culture and, in doing so, suggested the
power of cultural experts, such as Cole at the center, to select, analyze, and
represent objects and peoples from those sources. The resulting taxonomies
and the classification process itself contributed to imagining the nation, an
act of shared cultural formation.[31] This was also an imperial vision in the
sense that it followed Samuel Taylor Coleridge's and Matthew Arnold's
suggestions about collecting, studying, and applying the "best" of culture,
but threw the nets over a wider geographical and racial range than those
critics envisioned.[32] The formative act included people as well as art and literature, society in addition to culture. To some contemporary optimists,
the 1851 flow of peoples suggested "the follies of nationality" and the
utopian internationalist promises of free trade and colonial federation.[33]

Efforts to promote a diverse audience, including working-class, rural,
foreign, and colonial visitors, reflected and justified changes in the attitude
of both imperial and colonial elites towards popular forms of mass entertainment. Rather than continuing older policies to suppress or restrict tradi-

tional carnivals and amusements, such as that at Bartholomew in England and in various South Asian villages, the later Victorian-era officials promoted attendance by the general public at such venues. They helped reinvent those events and spaces. Exhibition commissioners and their allies moved away from the Benthamite "rational" side of rational recreation; they turned to the "recreational" component instead. Contemporary observers noted that zoos, museums, and exhibitions were replacing the older, often "exotic" minstrels, dancers, and outdoor fairs.[34] This was part of the sea change in attitudes towards popular entertainment. Earlier notions of "improvement" via moral reform gave way to ideas of "civilizing" by calling upon bread and circuses, or spectacles, and the beautiful.[35] Elites in England, Australia, and India increasingly viewed exhibitions, fairs, and other forms of popular amusement as vehicles for integrating those "masses," rather than as the previously feared agents of social disintegration. Large-scale entertainment might be a source of order, not disorder.

Cole remarked during a lecture in Liverpool in 1875 that every town should have public pleasure grounds, Working Men's Clubs, and musical festivals to "bring people together and give them innocent amusement."[36] Rather than fearing mass entertainment, Cole argued that "when a multitude is drawn together, the company exercises a restraining influence." International exhibitions and the purchase of their art works for permanent display at South Kensington were "almost indispensable to our national progress" and part of a more general plan to bring people "out of the public houses" and into "the Museums."[37] Exhibitions were the new Protestant churches; they forged national culture and civilized the masses. Cole testified at the time of the 1867 Paris Universal Exposition that the government should support exhibitions because "it is perfectly justifiable to try and civilize the people by any harmless means which you can induce them to adopt."[38]

Cole's views represented the growing consensus about mass entertainment. Standing at the opposite end of the political spectrum and in nearly complete and total agreement with him was Frederic Harrison. He considered such public festivals "great engines of civilization" and opportunities for "social cooperation."[39] Perhaps drawing upon his pleasant memories of the Great Exhibition, the prominent Positivist and author urged that Sunday and holiday lectures and museum visits would cultivate "national sympathies and common public convictions," rather than regional, religious, or class differences.[40] Favorable public opinion was further strengthened by the increasing power of the state to license and regulate cultural activities, and by the rise to prominence of entrepreneurial showmen, such as Imre Kiralfy in England and Jules Joubert in India and Australia.[41] They were supplanting "the almost extinct race of the old showmen."[42] Those new entertainers appealed to the government and aristocracy for patronage, providing regularized, orderly, and seemingly harmless forms of leisure.

This was not the Evangelical-Benthamite entertainment of the earlier nineteenth century, which sought to educate and transform; rather, here were Indian palaces, Australian bush scenes, and English machines offering the seduction of collective fantasy. The emphasis was less on individual self-control, more on the disciplining power of the group and spectacle. Members of the Revenue and Agriculture Department in India and the governing boards of Australian museums, libraries, and art galleries agreed. They opened their public collections at night, placed them in central locations, and encouraged visits by the "working classes" in the effort to educate and entertain "all classes of the community."[43] Provincial collections received additional government funds. By the mid-nineteenth century, colonial elites advocated visits to cultural institutions as agents for both nation building and social order.[44]

Australian and Anglo-Indian exhibition commissioners were among the strongest voices for those and other colonial applications of Cole's cultural antidote to social vices, such as drunkenness and political disorder. They joined social reformers in lobbying for Sunday and evening openings for museums, exhibitions, and art galleries. Those changes would offer the opportunity for the classes to mingle, since otherwise they might pursue their own highly differentiated forms of leisure and entertainment. Such collections and events would promote the sense of taste and national culture, which, Cole argued, Protestant churches once did in England and which, others contended, was the earlier role of public festivals.

Generally "good" behavior at the shows, except for a few charges of theft, vandalism, and drunkenness, continued to be used as justification for evening and Sunday openings. The superintendent of the Metropolitan Police reported in 1905 that "the conduct of the people on all occasions is quiet and orderly" at the Crystal Palace, Sydenham.[45] Over three million visitors toured the grounds during the preceding six years, but only thirteen were arrested for "drunkeness" [sic]. Metropolitan Police Reports for public attendance and behavior at the Crystal Palace for the 1869–1876 period listed only ten arrests for "drunkenness" among the more than sixteen million visitors. Such places of "resort and rational amusement" appeared to be "conducive to the good behaviour and soberness of the millions of people." In turn, that behavior contributed to the growing consensus in favor of mass entertainment.

IMPERIAL AND NATIONAL WORKERS

Public order at the exhibitions merged with the growing confidence in mass entertainment to encourage voluntary societies and elites to organize working-class visits to those shows.[46] In one well-documented case, the Prince of Wales, Royal Commission, and Royal Society of Arts coordinated and funded the visit of "206 selected Artisans" to the 1878 Paris Universal Exposition. Those workers represented over forty different branches of industry and reported on exhibits and factories in their fields after returning to Britain.[47] The collected findings were subsequently published with additional commentary on French aristanal life and institutions.[48] This was only one in a series of Royal Society–sponsored artisanal deputations to the French shows. The London Trades Council (L.T.C.) also participated in such projects, reporting the use of over four hundred thousand reduced-fare tickets at the time of the Colonial and Indian Exhibition. These were made available after a series of meetings among railway company officials, L.T.C. officers, and the Prince of Wales concerning "the best means of enabling the working population of London to visit" the exposition.[49] Negotiators finally agreed on reduced entrance prices for "workmen and their families." Those visitors joined other working-class families sponsored by "a scheme of workmen's clubs" and "the London School Board and other mediums."[50]

Workers were praised for attending the exhibitions and thus, by implication, for participating in nation- and empire-building at the shows. Francis Fuller noted in 1851 that "it was the . . . artificers who, by sending the produce of their industry, made the Exhibition."[51] His advocacy for using the Crystal Palace's proceeds to endow Schools of Design for the improvement of artisanal skills and national taste rested, in part, on the popularity of the event among laborers. Fuller concluded that the Great Exhibition would have been a financial failure without the mass attendance of working-class visitors on the one-shilling days. "It was among the working and middle classes that the undertaking found warm sympathy and support, at a time when the 'dandies' sneered from Rotten Row."

Exhibition commissioners who did not make special efforts to include working-class visitors often faced criticism. The editors of the *Working Man* supported the London International in 1862, but queried why "the Commissioners seem determined to show that working men are not wanted at the Exhibition?" They found it more than ironic that Saturday admissions were higher than those for weekdays. The five-shilling charge made the event rather expensive for the English working man, who, they argued, "stands more in need of visiting the exhibition" than others, but who could only attend on Saturdays. His studying other nation's exhibits not only would benefit English industry in general, but also would enable the worker to "contemplate the victories of labor, so as to rise in his own estimation."[52]

English exhibitions could celebrate both national wealth and working-class pride, but only if they were made available to the workers themselves. This integrated the working class into the national community, or sense of "Englishness." In this way, the exhibitions were perceived by some contemporaries as potential celebrations of what scholars consider "Radical patriotism," an alternative to the more common official nationalism.[53] If the London International Exhibition celebrated England, or the imagined community of the nation-state, then, according to the *Working Man*, it should include the majority of citizens, the workers, as both workers and citizens. The editors recommended that employers, railway companies, and exhibition commissioners work together to reduce transportation and admission prices for workers. A salary advance to cover exhibition expenses was also suggested. "The working man would then feel grateful, and at the same time, independent; and every one would gain."[54]

In this sense, the *Working Man* was suggesting the relevance of the exhibition experience to workers, but imputing to the commissioners either benign ignorance or malicious intent in preventing those same workers from participating. The exhibitions could offer an alternative to the public house, as organizers such as Cole proclaimed, but only if the commissioners saw fit to reduce the Saturday admissions to the more reasonable one charged on other days, so that the working man and his family could visit. At one level, then, the editors were only asking that the spectacle be made available to the workers on the same terms and with the same opportunities that it had been for others during the work week. But there was an important class-based coloring to these mid-summer editorials, written at the height of the exhibition. The editors argued that admissions should be reduced for workers, "the real power of the land," rather than for "the *gentle* idlers and loungers," who could enjoy the other, one-shilling days as the admission schedule now offered.[55] "The million" should be allowed to take their fair share, rather than provide for the pleasures of "the few," notably the "idle" aristocrats. This was a theme taken up by exhibition commissioners in the colonies as well.

COLONIAL WORKERS, COLONIAL NATIONS?

Australian and Indian government officers, exhibition officials, and newspaper editors also called for special provisions for working-class visitors, including delegations from labor organizations. Among the supportive measures were reduced rail fares and extended openings. Commissioners in Sydney, Melbourne, and Adelaide were anxious to provide gas and electrical lighting to encourage evening visits to exhibition buildings by those who labored during the day.[56] A deputation petitioned the colonial secretary to open the 1879 Sydney International Exhibition at night to "enable the Working and other classes who are engaged during the day to visit the Exhibition during their leisure time" and thus further promote the event's objectives.[57]

Sir Redmond Barry, executive commissioner for the colony of Victoria, invited visitors from South Australia, New South Wales, and other Australasian and Pacific colonies to Melbourne's Intercolonial Exhibition in 1866–67. Barry promised "grand" national results from the city's "Great Hall," which would house the most ambitious Australasian exhibition of its time. As the event approached, he asked those building it,

> Why should not our different guilds invite bands of their brethren of their respective trades to come from the adjoining colonies to visit us during the Exhibition? To exchange ideas respecting the objects of interest common to all of us, to explain practically in language which workmen understand better than Presidents, Commissioners, or Professional Lecturers can do, the excellencies or defects of the different materials on which they have to labour—to impart a knowledge of commodities which may become of immediate exchangeable value. But above all to break down the parochial little-mindedness, which, transplanted into these colonies, exaggerates itself into the contemptible form of colonial jealousy.[58]

The speech is particularly noteworthy not only for its articulation of the exhibition as a way to imagine and structure the *national* community, but also for its direct promotion of working-class attendance and participation to make the show a success and to fuse the nation.

Barry emphasized the interactive nature of this social experience and the value of local "knowledge" in guiding the interpretation of such exhibits. Visitors provided a "practical" guidebook for the displays and were thus part of the process by which the host colony and city were constructed and envisioned as a participatory picture defined, in part, by its relationship to the "adjoining" colonial societies in South Australia, New South Wales, and the Pacific region. Workers "from different guilds" were at the heart of this nationalist vision. Their participation broke down parochialism between the colonies and created the broader sense of Australian federation. Were Barry's "work-men" the first true Australian citizens?

Barry's colleague's in British India shared his enthusiasm for working-class participation. In one case, Anglo-Indian editors encouraged Indian princes to subsidize visits by South Asian artisans to the Calcutta International Exhibition.[59] Recalling the legendary influence of the Great Exhibition on English laborers, local proponents suggested "the same results will, we believe, in their degree, follow upon this Exhibition."

> The native artisan of India who shall see it, will be from that hour another man. It is the subject of common remark that a native of India who has once travelled by the railway, is no longer the same man; and a railway journey to Calcutta to this Exhibition as its consummation, will revolutionise the ideas of the masses of the native workmen, who are able to come and see it.

The Calcutta show would do so, they concluded, because exhibitions, originating with the Crystal Palace, "revolutionized" the workers and art of "the Western World." In keeping with this effort, the municipal leadership of a market town in Upper India voted funds to send to the exhibition "under the guidance of specially selected officers, bodies of . . . artizans and agriculturalists." Perhaps parochial barriers would be breached and local identities reconstructed to include wider social and political links?

One Anglo-Indian captured the power of such a national image at the time of the first Bengal Agricultural Exhibition in 1864. Indian princes, their retinues, and various castes entered the hall separately, comprising a "heterogeneous mass."[60] The contributor to the *Calcutta Review* continued,

> At first there was a marked distinction observed between the various native visitors, and each class kept carefully to itself. Each native Prince with his own retinue formed his own party . . . but in the eagerness to see the wonderful working of the machinery, of the fountains, and of the effects produced by steam power, all pressed forward, irrespective of position or rank. . . . and thus high and low, rich and poor, stood side by side.

These exhibitions allowed social groups to meet, mingle, and compare one another as "side by side" they did the exhibits. They suggested a momentary national integration across social, regional, political, and economic lines. The shows seemed to parallel the Indian railway, which also, according to its outspoken advocates, illustrated and constituted a national, rather than regional and caste-ridden, community. Here was the imagined and observable community of the Indian nation, a temporary prefiguration of a diverse people ordered, defined, policed, and exhibited. Some South Asians participated as active visitors and observers themselves, identified by local and social criteria as much if not more than by the transnational distinctions of race and rule. Commissioners invited South Asian subjects to display their costumes, crafts, wares, and themselves. They were to observe one another as they acted out an Indian taxonomy, or census.

THE ZENANA DAY CONTROVERSY

Exhibitions were agents for developing *national* economic, social, and cultural networks in India but, again, only with the attendance and participation of South Asian artisans, Indian princes, and on several occasions, local women in *purdah*. Proposals inviting South Asian women to visit exhibitions in India raised fundamental questions about their roles in local society and the Indian nation, as well as in the empire. Exhibitions revealed common nineteenth-century social tensions about inclusion and exclusion: who would be visible and invisible in the construction of national identity? Who could visit actively, and who should participate passively? Contests over the proposed inclusion of South Asian women revealed the contemporary understanding that exhibitions might be vehicles for transforming society, rather than only reflecting or indexing the community.

Visits by local women to major Indian shows, such as the Calcutta International Exhibition in 1883–84, "lifted the veil" in a variety of ways. Female participation momentarily suggested the integration of the private/invisible and the public/visible at the shows, and the new membership of old social groups in the nation and empire.[61] For a brief moment, the passive and observed object of the woman in the private space of *zenana* might become an active and observing subject in the public world of the exhibitions.[62] This cultural transition challenged traditionalist Indian society, as well as the delicate imperial and national political balance in India during the 1880s. Racial, gender, and, in essence, cultural, systems could be subverted by the suggestion of a public role for South Asian women, a public transposing of social relationships at the exhibitions. The intervention of imperial policy in the hands of exhibition commissioners at the shows was part of reconstructing local and national social relations. It was unconvincing at such moments to suggest that commissioners were only affecting imperial culture and not society at the periphery, as well, or that they were only preserving and not transforming India.

Painting this national picture at the exhibitions was a contested and controversial project, as Jules Joubert found out at the Calcutta International. "In order, if possible, to break through the impenetrable barrier of the zenana," Joubert wrote in his memoirs, a specific time and place was "set aside for the admission of 'females,'" but not without debate.[63] The executive commissioner confronted strong opposition in his attempt to invite wealthy South Asian women in *purdah* to leave their private sphere for a public walk through the exposition grounds. As was the case with Australian Aboriginals, the women of India had generally been represented at earlier exhibitions only by their wares or ethnographic models. Special arrangements for "Native Ladies" had been made at a few shows, but these were the exceptions. Two mornings were set aside for South Asian women at the Broach Exhibition in 1868, in which European ladies attended to explain the exhibits and "all males were excluded except those who were indispensable for showing the machines and tending some of the stalls."[64] Over nine hundred women attended the show. Commissioners also made arrangements for women to attend the Jeypore Exhibition "once every week" fifteen years later. Officials reported "the attendance on those occasions was large."[65]

No longer passive and invisible, South Asian women could now represent themselves for the moment at those exhibitions, as well as participate by observing, consuming, and manipulating exhibits. The government of India's official report for the Calcutta exhibition concluded that "a noticeable feature of the Exhibition was the large number of native females of all ranks who, in opposition to the restraints of caste and custom, were . . . visitors to its Courts."[66] The Revenue and Agriculture Department officer also recognized the social and religious controversies over this measure and added that "special arrangements had occasionally to be made for the visits of native ladies of high rank." Sunday afternoons were set aside for such women. All male attendants were removed, and screens were erected around the entrance gates to create a "special" protected space in this generally open public arena. Joubert attempted to satisfy the curious and suspicious members of the South Asian and Anglo-Indian communities by informing them in the local press that the direct management of these visits was "in the hands of a native gentleman," and not in those of a European.[67] "Several" thousand Indian women attended the exhibition and, in some cases, "native Princes purchased at a high figure the sole right of the Exhibition for a few hours" to enable their wives and mothers to view the show in "undisturbed" privacy.[68]

The invitation to women in *purdah* was made, in part, as one of Joubert's various schemes to increase the number of paying visitors from the local South Asian community. Despite extensive advertising, the show's attendance was far lower than expected and this resulted in significant and rather awkward financial troubles for Joubert and his company. Joubert also shared with other exhibition officials, both Anglo-Indian and South Asian, the confidence that the shows could educate, as well as entertain, and could provide for India a powerful agent for modern, national development. The executive commissioner intended to collect admission tickets but also to reform and preserve, that is, to offer social and political improvements without unrest. This included the breaking through of the *zenana* barrier. Never short of personal aggrandizement, Joubert considered himself the "liberator" of Indian women.[69]

Joubert's public speeches in support of his project complemented the views of influential Indian commissioners and Revenue and Agricultural Department officials, such as Sir Richard Temple, E. C. Buck, and John Forbes Royle.[70] Those architects of imperial cultural policy contended that exhibitions could serve to modernize the Raj and construct an Indian nation. Regional comparisons suggested national products and types, but also a recasting of the gender and class components of this social picture. Here was both a social picture of the Indian nation and that nation as a social picture. The image was painted in comprehensible ethnographic colors and shapes. This grammar made order out of variety and difference. It also provided a model for future postcolonial and multicultural visions of the Indian nation.

Joubert's "lifting of the veil" to include women generally outside of the English and Anglo-Indian image of the Indian nation can be considered one chapter in the long-term effort on the part of "reformers" and "modernizers" to improve the status of Indian women, but also to set the boundaries and terms of such colonial encounters. Reform precedents included literary societies for South Asian women and the struggles to terminate the rite of *sati*, or widow burning.[71] Whereas such encounters suggested cultural links between the Anglo-Indian, imperial, and indigenous elites, they also implied or represented divisions within the South Asian community. Wealthy women in *purdah*, for example, enjoyed their "special" day at the exhibitions, but other Indian females visited on a regular basis, mingling with visitors of both genders and of various races, castes, and classes. This distinction in the treatment of wealthy and common Indian women hardened existing class divisions while simultaneously challenging gender and political identities, as well as roles, for those of "high rank."

Zenana Days presented a potential reversal of the assumed ordering of

vision at the exhibitions. Colonial subjects and their world were usually
under observation and represented by someone else, but not in this case, at
least for upper-caste women. The colonial and gender subjects would in this
case observe, but, because only a few guides were allowed in at the same
time, their gaze on the special Sunday visits would not be returned. Yet, the
South Asian women assumed an active role, rather than being represented
by ethnographic models or an artistic product. Ironically, then, it was the
West and empire that were privatized, although not without disagreement.
After all, this effort to increase social intercourse and understanding—not
to mention gate receipts for the exhibition—unfolded within the fiery political context of the Ilbert Bill. Tensions over the latter contributed to the
war of words over Joubert's scheme.[72]

The proposal to invite women to the show was debated in Calcutta's
streets and press.[73] Modernizers, including many South Asians, applauded
Joubert's efforts and discerned a step towards national progress. Local nationalists, including one contributor to the press, noted that "female freedom has become a necessity, and it is for the reformer to watch with anxious
care its growth and development." One "Indian Gentleman" visited the exhibition and concluded that Joubert "with his Exhibition, has done more
in three months to break down Indian conservatism among our mothers,
wives, and daughters, than all the other would-be philanthropists who have
visited in India, have done for the past fifty years."[74] Other participants in
the public debate disagreed. Many officers of the Raj feared the inclusion of
women as a return to the days of "Liberal" reforms, which they continued
to blame for the violence and disorder of the Mutiny. Anglo-Indian and
South Asian traditionalists agreed that women should remain in *zenana*
for imperial and local social reasons.

Reaching into *purdah* to make public the native woman paralleled the
rhetoric of those who struggled to "save" ancient monuments from the Indian wilderness and local neglect: both "rescued" formerly invisible objects
and made them available for public observation, collection, and classification. Joubert's Zenana Day helped create the Indian woman as an active participant at the exhibitions and, in a sense, in the public culture of the Indian
nation. She was no longer only an exhibit, but might become an exhibitor:
both object and subject in the practice of imperial and national culture. Such
ambitious measures would be the agendas for some future exhibition commissioners and visitors, while others would act in defiance, securing a more
traditionalist role for women at the shows. Those contests were negotiated
by participating in the series of Womens' Buildings and Labor Courts.[75]

EXHIBITING SOUTH ASIANS:
ETHNOGRAPHIC SUBJECTS AND MODELS

The construction of the Indian nation and its constituent parts at the exhibitions also included the display of South Asians as observed exhibits rather than observing visitors. Commissioners collected South Asian social "types" and their material culture, transforming them into ethnographic objects and models at the shows. Essentially, Indian and local government officers as well as Anglo-Indian anthropologists and museum curators organized living persons to exhibit themselves. Human subjects were labeled, displayed, and studied much as were complementary commercial and artistic exhibits. Generally invisible aboriginal and hill tribes visited local shows; they were thus made a visible part of the national picture, although as an atavism from the past rather than as citizens of the future. Whereas Australian officials were reluctant to invite Aboriginals to exhibitions, their Indian counterparts were enthusiastic about including living "native types" in colonial shows during this period.

The use of South Asians as ethnographic exhibits was part of a more general Victorian-era project to construct an ethnographic survey of the subcontinent. Officials compiled census reports, photographic albums, and museum collections depicting the various castes, tribes, princes, and artisanal classes of the Raj during the later nineteenth century for a variety of intellectual and political purposes.[76] Exhibition commissioners, such as John Forbes Watson, were among those most active in developing such taxonomies for British India. Watson participated in this project as commissioner for India at a series of shows in the 1860s and 1870s and as part of his portfolio as reporter on products for the India Office. He took advantage of new photographic and publishing technologies to produce sample-books of Indian materials and comprehensive albums of ethnographic photography.[77]

Those and many similar projects received official support from the Indian government and the Council of India in London; they complemented various local ethnographic studies by, in one case, members of the Bombay Civil Service.[78] In turn, the publications filled exhibition courts. Several of Watson's ethnographic images were reproduced by the popular press at the time of the Colonial and Indian Exhibition to suggest the "varieties of the heterogeneous population in different provinces of India" and the realism of both the exhibition displays and the engravings.[79] Visitors could compare the Indian artisans and princes whom they observed at the show with the various forms of reproductions, such as photographs, engraved newsprint, and life-sized models.

Commissioners were not only pursuing political and scientific objectives by displaying living colonial subjects. They were also responding to critics who found exhibitions lifeless and dull, particularly after the novelty of the Crystal Palace had worn off. The editors of London's *Pall Mall Gazette* criticized the lack of "life, motion and reality" found at English exhibitions and called for "living specimens" of various colonial peoples at the South Kensington shows in the mid-1880s.[80] In comparison to ethnographic paintings and models, "living specimens of . . . native tribes" would provide more entertainment and education. Visitors could observe "our fellow subjects themselves, in the habits in which they live, following the pursuits in which they spend their existence, and inhabiting dwellings identical with those in which they reside when at home." Anglo-Indian organizers were among the early advocates of living displays and demonstrations at the exhibitions.

Ethnographic visitors often performed traditionalist dances and craftsmanship in reconstructed private dwellings, market bazaars, and carnival spaces. Exhibition commissioners appropriated the traditions of country and metropolitan fairs, including stock figures, such as Indian jugglers, Zulu warriors and Irish giants.[81] These and "wild Australia" shows with "the stirring episode of the last stand of Ned Kelly and his gang" were common attractions at the Crystal and Alexandra Palaces during the second half of the nineteenth century.[82] Commissioners at the Festival of Empire in 1911 continued such entertainment by presenting a "Giants of Empire" competition and display.[83] In those cases, the colonial subjects represented types; they were part of the shows as human exhibits, rather than as equal participants.

As such, those Australians and South Asians were passive actors in the spectacles of national and imperial entertainment, performers rather than visitors. Those ethnographic displays emphasized social distance, rather than the opportunity for seemingly simultaneous and integrative consumption, observation, and self-representation.[84] Distinctions and social distance were hardened not only between colonial subjects and imperial authorities, but also between "wild" and "civilized" colonial subjects, or indigenous participants in colonial public life. Here were South Asian and Australian "citizens" on one hand and their aboriginal communities on the other. Public identities included racial and social criteria in nineteenth-century colonial society. Distances were imperial and national, racial, social, and historical.

Officers of the Royal Asiatic Society in Calcutta proposed "wild" ethnographic exhibits, or "ethnological congresses," as early as the 1860s.[85] The society's leading members suggested exhibiting "typical examples of the races of the old world" for the shows in Calcutta, Jubbulpore, and Nagpore. Dr. Fayrer and J. Anderson, the curator of the society's museum, proposed inviting for observation and study the "aboriginal tribes" of the subcontinent and, if possible, examples of "the races of all Asia, Australia, and the Isles even to the farthest Pacific."[86] Fayrer intended to exhibit "a suitable number of individuals of pronounced type" in a manner similar to that of economic and natural history objects. Indigenous men and women would occupy booths or stalls, such as those found in theaters or Indian bazaars, and be classified according to races and tribes. Sitting in their specific boxes, the South Asians would then be available for observation, photographing, painting, casting, and "otherwise reasonably dealt with, in the interest of science." The society would provide interpreters to enable communication between the public and its exhibition objects. Ever mindful of budget concerns and the disciplining power of work, advocates suggested that the ethnographic subjects could be employed "to put in order the Exhibition grounds at certain times" when they were not on display.

The Royal Asiatic Society proposed as part of the 1868 Calcutta Agricultural Exhibition the display of "the various tribes of men . . . accompanied by sexual examples of their domestic breeds of cattle, sheep and goats, and of the implements which they use in the prosecution of their primitive agriculture."[87] Such subjects would not only offer contrasts to the Anglo-Indian and European visitors to the shows, but also to those South Asians, such as princes, merchants, and artisans invited into the imperial and national picture by the exhibition commissioners. The organizers also intended that such exhibits would provide the materials for a more permanent ethnological museum, contribute to the legitimacy and authority of colonial scientists and learned societies, and, in a sense, domesticate what one contemporary termed India's "wildest and curious tribes." By making public such generally distant or invisible subjects, the local scientists hoped to become "the Pioneers" in the science of anthropology and "earn for themselves a name in history" by addressing the racial concerns of the Anglo-Indian community.[88]

Twenty years later, Calcutta International Exhibition officials invited local governments to send representatives for "a gathering of living specimens of all the aboriginal tribes of India" in an effort to complete and expand the earlier proposed schemes. They once again differentiated "wild" from "civilized" subjects within the South Asian community.[89] Indian Museum officials and visiting commissioners took advantage of such opportunities to construct and photograph full-sized, lifelike models. George Watt, an official of the Revenue and Agriculture Department and one of the most prominent and active exhibition officers, oversaw the making of these models in Calcutta.[90] The Ethnological Court at the International Exhibition in 1883–84 offered a collection he "considered of exceptional value from a scientific point of view," and the various models, dwellings, and tools were either collected for permanent display in the city's government museum or exchanged for overseas exhibition displays.[91]

Fears of going "beyond the pale" and miscegenation captured the imagination of many Europeans in India. Rudyard Kipling's writings are just one example of that literary and social trope.[92] On the other hand, the ethnological congresses and their complementary exhibition displays created defensible cultural and scientific barriers. For the observers and the observed, here were living pictures of the Raj's diversity, but also its hierarchical order. Distinctions were recognized, and the exhibitions provided a process to establish their ordering and management, not their erasure. Identities were defined in ethnic, racial, cultural, and social, but generally not political, terms, distinctions being drawn between passive and active South Asian subjects, and between the two sides of Kipling's famous "pale." The shows organized the world of India according to generally accepted classifications and groups, enabling visitors and scientists to verify, observe, and thus make less threatening India's "wildest" groups. Exhibitions revealed the legendary social and cultural variety of India and, at the same time, the capacity of the Raj to order such multiculturalism and mediate difference and similarity. Participation at the exhibitions provided a moment to imagine nationhood for "civilized" South Asians in contrast to their excluded "wild" races, fundamentally a social, rather than racial, distinction.

ABORIGINALS AS VISITORS AND EXHIBITS

Overseas professional showmen with attachments to Australasia, such as R. E. N. Twopeny and Jules Joubert, agreed with their Anglo-Indian and English colleagues about living exhibits. They contended that human participation would not only make Australia's displays more complete at the shows, but also more popular. Weapons, clothes, utensils, and other "exhibits of native industry" grounded the ethnographic displays.[93] Those lacked the vitality that only living Australian Aboriginals could provide for visitors to both local and overseas shows. Entertainment was necessary. Exhibits needed to appeal to the eye and the imagination of visitors: "a living thing, speaking in distinct and unmistakable tones."[94] Even Redmond

Barry's brother wrote home before the 1862 London International Exhibition requesting that the Melbourne commissioners "get home a *Native* or two with his Boomerang" to accompany Victoria's collection of skins, feathers, and other natural history exhibits.[95] The dynamic addition of such living subjects would prevent colonial displays and exhibitions from becoming yet "one more dead museum" as many European ones threatened to become.

Most Australian government officials and reformers did not share that enthusiasm for inviting Aboriginals to participate at the exhibitions. They were wary about allowing Aboriginals to travel overseas. Officials might organize tours of Aboriginal cricket and rugby squads, but those were exceptional events, and the same public figures prohibited direct Aboriginal participation as visitors or displays in Paris, London, and other foreign cities.[96] Victoria's Aboriginal "Guardians" vetoed a request in 1860 for Aboriginals to perform on the English stage, and the colony's Board for the Protection of Aborigines later declined the request of the French anthropologist Charnay for one dozen Aboriginals for display in Paris.[97] Board members concluded that "blacks who have hitherto visited Europe have generally returned broken in health & deteriorated in other respects." Barry agreed, refusing to send Australian Aboriginals to the 1862 London International Exhibition, as his brother had requested.

The Australian decisions contrasted with those of the Indian government's officers and exhibition commissioners, who repeatedly forwarded artisans, performers, and waiters for the Raj's courts at overseas shows. But, this reluctance to display Aboriginals as part of Australian public culture at exhibitions was consistent with the commitment of local politicians and religious reformers to isolate "Natives" on Mission Stations.[98] Australian officials were not inclined to promote direct contact between Aboriginals and settlers, such as might result in the urban context and at exhibitions. Much of the official rhetoric suggested that cities were quickening the pace of cultural destruction, and thus Aboriginals should be isolated and "civilized" away from settler communities. Barry invited several Aboriginals to Melbourne as subjects for exhibition casts during the early 1860s, but he agreed with the protector of Aborigines that "the poor people should not be allowed to remain in town longer than is absolutely necessary."[99]

Government protectors and evangelical activists were struggling to "save" Aboriginals by resolving what one scholar sees as the duality of "Christianization" and "Civilization"; those reformers feared the evil influences of Adelaide, Melbourne, and Sydney.[100] Frederick W. Taplin, superintendent of the Point McLeay Mission Station in South Australia, was particularly concerned about Aboriginals "loitering about the townships" and adopting "a lazy life." He was confident that the stations promoted "industrious habits," whereas "the evils arising from Aboriginals frequenting the city and country town is great, and should be fully recognized by the authorities establishing ration depots away from these places where practicable."[101] Exhibitions and their various forms of entertainment and visitors offered a threat to, rather than promotion of, "the civilizing process."

The "modern" cities and expositions challenged the isolated education of the established Mission Stations. Proposals for "Black Townships" were made as early as 1838; the stations became a recognizable feature of the social landscape several decades later.[102] They were described in an official dispatch from Victoria in 1874 as "practically Hospitals and Houses of Refuge for the aged and infirm among the Aborigines, and industrial Schools for the children of both Sexes, where they receive the instruction usually given in primary schools, and also learn trades, or are fitted for employment by the agricultural and pastoral settlers."[103] Others mocked stations, such as the one in Coranderrk, Victoria, as "a Government breeding establishment," dominated by idleness and the artificial preservation of the race.[104] Their solution? Extinction, adaptation to modern methods of working and developing the land, or complete isolation, far away from "the temptations of the white man," which included exhibitions.

At the same time, settlers and the first generation of Australian-born politicians wanted to remove the uncomfortable memories of frontier warfare and conquest from public display for a variety of reasons, including the acquisition of land by outright dispossession. The exhibition of Aboriginals, rather than only their material culture or ethnographic models, brought noise to the desired "silence" about Australia's recent past, undermining the new legal notion of a previously unoccupied land.[105] On the other hand, exhibitions could also provide a temporary moment in which the Aboriginals and their reformers might become citizens, participants in Australia's public culture and history. Aboriginal visitors at the exhibitions would help advertise the civilizing process and its successful converts, the civilized Aboriginals, as "living" examples of cultural assimilation.

John Kruger visited a station in the colony of Victoria during the time of the Melbourne International and presented a picture quite distinct from that of the "savage" Aboriginals represented by ethnographic exhibition models and weapons, and from the depressing impressions of other station visitors. He concluded in 1886, "Some of the station residents dwell in cottages, and lead a partially civilised life, their children going to school, and they themselves performing work in the hop field or in the gardens."[106]

Was it not then ironic that when selected to participate at the exhibitions, these Aboriginals were expected to perform "savage" ceremonies and demonstrate "primitive" weapons and tools? Searching for a national past to authenticate the "progress" of white settler society, Australians turned to such rituals performed by converted survivors. Their activities suggested the threatening, yet controlled, atavism of savagery, which required continued discipline and isolation. The hybridity of savage and civilized reconfirmed the power of settlers and their state.

Organizers of the 1879 Sydney International collected and displayed living natives and other "aboriginal people" to satisfy demands for a total, entertaining, and authentic show and to address the place of the *indigene* in national public culture. Those displays included "specimens . . . of the great Australian continent," and "two small companies" from New Zealand and Fiji.[107] The Maoris and Fijians performed dances and other activities in houses specially constructed for the event. The Fijian war dance proved to be particularly popular and gained fame in the local and London press.[108] The "savage" performance, in the words of one journalist, was portrayed as an atavism and described with terms such as "lusty," "cannibalistic," and "war-like." The illustrator for a Sydney weekly added spears and skulls to his engraving of the performance to satisfy preconceptions of "savagery."[109] Who could miss that blunt reminder of the cultural mission yet to be accomplished in the region? This paralleled many of the "savage" exhibits from New Guinea that were collected and displayed at Australian and English shows in the mid-1880s by subimperial officials in Queensland. Those exhibits coincided with the various debates among English, Australian, and German authorities concerning expansion into and political control of that island.[110]

The "authentic" Australian Aboriginal clothes and rituals contrasted with the text of the official catalogue in 1879.[111] That volume's authors suggested that European clothes and ways were being adopted and that those groups that did not do so faced extinction. The vast collection of over five thousand costumes, weapons, and specimens in the Ethnological Court portrayed, according to Australian and English experts, a prehistoric or pre-European age, in contrast to that represented by overseas displays and those of local settlers.[112] The apparent disappearance of such aboriginal peoples was made to seem a "natural" evolutionary development at the exhibitions. Thus, officials advertised the Ethnological Court at Sydney as the last chance to see a collection of authentic wares: it "has, in every probability, never been got together before, and one which it would be scarcely possible to bring together again."[113] The objects' collective value was enhanced by claims that they had been "extremely difficult to procure, and . . . perhaps could not be obtained for display at any other time or place," since their makers were disappearing and assimilating. Here were relics signifying Australia's prehistoric past, the seemingly natural progress and domination of the settlers in contrast to the extinction of the Aborigines, and, later, a shared national identity.

Sydney's commissioners reminded visitors that they "had an opportunity of seeing . . . specimens of the aboriginal people of the great Australian continent" since the latter were admitted to the Garden Palace free of charge during the exhibition in 1879.[114] Although it appears that the Maoris and Fijians could be interviewed by visitors, including the *Graphic*'s local reporter, there is only limited commentary about the Aboriginals.[115] The *Official Catalogue* concluded that the Australian Aboriginal "appears to have few aspirations beyond the satisfying of the necessities of nature." In contrast, the exhibitions acted as "European settlements," stimulating "acquired, but questionable tastes" in such men, women, and children.[116] Their past was frozen in a timeless mode of ethnographic representation: weapons, "rude manufactures," pottery, and models were objects of gaze and classification at the exhibition, not subjects for exotic voyeurism, as were the Fijian dancers. The limited presence of Aboriginals reminded visitors that "the Australian black in his natural condition . . . is now only to be found in the most unfrequented parts of the recent Colony of Queensland, in the northern territory forming part of South Australia, and in Western Australia."[117] Aboriginal tools contrasted with the Australian settler and European courts' icons of national development, such as machinery, minerals, photography, and painting; indigenous tools were transformed into artifacts from the past, although still used by the Aboriginal Australians at the time of the exhibitions.

Colonial shows suggested the tension between Mission Stations and cities, simultaneously challenging and advertising the preservationist projects of experts and the continued efforts to exclude the Aboriginals from public Australian life. Aboriginals rarely attended such events, but perhaps because of that absence, they were considered potentially popular attractions by most local showmen. The promise of increased attendance at Melbourne's Zoological Gardens because of the Centennial Exhibition prompted its superintendent to "contemplate restoring the Native encampment" and to invite Aboriginals to become part of his diorama and model village.[118] He intended a living natural history picture to provide authenticity for the collection of Australian animals and to attract provincial, intercolonial, and overseas visitors to the zoo. Aboriginals were solicited to perform religious and hunting rites, including an "exhibition of boomerang and spear throwing."[119] The director of the Gardens reported that "all the details of the encampment of the aborigines who possessed the country where Melbourne now stands when the white man first arrived will be faithfully carried out."[120] The camp would include weapons, such as stone tomahawks, and Australian flora and fauna considered common components of the Aboriginals' daily lives.

Some Mission Station and religious leaders agreed with such professional showmen. Those reformers perceived an opportunity to advertise their charitable and educational works with the exhibition of "civilized and converted" Aboriginals. The latter had adopted European ways, including reading, Christianity, and clothing, in contrast to "savage" ethnographic displays and visitors. Superintendent Taplin generally agreed with the reluctance of other officials to let Aboriginals "frequent the centers of population," but by the late 1880s he had changed his tune. He suggested that a short-term visit to the major international exhibitions might educate and elevate Aboriginals. It would improve their spoken and written English, provide a religious education, and, as was the intended impact on non-Aboriginal visitors, "start the lad on the road to be a useful citizen instead of a nuisance and a pest to society."[121] Taplin concluded, "Although we strongly disapprove of natives being permitted to frequent the centres of population, an occasional opportunity of visiting the city may prove helpful in educating and elevating the young people." With a slight stretch of geography, these could have been Cole's words as he described a Manchester lad's preference for "gin-palaces" and gambling, and the prescribed antidotes of national education, museums, and exhibitions.[122]

One of the most notable inclusions of Aboriginal visitors occurred at Adelaide's International Exhibition, scheduled to celebrate the colony's and Queen Victoria's joint jubilees in 1887. Bitter debate about the visit raged between exhibition commissioners, Mission Station officers, religious leaders, and government officials.[123] There was concern about supplies and the impact of "a large number of Aboriginals in the City during the Exhibition Season." Many of the Aboriginals were eager to attend, but Taplin, in particular, reiterated the need for strict regulation of a relatively limited number. Members of the local branch of the Geographical Society of Australasia applauded the government's proposal for "Aborigines from the several Mission Stations" to visit the exhibition. They suggested the visitors "give illustrations of aboriginal life," including a *corroboree*, in the Adelaide Town Hall.[124] This argument highlighted the ironic twist in the debate: many Australians applauded the capacity of the state and its agents to isolate and civilize Aboriginals, but, in turn, wanted those same Aboriginals to perform traditional arts, dances, and rituals. Racial and philanthropic visions shaped the ways in which Aboriginals were represented or allowed to represent both themselves and Australia's past at the exhibition.

A short-term, well-organized trip resulted after extensive correspondence. Control of numbers, movement, and social contact was strictly enforced, thereby limiting the social integration encouraged in the case of other visitors, such as those from neighboring Australasian colonies and India. Joseph Hillier was among the Adelaide Exhibition's five thousand daily visitors and recorded in his diary impressions of the concert "given by 230 Aboriginals," including children and adults.[125] He noted that the group from one of the nearby Mission Stations also made mats and fires, fought mock battles, and recited stories to the audience in English. Contemporary newspaper accounts also emphasized the entertainment provided by the Aboriginal visitors; one journalist described their spectacle as a "tableaux illustrative of savage life."[126] This might have seemed a bit awkward, since over thirty of the Aboriginals had recently converted to Christianity. Nearly one hundred station residents took part in the theatrical scenes. With more than a twist of irony, the visitors recited "The British Flag" and performed a musical version of *Robinson Crusoe*. The South Australian deputation's performances appeared more "civilized" than those given by thirty Fraser Island Aboriginals at the Queensland International Exhibition ten years later. *Corroborees*, boomerang-throwing exhibitions and mock combat entertained visitors in Brisbane, emphasizing the persistence of "savage" culture at that event.[127]

The Point McLeay and Point Pearce Aboriginals returned to their Mission Stations away from Adelaide and the exhibition, but only after the "native scenes" and concerts had been prolonged by public demand.[128] Their pilgrimage had served to emphasize difference, rather than only similarity, distinction as well as temporary social integration. Their public presence confronted the "silence" about Aboriginals upon which much of Australian public history, the myth of *terra nullius*, and national identity had been grounded. The living Aboriginal was part of Australia's present as well as its past. Although performers, the Aboriginals also exercised their active vision: the observed could also be the observer at the exhibitions; the formerly invisible was now visible. This was in contrast to static collections of weapons and wax models representing Aboriginal society, culture, and history at most Australian shows.[129] For example, wax figures from Sydney occupied the "Aboriginal Camp" at the National Agricultural and Industrial Association exhibitions as late as the early 1890s in Brisbane.[130]

There is no doubt that the temporary transition to active participants at the Adelaide Exhibition was under the control of the protectors, Friends Association, and other non-Aboriginal groups. But the popular success of the Aborigines' visit served to assert their role in the colony's public life, to challenge the earlier historical silences. This did not mean that Aboriginals participated in that public culture on a level playing field with European settlers and emigrants. At the same time, though, reformers were confident that "the visit of the children and adults from the Point Macleay Mission . . . probably revealed to many, to an extent beyond their anticipation, the extent of improvement and instruction which the natives are capable of receiving, and created some additional interest in the work of the Association." [131] The representation of some "savage" atavisms reminded observers that such "work" was still necessary and required financial and political assistance.

The presence and participation of the Aboriginal visitors offers a parallel to the efforts of reform-minded Indian commissioners to include women in *purdah* at their shows. In both cases, formerly isolated or invisible social groups were invited to momentarily participate in public culture as members of a national community. Visitors reflected and shaped the potential contour of those nations; their physical presence at the shows suggested alternative national and imperial visions, but also reminded contemporaries about the contests over such political communities within the overarching imperial one. The exhibitions revealed both the opportunities and the limitations of public culture, a sphere which was defined by intertwining traditionalist and modern structures and ideas.

IMPERIAL BAZAARS

Imperial and national social groups at the exhibitions came into contact with one another within traditionalist venues. Those included the Indian Palace Courtyard at South Kensington in 1886, the Irish and Scottish villages common at many British shows, and Aboriginal encampments. The London press reported that the Colonial and Indian Exhibition's Courtyard offered visitors "a veritable Indian bazaar, at the various stalls of which brisk purchases of Indian tea and cigars, glowing fabrics, and glittering jewels and brass ornaments from Benares go on daily." [132] After entering under the Gwalior Gateway (Figure 8), visitors mingled around artisans (including silversmiths, weavers, potters, and screen-makers) and shops in "the busy courtyard" (Figure 16). Direct contact between English and South Asian visitors occurred amid the exhibits, models, gateways, and central fountain. At least one English visitor escaped the West and found his Orientalist fantasy in this recreated bazaar. "The whole makes a singularly beautiful interior, conveying a sense of repose which cheats one into the belief of being far away from the rattle and bustle of London." [133]

Commissioners from England and India built those idealized exhibition spaces in an attempt to reproduce what they considered authentic social environments. This was intended to attract British and European visitors, drawn by the apparent magic of the East, but also to assimilate and make popular with the subject population what was, after all, an imported and novel cultural institution. The exhibition was not exactly a bazaar, but many commissioners did what they could to conflate the two. The historicist appropriation of the mythical Eastern bazaar was part of that seemingly common nineteenth-century maneuver by which the new was made popular by appealing to the old, even if the latter was a product of the imagination, as much as, if not more than, the historical record. The Indian section at the Colonial and Indian Exhibition reminded visitors of those bazaars and festivals. "At a single step," wrote the *Times* during the show, "the visitor is carried from the wild, mad, whirl of the individual struggle for existence to which civilisation has been reduced in the ever changing West, into the stately splendour of the unchanging antique life of the East." [134] Thomas Hendley, exhibition commissioner and museum official in Jeypore, compared "the large number of visitors" at Indian museums and exhibitions, and their fascination with art works and relics, to South Asian pilgrims journeying among shrines and fairs. [135]

This Orientalist escape from representing exhibitions as modern markets, cities, and factories was informed by the work of Anglo-Indian antiquarians and officials, many of whom were also exhibition commissioners. They were busy reviving earlier studies of religious festivals and reconstructing both those events and their particular spaces, such as town squares. [136] F. S. Growse was an active member of that group in the later Victorian period. A prominent officer in the Department of Public Works in India and an exhibition commissioner, Growse considered the restoration of festival space to be an important part of rebuilding the town of Bulandshahr. [137] Its revived square could be used for traditional fairs and the Annual District Show, a local exhibition. Such projects during the second half of the century were part of the general scheme to reinvent traditionalist Indian society, culture, and political authority after the Sepoy Mutiny. Growse and his colleagues linked social relations, local history, and architectural space to recapture the allegedly "unchanging antique life" of India.

Exhibition commissioners and Indian government officials turned to festivals and their particular performance areas as moments in time and space

in which the various regions and castes of India merged in a varied but ordered experience, legitimized by its apparent continuity with the past. Val
Prinsep, artist for the official portrait of the Delhi Imperial Durbar, visited
India during the late 1870s and noted, "What a sight the bazaars of Bombay
offered to his artist's eyes. All sorts of Indian forms, from black to white;
all sorts of dresses, from nothing at all to tinsel and *kincaub;* colours of the
most entrancing originality, and forms of the wildest beauty." [138] Prinsep's
sense of color, variety, daze, and fantasy in the bazaar is also found in contemporary descriptions of museums and exhibitions appealing to analogies
outside of history and the West. Hendley compared exhibitions and museums to religious pilgrimages; participants in all cases were driven by "the
craving for excitement, and the love of the strange and curious," the mixing of various peoples marking those collective experiences. [139] Macaulay
ventured even further, grasping beyond historical time and space in pursuit of a precedent, or metaphor, for the Crystal Palace in 1851. The historian and politician voyaged to the imaginary realm of Orientalist fantasy,
where he reflected that the "sight" in Hyde Park on opening day was "beyond the dreams of the Arabian romances; I cannot think that the Caesars
ever exhibited a more splendid spectacle." [140]

Differences in time and space continued to be "annihilated" at these
shows as Whewell claimed they were at the Crystal Palace in 1851. [141] This
appeared to be the case with the gateways, tea gardens, and bazaars at the
International Health and Colonial and Indian Exhibitions in South Kensington over thirty years later. Differences in the images and styles from
several regions and periods were collapsed, integrated, and idealized in Orientalist fantasies, whether they were described as romances or bazaars. [142]
This presented a timeless, universal picture of the Indian "village community" and its occupants, both Indian princes and artisans, and thus provided
historically authentic craftsmanship for the sale items. Commissioners reconstructed the original aura of production in a world of rapidly mechanized
reproduction. They asserted that cultural power in the face of distance, in
terms of both time and space. Visiting artisans from various regions of the
Raj produced traditional Indian arts and crafts and met English, foreign,
and colonial visitors at South Kensington's traditionalist courts.

Consumption of "pure" and "authentic" South Asian teas, oils, coffee,
tobacco, and art provided a shared and integrative imperial experience. [143]
Traditional villages and artisans also provided the total environment necessary to create the sense of authenticity for the production, sale, and consumption of linens, pottery, teas, and other goods from the Celtic Fringe.
The most popular of those included brooches and bracelets displayed by the

Belfast School of Design at the 1853 Dublin Industrial Exhibition and Scottish crafts and clothes at South Kensington's "Highlands" stall in 1862.[144] Government officials and commercial establishments provided "authentic" objects for display and sale by reconstructing the seemingly unique context of original craftsmanship.[145]

Ironically, commissioners turned to modern forms of technology to construct such traditionalist exhibition courts. They also used new methods of crowd control to move, organize, and integrate the visitors occupying those spaces. Exhibitions offered bazaars from the past at the very same time that they introduced the uses of modern telegraphy and railway systems to a wider audience. Commissioners exercised the power to reconstruct and link communities at the exhibitions, mirroring the telegraph, steam, and rail systems uniting disparate parts of the empire and communities within specific national units.[146] The omnipresent electric telegraph was reconfiguring the Australian and Indian landscapes and conflating temporal and spatial distances both within and between such polities during those years. Exhibition displays and literature advertised the application of that new technology. South Australia's official "Sketch" for the distribution at the 1880 Melbourne International Exhibition boasted that there were "4,400 miles of telegraph lines, and 6,000 of wire open to the public" by the end of the preceding year.[147] The Raj's displays at the Melbourne show reminded visitors that there were two lines of telegraphic communication between India and England, and the Indian government telegraph had been operating for almost thirty years.[148]

The spread of information via telegraph cables and newspapers linked "national" and "imperial" events and identities. Nineteenth-century technology and the international exhibitions provided the sense of simultaneity necessary to transform "distant" into immediate events, as the former insulation of time and space dissolved. For example, Harriet Martineau noticed that the telegraph kindled the public outcry at the time of the Indian Mutiny in 1857–58, transforming the Indian empire into a concern for more than the English political elite and the small Anglo-Indian community.[149] Popular telegraph departments and displays illustrated to exhibition visitors the new technology's many public uses and capacity to create that sense of community. The electric telegraph at the Dublin Industrial Exhibition linked the Northern Gallery with the quay at which ships, visitors, and exhibits arrived. A contemporary noted that many men and women took "marked interest in its silent but instantaneous capabilities for communicating messages between these termini."[150]

An Australian visiting the Philadelphia Centennial Exhibition in 1876 remarked that the central telegraph display allowed "visitors [to] readily communicate with friends abroad" in all parts of the world.[151] The commissioners for the 1897 Queensland International Exhibition took those projects and goals an additional step. They proposed "full postal, telephonic, telegraphic, and banking facilities" for the use of visitors and exhibitors in the main buildings.[152] Those displays brought a sense of participation, simultaneity, and social integration to the event; they suggested the various technological and economic imperial connections organized by the commissioners and other experts. Communication displays not only demonstrated the power of the national and imperial States, but also the benefits of merging private initiative with governmental funding and organization for the effective diffusion of those new technologies.

Following the precedent of ambitious empire-builders, the exhibition officials also turned to the railways to bring people and exhibits to the shows. Australian rail authorities organized "special excursion trains" linking Sydney, Melbourne, and other cities during the exhibitions. These temporary connections were in addition to the ordinary railway runs. Richard Pope took advantage of such "cheap excursions" and visited the Melbourne International Exhibition in early 1881, and seven years later Ada Cambridge regularly traveled "nearly 200 miles" to attend concerts and admire the overseas paintings at Melbourne's Centennial Exhibition.[153] By the time of the Festival of Empire in 1911, exhibition commissioners were working with government officials to extend the South London elevated electric railway to the Crystal Palace, Sydenham.[154] Visitors could purchase special round-trip tickets (including admission to the exhibition) from any "tube" station in London.

POLICING THE EXHIBITION CROWD

Railway connections also assisted workers visiting the Crystal Palace in 1851. Over four million laborers, many of whom arrived by trains, toured the Great Exhibition with one-shilling tickets. Officials directed them around the galleries and then out, without allowing a return tour of the exhibits.[155] Lancashire artisans, for example, traveled to London, toured the Crystal Palace for five hours, and returned home by train within one day. Such organization and management was seen by one contemporary as a rival to Napoleon's ability to move and control "large masses" in the field of battle.[156] "It seems to be the fate of this extraordinary show to confound all predictions favourable and unfavourable," concluded Macaulay, upon noticing the absence of rioting and drunkenness among those working-class visitors.[157] The rational and orderly movement of visitors in the Crystal Palace encouraged and relieved contemporaries fearful of unrest and disorder at large-scale public events, particularly in the aftermath of Britain's Chartist demonstrations and Europe's revolutions of 1848.

Eleven years after the Great Exhibition, the bustle and hustle of London at the time of the International Exhibition was greeted with amusement, but not fear. The popular press provides a representative example of those changed perceptions. One *Times* reporter visited South Kensington at the height of the event, noting that "the crowds of gaily-dressed visitors, the busy hum of conversation, and jangle of musical instruments going in all directions gave a life and animation to the interior such as we have seldom seen before."[158] Among those creating that "life and animation" were British and European workers and the Japanese ambassadors and commissioners. The latter were "amongst the numerous foreign exhibitors . . . [who] have attracted more than ordinary attention."[159] Not surprisingly, the Japanese visitors were "the objects of unmeasured curiosity."[160]

The *Leisure Hour* also celebrated the energy and vitality of the host city in 1862, both a cause and reflection of the hectic world inside of the exhibition halls.[161] Its editors illustrated their account with an engraving full of the energetic chaos and urban vitality of mass society (Figure 17). The diverse and large exhibition crowd and its omnibuses presented a portrait of ordered social integration rather than the previously feared social disintegration. Visitors with organized deputations from provincial towns, schools, and cotton mills, "mingled" with men, women, and children from London, Europe, the colonies, and Asia.[162] "London, in 1862, was a sight never to be forgotten; the streets . . . became a thing to be contemplated with awe and doubt . . . and good-humour."[163]

Earlier English urban crowds and seeming floods of mid-Victorian Australasian miners and Indian subjects provoked fears of social dissolution and disintegration. The exhibitions, on the other hand, provided a popular and seemingly peaceful mode for political and social elites to categorize, identify, and thus make such "monsters" less threatening. Exhibitions offered images of order, rather than the feared Socialist, trade union, and foreign disturbances. "I saw none of the men of action with whom the Socialists were threatening us," remarked Macaulay in a letter at the time of the Great Exhibition.[164] Cole also admitted that earlier "fears" and "panics" about foreign disease and revolutionaries, as well as those about England's own working class in the wake of 1848, proved to be unfounded.[165]

Among the reasons for such order in 1851 might have been the unusually large number of policemen and soldiers in London and on the Crystal

Palace grounds during the show. Over six hundred metropolitan, foreign, and provincial police kept watch at the Crystal Palace during the day and arrested nearly twenty suspects for picking pockets and pilfering.[166] The *Edinburgh Review* reported that even the arrivals of foreigners by steam boat and railway were "carefully watched" in 1851.[167] One visiting American commissioner encountered "a well clad army of Police . . . stationed all over the city within sight of each other, constantly perambulating the streets, to keep all things in order and to give strangers every species of information they may desire." [168]

Chartists were well aware of that "army," but failed to share the American's interpretation of its seemingly benign purpose. Although the Crystal Palace offered the opportunity for large-scale direct action, even hardy "physical-force" Chartist leaders advised against rioting and protest. Among those was the Irishman Fergus O'Connor, who recommended restraint in the interests of self-protection and political capital after noting the concentration of police and soldiers in and around London.[169] This was not the revolutionary moment. Instead, O'Connor advised patience to protect "your liberty, your wives, and your children, and perhaps your lives." He implored workers "not to be led away by the folly of others when the Exhibition takes place."

Police were omnipresent and active at Indian and Australian exhibitions as well. The Nagpore Exhibition's commissioners provided a large force of over three hundred police to protect the exhibits and control the expected crowds in 1865. Sentries lined the large building in which were displayed jewels and "the most valuable property." [170] In the case of the Calcutta International Exhibition eighteen years later, special police precautions included soliciting detectives from Scotland Yard, although most of the routine guard duties were performed by the local Calcutta Police.[171] These officers retained order, but could not prevent "some thefts" and vandalism, the most significant of which was the "wrenching off [of] a piece of the gold throne" exhibited by one of the Indian princes.[172] Commissioners for Sydney's first international exhibition in 1879 drew up special regulations for attending police. Officers were required to watch over property, assist visitors with any questions about exhibits, and, in their movement around the displays, "to prevent overcrowding or blocking," remove intoxicated persons, and in general preserve "good order." [173]

Those large numbers of visible policemen and soldiers help explain the relatively peaceful exhibitions, which diminished much of the fear about public festivals in their respective host communities. Law enforcement personnel addressed the physical problems of rioting, drunkenness, and disorder at the exhibitions, but what about the cultural question of taming awe and anxiety, or the political one of using the sense of wonder to strengthen social order? After all, as one journal noted at the time of the London International Exhibition, "sixty-two thousand human beings collected under one roof is of itself a rare, grand . . . show," and one to be managed and controlled in new ways.[174] Commissioners applied various strategies to order, identify, measure, and control this "show." The exhibitions were opportunities to experiment with noncoercive ways to police the masses and modern forms of entertainment. They provided the experience and the language by which colonial subjects and domestic workers, almost the world itself, could be managed and governed.

Management included very practical developments. Charles Babbage suggested rail schemes, announcement boards, and guides for the many visitors at the time of the Great Exhibition.[175] Commissioners at the London International eleven years later prevented the carrying of sticks and "carpet bags or hampers" in the Picture Galleries.[176] Partitions and walls tended to reduce the frustrating sense of vastness often experienced at viewing the exhibition halls from the outside or upon one's entrance. One American's expectations "had been raised pretty high" when he first caught sight of the Crystal Palace, but the dimensions seemed comprehensible once inside, where "that sense of greatness, or vastness" was tamed and reduced by walkways and dividers.[177] These and other measures seem rather predictable today, but the exhibition commissioners were the first generation to confront the problem of organizing and managing such large-scale, indoor entertainments. They recognized the value of awe and wonder, but took novel measures to manage them as part of the spectacle.

Photography provided assistance. Organizers at several shows included a photograph of the visitor on his or her season pass. This practice was inaugurated at the 1867 Paris Universal Exposition and applied in both England and the colonies.[178] The photograph obviated the need for ticket holders to show their signatures each time they entered the building and made easier the differentiation between the many social and cultural types at the events. The editors of the *Photographic News* framed this problem of identification at the time of the next French exposition in 1878: "A Polish Jew succeeds an Englishman through the barrier, and the latter is perhaps followed by a provincial Frenchman and a Turk. How is the check-taker to know whether the outlandish name and more outlandish writing at the bottom of the ticket is that of the bearer?"[179] The photograph provided for this commentator the "trustworthy . . . the only test" to verify the visitor's identity upon entering the exhibition hall and created a personal souvenir of the show.

Automatic gates and turnstiles controlled the movement of visitors and, while doing so, counted the number of admissions.[180] Sydney's Garden Palace was among the first exhibition halls to use the recently patented, self-registering turnstiles, and from those the number of visitors could "readily be ascertained at any time" in 1879.[181] Sufficient exit gates were provided as well for "visitors to pass out easily," but designed to prevent their return. These substituted for direct supervision by exhibition attendants. Clocks, small-scale railways, turnstiles, and barriers directed the flow of visitors in a mode similar to the new processes which organized the movement of citizens in the growing cities of England and the colonies, and the time and labor of industrial workers at the new factories.[182] Here, as with the machinery-in-motion courts, the exhibition itself presented a self-regulating total social system, seemingly functioning without the necessity of visible human intervention.

In the case of the Nagpore Exhibition, organizers created two entrances to distinguish European from non-European visitors. Civil and military officers and European visitors entered the Nagpore Exhibition building from the West and, in an early Kiplingesque turn, princes, *zamindars*, and native artisans from the city entered at the East Door.[183] That scheme attempted to distinguish visitors by race and political authority. Once all were inside of the building, though, the resulting vision was of a more complex colonial society. Rudyard Kipling's "Twain" did meet, after all, in the exposition halls, forming fluid combinations of class, social status, and gender. Similar developments had unfolded at the 1854 Bombay Exhibition, where attendants admitted "the common public" at the front entrance and "Europeans, and Native Ladies and Gentlemen" at the south side of the Town Hall. No such structured distinctions prevented their intermingling once inside the building. Contact among "great numbers of all these classes" resulted in the exhibition gallery.[184]

THE DILEMMAS OF IMPERIAL SOCIAL INTERCOURSE

Exhibitions provided the sense of a seemingly shared and simultaneous experience, although it contained within it powerful oppositions and distinctions. Differentiated ticket prices encouraged such distinction and thus an ordered social hierarchy. There were season tickets, one-shilling days, different prices for women and children, and often free passes for government officials and commissioners. Editors of the *Working Man* praised commissioners in 1862 for lowering the admission charge on Saturdays, although they found the price still too high for most common laborers.[185] In a parallel to nineteenth-century rail travel, the promise of uniformity or equality was belied by such inequality. Various ticket prices, passenger cars, and waiting rooms created differences in the railway experience, as their complements did at exhibitions.[186] Further, critics of railways, cities, and exhibitions feared that all three could provoke social disintegration into anonymity, self-interest, and social distance. Lady Eastlake, for example, felt alone and accompanied only by nature on her rail travels. She abhorred railway stations because "no one [was] interested in his neighbor, all caring for self, no civilities as in old coaching days. People run against you." [187]

No one could doubt that millions of people literally ran "against" one another at the exhibitions, as well, or that it at least seemed as if millions did so. John Bright visited the Great Exhibition several times in 1851 and during one day met Sir J. Graham, the Duke of Newcastle, Rungor Bapojee ("the Vakeel of the late Rajah of Sattara"), Lord Broughton, and Charles Dickens.[188] This social intercourse could prove "too much" contact for others, such as Dickens himself. The novelist found the human mass and the vast cosmos of exhibits within the Crystal Palace both excessive and tiring. Writing to a friend, he admitted that "I have only been twice; so many things bewildered me. I have a natural horror of sights, and the fusion of so many sights in one has not decreased it." [189] The State of Maine's commissioner experienced a similar sense of distress and awe as he toured the Crystal Palace "amidst a moving mass of humanity, almost as varied as the objects of the Exhibition." [190] "It was extremely difficult to move from place to place," and after six hours in the North Gallery he was reconciled to having "hardly glimpsed at one tenth" of the exhibits. For some, then, the numbers of people and exhibits bewildered and frustrated, rather than amused and satisfied.

Rules and measures were not intended to prevent social contact or the impression of awe, but to manage and police them. The mingling of visitors and artisans in the Indian Courtyard at South Kensington, for example, was neither accidental nor random. Exhibition officials policed this space and its social dynamics. All of the visiting colonial artisans were daily lodged before and after the show in separate buildings, "known as the Compound, situated to the West of the Arcade," and thus rarely met English men, women, and children outside of the exhibition halls in "the rattle and bustle" of the city.[191] Inside those halls, though, the exhibition experience became part of the empire-wide project of promoting what one South Asian termed "social, political and religious intercourse" between colonial rulers and their subjects.[192] Such "intercourse" among the various classes in Britain, Australia, and India was also promoted. The practice of national and imperial culture provided the forms and boundaries for such public contact and knowledge.

At times, this social intercourse resulted in moments of humorous surprise, such as in the meeting of wealthy families and their servants, or employers and their workers at exhibitions. *Punch* illustrated this unexpected rendezvous in its famous cartoon about the one-shilling day in 1851: "The Pound and The Shilling—Whoever thought of meeting you here?"[193] On other occasions, the public presentation of unity mystified and even revealed undercurrents of dissent and conflict. Contact could produce a potential political mess, as it nearly did at the Calcutta International Exhibition. The local Executive Committee had followed the common practice at Indian exhibitions and invited various Indian princes and their retinues to attend the opening ceremony and tour the grounds. The attendance of the Nizam of Hyderabad, however, caused much anxiety, as he chose not to play the role of a loyal subject and, in the minds of some, was attempting to take advantage of the popular event to make a claim for greater authority.

The Nizam's behavior seemed particularly threatening in an atmosphere charged with the Ilbert Bill debates, when all claims apparently underscored or questioned the political, legal, and social relations between the Raj and its South Asian subjects.[194] The prince was housed in "a special residence," which included room for his nobles and famous African Body Guard.[195] He visited the exhibition on several occasions, but also addressed various local "native" political and social groups, and received a formal deputation from the nationalist Mahomedan Literary Society.[196] In this case, the colonial exhibition provided a venue for a member of the indigenous elite to publicly negotiate and claim new political authority. The viceroy took advantage of the event to realign the Nizam with the Raj and announce the prince would shortly assume direct administration of the Hyderabad State.[197]

The temporary mixing of races, classes, and other social groups in the exhibition buildings presented an alternative to common Victorian tropes of cultural contact and social intercourse. Popular literary representations included familial, captivity, and "beyond the pale" metaphors and narrative structures.[198] These often suggested the hazards and fears of racial contact. Colonial visitors, on the other hand, did not always act as such threatening characters or types in those spectacles of conciliation, not conflict. Such men and women were not only on display as possibly dangerous or wild "savages," as they were in many ethnographic dioramas and Alexandra Palace spectacles, but also temporarily participated as citizens of the nation and empire.[199] That was an economic, social, and cultural citizenship, but not a political one.

Exhibition courts were often constructed as antimodern, or traditionalist, cultural landscapes, such as Indian bazaars, seemingly without modern class and politics. They were idealized spaces in which pilgrims moved together and interacted in a moment of imperial and national liminality. Ironically, their construction and operation incorporated modern technologies, such as the railway and telegraph. Hierarchies were not reversed, as at the popular early-modern carnivals, but, in this case, English, Anglo-Indian, and Australian elite governance and commerce were clothed in the traditionalist dress of personal and historical rule.[200] Exhibitions implied a sense of cultural and economic participation, but not political equality. This was a participatory metaphor for the multicultural colonial nation and modern British Commonwealth of producers and consumers, a reworking of integrative mid-nineteenth-century liberalism. Some colonial visitors were also commissioners, or coarchitects of the vast imperial cultural network. Their participation provided a momentary reinvention of identities as artisans, settlers, "Australians," and "Indians," that is, national and imperial citizens. For some, that was a limited citizenship; others enjoyed a less restricted form.

The activities of colonial visitors and tourists suggested alternative aesthetic and commercial links. These men and women provided an example of the social intercourse that mediated national, imperial, and racial identities. Variety was not denied, but represented and managed as a form of cultural and social federation at the exhibitions. The commissioners' organization of visitors and the visitors' own activities illustrated and constituted this idea of empire as "federation," most particularly as a prepolitical form of commonwealth. Lyon Playfair, scientist and member of the 1851 Royal Commission, noted this distinction among types of federation during his trip to Canada in 1878. "I have always been a warm friend of what is called the federation of the Empire. Political federation may be in the dim and distant future, but unity of interests and of sentiment already exists, and can be readily promoted."[201] The process of creating, organizing, and visiting these English, Australian, and Indian exhibitions reflected and diffused this confidence in the unity of imperial and national "interests." It embodied a vision of imperial "sentiment."[202]

That form of social intercourse and its promise survived well after the turn of the century. Organizers of the Festival of Empire in 1911 promised "a Social Gathering of the British Family," in which men and women who emigrated years ago would return home to redefine and replant "the family tree," nurturing federation in the form of temporary and often imaginative familial reunification.[203] They would renew associations and relate to the "old people at home the wonders of those new-found lands," such as Australia. This suggested the ways in which the modern nation-states of Australia, India, and England would perceive, articulate, and confront later issues of postcolonial immigration, multiculturalism, and the "family" of the British Commonwealth of Nations.

8 The Imperial Pilgrims' Progress

Ceremonies, Tourism, and Epic Theater at the Exhibitions

Lord George Nathaniel Curzon, British India's fin de siècle viceroy and proudly "forward" imperialist, ambitiously invited Indian princes, Anglo-Indians, soldiers, local artisans, and English tourists to his Durbar Art Exhibition in 1903. Never bashful, Curzon produced an extravaganza, at least in his own mind.[1] In this case, others also agreed. One visiting British journalist noted that "a fortnight of splendour and pageantry" entertained the "kaleidoscope" of visitors to Delhi celebrating the new imperial monarch and the Raj's treasures.[2] All were "satiated with brilliant ceremonies and festive gatherings" by the end of the coronation ceremonies and exhibition.[3] Crowds had surrounded the Durbar halls and artware exhibits, "dazzled and bewildered" by fireworks, polo matches, and state processions as "the East clings to the last to her love for colour and display." However, it was not just "the East" clinging to a colorful ceremonial form, but also the architects of, and participants in, the British Empire's traditionalist social vision and political culture.

Curzon's marriage of state ceremony, traditional arts and crafts, and a formal exhibition points to the triumph of such forms and language in shaping and expressing public culture since the Crystal Palace in 1851. Although one domestic critic of the viceroy's "Imperial gathering" claimed there was among the English a "sturdy dislike" for "the semblance of theatrical display or of fancifulness," the Durbar ceremony concluded a half century of such imperial and national rituals at exhibitions in England, Australia, and India.[4] Those "gatherings" were popular and essential parts of political culture in the three societies in contrast to the editors' claims that they were "foreign" and only "found here and there." Was the Empire then "foreign?" Were Ireland, Australia, and India only "here and there?" Fanciful public theater fostered and illustrated the popular ideas of the British Empire, colonial nationalism, and their respective civil societies. Such rituals of integration and education linked constituent parts and subjects of the Victorian and Edwardian Empires. Among those activities were tourism, coronations, funerals, official processions, historical pageants, and opening and closing ceremonies for major public institutions and exhibitions.

Exhibition ceremonies complemented other English and colonial rituals; they created and reflected the ideas, images, and fantasies necessary for nationalism and imperialism. Participation at the exhibitions as visiting tourists and actors in pageants was part of the process of building those political, social, and cultural communities. This was not fantasy as escapism, but the fantasy which integrated experience and imagination, thereby linking citizens and subjects together in a seemingly viable, tangible way. Those participatory moments represented the idealized relationships between groups within the nation and empire, a utopian condition which could be envisioned at the shows and imagined afterwards. Simultaneity was observed and visually validated at the events as a reference point for social and personal narratives outside of the exhibition walls. Souvenirs and memory kept alive the connections and dreams.[5]

Visitors became part of the imperial, colonial, and national pictures along with economic products and works of art at the exhibitions, but they actively created their part of that picture by marching in ceremonies, traveling as tourists, and acting in historical pageants. Crowds came to look at themselves, as well as at the many commercial and artistic displays. Exhibitions offered visitors the opportunities to become participating citizens in newly reimagined and reenvisioned communities. While appearing to engage as equals in this public culture, they in fact did so in a hierarchical way. Parades illustrated not only the interconnectedness of groups and individuals within society, but also their respective places within that social order. As the Australian political scientist Donald Horne remarks, modern public culture includes rituals, such as exhibitions, "in which all the citizens are made to appear to be common, if differentiated, participants."[6]

Exhibition officials used ceremonies and historical pageants to establish hierarchies within and between communities. Here were the members of imperial, national, and colonial civil societies, arranged in order, everyone and every group in its proper niche.[7] These were illustrated according to which type or group represented itself in an active role at the shows and which were represented by exhibition commissioners and other experts in a generally passive form of display. Others, such as "the Irish Celt, the man whose blood and daring have done, do, and will do so much to conserve the fabric of Empire" were absent from ceremonies.[8] Such was the case at the

Colonial and Indian Exhibition's opening spectacle. The absence suggested the Celtic "He" was not part of this civil society or imperial "general group." This is a reminder that participation at the exhibitions revealed the tensions within public culture between inclusion and exclusion, those that were visible and those that were invisible, whether the polarities were imperial Britain and colonial Australia and India, or social classes of elites and commoners within the host country itself.

Traditionalist Indian visitors—including Indian princes and artisans—were common participants and often paid homage to Queen Victoria as the Empress of India at the shows and her Court during the Jubilee years. Their modern counterparts in South Asian industry and the Nationalist movements were not such visible members of this public culture. That distinction paralleled the dominance of the traditionalist Punjab and Frontier in the late-Victorian imagining of India. The village community and durbar displaced urban centers and the merchant house at the core of this vision.[9] Australia, as a "new" society without monuments and, in a sense, its own history or tradition, was represented by "bush" figures, pastoralists, and miners, as well as official commissioners, but generally not by "invisible" Aboriginals and convicts from its past.[10]

Official opening ceremonies were theaters of traditionalism, rituals of education and integration at both the center and the periphery. They called upon an imagined past to address the difficulties of the present. A variety of imperial pilgrims to ritual centers were invited to participate in the spectacles, including Indian princes and Australian commissioners. Those visitors marched in the processions, were among the official guests, and often gave public addresses to the crowd. This marked the national and imperial importance of the event. Others passively observed the exercise of imperial power. The Crown was displayed as the center of this new civil ritual, illustrating both the essence of imperial identity as allegiance to King and Queen, and the inherent hierarchy of imperial civil society.

Imperial ceremonies and exhibition halls were decorated with a new, self-consciously Imperial Feudal Gothic, or Royal, style to represent such political and social relations. Flags, banners, and other often medievalesque decorations ornamented the interior and exterior of exhibition halls; that was the case in cities as varied as London, Calcutta, Dublin, and Melbourne.[11] Over one hundred and sixty "Armorial bearings" for guilds, countries, cities, corporations, and prominent office holders decorated the walls during the 1853 Industrial Exhibition in Dublin.[12] Those decorations provided signs for the "international" character of the event, and were attempts on the part of its organizers and local political elites to suggest the show's historical connections and continuity with the Great Exhibition in Hyde Park. Flags and medieval banners also surrounded visitors and exhibits in the main halls at the 1870 Sydney Metropolitan and the 1875 Melbourne Intercolonial Exhibitions (Figure 18).[13] While these decorations were exhibits in their own right, they also provided a material and aesthetic reflection of the efforts by James Anthony Froude and Sir John Seeley, among other imperial historians and publicists. They sought to anchor the New Empire and British nationalism in the mythical periods of the Tudor *Oceana* and the reign of King Arthur.[14] On a more prosaic level, the traditionalist ornamentation was part of the battle to make attractive the rather utilitarian iron exhibition structures in Britain and the colonies.[15]

Historical pageants at major English exhibitions were a particularly popular form of participation, sometimes including thousands of costumed men, women, and children. In one of the largest pageants, over fifteen thousand local residents and colonial visitors reenacted various scenes from English history at the Crystal Palace's Festival of Empire in 1911. An enthusiastic supporter remarked that they represented events "with dignity and historical accuracy."[16] Among those historical moments were imperial discoveries, treaties, and early explorations, such as "Our Trade with the Indies."[17] This participatory drama was intended to "help in bringing about a more adequate realization of the extent and power of the Empire" and its heart, the city of London.[18] The original program likened London "to a great personality taking part in the clash and balance of forces and personalities which have gone to make the history of the Empire and the history of the world." Actors reenacted historical tableaux and scenes within "facsimiles" of Old London, The Tower, Westminster Abbey, and Roman forts. The final scene was the Imperial Masque.

Nation and empire were introduced as spectacle, but became personal and accessible at the Festival of Empire and other exhibitions by means of such participatory forms of public culture and entertainment. Ceremonies and pageants accompanying exhibitions reflected not only a picture of social order, but offered a vision of future cultural federation and created its citizens. The latter were at various times passive observers of, and active participants in, these shows. At other moments, they were the subjects of observation. They displayed and were the displays. Although not all groups participated on an equal basis or with the same amount of visibility, organizers in England, Australia, and India represented Empire and Nation as living pictures and rituals of participatory epic theater. They each addressed their particular social and political problems, such as relations between settlers and indigenous peoples.

Exhibition ceremonies and other human displays invited the participation of various groups in the growing imperial civil religion in England and the colonies.[19] This cultural system, with its rituals, language, and forms of social contact, was among the more prominent developments that marked the New Imperialism in contrast to the earlier era of "Free Trade" imperialism. Participation at the exhibitions defined social roles and activities in this network and, in doing so, legitimated various cultural, political, and social "centers." Visitors' experiences were framed as a shared, simultaneous moment at those centers. Momentary integration as participating visitors suggested the imagined and envisioned communities of nation and empire, citizen and subject, but not without controversy. George Julian Harney's *Friend of the People*, for example, attacked the Great Exhibition's "essentially aristocratic" opening ceremony.[20] The republican newspaper preferred to see the Crystal Palace "opened not in the presence of the richest, but of the worthiest of the nation, selected by popular election, to represent not a class, but *all*."

JOHN FORBES WATSON, HISTORIANS, AND THE EXHIBITIONS

Participatory activities at the exhibitions were both reflective mirrors and active agents of public culture, moments of negotiation and contest. Crowds and individuals participated in these selective constructions of the nation and empire, whether in the home country or colonies. Effective colonial rule and the mobilization of local opinion in favor of both national and imperial policies increasingly required the participation of subjects and citizens. The structure of the exhibition experiences, including ceremonies, pageants, and tourism, provided an exercise in a participatory style of public opinion. Those activities promoted the sense of grandeur, expectation, and participation among the visiting public, those whom John Forbes Watson termed, "the real actors in the Exhibitions."[21]

Exhibitions were not only reflections, mechanisms, or indices for society or the public. They constituted that civil society as a dynamic and contested process, sometimes with success, most notably in Australia and England, and less so in India. As Watson suggested, perhaps participation at the exhibitions created the public sphere. The reporter on products for the India Office articulated this symmetry between the shows and the public while serving as the official commissioner for India at English and overseas exhibitions during the 1860s and 1870s. Those included the popular London and Vienna Internationals. In a series of letters to the *Times*, later published as a single volume, Watson addressed changes in the exhibitions since the Crystal Palace over twenty years earlier affecting that symmetry.[22] He noted differences in public spirit, management, and the world of commerce which appeared to make the South Kensington shows in the 1870s less popular than their predecessors.

Commissioners could no longer appeal to mere novelty to attract visitors and exhibitors, since there had been many shows since 1851, and much of the shows' information was available via commercial, telegraphic, and written connections—often products of exhibitions themselves. "Everything is done in reference to the 'public' in general," Watson concluded, echoing the Victorians' obsession with public opinion and recognizing that the public was increasingly complex and sophisticated. There was a changed relationship with "the public," or civil society, because it had changed since 1851, and exhibitions mirrored and shaped both those changes and the internal dynamism of that public. Commissioners needed to address the relationship between exhibitions and this increasingly multifaceted public.

Watson's public included "well defined special classes" in society and at the exhibitions, such as producers, traders, and consumers, but also "in a wider sense," the public included the private community and the state itself. The commissioner suggested that there was a mirroring between society and exhibitions; to some degree, the latter created and shaped the former as the "public." The interests of the various sections of the public—economic, private, and state—were different and conflicting, but the exhibitions could appeal to and reconcile these special classes. "The promotion of every one of these interests may, and should, be made the subject of specially devised measures, while preserving harmony" in the working of the exhibition and society. The link was Watson's definition of the public: both inside and outside of the exhibition experience and space. Participation at the exhibitions formed and represented that public.

This is not to suggest that exhibitions elided the ideas and spaces of civil society and the public sphere, but that experiencing them helped mediate between the private sphere, those very public ones, and the mid-Victorian state.[23] Participation at the exhibitions helped create the sense of a Victorian public, particularly if we conceptualize the public as a process or, as Mary Poovey has argued about culture and cultural formation, as a social body being formed, rather than as a thing or a condition of stasis.[24] Exhibitions suggested one mode of civil society: open to policed participation, limited dissent, and qualified equality.

Historians have generally ignored Watson's point about the active nature of the exhibition experience. Instead, scholars tend to highlight the passive observation and enjoyment on the part of the millions of visitors to the shows, and thus their uncontested participation in the "civilizing" process.[25] Such events can then be perceived as elements in the pervasive schemes of "rational recreation" and "social control" to promote the dominant core ideologies of nationalism and imperialism in the later nineteenth century. The exhibitions are thus considered as one more event in a system of cultural hegemony in which "citizens" and consumers are made, but are not active partners in that social process. Public opinion is manipulated at the exhibitions; social categories are passively filled. This chapter argues, on the other hand, that the exhibitions provided moments in which visitors participated in the construction of social and cultural types and categories, becoming a part of the very process of creating the Victorian public and public opinion.

In a parallel to the creation of nineteenth-century administrative classifications (studied by Ian Hacking in the 1980s) and early-Victorian ethnographic groupings (analyzed by Harriet Martineau in the 1830s), the exhibition experience reinvented citizens and subjects during the nineteenth century.[26] This was an interactive and dynamic process for the individual and the masses.[27] Social types and their behavior coincided with the invention of categories labeling them as English, Australian, Indian, workers, consumers, subjects, and citizens at the exhibitions. Visitors' experiences shaped collective as well as personal values, behavior, and identity, paralleling Hacking's arguments about the ways in which statistical categories or "slots" were created and filled during the nineteenth century. He uses the term "dynamic nominalism" to describe the process by which "people spontaneously come to fit their categories" and in which subjects and objects interact at the moment of social construction.

Participation at exhibitions was such a dynamic experience, but also one that was very public and mass-oriented. Exhibitions were powerful rituals of socialization, not only because they were educative, but also because they were participatory; integration relied on participation at the imperial, national, and civic levels. The shows and their accompanying ceremonies constituted public opinion and civil society rather than merely acting as mechanisms for their representation. Commissioners invited visitors to purchase artwork and other souvenirs, consume food products, travel among the shows, embrace collective memory and nostalgia, march in ceremonies, and act in large-scale historical pageants. Those actions often celebrated nationalism, imperial pride, or some combination of the two, whether in England, Australia, or India. This was not a case of unilaterally imposing an official ideology, or worldview; rather, it was a seductive invitation to help build that view. Participation at the exhibitions helped create the sense of a Victorian public as a dynamic, contested, and participatory sphere.

This physical and political space became, then, a metaphor, or testing ground for general nineteenth-century experiments in liberal and sometimes democratic theory and practice. Among the popular displays explicitly illustrating those changing notions of politics and the public at exhibitions and beyond were new voting machines, ballot boxes, and other instruments of extended political participation. The State of Maine's commissioner toured the Crystal Palace in 1851 and recorded in detail the design and operation of "a Voting Machine" and "model ballot-box" which arrested his attention in the North Central Gallery.[28] He noted in his travel memoirs that the machines attracted numerous visitors, many of whom seemed fascinated by the promise that they prevented fraud in the "the exercise of the elective franchise." Ethnographic displays, large machines, and royal rituals emphasized the "distance" between visitors and objects; the participatory modes of electoral exhibits and other visitor activities annihilated that "distance."[29] They suggested an integrative ideology for the national and imperial communities. Participation at these events mediated the tensions between imperial and national civil societies, as well as the distinctions within them. Active visitors fulfilled various roles with an array of meanings in the construction of citizenship at the exhibitions.

Those shows offered a public sphere in which visitors intermingled and engaged in common pursuits of observation and consumption. They manipulated machines-in-motion, read materials about British and colonial public issues in reading rooms, and subscribed to art unions and lotteries. Journalists praised the reading room at South Kensington's International Health Exhibition in 1884, and colonial commissioners organized a similar Australian Reading Room and Library at the Chicago Columbian Exposition nine years later.[30] In the case of Australia, the art union projects were part of the more general efforts of colonial elites to acquire European paintings, thereby constructing an aesthetic canon for their "new" communities. The Adelaide International Jubilee Exhibition commissioners followed the patterns established at shows in London, Edinburgh, Paris, and Melbourne, offering an Art Union to "encourage a taste for the Fine Arts" in South Australia.[31] They distributed English engravings and paintings by lottery.[32]

The various modes of visitor participation remind us that the most successful exhibitions in terms of popularity and financial profit were those that entertained as well as educated. They appealed to the public, Watson's "real actors." These were the consumers, producers, traders, and private citizens whose interests constituted the shows. Echoing Watson, Jules Joubert advised Australian officials planning for the Melbourne Centennial Exhibition that they should follow the precedent of the South Kensington shows. The International Fisheries, International Health, and Colonial and Indian Exhibitions in the early and mid-1880s were places of amusement and education. They were open at night and included shops, lit gardens, and concerts. They invited visitors to participate. The Australian exhibition should be equally spectacular: "Everything should be done on a scale of magnificence in accordance with such a great event as the Centennial year of Australia & in such a city as Melbourne." [33]

EXHIBITION TOURISTS AS PILGRIMS

Colonial visitors played different social, political, and cultural roles at the exhibitions. Some were part of the exhibits. At more than one show, South Asian artisans and Australian miners produced and sold local products. Others acted as official representatives of their colonies and participated in conferences, scientific exchanges, and social festivities. For example, Sir Redmond Barry received commemorative illuminated charters authorizing him "to represent Victoria in connection with the [1862 London International] Exhibition" and to use his "temporary sojourn in Europe" for the "intellectual improvement of the Colony." [34] The council of the City of Melbourne and the Fitzroy Volunteer Rifle Company also charged him with explaining to overseas visitors and commissioners the colony's "physical condition, and its political, commercial and social progress" as part of his "honorable and important Mission."

A third prominent and discernible colonial group comprised Australians and South Asians who visited the exhibitions as part of their personal and professional travels. These shows and the exhibition buildings were among the major shrines in a growing empire-wide tourist pilgrimage. Alexander W. Dobbie, a prominent South Australian businessman and inventor, was just one among many nineteenth-century imperial pilgrims to these exhibitions.[35] He traveled overseas in the late 1870s and spent at least three days in 1878 completing a "great many notes re. Paris and the [Universal] Exhibition." [36] Anxious to tour the grounds and exhibits, Dobbie recorded that "immediately after breakfast I made straight for the Exhibition, and at once commenced to systematically 'do' it. I first gave it a hurried general survey for a few hours, and then commencing at the machinery department, examined it bit by bit for two solid days."

The South Australian had also "examined" Philadelphia's Centennial Exhibition two years before his tour in Paris, reminding us that nineteenth-century Australian tourists often visited more than one exposition. A traveling Melbourne citizen visited a series of such shows in the 1870s and 1880s, recording in the Visitors' Book at the 1887 Adelaide Jubilee International Exhibition that "I enjoyed this exhibition more than I did the Colinderies [1886], Fisheries [1883], Healtheries [1884], Philadelphia [1876] or Paris [1878]."[37] Colonial visitors followed the exhibitions around the world, often taking advantage of Thomas Cook's organized tours to such shows. There were special excursion trains and hotel accommodations arranged for the armies of provincial, overseas, and intercolonial tourists.[38] One Australian tried to travel from Bombay back home in late 1886, but was told he could "be booked only to Colombo as there was not a single berth available . . . both vessels being crammed with Australians on their return from the Colonial Exhibition in London."[39]

Visitors books for the 1862 London and 1880–81 Melbourne International Exhibitions offer comments by men and women who had traveled to shows in England, Europe, India, and Australasia. They compared expositions as they might museums, restaurants, and hotels. "Better than Paris," was a common refrain in the Melbourne volume. However, the colonial show faced stiffer competition when compared to the Great Exhibition of 1851 and to one Bombay visitor's own personal "bazaar and harem."[40] Visitors from Canada, Ireland, Scotland, and various English provincial cities toured the South Kensington buildings in 1862, and a Canadian visitor to Adelaide's Jubilee International Exhibition in 1887 claimed to "have been present at over 10 exhibitions in different parts of the world."[41] He found the South Australian show "the best Exhibition outside" of Europe.

Unlike the travels of John Bunyan's Christian, their seventeenth-century dissenting predecessor, the Victorian pilgrims progressed towards a worldly, albeit temporary, Celestial City: the Vanity Fair of nineteenth-century exhibitions and exhibition buildings. James Barnet, colonial architect in New South Wales, traveled to England and Europe during 1885 and twice visited the International Inventions Exhibition at South Kensington. He "spent the day" at the show and toured other museums and galleries in London.[42] Another tourist from New South Wales attended concerts and various temporary exhibitions at the Crystal Palace, Sydenham, before departing England for the 1873 Vienna International Exhibition.[43] These colonial pilgrims rarely traveled alone, as had the solitary eighteenth-century visitors from the New Worlds of America and the South Pacific.[44] At times, the Victorians had the world as their companions.

Dobbie and Edward D. S. Ogilvie were two of the more notable nineteenth-century Australian travel chroniclers.[45] Their memoirs included extended comments about exhibition buildings, English, colonial and European exhibits, and their roles as "native informants" at such shows. They both traveled to Europe and England twice and each time visited exhibitions.[46] Ogilvie, a wealthy pastoralist from New South Wales, prefaced his "Diary" with a reminder that his local friends had committed him to "writing, for their amusement, my impressions of the various scenes and wonders I was about to visit in the course of a pilgrimage which was to lead me over many of the most interesting portions of the Old World."[47] Exhibitions and exhibition buildings were among the "wonders" he hoped to see and experience overseas.

This sense of pilgrimage to the Old World and the experiences at the imperial center were important parts of the process of Australian nationalism during the Victorian era. Colonial subjects and citizens often invented their identities in contrast to the "Europe" and "England" discovered on such late nineteenth-century travels.[48] Imperial commissioners did not want colonial visitors to forget that they were, in fact, at the imperial center. Officials at South Kensington placed a "Great Map" designating imperial possessions in red, surmounted by five clock faces at the entrance to their exposition courts. The clocks simultaneously proclaimed the time in Greenwich, Ottawa, Calcutta, Sydney, and Cape Town. A panorama of London and Parliament House rested in the middle, or the "heart" of the surrounding illustrations.[49]

Australian, Anglo-Indian, and South Asian visitors and their exhibits made imperial distinctions in addition to similarities within the Empire public and visible at the exhibitions.[50] This duality underscored and represented the increasing tensions within the British Empire between developing colonial nationalisms and imperial unity. One English observer during the 1880s concluded that such growing cultural distinctions put increased pressures on the political and legislative ties among the imperial communities.[51] The seeds of cultural and social unity, or federation, however, were also being sown at the exhibitions with the participation of colonial visitors. This was particularly true of science and art experts, men of commerce, commissioners, and social elites. They found some social and intellectual commonalities within limits across political, racial, and geographic borders at the exhibitions. Shared migration and pilgrimage to and participation at the shows were thus forms of both national and imperial social and self-discovery. This is not to suggest that the Empire's social chain of being was not without contest and tension during these years; it most certainly was.

Visits to England had marked the sense of exile and distance for early settlers, many of whom still considered themselves temporary emigrants or "overseas Britons." Later Australian-born travelers' experiences abroad highlighted a hybrid of national pride, cultural, and social solidarity, perhaps even a separate political identity. The visits suggested economic and political distinctions, but also cultural similarities within the Empire. The migrant's diasporic spirit informed early excursions to Britain; the settler's sense of permanence marked later visits overseas. Sometimes this permanence was assumed by others. As Dobbie found out in Philadelphia, colonial visitors were often perceived as types or de facto representatives of their societies, although they were not hired to and did not intend to perform such social roles.[52] They might even be recent immigrants themselves. The travel experience constructed colonial distinctions, as well as imperial similarities, sometimes strengthening the roles of cultural centers and elites, such as those at South Kensington, and at other times challenging them.

England and Europe provided for Antipodean pilgrims a public and personal "History" in the forms of ancient monuments, High Culture, and family reunions. Exhibition halls, such as the Crystal Palace, were among these monuments marking the European and English landscape. Their scale awed Australasian visitors, who repeatedly remarked in travel memoirs and correspondence about the size of the structures and the vast numbers attending exhibitions and concerts. One colonial "Pioneer" recalled the 1859 Handel Festival at the Crystal Palace at which "the crowd was so enormous, filling every foot of that spacious building—I was almost dazed at the uncountable mass of faces; and my next impression was the pigmy appearance of the organist and principal vocalists."[53] A fellow Australian was astonished at sitting with over thirty-five thousand persons during a "concert of sacred music" at the Palace.[54] These dimensions reinforced a sense of colonial subordination, or at least cultural inferiority, on the part of such travelers and increased the pressure for colonial cities to build their own Crystal Palaces and British Museums.

On the other hand, visitors also repeatedly confronted misconceptions and myths about Australia. This experience seems to have increased the sense of distance and difference informing colonial national identity. Dobbie found that the label "South Australia" stimulated responses from visitors to the 1876 Philadelphia Centennial Exhibition, but that "the words Victoria and Queensland are not so advantageous," as they were seemingly unknown.[55] Photographs, exhibition displays, and popular panoramas appear to have had little impact on correcting public and private misconceptions about Australian culture and society. "The condition of our Australian colonies is singular and anomalous beyond conception," wrote William Howitt from the gold fields and Melbourne.[56] "And what is not the less extraordinary is, that it is totally unknown at home" in England.[57]

On the more positive side, Ogilvie noted the interest in Australian wines, timbers, and minerals at the Paris Exposition in 1855, recording favorable comments by the official judges for his colonial readers back home.[58] Twenty years later and across the Atlantic at the Philadelphia Centennial, Dobbie inspected machinery and public works which might be useful back home in Australia. He also provided a picture of his colony's position in terms of economic development for other visitors. Official commissioners from the various Australasian colonies pursued a similar path and returned with museum catalogues, railway plans, and schemes to introduce new labor-saving technologies. Reports from Victoria's commissioners at the Philadelphia Exhibition overflow with comments about American, Canadian, and European machinery, transportation systems, educational institutions, and laws.[59]

Such exhibition visits, however, were not all work and no play. Australians enjoyed food and entertainment at various English, European, and colonial shows. Barry wrote home during the 1862 London International Exhibition to inform a very close friend that "the work of the Exhibition is not finished & will keep me hard at work for some time longer."[60] He was organizing Victoria's exhibits and exchanges for Melbourne's various public institutions. The rest of his letter describes days filled with meeting "remarkable & distinguished scientific men of Europe," eating at extravagant feasts—one of which began with "15 kinds of fish"—and touring the foreign exhibits. The colonial commissioner traveled to Dublin on official business before returning home to Melbourne.

Barry's successors were treated even better. The Executive and Reception Committee for the 1886 Colonial and Indian Exhibition prepared travel itineraries for "official" and "unofficial" Australian and Indian visitors. Those included visits to the Isle of Wight, Oxford, Cambridge, various northern provincial centers, and a series of military reviews.[61] The chairman and directors of the Peninsular and Oriental Steam Navigation Company entertained "a large party of Colonists and Indians" during June and "visitors from the Colonies" were given special guided tours of the British Museum's ethnographic collections.[62] Additional social contacts were made at dinners sponsored by various professional and civic organizations, and at meetings of the Royal Society.

Australian visitors took advantage of those overseas events. They cultivated political and social connections, which added to their prestige at home. Advocates of steam lines linking Melbourne, Cape Town, and London in the late 1860s asserted that a visit to "the mother country" would provide Australians with "sobered senses, corrected tastes, and a better appreciation of the work to be done upon their return so that we can hope to rival the countries of the old world." [63] One Adelaide newspaper reported that Dobbie's overseas travel in 1876 "was fruitful in helpful and profitable business hints" and that "it was in connection with this journey that he unexpectedly blossomed into authorship." [64]

Indian and Australian exhibitions also included a variety of tours and festivities to encourage the construction of an imperial community, most notably among politicians, scientists, and businessmen. Chambers of Commerce in South Asian cities hosted Australian and English commissioners to create or strengthen direct economic links between the colonial units. This action on the part of the private commercial body was consistent with the public objective of the Indian government to promote "a reciprocal trade between India and Australia" at exhibitions.[65] The Calcutta dinner for the Australian commissioners in 1884 was part of this common effort. It was praised by the local Anglo-Indian press for the "likely" political and commercial results of closer ties between the colonies.[66] Australian banquets, museum visits, and excursions to provincial towns provided opportunities to further develop complementary national, intercolonial, and imperial alliances. Leading Australian public figures, such as Sir Samuel J. Way, South Australia's chief justice, met their colleagues from other colonies at those shows, sharing various official and unofficial dinners and conversations.[67]

George Frederick Belcher represented Denmark as vice consul at the 1888 Melbourne Centennial Exhibition, and he later recalled the opening ceremony, meetings with "notable personalities," and "an Excellent dinner" at the city's Melbourne Club.[68] He conversed with the Indian commissioner and various Australasian governors. A public dinner in the host city reunited "early" Australians visiting the exhibition. Those included William Westgarth and Francis Henty. Westgarth also rekindled his friendship with Robert Reid, president of the local Chamber of Commerce, whom he had originally met two years before at the Colonial and Indian Exhibition at the imperial center.[69]

The travel memoirs of T. N. Mukharji, one of the Australians' colleagues from India, include various direct cross-cultural encounters during the Colonial and Indian Exhibition.[70] The visiting South Asian exhibition commissioner made a point of discussing India and the Indian exhibits at the 1886 South Kensington show with English visitors. He recorded his impressions of their attitudes, dress, social styles, and eating habits. Those observations were framed in ethnographic terms—not unlike those that would be found in contemporaneous accounts of English travelers in India. Mukharji did not find the British unkind, but wrote that they were "wanting in family affection." The Indian visitor offered his views on England's "caste-system," including the Royal Family, titled nobility and those "near relations of nobility without any independent means," the hotly contested election of 1886, and England's own "ancient monuments." His active participation at the exhibition included conversations with "old Indian hands" stopping by the exhibition courts to reminisce and reconstruct the Anglo-Indian community.

These exhibition excursions were temporary imperial pilgrimages from the periphery to the core—and finally back again—after a momentary integrative and educational experience. Periodic migration to these national and imperial cultural "centers" solidified the common cultural ideas and practices of the science and art experts, among others, and provided political capital upon such visitors' return to Australia and India.[71] Connections formed at sessions with influential figures, including the Queen, prime ministers, and scientists at the imperial center strengthened the visitor's position in local politics and society. This was most notably the case with visiting Australians in contrast to their South Asian colleagues. Many of the latter perceived a cultural barrier to integration at the center, experiencing racial distinction as much as professional commonality. As Mukharji confided in his memoirs, even after spending time describing India and the exhibits in 1886, he was certain that at least one member of his intimate and "delighted" audience would return to her friends "to brag . . . of having actually seen and talked to a genuine 'Blackie.'"[72]

Mukharji's reflections remind us of the strong and persistent limitations structuring social encounters at the exhibitions. These were often parallels to the divisions found elsewhere in the Empire and within colonial societies themselves. Australians were not immune to criticism and self-doubt at the imperial center, sharing to some degree Mukharji's ambivalence about their place in the imperial world. Their active pursuit of approval and prestige at the exhibitions often drove them into the arms of the Queen, but at a price. Such behavior prompted dagger-like accusations of colonial snobbery. *Reynold's Newspaper* noted that many colonial commissioners boasted of "a C.M.G.'ship" and returned with the Queen's recognition of their own international exhibitions; thus, the republican editors concluded, the visitors had "not drivelled and grovelled in vain."[73]

OPENING CEREMONIES AND THE ROYAL TOUCH

Curzon's Durbar extravaganza in 1903 was both a recognition of the Crown's central role in imperial rituals even after Victoria's death and an echo of the Crystal Palace's official opening spectacle in 1851. That ceremony remained a model and reference for later shows, including the Colonial and Indian Exhibition in 1886. The editors of the *Craftsman*, a self-proclaimed journal for "conservative" workingmen, told their readers to expect an opening ceremony at South Kensington that year which would "certainly surpass in grandeur anything which has been seen in England since the inauguration of the Great Exhibition."[74] Rekindling memories of Victoria, Albert, and their family, the commissioners promised the Royal Family's attendance, an imperial ode from Tennyson, and official representatives from the colonies.

Exhibition visitors as different from one another as the Queen and a London clockmaker recorded in diaries and correspondence their impressions of the grand ceremonies opening the shows. Victoria described a moment of imperial triumph amidst her subjects in 1886, while the artisan marked with less passion, but equal regularity, the official openings of each London and Paris exhibition between 1851 and 1886.[75] The "visit of Colonial & Indian Representatives to Guildhall" highlighted his entry for the Colonial and Indian Exhibition—written dutifully at age 79! The clockmaker found the French capital inviting, as well, and traveled there to attend the state ceremony for the 1867 Universal Exposition and to tour the 1889 show. However, he ascended only to the Eiffel Tower's "second stage, owing to the crowd." The memoirs of these and other visitors inscribed imperial, national, and social impressions to those public spectacles which enhanced their lasting autobiographical meaning.

The Crown, traditionalist art forms, and social elites dominated the exhibition ceremonies. Queen Victoria or a member of the Royal Family officially opened and toured the English and colonial shows. Assisted by two thousand choristers and four hundred musicians, the Duke of Cambridge formally opened the 1862 London International Exhibition; he invited visitors to pay heed to Tennyson's exhibition ode.[76] When royalty was not available, the Queen's representatives—the viceroy and governor general in India, lord lieutenant in Ireland, and governors in the Australasian colonies—declared the exhibitions open and toured their courts. For example, Sir John Lawrence's speech as governor-general and the Queen's representative officially opened one of the popular agricultural exhibitions in Calcutta during the early 1880s.[77]

Royal visits to European and Irish exhibitions were also common during the nineteenth century. Victoria traveled to Dublin in 1853 for the first Irish exhibition.[78] Twelve years later, Palmerston recommended that "the loyal part of the Irish population should be gratified, and that their attachment to the Crown should be warmed and strengthened" by a visit from the Royal Family during Dublin's subsequent International Exhibition.[79] This was a time of Fenian challenges to English authority, and the prime minister suggested that the Prince of Wales officially open the event as a show of competing strength and attachment. The prince concurred. He subsequently declared the exhibition open in front of over ten thousand spectators.

Those exhibition ceremonies provided a ritualistic political and social "center" in the ideology and practice of imperial culture.[80] Official opening and closing rituals framed the sense of place, social roles, economic structure, and political authority of the empire in terms of a traditionalist commonwealth centered by the Crown. Such spectacles both encouraged and received authority from Albert's presence in and the later return of Queen Victoria to public life in England and the colonies.[81] Victoria and her authority were present in an often dizzying kaleidoscope of images and objects, including her person and family, artistic representations, royal displays of armor, and war booty. As one amateur poet and visitor to the Great Exhibition concluded in 1851,

> And 'ere Thy Race hath run,
> Emigrants shall thy children be;
> For Indian Emperors and Canadian Kings,
> And Princes o'er the Isles,
> Fair Queen, shall spring from Thee![82]

Colonial commissioners, visitors, and exhibits were among the planets spreading from "thy small Island like a Sun."

Victoria took advantage of the Great Exhibition to display herself and her family to visitors and "the world." The Queen, often "in company with the Prince Consort, and three of their little ones," attended the opening and closing ceremonies, repeatedly toured the Crystal Palace, and received various objects from colonial exhibitors and commissioners.[83] Similar actions were expected at the 1862 London International Exhibition, but the sudden death of the Prince Consort removed the Queen from the public sphere.

After Albert, successive Princes of Wales and other members of the Royal Family oversaw Royal Commissions for international exhibitions and officially opened with state ceremony shows in Great Britain. Those included the 1871 London International at South Kensington.[84] Victoria's retreat from public ceremony ended several years later. South Kensington's thematic exhibitions in the mid-1880s provided the spectacle of her triumphant return to visible political culture. Poor health prevented her from officially opening the 1883 International Fisheries Exhibition, but she centered the massive state ceremony at Albert Hall for the Colonial and Indian Exhibition three years later and toured South Kensington three more times during the show (see the cover illustration).[85]

In the case of the 1886 show, over fourteen thousand in Royal Albert Hall witnessed Tennyson's imperial ode, the singing of the second verse of the national anthem in Sanskrit by Professor Max Müller, official speeches by the Monarch and the Prince of Wales, and then a royal tour of the many South Kensington courts. The Queen marched between two restorations: the medieval entrance of Old London and the Scindia Gateway to the Durbar Palace. Victoria's path was flanked by contrasting but complementary traditionalist subjects: visiting Indian artisans and British Beefeaters.[86] They were connected across space and time by the Crown. The artisans greeted Victoria with the cry "Ram, Ram Al-Ahmad-ul-illah," which they repeated several times.[87] The Queen's chair of state for the Colonial and Indian Exhibition was placed on a dais and enveloped by a canopy of Indian cloth of gold. The throne itself was imperial war booty; it was taken during the capture of Lahore and now rested beneath the Imperial Crown and the monogram of Victoria, Queen and Empress of India.[88]

That opening ceremony reminded contemporaries of the Great Exhibition, also opened by Victoria. We "cannot fail to recall to memory that great and never-to-be-forgotten ceremonial in 1851," wrote the *Westminster Review*'s editors, "when, in the heyday of her popularity," the Queen was accompanied by her husband and children.[89] The memory centered upon the person of Victoria and the association of Prince Albert with the exhibition tradition; the exhibition itself was "the great monument." Here were signs of political and cultural power, enframed by the royal ceremonial and its nearly mythic precedent in 1851. At mid-century, opening ceremonies celebrated the power of England; in 1886, the Queen was "the monarch of a vast empire, presiding over the first gathering of her colonial subjects." Not everyone was favorably impressed with that celebration of Crown and Empire. William Morris and the Socialist League characterized South Kensington's opening ceremony as "that farce of all farces."[90]

The Queen's diary recalled in favorable detail her meetings in 1886 with South Asian, Australian, and other colonial visitors at Windsor Castle and in the exhibition halls.[91] Among those visitors were Indian princes and artisans in their "brilliant-coloured dresses," and Australian politicians. Several of the South Asian visitors sang for Victoria. Those meetings revived the traditionalist practice of receiving royal visitors from Europe and other overseas regions at Court.[92] Indian princes were also common visitors to court during Victoria's Jubilee celebrations the following year.[93] Such visits promoted the sense of personal, traditionalist, or "feudal," government. They paralleled the "curiosities, ancient arms, and specimens of local manufacture" given by Indian princes to the Prince of Wales as tokens of their feudal loyalty during his tour of India in 1875–76. Those were displayed as signs of imperial power and traditional society at subsequent exhibitions, including the Paris Universal two years later. The Indian "arms" at that show were intended to impress French visitors, in particular, with the Raj's grandeur and power and its subjects' personal and strong attachment to the Crown.[94]

Australian officials at the "Colinderies," as the Colonial and Indian Exhibition was commonly called, repeatedly mentioned the Queen's visits to their courts. They competed for the monarch's and Prince of Wales's attention and praise. With few exceptions—notably those with republican commitments or deep ties to their Irish Catholic heritage—Australian officers and attendants melted with enthusiasm before Victoria. The executive commissioner for New South Wales wrote home to his nephew that the monarch "was much interested in all she saw and asked me a great many questions regarding the Colony and expressed herself very much pleased with the Exhibit."[95] In an adjacent court, the colony of Victoria's Graham Berry and Joseph Bosisto telegraphed Melbourne that the Queen "expressed herself highly pleased with Exhibits & general arrangements." This visit followed that of the Prince of Wales, during which he "expressed his great satisfaction" with the colonial court at South Kensington.[96]

The royal opening ceremony and the Queen's subsequent visits, displays of imperial wealth, and the obsequiousness of colonial commissioners angered English republicans. *Reynold's Newspaper* charged the colonial representatives with "royal toadyism" and considered the official opening only an "Imperial Prologue" to further expenditures on "an army and navy and a costly civil service," which included the English exhibition commissioners.[97] The Republican paper was particularly indignant about Australian commissioners who "rushed in a sort of frenzy on a hurry-scurry visit to the

Queen at Windsor" and, in general, acted as "Colonial Snobs." [98] Although the editors noted that colonial societies "found out that they can get on very well without queens, kings, or princes," their commissioners turned to the Crown for personal honors and support for the upcoming Adelaide Jubilee International Exhibition. English Republicans found this sycophantic posturing more than comic and ironic; it was politically dangerous.

The Prince of Wales was often the recipient of this colonial flattery. He had been noticeably engaged with the Colonial and Indian Exhibition; that engagement was part of a larger trend. The prince and his successors donned the Prince Consort's exhibition mantle during the final years of the nineteenth century and successive colonial commissioners repeated their submissive public behavior towards the royal heirs. Albert's association with the Great Exhibition and the international exhibition assumed almost mythic proportions during these years as the time grew more distant from 1851. The Crystal Palace became part of the cult and memory of the Prince Consort; he was associated with the "neutral ground" of public science, art, and letters. [99] His heirs grabbed some of that magic by chairing Royal Commissions, negotiating funding and arrangements with the Royal Society of Arts, foreign commissioners, and host governments, and formally opening exhibitions in England and Europe.

The Princes of Wales also introduced and presented Queen Victoria to official colonial representatives at the exhibitions. [100] Victoria's sons thus appropriated the central role of an active imperial and national cultural voice, as Prince Charles has attempted to do with varying degrees of success during the 1980s and 1990s. In doing so, they not only acted as intermediaries between the Queen and her subjects, but were the focal point of both public praise and criticism. Once again, the republicans attacked in 1886, challenging the Prince of Wales to prove that he had done anything of "merit" for the Colonial and Indian Exhibition and the proposed Imperial Institute. [101] Rather, "any success that has attended the Indian and Colonial [sic] Exhibition is due to our kith and kin across seas, not to the Prince at all."

Nationalist displays by those "kith & kin" in the colonies were balanced against imperial attempts to reassert economic, social, and political links with Great Britain. Royal representatives opening shows in Australia reminded visitors of the political, as well as cultural and social, ties to England and Empire. A vice-regal party led by Sir William Wellington Cairns, governor of Queensland, formally opened Brisbane's Intercolonial Exhibition in 1876, and other representatives of the Crown led exposition processions of local military bands and elites. [102] Anxious to exploit that tradition, Australian politicians pleaded for "the presence of the Prince of Wales" and a "first class Man of War" from the Royal Navy to open the series of international exhibitions held in their major cities during the early 1880s.[103]

Royal participation sanctioned colonial events for the general public, reduced local opposition, except among republican and Irish settlers, and encouraged the participation of foreign states. The prince had recently opened a new railway bridge in Montreal, and Victoria's commissioners sought a similar act of linkage with the Crown and the Prince Consort's mythical 1851 Great Exhibition. The "Governor's Despatch" reminded the secretary of state of the Prince of Wales's exhibition lineage. "It is to the great mind and far-seeing wisdom of His Father the lamented Prince Consort that Exhibitions of this kind owe their origin."[104] The Royal Family created additional links by providing a series of popular objects for display at various Australasian international exhibitions. Among those were electrotype reproductions of the royal regalia in the Tower of London, including the sceptre and silver candlesticks, and paintings by modern masters (including Turner and Landseer) donated to the Adelaide Jubilee and Melbourne Centennial Exhibitions.[105]

The Crown was present in, or at least represented by, other forms as well. Statues of Victoria could not be missed at various colonial exhibition sites. A bronze figure of the Queen dressed in a classical gown dominated the circular space under the Garden Palace's central dome in Sydney, and a similar statue of Victoria decorated the exposition grounds in Brisbane.[106] Writing to her sister from Queensland, Helen Ferguson noted that the Queen's statue was "the first thing that caught" her eye when she visited the Exhibition Grounds in 1883.[107] In a parallel from the Celtic Fringe, the equestrian statue of the Queen at the entrance to the main hall at the Dublin exhibition in 1853 was later bronzed and reerected in Glasgow.[108] The Queen might not have attended the Australian exhibitions in person, but she "was then in all" the visitors' minds as they observed her official representatives and the many symbols of Empire attached to the Crown.[109]

Exhibition displays and statues of the Royal Family were among the many examples of the pervasive representation of the Crown in the Australian colonies, paralleling the actions of governors and other imperial officials who enacted laws in the Queen's name. The strong royal presence in these colonial societies persisted and sometimes found a popular form of expression and support at the exhibitions.[110] At other times, the royal presence was a focal point for dissent and nationalism. Many exhibition commissioners joined the imperial writers and publicists attempting to construct cultural and historical connections between the Empire's constituent parts and reassert the symbolic role of the Crown in imperial and English politics.[111] This was particularly urgent in a period of increasing colonial economic and political self-assertion. Uncertain about the grammar or forms of representation, exhibition officials turned to the "traditions" of royal gifts, ceremonies, and banners to picture the attachments to the center and past. This offered an idiom for the Empire to represent itself to itself, although sometimes in direct conflict with more nationalist exhibits at the Australian and Indian shows.

OPENING CEREMONIES AND COLONIAL CIVIL SOCIETY

Exhibition ceremonies also constituted and revealed the contours of colonial communities. These were participatory pictures of local, national, and imperial civil societies in Australia and India. Lord Harris, for example, opened "with a considerable degree of pomp and solemnity" the Madras Industrial Exhibition in 1855 and declared a public holiday to mark the importance of this event.[112] A royal salute fired at sunrise announced the proceedings and called for the participation of "a large number of Ladies and Gentlemen, including a good many of the Native community." Bands played as the official procession entered the Town Hall's Banquet Room. The crowd continued with prayers, a reading of the One Hundredth Psalm, speeches and comments from political and religious leaders, and the singing of the national anthem. A further royal salute prompted an inspection of "the costly and interesting products of art and nature" gathered together for exhibition.[113] This official ceremony helped reconstruct connections between imperial, Anglo-Indian, and South Asian elites in the host city and its region.

Similar festivities marked the opening of Australian exhibitions. Official representatives from the Crown, the host colony's legislature, neighboring colonies, and foreign countries marched in Australian exhibition parades.[114] William Macleay noted in his diary that September 17, 1879, was "a lovely day. . . . The [Sydney International] Exhibition was open[ed] with great eclat. Four Governors present & an immense concourse of people. It was a general holiday."[115] The opening procession in Sydney also included intercolonial commissioners and official visitors from Germany, Japan, Holland, and Italy.[116] Dressed "in their national costume," the Chinese commissioners were among the most notable foreign participants in the procession opening the Adelaide International Exhibition eight years later.[117] Such participants highlighted the colonial cities' ambitions for regional and worldly roles.

Officers of local voluntary societies and trade unions also participated. The president of the Trades and Labour Council of Adelaide stood on the dais for the opening ceremony of the Adelaide Exhibition in 1887, but this role paled in comparison to that of his colleagues in Victoria.[118] Masons, engineers, iron-molders, and other laborers stood with their union banners and formed a double line through which the colonial governors and other politicians passed at the opening of Melbourne's International Exhibition in 1880. The tradesmen subsequently followed four abreast through the exhibition building's door to tour the exhibits. There was one reminder of their status: participants had to purchase a ticket for the opening ceremony![119]

Eight years later, "The Orders of March" for Melbourne's Centennial Exhibition invited representatives from the Seamen, Tailors, Gas Stokers, and forty other labor societies from the influential Trades' Hall community.[120] Some of those participants were also on the Executive Committee for the event, and others, although not seated at the front, could "enjoy the music, and feast their eyes with the sight of the notabilities of the dais." They did not pay the "guineas and half-guineas" in contrast to the "time in the history of the colony—and that not so long ago either—when their [Labor's] view of the proceedings would have been limited by the outside walls of the building." Participation in the exhibition's opening ceremony was a sign of organized labor's inclusion in Victoria's and Melbourne's public culture and civil society.

The colonial processions thus defined and represented the national and civic communities, as well as their places in the wider imperial society. They marked internal colonial social progress, as well as external political changes. On the other hand, exhibition ceremonies also reminded Australians that theirs was a "new" country without precedents and traditional orderings for such public spectacles. The chief justice, speaker of the Legislative Assembly, and governor in Victoria faced the "unfortunate difficulty" of ranking themselves and other officials at the Centennial show without the colonial version of "a Herald's College."[121] The chief justice protested what he considered the usurpation of his proper rank by the speaker and "stayed away from the opening ceremony altogether."

Many other colonial visitors participated in the opening processions. Those ceremonies provided the picture of a cultural and political hierarchy—with the Crown or its representative at the top and center—and a celebration of the ordered and naturalized variety of citizens. The rituals of the growing imperial and national civil religions offered cognitive and participatory moments, suggesting unity and difference, as did other nineteenth-century civic ceremonies. Those included popular public funerals and parades.[122] The order of such processions suggested the ways in which groups and individuals were linked within those societies, while simultaneously hinting at divisions. Unlike political demonstrations and riots, which explicitly highlighted and perhaps even hardened those divisions, the opening ceremonies offered the image of and way to imagine a systematic, observable, mass social order. They provided momentary participation in that seemingly viable social vision. Time and place were conflated as types illustrated and suggested the ideal civil society. Visitors from England, India, and Australia represented the various interests within imperial and colonial society and the roles each played in the known past and uncertain future.

One visitor to the opening of the Calcutta Exhibition captured the traditionalist image of that ordered imperial and local community: "We witnessed the opening of the Great Exposition, under the auspices of the Viceroy, Lord Ripon, and the Duke and Duchess of Connaught, and attended by the native princes of India, who had come from all parts of the Empire."[123] Also in official attendance were the governors of Bombay and Madras, the social elite of Calcutta, and the heads of various civil and military establishments. According to one visiting South Australian official, the mixing of South Asians "dressed in oriental costume" and Anglo-Indians created "a grand effect in the quadrangle of the Imperial Museum."[124]

On closer inspection, however, this ritual of integration also represented current political divisions and the threat of disintegration. Anger at the proposed Ilbert Bill caused many local Europeans and English guests to decline the invitation to participate in the ceremony. They refused to sit on the podium with the viceroy and visiting Indian princes as part of the general Anglo-Indian opposition to the measure. This was then a self-selected and incomplete colonial civil society on display. Writing several years later, Rudyard Kipling remembered that "the European community were much annoyed. They went to the extremity of revolt—that is to say even the officials of the Service and their wives very often would not attend the functions and levees of the then Viceroy."[125] The failure of the electric light during the ceremony was at first attributed to some malicious person responding to this controversy. Later inspection of the wires revealed they were too small to carry the current required, rather than evidence of sabotage or vandalism.[126] As was the case with later Australian and Indian celebrations of the Queen's Jubilee and Empire Day, spectacles of apparent unity, such as opening ceremonies, revealed in their organization and unfolding the many social tensions and divisions within colonial societies.[127] The same could be said of the epic theatrical spectacles performed at the exhibitions by visitors from England around the Empire. Those reached a crescendo as Britain moved into the later Edwardian era and then celebrated the Festival of Empire in 1911.

IMPERIAL HISTORY AS EPIC THEATER

Organized in 1910, but delayed one year because of the Monarch's unexpected death, the Festival's pageant provides a suggestive example of these epic theaters. One contemporary saw them as a form of "visual instruction" to construct and teach the history of, in this case, London and its "gradual growth and importance as the centre" of the Empire and nation since pre-Roman times.[128] The pageant consisted of a cycle of four parts of eight scenes each, culminating in "The Gathering of the Overseas Dominions around the Mother Country." Among the scenes performed in 1911 at the Crystal Palace, Sydenham, were thirty two moments selected by "leading authorities on the history and antiquities of London." Those included "The Druids Prayer," "Merrie England May Day Revels," early Elizabethan discoveries and trade, such as "the Virginia colony," the Napoleonic Wars, and the Treaty of Waitangi.[129]

Provincial and neighborhood men and women, as well as "Indian visitors and ladies," performed for the King and Queen, overseas royal visitors, and exhibition ticket holders. "Many titled people are taking part," noted one local journalist in 1911, "while in some cases the characters of famous folk will be played by their descendants."[130] Residents of Sydenham, the host borough, were honored with the responsibility for acting out the initial "Beginnings of Empire" scene. This included "Pocahontas at [the] Court of James I." Hackney residents played "Ancient Britons" in recognition of the recent excavations of Paleolithic relics in that area.[131] At times, organizers striving for both mass participation and historical accuracy found the staging rather awkward. One actress recorded in her diary that "the crowd was too big to manipulate" and her colleague nearly drowned one day in the middle of the Merrie England scene.[132]

Britons, Canadians, Australians, South Africans, and South Asians alternated acting in the program.[133] This reflected the increasing presence of local pageants and town ceremonies—or, in the words of contemporaries, "human pictures" and "living panoramas"—on civic calendars in England and the colonies during the late nineteenth and early twentieth centuries.[134] The popularity of pageants was apparent in London in 1910, when visitors and city-dwellers could view the Pageant of the Army, the "living" story of the English soldier. Historical scenes from the previous five centuries were acted out against the backdrop of the post–Anglo-Boer War debates about the condition of the army and its recruits.[135]

Frank Lascelles and Margaret Baxter, among other "pageant-masters," created with these "epic theaters" a sense of national and imperial history. The sweep of costumes, colors, scenery, and dances offered a political parable to contemporaries attempting to assimilate the Edwardian Empire into the patterns and contours of English history with some continuity. Historical pageants were didactic rituals. They tended to limit the distance between the actors and their audience, comprised of other exhibition visitors, and suggested a unity and destiny in the unfolding of an invented past.[136] Covering a great span of time, pageants offered an imagined nation and empire, as well as the exercise of political will. They did so by seemingly democratizing culture. Pageant advocates argued that "painting and sculpture reserved their message for the trained eye. Literature opens her richest beauties only to the scholar."[137] On the other hand, the pageants were seemingly accessible to all citizens and created an "eager hospitality" for the past because of the sense of participation in that past.

Part of that enthusiasm rested on the illusion of mass culture, which stimulated the imagination, ensuring a sympathy with and remembrance of history. The Festival of Empire Pageant was a dramatic and large-scale movement of masses in contrast to spoken dialogue, intimate contact, or the observation of objects. The pageant transcended a "mere Exhibition's" capacity to visually convey the sense of history; it provided opportunities for direct participation.[138] Historical epics constituted the merging of democratic participation and traditionalist cultural forms. The experience of acting in the pageants represented this modern structure of mass social interaction.

Aston Webb and various other prominent architects provided imperial stages and amphitheaters for these pageants in England and India. Best known at the time for his scheme to imperialize Admiralty Way between the Arch and Buckingham Palace, Webb also prepared architectural designs for Curzon's Durbar site in Delhi. Those included a Memorial Park guarded by sculptured lions on pedestals and a water channel leading to an island portico. A Cleopatra needle arose from the center of the island. Marble paths and terraced walks encircled bronzed medals and tablets in a covered loggia.[139] Several years later, Webb built a grandstand in the "form of an ancient Greek ampitheatre" to accommodate ten thousand spectators at the Festival of Empire Exhibition.[140] Neoclassical decorations, ornamentation, and props constructed historical sites and links for weaving together individual events with an overarching sense of continuity and tradition. Greek temples and columns, "a pleasant meadow, wood-bounden" and rocky eminences presented types of environmental spaces to challenge explorers, warriors, missionaries, and tradesmen on the once-moved Crystal Palace's grounds in Sydenham.[141]

The pageant opened with a royal concert performed by the 4,500-member Imperial Choir and Festival of Empire Military Band. Visitors were entertained by forty-eight performances of the pageant over two months. Its scenes offered a selective vision of imperial history and anchored the Empire's evolution in the exploits of heroes and their heroic moments. Treaties and trade marked the relations between England and her subjects in contrast to the history of violence. The epic theater and its accompanying festivities integrated traditional Merrie England and the empire as part of the continued effort to paint current developments with historical and mythic colors. Like other exhibition commissioners, the pageant's organizers orchestrated a mode of participation which provided the historical grounding and sense of continuity for imperial and national political cultures. The pageant concluded with the "Imperial Masque" intended to suggest in allegory "the advantages of empire" and its role as an instrument of "perfection."[142] In contrast to the path of "old Empires," which had lost their direction and become "drunk with power, with pride besot," the masque's text envisioned "something more than brute content" for British colonial subjects and their imperial guides.

CLOSING CEREMONIES, NOSTALGIA, AND PUBLIC MEMORY

Exhibitions created their own lasting sense of mythology, history, and memory. This could be imaginative or material. For example, visitors purchased souvenir books illustrating and describing exhibition pageants, including the epic drama staged at the Festival of Empire.[143] These volumes included "historical" backgrounds to the scenes. Such permanence contrasts with the ephemeral nature of some of the exhibition buildings and displays, which were torn down and removed after the show. The Pageant of Empire, after all, unfolded alongside the Crystal Palace structure which had adorned Hyde Park before its speedy dismantling and removal to Sydenham. The exhibition experience remained a shared one, creating a lasting community of participants, including visitors, exhibitors, and commissioners. The literature, nostalgia for, and commemoration of those events helped anchor the collective memory of Victorian and Edwardian England, Australia, and India, and thus the sense of an historical public.

Melbourne's *Imperial Review* reviewed Queen Victoria's reign at the time of her Jubilee in 1887 and concluded: "The great English events of the reign are the Corn Laws Abolition, Exhibition of 1851, Crimean War, Indian Mutiny."[144] There seemed little doubt in the contributor's mind about the importance of the Crystal Palace show and its own burden of the past almost forty years later. But, contemporaries created the myth of 1851 before the exhibition was officially closed in odes, speeches, commemorative medals, children's' stories, and catalogues.[145] These manufactured the sense of importance echoed by future English and colonial exhibition visitors and commissioners, who brought to later shows their experiences and subsequent expectations about the ideal type of "exhibition."

A natural comparison with the "Great" Exhibition resulted. The 1851 event seemed so "harmonious" and "as much a part of the natural creation as the work of man's hand" because, in part, the following years had been filled with domestic, imperial, and international tensions; the Temple of Peace opened a decade marked by violent crises such as the Crimean War and Sepoy Mutiny. "At the same time," a commentator wrote eleven years later, "nobody doubts that were the old show to arise tomorrow and the new one to disappear, [South] Kensington would again be thronged with eager sightseers."[146] Perhaps this was a response to unfulfilled expectations both inside and outside of the shows. By the turn of the century, showmen in Sydenham were preparing a Grand Naval and Military Exhibition to commemorate "the opening of the Great Exhibition of '51."[147] The exhibition text was so thick that it had become self-referential. Major exhibitions were held to celebrate other exhibitions!

Personal memoirs were among the relics shaping memories of the exhibition experience. M. P. Noel, a pageant player at the 1911 Festival of Empire, compiled a personal scrapbook of photographs, leaflets, and her daily impressions of the event.[148] Postcards, coins, and other forms of memorabilia extended such nostalgic impressions and made the references of memory public, as well as personal. In Australia, commemorative medals were cast to honor Melbourne's exhibition halls and the events they housed, while other organizers manufactured and sold waves of competing souvenirs and seeming ephemera.[149] Recognizing the visitors' desire to send correspondence abroad which would also serve as souvenirs of the show, officials canceled letters and postcards from their own post office at Sydenham in 1911 with a stamp bearing the inscription "Festival of Empire Imperial Exhibition, Crystal Palace."[150] The advertising manager suggested that "an impression of this stamp . . . will make the letter bearing it worth keeping as a little memento of the Festival."

English and colonial exhibitions closed with formal ceremonies, echoing the opening spectacles. This was generally a faint echo, though, since there was never the same sound and fury at the end of the shows as had been expressed and experienced at the beginning. At the same time, those closing events also molded personal and collective memories about the exhibition. In a representative example, crowds filled the galleries and sang "God Save the Queen" at the official closing of the London International Exhibition in 1862.[151] As a form of epic theater and spectacle, exhibitions required such ceremonial closures; they helped shape the popular memory of the events. Those moments marked public and private calendars, but were generally more subdued and less fanciful than the opening ceremonies.

Closing ceremonies were popular, but colored by a flood of nostalgia rather than of expectations, as were the opening ones. That sentiment was provoked initially by observers and participants at the first closing ceremony in 1851. One visitor to the Crystal Palace remarked, "It is well that the new wonder of the world should have its close. But still the change . . . is one which leaves behind it that sort of sadness which we feel when we leave the joyous gatherings."[152] Macaulay also attended the official ceremony at which the Bishop of London provided a thanksgiving sermon. Reflecting upon the meaning of the Great Exhibition, the historian and politician wrote, "This will long be remembered as a singularly happy year, of peace, plenty, good feeling, innocent pleasure, national glory of the best and purest sort."[153] Much of the Great Exhibition's power, attraction, and effectiveness resulted from this interplay of temporary direct experience and selective long-term memory.

Not surprisingly, Thomas Carlyle's response to the closure of the Great Exhibition shared little with Macaulay's. The critic's reactions mirrored his earlier attacks on the event. Carlyle wrote his brother that the "blessed tranquility" of London's streets was the most appropriate antidote to the noisy Crystal Palace and the most meaningful sign that the show "has dissolved itself, all gone or going to the four winds."[154] Much to his pleasure, those winds would take the exhibition mania across the Channel to Paris four years later, but, alas, the storm would reverse itself for London's South Kensington in 1862. For now, though, Carlyle could return in his letters to his family, publications, and a growing interest in his brother's new land, America.

Colonial exhibitions closed with similar ceremonies. "Every foot of standing room was occupied" at the concert officially closing Melbourne's Intercolonial Exhibition in 1867.[155] An attending journalist considered the ceremony a "first class affair." In India, the viceroy formally closed the Calcutta International Exhibition in 1884 with a public speech and firings from the guns of Fort William.[156] The presentation of the jurors' reports and awards completed "a somewhat tame and unimpressive spectacle" in contrast to the opening ceremonies common at Indian exhibitions. There was a "fairly numerous, but not large, assemblage of spectators."

The Great Exhibition's commissioners had also limited "pomp or ceremonial at the close." Officers in Hyde Park allowed their event to continue in pleasant reflection in various commemorative forms. Lord Broughton "wandered about" the Crystal Palace after the small ceremony and considered "the building, already stripped of many of its treasures; a melancholy sight!"[157] Doubt and uncertainty filled these moments of seeming imperial and national euphoria. Noel noted that members of the Imperial Choir sang Kipling's "Recessional" to the tune of "God of our Fathers, Known of Old" at the end of the 1911 Festival of Empire.[158] New exhibition activities, such as tourism, combined with reconstructed older ones, including royal ceremonies, to provide moments of continuity, pictures of integration at times of perceived crises. The merging of the traditional and modern was most successful when it included direct participation; that was the case with historical pageants and official ceremonies. How long would such images and memories last? "And so we went home from that wonderful field of ghosts," concluded Noel in her personal scrapbook. "All the nice people are going, including us, and it was too good to last for ever. And here the Pageant ends."

Epilogue

*Recessional: Imperial Culture and
Colonial Nationalism*

Victorians at home and abroad were confident about the power of exhibitions. South Kensington's architect was no exception, writing in the 1860s that "Exhibitions . . . have had the object from their commencement of bringing to light all the novelties of manufacture and of Science, [and] are recussitating [*sic*] also that which was decaying and giving it fresh tone and renewed vigour." [1] Such shows were part of the general nineteenth-century obsession with discovering, or resuscitating, the authentic and the original in material culture, and applying those representations of the past for political and social purposes in England, Australia, and India. [2] The popularity of the British monarchy, Australian explorers and bush figures, and Indian artisans, princes, and durbar palaces, resulted, in some part, from the cultural policy to create and preserve those historical fantasies at the exhibitions. Such displays at almost every English and colonial exhibition between 1851 and 1914 expressed the traditionalist political culture of the host nation and the British Empire. Relics, machines, consumer goods, and ceremonies also reconstructed an imperial past for modern British identity and naturalized the presence and authority of "new" social groups, such as Australian settlers and Anglo-Indians. This "imperialist nostalgia" was not only an effort to reclaim "traditional" India—destroyed, in part, by intervention and rule—or create an historical Australia, but also an attempt to resolve local tensions within polities. [3]

Exhibitions offered the objects and activities of mass education and entertainment, providing the public culture necessary for the participatory remaking of history, memory, and identities. Traditionalist exhibits in this process included the "immense" cast of the Sanchi Tope, which dominated the Picture Gallery at the London International Exhibition of 1871; the Gwalior Gateway, inviting visitors into the Indian Court and Bazaar at South

Kensington in 1886; and, in a literary rather than architectural form, Sir Redmond Barry's dictionary of Aboriginal languages organized for the 1866–67 Melbourne Intercolonial Exhibition.[4] These were complemented by British royal ceremonies and the costuming of new metropolitan machines in the older gowns of art. In a suggestive parallel close to home, commissioners brought to Dublin's Industrial Exhibition in 1853 a series of twelfth-century stone crosses from Irish marketplaces and casts of "Irish Antiquities" from among "the most famous remains."[5] These filled a separate court as "a monument of the glories of ancient Ireland." Anglo-Irish landlords and military leaders were among the contributors of such relics. Their English parallels were the Irish villages constructed at various shows, including the Franco-British Exhibition in 1908.

Those preservationist projects played an important and visible role at the exhibitions. They were not only the physical representations of "traditional" culture during a period of self-conscious modernization, but also signs of the power of national and imperial elites to recreate that past, to construct and display visible and tangible links with it. The authority and expertise exercised in manipulating relics and art validated not only the commissioners and exhibitors, but also their sponsoring states. They acted "the part of a regenerator," which helped legitimate and naturalize that authority.[6] For the British and their colonists, then, it was not necessarily the attraction of the "exotic," as often marked the French universal expositions, but an obsession with the preservationist impulse—at home and abroad—in the face of seemingly "disappearing" and "new" races, economies, cultures, and arts that drove their exhibition mania.[7] In both cases, exhibitions attempted to mediate distance, but the French and British organizers and visitors understood that term in different ways. Traditional groups defined, in part, the nation and empire as a dialectic between the past and present, placing questions about imperial rule and colonial nationalism within the overriding cultural ambivalence about the modern condition. This tension was illustrated at the British and colonial exhibitions by contrasting "wild" and "civilized" South Asians, skilled and unskilled laborers, raw materials and manufactured goods; it constituted the driving dynamic of the tripartite imperial picture of modern England, traditional India, and new Australia, as well as the social divisions within each polity.

The opposition between past and present was institutionalized by the series of legislative acts in England and the colonies protecting "antiquarian" and "native" remains, relics, and art during the later nineteenth century.[8] Lubbock's original Parliamentary efforts to protect England's "Ancient Monuments" served as a precedent for later colonial statutes. In preserving these relics, however, exhibition organizers, political allies, and science and art colleagues throughout the Empire provided the symbols and language for colonial nationalism, as well as imperial identity and power. The exhibition form popularized traditional Indian art and labor, providing an effective vehicle to represent the Indian National Congress' *swadeshi* movement for independence, as well as the policies and ambitions of the imperialist British Raj.[9]

The effort to reconstruct traditionalist India revealed inconsistencies and contradictions in the imperial enterprise and, in the end, provided a vehicle and vision for twentieth-century Indian nationalism and political decolonization. Only temporary political links were created with traditionalist elites at the expositions, and these were often unpopular. This pattern was repeated in the recreation and diffusion by imperial figures of the Australian bush and settler imagery, which also, in the end, provided a sense of Australian identity as part of a continuing "neo-anti-colonial nationalism," rather than only the intended stronger link with England.[10] The exhibition structure and experience were claimed by both nationalists and imperial collaborators, by the National Congress as well as Indian princes. Colonial exhibitions during the second half of the nineteenth century offered such contests between nationalism and imperial cultural policy. Those shows and their displays of relics promoted a particular form of colonial nationalism which, in the twentieth century, has further provoked the prophecy of an imperial recessional marching to the tunes of Victorian science, art, and public history.

Late nineteenth- and twentieth-century overseas and colonial exhibitions represented these tensions and the pervasive cultural effects of imperial rule. Exhibitions continued to be a popular and influential mode of representing material and ideological inventories containing both political and social meanings. In Melbourne, the Victorian Trades Hall Council appropriated the exhibition form's classificatory and participatory nature to promote colonial industry and independent trade, implying the legitimacy of not only Australian goods, but Australian labor.[11] In 1904, the Council's president attacked "imported" manufactures, including the "use of a foreign made piano at the Exhibition of Australian Manufactures and Products."[12] The language, symbols, and relics of post–Great War national identity in the form of a traditionalist vision were also part of Congress exhibitions, the Festival of India in the early 1980s, and the Brisbane Bicentenary Exhibition in 1988.[13]

The Congress, for example, sponsored several exhibitions of Indian arts, crafts, and manufactures in Madras, Bombay, and Calcutta during the interwar period, drawing upon its series of shows around the turn of the century. The All-India Khadi and Swadeshi Exhibition of 1937–38 was a particularly notable example of this nationalist appropriation and reworking of the imperial vision and project, both its traditionalist ideology and the exhibitionary mode.[14] At the same time, imperial authorities and their colonial agents continued to represent India in the form of traditional pavilions, bazaars, and craftsmanship at the final "great" imperial exhibitions at Wembley (1924–25) and Glasgow (1938).[15] Once emblems of an imperial cultural and economic system, exhibits such as Doulton's impasto "types" at the Colonial and Indian Exhibition became symbols of national heroes in the historical vision shaping struggles for decolonization and postcolonial independence. Nationalists and imperialists battled over the past manufactured at the shows, choosing to represent their ideal societies within the exhibition's structure of material culture and participation. Those battles were also fought within colonial and postcolonial societies among competing Indian and Australian political and social groups.

Postwar exhibitions continued to represent common distinctions between Australia and India. This opposition was revealed by the contrasting architectural forms of national exhibition halls and galleries, such as those at the Wembley British Empire Exhibition. That show's pavilions reflected one editor's conclusion in 1924 that "building in its finest aspects reflects the character of a nation as a community."[16] Australia's exhibits were housed in a neoclassical structure, noted for "the simplicity" of its form, whereas visitors to the Indian section walked amid a "fantasy-like" reconstructed durbar palace or pseudo–Taj Mahal. The play of ornamentation and "atmosphere of romance" in the latter provided "a useful contrast" to its Commonwealth counterpart.[17] One official Wembley Exhibition publication described the Indian Pavilion as "stately . . . with its minarets and domes [it] is one of the most striking buildings in the Exhibition."[18] This was a neo-Victorian reworking (without reference to the Sepoy Mutiny) of Ruskin's contrast between the simple and natural Scottish hearth and "the delicate Indian palaces whose marble was pallied with horror" and sensuality.[19] Whereas an Australian architect designed his colony's pavilion, an English—not South Asian—artist crafted the Indian counterpart.

With the persistence of these cultural practices and images, it is clear that the emperor's clothes were becoming the gowns for twentieth-century forms of Australian and Indian nationalism, as well as for the persistent reimagining and reenvisioning of the British Commonwealth of Nations. The latter continued to balance similarity and difference, racial distinction and political linkage. Exhibitions suggested the strong cultural and moral role for the state in England and the colonies both during and after the Victorian and Edwardian eras. Art and industry exhibits, cognitive structures, and the role of science and art experts at the Festival of India and Brisbane International Exhibition during the 1980s reaffirmed this imperial sociocultural network and the authority of expositions, exhibitors, and commissioners to create and diffuse ideas, materials, and people.

The neoimperial network is alive and well. It links private associations, consumers, tourists, government offices, and public institutions within the Commonwealth. Australian, Indian, and English exhibitions continue to express and shape modern identities, but in doing so, they confront, appropriate, and remake the older national, imperial, and social ones formed at exhibitions between 1851 and 1914. The production of nationalism at contemporary shows invites us to consider the continuities of official cultural policy and both its bureaucratic managers and common consumers between the New Imperial and seemingly postcolonial eras.

Appendix A

Major Australian, English, and Indian Exhibitions, 1851–1914

Great Exhibition (Crystal Palace) (1851)

Melbourne Metropolitan (1854)

Sydney Metropolitan (1854)

Bombay Metropolitan (1854)

Madras Industrial (1855)

Victorian Exhibition (1861)

London International (1862)

Calcutta Agricultural (1864)

Punjab Art and Industry (1864)

Nagpore Arts, Manufactures, and Produce (1865)

Melbourne Intercolonial (1866–67)

Sydney Metropolitan and Intercolonial (1870)

London International (1871–74)

Melbourne Intercolonial (1875)

Queensland Intercolonial (1876)

Sydney Industrial and Intercolonial (1877)

Sydney International (1879)

Melbourne International (1880–81)

Adelaide Arts and Industries (1881)

Punjab Art and Industry (1881)

Calcutta International (1883–84)

Jeypore Art and Industrial (1883)

International Fisheries (South Kensington) (1883)

International Health (South Kensington) (1884)

Colonial and Indian (South Kensington) (1886)

Adelaide Jubilee International (1887)

Melbourne Centennial (1888)
Empire of India (1895)
Queensland International (1897)
Greater Britain (1899)
Delhi Durbar and Indian Art (1903)
Franco-British (1908)
Festival of Empire (1911)

Appendix B

Prominent Exhibition Commissioners,
1851–1914

BARRY, SIR REDMOND (1813–80). Justice and Chief Justice, Supreme Court of Victoria (1852–80); "unofficial standing counsel" (often without fee) for Australian Aboriginals in the Melbourne Courts; Chancellor, University of Melbourne; Founder, Melbourne Mechanics' Institute; Member, Philosophical Institute and Royal Society of Victoria; Trustee, Melbourne Public Library, Gallery, and Museum; Visiting Executive Commissioner for Victoria at London (1862), Dublin (1865), and Philadelphia (1876) Exhibitions; Executive Commissioner for Melbourne Intercolonial Exhibition (1866–67); Commissioner, Local Executive Committee for Melbourne exhibitions, including Victoria (1861) and Intercolonial (1875).

BIRDWOOD, SIR GEORGE CHRISTOPHER MOLESWORTH (1832–1917). Bombay Medical Service; Professor, Grant Medical College, Bombay; Curator of the Government Central Museum, Bombay; Honorary Secretary, Bombay branch of the Royal Asiatic Society; Honorary Secretary of the Agri-Horticultural Society of Western India; Special Assistant in the Revenue, Commerce, and Statistics Department of the India Office (1878–99); chaired sessions on India for the Royal Society of Arts (London); Commissioner, author, and editor of official catalogues and juror for Royal Commissions and Indian Government at major English and European exhibitions between London International (1862) and Paris Universal (1889); Special Commissioner for the Bombay Government at Paris Universal Exposition (1867); Co-Founder of Primrose Day. Author and editor: regular contributor to the *Journal of Indian Art and Industry; Catalogue of the Economic Products of the Presidency of Bombay: being a catalogue of the Government Central Museum, Division I* (1862); *Report on the Government Central Museum and the Agricultural and Horticultural Society of Western India for 1863. With Appendices, being the Establishment of the Victoria and Albert Museum and of the Victoria Gardens* (1864); *Paris Universal Exhibition of 1878. Handbook to the British Indian Section* (1878); *The Industrial Arts of*

India (1880); *Report on the Miscellaneous Old Records of the India Office* (1891); *First Letter Book of the East India Company* (1895); and *Sva* (1915).

BUCK, SIR EDWARD CHARLES (1838–1917).   Bengal Civil Service; Secretary to the Government of India in the Revenue and Agriculture Department (1882–97); Chairman of Indian Government Art Committee, Calcutta (1883); Co-Founder, *Journal of Indian Art and Industry* (1884–1917); Commissioner for Indian Government at Melbourne International (1880–81), Colonial and Indian (1886), and Paris Universal (1900) Exhibitions. Author and editor: government reports on education, agriculture, land revenue, tea trade, and artware; official dictionaries of Indian economic products; "The Utility of Exhibitions to India," *Asiatic Quarterly Review* 2 (1886); and *Historical Summaries of Administration Measures in the Several Branches of Public Business Administered in the Department of Revenue and Agriculture. Drawn up in 1896.*

COLE, SIR HENRY (1808–82).   Assistant Keeper of the Public Records; Officer of the Royal Society of Arts; General Superintendent of the Department of Practical Art and the Museum of Ornamental Art; Keeper of the Department of Science and Art; Executive Commissioner for the Great Exhibition (1851); Secretary and Chief Commissioner for the British Section at the Paris Universal Exposition (1855); Principal Adviser to the Commissioners for the London International Exhibition (1862); Executive Commissioner and Secretary of the Royal Commission for the Paris Universal Exposition (1867); Acting Commissioner for South Kensington International Exhibitions (1870–74). Author and editor: handbooks for public buildings and collections, including National Gallery, Westminster Abbey, and Tower of London (1839–45), and official reports and catalogues for English and European exhibitions (1851–74).

DAVENPORT, SIR SAMUEL (1818–1906).   Member of South Australian Legislative Council (1857–66); President, Royal Agricultural and Horticultural Society of South Australia and South Australian Branch of the Royal Geographical Society of Australia; Executive Commissioner for South Australia at Crystal Palace (1851), Philadelphia (1876), Sydney (1879), Melbourne International (1880), Colonial and Indian (1886), and Melbourne Centennial (1888) Exhibitions. Author and editor: various publications on olives, olive oil, silk, and tobacco production.

HENDLEY, THOMAS HOLBEIN (1847–1917).   Indian Medical Service and Resident Surgeon; Honorary Secretary of the Jeypore Museum; Honorary Secretary for the Exhibition of Indian Art Metal Work, Imperial Institute; Governor and Member of the Executive Council of the Imperial Institute; Chairman (Executive Committee) of the Jeypore Exhibition (1883);

Chairman (Jeypore Committee) for the Colonial and Indian Exhibition (1886). Author and editor: regular contributor to the *Journal of Indian Art and Industry,* including special issue on "Indian Museums" (1914); *Handbook to the Jeypore Museum* (1885); *Handbook for the Contributions of Jeypore to Colonial and Indian Exhibition* (1886); and *Ulwar and its Art Treasures* (1888).

JOUBERT, JULES (1824 – 1907). Professional showman and exhibition manager; Member and Secretary, Royal Agricultural Society of New South Wales; Commissioner of Annual Agricultural Society Shows (1870s); Secretary, New South Wales Commission to the Paris Universal Exposition (1878); Commissioner for New Caledonia, Sydney International Exhibition (1879); Executive Commissioner for the Calcutta International Exhibition (1883 – 84); Manager for Adelaide (1881), Launceston (1891 – 92) and Hobart (1894 – 95) Exhibitions. Author and editor: *Shavings and Scrapes from Many Parts* (1890).

KIPLING, JOHN LOCKWOOD (1837 – 1911). Architecture student at South Kensington; architectural sculptor at Bombay School of Art; Principal of the Mayo School of Art, Lahore; Curator at the Government Central Museum, Lahore; Government Reporter for Art and Industry in Northern India; Commissioner and Local Committee Member for Bombay or Lahore at various English, Indian, and European exhibitions, including London International (1871), Paris Universal (1878), Jeypore Art and Industry (1883), Calcutta International (1883 – 84), and Colonial and Indian (1886). Author and editor: editor and regular contributor to the *Journal of Indian Art and Industry;* author of *Beast and Man in India* (1891).

KNIGHT, JOHN GEORGE (1826 – 92). Founder and President, Victorian Institute of Architects; Lecturer in Civil Engineering, University of Melbourne; Chief Clerk of Works, Public Works Department, Melbourne; Founder and Manager of Melbourne's Athenaeum Club; First Secretary of Melbourne Mining Exchange; Secretary and Accountant to Government Resident, Northern Territory; Government Resident for Northern Territory; proponent and organizer of the Victorian Exhibition (1861); Secretary for Victoria at the London International Exhibition (1862); organized Victoria's contributions to the Dublin (1865) and Paris Universal (1867) Exhibitions; Executive Secretary and General Manager for the Melbourne Intercolonial (1866 – 67); Executive Secretary for Victoria at Sydney Intercolonial Exhibition (1873); and Commissioner for the Northern Territory at the Adelaide Jubilee (1887) and Melbourne Centennial (1888) shows. Designed a "miniature Crystal Palace" for the 1861 Victorian Exhibition and earned medals for a gilded pyramid representing the colony's gold output and collection of building stones in London (1862). Author and editor: *The Australasian Colonies at the International Exhibition, London, 1862. Extracts from the Reports of the Jurors and Other Information Taken from Official Sources* (1865); and *Companion to the Official Catalogue. Guide to the Inter-Colonial Exhibition of 1866* (1866).

LEVEY, GEORGE COLLINS (1835–1919). Journalist, editor, and member of the Legislative Assembly in Victoria; Secretary to Victoria's Commission at the Sydney International Exhibition (1879); Commissioner at Melbourne Intercolonial (1875) and International (1880–81), Vienna International (1873), South Kensington Annual (1873), Philadelphia Centennial (1876), Paris Universal (1878), and Amsterdam Colonial (1883) Exhibitions; Secretary to Host Commission for the Tasmanian (1894) and Royal Commission for the Paris Universal (1900) shows; lectured on Victoria's products and organized exchanges of exhibits at London (1873) and Philadelphia (1876) Exhibitions.

ROYLE, JOHN FORBES (1799–1858). Assistant Surgeon in Bengal; Superintendent of the Saharanpur Government Botanic Gardens; Keeper of Vegetable Products Museum at India House, London; Secretary to the British Association for the Advancement of Science; Fellow of the Royal, Linnaean, and Geological Societies; Acting Commissioner and Acting Agent for East Indies and Indian Archipelago at the Great Exhibition (1851); Superintendent for British contributions to Classes III and IV at the Great Exhibition (1851); General Commissioner and Keeper for India Section at the Great Exhibition (1851); Executive for Indian Department at Paris Universal Exposition (1855). Author and editor: *The Culture and Commerce of Cotton in India and Elsewhere, with an Account of the Experiments Made by the Hon. East India Company up to the Present Time* (1851); *The Fibrous Plants of India Fitted for Cordage, Clothing, and Paper, with an Account of the Cultivation and Preparation of Flax, Hemp, and their Substitutes* (1855); "Observations on Provincial Exhibitions and the Improvement of the Resources of the Several Districts of the Madras Presidency," *Madras Journal of Literature and Science* n.s. 2 (1857); *Paris Universal Exposition, 1855. Report on Indian and Colonial Products, Useful as Food and for Manufactures* (1857); and other volumes on fibrous plants, cotton, cinchona, and other natural history and economic topics, including *On the Productive Resources of India* (1840).

TEMPLE, SIR RICHARD (1826–1902). Chief Commissioner of the Central Provinces; Resident at Hyderabad; Foreign Secretary to the Government of India; Financial Member of Council of India; Lieutenant-Governor of Bengal and Famine Commissioner; Governor of Bombay; organizer of Nagpore (1865) and various other local Indian exhibitions during the 1860s and 1870s; Commissioner for India at Paris Universal Exposition (1878). Author and editor: *India in 1880* (1881); *Men and Events of My Time in India* (1882); and *The Story of My Life* (1896).

TWOPENY, RICHARD ERNEST NOWELL (1857–1915). Journalist and professional showman; representative of Australian Frozen Meat Export Association (to study Argentine meat trade and oversee meat marketing committee for colonial frozen meat in Britain); Secretary for South Australian Royal Commission at Paris (1878), Sydney (1879), and Melbourne International (1880) Exhibitions; New Zealand Commissioner at Melbourne Centennial Exhibition (1888); Executive Commissioner for New Zealand and South Seas Exhibition, Dunedin (1889–90); managed, with Jules Joubert, private venture exhibitions in Adelaide (1881), Perth (1881), and Christchurch, N.Z. (1892). Author and editor: *Town Life in Australia* (1883) and *A Proposal for Holding an Australasian Exhibition in London* (1883).

WATSON, JOHN FORBES (1827–92). Bombay Medical Service and Reporter on the Products of India for the India Office; Director, Indian Museum, London; Commissioner and Editor of Official Catalogues for India at London International (1862), New Zealand International (1865), Paris Universal (1867), Vienna International (1873), and South Kensington Annual (1870–74) Exhibitions. Author and editor: *The Textile Manufactures and Costumes of the People of India* (1866); *Index to the Native and Scientific Names of Indian and other Eastern Economic Plants and Products* (1868); *The People of India* (1868–72); and *International Exhibitions* (1873), a compilation of his letters to the *Times* in the early 1870s.

WATT, SIR GEORGE (1851–1930). Professor of Botany, Calcutta University; Scientific Assistant-Secretary to the Government of India; Reporter on Economic Products to Government of India; Commissioner for India at Colonial and Indian Exhibition (1886); Director, Indian Durbar Art Exhibition (1903). Author and editor: *Dictionary of the Economic Products of India* (1889); *Official Catalogue of Indian Art from Delhi Exhibition* (1903); and scientific reports on teas, pests, and grasses.

WHEWELL, WILLIAM (1794–1866). Master of Trinity College, Cambridge; Secretary and Member, British Association; Lecturer at Department of Practical Art, London. Added "Moral Sciences" and "Natural Sciences" to Triposes in 1848; delivered inaugural lecture on "The Results of the Great Exhibition" at the suggestion of the Prince Consort.

Sources: *Art-Journal; Australian Dictionary of Biography; Dictionary of National Biography; Illustrated Sydney News; Indian Biographical Dictionary, 1915; Journal of Indian Art and Industry; Madras Journal of Literature and Science; Times;* and *Town and Country* (Sydney).

Appendix C

Table 1. English Government (Direct) Expenditures in Sterling (£) and Overseeing Commissions for Selected Exhibitions, 1851–1914

Year	Exhibition	Amount	Commission
1853	New York International	2,432	(Royal Commission)
1855	Paris Universal	41,253	(Sci./Art Depart.)
1867	Paris Universal	120,556	(Royal Commission)
1873	Vienna International	30,352	(Royal Commission)
1876	Philadelphia Centennial	40,462	(Sci./Art Depart.)
1878	Paris Universal	73,712	(Royal Commission)
1879	Sydney International and		
1880–81	Melbourne International	9,203	(Royal Commission)
1887	Adelaide Jubilee	3,864	(Royal Commission)
1888	Melbourne Centennial	6,557	(Royal Commission)
1889	Paris Universal	98,000	(Society of Arts)
1893	Chicago Columbian	61,464	(Society of Arts)
1894	Tasmanian International	2,000	(Royal Commission)
1900	Paris Universal	97,033	(Royal Commission)
1904	St. Louis	128,000	(Royal Commission)
1907	New Zealand International	8,000	(Colonial Office / Board of Trade)

SOURCE: "Appendix: Return Showing Actual Expenditure from Public Funds in Respect of the Participation of this Country in International Exhibitions," Public Record Office, Kew, PRO BT 60/6/3 and BT 13/41/15.

Notes

PREFACE

   1. *Illustrated Weekly News*, October 12, 1862, p. 2.

   2. Ibid., p. 2.

   3. *Times*, December 28, 1872, p. 10.

   4. J. R. Seeley, *The Expansion of England* [1883], Chicago: University of Chicago Press, 1971.

   5. Edward Said, *Orientalism*, New York: Vintage Books, 1979; *Culture and Imperialism*, New York: Alfred A. Knopf, 1994; and "Orientalism Reconsidered," *Race and Class* 27 (1985), pp. 1–15.

   6. Bernard S. Cohn, "Social and Political Theory and the Symbols of Empire in Nineteenth-Century India: A Proposal for Research," *Journal of the Indian Anthropological Society* 8 (1973), pp. 117–22; *An Anthropologist among the Historians and Other Essays*, Ranajit Guha, ed., New York: Oxford University Press, 1990; and *Colonialism and Its Forms of Knowledge: The British in India*, Princeton, NJ: Princeton University Press, 1996.

   7. John M. MacKenzie, "General Introduction," in J. A. Mangan, *Making Imperial Mentalities: Socialisation and British Imperialism*, New York: St. Martin's Press, 1990, p. ix.

   8. John M. MacKenzie, *Propaganda and Empire: The Manipulation of British Public Opinion, 1880–1969*, Dover, NH: Manchester University Press, 1984; and MacKenzie, ed., *Imperialism and Popular Culture*, Dover, NH: Manchester University Press, 1986.

   9. Patrick Brantlinger, *Rule of Darkness: British Literature and Imperialism, 1830–1914*, Ithaca, NY: Cornell University Press, 1988; Antoinette Burton, *At the Heart of the Empire: Indians and the Colonial Encounter in Late-Victorian Britain*, Berkeley, CA: University of California Press, 1998; Annie E. Coombes, *Reinventing Africa: Museums, Material Culture, and Popular Imagination in Late Victorian and Edwardian England*, New Haven, CT: Yale University Press, 1994; Inderpal Grewal, *Home and Harem: Nation, Gender, Empire, and the*

Cultures of Travel, Durham, NC: Duke University Press, 1996; and Mrinalini Sinha, *Colonial Masculinity: The 'Manly Englishman' and the 'Effeminate Bengali' in the Late Nineteenth Century*, New York: St. Martin's Press, 1995.

10. Tony Bennett, "The Exhibitionary Complex," in Nicholas B. Dirks, Geoff Eley, and Sherry B. Ortner, eds., *Culture/Power/History: A Reader in Contemporary Social Theory*, Princeton, NJ: Princeton University Press, 1994, pp. 123–54; Robert Brain, "Going to the Exhibition," in Richard Staley, ed., *The Physics of Empire: Public Lectures*, Cambridge, England: Whipple Museum of the History of Science, 1994, pp. 113–42; Paul Greenhalgh, *Ephemeral Vistas: The Expositions Universelles, Great Exhibitions, and World's Fairs, 1851–1939*, New York: St. Martin's Press, 1988; Timothy Mitchell, *Colonising Egypt*, New York: Cambridge University Press, 1988, esp. Chapter 1, "Egypt at the Exhibition," pp. 1–33; Robert W. Rydell, *All the World's a Fair: Visions of Empire at American International Expositions, 1876–1916*, Chicago: University of Chicago Press, 1984, and *World of Fairs: The Century-of-Progress Expositions*, Chicago: University of Chicago Press, 1994.

11. Lewis Arnold, *An Early Encounter with Tomorrow: Europeans, Chicago's Loop, and the World's Columbian Exposition*, Urbana, IL: University of Illinois Press, 1997; Jeffrey A. Auerbach, *Exhibiting the Nation: British National Identity and the Great Exhibition of 1851*, New Haven, CT: Yale University Press, 1999; Penelope Harvey, *Hybrids of Modernity: Anthropology, The Nation State, and the Universal Exhibition*, New York: Routledge, 1996; and Keith Walden, *Becoming Modern in Toronto: The Industrial Exhibition and the Shaping of a Late Victorian Culture*, Buffalo: University of Toronto Press, 1997. Older exhibition reference texts include John Allwood, *The Great Exhibitions*, London: Studio Vista, 1977; John E. Findling, ed., *Historical Dictionary of World's Fairs and Expositions, 1851–1988*, New York: Greenwood Press, 1990; and Kenneth W. Luckhurst, *The Story of Exhibitions*, New York: The Studio Publications, 1951.

12. Manon Niquette and William J. Buxton, "Meet Me at the Fair: Sociability and Reflexivity in Nineteenth-Century World Expositions," *Canadian Journal of Communication* 22 (1997), pp. 81–113.

13. For example, see Janet Minihan, *The Nationalization of Culture: The Development of State Subsidies to the Arts in Great Britain*, New York: New York University Press, 1977.

14. Wolfgang Iser, *The Act of Reading: A Theory of Aesthetic Response*, Baltimore: Johns Hopkins University Press, 1981, and *The Implied Reader: Patterns of Communication in Prose Fiction from Bunyan to Beckett*, Baltimore: Johns Hopkins University Press, 1987.

15. Lord Askwith, "Exhibitions," *Journal of the Royal Society of Arts* 72 (1923), pp. 2–14. Askwith traced such a tradition to buttress support for the proposed British Empire Exhibition at Wembley.

16. Edward Huybers, *From Birth to Borderland (An Eighty-Five Year Life-Story)*, Mitchell Library, State Library of New South Wales, ML Mss. 1423, p. 45.

17. John L. Hordern to W. and C. Hordern, April 5, 1867, Royal Historical Society of Victoria, Melbourne, MS 000365, Box 127/2, ff. 2–10.

18. Rudyard Kipling, *Souvenirs of France*, London: Macmillan, 1938, pp. 1–6, 72.

19. Paul Morand, *1900*, New York: William Farquhar Payson, 1931, pp. 61–62.

20. Wolfgang Iser, "Interaction Between Text and Reader," in Susan R. Suleiman and Inge Crosman, eds., *The Reader in the Text: Essays on Audience and Interpretations*, Princeton, NJ: Princeton University Press, 1980, p. 106.

21. Sir Arthur Blyth to H. E. Bright, September 26, 1884, Mortlock Library, State Library of South Australia, V 991.

22. "Illustrated Catalogue of the Chinese Collection of Exhibits for the International Health Exhibition, London, 1884," *China, Imperial Maritime Customs. II — Miscellaneous Series: No. 12*, London: William Clowes and Sons, 1884.

23. Samuel Warren, *The Lily and the Bee: an apologue of the Crystal Palace*, Edinburgh: William Blackwood and Sons, 1851.

24. John Tallis, *Tallis's History and Description of the Crystal Palace and the Exhibition of the World's Industry in 1851*, vol. 1, London: London Printing and Publishing Company, 1852, pp. 207–8.

25. "Report of the Executive Commissioner Upon the Colonial and Indian Exhibition," *Queensland Legislative Assembly, Votes and Proceedings* 4 (1887), p. 3.

26. "Memorandum for the Members of the Australian Commission, Part 1, May 1914," *Papers of the Panama-Pacific Exposition, San Francisco, 1915*, Queensland State Archives, A/6335, Bundle 110.

27. Distinctions between "culture" and "society" are suggestively drawn by the anthropologist Clifford Geertz in "Ritual and Social Change: A Javanese Example," in *The Interpretation of Cultures*, New York: Basic Books, 1973, esp. pp. 144–45.

28. Eric Hobsbawm, "Introduction: Inventing Traditions," and "Mass-Producing Traditions: Europe, 1870–1914," in Hobsbawm and Terence Ranger, eds., *The Invention of Tradition*, New York: Cambridge University Press, 1984, pp. 1–14, 263–307.

CHAPTER 1. EXHIBITIONS AND THE
NEW IMPERIALISM

1. Joan Evans and John Howard Whitehouse, eds., *The Diaries of John Ruskin, 1848–1873*, Oxford: Clarendon Press, 1958, p. 468.

2. "Thursday, May 1, 1851," in *The Life and Letters of Lord Macaulay, By His Nephew, George Otto Trevelyan, M.P.*, vol. 2, London: Longmans, Green, 1876, pp. 292–93.

3. Lists of major international exhibitions are included in John Allwood, *The Great Exhibitions*, London: Studio Vista, 1977; Burton Benedict, ed., *The*

Anthropology of World's Fairs: San Francisco's Panama Pacific International Exposition of 1915, Berkeley: Scolar Press, 1983; and Kenneth W. Luckhurst, *The Story of Exhibitions*, New York: The Studio Publications, 1951.

4. Patrick Geddes, *Industrial Exhibitions and Modern Progress*, Edinburgh: David Douglas, 1887, p. 8; and *Report of the Royal Commission for the Colonial and Indian Exhibition, London, 1886*, English Parliamentary Papers, [c. 5083], xx. 1., p. xlvii.

5. Please see appendix A for the English, Australian, and Indian exhibitions included in this study.

6. *Art-Journal International Exhibition Supplement* n.s. 11 (1872), p. 1; and *Art-Journal* n.s. 25 (1873), p. 378.

7. "Report Upon the Agricultural Exhibits in the Queensland Court of the Greater Britain Exhibition, 1899," *Agriculture and Stock Department Papers*, Queensland State Archives, AGS/N 52, p. 1.

8. Sir Richard Temple, *The Story of My Life*, London: Cassell and Company, 1896, pp. 163, 165; *Report of the Nagpore Exhibition of Arts, Manufactures, and Produce, December 1865*, Nagpore: Central Provinces' Printing Press, 1866; and *Statesman and Friend of India*, January 17, 1883, p. 2.

9. *Annual Register*, 126 (1884), p. 366; and H. H. Risley, "Report on the Calcutta International Exhibition, October 1885," *Revenue and Agriculture Department Papers*, Oriental and India Office Collections, British Library, London, P/2490, p. 5.

10. *Prospectus of Melbourne Intercolonial Exhibition, 1875*, La Trobe Collection, State Library of Victoria, MS 11308/MSB 401.

11. *Age*, September 20, 1875, p. 3.

12. *Statesman and Friend of India*, January 17, 1883, p. 2.

13. *Town and Country Journal*, October 23, 1880, p. 780.

14. Benedict Anderson, *Imagined Communities: Reflections on the Origin and Spread of Nationalism*, New York: Verso, 1991.

15. Ibid., p. 6.

16. "The Paris Exhibition, 1878," *Sir Arthur Hodgson Papers, 1850–1889*, Queensland State Library, Film 0073 V2/C1, fol. 231.

17. *New South Wales. Official Catalogue of Exhibits from the Colony, forwarded to the Colonial and Indian Exhibition, London, 1886*, Sydney: Thomas Richards, Government Printer, 1886, pp. 9–10.

18. Sir Richard Temple, *Men and Events of My Time in India*, 2nd ed., London: John Murray, 1882, pp. 240–41.

19. Temple, *The Story of My Life*, pp. 163, 165.

20. "Report by the Chairman of the Sub-Committee for External Arrangements," in *Report of the Nagpore Exhibition*, pp. 21–28.

21. *Calcutta Review* 26 (1856), pp. 283–84.

22. *Calcutta Exhibition, 1923. Handbook*, Oriental and India Office Collections, T/11793, p. 34.

23. For an important exception, see the work of Paul Greenhalgh, including *Ephemeral Vistas: The Expositions Universelles, Great Exhibitions, and*

World's Fairs, 1851–1939, New York: St. Martin's Press, 1988, and "Education, Entertainment, and Politics: Lessons from the Great International Exhibitions," in Peter Vergo, ed., *The New Museology*, London: Reaktion Books, 1989, pp. 74–98. The latter provides a brief review of various "epic" and "serial" exhibitions in England between 1871 and 1914.

24. Thomas Hardy, "The Fiddler of the Reels," in *Life's Little Ironies: A Set of Tales with Some Colloquial Sketches Entitled A Few Crusted Characters*, New York: Harper and Brothers Publishers, 1905, pp. 165–85.

25. Lady Dorchester, ed., *Recollections of a Long Life by Lord Broughton (John Cam Hobhouse), with Additional Extracts from his Private Diaries, Volume VI. 1841–1852*, New York: Charles Scribners' Sons, 1911, pp. 279–80.

26. Asa Briggs, "The Crystal Palace and the Men of 1851," in *Victorian People: A Reassessment of Persons and Themes, 1851–1867*, Chicago: University of Chicago Press, 1972, pp. 15–51.

27. Frederic Harrison, *Autobiographic Memoirs, Volume I. (1837–1870)*, London: Macmillan, 1911, pp. 88–89.

28. *Journal of the Royal Society of Arts* 6 (1858), p. 333.

29. *Cornhill Magazine* 5 (1862), pp. 672–73.

30. George Frederick Pardon, ed., *A Guide to the International Exhibition; with Plans of the Building, An Account of its Rise, Progress and Completion and Notices of its Principal Contents*, London: Routledge, Warne and Routledge, 1862, p. 1.

31. *Bombay Times & Journal of Commerce*, May 26, 1855, p. 1049.

32. Derek Hudson and Kenneth W. Luckhurst, *The Royal Society of Arts, 1754–1954*, London: John Murray, 1954, p. 208.

33. *Calcutta Review* 26 (1856), pp. 269–70.

34. *Statesman and Friend of India*, January 5, 1883, p. 2.

35. *Journal of Applied Science, and Record of Progress in the Industrial Arts* 1 (1870), p. 137.

36. Benjamin Pierce Johnson, *Report on International Exhibition of Industry and Art, London, 1862*, Albany: Steam Press of C. Van Bethuysen, 1863, pp. 76–77, 92–93.

37. Geddes, *Industrial Exhibitions and Modern Progress*, p. 4.

38. *Great Exhibition of the Works of Industry of All Nations, 1851. Official Descriptive and Illustrated Catalogue*, London: William Clowes and Sons, 1851, p. 27.

39. Edward Cunliffe-Owen to Arthur Blyth, June 19, 1885, *Letter-Book, Colonial and Indian Exhibition, March 1885–March 1886, Volume I. Out-Letters of Executive Commissioner for South Australia*, South Australia Public Records Office, GRG 55/11/1, pp. 94–96.

40. *The Vagabond Papers, Sketches in New South Wales and Queensland*, 5th series, Melbourne: George Robertson, 1878, pp. 186–96.

41. Pardon, ed., *A Guide to the International Exhibition*, pp. 58–61.

42. *Morning Chronicle*, June 7, 1855, p. 3.

43. March 22, 1865, *Dispatches of Governor to the Secretary of State for the*

Colonies, vol. 5, Victoria Public Record Office, 1084, no. 39, pp. 540–41; and *Catalogue of Products from the Colony of Victoria, Australia at the Dublin International Exhibition, 1865*, Melbourne: Wilson & MacKinnon, Printers, 1865. Over one hundred cases were shipped to Dublin, including a "Cabinet Collection of Types of some of the Principal Industries of the Colony."

44. *Times*, May 19, 1886, p. 15.

45. *Graphic*, May 8, 1886, p. 495.

46. H. J. Scott to Jules Joubert, June 4, 1883, *Calcutta Exhibition Letterbook, Auditor-General Department*, South Australia Public Record Office, GRG 44/64, p. 19.

47. "Correspondence re. Paris Exhibition of 1900," *Curzon Collection*, Oriental and India Office Collections, MSS Eur. F. 112/8b, fols. 12 and 115.

48. Stephen Alomes, "Australian Nationalism in the Eras of Imperialism and 'Internationalism,'" *Australian Journal of Politics and History* 34 (1989), pp. 320–32; Douglas Cole, "'The Crimson Thread of Kinship:' Ethnic Ideas in Australia, 1870–1914," *Historical Studies* 14 (1971), pp. 511–25; Graeme Davison, J. W. McCarty, and Ailsa McLeary, eds., "The Imperial Connection," in *Australians/1888*, Fairfax, Sydney: Fairfax, Syme & Weldon Associates, 1987, pp. 403–25; John Eddy and Deryck Schreuder, eds., *The Rise of Colonial Nationalism: Australia, New Zealand, Canada, and South Africa First Assert Their Nationalities, 1880–1914*, Sydney: Allen and Unwin, 1988, esp. pp. 131–59; Luke Trainor, *British Imperialism and Australian Nationalism: Manipulation, Conflict, and Compromise in the Late Nineteenth Century*, New York: Cambridge University Press, 1995; and Richard White, *Inventing Australia: Images and Identity, 1688–1980*, Boston: George Allen & Unwin, 1988.

49. "Correspondence," *Exhibition Trustees, Paris International Exhibition, 1867*, September 28 and November 24, 1866, pp. 26–28, 45–46, Victoria Public Record Service, 927/6.

50. January 20, 1892, *Correspondence and Papers Relating to the World's Columbian Exposition, Chicago, 1891–1893*, Queensland State Archives, PRE/137.

51. Herbert Jeckyll to Sir Francis Knollys, August 3, 1898, "Correspondence re. Paris Exhibition of 1900," *Curzon Collection*, fols. 230–31.

52. *Art-Journal* 5 (1853), p. 299.

53. Ellis Lever, *Suggestions for a Grand International Exhibition of the Industrial Arts, Manufactures, Fine Arts, Scientific Inventions, Discoveries, and Natural Products of All Countries, to be held in Manchester, in the Year, 1882*, Manchester: Guardian Letterpress and Lithographic Works, 1881, p. 58.

54. *Bombay Builder* 3 (1868), p. 380.

55. Among such preliminary colonial exhibitions were those held in Sydney (1854, 1861, 1870), Melbourne (1854, 1861, 1866–67, 1875), and Bombay (1854). Anglo-Indian and Australian officials followed the precedent established by Mechanics' Institutes in Montreal and Toronto. Those organizations scheduled "grand industrial fairs," including grains, ores, canoes, and "accounts of the place where produced, and other information valuable to the merchant" before

forwarding selected displays to the Great Exhibition in 1851. *Art Journal* 3 (1851), p. 6; and *Journal of Design and Manufactures* 4 (1850–1851), p. 18.

56. William Westgarth, *The Colony of Victoria: Its History, Commerce and Gold Mining; its Social and Political Institutions; Down to the End of 1863. With Remarks, Incidental and Comparative, Upon the Other Australian Colonies,* London: Sampson Low, Son, and Marston, 1864, p. 391.

57. Graeme Davison, "Festivals of Nationhood: The International Exhibitions," in S. L. Goldberg and F. B. Smith, eds., *Australian Cultural History,* New York: Cambridge University Press, 1988, pp. 158–77; and Allwood, *The Great Exhibitions,* pp. 64–84.

58. *Journal of the Royal Society of Arts* 27 (1879), pp. 466–67.

59. B. R. Mitchell, ed., *International Historical Statistics: The Americas and Australasia,* Detroit: Gale Research Company, 1983, pp. 53, 109.

60. *The Official Record of the Centennial International Exhibition, Melbourne, 1888–1889,* Melbourne: Sands and McDougall, 1890, pp. 123–28.

61. Rudyard Kipling, *Something of Myself and Other Autobiographical Writings,* Thomas Pinney, ed. New York: Cambridge University Press, 1991, pp. 17, 132; and Charles Carrington, *Rudyard Kipling: His Life and Work,* 3rd ed., London: Macmillan, 1978, pp. 60–61.

62. Kipling, *Something of Myself,* p. 9.

63. John Forbes Watson, *International Exhibitions,* London: Henry S. King, 1873, pp. 20–21.

64. Thomas H. Hendley, "Indian Museums," *Journal of Indian Art and Industry* n.s. 16 (1914), pp. 53–54.

65. "Museums and Exhibition. Resolution from the Proceedings of the Government of India, in the Department of Revenue and Agriculture, dated Calcutta, the 14th March, 1883," *Journal of Indian Art and Industry* 1 (1884–1886), 6 pp.

66. George Collins Levey to Chief Secretary, July 29, 1876, *Chief Secretary's Supplemental Correspondence: Paris Exhibition Commissioners,* Victoria Public Record Office, 1226/77.

67. *Reports on the Government Central Museum, Madras, by Surgeon Edward Balfour, Madras Army, Officer in Charge of the Central Museum, 1853,* Madras: Fort St. George Gazette Press, 1853; and *Reports on the Government Central Museum, Madras, and on the Government Museums,* Madras: Asylum Press, 1855.

68. *Reports on the Government Central Museum, Madras . . . 1853,* pp. 9–10.

69. *Journal of the Proceedings of the United States Centennial Commission, at Philadelphia, 1872,* Philadelphia: E. C. Markley and Son, 1872, p. 63.

70. "Art. IX. Official Catalogue of the Great Exhibition of the Works of Industry of All Nations, 1851," *Edinburgh Review* 94 (1851), pp. 557–95.

71. *Journal of the Proceedings of the United States Centennial Commission,* p. 63.

72. *Proceedings of the Royal Asiatic Society of Bengal,* 1882, pp. 30–32.

73. July 8 and August 25, 1851, *The Correspondence of Thomas Carlyle and Ralph Waldo Emerson, 1834–1872*, vol. 2, London: Chatto and Windus, 1883, pp. 197, 473.

74. Charles Babbage, *The Exposition of 1851; or, Views of the Industry, the Science, and the Government of England*, 2nd ed., London: John Murray, 1851, p. 12.

75. *Bee-Hive*, November 15, 1862, p. 1.

76. For example, see *Address to the Workmen Employed in Building the Great Hall of the Melbourne Public Library and Museum, in Melbourne, Victoria. Delivered by Sir Redmond Barry, on Saturday, September 8, A.D. 1866*, Melbourne: Wilson and MacKinnon, 1866; and "The International Exhibition: Its Purpose and Prospects," *Blackwoods' Edinburgh Magazine* 91 (1862), pp. 473–75.

77. *Working Man*, June 1, 1862, pp. 141–42.

78. Jules Joubert, *Shavings & Scrapes From Many Parts*, Dunedin: J. Wilkie and Co., 1890, pp. 180–83.

79. *Intercolonial Exhibition, 1866. Official Catalogue*, Melbourne: Blundell and Ford, 1866, p. 104; and Frank W. Fenton, ed., *Guide to the Victorian Intercolonial Exhibition, 1875*, Melbourne: W. H. Williams, 1875, p. 60.

80. *Official Record of the Sydney International Exhibition, 1879*, Sydney: Thomas Richards, Government Printer, 1881, p. 171.

81. *South Australian Register*, August 29, 1887, p. 7 and *South Australian Advertiser*, September 7, 1887, p. 5, September 24, 1887, p. 6, and November 23, 1887, p. 5.

82. Michel Foucault, *Discipline and Punish: The Birth of the Prison*, trans. Alan Sheridan, New York: Vintage Books, 1979.

83. "Speaking to the Eye," *Illustrated London News*, May 24, 1851, pp. 451–52.

84. Tony Bennett, "The Exhibitionary Complex," in Nicholas B. Dirks, Geoff Eley, and Sherry B. Ortner, eds., *Culture / Power / History: A Reader in Contemporary Social Theory*, Princeton, NJ: Princeton University Press, 1994, pp. 123–54; and Robert Brain, "Going to the Exhibition," in Richard Staley, ed., *The Physics of Empire: Public Lectures*, Cambridge, England: Whipple Museum of the History of Science, 1994, pp. 113–42.

85. "Lecture I.—Dr. Whewell on the General Bearing of the Great Exhibition on the Progress of Art and Science," in *Lectures on the Progress of Arts and Science, Resulting from the Great Exhibition in London, delivered before the Society of Arts, Manufactures and Commerce, at the Suggestion of H.R.H. Prince Albert*, New York: A. S. Barnes, 1854, pp. 7–11.

86. *Builder*, 51 (1886), pp. 285–86.

87. *Reminiscences of the Colonial and Indian Exhibition. A Lecture Delivered by John McCarthy, Government Analyst and Professor of Chemistry, Trinidad. And Published for Use in the Schools of the Island, by Direction of His Excellency Sir W. Robinson, K.C.M.G., Governor, Etc.* Port-of-Spain: Government Printer, 1887, p. 4.

88. Edmund Gosse, *Sir Henry Doulton: The Man of Business as a Man of Imagination*, ed. Desmond Eyles, London: Hutchinson, 1970.

89. Doulton displayed and earned official prizes in 1851 (Crystal Palace), 1862 (London), 1867 (Paris), 1871–72 (London), 1873 (Vienna), 1876 (Philadelphia), 1878 (Paris), 1893 (Chicago), and 1900 (Paris). [Personal communication from Katharine Berry, Historical Information Officer, Royal Doulton (UK) Archives, Stoke-on-Trent, March 18, 1991.]

90. Martin Heidegger, "The Age of the World Picture," in William Lovitt, trans. and ed., *The Question Concerning Technology and Other Essays*, New York: Garland Publishing, 1977, p. 129.

91. Eric J. Hobsbawm, *Nations and Nationalism Since 1780: Programme, Myth and Reality*, New York: Cambridge University Press, 1990. Other recent influential studies of modern nationalism include the following: Anderson, *Imagined Communities*; Gopal Balakrishnan, ed., *Mapping the Nation*, New York: Verso, 1996; Partha Chatterjee, *The National and Its Fragments: Colonial and Postcolonial Histories*, Princeton, NJ: Princeton University Press, 1993; Prasenjit Dura, *Rescuing History from the Nation: Questioning Narratives of Modern China*, Chicago: University of Chicago Press, 1995; Geoff Eley and Ronald Grigor Suny, eds., *Becoming National: A Reader*, New York: Oxford University Press, 1996; Ernest Gellner, *Nations and Nationalism*, Ithaca, NY: Cornell University Press, 1983; Liah Greenfeld, *Nationalism: Five Roads to Modernity*, Cambridge, MA.: Harvard University Press, 1992; and Tzvetan Todorov, *On Human Diversity: Nationalism, Racism and Exoticism in French Thought*, Cambridge, MA.: Harvard University Press, 1994.

92. This phrase is from Preben Kaarsholm, "Reviews and Enthusiasms," *History Workshop* 16 (1983), pp. 157–60.

93. *Illustrated London News*, July 17, 1886, p. 81.

94. Debora L. Silverman, "The 1889 Exhibition: The Crisis in Bourgeois Individualism," *Oppositions* 8 (1977), pp. 70–91.

95. P. Burroughs, "John Robert Seeley and British Imperial History," *Journal of Imperial and Commonwealth History* 1 (1971), pp. 191–213; J. G. Greenlee, "'A Succession of Seeleys': The 'Old School' Re-examined," *Journal of Imperial and Commonwealth History* 4 (1976), pp. 266–82; and Robert T. Kitson, "John Robert Seeley and the Idea of a National Church," in Robert Robson, ed., *Ideas and Institutions of Victorian Britain: Essays in Honour of George Kitson Clark*, New York: Barnes and Noble, 1967, pp. 236–67.

96. *The Crystal Palace, and the Great Exhibition; an Historical Account of the Building, Together with a Descriptive Synopsis of its Content*, London: H. G. Clarke, 1851, p. 15.

97. For a discussion of the "market" as an explicative and representative system, see Simon Gunn, "The 'Failure' of the Victorian Middle Class," in Janet Wolff and John Seed, eds., *The Culture of Capital: Art, Power, and the Nineteenth-Century Middle Class*, Manchester: Manchester University Press, 1988, pp. 17–43.

98. Thomas Richards, *The Commodity Culture of Victorian England: Ad-*

vertising and Spectacle, 1851–1914, Stanford, CA: Stanford University Press, 1990, esp. chapter 1.

99. Ibid., p. 18.

100. Babbage, *The Exposition of 1851,* pp. 129–31.

101. Henry Cole, "Reductions in the French Tariff," *Henry Cole Papers, Miscellanies, Volume 10, 1852–1860,* National Art Library, London, fols. 60b–61.

102. Cole, "Reductions in the French Tariff," fol. 61.

103. *Paris Exhibition, 1855. Report Presented to the Bradford Chamber of Commerce, on the 26th November, 1855,* National Art Library, London, Box I.A.9.

104. J. Emerson Tennent to Under Secretary of State, January 25, 1867, *Board of Trade: Commercial Department Out-Letters, 1867,* Public Record Office, Kew, PRO BT 12/4.

105. Scholars pursuing questions of gendering might perceive the juxtapositioning of a masculine Britain (and Australia) with a feminine France (and India), noting that those characteristics were expressed at the exhibitions in economic terms.

106. *Graphic,* May 8, 1886, p. 495.

107. Alexander Hunter, *Suggestions for the Establishment of a School of Industrial Arts at Lahore, Prepared at the Request of His Excellency, Sir Robert Montgomery, K.C.B., Lieut.-Governor of the Punjab, 1863,* Oriental and India Office Collections, TR 633, p. 35.

108. "Lecture I.—Dr. Whewell on the General Bearing of the Great Exhibition," pp. 14–15.

109. George Donham Bearce, *British Attitudes Towards India, 1784–1858,* New York: Oxford University Press, 1961; and Allen J. Greenberger, *The British Image of India: A Study in the Literature of Imperialism, 1880–1960,* New York: Oxford University Press, 1969.

110. Hunter, *Suggestions for the Establishment of a School of Industrial Arts at Lahore,* p. 35.

111. "A Letter to the Board of Visitors of the Greenwich Royal Observatory, 1854," *Sheepshanks Papers,* University of London Library, fols. 69 and 75.

112. May 24, 1850, Lyon Playfair to General Charles Grey, *Lyon Playfair Correspondence,* Imperial College Archives, London, fol. 765.

113. "Draft to Secretary, July 6, 1861," *Lyon Playfair Correspondence,* fol. 371.

114. *Journal of the Royal Society of Arts* 34 (1887), p. 374.

115. For discussion of "social control" in historical context, see A. P. Donajgrodzki, ed., *Social Control in Nineteenth Century Britain,* Totowa, NJ: Rowman and Littlefield, 1977; Gareth Stedman Jones, "Class expression versus social control? A critique of recent trends in the social history of 'leisure'," in *Languages of Class: Studies in English Working Class History, 1832–1982,* New York: Cambridge University Press, 1983, pp. 76–89; and F. M. L. Thomp-

son, "Social Control in Victorian England," *Economic History Review* 2nd series, 34 (1981), pp. 189–208.

116. Edward Alsworth Ross, *Social Control; A Survey of the Foundations of Order*, New York: Macmillan, 1901; Michael Blanch, "Imperialism, Nationalism, and Organized Youth," in Richard Johnson, John Clarke, and Chas Critcher, eds., *Working-Class Culture: Studies in History and Theory*, London: Hutchinson, 1979, pp. 103–20; Richard Johnson, "Educational Policy and Social Control in Early Victorian England," *Past and Present* 49 (1970), pp. 96–119.

117. This distinction was drawn by Norman Birnbaum in "Work and Leisure in Industrial Society," *Past and Present* 30 (1965), p. 102.

118. For discussions of "Englishness" and the development of English national identity and political culture, see Robert Colls and Philip Dodd, eds., *Englishness: Politics, and Culture, 1880–1920*, New York: Methuen, 1987; Eric Hobsbawm and Terence Ranger, eds., *The Invention of Tradition*, New York: Cambridge University Press, 1984; and Raphael Samuel, ed., *Patriotism: The Making and Unmaking of British National Identity*, 3 vols., New York: Routledge, 1989. The relationships between imperialism and Australian national identity are discussed in Alomes, "Australian Nationalism in the Eras of Imperialism and 'Internationalism'"; Cole, "'The Crimson Thread of Kinship:' Ethnic Ideas in Australia, 1870–1914"; Trainor, *British Imperialism and Australian Nationalism*; and John Eddy and Deryck Schreuder, eds., *The Rise of Colonial Nationalism*. That comparative volume draws upon the ideas first articulated by Richard Jebb in *Studies in Colonial Nationalism*, London: Edward Arnold, 1905.

119. Annie E. Combes, "Museums and the Formation of National and Cultural Identities," *Oxford Art Journal* 11 (1988), pp. 57–68; Carol Duncan and Alan Wallach, "The Universal Survey Museum," *Art History* 3 (1980), pp. 448–69; and David K. van Keuren, "Museums and Ideology: Augustus Pitt-Rivers, Anthropological Museums, and Social Change in Later Victorian Britain," *Victorian Studies* 28 (1984), pp. 171–89.

120. *Nature* 5 (1871), p. 151; and *Graphic*, June 17, 1871, p. 564.

121. The distinction between "organic" and "arbitrary" ideologies was articulated by Antonio Gramsci in "The Philosophy of Praxis," in Quintin Hoare and Geoffrey Nowell Smith, eds. and trans., *Selections from the Prison Notebooks*, New York: International Publishers, 1983, esp. pp. 375–77. For a discussion of these and similar concepts, including "cultural hegemony" and "the dominant ideology," see Nicholas Abercrombie, Stephen Hill, and Bryan S. Turner, *The Dominant Ideology Thesis*, Boston: G. Allen & Unwin, 1980; and Jackson T. J. Lears, "The Concept of Cultural Hegemony: Problems and Possibilities," *American Historical Review* 90 (1985), pp. 567–93.

122. *Illustrated Sydney News*, April 20, 1874, p. 6.

123. Richard Hoggart, *The Uses of Literacy: Aspects of Working-Class Life with Special Reference to Publications and Entertainments*, New York: Oxford University Press, 1970.

124. *Times*, February 22, 1876, p. 9.

125. *Reminiscences of the Colonial and Indian Exhibition*, p. 8.

126. Patrick Brantlinger, *Rule of Darkness: British Literature and Imperialism, 1830–1914*, Ithaca, NY: Cornell University Press, 1988; Patrick A. Dunae, "Boy's Literature and the Idea of Empire, 1870–1914," *Victorian Studies* 24 (1980), pp. 106–20; J. A. Mangan, "Images of Empire in the Late Victorian Public School," *Journal of Educational Administration and History* 12 (1980), pp. 31–39; Henry Pelling, "British Labour and British Imperialism," in *Popular Politics and Society in Late Victorian England*, 2nd ed., New York: Macmillan, 1979, pp. 82–100; Richard Price, *An Imperial War and the British Working Class: Working-Class Attitudes and Reactions to the Boer War, 1899–1902*, Toronto: University of Toronto Press, 1972; Jeffrey Richards, "'Patriotism with Profit:' British Imperial Cinema in the 1930s," in James Curran and Vincent Porter, eds., *British Cinema History*, Totowa, NJ: Barnes & Noble, 1983, pp. 245–56; and Edward Said, *Culture and Imperialism*, New York: Alfred A. Knopf, 1993.

127. James Anthony Froude, *Oceana, or England and Her Colonies*, 2nd ed., London: Longman, Green, 1886, esp. pp. 383–96.

128. Goldwin Smith, *The Empire. A Series of Letters, Published in the 'Daily News,' 1862, 1863*, London: John Henry and James Parker, 1863; and R. Koebner, "The Emergence of the Concept of Imperialism," *Cambridge Journal* 5 (1952), pp. 726–41.

CHAPTER 2.   THE EXHIBITION WALLAHS

1. Thomas Richards, *The Imperial Archive: Knowledge and the Fantasy of Empire*, New York: Verso, 1993; and Roy Macleod, ed., *Government and Expertise: Specialists, Administrators, and Professionals, 1860–1919*, New York: Cambridge University Press, 1988.

2. Joules Joubert, *Shavings and Scrapes from Many Parts*, Dunedin: J. Wilkie, 1890, pp. 184–85.

3. John Eddy, "The Technique of Government: Governing Mid-Victorian Australia," in Macleod, ed., *Government and Expertise*, p. 181.

4. *Report of the Ballarat Agricultural and Pastoral Society for the Year Ending on May 5, 1877*, pp. 11–12; and *Report of the Ballarat Agricultural and Pastoral Society for the Year Ending on May 4, 1878*, pp. 12–14.

5. George W. Stocking, Jr., *Victorian Anthropology*, New York: The Free Press, 1987, p. 239.

6. Charles Babbage, *The Exposition of 1851; or Views of the Industry, the Science and the Government of England*, 2nd ed., London: John Murray, 1851, pp. 12–25.

7. William A. Drew, *Glimpses and Gatherings, During a Voyage and Visit to London and the Great Exhibition, in the Summer of 1851*, Augusta, ME: Homan and Manley, 1852, pp. i–ii.

8. Ferdinand von Mueller to Chief Secretary, July 4, 1861, *Chief Secretary's*

Office. Registered Inward Correspondence: "Exhibitions," *1856–58 and 1860–63,* Victoria Public Record Office, 1189/750.

9. Hooker to Von Mueller, December 24, 1862, Royal Historical Society of Victoria, MS 000012, Box 6/4, fol. 8.

10. James Fergusson, *Address on a National Gallery of Architectural Art,* London, 1857, p. 1.

11. Babbage, *Exposition of 1851,* pp. 12–13.

12. Clifford Geertz's anthropological definition provides helpful background. He writes that culture is "an ordered system of meaning and of symbols, in terms of which social interaction takes place, . . . the framework of beliefs, expressive symbols, and values in terms of which individuals [and social groups] define their world, express their feelings and make their judgments; . . . Culture is the fabric of meaning in terms of which human beings interpret their experience and guide their action." See "Ritual and Social Change: A Javanese Example," in *The Interpretation of Cultures,* New York: Basic Books, 1973, pp. 144–45. My usage adds the element of participatory dynamism to his construction of cultural symbols and language. Culture is the process of interaction as well as the framework for that interaction.

13. Ian Inkster, "Introduction: Aspects of the History of Science and Science Culture in Britain, 1780–1850 and Beyond," in Inkster and Jack Morrell, eds., *Metropolis and Province: Science in British Culture, 1780–1850,* London: Hutchinson, 1983, pp. 11–54; and Arnold Thackray, "Natural Knowledge in Cultural Context: The Manchester Model," *American Historical Review* 79 (1974), pp. 672–709.

14. Sir Redmond Barry, *Exhibition Correspondence,* La Trobe Collection, State Library of Victoria, Box 122/2, fol. 151.

15. Jules Joubert to Alfred Deakin, June 17 and December 15, 1886, *Alfred Deakin Papers,* Australian National Library, Manuscripts Section, Canberra, MS 1540/9/39–42 and 44–45.

16. J. C. Neild, *Report of the Executive Commissioner for New South Wales to the Adelaide Jubilee International Exhibition, 1887–1888,* Sydney: Charles Potter, Government Printer, 1890.

17. December 4, 1883, *John Lockwood Kipling Correspondence, Kipling Family Papers,* University of Sussex Archives, Box 1/ File 10.

18. "The Great Exhibition: A Tour Through the Manufacturing Districts," in Wemyss Reid, ed., *Memoirs and Correspondence of Lyon Playfair, First Lord Playfair of St. Andrews, P.C., G.C.B., LL.D., F.R.S., etc.,* London: Cassell and Company, 1899, pp. 109–45.

19. June–July 1875, *Agricultural Societies and the Philadelphia Exhibition,* Archives Office of New South Wales, 4/799.1.

20. Paul Greenhalgh discusses the "central" role of the Royal Society of Arts in *Ephemeral Vistas: The Expositions Universelles, Great Exhibitions and World's Fairs, 1851–1939,* New York: St. Martin's Press, 1988, pp. 55–56.

21. Noel G. Anan, "The Intellectual Aristocracy," in John Harold Plumb,

ed., *Studies in Social History: A Tribute to G. M. Trevelyan*, Freeport, NY: Books for Libraries Press, 1969, pp. 241–87.

22. Michel Foucault, *The Order of Things: An Archaeology of the Human Sciences*, New York: Random House, 1970, and *The Archaeology of Knowledge and the Discourse of Language*, A. M. Sheridan, trans. and ed., New York: Pantheon Books, 1972.

23. For example, see Barry's marginal note about Owen Jones as "an attentive observer" capable of using artistic specimens "to establish Ethnological and Ethnographic principles and to fix type of national or specific styles of decoration." Barry implies Jones's discussion of art and ethnography in *Grammar of Ornament*. Redmond Barry to Commodore Wilson, July 25, 1880, *President of Trustees Letter Book, 1879–1884*, Victoria Public Record Office, 4367/4, fols. 205–11.

24. "Sir Henry Cole, Appendix," *Papers Referring to the Proposed Contributions from India for the Industrial Exhibition of 1851, by J. Forbes Royle, 1849–1851*, National Art Library, London, pp. 585–607; and "Memo of Philip Cunliffe-Owen to Earl of Dufferin, Viceroy, Confidential Communication for Lord Reay, April 1, 1887," *Reay Papers: Bombay Files*, School of Oriental and African Studies Manuscript Collection, University of London, PP MS37/ no. 51.

25. Asa Briggs, "Prince Albert and the Arts and Sciences," in John A. S. Phillips, ed., *Prince Albert and the Victorian Age*, New York: Cambridge University Press, 1982, esp. pp. 67–71.

26. *Documents Illustrative of English History in the Thirteenth and Fourteenth Centuries, Selected from the Records of The Department of the Queen's Remembrance of the Exchequer; and edited by Henry Cole, of the Honourable Society of the Middle Temple, An Assistant Keeper of the Public Records*, London: George E. Eyre and Andrew Spottiswoode, 1844.

27. *Royal Society of Arts Correspondence and Papers*, Corporation of London Archives, A/RSA/2/G/50 [1847].

28. Henry Cole, "Some Thoughts on Hampton Court Palace, its Pictures, Tapestry, & Other Works of Decorative Art," *Sir Henry Cole File*, Victoria and Albert Museum Registry, File SF 233. Cole published 150 copies of this essay in 1859.

29. Michael Argles, *South Kensington to Robbins: An Account of English Technical and Scientific Education since 1851*, London: Longmans, Green, 1964, esp. pp. 16–56; and Janet Minihan, *The Nationalization of Culture: The Development of State Subsidies to the Arts in Great Britain*, New York: New York University Press, 1977, esp. pp. 112–19.

30. "The Exhibition Land," *Leisure Hour* 11 (1862), pp. 181–82; and "Memorandum by the Prince Consort as to the Disposal of the Surplus from the Great Exhibition of 1851," copy from Martin, *The Life of His Royal Highness*, vol. 2, pp. 569–73, in *Department of Education and Science, Private Office Papers, Museums: Science Museum*, Public Record Office, Kew, PRO ED 224/45.

31. Sir Henry Trueman Wood, *A History of the Royal Society of Arts*, Lon-

don: John Murray, 1913, pp. 375–77; and Reid, ed., *Memoirs and Correspondence of Lyon Playfair*, pp. 130–43.

32. Henry Cole, "Introductory Address on the Functions of the Science and Art Department," in *Fifty Years of Public Work of Sir Henry Cole, K.C.B., Accounted for in His Deeds, Speeches and Writings*, vol. 2, London: George Bell and Sons, 1884, pp. 285–95.

33. W. E. Forster to Secretary, HM. Treasury, May 27, 1873, *Sir Henry Cole File*, Victoria and Albert Museum Registry, London, SF 233.

34. "It may be admitted that Cole had in full measure the defects of his qualities. He liked having his own way, and he generally got it. He disliked opposition, and was ruthless with his opponents." Wood, *A History of the Royal Society of Arts*, p. 359.

35. *Report on the System of Circulation of Art Objects on Loan from the South Kensington Museum for Exhibition as Carried on by The Department from its First Establishment to the Present Time*, London: William Spottiswoode and George E. Eyre, 1881.

36. Sir Henry Cole, "The Purchase of Art Objects for Schools of Art. Copy of Board Minute of 9 February 1856," *Department of Education and Science, Victoria and Albert Museum Records*, Public Record Office, Kew, PRO ED 84/34.

37. "The Schools of Arts and Public Examinations," *Sydney Magazine of Science and Art* 2 (1859), pp. 21–22; "Dr. Wooley's Inaugural Address at the School of Arts," *Sydney Morning Herald*, May 2, 1860, p. 2; and Partha Mitter, *Art and Nationalism in Colonial India, 1850–1922: Occidental Orientations*, New York: Cambridge University Press, 1994, pp. 29–62.

38. James Craig, "John Lockwood Kipling: The Formative Years, Parts I and II," *Kipling Journal* 41 (1974), pp. 5–7, and 42 (1975), pp. 5–9; and Mahrukh Tarapor, "John Lockwood Kipling and Art Education in India," *Victorian Studies* 24 (1980), pp. 53–81.

39. Among the many official handbooks were those written by Peter L. Simmonds, including *Animal Products: Their Preparation, Commercial Uses, and Value. Published for the Committee of Council on Education*, London: Chapman and Hall, 1877; and *South Kensington Museum Science Handbooks. Branch Museum, Bethnal Green. Animal Products: Their Preparation, Commercial Uses, and Value. Published for the Committee of Council on Education*, London: Chapman and Hall, 1877.

40. George Birdwood, *The Industrial Arts of India*, London: Chapman and Hall, 1880.

41. Sir Henry Cole to Lord Mayo, March 15, 1870, *Correspondence with Sir Henry Cole, Lord Mayo Papers*, University of Cambridge Archives, ADD 7490/51 (XI), fol. 151.

42. *Fifty Years of Public Works of Sir Henry Cole*, vol. 2, p. 348.

43. *The Great Exhibition of the Works of Industry of All Nations, 1851. Official Descriptive and Illustrated Catalogue, Volume I*, London: W. Clowes and Sons, 1851; *Reports on Paris Universal Exposition, 1855, Parts I–III*, En-

glish Parliamentary Papers, 1856, [XXXVI]. 413; *Reports on Paris Universal Exposition, 1867, Volume I. Reports by Executive Commissioner; with Appendices,* English Parliamentary Papers, 1868–69, [XXX]. Pt. i. 1; and *A Special Report on the Annual International Exhibitions of the Years 1871, 1872, 1873 & 1874, Drawn Up by Sir Henry Cole, Acting Commissioner in 1873 and 1874, and Presented by the Commissioners for the Exhibition of 1851,* English Parliamentary Papers, 1878 [XXVII]. 139.

44. *Times,* May 19, 1886, p. 15; "Owen, Sir Francis Philip Cunliffe (1828–1894)," in *Dictionary of National Biography,* vol. 14, *Myllar–Owen,* ed. Sir Leslie Stephen and Sir Sidney Lee, New York: Oxford University Press, 1921–22, pp. 1300–1; and "Obituary: Sir Philip Cunliffe-Owen, K.C.B., K.C.M.G., C.I.E.," *Journal of the Royal Society of Arts* 42 (1893–94), pp. 406–7.

45. "Circular, 12 March 1875," *Colonial Secretary Files, Despatches,* Archives Office of New South Wales, 4/136; and *Journal of the Legislative Council of New South Wales* 13 (1865–66), pp. 181–200.

46. Sir Henry Cole, "Appendix," *Papers Referring to the Proposed Contributions from India for the Industrial Exhibition of 1851, by J. Forbes Royle, 1849–1851,* pp. 585–607.

47. *Catalogue of Contributions Transmitted from British Guiana to the Paris Universal Exposition of 1855,* Georgetown, Demerara: Royal Gazette Office, 1855.

48. "Board of Trade Correspondence Regarding Art Purchases, 1852," and "Items Retained and Purchased from Crystal Palace," *Board of Trade Correspondence,* Public Record Office, Kew, PRO BT 1/488; "Purchase of Art Objects for Schools of Art. Copy of Board of Trade Minutes, 1855–56," *Department of Education and Science, Victoria and Albert Museum Records, 1852–1870,* Public Record Office, Kew, PRO BT 84/34; and *Fifteenth Report of the Science and Art Department,* 1868, pp. xvi–xviii.

49. *Report of Select Committee on Advisability of Making Purchases for Benefit of Schools of Science and Art, etc.; with Proceedings, Minutes of Evidence, and Appendix,* English Parliamentary Papers, 1867, [X.]. 605; and "Purchase of Art Objects for the Schools of Art, Copy of Board Minutes of 5 March 1855 and 6 August 1857," *Department of Education and Science, Victoria and Albert Museum Records, Minutes Relative to the Acquisition of Art Objects for the Benefits of Schools of Art, 1852–1870,* Public Record Office, Kew, PRO ED 84/34.

50. "Testimony of Sir Henry Cole," *Report of Select Committee on Advisability of Making Purchases,* pp. 6 and 33.

51. H. H. Cole, *Science and Art Department of the Committee of Council on Education, South Kensington Museum. Catalogue of the Objects of Indian Art Exhibited in the South Kensington Museum,* London: George E. Eyre and William Spottiswoode, 1874.

52. "Testimony of Henry Cole, Science and Art Department," *Hyde Park Exhibition Services, Committee to Determine the Future of the Building and*

Site, Department of Public Works, Miscellanea, 1850–1859, Public Record Office, Kew, PRO WORKS 6/126/1/121–40, fols. 189–94.

53. Geoffrey Blainey, *The Tyranny of Distance: How Distance Shaped Australia's History,* Melbourne: Sun Books, 1966.

54. *Bee-Hive,* November 22, 1862, p. 7.

55. "The Genesis of the Indian Museum," *Indian Textile Journal* 14 (1904) pp. 147–49; and H. H. Risley, "Resolution: Calcutta Exhibition and Museum: Darjeeling, 4th October 1885," *Department of Revenue and Agriculture Proceedings,* Oriental and India Office Collections, P/2490, p. 5.

56. For example, see "Correspondence on Subject Presentations Made by Trustees," *Melbourne International Exhibition, 1880,* Victoria Public Record Office, 4363/12.

57. "If I were asked to name the most popular man in South Australia, I think it would be that of Sir Samuel Davenport." *Writings of Simpson Newland,* Mortlock Library of South Australiana, State Library of South Australia, PRG 288/10/4; and "Samuel Davenport, Esq., Executive Commissioner for South Australia," *Illustrated Sydney News,* November 1, 1879, p. 19.

58. Rev. James Ballantyne, *Homes and Homesteads in the Land of Plenty: A Handbook of Victoria as a Field for Emigration,* Melbourne: Mason, Firth and M'Cutcheon, 1871, p. 66.

59. Bowen to J. Hamilton Fish, Secretary of State, February 5, 1876, *Redmond Barry Collection,* La Trobe Collection, State Library of Victoria, MS 8380, 600/5(a).

60. "Combes, Edward (1830–1895)," in *Australian Dictionary of Biography,* vol. 3, *1851–1890: A–C,* Melbourne: Melbourne University Press, 1969, pp. 445–46.

61. William Westgarth, *The Colony of Victoria: Its History, Commerce and Gold Mining; Its Social and Political Institutions; Down to the End of 1863. With Remarks, Incidental and Comparative, Upon the Other Australian Colonies,* London: Sampson Low, Son and Marston, 1864, p. 391. Among Knight's various exhibition publications was *The Australasian Colonies at the International Exhibition, London, 1862. Extracts from the Reports of the Jurors and Other Information Taken from Official Sources. Compiled by J. G. Knight, F.R.I.B.A.,* Melbourne: John Ferres, Government Printer, 1865.

62. *Table-Talk* (Melbourne), October 27, 1894.

63. *Official Record of the Sydney International Exhibition, 1879,* Sydney: Thomas Richards, Government Printer, 1881, pp. 1030–32.

64. Margaret Willis, *By Their Fruits: A Life of Ferdinand von Mueller, Botanist and Explorer,* Sydney: Angus and Robertson, 1949, pp. 82–84, 88, 142.

65. Sir Henry Parkes to William Macarthur, March 6, 1866, *Sir William Macarthur, International Exhibitions, 1862–1879,* Macarthur Papers, vol. 45, Mitchell Library, State Library of New South Wales, A 2941.

66. "A Paper by Sir William Macarthur on the Products of New South Wales, Prepared for the Paris Universal Exposition of 1855, with Special Ref-

erence to the Production of Wine and Wool," *Macarthur Family Papers*, vol. 9, Mitchell Library, State Library of New South Wales, D 185, fols. 105–26.

67. Barbara Rose Atkins, *The Problem of the Representation of Australia in England: The Origins and Development of the Australian Agents-General During the Nineteenth Century*, University of Melbourne M.A. Thesis, 1960, Mitchell Library, State Library of New South Wales, ML FM 4/1448; and Clem Lack, "Some Queensland Agents-General: Horace Tozer and Those Who Followed Him," *Journal of the Royal Historical Society of Queensland* 8 (1966–67), pp. 246–85. For contemporary discussions of the Agents-General, see "Colonial Agents," *Colonial Magazine and Commercial-Maritime Journal* 2 (1840), pp. 354–56; and "Representatives for the Colonies—Colonial Agents in London," *Colonial Magazine and Foreign Miscellany* 9 (1846), pp. 303–19.

68. *Private and Confidential Letters. Letters of Sir Arthur Blyth, Agent-General, to Simpson Newland, Treasurer, 1885–1886*, Mortlock Library of South Australiana, State Library of South Australia, PRG 288/9/1–36. Emphasis in original.

69. Saul Samuel, Agent-General to Chief Secretary, July 13, 1882, *Fisheries Exhibition Bundle, 1882*, Archives Office of New South Wales, 4/840.2.

70. George Nadel, *Australia's Colonial Culture: Ideas, Men, and Institutions in Mid-Nineteenth-Century Eastern Australia*, Melbourne: F. W. Cheshire, 1957; and D. I. McDonald, "The Diffusion of Scientific and Other Useful Knowledge," *Journal of the Royal Australian Historical Society* 54 (1968), pp. 176–93.

71. Sir Redmond Barry to H. C. E. Childers, May 16, 1859, *Redmond Barry Papers*, La Trobe Collection, State Library of Victoria, MS 8380, Box 599/1(A).

72. Sir Redmond Barry to Hugh Childers, August 25, 1860, *Redmond Barry Papers*, MS 8380, Box 599/1 (B).

73. Sir Redmond Barry to Mrs. Louisa Barrows, May 20 and August 25, 1862, *Redmond Barry Correspondence*, La Trobe Collection, State Library of Victoria, MS 8380, Box 599/5. Emphasis in original letter.

74. Greenhalgh, *Ephemeral Vistas*, pp. 59–60.

75. C. Purdon Clarke, "Preface," in *Paris Universal Exhibition of 1878. Handbook to the British Indian Section by George C. M. Birdwood, C.S.I., M.D. Edin.*, 2nd ed., London: Offices of the Royal Commission, 1879, pp. iii–iv.

76. "Memo of Philip Cunliffe-Owen to Earl of Dufferin," fols. 2 and 5.

77. *Report on the Indian Section of the Franco-British Exhibition, London, 1908*, London: Eyre and Spottiswoode, 1908.

78. "On the Utility of Establishing a Reporter on Trade Products in the Colonial Office," *Proceedings, Royal Colonial Institute* 2 (1870), pp. 154–66.

79. For career outlines, please see the obituaries for "John Forbes Royle, M.D., F.R.S., F.G.S.," *Journal of Indian Art and Industry* 2 (1888), pp. 65–66, and "Dr. John Forbes Watson, M.A., M.D., LL.D.," *Journal of Indian Art and Industry* 3 (1890), pp. 25–27.

80. J. Forbes Royle, "Observations on Provincial Exhibitions and the Improvement of the Resources of the Several Districts of the Madras Presidency,"

Madras Journal of Literature and Science n. s. 2 (1857), pp. 64–79, and n.s. 3 (1857), pp. 171–72; and John Forbes Watson, *International Exhibitions*, London: Henry S. King, 1873.

81. J. Forbes Watson, "Preface," in *The International Exhibition of 1862. A Classified and Descriptive Catalogue of the Indian Department*, London: W. Clowes and Sons, 1862.

82. *New Zealand Exhibition, 1865*, Mitchell Library, State Library of New South Wales, CY Reel 100. A 28, fols. 12–15.

83. *Vienna Universal Exhibition. A Classified and Descriptive Catalogue of the Indian Department*, London: W. H. Allen, 1873.

84. Neil J. Markelyne [British Museum] to Sir Redmond Barry, November 22, 1862, *Letters from Persons of Distinction in Europe, 1860–1869*, La Trobe Collection, State Library of Victoria, MS 6333, Box 297/2, fol. 16.

85. *Register for Disposal of Exhibits, London International Exhibition, 1862*, Mitchell Library, State Library of New South Wales, M. L. Uncat., MSS set 508, Item 9.

86. *Correspondence, Volume 2, E. P. Ramsay Papers*, Mitchell Library, State Library of New South Wales, ML MSS 1370/2, fols. 291–315, 323–32 and 337–38.

87. "December 1884," *Papers from Botanical Gardens, 1878–1895*, Archives Office of New South Wales, 4/915, File 2873/84.

88. *Report of the Royal Commission for the Australian International Exhibitions, 1882*, English Parliamentary Papers, 1882 [c. 3099], xxviii.

89. "May 23, 1881," *Melbourne International Exhibition, 1880: Correspondence*, Victoria Public Record Office, 4363/12, Letter no. 39.

90. *Victorian Exhibition Commissioners Correspondence, 1861–1862*, La Trobe Collection, State Library of Victoria, Box 122/2, fols. 149–50.

91. "Intercolonial Exhibition of Australasia, 1866–67. Appendix, Containing Descriptive and Statistical Information Relating to the Colonies of New South Wales, Queensland, South Australia, Tasmania, New Zealand, Western Australia," in *Intercolonial Exhibition of Australasia, Melbourne, 1866–67. Official Record, Containing Introduction, Catalogues, Reports and Awards of the Jurors, Essays and Statistics on the Social and Economic Resources of the Australasian Colonies*, Melbourne: Blundell, 1867.

92. Willis, *By Their Fruits*, p. 82; and "Notes on the Vegetable Products in the Intercolonial Exhibition of 1866. By Ferdinand von Mueller, Ph.D., M.D., F.R.S., etc.," in *Intercolonial Exhibition of Australasia, Melbourne, 1866–67. Official Record, Containing Introduction . . .* , p. 221.

93. "Memo of Philip Cunliffe-Owen to Earl of Dufferin," fols. 2–4.

94. *Memorandum of Measures Adopted, and Expenditure Incurred, in India, for the Promotion of Literature, Science and Art, since the Assumption by Her Majesty, the Queen of the Direct Government of the Country*, Oriental and India Office Collections, V/27/900/1; and "Resolution on Museums and Exhibitions," *Journal of Indian Art and Industry* 1 (1884–86), pp. 1–6.

95. Sir Edward Buck, *(Confidential) Historical Summaries of Administra-*

tive Measures in the Several Branches of Public Business Administered in the Department of Revenue and Agriculture. Drawn up in 1896, Calcutta: Government Printing Office, 1897.

96. C. A. Bayly, "Knowing the Country: Empire and Information in India," Modern Asian Studies 27 (1993), pp. 3–43, and Empire and Information: Intelligence Gathering and Social Communication in India, 1780–1880, New York: Cambridge University Press, 1997; Deepak Kumar, Science and the Raj, 1857–1905, New York: Oxford University Press, 1995; and Marika Vicziany, "Imperialism, Botany and Statistics in early Nineteenth-Century India: The Surveys of Francis Buchanan, 1762–1829," Modern Asian Studies 20 (1986), pp. 625–60.

97. Times, June 11, 1886, p. 4.

98. Temple, Men and Events of My Time in India, pp. 360–61, 382–83.

99. E. C. Buck, "The Utility of Exhibitions to India," Asiatic Quarterly Review 2 (1886), p. 319.

100. "Employment of Natives in Scientific Investigations," in Buck, (Confidential) Historical Summaries of Administrative Measures, pp. 19–23; Kumar, Science and the Raj, 1857–1905, pp. 113–50; and Gauri Viswanathan, Masks of Conquest: Literary Study and British Rule in India, New York: Columbia University Press, 1989.

101. Among the government branches responsible for exhibitions were Industrial Art, Museums and Exhibitions (1871–72); Industry, Science and Arts (1873–79); Exhibitions (1881–82); Museum and Exhibitions (1882–1894); and Practical Arts and Museums (1895–1905). The formation, transportation, exchange, and sale of collections also interested other Indian government departments, such as Home, Commercial, and Education. This multiple coverage paralleled the English model in which the Board of Trade and the Science and Art Department of the Council of Education shared interest in exhibitions, since the shows were perceived to have educational, artistic, and commercial purposes.

102. For biographical information, please see C. Hayavadana Rao, ed., The Indian Biographical Dictionary, 1915, Madras: Pillar, 1915, pp. 70, 146.

103. Colonial and Indian Exhibition. Empire of India Catalogue, 1886, National Art Library, Victoria and Albert Museum, London, A. 23 (32), pp. 11–18.

104. Colonial and Indian Exhibition. Royal Commission and Government of India Silk Culture Court. Descriptive Catalogue, London: William Clowes & Sons, 1886.

105. Sir George Watt, The Commercial Products of India, Being An Abridgement of "The Dictionary of the Economic Products of India," New Delhi: Today and Tomorrow's Printers and Publishers, 1966 [reprint edition of 1908 original], and A Dictionary of The Economic Products of India, Six Volumes, Delhi: Cosmo Publications, 1972 [reprint of 1889 original].

106. "Memo of Philip Cunliffe-Owen to Earl of Dufferin," fols. 2–4.

107. Capt. W. A. Tate to Major Jervis, September 12, 1838, Address . . . Descriptive of the State, Progress and Prospects of the Various Surveys and Other

Scientific Enquiries Instituted by the East India Company, Torquay: Privately Printed, pp. 1–5; and George Everest, *Historical Records of the Survey of India, Volume 4, 1830–1842,* Dehra Dun (U.P.): Office of the Northern Circle, Survey of India, 1958, pp. 401–13.

108. File No. 1, Serial No. 4, January 26, 1886, *Government of India, Revenue and Agriculture Department Proceedings: Museums and Exhibitions, 1886 Section,* Oriental and India Office Collections, P/3490, pp. 4–5.

109. "Memo of Philip Cunliffe-Owen to Earl of Dufferin, Viceroy, April 1, 1887," fols. 13–14.

110. December 4, 1883, *John Lockwood Kipling Correspondence, Kipling Family Papers,* University of Sussex Archives, Box I, File 10.

111. *The Indian Museum: 1814–1914,* Calcutta Baptist Mission Press, 1914, pp. 9–10.

112. *Statesman and Friend of India,* January 17, 1883, p.2.

113. *A Hand-Book of Indian Products. (Art-Manufactures and Raw Materials.) by T. N. Mukharji, Author of "A Rough List of Indian Art-Ware" and "A Descriptive Catalogue of Indian Products Contributed to the Amsterdam Exhibition,"* Calcutta: C. J. A. Pritchard at the "Star" Press, 1883; *Government of India. Revenue and Agriculture Department, Classified List of Indian Produce Contributed to the Amsterdam Exhibition, 1883. Compiled by Trailokya Nath Mukharji, Officer in Charge of Indian Exhibits for the Amsterdam Exhibition,* Calcutta: Superintendent of Government Printing, 1883; and T. N. Mukharji, *Art-Manufactures of India, Specially Compiled for the Glasgow International Exhibition, 1888,* Calcutta: Superintendent of Government Printing, India, 1888.

114. *Statesman and Friend of India,* July 7, 1883, p. 2.

115. *Selections from the Records of the Government of India, Revenue and Agriculture Department, by the Reporter on Economic Products,* vol. 1, Calcutta: Superintendent of Government Printing, 1889, p. 169.

116. T. N. Mukharji, "The Exhibition and its Visitors," in *A Visit to Europe,* London: Edward Stanford, 1889, pp. 64–138.

117. *Report of the Royal Commission for the Colonial and Indian Exhibition, London, 1886,* Parliamentary Papers, 1887 [c. 5083], xx. 1; and "Memo of Philip Cunliffe-Owen to Earl of Dufferin," fols. 2–4 and 10.

118. Mukharji, *A Hand-Book of Indian Products. (Art-Manufactures and Raw Materials.)*

119. *A Rough List of Indian Art Ware, compiled by Babu T. N. Mukharji, In Charge of Work Connected with Exhibitions, Revenue and Agriculture Department, Government of India, 1883,* Oriental and India Office Collections, V/27/940/1.

120. "Preface," in *A Hand-Book of Indian Products,* p. 11.

121. Mukharji's opinions are included in various Indian government publications, such as the *Official Gazette of India* and George Watt and Percy Brown, eds., *Indian Art at Delhi, 1903, Being the Official Catalogue of the Delhi Exhibition, 1902–1903,* Calcutta: Superintendent of Government Printing, 1903.

122. Mukharji, *A Visit to Europe*, p. xii.

123. N. N. Ghose, "Preface," in Mukharji, *A Visit to Europe*, pp. vii–xii.

124. For example, see George Campbell, "The Employment of the Natives of India in Their Own Country," *Journal of the National Indian Association* 121 (1881), pp. 4–7; and Lepel Griffin, "The Public Service of India," *Asiatic Quarterly Review* 3 (1887), pp. 250–83.

125. Mukharji, *A Visit to Europe*, pp. 128–31.

126. Ibid., p. xii.

127. Ibid., pp. 128–31.

128. Ibid., p. x.

129. Edward Said, *Orientalism*, New York: Vintage Books, 1979, and "Orientalism Reconsidered," *Race and Class* 27 (1985), pp. 1–15; Said's first essay on "Orientalism" appeared in *Georgia Review* for Spring 1977. For a comprehensive and suggestive review of *Orientalism*, see James Clifford, "On *Orientalism*," in *The Predicament of Culture: Twentieth-Century Ethnography, Literature and Art*, Cambridge, MA: Harvard University Press, 1988, pp. 255–76.

130. Gyan Prakash, "Orientalism Now," *History and Theory* 34 (1995), pp. 199–212.

131. Aijaz Ahmad, "*Orientalism* and After: Ambivalence and Metropolitan Location in the Work of Edward Said," in *In Theory: Classes, Nations, Literatures*, New York: Verso, 1992, pp. 159–219; Lata Mani and Ruth Frankenberg, "The Challenge of Orientalism," *Economy and Society* 14 (1995), pp. 174–92; John M. MacKenzie, *Orientalism: History, Theory, and the Arts*, New York: Manchester University Press, 1995; and Michael Richardson, "Enough Said: Reflections on Orientalism," *Anthropology Today* 6 (1990), pp. 16–19.

132. Bernard S. Cohn, "Social and Political Theory and the Symbols of Empire in Nineteenth-Century India: A Proposal for Research," *Journal of the Indian Anthropological Society* 8 (1973), pp. 117–22; *An Anthropologist Among the Historians and Other Essays*, New York: Oxford University Press, 1990; "Representing Authority in Victorian India," in Eric Hobsbawm and Terence Ranger, eds., *The Invention of Tradition*, New York: Cambridge University Press, 1984, pp. 165–209; and *Colonialism and Its Forms of Knowledge: The British in India*, Princeton, NJ: Princeton University Press, 1996.

133. Cohn, "Social and Political Theory and the Symbols of Empire," p. 117.

134. Scholars of the Subaltern School of Indian historiography have addressed a strikingly similar top-down or elitist view of the subcontinent's political and social history. They have argued that the emphasis on South Asian elites, including members of the Congress Party, has mystified our understanding of the struggle for Indian independence and nationalism, removing the peasant and worker from the historical equation. Perhaps their social subalterns share an historiographical fate not unlike the cultural and professional subalterns who worked with exhibition committees. For an introduction to the Subaltern School, see Ranajit Guha and Gayatri Chakravorty Spivak, eds., *Selected Subaltern Studies*, New York: Oxford University Press, 1988; and Gyan

Prakash, "AHR Forum: Subaltern Studies as Postcolonial Criticism," *American Historical Review* 99 (1994), pp. 1475–90.

135. Bernard S. Cohn, "The Transformation of Objects into Artifacts, Antiquities, and Art in Nineteenth-Century India," in *Colonialism and Its Forms of Knowledge*, pp. 76–105.

136. Deepak Kumar, "Patterns of Colonial Science in India," *Indian Journal of History of Science* 15 (1980), p. 105; and Michael Adas, "A Field Matures: Technology, Science, and Western Colonialism," *Technology and Culture* 38 (1997), pp. 478–87.

137. Roy Macleod discusses the development of imperial and colonial science in Australia in "On Visiting the 'Moving Metropolis:' Reflections on the Architecture of Imperial Science," in Nathan Reingold and Marc Rothenberg, eds., *Scientific Colonialism: A Cross Cultural Comparison*, Washington, DC: Smithsonian Institution Press, 1987, pp. 1–16; and "Passages in Imperial Science: From Empire to Commonwealth," *Journal of World History* 4 (1993), pp. 117–50.

138. For discussion of the relationships between the study and practice of Indian art and imperial rule, see Patrick Brantlinger, "A Postindustrial Prelude to Postcolonialism: John Ruskin, William Morris, and Gandhism," *Critical Inquiry* 22 (1996), pp. 466–85; Thomas R. Metcalf, *An Imperial Vision: Indian Architecture and Britain's Raj*, Berkeley: University of California Press, 1989, pp. 141–75; Partha Mitter, *Art and Nationalism in Colonial India, 1850–1922: Occidental Orientations*, New York: Cambridge University Press, 1994; and John M. MacKenzie, "Art and the Empire," in P. J. Marshall, ed., *The Cambridge Illustrated History of the British Empire*, New York: Cambridge University Press, 1996, pp. 296–315.

139. Gyan Prakash, "Science 'Gone Native' in Colonial India," *Representations* 40 (1992), pp. 153–78.

140. "Committees," *Journal of Royal Asiatic Society of Bengal* 1886, pp. 56–57.

141. Mitter, *Art and Nationalism in Colonial India*, pp. 215, 249, 284–86.

142. *Calcutta Review* 19 (1853), p. 250; and Harry Rivett-Carnac, "Memorandum on the Measures Adopted in India to Select Contributions for the International Exhibition of 1871," in *Circulars Relating to the Kensington International Exhibition of 1871. Temple Papers*, Oriental and India Office Collections, MSS Eur. F. 86/119.

143. *Empire of India Catalogue*, p. 11.

144. S. N. Sen, "The Character of the Introduction of Western Science in India During the Eighteenth and Nineteenth Centuries," *Indian Journal of History of Science* 1 (1966), pp. 112–22; and Kumar, *Science and the Raj*, pp. 180–227.

145. *A Hand-Book of Indian Products*, pp. 1–2.

146. *Report of the Industrial and Agricultural Exhibition of the Punjab, N.–W. F. Province and Kashmir, 1909–1910*, Lahore: Lahore: "Tribune" Press, 1911, p. 17.

147. Ronald Robinson, "Non-European Foundations of European Imperialism: Sketch for a Theory of Collaboration," in Roger Owen and Bob Sutcliffe, eds., *Studies in the Theory of Imperialism*, London: Longman Group, 1971, pp. 117–42.

148. Burton Benedict, "International Exhibitions and National Identity," *Anthropology Today* (U.K.) 17 (1991), pp. 5–9.

149. C. F. G. Masterman, *The Condition of England*, 4th ed., London: Methuen, 1909, p. 58.

CHAPTER 3. COMMISSIONERS AND THE STATE

1. Sydney Checkland, *British Public Policy, 1776–1939: An Economic, Social, and Political Perspective*, New York: Cambridge University Press, 1985; Roy Macleod, ed., *Government and Expertise: Specialists, Administrators, and Professionals, 1860–1919*, New York: Cambridge University Press, 1988; and Harold Perkin, *The Rise of Professional Society: England Since 1880*, New York: Routledge, 1990.

2. The term was used by Samuel Taylor Coleridge as a label for cultural experts responsible for cultivating ideas, maintaining intellectual life, connecting the state and the professions, and forging a new Establishment. Theirs was a new gentleman class. See Samuel Taylor Coleridge, *On the Constitution of the Church and State* (1830), ed. John Barrell, London: J. M. Dent & Sons, 1972.

3. *Fifty Years of Public Work of Sir Henry Cole, K.C.B., Accounted for in His Deeds, Speeches and Writings*, 2 vols., London: George Bell and Sons, 1884.

4. Miriam R. Levin, *Republican Art and Ideology in Late-Nineteenth-Century France*, Ann Arbor: University of Michigan Research Press, 1986; Daniel J. Sherman, *Worthy Monuments: Art Museums and the Politics of Culture in Nineteenth-Century France*, Cambridge, MA.: Harvard University Press, 1989; Debora L. Silverman, "The 1889 Exhibition: The Crisis in Bourgeois Individualism," *Oppositions* 8 (1977), pp. 70–91, and *Art Nouveau in Fin-de-Siecle France: Politics, Psychology, and Style*, Berkeley: University of California Press, 1989. Charles Babbage praised the roles of the French government in "the promotion of the arts connected with commerce and manufactures," including the establishment of the "Conservatoire des Arts et Metiers" and "the juxtaposition, at proper intervals of time, in one large building, of selected specimens of all the produce of national industry." *The Exposition of 1851; or, Views of the Industry, the Science, and the Government of England*, 2nd ed., London: John Murray, 1851, pp. 21–25.

5. Lady Dilke, *Art in the Modern State*, London: Chapman and Hall, 1888. A review of her commentary on "the organization of Art in France" was published in *Art-Journal* 51 (1889), pp. 63–64.

6. Carol A. Breckenridge, "The Aesthetics and Politics of Colonial Collecting: India at World Fairs," *Comparative Studies in Society and History* 31 (1989), pp. 195–216; and Bernard S. Cohn, "The Transformation of Objects into Artifacts, Antiquities, and Art in Nineteenth-Century India," in *Colonialism*

and Its Forms of Knowledge: The British in India, Princeton, NJ: Princeton University Press, 1996, pp. 76–105.

7. Mary Poovey, *Making a Social Body: British Cultural Formation, 1830–1864,* Chicago: The University of Chicago Press, 1995, esp. chapter 2.

8. Tony Bennett, "The Exhibitionary Complex," in Nicholas B. Dirks, Geoffrey Eley, and Sherry B. Ortner, eds., *Culture/Power/History: A Reader in Contemporary Social Theory,* Princeton, NJ: Princeton University Press, 1994, pp. 123–54.

9. Pierre Bourdieu, *Distinction: A Critique of the Judgement of Taste,* Richard Nice, trans. Cambridge, MA: Harvard University Press, 1984.

10. *Westminster Review,* 126 (1886), pp. 35–37.

11. This phrase is from *United Empire* 14 (1923), pp. 543–46.

12. *Bee-Hive,* November 15, 1862, p. 1, and May 5, 1865; and *Hansard's Parliamentary Debates,* series 3, vol. 178, p. 1560.

13. "Close of the Exhibition—Its Failure," *Bee-Hive,* November 1, 1862, p. 1.

14. *Victoria Parliamentary Debates,* 1866 (vol. 2), p. 361.

15. Daniel J. Sherman, "Art Museums, Inspections, and the Limits to Cultural Policy in the Early Third Republic," *Historical Reflections/Réflexions Historiques* 15 (1988), pp. 339–59.

16. George Cornewall Lewis, *An Essay on the Influence of Authority in Matters of Opinion,* 2nd ed., London: Longmans, Green, 1875, esp. pp. 219–22. For contemporary information about Lewis, see "Sir George Cornewall Lewis," *Macmillan's Magazine* 2 (1870), pp. 470–71; and *Edinburgh Review* 91 (1849–50), pp. 508–58.

17. *Quarterly Review* 101 (1857), pp. 563–66.

18. *Royal Colonial Institute Yearbook,* 1912, pp. x, 2, 23.

19. "Proceedings of the Colonial Society's Inaugural Dinner on March 10, 1869 and 1st Meeting, March 15, 1869," *British Library Tracts, 1856–1871,* British Library Printed Books Collection, London, CT. 302, pp. 2, 34–36.

20. *The Exhibition—Has It Had a Beneficial Tendency?* National Art Library, London, 86 QQ Box I (vi).

21. For example, see John R. Seeley, *The Expansion of England* [1883], Chicago: University of Chicago Press, 1971.

22. John R. Seeley, "Introduction," in *Colonial and Indian Exhibition, 1886. Her Majesty's Colonies. A Series of Original Papers Issued Under the Authority of the Royal Commission,* London: William Clowes and Sons, 1886, pp. vii–xxv.

23. John R. Seeley to Macmillan, *Macmillan Papers,* British Library Manuscripts Department, Add. MS 55,074, fols. 43, 47–48 and 57.

24. Daniel Duman, "The Creation and Diffusion of a Professional Ideology in Nineteenth-Century England," *Sociological Review* n.s. 27 (1979), pp. 113–38.

25. The parallel development among British writers and critics is discussed by Raymond Williams in *Culture and Society: 1780–1850,* New York: Colum-

bia University Press, 1983. For an extended discussion and analysis of the professional ideal, see Perkin, *The Rise of Professional Society*. In many ways, these cultural experts represented and practiced the "professional ideal" discussed in that volume.

26. John Ruskin, *The Political Economy of Art; Being the Substance with Additions of Two Lectures*, London: Smith, Elder, 1857.

27. Walter Benjamin, "The Work of Art in the Age of Mechanical Reproduction," in Hannah Arendt, ed., *Illuminations: Essays and Reflections*, New York: Schocken Books, 1978, p. 224.

28. *Quarterly Review* 37 (1828), p. 486.

29. John Lockwood Kipling, "General Reports of Results," in *Punjab Exhibition Official Report, 1881*, National Art Library, London, 098956 (19a); and "Relics of Ancient Art," in *Official Catalogue of the Great Industrial Exhibition (In Connection with the Royal Dublin Society), 1853*, 4th ed., Dublin: John Falconer, 1853, esp. pp. 131–56.

30. John Stuart Mill, "Civilization," in J. B. Schneewind, ed., *Essays on Literature and Society*, New York: Collier Books, 1965, pp. 171–72.

31. "Convention for Promoting Universally Reproductions of Works of Art for the Benefit of Museums of All Countries," *Fifteenth Report of the Department of Science and Art*, 1868, pp. 24–25; and Sir Henry Cole to Lord Mayo, September 6, 1869, *Correspondence with Sir Henry Cole*, Mayo Papers, University of Cambridge Archives, Add. 7490/51 (XI), fol. 148.

32. Francis Turner Palgrave, "Lost Treasures," in *Essays on Art*, London: Macmillan, 1866, pp. 211–16.

33. This phrase is from a review article on "the gentleman" in *Colonial Magazine and Commercial-Maritime Journal* 2 (1840), pp. 237–38.

34. Peter Allen, "S. T. Coleridge's 'Church and State' and the Idea of an Intellectual Establishment," *Journal of the History of Ideas* 46 (1985), pp. 89–106; and Ben Knights, *The Idea of the Clerisy in the Nineteenth Century*, New York: Cambridge University Press, 1978.

35. Coleridge, *On the Constitution of the Church and State*, p. 34.

36. Karl Marx, "Preface to the First Edition," in *Capital: A Critique of Political Economy*, vol. 1, New York: Vintage Books, 1977, p. 91.

37. Frank A. L. James, "Science in the Pits," paper delivered at the Third British–North American History of Science Meeting, Edinburgh, Scotland, July 1996, MSS; see F. James and Margaret Ray, "Science in the Pits: Michael Faraday, Charles Lyell, and the Home Office Enquiry into the Explosion at Haswell Colliery, County Durham, in 1844," *History and Technology* 15 (1999), pp. 213–31.

38. *Great Exhibition of the Works of Industry of All Nations, 1851. Official Descriptive and Illustrated Catalogue, Volume I*, London: W. Clowes and Sons, 1851, pp. 22–23.

39. *Intercolonial Exhibition of Australasia, Melbourne, 1866–67. Official Record, Containing Introduction, Catalogues, Reports and Awards of the Ju-*

rors, *Essays and Statistics on Social and Economic Resources of the Australasian Colonies*, Melbourne: Blundell, 1867, p. ii.

40. *Statesman and Friend of India*, December 27, 1883, p. 2.

41. Robert Brain, "Going to the Exhibition," in Richard Staley, ed., *The Physics of Empire: Public Lectures*, Cambridge, England: The Whipple Museum of the History of Science, 1994, pp. 113–42.

42. John Ruskin, *The Inaugural Address Delivered at the Cambridge School of Art*, Kent: George Allen, 1879, p. 7.

43. Bennett, "The Exhibitionary Complex," pp. 123–54.

44. Susan Sontag, *On Photography*, New York: Viking Penguin, 1986.

45. William A. Drew, *Glimpses and Gatherings, During a Voyage and Visit to London and the Great Exhibition, in the Summer of 1851*, Augusta, ME: Homan & Manley, 1852, p. 336.

46. "Lecture I.—Dr. Whewell on the General Bearing of the Great Exhibition on the Progress of Art and Science," in *Lectures on the Progress of Arts and Science, Resulting from the Great Exhibition in London*, New York: A. S. Barnes, 1854, pp. 7–11.

47. *Report on the Government Central Museum, and on the Agricultural and Horticultural Society of Western India, for 1863. With Appendices, being the Establishment of the Victoria and Albert Museum and of the Victoria Gardens*, Bombay: Education Society's Press, 1864, pp. 16–18.

48. Ibid., p. 30.

49. James E. Sherrard, *Official Catalogue of Exhibits*, Melbourne: Firth and M'Cutcheon, 1885.

50. *Art-Journal* 43 (1891), pp. 120–22; and "Montefiore, Eliezer Levi," in *Australian Dictionary of Biography, Volume 5, 1851–1890: K–Q*, Melbourne: Melbourne University Press, 1974, p. 269.

51. George Verdon to Eliezer Montefiore, May 4, 1881, *Australian Autograph Collection*, La Trobe Collection, State Library of Victoria, M 4970; and *Eliezer Montefiore Correspondence to Victorian Academy of Arts, 1870–72*, La Trobe Collection, MS 7593, Box 580/1(A).

52. May 5, 1865, *Hansard's Parliamentary Debates*, 3rd series, vol. 178 (1865), pp. 1543–44.

53. Sir Charles Locke Eastlake, "How To Observe," in *Contributions to the Literature of the Fine Arts*, 2nd series, London: John Murray, 1870.

54. John Ruskin, "Lecture II. The Unity of Art. Delivered in Manchester, 14 March, 1859," in *The Two Paths: Being Lectures on Art and its Application to Decoration and Manufacture, Delivered in 1858–1859*, London: Smith, Elder, 1859, p. 40; emphasis in original.

55. *Reminiscences of the Crystal Palace, with a full description of the principal objects exhibited. And a plan, showing the arrangements of the various departments*, 2nd ed., London: George Routledge, 1852, pp. v–vi.

56. Harriet Martineau, *How to Observe Morals and Manners* [1838], ed. Michael R. Hill, New Brunswick, NJ: Transaction Publishers, 1989, p. 13.

57. This phrase is from a discussion of the British Empire Exhibition in *Round Table* 55 (1924), pp. 541–42.

58. Martin Heidegger, "The Age of the World Picture," in William Lovitt, trans. and ed., *The Question Concerning Technology and Other Essays*, New York: Garland Publishing, 1977, pp. 115–54.

59. Timothy Mitchell, "The World as Exhibition," *Comparative Studies in Society and History* 31 (1989), pp. 217–36, and *Colonising Egypt*, Berkeley, CA: University of California Press, 1991.

60. Ruskin, *Inaugural Address Delivered at the Cambridge School of Art*, p. 6.

61. John Allwood, "International Exhibitions and the Classification of Their Exhibits," *Journal of the Royal Society of Arts* 128 (1980), pp. 450–55; Arjun Appadurai, "Introduction: Commodities and the Politics of Value," in Appadurai, ed., *The Social Life of Things: Commodities in Cultural Perspective*, New York: Cambridge University Press, 1986, pp. 3–63; and Mary Douglas and Baron Isherwood, *The World of Goods*, New York: Basic Books, 1979.

62. Thomas Richards, *The Commodity Culture of Victorian England: Advertising and Spectacle, 1851–1914*, Stanford, CA: Stanford University Press, 1990.

63. George Birdwood, *The Industrial Arts of India*, vol. 1, London: Chapman and Hall, 1880.

64. Ruskin, *The Two Paths*, pp. 78–80.

65. "Experiments on Colonial Woods," *Builder* 51 (1886), pp. 548–49; Arthur Beckwith, *International Exhibition, London, 1871. Pottery. Observations on the Materials and Manufacture of Terra-Cotta, Stone-Ware, Fire-Brick, Porcelain, Earthen-Ware, Brick, Majolica, and Encaustic Tiles, with Remarks on the Products Exhibited*, New York: D. Van Nostrand, Publisher, 1872, p. 50; and Edward Lonsdale Beckwith, *Practical Notes on Wine, Reprint of Report on Wines for Royal Commissioners for Paris Exposition, 1867*, London: Smith and Elder, 1868, pp. 63–67.

66. *The International Exhibition of 1862. The Illustrated Catalogue of the Industrial Department, Volume II. Colonial and Indian Divisions*, London: Eyre and Spottiswoode, 1862, pp. 51, 53.

67. "The Mineral Trophy in Front of the Garden Palace," *Illustrated Sydney News*, October 4, 1879, p. 5.

68. *An Illustrated Souvenir of the First Adelaide Exhibition held during the months of July, August, and September, 1881*, Adelaide: Frearson and Brother, 1881, p. 7.

69. W. and C. Hordern to John L. Hordern, April 5, 1867, Royal Historical Society of Victoria, Melbourne, MS 000365, Box 127/2, fols. 4–5.

70. Debates about the value of exhibition displays represented general nineteenth-century concerns about representation, the meaning of material objects, and the subjectivity of measurements. Much of the Victorian-era literature about "value" recalled the publications and discourse of the first-generation political economists. For example, see Adam Smith, *The Wealth of*

Nations: "In order to investigate the principles which regulate the exchangeable value of commodities, I shall endeavour to show, First, what is the real measure of this exchangeable value; or wherein consists the real price of all commodities. Secondly, what are the different parts of which this real prices is composed or made up" (book 1, chapter 4: "On the Origin and Use of Money").

71. *Reports on the Paris Universal Exposition, 1867, Volume I: Reports by Executive Commissioner; with Appendices,* English Parliamentary Papers, 1868–69. [xxx]. Pt. i. 1, pp. 36–37; and *A Special Report on the Annual International Exhibitions of the Years 1871, 1872, 1873, and 1874, Drawn up by Sir Henry Cole, Acting Commissioner in 1873, and 1874, and Presented by the Commissioners for the Exhibition of 1851,* English Parliamentary Papers, 1878 [XXVII]. 139, pp. xxix–xxxi.

72. Sir Francis Philip Cunliffe-Owen to Sir Henry Cole, August 31, 1871, *Henry Cole Correspondence,* National Art Library, London, Box 15.

73. Cited in *Club and Institute Journal* (1885), p. 41.

74. *Illustrated Melbourne Post,* 1867, p. 38.

75. *Victoria Parliamentary Debates,* vol. 58 (1888), p. 1634.

76. Babbage, *The Exposition of 1851,* pp. 129–31.

77. Ibid., pp. 112–24.

78. Ibid., p. 21.

79. Ibid., p. 79.

80. Michael B. Miller, *The Bon Marche: Bourgeois Culture and the Department Store, 1869–1920,* Princeton, NJ: Princeton University Press, 1981; and Rosalind H. Williams, *Dream Worlds: Mass Consumption in Late-Nineteenth-Century France,* Berkeley: University of California Press, 1982.

81. *Nineteenth Century* 20 (1886), p. 641.

82. *Art-Journal* n.s. 17 (1878), pp. 7–8.

83. Walter Benjamin, "Grandville, or the World Exhibitions," in Peter Demetz, ed., and Edmund Jephcott, trans., *Reflections: Essays, Aphorisms, Autobiographical Writings,* New York: Schocken Books, 1986, pp. 151–53.

84. John Ruskin, *"Unto this Last": Four Essays on the First Principles of Political Economy,* Lincoln: University of Nebraska Press, 1967, p. 78.

85. Lawrence Weaver, *Exhibitions and the Art of Display,* London: Country Life, 1925.

86. "Greater Britain Exhibition, 1899: Report Upon the Agricultural Exhibits in the Queensland Court of the Greater Britain Exhibition," *1899 Queensland Votes and Proceedings,* Queensland State Archives, AGS/N52, pp. 1–8; and Horace Tozer to Colonial Secretary, October 25, 1907, *Premier's Department Letters and Papers re. Franco-British Exhibition, 1908–1911,* Queensland State Archives, A/6321, pp. 7–8.

87. Sandra B. Freitag, "Visions of the Nation: Theorizing the Nexus between Creation, Consumption, and Participation in the Public Sphere," paper delivered at the S.O.A.S. Popular Culture Conference, 1995, MSS; and Gyan Prakash, "Science 'Gone Native' in Colonial India," *Representations* 40 (1992), pp. 153–78.

88. *Journal of Applied Science, and Record of Progress in the Industrial Arts* 1 (1870), p. 1.

89. A complaint noted by R. E. N. Twopeny in "A Proposal for Holding an Australasian Exhibition in London," Sydney, 1883, *Australia Pamphlets* no. 20, Foreign and Commonwealth Office Library, London, p. 7.

90. *Adelaide Jubilee International Exhibition, 1887–1888. Letter Book of the South Australia Commissioners, Volume I, December 1886–August 1887*, Public Record Office of South Australia, GRG 47/7/1, p. 230.

91. *Adelaide Jubilee International Exhibition, 1887–1888. Finance Committee Minutes, 1883–1887*, Public Record Office of South Australia, GRG 47/5/1, pp. 232–33.

92. Ibid., pp. 263, 306, 361.

93. Ibid., p. 261.

94. *Statesman and Friend of India*, September 28, 1883, p. 3.

95. *Key*, June 10, 1871, p. 6, in *Francis Fowke Papers and Manuscripts*, National Art Library, London, 86 JJ Box II (iii).

96. *Report of the Royal Commission for the Colonial and Indian Exhibition, London, 1886*, English Parliamentary Papers 1887 [c. 5083], xx. 1., p. 106.

97. *Report on the Indian Section, Franco-British Exhibition 1908*, London: Eyre and Spottiswoode, 1909, pp. 23–24.

98. "Fifteen Thousand Authors and Their Book: Official Descriptive, and Illustrated Catalogue of the Great Exhibition," *Chambers' Edinburgh Journal* 16 (1851), pp. 391–93; and Nancy B. Keeler, "Illustrating the 'Reports by Juries' of the Great Exhibition of 1851: Talbot, Henneman, and Their Failed Commission," *History of Photography* 6 (1982), pp. 257–72.

99. John Tallis, *Tallis's History and Description of the Crystal Palace and the Exhibition of the World's Industry in 1851*, vol. 3, London: The London Printing and Publishing Company, 1852, p. 3.

100. *Calcutta Review* 26 (1856), p. 270.

101. *Views of the International Exhibition: The Interior*, London: T. Nelson and Sons, 1862, pp. 1–2.

102. Ibid., p. 3.

103. November 23, 1861, Royal Commission to Chief Secretary, *Chief Secretary's Office, Registered Inward Correspondence: Exhibitions, 1856–58 and 1860–63*, Victoria Public Record Office, 1189/750.

104. George C. M. Birdwood, *Paris Universal Exhibition of 1878. Handbook to the British Indian Section*, London: Offices of the Royal Commission, 1878.

105. *Illustrated London News*, July 13, 1878, p. 42.

106. *Delhi Indian Art Exhibition, 1902–1903. Indian Art at Delhi, 1903, Being the Official Catalogue of the Delhi Exhibition, 1902–1903*, Calcutta: Superintendent of Government Printing, 1903; and "Indian Art Manufactures," *Times*, September 4, 1903, p. 11.

107. *Catalogue of the Natural and Industrial Products of New South Wales Forwarded to the Paris Universal Exhibition of 1867, by the New South Wales*

Exhibition Commissioners, Sydney: Thomas Richards, Government Printer, 1867.

108. *Calcutta Review* 32 (1859), pp. 136–38.

109. Thomas H. Hendley and John Lockwood Kipling, "Introduction," in *Memorials of the Jeypore Exhibition*, vol. 1, National Art Library, London, pp. i–x.

110. *Letter Book, Colonial and Indian Exhibition, Volume I, March 1885–March 1886*, Public Record Office of South Australia, GRG 55/11/1, fols. 328–30.

111. Ibid., fols. 368–69.

112. "Further Correspondence Respecting the Colonial and Indian Exhibition," *Queensland Votes and Proceedings*, 1885 (vol. 1), p. 4.

113. *The Illustrated Paris Universal Exposition*, May 7, 1878, p. 4.

114. *Annual Report of the Bombay Chamber of Commerce*, 1887, p. 255.

115. June 20 and September 19, 1884, and December 6, 1886, *Agents-General and Public Institution's Correspondence*, Public Record Office of South Australia, GRG 19/ser. 256, fols. 68, 72, 92.

116. George Dodd, *Dictionary of Manufactures, Mining, Machinery, and the Industrial Arts*, New York: Virtue and Yorston, 1869. References were made to the "Hyde Park" (1851), New York Crystal Palace (1853), Paris Universal (1855), and London International (1862) Exhibitions.

117. *Catalogue of Books on Australasia, Francis Edwards Bookseller*, Bancroft Library, University of California, Berkeley.

118. Paul Greenhalgh discusses the interplay between "funding, politics and society" at English, French, and American exhibitions in *Ephemeral Vistas: The Expositions Universelles, Great Exhibitions and World's Fairs, 1851–1939*, New York: St. Martin's Press, esp. pp. 27–51.

119. See appendix C.

120. Lewis, *Influence of Authority in Matters of Opinion*, pp. 219–22.

121. Henry Cole, "The Duty of Governments Towards Education, Science and Art," October 25, 1875, National Art Library, London, p. 7.

122. "The Collections of Indian Princes," *Journal of Indian Art and Industry* 16 (1914), pp. 38–39.

123. Alan Atkinson, "Time, Place, and Paternalism: Early Conservative Thinking in New South Wales," *Australian Historical Studies* 23 (1988), pp. 1–18.

124. On the other hand, there were financial limits as well. For example, New South Wales proved reluctant to help fund the proposed Colonial Annexe at South Kensington after the International Exhibition in 1873. Sir Henry Parkes, the Premier, supported funding, but the local assembly twice refused his requests for a grant. Source: *Times*, October 1, 1873, p. 8.

125. *Calcutta Review* 40 (1864–65), p. 237.

126. *Report on the Melbourne International Exhibition*, Oriental and India Office Collections, W2012, p. 1.

127. *Journal of Indian Art and Industry* 1 (1886), p. 48.

128. *Statesman and Friend of India,* March 14, 1884, p. 3.

129. H. H. Risley, "Report on the Calcutta International Exhibition, October 1885," in *Revenue and Agriculture Department Proceedings,* Oriental and India Office Collections, P/2490, p. 2; and *Memorandum of Measures Adopted, and Expenditure Incurred, in India, for the Promotion of Literature, Science and Art, since the Assumption by Her Majesty the Queen of the Direct Government of the Country,* Oriental and India Office Collections, V/27/900/1, pp. 46–48.

130. *Calcutta Review* 26 (1856), p. 282.

131. *International Exhibition, Saint Louis, 1904. Reports of the Art Committee and Sub-Committee for Applied Art,* London: William Clowes and Sons, 1906, p. 5.

132. Derek Hudson and Kenneth W. Luckhurst, *The Royal Society of Arts, 1754–1954,* London: John Murray, 1954, pp. 187–205.

133. Keeler, "Illustrating the 'Reports by Juries' of the Great Exhibition of 1851," p. 264.

134. "International Health Exhibition File," *Royal Society of Arts Papers,* Greater London Council Office, London.

135. (Confidential Letter no. 6543) Walter H. Harris to Sir Henry Bergne, December 20, 1894, *Foreign Office Correspondence: List of Confidential Papers Relating to Foreign Affairs,* Public Record Office, Kew, PRO F.O. 881/6543.

136. *Report of the Committee Appointed by the Board of Trade to Make Enquiries with Reference to the Participation of Great Britain in Great International Exhibitions,* London: William Spottiswoode and George E. Eyre, 1907.

137. *The Industrial Progress of New South Wales; Being a Report of the Intercolonial Exhibition of 1870 at Sydney; Together with a Variety of Papers Illustrative of the Industrial Resources of the Country,* Sydney: Thomas Richards, Government Printer, 1871, pp. 3 and 8.

138. *Report of the Royal Commission for the Colonial and Indian Exhibition, London, 1886,* English Parliamentary Papers, 1887 [c. 5083], xx., 1., p. xxxv.

139. "Arrangements Made by the Board of Customs to Admit Foreign and Colonial Productions, for the Purposes of the Exhibition of 1851, Without Payment of Duty," *Exhibition of Industry of All Nations. To Be Held in 1851. Information for the Use of Foreign Exhibitors,* July 1850, Archives Office of New South Wales, 4/1334.

140. Sir Henry Cole, "Speech at the Distribution of Prizes to the Students of the Nottingham School of Art, 15th January, 1873," in *Fifty Years of Public Work of Sir Henry Cole,* vol. 2, p. 347.

141. *The Industrial Progress of New South Wales,* p. 8.

142. Edward Huybers, *From Birth to Borderland (An Eighty-Five Year Life-Story),* Mitchell Library, State Library of New South Wales, MSS 1423, pp. 93–95.

143. Harold Hartley, *Eighty-Eight Not Out: A Record of Happy Memories,* London: Frederick Muller, 1939, pp. 57–63.

144. *Statesman and Friend of India,* March 13, 1884, p. 2, and March 16, 1884, p. 2. Joubert was defended by "A Native of Bengal" in *Statesman and Friend of India,* March 14, 1884, p. 2.

145. *Statesman and Friend of India,* February 28, 1884, p. 3.

146. December 4, 1883, *Kipling Correspondence, John Lockwood Kipling Papers,* Sussex University Archives, Sussex University Library, Box 3/File 8.

147. "List of Promoters," *Adelaide Jubilee International Exhibition, 1887. Report of Juries and Official List of Awards,* Adelaide: H. F. Leader, 1889, p. 6; and "List of Subscribers," *Sydney International Exhibition, 1879, Papers,* Mitchell Library, State Library of New South Wales.

148. *Journal of the Royal Society of Arts* 33 (1886), p. 1132.

149. *Report of the Royal Commission for the Colonial and Indian Exhibition,* p. xxviii; and "Further Correspondence Respecting the Colonial and Indian Exhibition: Preliminary List of Guarantors," *Queensland Votes and Proceedings,* 1885 (vol. 1), pp. 7–9.

150. *Royal Society of Arts Correspondence and Papers,* Corporation Library of London, A/RSA/3/D/9 [1862], pp. 36–37.

151. A. J. P. Taylor, "William Cobbett," in *Essays in English History,* New York: Penguin Books, 1976, pp. 49–53.

152. *North British Review* 15 (August 1851), pp. 273–94.

153. Anthony Hyman, *Charles Babbage, Pioneer of the Computer,* Princeton, NJ: Princeton University Press, 1982; and "Babbage, Charles (1792–1871)," in *Dictionary of National Biography,* vol. 1, New York: Cambridge University Press, 1921–22, pp. 776–78.

154. Babbage, *The Exposition of 1851,* pp. v–vi.

155. Ibid., pp. vii–viii, 189.

156. Charles Babbage, *Passages from the Life of a Philosopher,* London: Longman, Green, Longman, Roberts, and Green, 1864, pp. 158–61; emphasis in original.

157. *Bee-Hive,* November 15, 1862, p. 1.

158. *Passages from the Life of a Philosopher,* pp. 158–61.

159. *Mechanics' Magazine,* February 2, 1850, pp. 29–33, and March 2, 1850, pp. 168–69.

160. Richard Yeo, "Science and Intellectual Authority in Mid-Nineteenth Century Britain: Robert Chambers and *Vestiges of the Natural History of Creation,*" *Victorian Studies* 28 (1984), pp. 5–31.

161. "An Exhibition of the Society of Arts," *Mechanics' Magazine,* April 12, 1861, pp. 243–44.

162. The editors overcame their disgust for the commissioners and provided "Notes" from South Kensington on a variety of exhibition topics, such as the opening ceremonies, colonial raw materials, and machinery. The mechanical and industrial advantages to be gained were promised "in spite of blunders, incapacity, and folly" on the part of organizers, contractors, and commissioners (April 18, 1862, p. 270).

163. *Bee-Hive*, November 15, 1862, p. 1.

164. *Bee-Hive*, October 4, 1862, p. 7.

165. *Bee-Hive*, November 15, 1862, p. 1.

166. *Reynold's Newspaper*, May 9, 1886, p. 4, September 26, 1886, p. 4, and November 21, 1886, p. 4.

167. *Clarion*, April 28, 1911, p. 4, and May 26, 1911, p. 4.

168. W. L. Burn, *The Age of Equipoise: A Study of the Mid-Victorian Generation*, New York: W. W. Norton, 1965; Philip Corrigan and Derek Sayer, *The Great Arch: English State Formation as Cultural Revolution*, New York: Basil Blackwell, 1985; Poovey, *Making a Social Body*; and F. M. L. Thompson, *The Rise of Respectable Society: A Social History of Victorian Britain, 1830–1900*, Cambridge, MA: Harvard University Press, 1988.

169. "At the Great Exhibition," *Cornhill Magazine* 5 (1862), p. 666.

170. Graeme Davison, "Festivals of Nationhood: the International Exhibitions," in S. L. Goldberg and F. B. Smith, eds., *Australian Cultural History*, New York: Cambridge University Press, 1988, pp. 158–77.

171. Victor G. Kiernan, "After Empire," in Harvey J. Kaye, ed., *Imperialism and Its Contradictions*, New York: Routledge, 1995, p. 198.

CHAPTER 4.   CONSUMERS, PRODUCERS, AND MARKETS

1. *Proceedings, Royal Colonial Institute* 10 (1878–79), pp. 6–7.

2. More pragmatic and cool-headed politicians, including William Gladstone, also visited and enjoyed the exhibition, but responded that it could not be easily "turned" in such a direction. March 22, 1886, *Hansard's Parliamentary Debates*, 3rd series, vol. 303 (1886), pp. 1500–1.

3. John Forbes Watson, *International Exhibitions*, London: Henry S. King, 1873; and John Forbes Royle, *Paris Universal Exhibition. Report of Indian and Colonial Products, Useful as Food and For Manufactures*, London: George E. Eyre and William Spottiswoode, 1857, p. 5.

4. *Journal of Industry* (Adelaide), March 1911, p. 5.

5. John G. Knight, *Companion to the Official Catalogue. Guide to the Inter-Colonial Exhibition of 1866*, Melbourne: Blundell and Ford, 1866, p. 11.

6. E. C. Buck, "On the Utility of Exhibitions to India," *Asiatic Quarterly Review* 2 (1886), pp. 306–23.

7. *A Hand-Book of Indian Products. (Art-Manufactures and Raw Materials.) by T. N. Mukharji, Author of "A Rough List of Indian Art-Ware" and "A Descriptive Catalogue of Indian Products contributed to the Amsterdam Exhibition,"* Calcutta: C. J. A. Pritchard at the "Star" Press, 1883, pp. 1–2.

8. *Report of the Bombay Chamber of Commerce, 1881–1882*, pp. 137–38, 248–50.

9. Walter H. Harris to Sir Henry Bergne, Foreign Office, December 20, 1894, *List of Confidential Papers Relating to Foreign Affairs*, Public Record Office, Kew, PRO FO 881/6543, no. 6543. Harris was a former Sheriff of London, a royal commissioner for the 1893 Chicago Columbian Exposition, and a mem-

ber of the official committees for the Antwerp and Tasmanian International Exhibitions in the early 1890s.

10. Charles Babbage, *The Exposition of 1851; or, Views of the Industry, the Science, and the Government of England*, 2nd ed., London: John Murray, 1851, p. 42.

11. "The International Exhibition: Its Purposes and Prospects," *Blackwood's Edinburgh Magazine* 91 (1862), pp. 473–78.

12. *Imperial Federation Journal* 1 (1886), p. 291.

13. Patrick Geddes, *Industrial Exhibitions and Modern Progress*, Edinburgh: David Douglas, 1887, p. 7.

14. *Proceedings, Royal Colonial Institute* 10 (1878–79), p. 12.

15. *Bombay Telegraph and Courier*, March 1, 1855, p. 415.

16. Alexander Hunter, *Suggestions for the Establishment of a School of Industrial Arts at Lahore, Prepared at the Request of His Excellency Sir Robert Montgomery, K.C.B., Lieut.-Governor of the Punjab, 1863*, Oriental and India Office Collections, British Library, TR 633, p. 35.

17. *Times*, July 16, 1886, p. 8; and *Reminiscences of the Colonial and Indian Exhibition. A Lecture Delivered by John McCarthy, Government Analyst and Professor of Chemistry, Trinidad. And published for use in the schools of the Island, by direction of His Excellency, Sir W. Robinson, K.C.M.G., Governor, etc.*, Port-of-Spain: Government Printer, 1887, p. 4.

18. For the imperial contours and consequences of the nineteenth-century world economy, see Eric J. Hobsbawm, *Industry and Empire: From 1750 to the Present Day*, New York: Penguin Books, 1990; Barrie M. Ratcliffe, ed., *Great Britain and Her World, 1750–1914. Essays in Honour of W. O. Henderson*, Manchester: Manchester University Press, 1975; and Luke Trainor, *British Imperialism and Australian Nationalism: Manipulation, Conflict and Compromise in the Late Nineteenth Century*, New York: Cambridge University Press, 1994.

19. "Collection of Specimens for Great Exhibition, 1862," *Exhibition Correspondence, Department of Public Works*, Victorian Public Record Office, 2/585.

20. *Catalogue of the Victorian Exhibition, 1861; with Prefatory Essays, Indicating the Progress, Resources, and Physical Characteristics of the Colony*, Melbourne: John Ferres, Government Printer, 1861, pp. 9–10.

21. *Proceedings of the Madras Central Committee, for the Exhibition of the Industry and Art of All Nations, held in London in the Year 1851*, Madras: Fort St. George Gazette Press, 1853, pp. 1–2.

22. John Forbes Royle, "Observations on Provincial Exhibitions and the Improvement of the Resources of the Several Districts of the Madras Presidency," *Madras Journal of Literature and Science* n.s. 2 (1857), pp. 64–79, 171–72.

23. John Forbes Royle, *The Fibrous Plants of India Fitted for Cordage, Clothing, and Paper, with an Account of the Cultivation and Preparation of Flax, Hemp, and their Substitutes*, London: Smith, Elder, 1855, pp. v–ix.

24. John Forbes Royle, *Paris Universal Exposition. Report on Indian and*

Colonial Products, Useful as Food and for Manufactures, London: Eyre and Spottiswoode, 1857.

25. For example, see "Report by the Chairman of the Sub-Committee for External Arrangements," in *Report of the Nagpore Exhibition of Arts, Manufactures, and Produce, December 1865,* Nagpore: Central Provinces' Printing Press, 1866, pp. 21–28.

26. Lyall to Rivett-Carnac, April 14, 1969, *Lyall Papers,* Oriental and India Office Collections, MSS Eur. F 132/13A (Part I).

27. *Illustrated London News,* August 9, 1862, p. 168.

28. *Correspondence re. Victorian Exhibition, 1861,* La Trobe Collection, State Library of Victoria, Box 122/2, fols. 84–85, 90–91, 97.

29. Edward D. S. Ogilvie, *Diary of Travels in Three Quarters of the Globe, by an Australian Settler,* vol. 2, London: Saunders and Otley, 1856, p. 381.

30. "The Great International Exhibition of 1862," in William Westgarth, *The Colony of Victoria: Its History, Commerce and Gold Mining; Its Social and Political Institutions; Down to the End of 1863. With Remarks, Incidental and Comparative, Upon the Other Australian Colonies,* London: Sampson Low, Son, and Marston, 1864, pp. 388–93.

31. "Geology of Queensland as Represented at London Exhibition, 1871," *Queensland Votes and Proceedings,* 1st session, 1871–72, p. 3.

32. *Graphic,* June 5, 1886, pp. 602, 609.

33. *Colonial and Indian Exhibition Letterbook, Volume I, 1885–1886. Out-Letters of Executive Commissioner for South Australia,* Public Record Office of South Australia, GRG 55/11/1, fols. 23, 40–41, 50–55.

34. *Minutes of the Meetings of the Executive Committee for the Greater Britain and Paris Exhibitions, 1898–1901,* Victoria Public Record Office, 1565, p. 126.

35. Ibid., pp. 99–100, 113.

36. November 30, 1850, *Despatches to the Court of Directors, London from New South Wales, 1850–1852,* Australian Agricultural Company Papers, Noel Butlin Archives Center, Australian National University, Canberra, 78/1/20, fols. 37–38.

37. Court of Directors to General Superintendent, May 27, 1861, *Despatches to New South Wales,* Australian Agricultural Company Papers, 78/3/5, no. 146, fols. 228–29.

38. Despatch No. 148, July 26, 1861, ibid., fol. 257.

39. Despatch No. 169, November 26, 1862, ibid., fol. 451.

40. May 22, September 21, November 22 and enclosure, 1866, *Despatches to London Secretary from New South Wales, 1866,* Australian Agricultural Company Papers, 78/1/39, fols. 113, 232–33, 274–78.

41. R. Edmond Malone, *Three Years' Cruise in the Australasian Colonies,* London: Richard Bentley, 1854, p. 129.

42. Ogilvie, *Diary of Travels in Three Quarters,* vol. 2, p. 381.

43. James King, "On the Growth of Wine in New South Wales," *Journal of the Royal Society of Arts* 4 (1856), pp. 575–78.

44. *Royal Society of Arts Correspondence and Papers,* Corporation of London Library, A/RSA/24/W/3–15.

45. "A Paper by Sir William Macarthur on the Products of New South Wales, Prepared for the Paris Universal Exposition of 1855, with Special Reference to the Production of Wine and Wool," Macarthur Papers, vol. 16, Mitchell Library, State Library of New South Wales, D 185, fols. 105–26; *Second Annual Report of the Australasian Botanic and Horticultural Society, 1850,* pp. 1–6; and "Historical Summary of Hunter River," *Colonial Secretary Bundle,* Archives Office of New South Wales, 4/409, pp. 12–13, 22–23.

46. *Sydney Magazine of Science and Art* 1 (1858), pp. 13–14.

47. "Colonial Wines," in *Catalogue of the Natural and Industrial Products of New South Wales Exhibited in the Australian Museum by the Paris Exhibition Commissioners. Sydney, November, 1854,* Sydney: Reading and Wellbank, 1854, p. 83.

48. *International Exhibition, 1862. Report to the Commissioners of Her Majesty's Customs of the Results Obtained in Testing Samples of the Various Wines Exhibited,* London: George E. Eyre and William Spottiswoode, 1863, pp. 5–6.

49. "Class III. Section C.—Wines, Spirits, Beer, and Other Drinks, and Tobacco," in *International Exhibition, 1862. Reports by the Juries of the Subjects in the Thirty-Six Classes Into Which the Exhibition was Divided,* London: William Clowes, 1863, p. 6.

50. "Wine and the Wine Trade," *Edinburgh Review* 126 (1867), pp. 179–204; and Asa Briggs, *Wine for Sale: Victoria Wine and the Liquor Trade, 1860–1984,* Chicago: University of Chicago Press, 1986.

51. *International Exhibition, 1862. Reports by the Juries of the Subjects,* p. 12.

52. "June 14, 1879," and "August 11, 1879," *William Macleay Diary for 1879,* Macleay Museum, University of Sydney, Sydney, pp. 74, 95.

53. "WINE. Some Remarks upon Wine as a Food, and its Production. Paper by Dr. W. L. Cleland, of Adelaide, Read Before The Royal Agricultural and Horticultural Society, Friday, August 27th, 1880," in *Report of the Royal Agricultural and Horticultural Society of South Australia, 1880–1881,* pp. 81–87.

54. Caroline Clark wrote her relatives in England about the success of Australian wines and forwarded one of Bleasdale's essays about the medicinal qualities of the local product. "Things are different now. Thoroughly good wine is made, wine that can be carried freely in our own range of temperature and some that have crossed the tropics and reached England and France and still been very good. We all drink Colonial wine now in preference to any other." December 28, 1867, and April 24, 1868, *Letters written by Francis Clark and his Wife Caroline to their Relatives in England, 1850–1871,* Mortlock Library, State Library of South Australia, PRG 389/1, pp. 11–12.

55. "Wine," in *A Sketch of South Australia for the Melbourne International Exhibition, 1880. Published by Direction of the Royal Commissioners*

for South Australia. With Maps and Statistical Diagrams, Adelaide: E. Spiller, Government Printer, 1880, p. 38.

56. *Proceedings of the Royal Agricultural and Horticultural Society of South Australia, 1883*, p. xiv.

57. "Department 4. Wine," in *By Authority of the Commissioners. Victorian Intercolonial Exhibition, 1875. Preparatory to the Philadelphia Exhibition, 1876. Opened 2nd September, 1875. Official Catalogue of Exhibits*, Melbourne: M'Carron, Bird, 1875, pp. 73–87.

58. "Classes 635–638. Wines, Spirits, Fermented, and other Drinks," in *Official Record of the Sydney International Exhibition, 1879*, Sydney: Thomas Richards, Government Printer, 1881, pp. 863–65.

59. Edward Lonsdale Beckwith, *Practical Notes on Wine, Reprint of Report on Wines for Royal Commissioners for Paris Exposition, 1867*, London: Smith and Elder, 1868, pp. 67–68.

60. Arthur Hodgson, "The Paris Exhibition," and "Australia Revisited, 1874–1889," *Sir Arthur Hodgson Papers, 1850–1889*, vol. 2, Queensland State Library, Film 0073, fols. 230–65.

61. *South Australia Parliamentary Debates*, 1893, pp. 2730, 3878–80, 3895, 3992; and *South Australia Parliamentary Debates*, 1898, p. 257.

62. *Correspondence of Department of Agriculture, Adelaide, to South Australia Wine and Produce Depot, London, 1895–1902*, Mortlock Library, State Library of South Australia, SRG 55/10, pp. 8–9, 124–25.

63. *Report of the Bombay Chamber of Commerce, 1903*, pp. 647–48.

64. *A Hand-Book of Indian Products. (Art-Manufactures and Raw Materials.) by T. N. Mukharji; Government of India, Revenue and Agriculture Department, Classified List of Indian Produce Contributed to the Amsterdam Exhibition, 1883, Compiled by Trailokya Nath Mukharji, Officer in Charge of Indian Exhibits for the Amsterdam Exhibition*, Calcutta: Superintendent of Government Printing, 1883; and T. N. Mukharji, *Art-Manufactures of India, Specially Compiled for the Glasgow International Exhibition, 1888*, Calcutta: Superintendent of Government Printing, 1888.

65. *A Hand-Book of Indian Products*, pp. 1–2.

66. Mukharji, *Art-Manufactures of India*, pp. 7–8.

67. For example, see H. M. Ross, "The Impurity of Indian Wheat," *Calcutta Review* 89 (1889), pp. 64–74; and "Impurities in Indian Wheats," *Board of Trade Journal* 6 (1889), pp. 556–57.

68. John Forbes Royle, *Essay on the Productive Resources of India*, London: W. H. Allen, 1840.

69. *Chambers' Journal of Popular Literature, Science and Arts* 5 (1889), p. 478.

70. Peter Harnetty, "The Cotton Improvement Program in India, 1865–1875," *Agricultural History* 44 (1970), pp. 379–92.

71. John Forbes Royle, *Review of the Measures Which Have Been Adopted in India for the Improved Culture of Cotton*, London: Smith, Elder, 1857,

pp. 84–94; and Sir Richard Temple, *India in 1880*, 3rd ed., London: John Murray, 1881, p. 293.

72. Royle, "Observations on Provincial Exhibitions and the Improvement of the Several Districts of the Madras Presidency," pp. 3–4.

73. D. A. Farnie, "The Cotton Famine in Great Britain," in Ratcliffe, ed., *Great Britain and Her World, 1750–1914*, pp. 153–78.

74. *Bombay Miscellany* 4 (1862), pp. 361, 411–19; and 5 (1863), pp. 458–59.

75. *The Practical Mechanic's Journal Record of the Great Exhibition, 1862*, London: Longman, Green, Longman, and Roberts, 1862, pp. 87–88.

76. *Times*, August 11, 1862, p. 5.

77. *Colonial and Indian Exhibition. Royal Commission and Government of India Silk Court. Descriptive Catalogue*, London: William Clowes and Sons, 1886, pp. 17–18.

78. For a review of the "Swadeshi Movement," see C. A. Bayly, "The Origins of Swadeshi (Home Industry): Cloth and Indian Society, 1700–1930," in Arjun Appadurai, ed., *The Social Life of Things: Commodities in Cultural Perspective*, New York: Cambridge University Press, 1986, pp. 285–321. My thanks to Prof. Antoinette Burton for bringing this essay to my attention.

79. *Indian Textile Journal* 14 (1903), pp. 82, 99; and Partha Mitter, *Art and Nationalism in Colonial India, 1850–1922: Occidental Orientations*, New York: Cambridge University Press, 1994, pp. 249, 284–86.

80. Deepak Kumar, *Science and the Raj, 1857–1905*, New York: Oxford University Press, 1995, esp. pp. 180–227.

81. "Tea, Coffee and Tobacco," in Frank Cundall, ed., *Reminiscences of the Colonial and Indian Exhibition, illustrated by Thomas Riley, Designer of the Exhibition Diploma*, London: William Clowes and Sons, 1886, p. 34; and Benjamin Rose, ed., *Paris Universal Exhibition, 1900. Report of the Indian Section*, London: George E. Eyre and William Spottiswoode, 1901, pp. 87–88.

82. *The International Health Exhibition, 1884. The District Railway Exhibition Guide: A Popular Summary and Review*, London: Alfred Boot and Son, 1884, pp. 56, 59–63.

83. *Annual Report of the Calcutta Chamber of Commerce, 1880–1881*, pp. 9–10; and *Report of the Committee of the Bengal Chamber of Commerce, 1880*, pp. 165–71.

84. Indian coffee planters argued before the 1900 Paris Universal Exposition that they were "of almost equal importance to the tea industry" and therefore should receive similar "liberal" government grants for exhibition displays. Trade created by exhibits and samples might help pull the coffee industry out of its "state of extraordinary depression." "Representation of the Indian Coffee Industry at Paris Exhibition, 1900, Madras, 19th December 1899," *Proceedings of the Department of Revenue and Agriculture*, Oriental and India Office Collections, P/5902, pp. 11–12.

85. *Assam Company. Minutes of Proceedings in India, Volume 5, 1849–1851*, Guildhall Library, London, MS 9925/5.

86. *Assam Company. Minutes of Proceedings in India, Volume 6, 1851–1853,* Guildhall Library, MS 9925/6; and "Lecture VI. On Substances Used as Food, Illustrated by the Great Exhibition by John Lindley, Ph.D., F.R.S.," in *Lectures on the Progress of Arts and Science, Resulting from the Great Exhibition in London, delivered before the Society of Arts, Manufactures and Commerce, at the Suggestion of H.R.H. Prince Albert,* New York: A. S. Barnes, 1854, pp. 174–75.

87. *Madras Journal of Literature and Science* n.s. 2 (1857), p. 169.

88. *Indian Tea Association Papers and Annual Reports,* Oriental and India Office Collections, MSS Eur. F. 174/1–11; and Percival Joseph Griffiths, *The History of the Indian Tea Industry,* London: Weidenfeld and Nicolson, 1967.

89. *Report on the Indian Section, Franco-British Exhibition 1908,* London: Eyre and Spottiswoode, 1909, pp. 18–19.

90. Indian Tea Exports to Australia in lbs./annum:

1883	696,474
1884	1,029,463
1885	1,867,925

Source: *Indian Tea Districts Association Fourth Annual Report,* February 21, 1884, p. 3; *Indian Tea Districts Association Fifth Annual Report,* March 6, 1885, p. 3; and *Indian Tea Districts Association Sixth Annual Report,* March 30, 1886, p. 3.

91. *The International Health Exhibition. The District Railway Exhibition Guide,* pp. 56, 59–63.

92. *Times,* April 7, 1884, p. 5.

93. *Graphic,* June 14, 1884, p. 570.

94. *Indian Tea Districts Association Fourth Annual Report,* February 21, 1884, pp. 3–4; and *Indian Tea Districts Fifth Annual Report,* March 6, 1885, pp. 2–3.

95. *The International Health Exhibition, 1884. The District Railway Guide to the Exhibition,* p. 63.

96. *Report on the Indian Section, Colonial and Indian Exhibition, 1886,* Oriental and India Office Collections, P/W 812, pp. 13–14.

97. *Indian Tea Districts Association Sixth Annual Report,* March 30, 1886, p. 3; and *Indian Tea Districts Association Seventh Annual Report,* March 29, 1887, p. 2.

98. *Colonial and Indian Exhibition, 1886. Official Catalogue,* London: William Clowes and Sons, 1886, pp. 84–85.

99. "The Indian Tea Association" (London) and "American and Foreign Tea Committee" Papers for 1896, *Indian Tea Association Papers,* Oriental and India Office Collections, MSS Eur. F. 174/11; and *Indian Tea Districts Association Tenth Annual Report,* June 16, 1890, pp. 2–3.

100. *Assam Company. Minutes of Proceedings in India, Volume 6, 1851–1853,* pp. 94–95.

101. *James Inglis Papers*, Mitchell Library, State Library of New South Wales, MSS 2331; and "Inglis, James (1845–1908)," in *Australian Dictionary of Biography, Volume 4, 1851–1890: D–J*, Melbourne: Melbourne University Press, 1972, pp. 457–58.

102. *Sydney International Exhibition, 1879. Official Catalogue of Exhibits*, Sydney: Foster and Fairfax, 1879, p. 19; and May 23 and October 27, 1881, *Correspondence, Melbourne International Exhibition, 1880*, Victoria Public Record Office, 4363/12, Letters nos. 39 and 70.

103. James Inglis, *The Story of the Tea Trade*, Sydney: William Brooks, 1901, esp. pp. 48–55.

104. *Report on the Melbourne International Exhibition, 1880–1881*, Oriental and India Office Collections, W2012, p. 1.

105. Tea exports from Indian Tea Association members to Australia in lbs./year:

1870	52,002
1880	807,608
1885	1,766,447
1890	5,118,714
1895	10,438,984

Source: *Detailed Report of the General Committee of the Indian Tea Association for the Year 1911*, Calcutta: Criterion Printing Works, 1912, p. 208; *Indian Tea Association Papers*, Oriental and India Office Collections, MSS Eur. F. 174/14.

106. G. Bidie, *Catalogue of Articles Collected and Forwarded, Under the Orders of the Government of Madras, to the Melbourne International Exhibition of 1880*, Madras: E. Keys, 1880.

107. *Statesman and Friend of India*, December 23, 1892, p. 2.

108. *Indian Tea Districts Association Tenth Annual Report*, June 16, 1890, p. 3; and *Indian Tea Districts Association Thirteenth Annual Report*, July 17, 1893, p. 2.

109. *Indian Tea Districts Association Fourteenth Annual Report*, June 11, 1894, pp. 2–3.

110. *The 30th Annual Report by the Committee of the Melbourne Chamber of Commerce, May 1881*, Melbourne: Mason, Firth and Mc'Cutcheon, 1881, pp. 15–16.

111. *Sydney International Exhibition, 1879. India: Official Catalogue of Exhibits*, Sydney: Foster and Fairfax, 1879, esp. pp. 7, 21–24.

112. Jules Joubert, *Shavings and Scrapes in Many Parts*, 2nd ed., Hobart: A. S. Gordon, 1894, pp. 198–99.

113. *Town and Country Journal* (Sydney), April 17, 1875, p. 6.

114. Joubert, *Shavings and Scrapes*, p. 221.

115. H. H. Risley, "Report on the Calcutta International Exhibition, October, 1885," *Revenue and Agriculture Department Proceedings*, Oriental and India Office Collections, P/2490, p. 2.

116. *Statesman and Friend of India,* January 18, 1883, p. 2.

117. *Melbourne Chamber of Commerce Minute Book, 1878–1886,* La Trobe Collection, State Library of Victoria, MS 10917, pp. 329–30, 333.

118. "Chairman's Address," *Thirty-Third Annual Report of the South Australian Chamber of Commerce, April 1883,* p. 8.

119. *Calcutta Review* 78 (1884), pp. 348–49.

120. Ibid., p. 358.

121. P. G. King to Sir Edward C. Buck, November 2, 1888, *Peel River Land and Mineral Company Correspondence,* Noel Butlin Archives Center, 78/15/27.

122. Governor Loftus to Earl of Derby, Secretary of State for the Colonies, October 2, 1883, *Home Correspondence,* volume 39, no. 179, Archives Office of New South Wales, 4/1647, fol. 40.

123. *Calcutta Exhibition Letterbook, 1883. Auditor-General's Department,* Public Record Office of South Australia, GRG 44/64, pp. 28–29, 80–81.

124. *Report to the Hon. R. D. Ross, Chairman of the South Australian Committee for the Calcutta International Exhibition, 1883–1884,* Mortlock Library, State Library of South Australia.

125. "Paris Exhibition of 1867. Jury Reports on the New South Wales Products," *New South Wales Legislative Assembly Votes and Proceedings,* 1868–69 (vol. 2), p. 2.

126. Marc Rothenberg and Peter Hoffenberg, "Australia at the 1876 Exhibition in Philadelphia," *Historical Records of Australian Science* 8 (1990), pp. 55–62.

127. *Catalogue of Victorian Exhibits Prepared for the New Orleans Universal Exposition and World's Fair, 1884–1885,* Melbourne: John Ferres, 1885.

128. "The Imperial Connection," *Colonial Magazine* (Melbourne) 4 (1869), p. 108.

129. *Sydney International Exhibition, Executive Commissioner's Letter Book, No. 3, 1879–1881,* Archives Authority of New South Wales, 7/404, pp. 484–86.

130. "Outward Correspondence, 1873–1880," *Melbourne Chamber of Commerce Papers,* La Trobe Collection, State Library of Victoria, MS 485289, pp. 396–98, 400–1.

131. *Melbourne Chamber of Commerce Minute Book, 1878–1886,* La Trobe Collection, MS 10917.

132. "Outward Correspondence, 1873–1880," *Melbourne Chamber of Commerce Papers,* pp. 402–3.

133. Lord Granville to Lord Odo Russell, June 23, 1880, *British Embassy, Berlin: Commercial, 1880, Foreign Office Correspondence, Prussia and Germany,* Public Record Office, Kew, PRO FO 64/965; and Colonial Office to Foreign Office, June 21, 1880, *Various: Commercial and Domestic, Foreign Office Correspondence, Prussia and Germany,* Public Record Office, Kew, PRO FO 64/969.

134. Foreign Office to W. Beauclerk, August 14, 1889, *To British Embassy,*

Berlin: Commercial, Foreign Office, Correspondence, Prussia and Germany, Public Record Office, Kew, PRO FO 64/1217.

135. September 30, 1891, Chamber of Manufactures to Premier, *Papers in Connection with Chicago Exhibition,* Archives Authority of New South Wales, 1226/33.

136. *General Correspondence of the London Office, September–October, 1898, Archives of the Commission, Paris Exhibition, 1900,* Foreign Office Papers, Public Record Office, Kew, PRO FO 311/1A/10, fols. 8–9.

137. H. W. Venn to Royal Commission, August 18, 1900, *General Correspondence of the London Office, February–August, 1900. Archives of the Commission, Paris Exhibition, 1900,* PRO FO 311/1A/12.

138. Paul Greenhalgh, "Art, Politics, and Society at the Franco-British Exhibition of 1908," *Art History* 8 (1985), pp. 434–52; and Annie E. Coombes, *Reinventing Africa: Museums, Material Culture and Popular Imagination in Late Victorian and Edwardian England,* New Haven, CT: Yale University Press, 1994, pp. 187–213.

139. *Chambers' Edinburgh Journal* n.s., 15 (1851), p. 337.

140. *Victoria Parliamentary Debates,* 1867, p. 1357.

141. *Report of the Committee of the Bengal Chamber of Commerce, 1880,* pp. 165–71.

142. "The Imperial Connection," pp. 107–8.

143. Critics drew upon the cultural and intellectual traditions discussed in Stefan Collini, *Public Moralists: Political Thought and Intellectual Life in Britain, 1850–1930,* New York: Oxford University Press, 1991; and Raymond Williams, *Culture and Society: 1780–1950,* 2nd ed., New York: Columbia University Press, 1983.

144. Thomas Carlyle to Alexander Carlyle, October 10, 1851, in Edwin W. Marrs, Jr., ed., *The Letters of Thomas Carlyle to His Brother Alexander, with Related Family Matters,* Cambridge, MA: The Belknap Press of Harvard University Press, 1968, p. 684.

145. Carlyle to Emerson, July 8, 1851, in Slater, ed., *The Correspondence of Emerson and Carlyle,* p. 468.

146. Carlyle to Emerson, August 25, 1851, ibid., p. 473.

147. Thomas Carlyle to Alexander Carlyle, October 10, 1851, *The Letters of Thomas Carlyle to His Brother Alexander,* pp. 683–87.

148. Thomas Carlyle to Alexander Carlyle, October 24, 1851, ibid., p. 687.

149. *Friend of the People,* December 7, 1850, p. 2.

150. *Friend of the People,* May 10, 1851, pp. 189–90; emphasis in original.

151. *Friend of the People,* March 29, 1851, p. 123.

152. *Friend of the People,* February 1851, p. 59.

153. *Friend of the People,* March 1, 1851, p. 92.

154. There are two interesting footnotes on the relationship between Harney and exhibitions: he applied for a position with Owen Jones at the rebuilt Crystal Palace in Sydenham, turning to Louis Blanc for the necessary letter of introduction, and, several years later, he wrote Engels that he looked forward

to attending the Colonial and Indian Exhibition at South Kensington. Harney extended his stay in London for that purpose. See Louis Blanc to G. Julian Harney, March 10, 1854, and G. Julian Harney to Frederick Engels, August 26, 1886, in Frank Gees Black and Renee Metivier Black, eds., *The Harney Papers*, Assen: Van Gorcum, 1969, pp. 12, 312–13.

155. *Commonweal, the Official Journal of the Socialist League* 2 (1886), pp. 49–50.

156. Edward W. Said, *Culture and Imperialism*, New York: Alfred A. Knopf, 1993, p. 241; Edward Palmer Thompson, *William Morris: Romantic to Revolutionary*, 2nd ed., New York: Pantheon Books, 1977, pp. 296–305, 451–460; and Merryn Williams, "The Prophet of Kelmscott," *New Left Review* 212 (1995), p. 125.

CHAPTER 5.   *TERRAE NULLIUS?*

1. *Athenaeum* no. 1420 (January 13, 1855), p. 53.

2. John Tallis, *Tallis's History and Description of the Crystal Palace and the Exhibition of the World's Industry in 1851*, vol. 1, London: The London Printing and Publishing Company, 1852, p. 53.

3. "V. British Possessions in Australasia," in *Great Exhibition of the Works of Industry of All Nations, 1851. Official Descriptive and Illustrated Catalogue, Volume II. Section IV., Colonies*, London: W. Clowes and Sons, Printers, 1851, pp. 988–92.

4. For example, see Sir T. L. Mitchell to General Blunt, December 30, 1854, *Mitchell Papers, Volume 5, 1850–57*, Mitchell Library, State Library of New South Wales, Sydney, A 294 and "Colonial Division," in *Paris Universal Exposition, 1855. Catalogue of the Works Exhibited in the British Section of the Exhibition*, London: Chapman and Hall, 1855, esp. pp., 99, 132, 135.

5. William Westgarth, *Victoria and The Australian Gold Mines in 1857; With Notes on the Overland Route from Australia, via Suez*, London: Smith, Elder, 1857, pp. 97–99.

6. *Athenaeum* no. 1420, p. 53.

7. *Calcutta Review* 26 (1856), pp. 265–66. The editors concluded, "These defects appear to have been in a great measure remedied at the Paris Exhibition of 1855."

8. Sir Richard Temple, *Men and Events of My Time in India*, 2nd ed., London: John Murray, 1882, pp. 163, 165.

9. For example, see George Frederick Pardon, ed., *A Guide to the International Exhibition; with Plans of the Building, An Account of its Rise, Progress and Completion, and Notices of its Principal Contents*, London: Routledge, Warne and Routledge, 1862, pp. 58–61.

10. *Proceedings, Royal Colonial Institute* 10 (1878–79), pp. 14–18, 21.

11. *Illustrated London News*, May 8, 1886, p. 495.

12. For example, compare the descriptions of Canada, New Zealand, and India in Goldwin Smith, *The Empire. A Series of Letters Published in 'The Daily*

News,' *1862, 1863*, London: John Henry and James Parker, 1863, pp. 95–203, 257–97; and J. R. Seeley, *The Expansion of England* [1883], Chicago: University of Chicago Press, 1971, pp. 143–215.

13. John Ruskin, *The Two Paths; Being Lectures on Art, and its Application to Decoration and Manufacture, Delivered in 1858–1859*, London: Smith, Elder, 1859.

14. Ibid., esp. "Lecture I: The Deteriorative Power of Conventional Art Over Nations. An Inaugural Lecture, Delivered at the Kensington Museum, 1858."

15. Ibid., p. 16.

16. Ibid., p. 14.

17. Sir William Thomas Denison, *Address to Members of Australian Agricultural and Horticultural Societies*, Sydney: Reading and Wellbank, 1855.

18. For example, see the exhibition correspondence and papers collected in *Journal of the Legislative Council of New South Wales* 13 (1865–66), pp. 181–200.

19. Samuel Davenport to Sir Henry Young, Letter A (1850), Public Record Office of South Australia, GRG 24/1.

20. "Canada and Australia," in *A Visit to the Great Exhibition, 1851*, National Art Library, Victoria and Albert Museum, London, 400.A.16, p. 10; and Robert Hunt, Esq., "The Science of the Exhibition," in *The Art-Journal Illustrated Catalogue of the Industry of Nations, 1851*, London: George Virtue, 1851, p. IV* (page no. as in source).

21. *Catalogue of Exhibits in the New South Wales Annexe of the Exhibition, London International, 1871*, Sydney: Government Printer, 1871.

22. Sir Daniel Cooper to Charles Kemp, September 26, 1862, Mitchell Library, State Library of New South Wales, AK 43/3.

23. *Argus*, October 12, 1850, p. 3.

24. *Paris Universal International Exhibition Letterbook*, vol. 6, Victoria Public Record office, 927, pp. 1–6.

25. *Illustrated London News*, July 3, 1862, p. 21; *Paris Universal Exhibition of 1867. Catalogue of Contributions from the Colony of Natal*, London: Jarrold and Sons, 1868; and *Reminiscences of the Colonial and Indian Exhibition. A Lecture Delivered by John McCarthy, Government Analyst and Professor of Chemistry, Trinidad. And Published for Use in the Schools of the Island, by Direction of His Excellency, Sir W. Robinson, KCMG, Governor, Etc.*, Port-of-Spain: Government Printing Office, 1887, pp. 15–17.

26. Yankee and Saxon books, machinery, tools, woods, and grains in the Canadian court were contrasted with "rather useless [Indian] articles" at the Colonial and Indian Exhibition; see *Reminiscences of the Colonial and Indian Exhibition*, pp. 15–17.

27. *The International Exhibition of 1862. The Illustrated Catalogue of the Industrial Department. Volume III. Colonial and Foreign Divisions*, London: George E. Eyre and William Spottiswoode, 1862, pp. 52, 68, 70.

28. "We flatter ourselves that what with the Gold Nuggets-wool-cotton-

iron-copper-and coal-not to mention the Australian Propellor-(Still thought highly of here)-we shall make a goodly display." Mitchell to Blunt, December 30, 1854, *Mitchell Papers*, p. 419.

29. "Report on the 1862 London International Exhibition," *Chief Secretary's Office, Registered Inward Correspondence re. Exhibitions, 1856–1858 and 1860–1863*, Victoria Public Record Office, 1189/750.

30. *Times*, November 10, 1886, p. 4.

31. *Brisbane Courier*, August 10, 1886, p. 5, and September 14, 1886, p. 5.

32. *Illustrated London News*, August 28, 1886, pp. 236–37.

33. "Energy," in Graeme Davison, J. S. McCarty, and Ailsa McLeary, eds., *Australians/1888*, Sydney: Fairfax, Syme, and Weldon Associates, 1987, pp. 69–76; and "Mining," *Australians/1888*, pp. 169–83.

34. *Chamber's Edinburgh Journal*, 15 (1851), p. 339; and *Great Exhibition of the Works of Industry of All Nations, 1851. Official Descriptive and Illustrated Catalogue, Volume I*, London: W. Clowes and Sons, 1851, p. 110. For more extended descriptions and discussions of British India's displays at the Great Exhibition, see "British Possessions in Asia. India-Ceylon. East Indies," in *Official Descriptive and Illustrated Catalogue. Volume II, Section IV. Colonies*; A. M. Dowleans, ed., *Catalogue of the East Indian Productions Collected in the Presidency of Bengal, and Forwarded to the Exhibition of Works of Art and Industry to be held in London in 1851*, London: W. Thacker, 1851; *Proceedings of the Madras Central Committee, for the Exhibition of the Industry and Art of All Nations, held in London in the Year 1851*, Madras: St. George Gazette Press, 1853; and "Chapter VI. Colonial Departments—India," in Tallis, *Tallis's History and Description of the Crystal Palace*, vol. 1, pp. 31–38.

35. *Aunt Busy-Bee's The Fine Crystal Palace the Prince Built*, London: Dean and Son, 1851, p. 6.

36. *Times*, May 3, 1851, p. 3.

37. *Illustrated London News*, August 11, 1855, pp. 169–70.

38. *Catalogue of the Natural and Industrial Products of New South Wales Exhibited in the Australian Museum by the Paris Exhibition Commissioners. Sydney, November 1854*, Sydney: Reading and Wellbank, 1854, p. 5.

39. Alan Beever, "From a Place of 'Horrible Destitution' to a Paradise of the Working Class: The Transformation of British Working Class Attitudes to Australia, 1841–1851," *Labour History* (Australia) 40 (1981), pp. 1–15; Patrick Brantlinger, "Black Swans; or, Botany Bay Eclogues," in *Rule of Darkness: British Literature and Imperialism, 1830–1914*, Ithaca, NY: Cornell University Press, 1990, pp. 109–33; and Crauford D. W. Goodwin, *The Image of Australia: British Perception of the Australian Economy from the Eighteenth to the Twentieth Century*, Durham, NC: Duke University Press, 1974.

40. Thomas De Quincey, "California and the Gold Mania," in *The Works of Thomas De Quincey*, vol. 10, *Politics and Political Economy*, Boston: Houghton, Mifflin, 1877, pp. 304–46.

41. "Lecture III. On the Raw Materials from the Animal Kingdom by Rich-

ard Owen, F.R.S.," in *Lectures on the Progress of Arts and Science, Resulting from the Great Exhibition in London, delivered before the Society of Arts, Manufactures and Commerce, at the Suggestion of H.R.H. Prince Albert,* New York: A. S. Barnes, 1854, p. 63.

42. Ibid., p. 72.

43. R. E. N. Twopeny, "A Proposal for Holding an Australian Exhibition in London," Sydney, 1883, *Australia Pamphlets,* no. 20, Foreign and Commonwealth Office Library, London, p. 7.

44. William Westgarth, *The Colony of Victoria: Its History, Commerce and Gold Mining; its Social and Political Institutions; Down to the End of 1863. With Remarks, Incidental and Comparative, Upon the Other Australian Colonies,* London: Sampson Low, Son and Marston, 1864, p. 391.

45. *Correspondence re. Victorian Exhibition, 1861,* La Trobe Collection, State Library of Victoria, Box 122/2, fols. 100–2.

46. Sir Redmond Barry to Sir Henry Cole, June 17, 1872, *Redmond Barry Collection,* La Trobe Collection, State Library of Victoria, MS 8380, Box 599/ENV 2; Sir Redmond Barry to Major General Scott, March 21, 1873, *Redmond Barry Collection,* MS 8380, Box 599/2(M); and Sir Redmond Barry to Captain B. Burgess, December 4, 1873, *Redmond Barry Letterbook, 1872–1874,* Victoria Public Record Service, 4367/2, fols. 463–69.

47. William Westgarth, *Victoria; Late Australia Felix, or Port Phillip District of New South Wales; Being An Historical and Descriptive Account of The Colony and its Gold Mines,* London: Simpkin, Marshall, 1863, pp. 340–41.

48. *Department of Public Works. Exhibitions Correspondence: Collection of Specimens for Great Exhibition, 1862,* Victoria Public Record Office, 2/585.

49. *Redmond Barry Letterbook, 1872–1874,* Victoria Public Record Office, 4367/2, fols. 193–94, 207–11, 241–44.

50. *Catalogue of the Natural and Industrial Products of New South Wales, forwarded to the Paris Universal Exposition of 1867, by the New South Wales Exhibition Commissioners,* Sydney: Thomas Richards, Government Printer, 1867, p. 33; and *Paris Universal Exhibition of 1867. Part II. Catalogue of the Works Exhibited in the British Section of the Exhibition,* London: Spottiswoode, 1868, p. 384.

51. After studying frescoes in Rome, Ironside returned to England and painted works purchased by the Prince of Wales. The Dublin Fine Arts Department was "most happy" to exhibit her pictures. For further information, see *Ironside Family Papers,* Mitchell Library, State Library of New South Wales, ML MSS 272.

52. T. A. Murray to Rev. John Lang, June 16, 1866, *Ironside Family Papers,* fols. 133–35.

53. Rev. John Lang to Adelaide E. S. Ironside, June 23 and July 18, 1866, *Ironside Family Papers,* fols. 131, 145.

54. Peter Quartermaine, "International Exhibitions and Emigration: The Photographic Enterprise of Richard Daintree, Agent-General for Queensland,

1872–1876," *Journal of Australian Studies* 13 (1973), pp. 40–55; and *Australasian Sketcher* (Melbourne), April 19, 1873, p. 3, and May 17, 1893, pp. 1, 19.

55. Neil J. Markelyne to Redmond Barry, November 22, 1862, *Letters from Persons of Distinction in Europe, 1860–1869. Redmond Barry Papers*, La Trobe Collection, State Library of Victoria, MS 6333, Box 297/2, fol. 16.

56. *Official Catalogue of the Great Exhibition of the Works of Industry of All Nations, 1851*, London: W. Clowes & Sons, 1851, p. 177; and Colonial Secretary to Surveyor-General, July 6, 1854, *Colonial Secretary Correspondence, 1854*, Archives Office of New South Wales, 2/1506.

57. *Australasian Sketcher* (Melbourne), April 15, 1873, p. 8.

58. "Circular, April 1866," *Exhibition Trustees, Paris International Exhibition Letterbook*, Victoria Public Record Office, 927/6, p. 63.

59. "International Exhibition, 1862. Reports and Enclosures from Commissioners," *Victoria Parliamentary Papers*, 1862–1863 (volume 4).

60. Arthur Blyth to J. F. Conigrave, March 24, 1885, *Letter Book, Colonial and Indian Exhibition, March 1885–March 1886, Volume I*, South Australia Public Records Office, GRG 55/11/1, fols. 16–17.

61. See for example, "Canada and Australia," in *A Visit to the Great Exhibition*, pp. 9–10.

62. "Colonial Contributions," *Colonial Magazine and East India Review* 21 (1851), pp. 521–24.

63. *Reminiscences of the Crystal Palace*, 1852, National Art Library, London, 400.A.114, pp. 118–20.

64. H. Gordon Graham to Under Secretary, Lands Department, July 9, 1908, *Lands Department Correspondence, Queensland Court, Franco-British Exhibition, School Essay on Exhibit*, Queensland State Archives, LAN/AK 40 (B) Batch 16.

65. Twopeny, "A Proposal for Holding an Australian Exhibition in London," pp. 6–7.

66. *Queensland (Australia). The Exhibits and Exhibitors, and Description of the Colony*, Brisbane: James C. Beal, 1878, p. 33.

67. *Paris Universal Exposition Papers, Communications with Intending Exhibitors, 1854*, Archives Authority of New South Wales, 4/411, pp. 9–10; and William Westgarth, ed., *Paris Universal Exposition, 1867. Catalogue of the Victorian Court*, Melbourne: Government Printer, 1968.

68. Westgarth, ed., *Paris Universal Exposition, 1867. Catalogue of the Victorian Court*, p. vii.

69. Robert Colls and Philip Dodd, eds., *Englishness: Politics and Culture, 1880–1920*, New York: Methuen, 1987; and Colin McArthur, "The Dialectic of National Identity: The Glasgow Empire Exhibition of 1938," in Tony Bennett, Colin Mercer, and Janet Wollacott, eds., *Popular Culture and Social Relations*, Milton Keynes: Open University Press, 1986, pp. 117–34.

70. For example, see F. Max Müller, "Cornish Antiquities, 1867," in *Chips from a German Workshop*, vol. 3, New York: Charles Scribner, 1871, pp. 238–

86; and "Remains of the Aboriginal Inhabitants of Ireland," *Gentleman's Magazine and Historical Review* 218 (1865), pp. 707–10.

71. T. A. Murray, "A Description of the Natural and Industrial Products of New South Wales, As Forwarded to the Paris Universal Exposition of 1867 By the New South Wales Commissioners," p. 8, in *Intercolonial Exhibition of Australasia, Melbourne, 1866–67. Official Record, Containing Introduction, Catalogues, Reports, and Awards of the Jurors, Essays and Statistics on the Social and Economic Resources of the Australasian Colonies*, Melbourne: Blundell, 1867.

72. David K. van Keuren, "Museums and Ideology: Augustus Pitt-Rivers, Anthropological Museums, and Social Change in Later Victorian Britain," *Victorian Studies* 28 (1984), pp. 171–89.

73. Twopeny, "A Proposal for Holding an Australian Exhibition in London," p. 6.

74. "London International Exhibition of 1871," *Papers Connected with the Representation of Queensland at the Exhibition. Votes and Proceedings of the Legislative Assembly*, 1871, 2nd session, p. 6.

75. Queensland's commissioners toured the courts at later overseas exhibitions for additional English educational models, curricula, and school architecture. "Report on the Education Section of the Health Exhibition of 1884, Addressed to the Government of Queensland," *Home Office, Despatches Written by the Agent-General, London, 1884*, Queensland State Archives, COL/91/ Files 7313, 7314, 8086.

76. *London International Exhibition, 1862. Catalogue of the Natural and Industrial Products of New South Wales; with a Map and Introductory Account of its Population, Commerce, and General Resources*, London: William Clowes and Sons, 1862, pp. 3–16.

77. *Age*, April 23, 1877, p. 2.

78. *Illustrated Sydney News*, September 7, 1878, p. 10.

79. "Preface," in *Official Catalogue of the Natural and Industrial Products of New South Wales, Forwarded to the International Exhibition of 1876, at Philadelphia*, Sydney: Thomas Richards, Government Printer, 1876.

80. *Age*, April 23, 1877, p. 2.

81. *District Railway, Time Tables and Illustrated Guide, 1886*, Guildhall Library, London, PAM 12494, p. 10.

82. "London International Exhibition, 1874. The Ethnology and Geography of the British Empire," *New South Wales Colonial Secretary Bundle: London International Exhibition*, Archives Office of New South Wales, 4/819.1.

83. Bernth Lindfors, "'The Hottentot Venus' and Other African Attractions in Nineteenth-Century England," *Australasian Drama Studies* 1 (1983), pp. 83–104; and Richard Altick, *The Shows of London*, Cambridge, MA: Harvard University Press, 1978, pp. 268–87.

84. John Conolly, *The Ethnological Exhibitions of London*, London: John Churchill, 1855, 44 pp. This is the text of a paper read at a meeting of the Eth-

nological Society of London and catalogued as Pamphlet 43, *Forster Collection,* National Art Library, London.

85. William A. Drew, *Glimpses and Gatherings, During a Voyage and Visit to London and the Great Exhibition, in the Summer of 1851,* Augusta, ME: Homan and Manley, 1852, p. 328.

86. *Great Exhibition of the Works of Industry of All Nations, 1851. Official Descriptive and Illustrated Catalogue,* vol. 2, London: William Clowes and Sons, 1851, pp. 833–34; and *Morning Chronicle,* February 13, 1855, p. 3.

87. H. H. Cole, *Science and Art Department of the Committee of Council on Education., South Kensington Museum. Catalogue of the Objects of Indian Art Exhibited in the South Kensington Museum,* London: George E. Eyre and William Spottiswoode, 1874, pp. 216A, 218A.

88. "Part I. Ethnology. The Natural History Court," in *Crystal Palace Guidebook, No. 6,* 1854, pp. 5–6, Guildhall Library, London.

89. *Anthropological Review* 5 (1867), pp. 241–42.

90. M. Digby Wyatt, *Views of the Crystal Palace and Park, Sydenham. From Drawings by Eminent Artists, and Photographs by P. H. Delamotte, with a title page and literary notices,* 1st series, London: Day and Son, 1854, p. 12.

91. Paul Greenhalgh, "Human Showcases," in *Ephemeral Vistas: The Exposition Universelles, Great Exhibitions and World's Fairs, 1851–1939,* Dover, NH: Manchester University Press, 1988, pp. 112–41.

92. *District Railway, Time Tables and Illustrated Guide,* p. 20.

93. Rowland Ward to Sir Arthur Blyth, July 20, 1885, *Letter Book, Colonial and Indian Exhibition, March 1885–1886, Volume I. Out-Letters of the Executive Commissioner,* Public Record Office of South Australia, GRG 55/11/1, pp. 130–31.

94. *Graphic,* June 5, 1886, pp. 602, 609.

95. *Graphic,* June 26, 1886, p. 689.

96. Redmond Barry to J. Thomas, August 27 and October 9, 1861, *Exhibition Correspondence,* La Trobe Library, State Library of Victoria, Box 122/2, fols. 162, 189–90.

97. Tom Griffiths, "Past Silences: Aborigines and Convicts in Our History-Making," *Australian Cultural History* 6 (1987), pp. 18–32.

98. "The Exhibits sent from Queensland," in *Queensland (Australia). The Exhibits and Exhibitors, and Description of the Colony,* p. 37.

99. "Section K. Ethnology, Archaeology, and Natural History," in *New South Wales. Official Catalogue of Exhibits from the Colony forwarded to the International Exhibition of 1883–84 at Calcutta,* Sydney: Thomas Richards, Government Printer, 1883, pp. 159–69.

100. Truganini, the last full-blooded Tasmanian, died in 1876, the same year as Custer's Last Stand, the Philadelphia Centennial, and Stanley's voyage down the Congo. For a discussion of Truganini and her death's impact, see Bernard Smith, *The Spectre of Truganini,* Sydney: Australian Broadcasting Commission, 1981.

101. "Ethnological Court and Groups," in *Colonial and Indian Exhibition,*

1886. Official Guide for the Indian Empire, London: William Clowes and Sons, 1886; and *District Railway, Time Tables and Illustrated Guide,* pp. 16–17.

102. *District Railway, Time Tables and Illustrated Guide,* p. 17.

103. "Museums and Exhibitions Branch," *Revenue and Agriculture Department Proceedings,* Oriental and India Office Collections, P/2981, pp. 75–83.

104. "Report of J. C. Tache, Esq., Canadian Commissioner to Paris in 1855," in *Canada at the Universal Exhibition of 1855,* Toronto: John Lovell, 1856, pp. 265–66.

105. *Bombay Telegraph and Courier,* November 20, 1854, p. 2207.

106. *Illustrated London News,* July 13, 1878, pp. 41, 42; and George C. M. Birdwood, *Paris Universal Exhibition of 1878. Handbook to the British Indian Section,* 2nd ed., London: Offices of the Royal Commission, 1878.

107. *Minute Book, United Kingdom. Colonial and Indian Exhibition, 1886,* Registry Papers, Victoria and Albert Museum, London.

108. *Official Report of the Calcutta International Exhibition, 1883–1884,* vol. 2, Calcutta: Bengal Secretariat Press, 1885, p. 110.

109. *Graphic,* March 9, 1878, p. 238; and *Illustrated London News,* July 17, 1886, p. 92.

110. Bernard S. Cohn, "The Transformation of Objects into Artifacts, Antiquities and Art in Nineteenth-Century India," in *Colonialism and Its Forms of Knowledge: The British in India,* Princeton, NJ: Princeton University Press, 1996, pp. 76–105.

111. Sir Archibald Michie, *Readings in Melbourne; with an Essay on the Resources and Prospects of Victoria,* London: Sampson Low, Marston, Searle, and Rivington, 1879, p. 199.

112. Colesworthy Grant, *Anglo-Indian Domestic Life. A Letter from an Artist in India to His Mother in England,* Calcutta: Thacker, Spink, 1862, p. 67.

113. *The Empire of India Exhibition, Earl's Court, S.W., 1895. Illustrated Official Catalogue,* London: J. J. Keliher, 1895, p. 53–67; and *Journal of Indian Art and Industry* 6 (1896), pp. 89–90.

114. Imre Kiralfy, "General Introduction," in *The Empire of India Exhibition,* p. 11.

115. *Indian Court, Festival of Empire, 1911. Guide Book and Catalogue,* London: Bemrose and Sons, 1911, pp. ix–x.

116. *Fifty Years of Public Work of Sir Henry Cole, K.C.B., Accounted for in His Deeds, Speeches and Writings,* vol. 2, London: George Bell and Sons, 1884, p. 348; and Sir Henry Cole, "Suggestions for Collecting Information About the Ancient Architecture of India," in *Miscellanies,* vol. 14, 1865–1868, National Art Library, London, 55 AA 59, fols. 49–51.

117. Cole, "Suggestions for Collecting Information"; and Sir Henry Cole to Lord Mayo, June 10, September 6, and October 22, 1869, *Correspondence with Sir Henry Cole, Mayo Papers,* University of Cambridge Archives, ADD 7490/51 (XI), fols. 147–53.

118. *Fifteenth Report of the Science and Art Department of the Committee of Council on Education,* 1868, pp. xiv, 27–34; *Sixteenth Report of the Sci-*

ence and Art Department of the Committee of Council on Education, 1869, pp. xvi, 50–54; and *Memorandum of Measures Adopted, and Expenditure Incurred, in India, for the Promotion of Literature, Science and Art, Since the Assumption by Her Majesty the Queen of the Direct Government of the Country*, Oriental and India Office Collections, V/27/900/1, pp. 12–13.

119. *Calcutta Review* 11 (1849), p. 92.

120. *Colonial and Indian Exhibition, 1886. Official Guide*, p. 23; and *Graphic*, May 15, 1886, p. 533.

121. *Illustrated London News*, March 5, 1870, pp. 240–41.

122. "Report of the General Superintendent and Director, 1870," and "Report of the General Superintendent and Director, 1871," in *Sir Henry Cole Papers, Miscellanies, Volume 17, 1845–1875*, National Art Library, London, 55 AA 62, fols. 52–53, 69.

123. *Nelson's Pictorial Guide-Books. The International Exhibition, 1871*, London: T. Nelson and Sons, 1871, p. 13; and *Graphic*, May 6, 1871, p. 423.

124. Mr. T. Rogers, "Report on Architectural Designs," in *Reports on the International Exhibition of 1871, Part III*, London: George E. Eyre and William Spottiswoode, 1872, pp. 62–63.

125. *Memorandum of Measures Adopted, and Expenditure Incurred, in India, for the Promotion of Literature, Science and Art*, pp. 12–13. Facing financial limitations, the government of India reduced its contributions, and only four casts were constructed. South Kensington received three (since the Science and Art Department contributed 75 percent of the funds) and officers of the government of India presented the fourth cast to their French colleagues. Herman Merivale offered assistance with the castings, if copies could be "done well, cheaply and promptly." He reminded Cole that the Raj faced a variety of demands (including famine relief) on its financial resources. Herman Merivale to Henry Cole, December 7, 1869, *Correspondence with Sir Henry Cole, Lord Mayo Papers*, University of Cambridge Archives, ADD MS 7490/51 (XI), fols. 152a–b.

126. Sir Henry Cole to Lord Mayo, October 22, 1869, *Correspondence with Sir Henry Cole, Lord Mayo Papers*, University of Cambridge Archives, ADD 7490/51 (XI), fol. 150.

127. *Illustrated London News*, July 10, 1886, p. 54; and *Journal of Indian Art and Industry* 2 (1888), p. 111–12.

128. *Builder*, 51 (1886), p. 10A.

129. *Colonial and Indian Exhibition, 1886. Official Guide*, London: William Clowes and Sons, 1886, pp. 15–17.

130. "In his grammar of ornament Jones declares that it is an anachronism to reproduce the forms of the past into the art of the present." J. B. Keith in *Journal of Indian Art and Industry* 2 (1888), p. 111.

131. Thomas R. Metcalf, *The Aftermath of Revolt India, 1857–1870*, New Delhi: Manohar, 1990.

132. *Journal of Indian Art and Industry* 2 (1888), pp. 110–12.

133. Sir Henry Maine, *The Effects of the Observation of India on Modern European Thought. Rude Lectures, May 22, 1875,* London: John Murray, 1875. For changes in the idea and image of "the village community," see Clive Dewey, "Images of the Village Community: A Study in Anglo-Indian Ideology," *Modern Asian Studies* 6 (1972), pp. 291–328; and Louis Dumont, "The 'Village Community' from Munro to Maine," *Contributions to Indian Sociology* 9 (1966), pp. 67–89.

134. George M. Birdwood, *Report on the Government Central Museum and the Agricultural and Horticultural Society of Western India for 1863. With Appendices, being the Establishment of the Victorian and Albert Museum and of the Victorian Gardens,* Bombay: Education Society's Press, 1864, pp. 8–9.

135. Colonel H. B. Hanna, *Catalogue of Twenty Original Indian Pictures Illustrating the Manner of Life of the Greatest of the Moghul Emperors. Painted in the Sixteenth and Seventeenth Centuries by Native Artists,* 1911, National Art Library, London, 4.D.74.

136. Temple, *Men and Events in My Time,* pp. 297–98.

137. *Preservation of National Monuments, Rajputana: Mount Abur, Ajmir, Jaipur and Ulwar,* Simla: Government Central Branch Press, 1881, pp. 8–9.

138. T. Holbein Hendley, *Ulwar and its Art Treasures,* London: W. Griggs, 1888.

139. Clements R. Markham, "The Archaeological Survey," in *A Memoir on the Indian Surveys,* London: By Order of Her Majesty's Secretary of State for India, 1871, pp. 198–203. Alexander Cunningham, H. H. Cole, James Burgess, and James Fergusson were among the experts overseeing these surveys.

140. *Proceedings of the Royal Asiatic Society of Bengal,* 1875, p. 42; and *Bombay Builder,* 4 (1868), p. 79. Rajendralall [or Rajendralala] Mitra was among the most active South Asians in these preservationist projects.

141. *Journal of Indian Art and Industry* 2 (1888), pp. 110–12.

142. *Journal of Indian Art and Industry* 1 (1888), p. 64.

143. *Journal of Indian Art and Industry* 2 (1888), p. 111.

144. *Quarterly Review* 106 (1859), pp. 325–26.

145. Griffiths, "Past Silences," pp. 18–32.

146. *Imperial Arts League Journal* (London), November 1912, pp. 12–14.

147. Cole, "Suggestions for Collecting Information."

148. Sir Henry Cole to Lord Mayo, September 6, 1869, *Correspondence with Sir Henry Cole, Lord Mayo Papers,* University of Cambridge Archives, Add. 7490/51 (XI), fol. 148.

149. "Lecture XI. The Arts and Manufactures of India by Professor J. F. Royle, M.D., F.R.S.," in *Lectures on the Progress of Arts and Science,* p. 396.

150. *Calcutta Review* 40 (1864–65), pp. 229–31.

151. Konrad Specker, "Madras Handlooms in the Nineteenth Century," *Indian Economic and Social History Review* 26 (1989), pp. 131–66.

152. "Paris Minute, December 30, 1865," *Department of Education and Science, Victoria and Albert Museum Records: Correspondence and Papers Re-*

lating to the Paris International Exhibition, 1865–1867, Public Record Office, Kew, PRO ED 84/18.

153. *Calcutta Review* 40 (1864–65), pp. 229–31.

154. "Lecture XI. The Arts and Manufactures of India," pp. 345–46.

155. *Primrose Record* 2 (1886), p. 87.

156. *Report on the Indian Section, Franco-British Exhibition, 1908,* London: Eyre and Spottiswoode, 1909, p. 23.

157. *Official Catalogue of the Great Exhibition of the Works of All Nations, 1851,* London: William Clowes and Sons, 1851, pp. 158–59.

158. The "sum realised [from sales] was about one-fourth the cost price of the articles" at the Franco-British Exhibition in 1908. *Report on the Indian Section, Franco-British Exhibition,* p. 23.

159. J. F. Watson to George Birdwood, June 3, 1889, *Birdwood Collection,* Oriental and India Office Collections, MSS Eur. F. 216/19, fol. 2.

160. *British Section Handbook, Paris Universal Exposition, 1889,* London: George E. Eyre and William Spottiswoode, 1889, pp. 124–25.

161. Whitworth, ed., *Messina's Popular Guide to the Melbourne International Exhibition of 1880–1881,* pp. 17–18.

162. Cundall, ed., *Reminiscences of the Colonial and Indian Exhibition,* pp. 26–27; and "The Indian Bazaar at the Paris Exhibition," *Graphic,* February 9, 1889, pp. 137–38.

163. *The Empire of India Exhibition, 1895. General Introduction,* Oriental and India Office Collections, T 10283; and Harold Hartley, *Eighty-Eight Not Out: A Record of Happy Memories,* London: Frederick Muller, 1939, p. 71.

164. C. Purdon Clarke to George Birdwood, July 29, August 7, and September 18, 1894, *George Birdwood Collection,* Oriental and India Office Collections, MSS Eur. F. 216/66, fols. 47–50, 55–56.

165. Cundall, ed., *Reminiscences of the Colonial and Indian Exhibition,* pp. 27–28.

166. Ibid., pp. 26–27.

167. Walter Benjamin, "The Work of Art in the Age of Mechanical Reproduction," in Hannah Arendt, ed., *Illuminations: Essays and Reflections,* New York: Schocken Books, 1978, pp. 217–51.

168. *George Birdwood Collection,* Oriental and India Office Collections, MSS Eur. F. 216/66, fols. 66–67.

169. *Official Guide to the Alexandra Palace and Park,* 1875, p. 2.

170. H. H. Cole, *Catalogue of the Objects of Indian Art Exhibited in the South Kensington Museum,* pp. 2–4.

171. *Primrose Record* 2 (1886), p. 87.

172. For a comprehensive study of the sociology and history of collecting, see John Elsner and Roger Cardinal, eds., *The Cultures of Collecting,* Cambridge, MA: Harvard University Press, 1994.

173. For a discussion of "Art" as a denial of the economic sphere and symbol of "culture" without party and class interest, please see "Class and Culture:

The Work of Bourdieu," *Media, Culture and Society* 2 (1980); and Raymond Williams, *Culture and Society: 1780–1950*, New York: Columbia University Press, 1983.

174. "Report of J. C. Tache, Esq., Canadian Commissioner to Paris in 1855," p. 152.

175. *Colonial Reports-Miscellaneous, No. 84. Papers Relating to the Preservation of Historic Sites and Ancient Monuments and Buildings in the West Indian Colonies. Presented to Parliament by Commend of His Majesty, November 1912.* London, 1912.

176. For a discussion of Pugin's Neo-Gothic contributions to the 1851 Great Exhibition, see Benjamin Ferrey, *Recollections of A. N. Welby Pugin, And His Father, Augustus Pugin, With Notices of their Works*, London: Edward Stanford, 1861, pp. 257–64. For information about Stone's career and photographs, see Bill Jay, *Customs and Faces: Photographs by Sir Benjamin Stone, 1838–1914*, London: Academy Editions, 1972; and Michael MacDonagh, ed., *Sir Benjamin Stone's Pictures. Records of National Life and History: Parliamentary Scenes and Portraits*, London: Cassell and Company, 1906.

177. J. B. Stone, *A History of Lichfield Cathedral, from its Foundation to the Present Time. With a Description of its Architecture and Monuments. With Photographic Illustrations*, London: Longmans, Green, Reader, and Dyer, 1870. For nineteenth-century Indian photography, see Ray Desmond, "Photography in India During the Nineteenth Century," *India Office Library and Records*, 1974, pp. 16–25; and Rev. Joseph Mullins, "On the Applications of Photography in India," *Journal of the Photographic Society of Bengal* 2 (1857), pp. 33–38. James R. Ryan discusses the various interplays between photography and British imperialism in *Picturing Empire: Photography and the Visualization of the British Empire*, Chicago: University of Chicago Press, 1997.

178. *Art-Journal* 52 (1900), p. 254.

179. "Catalogue of the Pictures in the Exhibition of the Photographic Society of Bengal," *Journal of Indian Art, Science, and Manufacture* 2nd series, 1 (1857), pp. 136, 173–79. Alexander Hunter, a doctor and superintendent of the School of Industrial Arts, Madras, was among the organizers of this exhibition.

180. *Burgess's Illustrated and Descriptive Guide to the International Health Exhibition, 1884*, 3rd ed., Guildhall Library, London, PAM 5023, pp. 3, 24–30.

181. *Leisure Hour* (1887), pp. 245–50.

182. For example, see "Conservation of Ancient Monuments and Remains," *Royal Institute of British Architects* 1864 and 1888, National Art Library, London, Box 35B.

183. *Fifty Years of Public Work*, vol. 2, pp. 393–93.

184. "Chapter XXVIII. Contributions from the Highlands," in Tallis, *Tallis's History and Description of the Crystal Palace*, vol. 1, pp. 175–82.

185. Henry Y.D. Scott, "International Exhibition of 1872. Representation of Peasant Jewelry," *Exhibition Pamphlets*, La Trobe Collection, State Library of Victoria.

186. *Catalogue of Works of Art and Design Contributed to the International Exhibition, 1873,* Calcutta: Office of the Superintendent of Government Printing, 1873.

187. Sir Richard Temple, *The Story of My Life,* London: Cassell and Company, 1896, pp. x–xi.

188. *Report of the Royal Commission for the Colonial and Indian Exhibition, London, 1886,* p. xxxiii.

189. Maine, *Effects of Observation of India on Modern European Thought,* p. 37.

190. Sir Henry Maine, "Lecture 8: Sovereignty and Empire," *Lectures on the Early History of Institutions,* New York: Holt and Company, 1875, p. 383.

191. Ainslie T. Embree, "The Rulers and the Ruled," in Clark Worswick and Ainslie T. Embree, eds., *The Last Empire: Photography in British India, 1855–1911,* London: The Gordon Fraser Gallery, 1976, pp. 145.

192. *Sir Henry Cole Papers, Miscellanies, Volume 17, 1845–1875,* National Art Library, London, 55 AA 62, fol. 69.

CHAPTER 6.   MACHINES-IN-MOTION

1. Alexander Dobbie, *Rough Notes of a Traveller Taken in England, Scotland, France, Holland, . . . Greece, Egypt, Ceylon, and Elsewhere,* 2nd series, London: Simpkin, Marshall, Hamilton, Kent, 1890, pp. 187–92.

2. For information about Dobbie's industrial and manufacturing background, see George E. Loyau, "Alexander Williamson Dobbie," in *Notable South Australians,* Adelaide: Carey, Page, 1885, pp. 117–19; and *Christian Weekly and Methodist Journal* (Adelaide), June 7, 1889, p. 3.

3. "Classes 653–658. Machines, Implements, and Processes of Manufactures," in *Official Record of the Sydney International Exhibition, 1879,* Sydney: Thomas Richards, Government Printer, 1881, p. 993.

4. Edward Combes to Colonial Secretary, June 19, 1878, *Colonial Secretary Letters, 1878,* Archives Office of New South Wales, Sydney, 1/2416.

5. P. L. Brown, ed., *The Narrative of George Russell of Golf Hill with Russellania and Selected Papers,* New York: Oxford University Press, 1935, p. 295. Many thanks to Dr. Nick Fisher for pointing out this helpful volume.

6. Sir Arthur Blyth to H. E. Bright, September 26, 1884, Mortlock Library, State Library of South Australia, V 991.

7. October 18, 1886, *National Agricultural and Industrial Association Minutes, 1883–1888,* John Oxley Library, State Library of Queensland, OM AB/1/4, fol. 292.

8. For example, please see "Appendix XX. Machinery, 1871," *A Special Report on the Annual International Exhibitions of the Years 1871, 1872, 1873 and 1874, Drawn up by Sir Henry Cole, Acting Commissioner in 1873 and 1874, and Presented by the Commissioners for the Exhibition of 1851,* English Parliamentary Papers 1878 [XXVII.] 139., pp. 109–10.

9. *Illustrated Weekly News,* October 12, 1862, p. 3; and E. V. B., *A London*

Sparrow at the Colinderies, London: Sampson, Low, Marston, Searle, and Rivington, 1887, p. 22.

10. Brown, ed., *Narrative of George Russell,* p. 295.

11. Horace Tozer to Colonial Secretary, October 25, 1907, *Premier's Department Letters and Papers Re. Franco-British Exhibition, 1908–1911,* Queensland State Archives, QSA A/6321, pp. 7–8.

12. David S. Landes, *The Unbound Prometheus: Technological Change and Industrial Development in Western Europe from 1759 to the Present,* New York: Cambridge University Press, 1980, esp. pp. 1–40.

13. Lewis D. B. Gordon, "Machinery of the Exhibition: As Applied to Textile Manufactures," in *The Industry of All Nations: The Art-Journal Illustrated Catalogue,* London: George Virtue, 1851, pp. I**–VIII** (page nos. as in source).

14. For background on industrialism and the introduction of machinery, see Landes, *Unbound Prometheus;* Robert W. Gray, *The Factory Question and Industrial England, 1830–1860,* New York: Cambridge University Press, 1996; Dolores Greenberg, "Energy, Power and Perceptions of Social Change in the Early Nineteenth Century," *American Historical Review* 95 (1990), 693–714; John F. Kasson, *Civilizing the Machine: Technology and Republican Values in America, 1776–1900,* New York: Viking Press, 1976; and Barry A. Turner, *Industrialism,* New York: Longman, 1975.

15. Jan Todd, *Colonial Technology: Science and the Transfer of Innovation to Australia,* New York: Cambridge University Press, 1995, esp. pp. 26–28.

16. "Correspondence: Agricultural Education," *Journal of the Agricultural Society of New South Wales* 2 (1875), pp. 229–32.

17. Lewis Mumford, "Authoritarian and Democratic Technics," *Technology and Culture* 5 (1964), pp. 1–8. For a fuller discussion of the connections between technology and culture, or "technics," see Mumford's *Technics and Civilization* (1934), *Art and Technics* (1952), *The Myth of the Machine: I. Technics and Human Development* (1967), and *The Myth of the Machine: II. The Pentagon of Power* (1970).

18. For Indian perspectives on industrialization, see Sudip Chaudhuri, "Debates on Industrialization," in Terence J. Byres, ed., *The Indian Economy: Major Debates since Independence,* Delhi: Oxford University Press, 1998, pp. 249–94.

19. Ernest Samuels, ed., *The Education of Henry Adams,* Boston: Houghton Mifflin, 1974, pp. 379–90.

20. Lynn White, Jr., "Dynamo and Virgin Reconsidered," in *Dynamo and Virgin Reconsidered: Essays in the Dynamism of Western Culture,* Cambridge, MA: MIT Press, 1968, pp. 57–73.

21. See the discussion of early anti-industrial activity (for example, Luddism and "machine-breaking") in Eric J. Hobsbawm and George Rude, *Captain Swing: A Social History of the Great English Agricultural Uprising of 1830,* New York: W. W. Norton, 1975; Kirkpatrick Sale, *Rebels Against the Future: The Luddites and Their War on the Industrial Revolution. Lessons for the Com-*

puter Age, New York: Addison-Wesley, 1995; and Edward Palmer Thompson, *The Making of the English Working Class,* New York: Pantheon Books, 1963. The introduction and diffusion of new technology in India is considered in M. D. Morris, "Towards a Reinterpretation of Nineteenth-Century Indian Economic History," *Journal of Economic History* 23 (1963), pp. 606–18; M. D. Morris et al., "A Reinterpretation of Nineteenth-Century Indian Economic History," *The Indian Economic and Social History Review* 5 (1968), pp. 1–100; and Frank Perlin, "Proto-Industrialization and Pre-Colonial South Asia," *Past and Present* 98 (1983), pp. 30–95. These essays emphasize the differences in technological innovation between the manufacturing and agricultural sectors of the South Asian economy. Changes in Australian power and energy sources are discussed in "Energy," Graeme Davison, in J. S. McCarty and Ailsa McLeary, eds., *Australians/1888,* Sydney: Fairfax, Syme, and Weldon Associates, 1987, pp. 69–89.

22. *Graphic,* June 17, 1871, pp. 563–64.

23. For example, see the discussion of machinery exhibits in "Report of C. Bernard Shaw, Secretary to the Chief Commissioner, Central Provinces," in *Report of the Nagpore Exhibition of Arts, Manufactures, and Produce, December 1865,* Nagpore: Central Provinces' Printing Press, 1865.

24. A. Lyall to J. H. Rivett-Carnac, November 18, 1867, *Lyall Papers,* Oriental and India Office Collections, MSS Eur. C. 265.

25. Toshio Kusamitsu, "Great Exhibitions Before 1851," *History Workshop* 9 (1980), pp. 70–89.

26. Charles Babbage, *The Exposition of 1851; or, Views of the Industry, the Science and the Government of England,* 2nd ed., London: John Murray, 1851, p. 18; and *Manchester Guardian,* December 9, 1837, p. 3.

27. Jeremy Black, "Agricultural Improvements in 1763: The Role of Foreign Examples," *Agricultural History* 64 (1990), pp. 90–91.

28. *Times,* May 8, 1884, p. 6.

29. *Reports from the Parliamentary Selection Committee on the Paris Exhibition, 1867, Volume I: Reports by Executive Commissioner; with Appendices,* English Parliamentary Papers, 1868–69 [xxx]. Pt. i. 1.

30. Ibid., p. 23.

31. Ibid., p. 33.

32. *Paris Exhibition, 1855. Report Presented to the Bradford Chamber of Commerce, on the 26th November 1855,* National Art Library, London, Box I.A.9, pp. 11 and 14.

33. *Minutes of the South Australian Commissioners, 1879–1882. Sydney International Exhibition, 1879. Auditor-General's Department,* Public Record Office of South Australia, GRG 44/60, pp. 22–29.

34. Harriet Ritvo, *The Animal Estate: The English and Other Creatures in the Victorian Age,* Cambridge, MA: Harvard University Press, 1987, pp. 45–81.

35. Rondo Cameron, "The Industrial Revolution: Fact or Fiction?" *Contention* 4 (1994), pp. 163–88; and Patrick K. O'Brien, "Introduction: Modern Conceptions of the Industrial Revolution," in O'Brien and Roland Quinault,

eds., *The Industrial Revolution and British Society*, New York: Cambridge University Press, 1993, pp. 1–30.

36. *Illustrated London News*, July 19, 1851, p. 88.

37. William Drew, *Glimpses and Gatherings, During a Voyage and Visit to London and the Great Exhibition, in the Summer of 1851*, Augusta, ME: Homan and Manley, 1852, p. 330.

38. Herbert N. Casson, *Cyrus Hall McCormick: His Life and Work*, Chicago: A. C. McClurg, 1909, pp. 123–28.

39. "Trial of Steam Plows, Yorkshire Show, York, England, August 5, 1862," *Journal of the Royal Agricultural Society* 12 (1851), pp. 160 and 644–51; and Benjamin Pierce Johnson, *Report of International Exhibition of Industry and Art, London, 1862*, Albany: Steam Press of C. van Bethuysen, 1863, pp. 67–69.

40. William T. Hutchinson, *Cyrus Hall McCormick, Volume II: Harvest, 1856–1884*, New York: D. Appleton-Century, 1935, pp. 418–31.

41. *Mechanics' Magazine*, January 8, 1864, p. 17.

42. The displays and demonstrations of threshers, reapers, drills and other farming machines can be added to the "interplay of economic, geographical and social facts" influencing the diffusion of agricultural technology. The size of farms, influence of local agricultural societies, access to information and modes of advertising were among the factors shaping the process of agricultural mechanization in England. See John R. Walton, "Mechanization in Agriculture: A Study of the Adoption Process," in H. S. A. Fox and R. A. Butlin, eds., *Change in the Countryside: Essays on Rural England, 1500–1900*, London: Institute of British Geographers, 1979, pp. 23–42.

43. Richard S. Rosenbloom, "Men and Machines: Some Nineteenth-Century Analyses of Mechanization," *Technology and Culture* 5 (1964), pp. 489–511; and Charles Babbage, "The Economy of Machinery and Manufactures," in Martin Campbell-Kelly, ed., *The Works of Charles Babbage*, vol. 8, New York: New York University Press, 1989.

44. George Wilson, *What Is Technology? An Inaugural Lecture Delivered in the University of Edinburgh, on November 7, 1855*, Edinburgh: Sutherland and Knox, 1855, pp. 6–7.

45. "Lecture V. On the Chemical Principles Involved in the Manufactures of the Exhibition as Indicating the Necessity of Industrial Instruction. by Prof. Lyon Playfair," in *Lectures on the Progress of Arts and Science, Resulting from the Great Exhibition in London, delivered Before the Society of Arts, Manufactures and Commerce, at the Suggestion of H.R.H. Prince Albert, President of the Society*, New York: A. S. Barnes & Co., 1854, p. 120.

46. "Arrangements for Exhibiting Manufactures in Each of the Seven Exhibitions to Follow That of 1873," *Exhibition Folio Pamphlets*, vol. 2, La Trobe Library Pamphlets Collection, State Library of Victoria, fol. 21; and John Allwood, "General Notes: International Exhibitions and The Classification of Their Exhibits," *Journal of the Royal Society of Arts*, 128 (1980), pp. 450–55.

47. *Official Catalogue of the Great Exhibition of the Works of Industry of All Nations, 1851*, 3rd ed., London: W. Clowes and Sons, 1851, p. 4.

48. Drew, *Glimpses and Gatherings*, p. 345.

49. Ibid., pp. 354–55.

50. *Illustrated London News*, September 20, 1851, p. 380.

51. *Cornhill Magazine* 4 (1861), pp. 96–97.

52. *Illustrated London News*, August 9, 1862, p. 169, and August 23, 1862, p. 217.

53. Arthur Beckwith, *International Exhibition, London, 1871. Pottery. Observations on the Materials and Manufacture of Terra-Cotta, Stone-Ware, Fire-Brick, Porcelain, Earthen-Ware, Brick, Majolica, and Encaustic Tiles, with Remarks on the Products Exhibited*, New York: D. Van Nostrand, 1872.

54. C. W. Yapp, *Popular Guide to the London International Exhibition of 1871*, London: J. M. Johnson and Sons, 1871, pp. 27–28.

55. Allwood, "General Notes: International Exhibitions and The Classification of their Exhibits," pp. 450–55; and Bruce Sinclair, "Technology on its Toes: Late Victorian Ballets, Pageants and Industrial Exhibitions," in Stephen H. Cutliffe and Robert C. Post, eds., *In Context: History and the History of Technology. Essays in Honor of Melvin Kranzberg*, Research in Technology Series, vol. 1, Bethlehem, PA.: Lehigh University Press, 1989, pp. 71–87.

56. *Report of the Canadian Commissioner at the Exhibition of Industry, held at Sydney, New South Wales, 1877*, Ottawa: Department of Agriculture, 1878, p. 19.

57. William Westgarth, *Half a Century of Progress, A Personal Retrospect*, London: Sampson Low, Marston, Searle & Rivington, 1889, pp. 60–62.

58. Frank W. Fenton, *The Exhibition (1875) and How to See It! A Complete Guide, with Plan of Building and Grounds*, Melbourne: W. H. Williams, 1875, pp. 30–31.

59. *Centennial International Exhibition, Melbourne 1888–1889. The Official Catalogue of Exhibits, Volume I*, Melbourne: Firth and M'Cutcheon, 1888, p. 42.

60. Michael Adas, *Machines as the Measure of Men: Science, Technology, and Ideologies of Western Dominance*, Ithaca, NY: Cornell University Press, 1989.

61. *Bradshaw's Hand-Book to the Paris International Exhibition of 1867*, London: W. J. Adams, 1867, pp. 31, 111.

62. Debora L. Silverman, "The 1889 Exhibition: The Crisis in Bourgeois Individualism," *Oppositions* 8 (1977), pp. 70–91.

63. Beckwith, "Preface," in *International Exhibition, London, 1871. Pottery. Observations on the Materials and Manufacture of Terra-Cotta, . . . with Remarks on the Products Exhibited*, p. i.

64. "Patents, Designs and Trade Marks Act, 1883," in *Report of the Royal Commission for the Colonial and Indian Exhibition, London, 1886*, English Parliamentary Papers, 1887 [c. 5083] xx.1., pp. 160–61.

65. *Report of the Canadian Commissioner at the Exhibition of Industry*, p. 19.

66. Gray, *The Factory Question and Industrial England, 1830–1860*, esp.

pp. 131–59; and Herbert L. Sussman, *Victorians and the Machine: The Literary Responses to Technology*, Cambridge, MA: Harvard University Press, 1968.

67. Drew, *Glimpses and Gatherings*, p. 354.

68. Ibid., p. 356.

69. "Energy," in *Australians/1888*, p. 86.

70. *Concluding Address, Official Ending of the 1888 Melbourne Centennial Exhibition*, Victoria Public Record Service, 1095, Bundle 18: "Melbourne Exhibition, 1888," no. 2.

71. E. P. Thompson, "Time, Work-Discipline, and Industrial Capitalism," in M. W. Flinn and T. C. Smout, eds., *Essays in Social History*, New York: Oxford University Press, 1979, pp. 39–77; and Sidney Pollard, "Factory Discipline in the Industrial Revolution," *Economic History Review* 2nd series, 16 (1963), pp. 254–71.

72. J. P. Roberts, *An Intercolonial Visit to Victoria and Tasmania, December 4, 1866 — January 13, 1867*, Mortlock Library, State Library of South Australia, PRG 271/6.

73. Andrew Ure, *The Philosophy of Manufactures: or, An Exposition of the Scientific, Moral and Commercial Economy of the Factory System of Great Britain*, London: Charles Knight, 1835; and Charles Babbage, *On the Economy of Machinery and Manufactures*, London: John Murray, 1846. For a discussion of early nineteenth-century political economy, machinery, and industrialism, see Maxine Berg, *The Machinery Question and the Making of Political Economy, 1815–1848*, New York: Cambridge University Press, 1980.

74. *Illustrated London News*, August 23, 1851, pp. 247–48.

75. Ure, *The Philosophy of Manufactures*, pp. 7, 21.

76. *Reminiscences of the Crystal Palace, 1852*, National Art Library, London, 400.A.114, p. 29.

77. Raphael Samuel, "The Workshop of the World: Steam Power and Hand Technology in Mid-Victorian Britain," *History Workshop* 3 (1977), pp. 57–58.

78. Twenty weekly construction images were photographed between March 17 and September 29, 1879. They are collected in "Sydney Exhibition Album, Volume I," Mitchell Library, State Library of New South Wales, Sydney, ML Q606/5.

79. *1862 Exhibition. Photos Showing the Progress of the Building, Presented by C. W. Dilke*, Photographic Department, National Art Library, London, Album X93.

80. *Friend of the People*, December 7, 1850, p. 8, and December 14, 1850, p. 8.

81. *Official Record of the Sydney International Exhibition*, Sydney: Thomas Richards, Government Printer, 1881, pp. xxxi–xxxiii.

82. The carpenters demanded an increase of 3d. per hour from the salary of 1s. 3d. The strike failed because of the colony's mass unemployment and the resulting plentiful supply of strike-breaking skilled craftsmen. Peter Bridges, "The Sydney International Exhibition of 1879: The Translation of Ideas Into Reality," unpublished MSS, 1986, p. 6; and *Town and Country Journal* (Sydney), April 26, 1879, p. 778.

83. *Illustrated London News*, March 15, 1862, p. 269.

84. *Report of the Commissioners for the Exhibition of 1862, to the Right Hon. Sir George Gray, Bart., G.C.B., etc., etc.*, London: George E. Eyre and William Spottiswoode, 1863, p. xl.

85. *Australasian Sketcher*, August 14, 1880, pp. 129–30.

86. "Testimony of Sir Henry Cole, July 9, 1867," in *Reports from the Parliamentary Selection Committee on the Paris Exhibition, 1867*, p. 37.

87. H. C. Kent, "Reminiscences of Building Methods in the Seventies under John Young," *Architecture* (Australia) 13 (1924) pp. 5–13.

88. *Journal of the Royal Society of Arts* 27 (1879), p. 425.

89. P. G. King to Board of Directors, March 15, 1879, *Peel River Land and Mineral Company Correspondence*, Noel Butlin Archives Center, Australian National University, Canberra, 78/15/18.

90. James Barnet, the Colonial Architect for New South Wales, also questioned the use of electrical lighting at the Garden Palace construction site. He concluded that "the cost [of the arc lights and wages for extended hours] is not justified by the extra benefit." April 30, 1879, *Colonial Secretary Minutes, 1879*, Archives Office of New South Wales, Sydney, 1/2467.1.

91. *Morning Chronicle*, January 10, 1862, p. 3, and January 17, 1862, p. 3.

92. *Morning Chronicle*, January 25, 1862, p. 4.

93. *Building News* 8 (1862), p. 97.

94. Kent, "Reminiscences of Building Methods in the Seventies under John Young," p. 11.

95. *Illustrated Sydney News*, August 3, 1870, pp. 19–20.

96. *Voices from the Workshop on the Exhibition of 1851*, National Art Library, London, 400.A.103–4.

97. "The Great International Exhibition of 1862," *Working Man*, June 1, 1862, p. 142. Emphasis in original.

98. *Leisure Hour* 14 (1865), pp. 31–32.

99. Ibid., p. 31.

100. *Leisure Hour* 11 (1862), p. 792. Emphasis in original.

101. Raphael Samuel, "The Workshop of the World: Steam Power and Hand Technology in Mid-Victorian Britain"; and "Energy," in *Australians/1888*, esp. pp. 69–76.

102. Greenberg, "Energy, Power, and Perceptions of Social Change in the Early Nineteenth Century," p. 697.

103. *Leisure Hour* 14 (1865), p. 32.

104. *Working Man: A Record of Social and Industrial Progress* 1 (1866), pp. 12, 20, 51, 158, 169.

105. "Extracts from the Minute Books of the London Trades Council relating to the National Workmens Exhibition, December 8, 1892," Trades Union Council Archives, London, pp. 7–8.

106. Sir M. Digby Wyatt, "Orientalism in European Industry," *Macmillan's Magazine* 21 (1870), pp. 551–56.

107. *Building News* 50 (1886), p. 855.

108. Drew, *Glimpses and Gatherings*, pp. 378–79.

109. *The First Australian Exhibition of Women's Work, 1907*, University of Melbourne Archives, Parkville, Victoria.

110. For example, see discussion of the Women's Industrial Section in *Adelaide Jubilee International Exhibition, 1887–1888. Finance Committee Minutes, 1883–1887*, vol. 2, Public Record Office of South Australia, GRG 47/5/2, p. 24. For more general discussion of Women's Buildings and the various roles of women at exhibitions, see Paul Greenhalgh, "Women: Exhibited and Exhibiting," in *Ephemeral Vistas: The Expositions Universelles, Great Exhibitions and World's Fairs, 1851–1939*, New York: St. Martin's Press, 1988, pp. 174–97; and E. Heaman Try, "'Taking the World by Show': Women Exhibitors During the Nineteenth Century," *Canadian Historical Review* 78 (1997), pp. 599–631.

111. John Forbes Royle, *Report on the Indian Section, Colonial and Indian Exhibition, 1886*, Oriental and India Office Collections, P/W 812, p. 14; and "Indian Artisans," *Graphic*, May 15, 1886, p. 535.

112. Frank Cundall, ed., *Reminiscences of the Colonial and Indian Exhibition, Illustrated by Thomas Riley, Designer of the Exhibition Diploma*, London: William Clowes and Sons, 1886, pp. 5, 114–15.

113. *Report of the Royal Commission for the Colonial and Indian Exhibition, London, 1886*, p. xlv.

114. "Memo of Sir Philip Cunliffe-Owen to Earl of Dufferin, Viceroy, Confidential Communication for Lord Reay, 1 April 1887," *Reay Papers: Bombay Files*, School of Oriental and African Studies Archives, University of London, PP MS 37/No. 51, fol. 18.

115. *Illustrated London News*, June 17, 1886, p. 88.

116. Clive Dewey, "Images of the Village Community: A Study in Anglo-Indian Ideology," *Modern Asian Studies* 6 (1972), pp. 291–328; and Louis Dumont, "The 'Village Community' from Munro to Maine," *Contributions to Indian Sociology* 9 (1966), pp. 67–89.

117. The engraving is reproduced in John Allwood, *The Great Exhibitions*, New York: Macmillan, 1977, p. 77. The illustration was originally published in *L'Exposition de Paris*, a four-volume popular catalogue for the 1889 Paris Universal Exposition.

118. J. C. Neild, *Report of the Executive Commissioner for New South Wales to the Adelaide Jubilee International Exhibition, 1887–1888*, Sydney: Charles Potter, Government Printer, 1890, p. 42.

119. *Report of the Nagpore Exhibition of Arts, Manufactures, and Produce*, pp. 14, 19; and *Bombay Builder* 1 (1865), p. 102.

120. *Bombay Builder* 3 (1868), p. 283.

121. *Report of the Canadian Commissioner at the Exhibition of Industry*, esp. pp. 35–36.

122. I. W. McLean, "The Adoption of Harvest Machinery in Victoria in the Late Nineteenth Century," *Australian Economic History Review* 13 (1973), pp. 41–56.

123. T. G. Parsons, "Technological Change in the Melbourne Flour-Milling

and Brewing Industries, 1870–1890," *Australian Economic History Review* 11 (1971), pp. 135–36.

124. *Town and Country Journal* (Sydney), May 4, 1872, p. 556; and "The Sydney Exhibition of 1878," in *The Vagabond Papers, Sketches in New South Wales and Queensland*, 5th series, Melbourne: George Robertson, 1878, pp. 186–96.

125. *National Agricultural and Industrial Association Letterbook, 1878*, John Oxley Library, State Library of Queensland, OM AB/7/1, pp. 154–56, 163–64, 180–81, 193, 618, 646, 660.

126. "Notice to Exhibitors of Machinery," in *Report of the Executive Commissioner for New South Wales to the Adelaide Jubilee International Exhibition*, pp. 174–75.

127. William Thomas Denison, *Address to Members of the Australian Agricultural and Horticultural Societies*, Sydney: Reading and Wellbank, 1856.

128. For example, see "Artizans' Prizes . . . to encourage mechanical genius [and] excellence of workmanship," in *The National Agricultural and Industrial Association of Queensland. Catalogue of the Intercolonial Exhibition*, Brisbane: William Thorne, 1877, pp. 92–93; and "The Mayor's Prizes. Open to Australasian Exhibitors," in Neild, *Report of the Executive Commissioner for New South Wales to the Adelaide Jubilee International Exhibition, 1887–1888*, pp. 188–89.

129. "Second Department—Non-Agricultural," in *Metropolitan Intercolonial Exhibition, 16th August, 1870*, Sydney: Gibbs, Shallard, Lithographic and Letterpress by Steam, 1870; "Division 2.—Non-Agricultural," *Journal of the Agricultural Society of New South Wales* 1 (1874), pp. 16–17; and "Class VI.—Section 24. Reports and Awards of the Jurors," in *Intercolonial Exhibition of Australasia, Melbourne, 1866–67. Official Record, Containing Introduction, . . . Resources of the Australasian Colonies*, pp. 379–83.

130. *Calcutta Review* 19 (1853), p. 246; 26 (1856), pp. 269–70, 283–84; and 40 (1864–65), pp. 231–45.

131. Sir Richard Temple, *Men and Events of My Time in India*, 2nd ed., London: John Murray, 1882, p. 314.

132. Sir Richard Temple, *The Story of My Life*, London: Cassell and Company, 1896, pp. 163, 165; and John Forbes Royle, "Observations on Provincial Exhibitions and the Improvement of the Resources of the Several Districts of the Madras Presidency," *Madras Journal of Literature and Science* n.s. 2 (1857), pp. 64–79, 171–73.

133. "Report of C. Bernard, Secretary to the Chief Commissioner, Central Provinces, Department II.–Machinery and Implements," in *Report of the Nagpore Exhibition of Arts, Manufactures and Produce*, pp. 12, 13.

134. Ibid., p. 27.

135. Ibid., p. 14.

136. Ibid., p. 24.

137. *Times*, January 21, 1884, p. 5.

138. For studies concerning the interplay among imperialism, science, and

technology, see Adas, *Machines as the Measure of Men: Science, Technology and Ideologies of Western Dominance;* Winfried Baumgart, *Imperialism: The Idea and Reality of British and French Colonial Expansion, 1880–1914,* New York: Oxford University Press, 1982, esp. pp. 21–32; Daniel R. Headrick, *The Tools of Empire: Technology and European Imperialism in the Nineteenth Century,* New York: Oxford University Press, 1981; and *The Tentacles of Progress: Technology Transfer in the Age of Imperialism, 1850–1940,* New York: Oxford University Press, 1988; and Deepak Kumar, *Science and the Raj, 1857–1905,* New York: Oxford University Press, 1995.

139. For an example of that nineteenth-century optimism, see George Dodd, *Railways, Steamers and Telegraphs: A Glance At Their Recent Progress and Present State,* London: W. R. Chambers, 1867, esp. pp. 63–65.

140. *Edinburgh Review* 107 (1858), p. 43.

141. Harriet Martineau, *British Rule in India; a Historical Sketch,* London: Smith, Elder, 1857, pp. 338–41.

142. John Lockwood Kipling, "Indian Architecture of To-Day," *Journal of Indian Art and Industry* 1 (1884–1886), pp. 1–5.

143. Two events in mid-century Bombay illustrate this project. Government and railway officials inaugurated the East Indian Railway in early 1855 with a scene that, according to one contemporary account, added "another story to the thousand and one Arabian Nights' Entertainments." Several thousand South Asians and Englishmen witnessed a state ceremony similar to those officially opening local exhibitions. After speeches, the Royal Salute was fired from Fort William, and the "well-filled" train departed. Local English and Indian elites also introduced steam power into Bombay's Colaba Press Company's factory with a similar traditionalist ceremony. Royal proclamations and a procession preceded the laying of the foundation stone for the first steam engine in 1853. Coins and copies of the local newspaper were dropped into the stone's cavity and suggested a local sense of history, continuity, and public memory. *Bombay Telegraph & Courier,* August 5, 1853, p. 1478, and February 17, 1855, p. 331.

144. *Calcutta Review* 40 (1864–65), p. 239.

145. Jules Joubert, *Shavings and Scrapes from Many Parts,* Dunedin, New Zealand: Wilkie, 1890, p. 215.

146. *Report of the Industrial and Agricultural Exhibition of the Punjab, North-West Frontier Province and Kashmir, 1909–1910, Lahore,* Lahore: "Tribune" Press, 1911.

147. Ibid., p. 17.

148. *Edinburgh Review* 89 (1849), pp. 47–83.

149. *Statesman and Friend of India,* January 2, 1883, p. 3.

150. "Report of C. Bernard, Secretary to the Chief Commissioner," in *Report of the Nagpore Exhibition of Arts, Manufactures and Produce, December, 1865,* p. 27.

151. Alexander Hunter, *Suggestions for the Establishment of a School of Industrial Arts at Lahore, Prepared at the Request of His Excellency Sir Robert*

Montgomery, K.C.B., Lieut.-Governor of the Punjab, 1863, Oriental and India Office Collections, TR 633.

152. Ibid., pp. 35, 43.

153. Alexander Hunter, *Report of the School of Industrial Arts, Madras, 1862,* Oriental and India Office Collections, TR 633, p. 33.

154. "Lecture XI. The Arts and Manufactures of India by Professor J. F. Royle, M.D., F.R.S.," in *Lectures on the Progress of Arts and Science, Resulting from the Great Exhibition in London,* pp. 396–97.

155. "Prof. Archer, Report on Pottery and Porcelain," in *Reports on the Vienna International Exhibition of 1873, Part II,* London: George E. Eyre and William Spottiswoode, 1874, pp. 153, 158–65.

156. For example, see "Correspondence and Papers Relative to the Manufacture of Glass and Earthen-wares and Fire Bricks in India: Received from the Government," *Calcutta Journal of Natural History and Miscellany of the Arts and Sciences in India* 2 (1842), pp. 589–609.

157. Sir E. C. Buck, *Report on Practical and Technical Education,* Calcutta: Office of the Superintendent of Government Printing, India, 1901, p. 26.

158. *The Indian Museum, 1814–1914,* Calcutta: Baptist Mission Press, 1914, p. 15.

159. *Bombay Times & Journal of Commerce,* August 11, 1855, p. 1575.

160. Sir William Wilson Hunter, *Bombay, 1885–1890: A Study in Indian Administration,* London: Henry Frowde, 1892, pp. 174–75.

161. *Sydney Magazine of Science and Art* 2 (1858), p. 146.

162. *Address on the Opening of the School of Mines at Ballarat, Victoria. Delivered by Sir Redmond Barry, on Wednesday, October 26th, A.D. 1870,* Melbourne: Firth and M'Cutcheon, 1870.

163. John Forbes Watson, *International Exhibitions,* London: Henry S. King, 1873, p. 19. This volume was a compilation of Watson's letters concerning "International Exhibitions," published in the *Times* December 28, 1872, p. 10, December 30, 1872, p. 8, and June 9, 1873, p. 6.

164. *Official Record of the Sydney International Exhibition,* p. cix.

165. *Ninth Annual Report of the Standing Committee of the South Australia Chamber of Manufactures, for the Year Ending July 24, 1878,* pp. 3–5.

166. Watson, *International Exhibitions,* p. 19.

167. *Illustrated London News,* June 30, 1855, p. 645.

168. Kasson, *Civilizing the Machine,* p. 158.

169. Hutchinson, *Cyrus Hall McCormick,* vol. 2, pp. 418–39, 444–45, 660–72.

170. Walter Benjamin, "Paris, Capital of the Nineteenth Century," in Edmund Jephcott, ed., *Reflections: Essays, Aphorisms, Autobiographical Writings,* New York: Schocken Books, 1978, p. 159.

171. Drew, *Glimpses and Gatherings,* p. 320.

172. *Fowke Family Letters and Papers, c. 1865–1927,* National Art Library, London, MSS English, 86 JJ Box II (iii).

173. David A. L. Saunders, *Joseph Reed; Architect, Melbourne, 1852–1890:*

His Life and Work and the Practice He Established, unpublished manuscript; 1950, La Trobe Collection, State Library of Victoria, MS H15360/Box 139/33; and "Joseph Reed, 1822–1890," in Howard Tanner, ed., *Architects of Australia,* South Melbourne: Macmillan, 1981, pp. 59–65.

174. *Building News* 37 (1879), p. 397.

175. *Fifty Years of Public Work of Sir Henry Cole, K.C.B., Accounted for in His Deeds, Speeches, and Writings,* vol. 1, London: George Bell and Sons, 1884, p. 253.

176. *Journal of the Royal Society of Arts* 15 (1866), p. 76.

177. *Macmillan's Magazine* 17 (1867), pp. 87–88.

178. Montgomery Schuyler, "Last Words About the World's Fair," in William H. Jordy and Ralph Coe, eds., *American Architecture and Other Writings,* vol. 2, Cambridge, MA: Harvard University Press, 1961, pp. 560–66.

179. Justus D. Doenecke, "Myths, Machines, and Markets: The Columbian Exposition of 1893," *Journal of Popular Culture* 6 (1973), p. 540–41.

180. For example, Colt revolving pistols were engraved so that visitors would not confuse them with other, similar objects considered by the exhibitors "simple in style" and strictly utilitarian; see, *The Exhibition of Art-Industry in Dublin,* London: Virtue, 1853, p. 24.

181. *Sixpenny Magazine,* 1862, pp. 8–9.

182. "At the Great Exhibition," *Cornhill Magazine* 5 (1862), p. 676.

183. Exhibitions on the continent were no different. One English visitor at the 1889 Paris Universal Exposition noted that the "elegant" Ministry of War building housed various guns, shells, and other "death-dealing explosives," which were, after all, among the "benefits we—French, English, Germans, Dutch, everybody—confer upon less civilised peoples when we take them under our protection." *All the Year Round* 1, 3rd series (1889), p. 520.

184. "Class XI. Military Engineering, Armour and Accoutrements, Ordnance, and Small Arms," in *International Exhibition, 1862. Reports by the Juries on the Subjects in the Thirty-Six Classes into which the Exhibition was Divided,* London: William Clowes and Sons, 1863.

185. H. J. Habbakuk, *American and British Technology in the Nineteenth Century: The Search for Labour-Saving Inventions,* New York: Cambridge University Press, 1962, p. 195.

186. "Ground Plan of the Intercolonial Exhibition, 1866," in *Companion to the Official Catalogue. Guide to the Intercolonial Exhibition of 1866,* Melbourne: Blundell and Ford, 1866; and *Statesman and Friend of India,* November 17, 1883, p. 3.

187. *Westminster Review* 126 (1886), pp. 58.

188. Tom Griffiths, "Past Silences: Aborigines and Convicts in Our History-Making," *Australian Cultural History* 6 (1987), pp. 237–54. Without any sense of irony, exhibition commissioners wrote, "Up to the present time the art of man-killing in open warfare is on this side of the globe merely in its theoretical form. Our Volunteer Army has been taught how to kill an enemy scientifically, but no opportunity has yet been given it to turn theory into practice, conse-

quently there has been no call upon such of our artizans as are able to invent and manufacture murderous weapons and projectiles." *By Authority of the Commissioners. Victorian Intercolonial Exhibition, 1875. Preparatory to the Philadelphia Exhibition, 1876. Opened 2nd September, 1875. Official Catalogue of Exhibits,* Melbourne: M'Carron, Bird, 1875, p. 164.

189. "At the Great Exhibition," *Cornhill Magazine*, p. 677. Emphasis in original.

190. *Illustrated London News*, June 14, 1862, pp. 618–19.

191. Philip Bright, ed., *The Diaries of John Bright*, London: Cassell and Company, 1930, pp. 126, 133, 151, 196, 395.

192. Ibid., pp. 676–77.

193. *Punch* 42 (1862), p. 177.

194. Sir Henry Trueman Wood, "Exhibitions," *Nineteenth Century* 20 (1886), p. 634.

CHAPTER 7.   IMPERIAL AND NATIONAL TAXONOMIES

1. Thursday, May 1, 1851, *The Life and Letters of Lord Macaulay, By His Nephew, George Otto Trevelyan, M.P.,* vol. 2, London: Longmans, Green, 1876, pp. 292–93.

2. *Aunt Busy-Bee's The Fine Crystal Palace the Prince Built,* London: Dean and Son, 1851, p. 5.

3. Tony Bennett, "The Exhibitionary Complex," in Nicholas B. Dirks, Geoffrey Eley, and Sherry B. Ortner, eds., *Culture/Power/History: A Reader in Contemporary Social Theory,* Princeton, NJ: Princeton University Press, 1988, pp. 123–54; and Robert Brain, "Going to the Exhibition," in Richard Staley, ed., *The Physics of Empire: Public Lectures,* Cambridge, England: Whipple Museum of the History of Science, 1994, pp. 113–42.

4. Thomas Babington Macaulay to Margaret Trevelyan, September 18, 1851, in Thomas Pinney, ed., *The Letters of Thomas Babington Macaulay, Volume 5: January 1849 to December 1855,* New York: Cambridge University Press, 1981, pp. 193–94.

5. *Punch* 21 (1851), p. 38.

6. Manon Niquette and William J. Buxton, "Meet Me at the Fair: Sociability and Reflexivity in Nineteenth-Century World Expositions," *Canadian Journal of Communication* 22 (1997), pp. 81–113.

7. Charles Babbage, *The Exposition of 1851; or, Views of the Industry, the Science, and the Government of England,* 2nd ed., London: John Murray, 1851, pp. v–vi.

8. Ibid., p. vi.

9. Ibid., pp. 5, 10–11.

10. "Lecture I.—Dr. Whewell on the General Bearings of the Great Exhibition," in *Lectures on the Progress of Arts and Science, Resulting from the Great Exhibition in London, delivered before the Society of Arts, Manufac-*

tures and Commerce, at the Suggestion of H.R.H. Prince Albert, New York: A. S. Barnes, 1854, pp. 5–15.

11. Harold Perkin, *The Origins of Modern English Society, 1780–1880,* Buffalo, NY: University of Toronto Press, 1981.

12. Edward Huybers, *"From Birth to Borderland" (An Eighty-Five Year Life-Story),* Mitchell Library, State Library of New South Wales, ML Mss 1423, pp. 45–46.

13. *Westminster Review* n.s. 126 (1886), pp. 29–30.

14. *Edinburgh Review* 93 (1851), p. 488.

15. *Westminster Review* n. s. 126, (1886), p. 31.

16. "Anthropological Conferences on the Native Races of the British Possessions: Being a Series of Special Meetings of the Anthropological Institute held in the Conference Hall of the Colonial and Indian Exhibition," *Journal of the Royal Anthropological Institute* 16 (1886), pp. 174–236.

17. Ibid., p. 175.

18. *Diaries of John Mills Hughes,* La Trobe Collection, State Library of Victoria, MS 10718, fols. 98–99.

19. *Visitors' Register, Melbourne International Exhibition, 1880–1881,* La Trobe Library, State Library of Victoria, MS 9306; *Visitors' Book, Exhibition Building Trustees,* 2 vols., Victoria Public Record Office, 839/1–2; and *Visitors' Books, Old Colonists' Court, Adelaide Jubilee International Exhibition, 1887,* 2 vols., Public Record Office of South Australia, GRG 47/17/1–2.

20. Robert P. Whitworth, ed., *Massina's Popular Guide to the Melbourne International Exhibition of 1880–81,* Melbourne: A. H. Massina, 1880, pp. 16–17.

21. Graeme Davison, "Festivals of Nationhood: the International Exhibitions," in S. L. Goldberg and F. B. Smith, eds., *Australian Cultural History,* New York: Cambridge University Press, 1988, pp. 167–69.

22. *Calcutta Review* 40 (1864–65), pp. 236–37.

23. *Times,* June 25, 1883, p. 5, and December 20, 1883, p. 3.

24. Thomas R. Metcalf, *Ideologies of the Raj,* New York: Cambridge University Press, 1997.

25. The ways in which cultural experts create taxonomies of knowledge and how such taxonomies function in modern society are two of the issues discussed in Pierre Bourdieu, *Distinction: A Critique of the Judgement of Taste,* trans. Pierre Nice, Cambridge, MA: Harvard University Press, 1984; Michel Foucault, *The Order of Things: An Archaeology of the Human Sciences,* New York: Vintage Books, 1970, and *The Archaeology of Knowledge,* ed. and trans. A. M. Sheridan, New York: Pantheon Books, 1972.

26. George Augustus Sala, *Notes and Sketches of the Paris Exhibition,* London: Tinsley Brothers, 1868, p. 18.

27. Umberto Eco, "A Theory of Expositions," in *Travels in Hyper-Reality,* London: Pan Books, 1987, pp. 291–307.

28. *Sydney Morning Herald,* April 12, 1877, reprinted in *Report of the*

Canadian Commissioner at the Exhibition of Industry, held at Sydney, New South Wales, 1877, Ottawa: Department of Agriculture, 1878, p. 19.

29. William A. Drew, *Glimpses and Gatherings, During a Voyage and Visit to London and the Great Exhibition, in the Summer of 1851*, Augusta, ME: Homan and Manley, 1852, pp. 321, 336.

30. "Lecture XX. 2nd series. December 1, 1852. On the International Results of the Exhibition of 1851," in *Fifty Years of Public Work of Sir Henry Cole, K.C.B., Accounted for in his Deeds, Speeches and Writings*, vol. 2, London: George Bell and Sons, 1884, pp. 233–34.

31. Benedict Anderson, *Imagined Communities: Reflections on the Origin and Spread of Nationalism*, New York: Verso, 1994; and Mary Poovey, *Making a Social Body: British Cultural Formation, 1830–1864*, Chicago: University of Chicago Press, 1995.

32. For example, Matthew Arnold, *Culture and Anarchy*, New York: Cambridge University Press, 1981; and Samuel Taylor Coleridge, *On the Constitution of the Church and State*, ed. John Barrell, London: J. M. Dent & Sons, 1972.

33. Quoted from the *Times* in "Lecture XX. 2nd Series. December 1, 1852. On the International Results of the Exhibition of 1851," in *Fifty Years of Public Work of Sir Henry Cole*, vol. 2, p. 234.

34. Thomas Frost, *The Old Showmen and the Old London Fairs*, London: Tinsley Brothers, 1874.

35. Peter Bailey, *Leisure and Class in Victorian England: Rational Recreation and the Contest for Control, 1830–1885*, London: Methuen, 1987; J. M. Golby and A. W. Purdue, *The Civilisation of the Crowd: Popular Culture in England, 1750–1900*, London: B. T. Batsford, 1984; and R. W. Malcolmson, *Popular Recreations in English Society, 1700–1850*, New York: Cambridge University Press, 1973.

36. Henry Cole, "National Culture and Recreation: Antidotes to Vice. An Address Delivered in the Liverpool Institute, 8th December, 1875," in *Sir Henry Cole Papers, Miscellanies, Volume 17, 1845–1875*, National Art Library, London, 55 AA 62, fols. 300–5.

37. "Testimony of Sir Henry Cole," in *Reports on the Paris Universal Exposition, 1867, Volume I: Reports by Executive Commissioner; with Appendices*, English Parliamentary Papers. 1868–69. [xxx]. Pt. i. 1, pp. 729–30.

38. Ibid., p. 41. In contrast to such bold claims, we are reminded of the popular tale told in 1851 about how one man had "made various attempts to visit the Great Exhibition, but had found so many public-houses on the road that he never got there at all!" See W. E. Adams, *Memoirs of a Social Atom*, London: Hutchinson, 1903, p. 335.

39. Frederic Harrison, *Sunday Evenings for the People. Sundays and Festivals, a Lecture*, London: Trubner and Company, 1867.

40. Frederic Harrison, "1851—Great Exhibition—Switzerland," in *Autobiographic Memoirs, Volume I (1831–1870)*, London: Macmillan, 1911, pp. 88–89.

41. Hugh Cunningham, "The Metropolitan Fairs: A Case Study in the Social Control of Leisure," in A. P. Donajgrodzki, ed., *Social Control in Nineteenth Century Britain*, Totowa, NJ: Rowman and Littlefield, 1977, pp. 163–82.

42. Frost, *The Old Showmen and the Old London Fairs*, pp. 20–21.

43. "The Library and Museum," *Australian Magazine* 1 (1859), pp. 119–24; and *Statesman and Friend of India*, November 14, 1883, p. 2, and December 15, 1883, p. 2. The development of "central" collections was not always without contest. For a discussion of the debate over Melbourne's National Museum, see Ian Wilkinson, "The Battle for the Museum: Frederick McCoy and the Establishment of the National Museum of Victoria at the University of Melbourne," *Historical Records of Australian Science* 11 (June 1996), pp. 1–11.

44. George Nadel, *Australia's Colonial Culture: Ideas, Men and Institutions in Mid-Nineteenth Century Australia*, Cambridge, MA: Harvard University Press, 1957; and "Opening Museum and Free Library on Sundays," *Sydney Magazine* 1 (1878), p. 66.

45. *Metropolitan Police Report, Crystal Palace Attendance*, John Burns Collection, Greater London Record Office, 18.49 (BUR).

46. Audrey Short discusses the Great Exhibition's working-class visitors and their sponsors in "Workers Under Glass in 1851," *Victorian Studies* 10 (1966), pp. 194–202.

47. *Journal of the Royal Society of Arts* 27 (1878–79), pp. 5, 682–83, 753–55, 929, 945, 953, 981.

48. *Artisans Reports, Royal Society of Arts to 1867 Paris Exposition*, London: W. Trounce, 1867.

49. August 5 and November 4, 1886, *London Trades Council Minute Book, No. 5, March 1883–December 1888*, Trades Union Congress Archives, London, pp. 325–26, 334–35.

50. Frank Cundall, ed., *Reminiscences of the Colonial and Indian Exhibition, illustrated by Thomas Riley, Designer of the Exhibition Diploma*, London: William Clowes and Sons, 1886, p. 6.

51. Francis Fuller, *Shall We Spend £100,000 on a Winter Garden for London, or in Endowing Schools of Design?* London: John Ollivier, 1851.

52. *Working Man*, July 1, 1862, pp. 173–74, and August 1, 1862, pp. 197–98.

53. John Belchem, "Britishness, the United Kingdom, and the Revolutions of 1848," *Labour History Review* 64 (1999), pp. 143–58; Victor Kiernan, "Working Class and Nation in Nineteenth-Century Britain," in Harvey J. Kaye, ed., *History, Classes and Nation-States: Selected Writings of V. G. Kiernan*, New York: Basil Blackwell, 1988, pp. 186–98; and Margot Finn, "'A Vent Which Has Conveyed Our Principles': English Radical Patriotism in the Aftermath of 1848," *Journal of Modern History* 64 (1992), pp. 637–59.

54. *Working Man*, August 1, 1862, p. 198.

55. Ibid., p. 197.

56. Neild, *Report of the Executive Commissioner for New South Wales to*

the *Adelaide Jubilee International Exhibition, 1887–1888;* October 14 and 18, 1880; *Governor's Minute Book,* vol. 2, Victoria Public Record Office, 1093/2, pp. 185–92; and *Age,* September 16, 1875, p. 3.

57. Secretary of Trades and Labour Council of New South Wales to Colonial Secretary, October 4 and October 7, 1879, *New South Wales Colonial Secretary Letters, 1879,* Archives Office of New South Wales, Sydney, 1/2456.

58. *Address to the Workmen Employed in Building The Great Hall of the Melbourne Public Library and Museum, in Melbourne, Victoria. Delivered by Sir Redmond Barry, on Saturday, September 8, A.D. 1866,* Melbourne: Wilson and MacKinnon, 1866, p. 38.

59. *Statesman and Friend of India,* December 15, 1883, p. 2.

60. "The First Bengal Agricultural Exhibition," *Calcutta Review* 40 (1864–65), pp. 240–41.

61. For a discussion of the written representations of such tensions in the *zenana,* see Janaki Nair, "Uncovering the Zenana: Visions of Indian Womanhood in Englishwomen's Writings, 1813–1940," *Journal of Women's History* 2 (1990), pp. 8–34.

62. "ZENANA s. Pers. zanana, from zan, 'woman'; the apartments of a house in which the women of the family are secluded. This Mahommedan custom has been largely adopted by the Hindus of Bengal and the Mahrattas." Col. Henry Yule and A. C. Burnell, *Hobson-Jobson, A Glossary of Colloquial Anglo-Indian Words and Phrases, and of Kindred Terms, Etymological, Historical Geographical and Discursive,* ed. William Crooke, Delhi: Munshiram Manoharlal, 1903, p. 981.

63. Jules Joubert, *Shavings and Scrapes from Many Parts,* Dunedin: J. Wilkie, 1890, pp. 180–83.

64. *Report on the Broach Exhibition, 1868–69. With Appendices A. to H.,* Bombay: Education Society's Press, 1869, p. 9.

65. *Statesman and Friend of India,* January 17, 1883, p. 2.

66. H. H. Risley, "Report on the Calcutta International Exhibition, October 1885," *Revenue and Agriculture Department Proceedings,* Oriental and India Office Collections, P/2490, p. 5.

67. *Statesman and Friend of India,* March 1, 1884, p. 2.

68. Joubert, *Shavings and Scrapes,* pp. 182–83.

69. Ibid., p. 183.

70. Sir Richard Temple, *Men and Events of My Time in India,* 2nd ed., London: John Murray, 1882, pp. 163, 165, 240–41; John Forbes Royle, "Observations on Provincial Exhibitions and the Improvement of the Resources of the Several Districts of the Madras Presidency," *Madras Journal of Literature and Science* n.s. 2 (1857), pp. 64–79, 171–72; and E. C. Buck, "The Utility of Exhibitions to India," *Asiatic Quarterly Review* 2 (1886), pp. 306–23.

71. V. N. Datta, *Sati: A Historical, Social and Philosophical Enquiry into the Hindu Rite of Widow Burning,* London: Sangam Books, 1988; Lata Mani, "Contentious Traditions: The Debate on *Sati* in Colonial India," in Abdul R. JanMohamed and David Lloyd, eds., *The Nature and Context of Minority Dis-*

course, New York: Oxford University Press, 1990, pp. 319–56, and *Contentious Traditions: The Debate on Sati in Colonial India,* Berkeley, CA: University of California Press, 1998; and Anand A. Yang, "Whose Sati? Widow Burning in Early Nineteenth-Century India," *Journal of Women's History* 1 (1989), pp. 8–33.

72. The Ilbert, or Criminal Jurisdiction, Bill of 1883, named after Sir Courtney Ilbert, Ripon's new Law Member, was intended to remove racial restrictions codified in 1872. Those prevented Indians in the British Judicial Service from trying cases involving Europeans charged with minor or major offenses. Anglo-Indian associations quickly organized and attacked the Viceroy and the Bill's proponents; they succeeded in having the legislation diluted. Public pressure, including a widespread newspaper campaign, resulted in a bill which permitted Europeans tried in a court presided over by a South Asian to demand a jury at least half European in its composition. The "outdoors" campaign of public opinion and petitions provided an example for future nationalist protest movements on the part of the Indian National Congress and other organizations. Stanley Wolpert, *A New History of India,* 6th ed., New York: Oxford University Press, 2000, p. 257.

73. *Statesman and Friend of India,* February 14, 1884, p. 2, February 23, 1884, p. 2, February 29, 1884, p. 2, March 1, 1884, p. 2, and March 23, 1884, p. 2.

74. *Statesman and Friend of India,* February 29, 1884, p. 2.

75. For a discussion of Womens' Buildings and the various roles of women at international exhibitions, see "Women: Exhibited and Exhibiting," in Paul Greenhalgh, *Ephemeral Vistas: The Expositions Universelles, Great Exhibitions and World's Fairs 1851–1939,* New York: St. Martin's Press, 1988, pp. 174–97; and E. Heaman Try, "'Taking the World by Show': Women Exhibitors During the Nineteenth Century," *Canadian Historical Review* 78 (1997), pp. 599–631.

76. John Falconer, "Ethnographical Photography in India, 1850–1900," *Photographic Collector* 5 (1984), esp. pp. 30–32; Metcalf, *Ideologies of the Raj,* esp. pp. 66–159; and Christopher Pinney, "Classification and Fantasy in the Photographic Construction of Caste and Tribe," *Visual Anthropology* 3 (1990), pp. 258–88.

77. J. Forbes Watson and John William Kaye, *The People of India. A Series of Photographic Illustrations, With Descriptive Letterpress, of the Races and Tribes of Hindustan, Originally Prepared under the Authority of the Government or India, and Reproduced by Order of the Secretary of State for India in Council,* vol. 1, Delhi: B. R. Publishing Corporation, 1987. Original volumes were published between 1868 and 1875 with the direct patronage of the Viceroy of India.

78. Ray Desmond, "Photography in India During the Nineteenth Century," *India Office Library and Records Report,* 1974, pp. 11–13.

79. *Illustrated London News,* July 17, 1886, p. 83.

80. *Pall Mall Gazette,* May 4, 1886, p. 2.

81. Mark Judd, "'The Oddest Combination of Town and Country': Popular Culture and the London Fairs, 1800–1860," in John K. Walton and James

Walvin, eds., *Leisure in Britain, 1780–1939*, Manchester: Manchester University Press, pp. 11–30; and Ben Shephard, "Showbiz Imperialism: The Case of Peter Lobengula," in John M. MacKenzie, ed., *Imperialism and Popular Culture*, Manchester: Manchester University Press, 1986, pp. 94–112.

82. *Crystal Palace District Advertiser*, September 2, 1911, p. 4.

83. *Crystal Palace District Advertiser*, April 22, 1911, p. 3.

84. Burton Benedict, "The Display of People," in *The Anthropology of World's Fairs: San Francisco's Panama Pacific Exposition of 1915*, Berkeley, CA: Scolar Press, 1983, pp. 43–48; and Robert Bogdan, *Freak Show: Presenting Human Oddities for Amusement and Profit*, Chicago: The University of Chicago Press, 1988.

85. *Proceedings of the Royal Asiatic Society of Bengal*, August 1865, pp. 148–49, March 1866, pp. 70–73, April 1866, pp. 80–95, August 1866, pp. 181–85, September 1866, pp. 188–91, and December 1866, 243–45.

86. *Proceedings of the Royal Asiatic Society of Bengal*, April 1866, p. 88.

87. *Calcutta Review* 43 (1866), p. 446.

88. "Papers on Indian Ethnology," *Huxley MSS, Notes and Correspondence — Anthropology*, vol. 12, XVI, pp. 96, 115–17 and verso, Imperial College of Science Archives, London; "Correspondence between Huxley and Fayrer," *Huxley Papers, Scientific and General Correspondence*, vol. 16, General Letters: F., 16.57–16.64, Imperial College of Science Archives; and *Proceedings of the Royal Asiatic Society of Bengal*, September 1866, pp. 188–90.

89. *Statesman and Friend of India*, July 30, 1883, p. 4.

90. Ibid., p. 4.

91. "Progress Report of the Bengal Economic Museum for the Year 1884–1885 by Horace A. Cokerell, Chairman, Bengal Economic Museum," *Revenue and Agriculture Department Proceedings*, Oriental and India Office Collections, P/2800, pp. 2–4.

92. For example, see Rudyard Kipling, "Beyond the Pale," in *Plain Tales from the Hills*, New York: The Greenwood Press, 1917, pp. 233–42.

93. *Intercolonial Exhibition Letterbook, 1866–67*, Victoria Public Record Service, 927/6, p. 203.

94. R. E. N. Twopeny, *A Proposal for Holding an Australasian Exhibition in London*, Sydney, 1883, Australia Pamphlets, no. 20, Foreign and Commonwealth Office Library, London, pp. 6–7.

95. James Barry to Redmond Barry, July 1, 1861, *Redmond Barry Collection*, La Trobe Collection, State Library of Victoria, MS 8380, 601/2 (A).

96. The forty-seven-match tour of England by thirteen Aboriginal cricketers in 1868 was a notable exception to this policy. See John Mulvaney, "Aboriginal Australians Abroad, 1606–1875," *Aboriginal History* 12 (1988), pp. 41–47; and Greg Ryan, "'Handsome Physiognomy and Blameless Physique': Indigenous Colonial Sporting Tours and British Racial Consciousness, 1868 and 1888," *International Journal of the History of Sport* 14 (1997), pp. 67–81.

97. February 17, 1860, "William Thomas Correspondence as Guardian of Aborigines, Victoria," *Surveyor-General, Board of Land and Works Re. Aboriginal Affairs, Department of Crown Lands and Survey, Registered Inward Correspondence,* Victoria Public Record Office, 2896/Box 4, B 1860/767; and "Papers re. D. Charnay, Mission Scientifique du Ministere de l'Instruction Publique," *Joseph Anderson Panton Papers,* Royal Historical Society of Victoria Archives, Melbourne, MS 000336, Box 118/13.

98. Bain Attwood, *The Making of the Aborigines,* Boston: Allen & Unwin, 1989, and *A Life Together, A Life Apart: A History of Relations Between Europeans and Aborigines,* Carlton, Victoria: Melbourne University Press, 1994; and *Aborigines' Friends Association Papers,* Mortlock Library, South Australia, PRG 186.

99. Sir Redmond Barry to J. Thomas, August 27, 1861, *Exhibition Correspondence,* La Trobe Collection, State Library of Victoria, Box 122/2, fol. 162.

100. Jean Woolmington, "The Civilisation/Christianisation Debate and the Australian Aborigines," *Aboriginal History* 10 (1986), pp. 90–98.

101. *Twentieth Annual Report of the Aborigines' Friends Association,* 1886, p. 10.

102. Stephen G. Foster, "'The Purposes, Duties and Arts of Life': Judge Burton's Plan for Black Villages," *Push From the Bush* 9 (1981), pp. 44–55.

103. August 22, 1874, *Despatch Book: Governor to Secretary of State,* vol. 8, no. 97, Victoria Public Record Office, 1084, pp. 137–40.

104. Julian Thomas, "A Peep at 'The Blacks,'" in *The Vagabond Papers,* 4th series, Melbourne: George Robertson, 1877, pp. 56–63.

105. Tom Griffiths, "Past Silences: Aborigines and Convicts in our History-Making," *Australian Cultural History* 6 (1987), pp. 18–32; and Henry Reynolds, *Law of the Land,* New York: Penguin Books, 1987.

106. *Australasian Sketcher* (Melbourne), April 7, 1886, p. 51.

107. *Official Record of the Sydney International Exhibition, 1879,* Sydney: Thomas Richards, Government Printer, 1881, p. 171.

108. *Graphic,* December 13, 1879, p. 579.

109. *Illustrated Sydney News,* 1879, pp. 6–7, 16.

110. For example, see Peter Overlack, "Queensland's Annexation of Papua: A Background to Anglo-German Friction," *Journal of the Royal Historical Society of Queensland* 10 (1978–79), pp. 123–37.

111. "General Report. Classes 200–294. Manufactures," and "General Report. Classes 300–329. Education and Science," in *Official Record of the Sydney International Exhibition,* pp. 171, 364–66.

112. "The Ethnological Court," in *Notes on the Sydney International Exhibition of 1879, with Photo-Type Illustrations,* Sydney: Government Printing Office, 1880, pp. 142–67.

113. Ibid., pp. lxxiv–lxxvii.

114. Ibid., p. 171.

115. *Graphic,* December 13, 1879, p. 579.

116. *Official Record of the Sydney International Exhibition,* pp. 171, 364–66.

117. Ibid., p. 171.

118. *Zoological and Acclimatisation Society of Victoria Minute Book, 1884–1888,* Victoria Public Record Office, 2223/8, p. 169.

119. "Report of the Director to the Council, 1888," ibid., p. 4.

120. "Report of the Director to the Council, 1887," ibid., p. 184.

121. *Minute Book, Volume 2, 1871–1889, Aborigines' Friends Association,* Mortlock Library, State Library of South Australia, SRG 139/2/2.

122. Henry Cole, "National Culture and Recreation: Antidotes to Vice," *Sir Henry Cole Papers, Miscellanies, Volume 17, 1845–1875,* National Art Library, London, 55 AA 62, fols. 300–5.

123. *Correspondence Files, Department of Aboriginal Affairs,* 1887, Public Record Office of South Australia, Dockets Nos. 177, 179, and 202; and *Protector of Aborigines Letterbook, 1885–1892,* Public Record Office of South Australia, GRG 52/7/6, pp. 361, 372.

124. August 19, 1887, *Minute Book, 1885–1910, Geographical Society of Australasia, South Australia Branch,* Mortlock Library, State Library of South Australia, p. 50.

125. November 22, 1887, Joseph Hillier, *Diary: A Visit to Adelaide, 1887,* La Trobe Collection, State Library of Victoria, MS 8915, Bay 5.

126. *South Australian Register,* August 29, 1887, p. 7; *South Australian Advertiser,* September 7, 1887, p. 5, September 24, 1887, p. 6, and November 23, 1887, p. 5; and Carmel McKeough and Norman Etherington, "Jubilee 50," *Journal of the Historical Society of South Australia* 12 (1984), p. 14.

127. *Brisbane Courier,* August 3, 1897, p. 5.

128. *Finance Committee Minutes, Adelaide Jubilee International Exhibition, 1887–1888,* Public Record Office of South Australia, GRG 47/5/1, pp. 314, 346, 380.

129. For example, "Department 18. Firearms, Ordnance and Other Instruments and Apparatus for the Destruction of Life, for Hunting, Trapping, Fishing, Military Engineering," in *By Authority of the Commissioners. Victorian Intercolonial Exhibition, 1875. Presented to the Philadelphia Exhibition, 1876. Opened 2nd September, 1875. Official Catalogue of Exhibits,* Melbourne: M'Carron, Bird, 1875, pp. 165–66.

130. *NAIA Committee Minutes, 1891–1893,* John Oxley Library, State Library of Queensland, OM AB/2/2.

131. *Aborigines' Friends Association, South Australia, Minute Book,* vol. 2, 1871–1889, Mortlock Library, State Library of South Australia, SRG 139/2/2.

132. *Illustrated London News,* July 17, 1886, p. 82.

133. *Builder* 50 (1886), p. 666.

134. *Times,* May 22, 1886, p. 5.

135. Thomas H. Hendley, "Indian Museums," *Journal of Indian Art and Industry* 16 (1914), pp. 39–40.

136. For example, see "The Festival of Kutub Mohedin," *Orientalist* 3

(1888–1889), pp. 167–68; "Art. VI—The Fair at Sakhi Sarwar," *Calcutta Review* 60 (1875), pp. 78–102; and "The Samlaj Fair," *Indian Antiquary* 1 (1872), p. 192 [reprinted from *Times of India*].

137. F. S. Growse, *Bulandshahr: or, Sketches of an Indian District; Social, Historical and Architectural,* Benares: Medical Hall Press, 1884, pp. 65–82.

138. Val C. Prinsep, *Glimpses of Imperial India* [1878], Delhi: Mittal Publications, 1979.

139. Thomas H. Hendley, "Indian Museums," *Journal of Indian Art and Industry* 16 (1914), pp. 39–40.

140. *Life and Letters of Lord Macaulay,* vol. 2, p. 226.

141. "Lecture I.—Dr. Whewell on the General Bearings of the Great Exhibition," in *Lectures on the Progress of Arts and Science,* pp. 5, 10–11.

142. For descriptions of the Indian exhibition courts, see *Graphic,* May 17, 1884, p. 483; *International Health Exhibition. The District Railway Exhibition Guide: A Popular Summary and Review,* London: Alfred Boot and Son, 1884, p. 56; and *Building News and Engineering Journal,* 49 (1886), p. 272.

143. Cundall, ed., *Reminiscences of the Colonial and Indian Exhibition,* p. 34.

144. *The Exhibition of Art-Industry in Dublin, 1853. The Art-Journal Illustrated Catalogue,* London: Virtue, 1853, p. 34; and *Illustrated London News,* July 12, 1862, pp. 41–42, 45.

145. The Irish villages at the 1908 Franco-British Exhibition are discussed in Annie E. Coombes, *Reinventing Africa: Museums, Material Culture, and Popular Imagination in Late Victorian and Edwardian England,* New Haven, CT: Yale University Press, 1994, pp. 207–13.

146. K. S. Inglis, "The Imperial Connection: Telegraphic Communication between England and Australia, 1872–1902," in A. F. Madden and W. H. Morris-Jones, eds., *Australia and Britain: Studies in a Changing Relationship,* London: Frank Cass and the Institute of Commonwealth Studies, University of London, 1980, pp. 21–38; and Daniel R. Headrick, *The Tools of Empire: Technology and European Imperialism in the Nineteenth Century,* New York: Oxford University Press, 1981.

147. "Telegraphs," in *A Sketch of South Australia for the Melbourne International Exhibition, 1880. Published by Direction of the Royal Commissioners for South Australia. With Maps and Statistical Diagrams,* Adelaide: E. Spiller, Government Printer, 1880, pp. 48–49.

148. Sir Richard Temple, *India in 1880,* 3rd ed., London: John Murray, 1881, pp. 279–80.

149. Harriet Martineau, *British Rule in India; a Historical Sketch,* London: Smith, Elder, 1857.

150. *Illustrated London News,* May 28, 1853, p. 415.

151. Alexander W. Dobbie, *Rough Notes of a Traveller,* 1st ed., Adelaide, 1877, p. 101.

152. *Prospectus, Queensland International Exhibition, 1897,* Queensland State Archives, QSA 11 CHA/25, pp. 3–4.

153. February, 1881, *Richard Pope Diary, 1879–1884,* La Trobe Collection, State Library of Victoria, Box 2470, fols. 64–70; and Ada Cambridge, *Thirty Years in Australia,* London: Methuen, 1903, pp. 186–87.

154. *Crystal Palace District Advertiser,* August 20, 1910, p. 3.

155. Audrey Short, "Workers under Glass," *Victorian Studies* 10 (1966), pp. 193–202.

156. John Tallis, *Tallis's History and Description of the Crystal Palace and the Exhibition of the World's Industry in 1851,* vol. 3, London: The London Printing and Publishing Company, 1852, pp. 49–51.

157. *The Life and Letters of Lord Macaulay,* vol. 2, pp. 292–94.

158. *Times,* July 7, 1862, p. 7.

159. *Leisure Hour* 12 (1862), p. 615.

160. *Times,* April 29, 1862, p. 7, April 30, 1862, p. 5, May 2, 1862, p. 11, and May 3, 1862, p. 11.

161. *Leisure Hour* 12 (1862), pp. 791–794.

162. *Macmillan's Magazine* 7 (1862), p. 120.

163. Ibid., p. 122.

164. *The Life and Letters of Lord Macaulay,* vol. 2, p. 292.

165. "Some Various Panics During 1850–51," in *Fifty Years of Public Work of Sir Henry Cole, K.C.B., Accounted For in His Deeds, Speeches and Writings,* vol. 1, London: George Bell and Sons, 1884, pp. 185–93. The political satirist "E. M. G." penned a more lyrical fear: "Lo! They come! on happy Britain's shore / The locust hordes of foreign nations poor, / Ripe for sedition, prompt to lend their aid / And teach John Bull the arts of Barricade." Source: *The Crystal Palace; a Satire for the Time,* National Art Library, London, 400.A.126(2), p. 2.

166. *Edinburgh Review* 96 (1852), pp. 8.

167. Ibid., pp. 20–21.

168. Drew, *Glimpses and Gatherings,* p. 195.

169. "To The Working Classes," *Northern Star,* April 19, 1851, p. 1.

170. "Report by the Chairman of the Sub-committee for External Arrangements," in *Report of the Nagpore Exhibition of Arts, Manufactures, and Produce, December 1865,* Nagpore: Central Provinces' Printing Press, 1866, pp. 19–21.

171. *Statesman and Friend of India,* November 6, 1883, p. 2.

172. Risley, "Report on the Calcutta International Exhibition," p. 5.

173. "Regulations to be Observed By Police on Duty at International Exhibition," *Colonial Secretary Letters, 1879,* Archives Office of New South Wales, 1/2451. Sir Henry Parkes approved these regulations with a marginal note: "There appears to be nothing objectionable in these Regulations."

174. *Macmillan's Magazine* 7 (1862), p. 122.

175. Babbage, *The Exposition of 1851,* pp. 30–41.

176. *Times,* August 11, 1862, p. 5, and August 29, 1862, p. 7.

177. Zadock Thompson, *Journal of a Trip to London, Paris, and the Great Exhibition, in 1851,* Burlington, VT: Nichols and Warren, 1852, pp. 66–67.

178. *Photographic News* 2 (1867), p. 39.

179. *Photographic News* 22 (1878), pp. 168–69.

180. John Allwood, *The Great Exhibitions*, London: Studio Vista, 1977, p. 70.

181. *Official Record of the Sydney International Exhibition, 1879*, p. cxv.

182. E. P. Thompson, "Time, Work-Discipline, and Industrial Capitalism," in M. W. Flinn and T. C. Smout, eds., *Essays in Social History*, Oxford: Clarendon Press, 1979, pp. 39–77.

183. "Report by the Chairman of the Sub-Committee for External Arrangements," in *Report of the Nagpore Exhibition*, pp. 19–20.

184. *Bombay Telegraph and Courier*, November 20, 1854, p. 2207.

185. *Working Man*, August 1, 1862, pp. 197–98.

186. Jeffrey Richards and John D. MacKenzie, *The Railway Station: A Social History*, New York: Oxford University Press, 1986; and Jack Simmons, *The Victorian Railway*, London: Thames and Hudson, 1991.

187. June 19, 1846, *Journals and Correspondence of Lady Eastlake*, vol. 1, ed. Charles Eastlake Smith, London: John Murray, 1895, p. 196.

188. Philip Bright, ed., *The Diaries of John Bright*, Toronto: Cassell and Company, 1930, p. 126.

189. Charles Dickens to Mrs. Watson, July 11, 1851, *The Letters of Charles Dickens, Edited by His Sister-in-Law and His Eldest Daughter, Volume I, 1833 to 1856*, London: Chapman and Hall, 1880, p. 257.

190. Thompson, *Journal of a Trip to London, Paris and the Great Exhibition*, p. 95.

191. *Report of the Royal Commission for the Colonial and Indian Exhibition, London, 1886*, p. xlv.

192. R. Ragoonath Row, "Social Intercourse Between the Ruled and the Rulers in India," *Asiatic Quarterly Review* 3 (1887), pp. 241–49.

193. *Punch* 20 (1851), p. 247.

194. *Statesman and Friend of India*, December 27, 1883, p. 2. The editorial concludes: "The claim of the Nizam is unanswerable."

195. *Times*, October 22, 1883, p. 7.

196. *Statesman and Friend of India*, January 15, 1884, p. 3.

197. Ibid., January 7, 1884, p. 5.

198. Patrick Brantlinger, *Rule of Darkness: British Literature and Imperialism, 1830–1914*, Ithaca, NY: Cornell University Press, 1990; Henry Louis Gates, Jr., ed., *"Race," Writing, and Difference*, Chicago: University of Chicago Press, 1986; Edward Said, *Orientalism*, New York: Vintage Books, 1979; and *Culture and Imperialism*, New York: Alfred A. Knopf, 1993.

199. For example, see *The Nubian Caravan at the Alexandra Palace* [1877], National Art Library, London, Pamphlet 200.B.5 (D), 9 pp.

200. For a discussion of the carnivalesque mode in which authority is symbolically overturned, or temporarily destroyed and replaced by subordinate classes, see Mikhail Bakhtin, *Rabelais and His World*, trans. Helene Iswolsky, Bloomington: Indiana University Press, 1984; Natalie Zemon Davis, *Society and Culture in Early Modern France*, Stanford, CA: Stanford University Press,

1975; and Victor Turner, *The Ritual Process: Structure and Anti-Structure,* Ithaca, NY: Cornell University Press, 1979.

201. Wemyss Reid, ed., *Memoirs and Correspondence of Lyon Playfair, First Lord Playfair of St. Andrews, P.C., G.C.B., LL.D., F.R.S., etc.,* New York: Harper & Brothers, 1899, p. 248.

202. "All of us are united at present by the invisible bonds of relationship and of affection for our common country, for our common sovereign, and for our joint spiritual inheritance. . . . We laugh at sentiment, but every generous and living relationship between man and man, or between men and their country, is sentiment and nothing else." James Anthony Froude, *Oceana; or, England and Her Colonies,* 2nd ed., London: Longman, Green, 1886, pp. 383–96.

203. "Preface," in *Official Programme, Festival of Empire Exhibition, 1911,* Guildhall Library, London, p. 1.

CHAPTER 8.   THE IMPERIAL PILGRIMS' PROGRESS

1. "Opening of the Indian Art Exhibition at Delhi," *Speeches by H.E. the Lord Curzon of Kedleston,* Oriental and India Office Collections, MSS Eur. F. 111/561, pp. 86–91.

2. *Manchester Guardian,* January 10, 1903, p. 7.

3. *Manchester Guardian,* January 27, 1903, p. 9.

4. "The Delhi Durbar: A Retrospect," *Blackwood's Edinburgh Magazine* 173 (1903), p. 315.

5. Benedict Anderson, *Imagined Communities: Reflections on the Origin and Spread of Nationalism,* New York: Verso, 1991; Paul Connerton, *How Societies Remember,* New York: Cambridge University Press, 1991; and Jacqueline Rose, *States of Fantasy,* Oxford: Clarendon Press, 1997.

6. Donald Horne, *Ideas for a Nation,* Sydney: Pan Books, 1989, p. 81.

7. Graeme Davison, "Festivals of Nationhood: The International Exhibitions," in S. L. Goldberg and F. B. Smith, eds., *Australian Cultural History,* New York: Cambridge University Press, 1988, p. 164.

8. *Pall Mall Gazette,* May 5, 1886, p. 3.

9. Ainslie T. Embree, "Bengal as the Western Image of India," in Mark Juergensmeyer, ed., *Imagining India: Essays on Indian History,* New York: Oxford University Press, 1989, pp. 101–9.

10. Tom Griffiths, "Past Silences: Aborigines and Convicts in our History-Making," *Australian Cultural History* 6 (1987), pp. 18–32.

11. Similar decorations celebrated the formal proclamation of Queen Victoria as "Empress of India" at the Royal Durbar in Delhi on January 1, 1877; see Owen Tudor Burne, "The Empress of India," *Asiatic Quarterly Review* 3 (1887), pp. 11–31; and Bernard S. Cohn, "Representing Authority in Victorian India," in Eric Hobsbawm and Terence Ranger, eds., *The Invention of Tradition,* New York: Cambridge University Press, 1983, pp. 165–209.

12. "List of Armorial Bearings: Centre Hall, Northern Hall and Southern Hall," in *Official Catalogue of the Great Industrial Exhibition (In Connection*

with the Royal Dublin Society), 1853, 4th ed., Dublin: John Falconer, 1853, pp. 5–6.

13. *Australasian Sketcher* (Melbourne), October 2, 1875, p. 105.

14. J. W. Burrow, *A Liberal Descent: Victorian Historians and the English Past,* New York: Cambridge University Press, 1983.

15. The executive commissioner for New South Wales was shocked when local officials at Adelaide's Jubilee International Exhibition in 1887 made no efforts to provide flags, banners, or other ornamentation to cover "the hideousness of . . . the galvanized iron walls and roof" in the display areas of their new exhibition building and its Western Annexe. J. C. Neil, *Official Report of the Executive Commissioner for New South Wales to the Adelaide Jubilee International Exhibition, 1887–1888,* Sydney: Charles Potter, Government Printer, 1890, p. 46.

16. ("Private and Confidential Letter") Chairman of Provisional Council [Lord Plymouth] to Lord Avebury, *Avebury Papers,* vol. 29, British Library Manuscript Department, London, Add. MSS 49, 676, fols. 154–55.

17. *Crystal Palace District Advertiser,* March 18, 1911, p. 3, and April 22, 1911, p. 3.

18. *Festival of Empire: The Pageant of London, May to July, 1910,* 2nd ed., Guildhall Library, London, Pamphlet PAM 10909, 24 pp.

19. For discussion of the concept and structures of "civil religion," see Robert N. Bellah, "Civil Religion in America," in William G. McLoughlin and Robert N. Bellah, eds., *Religion in America,* Boston: Beacon Press, 1968, pp. 3–23; John A. Coleman, "Civil Religion," *Sociological Analysis* 31 (1970), pp. 67–77; and Phillip E. Hammond, "The Rudimentary Forms of Civil Religion," in Robert N. Bellah and Phillip E. Hammond, eds., *Varieties of Civil Religion,* San Francisco: Harper and Row, 1980, pp. 121–37.

20. *Friend of the People,* May 10, 1851, pp. 189–90; emphasis in original.

21. *Times,* December 28, 1872, p. 10.

22. John Forbes Watson, *International Exhibitions,* London: Henry S. King, 1873.

23. The relationships between exhibitions and the various private and public spheres, such as civil society, are discussed in Tony Bennett, "The Exhibitionary Complex," in Nicholas B. Dirks, Geoffrey Eley, and Sherry B. Ortner, eds., *Culture/Power/History: A Reader in Contemporary Social Theory,* Princeton, NJ: Princeton University Press, 1994, 123–54; and Debora Silverman, "The 1889 Exhibition: The Crisis in Bourgeois Individualism," *Oppositions* 8 (1977), pp. 71–91. These and similar studies draw upon Jürgen Habermas, *The Structural Transformation of the Public Sphere: An Inquiry into a Category of Bourgeois Society,* originally published in 1962, and various works by Michel Foucault, including *The Order of Things: An Archaeology of the Human Sciences* (English translation in 1970), and *Discipline and Punish: The Birth of the Prison* (English translation in 1979).

24. Mary Poovey, *Making a Social Body: British Cultural Formation, 1830–1864,* Chicago: University of Chicago Press, 1995.

25. Paul Greenhalgh, *Ephemeral Vistas: The Expositions Universelles, Great Exhibitions and World's Fairs, 1851–1939*, Dover, NH: Manchester University Press, 1988; John M. MacKenzie, *Propaganda and Empire: The Manipulation of British Public Opinion, 1880–1960*, Dover, NH: Manchester University Press, 1985, esp. pp. 96–120; Robert Rydell, *All the World's a Fair: Visions of Empire at American International Exhibitions, 1876–1916*, Chicago: The University of Chicago Press, 1984; and *World of Fairs: The Century-of-Progress Expositions*, Chicago: The University of Chicago Press, 1993.

26. Harriet Martineau, *How to Observe. / Morals Manners*, London: Charles Knight, 1838; and Ian Hacking, "Making Up People," in Thomas C. Heller, Morton Sosna, and David E. Wellbery, eds., *Reconstructing Individualism: Autonomy, Individuality, and the Self in Western Thought*, Stanford, CA: Stanford University Press, 1986, pp. 222–36, 347–48.

27. Manon Niquette and William J. Buxton, "Meet Me at the Fair: Sociability and Reflexivity in Nineteenth-Century World Expositions," *Canadian Journal of Communications* 22 (1977), pp. 81–113.

28. William Drew, *Glimpses and Gatherings, During A Voyage and Visit to London and the Great Exhibition, in the Summer of 1851*, Augusta: Homan and Manley, 1852, pp. 376–77.

29. Burton Benedict, "International Exhibitions and National Identity," *Anthropology Today* (U.K.) 17 (1991), pp. 5–9.

30. *Times*, April 3, 1884, p. 10; and *Papers in Connection with Chicago Exhibition*, Archives Office of New South Wales, Sydney, 1226/33.

31. *Adelaide Jubilee International Exhibition, 1887–1888. Finance Committee Minutes, 1883–1887*, Public Record Office of South Australia, GRG 47/5/2, p. 24.

32. *International Exhibition, 1886. Minute Book of the Executive Committee, 31 July 1883 to 9 June 1888*, Public Record Office of South Australia, GRG 47/3, fol. 42; and *Adelaide Jubilee International Exhibition, 1887. Art Union Distribution Rules and Regulations, 1886*, Mortlock Library, State Library of South Australia, Pamphlet Z 606 A 228.

33. Jules Joubert to Alfred Deakin, December 15 and June 17, 1886, *Alfred Deakin Papers*, National Library Manuscripts Section, Australian National Library, Canberra, MS 1540/9/39–42, 44–45.

34. January 12 and 24, 1862, *Redmond Barry Collection*, La Trobe Collection, State Library of Victoria, MSS 605/7(A) and (B).

35. George E. Loyau, "Alexander William Dobbie," in *Notable South Australians*, Adelaide: Carey, Page & Co., 1885, pp. 117–19.

36. Alexander W. Dobbie, *Rough Notes of a Traveller Taken in England, Scotland, France, Holland, . . . Greece, Egypt, Ceylon and Elsewhere*, 2nd series, London: Simpkin, Marshall, Hamilton Kent, 1890, pp. 187–88.

37. *Visitors' Books, Old Colonists' Court, Adelaide Jubilee International Exhibition, 1887*, vol. 2, Public Record Office of South Australia, GRG 47/17/2, pp. 402–3.

38. W. Fraser, *The Business of Travel: A Fifty Years' Record of Progress*,

London: Thomas Cook and Son, 1891, esp. pp. 43–52, 141–48, 161–72, 287–94; and George Augustus Sala, *Life of George Augustus Sala, Written By Himself, Volume 2*, New York: Charles Scribner's Sons, 1895, pp. 186–89, 333–51.

39. November 12, 1886, *Journal of F. Kempson-Kelly: A Trip from Burma to Australia*, Mortlock Library, State Library of South Australia, D. 5588/1 (L.)

40. *Visitors' Register, Melbourne International Exhibition, 1880–1881*, La Trobe Collection, State Library of Victoria, MS 9306; and *Visitors' Book, Exhibition Building Trustees*, 2 volumes, Victoria Public Record Office, 839/1–2.

41. *Visitors to the Buildings for the International Exhibition of 1862*, National Art Library Archives, London, 86 NN 58; and *Visitors' Books, Old Colonists' Court, Adelaide Jubilee International Exhibition, 1887*, 2 volumes.

42. August 29 and June 10, 1885, London, *James Barnet Papers, 1852–1898*, Mitchell Library, State Library of New South Wales, ML MSS 726.

43. June 13 and April 17, 1873, *Personal Correspondence, 1873–1876, Knox Family Papers*, Mitchell Library, State Library of New South Wales, ML MSS 98/6, fols. 4 and 7.

44. E. H. McCormick, *Omai: Pacific Envoy*, Auckland: Auckland University Press, 1977; and Daniel J. Peacock, *Lee Boo of Belau: A Prince in London*, Honolulu: University of Hawaii Press, 1987. The reluctance on the part of Australian officials to send Aboriginals overseas might have been influenced, in part, by the problems encountered by such Pacific Islanders during the visit to England and upon their return. Early travelers faced smallpox, measles, and social alienation in Britain and after their return home.

45. References to Ogilvie's early days in New South Wales are found in Robert Leycester Dawson, "Pioneering Days in the Clarence River District," *Journal and Proceedings, Royal Australian Historical Society* 20 (1934), pp. 73–98. A more general biography is "Ogilvie, Edward David Stewart (1814–1896)," in *Australian Dictionary of Biography, Volume 5, 1851–1890: K–Q*, Melbourne: Melbourne University Press, 1974, pp. 358–59.

46. Edmund S. Ogilvie, *Diary of Travels in Three Quarters of the Globe. By an Australian Settler. In Two Volumes*, London: Saunders and Otley, 1856; Alexander W. Dobbie, *Rough Notes of a Traveller*, 1st ed., Adelaide: n.p., 1877; and *Rough Notes of a Traveller Taken in England, Scotland, France, Holland, . . . Greece, Egypt, Ceylon and Elsewhere*, 2nd series.

47. Ogilvie, *Diary of Travels*, pp. iii–iv.

48. For discussion of Australian travel and travelers, see Andrew Hassam, "Double Visions and the Desire for Recognition on Foreign Shores," *Journal of Australian Studies* 53 (1997), pp. 89–98; Charles Higham and Michael Wilding, eds., *Australians Abroad*, Sydney: F. W. Cheshire, 1967; and "Travellers, Journeys, Tourists," *Australian Cultural History* 10 (1991).

49. *Pall Mall Gazette*, May 4, 1886, p. 2; and *Colonial and Indian Exhibition Railway Guide and Route Book*, London: William Clowes and Sons, 1886, pp. 26–27.

50. Antoinette Burton, "Making a Spectacle of Empire: Indian Travellers in Fin-de-Siecle London," *History Workshop Journal* 42 (1996), pp. 127–46; and

At the Heart of the Empire: Indians and the Colonial Encounter in Late-Victorian Britain, Berkeley, CA: University of California Press, 1998.

51. C. J. Rowe, *An Englishman's Views on Questions of the Day in Victoria*, London: n.p., 1882, pp. 116–22.

52. Dobbie, *Rough Notes of a Traveller*, 1st ed., pp. 77–78.

53. "Reminiscences of a Pioneer in N.S.W.," *Morey Papers, 1893–1905*, Mitchell Library, State Library of New South Wales, ML MSS 883, fol. 465.

54. June 13 and April 17, 1873, *Personal Correspondence, 1873–1876, Knox Family Papers*, fols. 4 and 7.

55. Dobbie, *Rough Notes of a Traveller*, 1st ed., pp. 77–78.

56. William Howitt, *Land, Labour and Gold: or, Two Years in Victoria with Visits to Sydney and Van Diemen's Land* [1855], Kilmore: Lowden Publishing Company, 1972, p. vii.

57. Edmund Morey recalled how English men and women always asked about the roughness of living as a squatter. They showed no interest during the late 1850s in any of Australia's growing cities. "Memoirs of Edmund Morey (1859)," *The Morey Papers, 1893–1908*, Mitchell Library, State Library of New South Wales, ML MSS 1456, pp. 150–51.

58. Ogilvie, *Diary of Travels*, vol. 2, p. 381.

59. *International Exhibition at Philadelphia, 1876. Report of The Commissioners For Victoria to His Excellency the Governor*, Melbourne: John Ferres, Government Printer, 1877.

60. Sir Redmond Barry to Mrs. Louis Barrows, May 20, May 29, June 7, and August 25, 1862, *Redmond Barry Correspondence*, La Trobe Collection, State Library of Victoria, MS 8380, Box 599/5.

61. *Illustrated London News*, July 17, 1886, p. 59; Frank Cundall, ed., *Reminiscences of the Colonial and Indian Exhibition, illustrated by Thomas Riley, Designer of the Exhibition Diploma*, London: William Clowes and Sons, 1886, p. 6; and *Report of the Royal Commission for the Colonial and Indian Exhibition, 1886*, English Parliamentary Papers, 1887 [c. 5083] xx. 1, pp. xlviii–xlix and 355–68.

62. *Graphic*, June 12, 1886, pp. 621, 623; and "August, 5, 1886," *Minutes of the Museum Trustees Board Meetings, Department of Ethnography*, Museum of Mankind, British Museum, London, pp. 17, 289.

63. "The Imperial Connection," *Colonial Magazine* 4 (1869), p. 123.

64. *Christian Weekly and Methodist Journal*, June 7, 1889, p. 3.

65. "Circular No. 32EX. Extract from the Proceedings of the Government of India, in the Revenue and Agricultural Department (Exhibitions),—dated Simla, the 28th July 1882," in *Report on the Melbourne International Exhibition*, Oriental and India Office Collections, W 2012, pp. 1–2.

66. *Statesman and Friend of India*, April 6, 1884, p. 3.

67. *Diary of Sir S. J. Way*, Mortlock Library, State Library of South Australia, PRD 30/series 1.

68. January 1, 1887–February 23, 1889, *George Frederick Belcher Diary*,

vol. 10, La Trobe Collection, State Library of Victoria, MS 6219/Box 234 (3 and 4).

69. William Westgarth, *Half a Century of Australasian Progress, A Personal Retrospect*, London: Sampson Low, Marston, Searle, & Rivington, 1889, p. 41.

70. T. N. Mukharji, *A Visit to Europe*, London: Edward Stanford, 1889, pp. 64–138; and Antoinette Burton, *At the Heart of the Empire: Indians and the Colonial Encounter in Late-Victorian Britain*, Berkeley, CA: University of California Press, 1998.

71. Victor Turner, "The Center Out There: Pilgrim's Goal," *History of Religions* 12 (1973), pp. 191–230; and Edward Shils, "Center and Periphery," in *Center and Periphery: Essays in Macrosociology*, Chicago: University of Chicago Press, 1975, pp. 3–16.

72. Mukharji, *A Visit to Europe*, p. 105.

73. *Reynold's Newspaper*, July 11, 1886, p. 4.

74. *Craftsman* 4 (May 1886), p. 3.

75. George Earle Buckle, ed., "Extract from the Queen's Journal, Buckingham Palace, 4th May 1886," *The Letters of Queen Victoria, 3rd series, A Selection From Her Majesty's Correspondence and Journal, Between The Years 1886 and 1901, Volume I, 1886–1890*, New York: Longmans, Green, 1930, pp. 114–16; and *Diary of S. E. Atkins*, Guildhall Library, London, MS 15, 819. The entry for 1851 (age 44) begins with "Great Exhibition opened in Hyde park by Prince Albert. Sent two 2-days chronometers as Exhibits, but as the Council would not grant Free Admissions to Exhibitors altho' a great agitation was got up by a meeting of that Body, I determined not to enter the Building on payment."

76. *Philadelphia International Exhibition, 1876. Official Catalogue of the British Section, Part I.*, London: George E. Eyre and William Spottiswoode, 1876, pp. 66–67; and *Report of the Commissioners for the Exhibition of 1862, to The Right Hon. Sir George Grey, Bart., G.C.B., etc., etc.*, London: George E. Eyre and William Spottiswoode, 1863, pp. xli–xliii.

77. Richard Temple, *Men and Events of My Time in India*, 2nd ed., London: John Murray, 1882, p. 314.

78. "The Queen in Ireland," *Illustrated London News*, September 3, 1853, pp. 181–82. For discussion of the Dublin show, see Alun C. Davies, "The First Irish Industrial Exhibition: Cork 1852," *Irish Economic and Social History* 2 (1975), pp. 46–59; and "Ireland's Crystal Palace, 1853," in J. M. Goldstrom and L. A. Clarkson, eds., *Irish Population, Economy, and Society*, Oxford: Clarendon Press, 1981, pp. 249–70.

79. George Earle Buckle, ed., *The Letters of Queen Victoria, 2nd series, A Selection from Her Majesty's Correspondence and Journal, Between the Years 1862 and 1878, Volume I, 1862–1869*, London: John Murray, 1926, pp. 250–52.

80. Clifford Geertz, "Centers, Kings, and Charisma: Reflections on the Symbolics of Power," in *Local Knowledge: Further Essays in Interpretive An-*

thropology, New York: Basic Books, 1983; and Shils, "Center and Periphery," pp. 3–16.

81. David Cannadine, "Splendor out of Court: Royal Spectacle and Pageantry in Modern Britain, c. 1820–1977," in Sean Wilentz, ed., *Rites of Power: Symbolism, Ritual and Politics Since the Middle Ages,* Philadelphia: University of Pennsylvania Press, pp. 206–43.

82. W. Shuckard, "Ode on the Great Exhibition, 1851," National Art Library, London, 400.A.13 (1).

83. Drew, *Glimpses and Gatherings,* pp. 336–38.

84. *Graphic,* May 6, 1871, pp. 421–22; and *A Special Report on the Annual International Exhibitions of the Years 1871, 1872, 1873 and 1874, Drawn up by Sir Henry Cole, Acting Commissioner in 1873 and 1874, and Presented by the Commissioners for the Exhibition of 1851,* English Parliamentary Papers, 1878 [XXVII]. 139, p. xl.

85. *Illustrated London News,* May 19, 1883, p. 486, and May 8, 1886, p. 497; and "XVIII.—Royal Visits," in *Report of the Royal Commission for the Colonial and Indian Exhibition, London, 1886,* English Parliamentary Papers, 1887 [c. 5083] xx. 1., pp. 180–82.

86. *Journal of Indian Art and Industry* 1 (1886), p. 63; "The Queen Opening the Colonial and Indian Exhibition," *Graphic,* May 8, 1886, p. 487; *Westminster Review,* n.s. 46 (1886), pp. 29–30; and *Times,* May 5, 1886, pp. 5–6.

87. Mukharji, *A Visit to Europe,* pp. 66–67.

88. Cundall, ed., *Reminiscences of the Colonial and Indian Exhibition,* p. 9.

89. *Westminster Review* 126 (1886), pp. 29–30.

90. *Commonweal, The Official Journal of the Socialist League* 2 (1886), pp. 49–50.

91. "Extract from the Queen's Journal: Buckingham Palace, 4th May 1886," Buckle, ed., *The Letters of Queen Victoria, 3rd series,* pp. 114–16.

92. For early examples, see "Visits of Foreign Princes to England," *Asiatic Journal* 3rd series, 4 (1845), pp. 74–78.

93. "Indian Princes at Court," *Asiatic Quarterly Review* 4 (1887), pp. 241–55.

94. *Illustrated London News,* July 13, 1878, pp. 41–42.

95. Sir Alexander Stuart to W. E. Wilson, May 21, 1886, *Sir Alexander Stuart Family Correspondence,* vol. 3, Mitchell Library, State Library of New South Wales, ML MSS 1279/15, fols. 13–15.

96. "Colonial and Indian Exhibition, 1886," *Governors' Records,* Victoria Public Record Service, 1095/Bundle 17/no. 3.

97. *Reynold's Newspaper,* May 9, 1886, p. 4.

98. Ibid., July 11, 1886, p. 4.

99. "The Late Prince Consort," *Quarterly Review* 111 (1862), pp. 176–200.

100. Mukharji, *A Visit to Europe,* p. 65.

101. "The Heir-Apparent's Latest Move," *Reynold's Newspaper,* October 3, 1886, p. 4.

102. *Brisbane Courier*, August 23, 1876, p. 5, and August 25, 1876, p. 3.

103. *Journal of the Royal Society of Arts* 26 (1877), p. 72; and Despatches No. 56 (April 16, 1879) and No. 139 (November 27, 1879), *Despatch Book: Governor to Secretary of State*, vol. 9, Victoria Public Record Office, 1084, pp. 412–14, 459–60.

104. *Despatch Book: Governor to Secretary of State*, vol. 9, Victoria Public Record Office, 1084, pp. 459–60.

105. *Imperial Federation Journal* 3 (1888), p. 102.

106. *International Exhibition, Sydney, 1879–1880. Photographic Album*, Mitchell Library, State Library of New South Wales, p. 4.

107. July 28, 1883, *Helen Ferguson Diary, 1882–1888*, John Oxley Library, State Library of Queensland, OM 75–91.

108. *Official Catalogue of the Great Industrial Exhibition (In Connection with the Royal Dublin Society), 1853*, p. 17.

109. Westgarth, *Half a Century of Australasian Progress*, p. 60.

110.

> The Queen reigns in Victoria as veritably as she does in England, but as she cannot be on the spot to do those formal acts which in theory are required of her, and as delay in many cases might be inconvenient, she, trusting to the discretion of her representative, permits laws, passed in her name without her cognizance, to have temporary force and validity, until such time as her responsible advisers have had an opportunity of judging of their fitness and desirability. (*Colonial Magazine* [Melbourne], 4 [1869], p. 116)

111. David Cannadine, "The Context, Performance and Meaning of Ritual: The British Monarchy and the 'Invention of Tradition', c. 1820–1977," in Hobsbawm and Ranger, eds., *The Invention of Tradition*, pp. 101–64; and Asa Briggs, "Saxons, Normans and Victorians," in *The Collected Essays of Asa Briggs*, vol. 2, *Images, Problems, Standpoints and Forecasts*, Urbana: University of Illinois Press, 1988, pp. 215–35.

112. *Calcutta Review* 26 (1856), p. 268.

113. *Bombay Telegraph & Courier*, March 1, 1855, p. 415.

114. "The Opening Procession," in Westgarth, *Half a Century of Australasian Progress*, pp. 59–60.

115. Wednesday, 17 September 1879, *William Macleay Diary for 1879*, Macleay Museum, University of Sydney.

116. *Official Record of the Sydney International Exhibition, 1879*, Sydney: Thomas Richards, Government Printer, 1881, pp. xlvii–lxiv.

117. *Australasian Sketcher*, July 12, 1887, p. 103.

118. Carmel McKeough and Norman Etherington, "Jubilee 50," *Journal of the Historical Society of South Australia* 12 (1984), p. 14.

119. *Australasian Sketcher*, September 11, 1880, p. 147.

120. *Trades' Hall Gazette and Library Journal* (Melbourne), August 4, 1888, p. 5.

121. Edward E. Morris, ed., *A Memoir of George Higinbotham: An Australian Politician and Chief Justice of Victoria,* New York: Macmillan, 1895, p. 284.

122. Avner Ben-Amos, "The Other World of Memory: State Funerals of the French Third Republic as Rites of Commemoration," *History and Memory* 1 (1989), pp. 85–108; and Mary Ryan, "The American Parade: Representations of the Nineteenth-Century Social Order," in Lynn Hunt, ed., *The New Cultural History,* Berkeley, CA: University of California Press, pp. 131–53.

123. George E. Raum, *A Tour Around the World, Being a Brief Sketch of the Most Interesting Sights Seen in Europe, Africa, Asia, and America, While on a Two Year's Ramble,* New York: William S. Gottsberger, 1886, p. 361.

124. H. J. Scott, *Report to The Hon. R. D. Ross, Chairman of the South Australian Committee for the Calcutta International Exhibition, 1883–1884,* Mortlock Library, State Library of South Australia, p. 4.

125. Rudyard Kipling, *Something of Myself, for My Friends, Known and Unknown,* ed. Thomas Pinney, New York: Cambridge University Press, 1991, p. 31.

126. *Times,* December 10, 1883, p. 5.

127. Maurice French, "'One People, One Destiny'—A Question of Loyalty: the Origins of Empire Day in New South Wales, 1900–1905," *Journal of the Royal Australian Historical Society* 61 (1975), pp. 236–48.

128. *Festival of Empire: The Pageant of London, June, 1910,* 2nd ed., Guildhall Library, London, Pamphlet PAM 10909, 24 pp.

129. M. P. Noel, *Scrapbook Containing Material Relating to the Pageant of London, Which was Given as Part of the Festival of Empire, 1911,* National Art Library, London, MSS (Eng) 86 HH 16.

130. *Crystal Palace District Advertiser,* April 22, 1911, p. 3.

131. *Crystal Palace District Advertiser,* February 19, 1910, p. 3.

132. Noel, *Scrapbook.*

133. *Crystal Palace District Advertiser,* March 18, 1911, p. 3.

134. Earl of Darnley, ed., *Frank Lascelles: Our Modern Orpheus,* New York: Oxford University Press, 1932; and *Crystal Palace District Advertiser,* September 16, 1911, p. 3. As late as 1923, over 3,600 Harrow residents recreated ten scenes of local history, including "the Court of King Charles the First." One participant nearly found himself in two fights during these "historical" recreations: "first with a rake-hell from the Court of King Charles the First, who was ogling my lawful wedded wife with a too exact historical accuracy, and secondly with a carle in a sheepskin who rode his motorcycle, with too little historical accuracy, over my toes." *Clarion,* June 29, 1923, p. 7.

135. *Review of Reviews* 41 (1910), p. 219.

136. Walter Benjamin, "What Is Epic Theater?" in Hannah Arendt, ed., *Illuminations: Essays and Reflections,* New York: Schocken Books, 1978, pp. 147–54.

137. Darnley, *Frank Lascelles,* p. 167.

138. Ibid., pp. 49–52.

139. "Proposed Architectural Treatment of the Durbar Site, Delhi," Oriental and India Office Collections, MSS Eur. F. 112/431, fols. 1–3.

140. *Building News* 100 (1911), p. 226.

141. *Crystal Palace District Advertiser,* January 1, 1910, p. 3.

142. *Journal of Indian Art and Industry* 15 (1912–1913), p. 111.

143. Sophie C. Lomas, ed., *Festival of Empire. Souvenir of the Pageant of London,* London: Bemrose and Sons, 1911. This volume was praised for surpassing previous pageant books "in numbers, historical accuracy, and breadth of display." *Athenaeum,* no. 4370 (1911), p. 129.

144. *Imperial Review* (Melbourne), October 1887, p. 27.

145. For example, see "Dirge for the Exhibition of 1851," *New Monthly Magazine and Humorist* 93 (1851), p. 364; and Peter Berlyn, *A Popular Narrative of the Origin, History, Progress and Prospects of the Great Industrial Exhibition, 1851,* London: James Gilbert, 1851.

146. *Cornhill Magazine* 5 (1862), p. 673.

147. "Grand Naval and Military Exhibition in Commemoration of the Jubilee of the Great Exhibition," *Crystal Palace Magazine,* 1901, pp. 128–29, 156–57, 206–7, 233–36.

148. Noel, *Scrapbook.*

149. Isaac Selby, *The Old Pioneers' Memorial History of Melbourne From the Discovery of Port Phillip Down to the World War. Two Hundred and Eighty Photo Engravings from Original Pictures and Maps,* Melbourne: The Old Pioneers' Memorial Fund and McCarron, Bird, 1924, p. 17.

150. *Crystal Palace District Advertiser,* June 3, 1911, p. 3.

151. *Macmillan's Magazine* 7 (1862), pp. 123–25.

152. *Ecclesiologist* 12 (1851), p. 351.

153. Thomas Babington Macaulay to Margaret Trevelyan, October 14, 1851, in Thomas Pinney, ed., *The Letters of Thomas Babbington Macaulay, Volume 5, January 1849–December 1855,* New York: Cambridge University Press, 1981, pp. 203–4.

154. Thomas Carlyle to Alexander Carlyle, October 10, 1851, in Edwin W. Marrs. Jr., ed., *The Letters of Thomas Carlyle to His Brother Alexander, with Related Family Matters,* Cambridge, MA: Belknap Press of Harvard University Press, 1968, p. 687.

155. *Illustrated Melbourne Post,* 1867, p. 38.

156. *Times,* March 10, 1884, p. 5, and March 11, 1884, p. 5.

157. Lady Dorchester, ed., *Recollections of a Long Life by Lord Broughton (John Cam Hobhouse), with Additional Extracts from his Private Diaries, Volume VI, 1841–1852,* New York: Charles Scribner's Sons, 1911, p. 285.

158. Noel, *Scrapbook.*

EPILOGUE

1. *Fowke Family Letters and Papers, c. 1865–1927,* MSS English 86 JJ Box III (iii), National Art Library, London.

2. Stephen Bann, *The Clothing of Clio: A Study of the Representation of History in Nineteenth-Century Britain and France,* New York: Cambridge University Press, 1984; and J. W. Burrow, *A Liberal Descent: Victorian Historians and the English Past,* New York: Cambridge University Press, 1983.

3. This phrase is from Renato Rosaldo, "Imperialist Nostalgia," *Special Issue: Memory and Counter-Memory. Representations* 26 (1989), pp. 107–22. Rosaldo is particularly interested in the positioning in relation to traditional societies of anthropologists and their allegedly neutral scientific practices. As he points out, "agents of colonialism" often mourned the culture that they helped destroy, but such a remembrance invented as much as chronicled those communities.

4. *Intercolonial Exhibition, 1866. Vocabulary of Dialects Spoken by Aboriginal Natives in Australia,* Melbourne: Masterman, Printer, 1867.

5. *Official Catalogue of the Great Industrial Exhibition (In Connection with the Royal Dublin Society), 1853,* 4th ed., Dublin: John Falconer, 1853, p. 24; and *Dublin Exhibition, 1853, Art-Journal Catalogue,* p. vii.

6. *Westminster Review* 126 (1886), pp. 35–37.

7. Lisa Lowe, "Nationalism and Exoticism: Nineteenth-Century Others in Flaubert's *Salammbo* and *L'Education sentimentale,*" in Jonathan Arc and Harriet Ritvo, eds., *Macropolitics of Nineteenth-Century Literature: Nationalism, Exoticism, and Imperialism,* Philadelphia: University of Pennsylvania Press, 1991, pp. 213–42; Panivong Norindr, *Phantasmatic Indochina: French Colonial Ideology in Architecture, Film, and Literature,* Durham, NC: Duke University Press, 1996; and William Schneider, *An Empire for the Masses: The French Popular Image of Africa, 1870–1900,* Westport, CT: Greenwood Press, 1982.

8. For example, see "Protection of Antiquarian Remains," *Indian Antiquary* (1879), pp. 105–6.

9. Partha Mitter, *Art and Nationalism in Colonial India, 1850–1922: Occidental Orientations,* New York: Cambridge University Press, 1994, esp. pp. 215, 249, 284–86.

10. Donald Horne, *Ideas for a Nation,* Sydney: Pan Books, 1989.

11. *Victorian Trades Hall Council Minutes, 1888–1893,* Melbourne University Archives, 1/1/1/3, pp. 2, 5, 24.

12. October 14, 1904, *Victorian Trades Hall Council Minutes, 1903–1905,* Melbourne University Archives, 1/1/1/3, p. 359.

13. Brian Durrans, "Handicrafts, Ideology and the Festival of India," *South Asia Research* 2 (1982), pp. 13–22; and Susan Janson and Stuart Macintyre, eds. *Making the Bicentenary,* special issue, *Australian Historical Studies* 23 (1988).

14. *Handbook on Swadeshi, Guide and Directory. All India Khadi and Swadeshi Exhibition, 1937–1938,* Madras, 1938.

15. John M. MacKenzie, *Propaganda and Empire: The Manipulation of British Public Opinion, 1880–1960,* Dover, NH: Manchester University Press, 1985, pp. 96–120.

16. *Builder,* May 30, 1924, p. 868.

17. *Journal of the Royal Institute of British Architects* 31 (1924), pp. 653–65; and *Board of Trade Journal* 112 (1924), pp. 34–35.

18. G. C. Lawrence, ed., *British Empire Exhibition, 1925. Official Guide,* 2nd ed., London: Fleetway Press, 1925, pp. 74–75.

19. John Ruskin, "Lecture I: The Deteriorative Power of Conventional Art Over Nations. An Inaugural Lecture. Delivered at the Kensington Museum, January 1858," in *The Two Paths; being Lectures on Art, and its Application to Decoration and Manufacture, Delivered in 1858–1859,* London: Smith, Elder, 1859, esp. pp. 10–18.

Select Bibliography

The bibliography is organized as follows:

Manuscripts and Private Papers
General Government Correspondence, Papers, and Proceedings
Published Government Documents and Reports
Society and Association Papers and Correspondence
Exhibition Catalogues, Commentaries, Guidebooks, and Papers by Event
General Books, Essays, and Pamphlets
Secondary Sources

MANUSCRIPTS AND PRIVATE PAPERS

Redmond Barry Letterbooks. Victoria Public Record Office, Melbourne.
Redmond Barry Papers and Correspondence. La Trobe Collection, State Library of Victoria, Melbourne.
Sir George C. M. Birdwood Papers. Oriental and India Office Collections, British Library, London.
Sir Henry Cole Papers. National Art Library, London.
Curzon Collection. Oriental and India Office Collections, British Library, London.
Sir Samuel Davenport Papers. Mortlock Library of South Australiana, State Library of South Australia, Adelaide.
Fowke Family Letters and Papers, c. 1865–1927. National Art Library, London.
Sir Arthur Hodgson Papers, 1850–1889. Queensland State Library, Brisbane.
Huxley Papers. Imperial College of Science Archives, London.
James Inglis Papers. Mitchell Library, State Library of New South Wales, Sydney.
Ironside Family Papers. Mitchell Library, State Library of New South Wales, Sydney.

John Lockwood Kipling Correspondence and Files. Kipling Family Papers. Archives Department, University of Sussex, Brighton.

Macarthur Family Papers. Mitchell Library, State Library of New South Wales, Sydney.

William Macleay Diary. Macleay Museum, University of Sydney, Sydney.

Macmillan Papers. Manuscripts Department, British Library, London.

Lord Mayo Papers. University of Cambridge Archives, Cambridge.

E. P. Ramsay Papers and Correspondence. Mitchell Library, State Library of New South Wales, Sydney.

Sir Richard Temple Papers. Oriental and India Office Collections, British Library, London.

Von Mueller Correspondence. Royal Historical Society of Victoria, Melbourne.

GENERAL GOVERNMENT CORRESPONDENCE,
PAPERS, AND PROCEEDINGS

Australian Museum Correspondence and Minute Books. Australian Museum, Sydney.

Board of Trade Papers and Correspondence. Public Record Office, Kew.

Chief Secretary's Correspondence and Files. Victoria Public Record Office, Melbourne.

C.S.O. Letterbooks of Letters to Agent-General, London. Queensland State Archives, Brisbane.

Colonial Secretary's Letters and Files. Archives Office of New South Wales, Sydney.

Correspondence re. Miscellaneous Exhibitions, Board of Trustees, Melbourne Public Library. Victoria Public Record Office, Melbourne.

Council of India Minutes and Papers. Oriental and India Office Collections, British Library, London.

Department of Aboriginal Affairs, Correspondence Files. Public Record Office of South Australia, Adelaide.

Department of Education and Science Papers. Public Record Office, Kew.

Department of Lands Papers. Queensland State Archives, Brisbane.

Despatches Written by the Agent-General, London. Queensland State Archives, Brisbane.

Exhibition Commissioners Letterbooks, South Australian Commissions. Public Record Office of South Australia, Adelaide.

Exhibition Correspondence, Department of Public Works. Victoria Public Record Office, Melbourne.

Exhibition Folio Pamphlets. La Trobe Collection, State Library of Victoria, Melbourne.

Government of India, Revenue and Agriculture Department. Proceedings and Papers: Museums and Exhibitions Branch. Oriental and India Office Collections, British Library, London.

Industrial and Technological Museum and Library Letterbooks and Papers. Victoria Public Record Office, Melbourne.

Melbourne Public Library, Museum, and Art Gallery, Board of Trustees Correspondence. Victoria Public Record Office, Melbourne.

Memorandum of Measures Adopted, and Expenditures Incurred, in India, for the Promotion of Literature, Science, and Art, since the Assumption by Her Majesty the Queen of the Direct Government of the Country. Oriental and India Office Collections, British Library, London.

Papers from Botanical Gardens, 1878–1895. Archives Office of New South Wales, Sydney.

Protector of Aborigines Letterbooks. Public Record Office of South Australia, Adelaide.

Victorian Exhibition Commissioners Correspondence. La Trobe Collection, State Library of Victoria, Melbourne.

PUBLISHED GOVERNMENT DOCUMENTS AND REPORTS

Annual Reports of the Department of Science and Art. Parliamentary Papers, England.

Buck, Sir Edward C. *(Confidential) Historical Summaries of Administrative Measures in the Several Branches of Public Business Administered in the Department of Revenue and Agriculture. Drawn up in 1896.* Calcutta: Government Printing Office, 1897.

Cole, H. H. *Science and Art Department of the Committee of Council on Education, South Kensington Museum. Catalogue of the Objects of Indian Art Exhibited in the South Kensington Museum.* London: George E. Eyre and William Spottiswoode, 1874.

Hansard's Parliamentary Debates. 3rd series. London.

Journal of the Legislative Council of New South Wales.

Queensland Parliamentary Votes and Proceedings.

Report of the Committee Appointed by the Board of Trade to Make Enquiries with Reference to the Participation of Great Britain in Great International Exhibitions. London: William Spottiswoode and George E. Eyre, 1907.

Reports of the Trustees for the Melbourne Public Library, Museum and National Gallery.

South Australia Parliamentary Debates and Papers.

Victoria Parliamentary Debates and Papers.

SOCIETY AND ASSOCIATION PAPERS AND
CORRESPONDENCE

Aborigines' Friends Association Papers. Mortlock Library of South Australiana, State Library of South Australia, Adelaide.

Adelaide Chamber of Commerce Minute Books and Minutes of Committee Meetings. Mortlock Library, State Library of South Australia, Adelaide.

Assam Company, Minutes of Proceedings in India. Guildhall Library, London.

Australian Agricultural Company Papers. Noel Butlin Archives Center, Australian National University, Canberra.

Indian Tea Association Papers and Annual Reports. Oriental and India Office Collections, British Library, London.

London Trades Council Minute Books. Trades Union Congress Archives, London.

Melbourne Chamber of Commerce Minute Book. La Trobe Collection, State Library of Victoria, Melbourne.

National Agricultural and Industrial Association Letterbooks. John Oxley Library, State Library of Queensland, Brisbane.

Peel River Land and Mineral Company Papers. Noel Butlin Archives Center, Australian National University, Canberra.

Royal Society of Arts Correspondence and Papers. Corporation of London Archives, London.

Victorian Trades Hall Council Minutes. Melbourne University Archives.

Zoological and Acclimatisation Society of Victoria Minute Books. Victoria Public Record Office, Melbourne.

EXHIBITION CATALOGUES, COMMENTARIES,
GUIDEBOOKS, AND PAPERS BY EVENT

The Great Exhibition (Crystal Palace, 1851)

"Art. IX. Official Catalogue of the Great Exhibition of the Works of Industry of All Nations." *Edinburgh Review* 94 (1851).

The Art-Journal Illustrated Catalogue of the Industry of Nations, 1851. London: George Virtue, 1851.

Aunt Busy-Bee's The Fine Crystal Palace the Prince Built. London: Dean and Son, 1851.

Babbage, Charles. *The Exposition of 1851; or, Views of the Industry, the Science, and the Government of England.* 2nd ed. London: John Murray, 1851.

Berlyn, Peter. *A Popular Narrative of the Origin, History, Progress and Prospects of the Great Industrial Exhibition, 1851.* London: James Gilbert, 1851.

The Crystal Palace, and the Great Exhibition; an Historical Account of the Building, Together with a Descriptive Synopsis of its Content. London: H. G. Clarke, 1851.

The Crystal Palace; a Satire for the Time. National Art Library, London.

Dowleans, A. M., ed. *Catalogue of the East Indian Productions Collected in the Presidency of Bombay, and Forwarded to the Exhibition of Works of Art and Industry to be held in London in 1851.* London: W. Thacker, 1851.

The Exhibition — Has It Had a Beneficial Tendency? National Art Library, London.

Exhibition of Industry of All Nations. To Be Held in 1851. Information for the

Use of Foreign Exhibitors, July, 1850. Archives Office of New South Wales, Sydney.

"Fifteen Thousand Authors and Their Book: Official Descriptive, and Illustrated Catalogue of the Great Exhibition." *Chambers' Edinburgh Journal* 16 (1851).

Great Exhibition of the Works of Industry of All Nations, 1851. Official Descriptive and Illustrated Catalogue. London: William Clowes and Sons, 1851.

Lectures on the Progress of Arts and Science, Resulting from the Great Exhibition in London, delivered before the Society of Arts, Manufactures and Commerce, at the Suggestion of H.R.H. Prince Albert. New York: A. S. Barnes, 1854.

Official Catalogue of the Great Exhibition of the Works of Industry of All Nations, 1851. 3rd ed. London: William Clowes and Sons, 1851.

Papers Referring to the Proposed Contributions from India for the Industrial Exhibition of 1851, by J. Forbes Royle, 1849–1851. National Art Library, London.

Proceedings of the Madras Central Committee, for the Exhibition of the Industry and Art of All Nations, held in London in the Year 1851. Madras: Fort St. George Gazette Press, 1853.

Shuckard, William. "Ode on the Great Exhibition, 1851." National Art Library, London.

Tallis, John. *Tallis's History and Description of the Crystal Palace and the Exhibition of the World's Industry in 1851.* Vols. 1–3. London: The London Printing and Publishing Company, 1852.

A Visit to the Great Exhibition. National Art Library, London.

Voices from the Workshop on the Exhibition of 1851. National Art Library, London.

Warren, Samuel. *The Lily and the Bee: an apologue of the Crystal Palace, 1851.* National Art Library, London.

The Great Industrial Exhibition (Dublin, 1853)

The Exhibition of Art-Industry in Dublin. 1853. London: Virtue, 1853.

Official Catalogue of the Great Industrial Exhibition (In Connection with the Royal Dublin Society), 1853. 4th ed. Dublin: John Falconer, 1853.

Sydney Metropolitan Exhibition (1854)

Catalogue of the Natural and Industrial Products of New South Wales Exhibited in the Australian Museum by the Paris Exhibition Commissioners. Sydney, November, 1854. Sydney: Reading and Wellbank, 1854.

Paris Universal Exposition (1855)

Canada at the Universal Exhibition of 1855. Toronto: John Lovell, 1856.

Catalogue of Contributions Transmitted from British Guiana to the Paris Uni-

versal Exposition of 1855. Georgetown, Demerara: Royal Gazette Office, 1855.

"A Paper by Sir William Macarthur on the Products of New South Wales, Prepared for the Paris Universal Exposition of 1855, with Special Reference to the Production of Wine and Wool." Mitchell Library, State Library of New South Wales, Sydney.

Paris Exhibition, 1855. Report Presented to the Bradford Chamber of Commerce, on the 26th November, 1855. National Art Library, London.

Paris Universal Exposition, 1855. Catalogue of the Works Exhibited in the British Section of the Exhibition. London: Chapman and Hall, 1855.

Paris Universal Exposition Papers. Communications with Intending Exhibitors, 1854. Archives Office of New South Wales, Sydney.

Royle, John Forbes. *Paris Universal Exposition, 1855. Report on Indian and Colonial Products, Useful as Food and for Manufactures.* London: George E. Eyre and William Spottiswoode, 1857.

Victorian Exhibition (Melbourne, 1861)

Catalogue of the Victorian Exhibition, 1861; with Prefatory Essays, Indicating the Progress, Resources, and Physical Characteristics of the Colony. Melbourne: John Ferres, Government Printer, 1861.

Victorian Exhibition Commissioners Correspondence, 1861–62. La Trobe Collection, State Library of Victoria, Melbourne.

London International Exhibition (South Kensington, 1862)

1862 Exhibition. Photos Showing the Progress of the Building, Presented by C. W. Dilke. Photographic Department, National Art Library, London.

The Australasian Colonies at the International Exhibition, London, 1862. Extracts from the Reports of the Jurors and Other Information Taken from Official Sources. Compiled by J. G. Knight, F.R.I.B.A. Melbourne: John Ferres, Government Printer, 1865.

"Collection of Specimens for Great Exhibition, 1862." Exhibition Correspondence, Department of Public Works. Victoria Public Record Office, Melbourne.

"The International Exhibition: Its Purpose and Prospects." *Blackwood's Edinburgh Magazine* 91 (1862).

The International Exhibition of 1862. A Classified and Descriptive Catalogue of the Indian Department. London: William Clowes and Sons, 1862.

The International Exhibition of 1862. The Illustrated Catalogue of the Industrial Department, Volume II. Colonial and Indian Divisions. London: George E. Eyre and William Spottiswoode, 1862.

International Exhibition, 1862. Report to the Commissioners of Her Majesty's Customs of the Results Obtained in Testing Samples of the Various Wines Exhibited. London: George E. Eyre and William Spottiswoode, 1863.

International Exhibition, 1862. Reports by the Juries of the Subjects in the Thirty-Six Classes Into Which the Exhibition was Divided. London: William Clowes and Sons, 1863.

Johnson, Benjamin Pierce. *Report on International Exhibition of Industry and Art, London, 1862.* Albany: Steam Press of C. Van Bethuysen, 1863.

Pardon, George Frederick, ed. *A Guide to the International Exhibition; with Plans of the Building, An Account of its Rise, Progress and Completion, and Notices of its Principal Contents.* London: Routledge, Warne and Routledge, 1862.

The Practical Mechanic's Journal Record of the Great Exhibition, 1862. London: Longman, Green, Longman, and Roberts, 1862.

Register for Disposal of Exhibits, London International Exhibition, 1862. Mitchell Library, State Library of New South Wales.

Report of the Commissioners for the Exhibition of 1862, to the Right Hon. Sir George Gray, Bart., G.C.B., etc., etc. London: George E. Eyre and William Spottiswoode, 1863.

Views of the International Exhibition: The Interior. London: T. Nelson and Sons, 1862.

Visitors to the Buildings for the International Exhibition of 1862. National Art Library, London.

Calcutta Agricultural (1864)

"The First Bengal Agricultural Exhibition." *Calcutta Review* 40 (1864–65).

Dublin International Exhibition of Arts and Manufactures (1865)

Catalogue of Products from the Colony of Victoria, Australia, at Dublin International Exhibition, 1865. Melbourne: Wilson and MacKinnon Printers, 1865.

Nagpore Exhibition of Arts, Manufactures, and Produce (1865)

Report of the Nagpore Exhibition of Arts, Manufactures, and Produce, December, 1865. Nagpore: Central Provinces' Printing Press, 1866.

Melbourne Intercolonial Exhibition (1866–67)

Exhibition Trustees Letterbook for Intercolonial Exhibition. Victoria Public Record Office, Melbourne.

Intercolonial Exhibition Correspondence, 1866–67. Victoria Public Record Office, Melbourne.

Intercolonial Exhibition, 1866. Official Catalogue. Melbourne: Blundell and Ford, 1866.

Intercolonial Exhibition of Australasia, Melbourne, 1866–67. Official Record,

Containing Introduction, Catalogues, Reports and Awards of the Jurors, Essays and Statistics on the Social and Economic Resources of the Australasian Colonies. Melbourne: Blundell, 1867.

Intercolonial Exhibition, 1866. Vocabulary of Dialects Spoken by Aboriginal Natives of Australia. Melbourne: Masterman, Printer, 1867.

Knight, John G. *Companion to the Official Catalogue. Guide to the Inter-Colonial Exhibition of 1866.* Melbourne: Blundell and Ford, 1866.

Paris Universal Exposition (1867)

Artisans Reports, Royal Society of Arts to 1867 Paris Exposition. London: W. Trounce, 1867.

Beckwith, Edward Lonsdale. *Practical Notes on Wine. Reprint of Report on Wines for Royal Commissioners for Paris Exposition, 1867.* London: Smith and Elder, 1869.

Bradshaw's Hand-Book to the Paris International Exhibition of 1867. London: W. J. Adams, 1867.

Catalogue of the Natural and Industrial Products of New South Wales Forwarded to the Paris Universal Exhibition of 1867, by the New South Wales Exhibition Commissioners. Sydney: Thomas Richards, Government Printer, 1867.

Paris Universal Exposition of 1867. Catalogue of Contributions from the Colony of Natal. London: Jarrold and Sons, 1868.

Paris Universal Exposition, 1867. Catalogue of the Victorian Court. William Westgarth, ed. Melbourne: Government Printer, 1868.

Paris Universal Exposition, 1867. Part II. Catalogue of the Works Exhibited in the British Section of the Exhibition. London: George E. Eyre and William Spottiswoode, 1868.

Reports on the Paris Universal Exposition, 1867, Volume I: Reports by Executive Commissioner; with Appendices. English Parliamentary Papers. 1868–69. [xxx]. Pt. i. 1.

Sala, George Augustus. *Notes and Sketches of the Paris Exhibition.* London: Tinsley Brothers, 1868.

Broach Exhibition (1868–69)

Report on the Broach Exhibition, 1868–69. With Appendices A. to H. Bombay: Education Society's Press, 1969.

Sydney Metropolitan and Intercolonial Exhibition (1870)

The Industrial Progress of New South Wales; Being A Report of the Intercolonial Exhibition of 1870 at Sydney; Together with a Variety of Papers Illustrative of the Industrial Resources of the Country. Sydney: Thomas Richards, Government Printer, 1871.

Metropolitan Intercolonial Exhibition, 16th August 1870. Sydney: Gibbs, Shallard, Lithographic and Letterpress by Steam, 1870.

London International Exhibitions (South Kensington, 1871–74)

Beckwith, Arthur. *International Exhibition, London, 1871. Pottery. Observations on the Materials and Manufacture of Terra-Cotta, Stone-Ware, Fire-Brick, Porcelain, Earthen-ware, Brick, Majolica, and Encaustic Tiles, with Remarks on the Products Exhibited*. New York: D. Van Nostrand, 1872.

Catalogue of the Exhibits in the New South Wales Annexe of the Exhibition, London International, 1871. Sydney: Government Printer, 1871.

Nelson's Pictorial Guide-Books. The International Exhibition, 1871. London: T. Nelson and Sons, 1871.

New South Wales Colonial Secretary Bundle: London International Exhibition. Archives Office of New South Wales, Sydney.

Reports on the International Exhibition of 1871, Parts I, II and III. London: George E. Eyre and William Spottiswoode, 1872.

Rivett-Carnac, Harry. "Memorandum on the Measures Adopted in India to Select Contributions for the International Exhibition of 1871." Temple Papers, Oriental and India Office Collections, British Library, London.

A Special Report on the Annual International Exhibitions of the Years 1871, 1872, 1873 and 1874, Drawn up by Sir Henry Cole, Acting Commissioner in 1873 and 1874, and Presented by the Commissioners for the Exhibition of 1851. English Parliamentary Papers. 1878 [XXVII]. 139.

Yapp, C. W. *Popular Guide to the London International Exhibition of 1871*. London: J. M. Johnson and Sons, 1871.

Vienna International Exhibition (1873)

Reports on the Vienna International Exhibition of 1873. London: George E. Eyre and William Spottiswoode, 1874.

Vienna Universal Exhibition. A Classified and Descriptive Catalogue of the Indian Department. London: W. H. Allen, 1873.

Melbourne Intercolonial Exhibition (1875)

By Authority of the Commissioners. Victorian Intercolonial Exhibition, 1875. Preparatory to the Philadelphia Exhibition, 1876. Opened 2nd September, 1875. Official Catalogue of Exhibits. Melbourne: M'Carron, Bird, 1875.

Fenton, Frank W. *The Exhibition (1875) and How to See It! A Complete Guide, with Plan of Building and Grounds*. Melbourne: W. H. Williams, 1875.

———, ed. *Guide to the Victorian Intercolonial Exhibition, 1875*. Melbourne: W. H. Williams, 1875.

Prospectus of Melbourne Intercolonial Exhibition, 1875. La Trobe Collection, State Library of Victoria, Melbourne.

Philadelphia Centennial Exhibition (1876)

Agricultural Societies and the Philadelphia Exhibition. Archives Office of New South Wales, Sydney.

International Exhibition at Philadelphia, 1876. Report of the Commissioners for Victoria to His Excellency the Governor. Melbourne: John Ferres, Government Printer, 1877.

Journal of the Proceedings of the United States Centennial Commission, at Philadelphia, 1872. Philadelphia: E. C. Markley and Sons, 1872.

Official Catalogue of the Natural and Industrial Products of New South Wales, Forwarded to the International Exhibition of 1876, at Philadelphia. Sydney: Thomas Richards, 1876.

Philadelphia International Exhibition, 1876. Official Catalogue of the British Section, Part I. London: George E. Eyre and William Spottiswoode, 1876.

Sydney Industrial and Intercolonial Exhibition (1877)

Report of the Canadian Commissioner at the Exhibition of Industry, held at Sydney, New South Wales, 1877. Ottawa: Department of Agriculture, 1878.

Queensland Intercolonial (1877)

National Agricultural and Industrial Association of Queensland. Catalogue of the Intercolonial Exhibition. Brisbane: William Thorne, 1877.

Paris Universal Exposition (1878)

Minutes of the South Australian Commission, 1877–1882. Paris Universal Exposition, 1878. Auditor-General's Department Papers. Public Record Office of South Australia, Adelaide.

Paris Universal Exhibition of 1878. Handbook to the British Indian Section. by George C. M. Birdwood, C.S.I., M.D. Edin. 2nd ed. London: Offices of the Royal Commission, 1878.

Queensland (Australia). The Exhibits and Exhibitors, and Description of the Colony. Brisbane: James C. Beal, 1878.

Sydney International Exhibition (1879)

International Exhibition, Sydney, 1879–1880. Photographic Album. Mitchell Library, State Library of New South Wales, Sydney.

Minutes of the Meetings Held by the Committee of Foreign and Colonial Commissioners at the Sydney International Exhibition, 1879. Sydney: H. H. Kingsbury, 1879.

Minutes of the South Australian Commissioners, 1879–1882. Sydney International Exhibition, 1879. Auditor-General's Department Papers. Public Record Office of South Australia, Adelaide.

Notes on the Sydney International Exhibition of 1879, with Photo-Type Illustrations. Sydney: Government Printing Office, 1880.

Official Record of the Sydney International Exhibition, 1879. Sydney: Thomas Richards, Government Printer, 1881.

Report of the Royal Commission for the Australian International Exhibitions, 1879–1881. English Parliamentary Papers. 1882. [c. 3099]. xxviii.

Sydney International Exhibition, Executive Commissioner's Letter Book. Archives Office of New South Wales, Sydney.

Sydney International Exhibition, 1879. India: Official Catalogue of Exhibits. Sydney: Foster and Fairfax, 1879.

Sydney International Exhibition, 1879. Official Catalogue of Exhibits. Sydney: Foster and Fairfax, 1879.

Sydney International Exhibition, 1879. Papers. Mitchell Library, State Library of New South Wales, Sydney.

Melbourne International Exhibition (1880 – 81)

Bidie, G. *Catalogue of the Articles Collected and Forwarded Under the Orders of the Government of Madras, to the Melbourne International Exhibition of 1880.* Madras: E. Keys, 1880.

Melbourne International Exhibition, 1880. Catalogue of Exhibits in the Tasmanian Court. Foreign and Commonwealth Office Library, London.

Melbourne International Exhibition, 1880. Correspondence. Victoria Public Record Office, Melbourne.

Melbourne International Exhibition, 1880–1881. Official Record and Catalogue of Exhibits. Melbourne: Mason, Firth, and M'Cutcheon, 1882.

Melbourne International Exhibition, 1880–81. Papers and Correspondence. Victoria Public Record Office, Melbourne.

Report on the Melbourne International Exhibition, 1880–1881. Oriental and India Office Collections, British Library, London.

A Sketch of South Australia for the Melbourne International Exhibition, 1880. Published by Direction of the Royal Commissioners for South Australia. With Maps and Statistical Diagrams. Adelaide: E. Spiller, Government Printer, 1880.

Visitors' Register, Melbourne International Exhibition, 1880–1881. La Trobe Collection, State Library of Victoria, Melbourne.

Whitworth, Robert P., ed. *Messina's Popular Guide to the Melbourne International Exhibition of 1880–1881.* Melbourne: A. H. Messina, 1880.

Adelaide Exhibition of Arts and Industries (1881)

Careeg's Official Catalogue of the Adelaide Exhibition of Arts and Industries of All Nations, 1881, Including a List and a Description of the Pictures. Adelaide: R. Kyffin Thomas, 1881.

An Illustrated Souvenir of the First Adelaide Exhibition, held during the months of July, August, and September, 1881. Adelaide: Frearson and Brother, 1881.

Punjab Art and Industry Exhibition (1881)

Official Report of the Punjab Exhibition, 1881. National Art Library, London.
Punjab Exhibition Report, 1881. General Report of Results. National Art Library, London.

Calcutta International Exhibition (1883–84)

Calcutta Exhibition, Letterbook, 1883. Auditor-General's Department. Public Record Office of South Australia, Adelaide.
New South Wales. Official Catalogue of Exhibits from the Colony forwarded to the International Exhibition of 1883–84 at Calcutta. Sydney: Thomas Richards, Government Printer, 1883.
Official Report of the Calcutta International Exhibition, 1883–84. Calcutta: Bengal Secretariat Press, 1885.
Report to the Hon. R. D. Ross, Chairman of the South Australian Committee for the Calcutta International Exhibition, 1884–1884. Mortlock Library, State Library of South Australia, Adelaide.
Risley, H. H. *Report on the Calcutta International Exhibition.* Oriental and India Office Collections, British Library, London.

Amsterdam International Exhibition (1883)

Government of India. *Revenue and Agriculture Department, Classified List of Indian Produce Contributed to the Amsterdam Exhibition, 1883. Compiled by Trailokya Nath Mukharji, Officer in Charge of Indian Exhibits for the Amsterdam Exhibition.* Calcutta: Superintendent of Government Printing, 1883.
A Hand-Book of Indian Products. (Art-Manufactures and Raw Materials.) by T. N. Mukharji, Author of "A Rough List of Indian Art-Ware" and "A Descriptive Catalogue of Indian Products Contributed to the Amsterdam Exhibition." Calcutta: C. J. A. Pritchard at the "Star" Press, 1883.

International Fisheries Exhibition (South Kensington, 1883)

Fisheries Exhibition Bundle. Archives Office of New South Wales, Sydney.

International Health Exhibition (South Kensington, 1884)

Burgess's Illustrated and Descriptive Guide to the International Health Exhibition, 1884. 3rd ed. Guildhall Library Pamphlets, London.

"Illustrated Catalogue of the Chinese Collection of Exhibits for the International Health Exhibition, London, 1884." In *China, Imperial Maritime Customs. II — Miscellaneous Series: No. 12*. London: William Clowes and Sons, 1884.

International Health Exhibition. The District Railway Exhibition Guide: A Popular Summary and Review. London: Alfred Boot and Son, 1884.

Colonial and Indian Exhibition (South Kensington, 1886)

Colonial and Indian Exhibition. Empire of India Catalogue, 1886. National Art Library, London.

Colonial and Indian Exhibition, 1886. Her Majesty's Colonies. A Series of Original Papers Issued Under the Authority of the Royal Commission. London: William Clowes and Sons, 1886.

Colonial and Indian Exhibition Letterbooks. Public Record Office of South Australia, Adelaide.

Colonial and Indian Exhibition, 1886. Official Guide. London: William Clowes and Sons, 1886.

Colonial and Indian Exhibition Railway Guide and Route Book. London: William Clowes and Sons, 1886.

Colonial and Indian Exhibition. Royal Commission and Government of India Silk Court. Descriptive Catalogue. London: William Clowes and Sons, 1886.

Cundall, Frank, ed. *Reminiscences of the Colonial and Indian Exhibition, illustrated by Thomas Riley, Designer of the Exhibition Diploma*. London: William Clowes and Sons, 1886.

International Exhibition, 1886. Minute Books of the Executive Committee. Public Record Office of South Australia, Adelaide.

"Memo of Philip Cunliffe-Owen to Earl of Dufferin, Viceroy, Confidential Communication for Lord Reay, 1 April 1887." Baron Reay Papers: Bombay Files. School of Oriental and African Studies Archives, University of London.

Minute Book, United Kingdom. Colonial and Indian Exhibition, 1886. Registry Papers, Victoria and Albert Museum, London.

New South Wales. Official Catalogue of Exhibits from the Colony, forwarded to the Colonial and Indian Exhibition, London, 1886. Sydney: Thomas Richards, Government Printer, 1886.

Reminiscences of the Colonial and Indian Exhibition. A Lecture Delivered by John McCarthy, Government Analyst and Professor of Chemistry, Trinidad. And Published for Use in the Schools of the Island, by Direction of His Excellency Sir W. Robinson, K.C.M.G., Governor, Etc. Port-of-Spain: Government Printer, 1887.

Report of the Royal Commission for the Colonial and Indian Exhibition, London, 1886. English Parliamentary Papers. 1887. [c. 5083], xx. 1.

Adelaide Jubilee International Exhibition (1887)

Adelaide Jubilee International Exhibition, 1887. Art Union Distribution Rules and Regulations, 1886. Mortlock Library, State Library of South Australia, Adelaide.

Adelaide Jubilee International Exhibition, 1887–1888. Finance Committee Minutes, 1883–1887. Public Record Office of South Australia, Adelaide.

Adelaide Jubilee International Exhibition, 1887–1888. Letter Book of the South Australia Commissioners. Volume I. December 1886–August 1887. Public Record Office of South Australia, Adelaide.

Adelaide Jubilee International Exhibition, 1887. Reports of Juries and Official List of Awards. Adelaide: H. F. Leader, Government Printer, 1889.

Neild, J. C. *Official Report of the Executive Commissioner for New South Wales to the Adelaide Jubilee International Exhibition, 1887–1888.* Sydney: Charles Potter, Government Printer, 1890.

Report of the Royal Commission for the Adelaide Jubilee International Exhibition of 1887. English Parliamentary Papers. 1888. [c.5440].

Visitors' Books, Old Colonists' Court, Adelaide Jubilee International Exhibition, 1887. 2 vols. Public Record Office of South Australia, Adelaide.

Melbourne Centennial Exhibition (1888)

Centennial International Exhibition, Melbourne 1888–89. The Official Catalogue of Exhibits. Melbourne: Firth and M'Cutcheon, 1888.

Concluding Address, Official Ending of the 1888 Melbourne Centennial Exhibition. Victoria Public Record Office, Melbourne.

The Official Record of the Centennial International Exhibition, Melbourne, 1888–1889. Melbourne: Sands and McDougall, 1890.

Glasgow International Exhibition (1888)

Mukharji, T. N. *Art-Manufactures of India, Specially Compiled for the Glasgow International Exhibition, 1888.* Calcutta: Superintendent of Government Printing, 1888.

Paris Universal Exposition (1889)

British Section Handbook, Paris Universal Exposition, 1889. London: George E. Eyre and William Spottiswoode, 1889.

Empire of India Exhibition (London, 1895)

The Empire of India Exhibition, 1895. General Introduction. Oriental and India Office Collections, British Library, London.

The Empire of India Exhibition, Earl's Court, S.W., 1895. Illustrated Official Catalogue. London: J. J. Keliher, 1895.

Queensland International (1897)

Prospectus, Queensland International Exhibition, 1897. Queensland State Archives, Brisbane.

Greater Britain Exhibition (London, 1899)

Greater Britain Exhibition, 1899 Papers. Queensland State Archives, Brisbane.
Minutes of the Meetings of the Executive Committee for the Greater Britain and Paris Exhibitions, 1898–1901. Victoria Public Record Office, Melbourne.
"Report upon the Agricultural Exhibits in the Queensland Court of the Greater Britain Exhibition, 1899." Agriculture and Stock Department Papers. Queensland State Archives, Brisbane.

Paris Universal Exposition (1900)

Foreign Office Papers. General Correspondence of the London Office, 1900. Archives of Commissions, Paris Exhibition, 1900. Public Record Office, Kew.
Rose, Benjamin. *Paris Universal Exposition, 1900. Report of the Indian Section.* London: Charles E. Eyre and William Spottiswoode, 1901.

Durbar Art Exhibition (Delhi, 1903)

"The Delhi Durbar: A Retrospect." *Blackwood's Edinburgh Magazine* 173 (1903).
Delhi Indian Art Exhibition, 1902–1903. Indian Art at Delhi, 1903, Being the Official Catalogue of the Delhi Exhibition, 1902–1903. Calcutta: Superintendent of Government Printing, 1903.

St. Louis International (Louisiana Purchase) Exposition (1904)

Fletcher, Herbert Phillips. *The St. Louis Exhibition, 1904.* London: B. T. Batsford, 1905.
International Exhibition, St. Louis, 1904. Reports of the Art Committee and Sub-Committee for Applied Art. London: William Clowes and Sons, 1906.

Franco-British Exhibition (1908)

Lands Department Correspondence, Franco-British Exhibition. Queensland State Archives, Brisbane.

Papers Relating to the Franco-British Exhibition, 1908–1911. Queensland State Archives, Brisbane.

Premier's Department Letters and Papers Re. Franco-British Exhibition, 1908–1911. Queensland State Archives, Brisbane.

Report on the Indian Section of the Franco-British Exhibition, London, 1908. London: Eyre and Spottiswoode, 1908.

Festival of Empire Exhibition (Crystal Palace, Sydenham, 1911)

Catalogue of Twenty Original Indian Pictures Illustrating the Manner of Life of the Greatest of the Mughal Emperors. Painted in the Sixteenth and Seventeenth Centuries by Native Artists. National Art Library, London.

Festival of Empire: The Pageant of London. Guildhall Library, London.

Indian Court, Festival of Empire, 1911. Guide Book and Catalogue. London: Bemrose and Sons, 1911.

Lomas, Sophie C., ed. *Festival of Empire. Souvenir of the Pageant of London.* London: Bemrose and Sons, 1911.

Noel, M. P. *Scrapbook Containing Materials Relating to the Pageant of London, Which was Given as Part of the Festival of Empire, 1911.* English Manuscripts, National Art Library, London.

Official Programme, Festival of Empire Exhibition, 1911. Guildhall Library, London.

GENERAL BOOKS, ESSAYS, AND PAMPHLETS

An Account of the Celebration of the Jubilee Year of South Australia, 1886. Adelaide: W. K. Thomas, 1887.

Address on the Opening of the Free Public Library of Ballarat East, by Sir Redmond Barry, on Friday, 1st January, 1869. Melbourne: H. T. Dwight, 1869.

Address on the Opening of the School of Mines, at Ballarat, Victoria. Delivered by Sir Redmond Barry, on Wednesday, October 26th, A.D. 1870. Melbourne: Mason, Firth & M'Cutcheon, General Printers, 1870.

Address to the Workmen Employed in Building the Great Hall of the Melbourne Public Library and Museum, in Melbourne, Victoria. Delivered by Sir Redmond Barry, on Saturday, September 8, A.D. 1866. Melbourne: Wilson and MacKinnon, 1866.

Aunt Busy-Bee's The Fine Crystal Palace the Prince Built. London: Dean and Son, 1851.

Babbage, Charles. *The Exposition of 1851; or, Views of the Industry, the Science, and the Government of England.* 2nd ed. London: John Murray, 1851.

———. *On the Economy of Machinery and Manufactures.* London: John Murray, 1846.

Birdwood, George M. *The Arts of India as Illustrated by the Collection of H.R.H. Prince of Wales.* London: R. Clay, Sons, and Taylor, 1881.

―――. *Competition and the Indian Civil Service.* London: Henry S. King, 1872.

―――. *The Industrial Arts of India.* 2 vols. London: Chapman and Hall, 1880.

―――. *Report on the Government Central Museum and the Agricultural and Horticultural Society of Western India for 1863. With Appendices, being the Establishment of the Victoria and Albert Museum and of the Victoria Gardens.* Bombay: Education Society's Press, 1864.

Bright, Philip, ed. *The Diaries of John Bright.* Toronto: Cassell, 1930.

Buck, Sir Edward C. "The Utility of Exhibitions to India." *Asiatic Quarterly Review* 2 (1886).

Buckle, George Earle, ed. *The Letters of Queen Victoria. A Selection of Her Majesty's Correspondence and Journal.* 2nd and 3rd series. London: John Murray, 1926.

Coleridge, Samuel Taylor. *On the Constitution of the Church and State.* Ed. John Barrel. London: J. M. Dent and Sons, 1972.

Denison, Sir William Thomas. *Address to Members of Australian Agricultural and Horticultural Societies.* Sydney: Rading and Wellbank, 1855.

Dobbie, Alexander W. *Rough Notes of a Traveller.* 1st ed. Adelaide: n.p., 1877.

―――. *Rough Notes of a Traveller Taken in England, Scotland, France, Holland, . . . Greece, Egypt, Ceylon, and Elsewhere.* 2nd series. London: Simpkin Marshall, Hamilton Kent, 1890.

Drew, William A. *Glimpses and Gatherings, During a Voyage and Visit to London and the Great Exhibition, in the Summer of 1851.* Augusta, ME: Homan and Manley, 1852.

Eastlake, Sir Charles Lock. "How to Observe." In *Contributions to the Literature of the Fine Arts.* 2nd series. London: John Murray, 1870.

Fergusson, James. *Introductory Addresses on the Science and Art Department: On a National Collection of Architectural Art.* London: Chapman and Hall, 1857.

―――. *Observations on the British Museum, National Gallery, and National Record Office, with Suggestions for their Improvement.* London: John Weale, 1849.

Fifty Years of Public Work of Sir Henry Cole, K.C.B., Accounted for in His Deeds, Speeches and Writings. 2 vols. London: George Bell and Sons, 1884.

Froude, James Anthony. *Oceana, or England and Her Colonies.* 2nd ed. London: Longman, Green, 1886.

Fuller, Francis. *Shall We Spend £100,000 on a Winter Garden for London, or in Endowing Schools of Design?* London: John Olliver, 1851.

Geddes, Patrick. *Industrial Exhibitions and Modern Progress.* Edinburgh: David Douglas, 1887.

Hendley, Thomas H. *Handbook to the Jeypore Museum.* Calcutta: Central Press Company, 1885.

Hunter, Alexander. *Suggestions for the Establishment of a School of Industrial Arts at Lahore, Prepared at the Request of His Excellency Sir Robert Mont-*

gomery, K.C.B., Lieut.-Governor of the Punjab, 1863. Oriental and India Office Collections, British Library, London.

Inglis, James. The Story of the Tea Trade. Sydney: Williams Brooks, 1901.

Joubert, Jules. Shavings & Scrapes From Many Parts. Dunedin: J. Wilkie, 1890.

Kipling, Rudyard. Something of Myself, For My Friends, Known and Unknown. Ed. Thomas Pinney. New York: Cambridge University Press, 1991.

Lecture on the History of the Art of Agriculture, Delivered Before the Melbourne Mechanics' Institution, Friday, May 1, 1840, by Redmond Barry, Esquire, Barrister-at-Law. Melbourne: Lucas Brothers, 1854.

Lever, Ellis. Suggestions for a Grand International Exhibition of the Industrial Arts, Manufactures, Fine Arts, Scientific Inventions, Discoveries, and Natural Products of All Countries, to be Held in Manchester, in the Year, 1882. Manchester: Guardian Letterpress and Lithographic Works, 1881.

Lewis, George Cornewall. An Essay on the Influence of Authority in Matters of Opinion. 2nd ed. London: Longmans, Green, 1875.

The Life and Letters of Lord Macaulay, By His Nephew, George Otto Trevelyan, M.P. Oxford: The Clarendon Press, 1958.

Maine, Sir Henry. The Effects of Observation of India on Modern European Thought. Rude Lectures, May 22, 1875. London: J. Murray, 1875.

Martineau, Harriet. British Rule in India; a Historical Sketch. London: Smith, Elder, 1857.

———. How To Observe. / Morals and Manners. London: Charles Knight, 1838.

Masterman, C. F. G. The Condition of England. 4th ed. London: Methuen, 1909.

Michie, Sir Archibald. Readings in Melbourne; with an Essay on the Resources and Prospects of Victoria. London: Sampson, Low, Marston, Searle, and Rivington, 1879.

Mill, John Stuart. "Civilization." In J. B. Schneewind, ed., Essays on Literature and Society. New York: Collier Books, 1965.

Mukharji, T. N. A Visit to Europe. London: Edward Stanford, 1889.

The Objects of a Botanic Garden in Relation to Industries. A Lecture Delivered at the Industrial and Technological Museum, Melbourne, by Baron Ferdinand von Mueller, on 23rd November, 1871. Melbourne: Mason, Firth and McCutcheon, 1871.

Ogilvie, Edmund S. Diary of Travels in Three Quarters of the Globe. By an Australian Settler. In Two Volumes. London: Saunders and Otley, 1856.

The Old Colonists' Association Jubilee Commemoration Catalogue. Adelaide: Burden & Bonython, 1887.

Reid, Wemyss, ed. Memoirs and Correspondence of Lyon Playfair, First Lord Playfair of St. Andrews, P.C., G.C.B., LL.D., F.R.S., etc. London: Cassell, 1899.

Rowe, C. J. An Englishman's Views on Questions of the Day in Victoria. London: n.p., 1882.

Royle, John Forbes. The Culture and Commerce of Cotton in India and Elsewhere, with an Account of the Experiments Made by the Hon. East India Company up to the Present Time. London: Smith, Elder, 1851.

————. *The Fibrous Plants of India Fitted for Cordage, Clothing, and Paper, with an Account of the Cultivation and Preparation of Flax, Hemp, and their Substitutes.* London: Smith, Elder, 1855.

————. "Observations on Provincial Exhibitions and the Improvement of the Resources of the Several Districts of the Madras Presidency." *Madras Journal of Literature and Science* n.s. 2 (1857).

————. *Review of the Measures Which Have Been Adopted in India for the Improved Culture of Cotton.* London: Smith, Elder, 1857.

Ruskin, John. *Inaugural Address Delivered at the Cambridge School of Art.* Kent: George Allen, 1879.

————. *The Political Economy of Art; Being the Substance with Additions of Two Lectures.* London: Smith, Elder, 1857.

————. *The Two Paths; being Lectures on Art, and its Application to Decoration and Manufacture, Delivered in 1858–1859.* New York: John Wiley, 1859.

————. *"Unto this Last:" Four Essays on the First Principles of Political Economy.* Lincoln: University of Nebraska Press, 1967.

Sala, George Augustus. *Paris Herself Again.* 9th ed. London: Vizetelly, 1887.

Seeley, John R. *The Expansion of England.* Chicago: University of Chicago Press, 1971.

Smith, Goldwin. *The Empire. A Series of Letters Published in 'The Daily News,' 1862, 1863.* London: John Henry and James Parker, 1863.

Temple, Sir Richard. *India in 1880.* 3rd ed. London: John Murray, 1881.

————. *Men and Events of My Time in India.* 2nd ed. London: John Murray, 1882.

————. *The Story of My Life.* London: Cassell, 1896.

Thomas, Julian. *The Vagabond Papers.* 4th series. Melbourne: George Robertson, 1877.

Thompson, Zadock. *Journal of a Trip to London, Paris, and the Great Exhibition, in 1851.* Burlington, VT: Nichols and Warren, 1852.

Twopeny, R. E. N. *A Proposal for Holding an Australasian Exhibition in London* [1883]. Australia Pamphlets. No. 20. Foreign and Commonwealth Office Library, London.

Ure, Andrew. *The Philosophy of Manufactures: or, An Exposition of the Scientific, Moral and Commercial Economy of the Factory System of Great Britain.* London: Charles Knight, 1835.

Visitors' Books, Exhibition Building Trustees. 2 vols. Victoria Public Record Office, Melbourne.

Watson, John Forbes. *International Exhibitions.* London: Henry S. King, 1873.

Westgarth, William. *The Colony of Victoria: Its History, Commerce and Gold Mining; its Social and Political Institutions; Down to the End of 1863. With Remarks, Incidental and Comparative, Upon the Other Australian Colonies.* London: Sampson Low, Son and Marston, 1864.

————. *Half a Century of Australasian Progress, A Personal Retrospect.* London: Sampson Low, Marston, Searle & Rivington, 1889.

———. *Personal Recollections of Early Melbourne and Victoria.* Melbourne: George Robertson, 1888.

———. *Victoria; Late Australia Felix, or Port Phillip District of New South Wales; Being An Historical and Descriptive Account of the Colony and its Gold Mines.* London: Simpkin, Marshall, 1863.

Wood, Henry Trueman. "Exhibitions." *Nineteenth Century* 20 (1886).

Worsnop, Thomas. *The Prehistoric Arts of the Aborigines of Australia.* Adelaide: E. Spiller, 1887.

SECONDARY SOURCES

Adas, Michael. *Machines as the Measure of Men: Science, Technology, Ideologies of Western Dominance.* Ithaca, NY: Cornell University Press, 1989.

Allwood, John. *The Great Exhibitions.* London: Studio Vista, 1977.

———. "General Notes: International Exhibitions and the Classification of Their Exhibits." *Journal of the Royal Society of Arts* 128 (1980).

Alomes, Stephen. "Australian Nationalism in the Eras of Imperialism and 'Internationalism.'" *Australian Journal of Politics and History* 34 (1989).

Anderson, Benedict. *Imagined Communities: Reflections on the Origin and Spread of Nationalism.* New York: Verso Books, 1991.

Bailey, Peter. *Leisure and Class in Victorian England: Rational Recreation and the Contest for Control, 1830–1850.* London: Methuen, 1987.

Beever, Alan. "From a Place of 'Horrible Destitution' to a Paradise of the Working Class: The Transformation of British Working Class Attitudes to Australia, 1841–1851." *Labour History* (Australia) 40 (1981).

Benedict, Burton. "International Exhibitions and National Identity." *Anthropology Today* (U.K.) 17 (1991).

———, ed. *The Anthropology of World's Fairs: San Francisco's Panama Pacific International Exposition of 1915.* Berkeley, CA: Scolar Press, 1983.

Benjamin, Walter. "The Work of Art in the Age of Mechanical Reproduction" and "What Is Epic Theater?" In Hannah Arendt, ed., *Illuminations: Essays and Reflections.* New York: Schocken Books, 1978.

Bennett, Tony. "The Exhibitionary Complex." In Nicholas B. Dirks, Geoffrey Eley, and Sherry B. Ortner, eds., *Culture/Power/History: A Reader in Contemporary Social Theory.* Princeton, NJ: Princeton University Press, 1994.

Brantlinger, Patrick. *Rules of Darkness: British Literature and Imperialism, 1830–1914.* Ithaca, NY: Cornell University Press, 1988.

Breckenridge, Carol A. "The Aesthetics and Politics of Colonial Collecting: India at World Fairs." *Comparative Studies in Society and History* 31 (1989).

Brain, Robert. "Going to the Exhibition." In Richard Staley, ed., *The Physics of Empire: Public Lectures.* Cambridge, England: Whipple Museum of the History of Science, 1994.

Bridges, Peter. "*The Sydney International Exhibition of 1879: The Translation of Ideas into Reality.*" Unpublished MSS., 1986.

Burton, Antoinette. "Making a Spectacle of Empire: Indian Travellers in Fin-de-Siecle London." *History Workshop* 42 (1996), and *At the Heart of the Empire: Indians and the Colonial Encounter in Late-Victorian Britain*. Berkeley, CA: University of California Press, 1998.

Cannadine, David. "Splendor out of Court: Royal Spectacle and Pageantry in Modern Britain, c. 1820–1977." In Sean Wilentz, ed., *Rites of Power: Symbolism, Ritual and Politics Since the Middle Ages*. Philadelphia: University of Pennsylvania Press, 1985.

Cohn, Bernard S. "Social and Political Theory and the Symbols of Empire in Nineteenth-Century India: A Proposal for Research." *Journal of the Indian Anthropological Society* 8 (1973).

———. "The Transformation of Objects into Artifacts, Antiquities, and Art in Nineteenth-Century India." In *Colonialism and Its Forms of Knowledge: The British in India*. Princeton, NJ: Princeton University Press, 1996.

———. "Notes on the History of the Study of Indian Society and Culture." In *An Anthropologist Among the Historians and Other Essays*. New York: Oxford University Press, 1990.

Cole, Douglas. "'The Crimson Thread of Kinship': Ethnic Ideas in Australia, 1870–1914." *Historical Studies* 14 (1971).

Coombes, Annie E. "Museums and the Formation of National and Cultural Identities." *Oxford Art Journal* 11 (1988).

———. *Reinventing Africa: Museums, Material Culture and Popular Imagination in Late Victorian and Edwardian England*. New Haven, CT: Yale University Press, 1994.

Curti, Merle. "America at the World Fairs, 1851–1893." *American Historical Review* 55 (1955).

Darnley, Earl of, ed. *Frank Lascelles: Our Modern Orpheus*. New York: Oxford University Press, 1932.

Davison, Graeme. "Festivals of Nationhood: the International Exhibitions." In S. L. Goldberg and F. B. Smith, eds., *Australian Cultural History*. New York: Cambridge University Press, 1988.

———. *The Rise and Fall of Marvelous Melbourne*. Carlton, Victoria: Melbourne University Press, 1979.

Desmond, Ray. "Photography in India During the Nineteenth Century." *India Office Library and Records Report*, 1974.

Dewey, Clive. "Images of the Village Community: A Study in Anglo-Indian Ideology." *Modern Asian Studies* 6 (1972).

Doenecke, Justus D. "Myths, Machines, and Markets: The Columbian Exposition of 1893." *Journal of Popular Culture* 6 (1973).

Donajgrodzki, A. P., ed. *Social Control in Nineteenth-Century Britain*. Totowa, NJ: Rowman and Littlefield, 1977.

Durrans, Brian. "Handicrafts, Ideology and the Festival of India." *South Asia Research* 2 (1982).

Dumont, Louis. "The 'Village Community' from Munro to Maine." *Contributions to Indian Sociology* 9 (1966).

Eco, Umberto. "A Theory of Expositions." *Travels in Hyper-Reality*. London: Pan Books, 1987.

Eddy, John, and Deryck Schreuder, eds. *The Rise of Colonial Nationalism: Australia, New Zealand, Canada and South Africa First Assert Their Nationalities, 1880–1914*. Boston, MA: Allen and Unwin, 1988.

Embree, Ainslie T. *Imagining India: Essays on Indian History*. Ed. Mark Juergensmeyer. New York: Oxford University Press, 1989.

Falconer, John. "Ethnological Photography in India, 1850–1900." *Photographic Collector* 5 (1984).

Farnie, D. A. "The Cotton Famine in Great Britain." In Barrie M. Ratcliffe, ed., *Great Britain and Her World, 1750–1914. Essays in Honour of W. O. Henderson*. Manchester: Manchester University Press, 1975.

Foucault, Michel. *The Order of Things: An Archaeology of the Human Sciences*. New York: Vintage Books, 1970.

———. *The Archaeology of Knowledge*. Trans. and ed. A. M. Sheridan. New York: Pantheon Books, 1972.

French, Maurice. "'One People, One Destiny'—A Question of Loyalty: the Origins of Empire Day in New South Wales, 1900–1905." *Journal of the Royal Australian Historical Society* 61 (1975).

Geertz, Clifford. "Ritual and Social Change: A Javanese Example." In *The Interpretation of Cultures*. New York: Basic Books, 1973.

———. "Centers, Kings and Charisma: Reflections on the Symbolics of Power." In *Local Knowledge: Further Essays in Interpretive Anthropology*. New York: Basic Books, 1983.

Greenberg, Dolores. "Energy, Power and Perceptions of Social Change in the Early Nineteenth Century." *American Historical Review* 90 (1985).

Greenhalgh, Paul. "Art, Politics, and Society at the Franco-British Exhibition of 1908." *Art History* 8 (1985).

———. *Ephemeral Vistas: The Exposition Universelles, Great Exhibitions and World's Fairs, 1851–1939*. Dover, NH: Manchester University Press, 1988.

Griffiths, Tom. "Past Silences: Aborigines and Convicts in Our History-Making." *Australian Cultural History* 6 (1987).

———. "In Search of Classical Soil: A Bicentennial Reflection." *Victorian Historical Journal* 59 (1988).

Hacking, Ian. "Making Up People." In Thomas C. Heller, Morton Sosna, and David E. Wellbery, eds., *Reconstructing Individualism: Autonomy, Individuality, and the Self in Western Thought*. Stanford, CA: Stanford University Press, 1986.

Harvey, Penelope. *Hybrids of Modernity: Anthropology, the Nation State, and the Universal Exhibition*. New York: Routledge, 1996.

Heidegger, Martin. *The Question Concerning Technology and Other Essays*. Trans. and ed. William Lovitt. New York: Garland Publishing, 1977.

Hobsbawm, Eric J. *Nations and Nationalism Since 1780: Programme, Myth and Reality*. New York: Cambridge University Press, 1990.

Hobsbawm, Eric J., and Terence Ranger, eds. *The Invention of Tradition.* New York: Cambridge University Press, 1983.

Hoggart, Richard. *The Uses of Literacy: Aspects of Working-Class Life with Special Reference to Publications and Entertainments.* New York: Oxford University Press, 1970.

Horne, Donald. *Ideas for a Nation.* Sydney: Pan Books, 1989.

———. *The Public Culture: The Triumph of Industrialism.* London: Pluto Press, 1986.

Hudson, Derek, and Kenneth W. Luckhurst. *The Royal Society of Arts, 1754 – 1954.* London: John Murray, 1954.

The Indian Museum, 1814 –1914. Calcutta: Baptist Mission Press, 1914.

Inkster, Ian, and Jack Morrell, eds. *Metropolis and Province: Science in British Culture, 1780 –1850.* London: Hutchinson, 1983.

Iser, Wolfgang. *The Act of Reading: A Theory of Aesthetic Response.* Baltimore, MD: Johns Hopkins University Press, 1981.

———. *The Implied Reader: Patterns of Communication in Prose Fiction from Bunyan to Beckett.* Baltimore, MD: Johns Hopkins University Press, 1987.

Kasson, John F. *Civilizing the Machine: Technology and Republican Values in America, 1776 –1900.* New York: Viking Press, 1976.

Kidd, A. J., and K. W. Roberts, eds. *City, Class, and Culture: Studies of Cultural Production and Social Policy in Victorian Manchester.* Dover, NH: Manchester University Press, 1985.

Knights, Ben. *The Idea of the Clerisy in the Nineteenth Century.* New York: Cambridge University Press, 1978.

Kusamitsu, Toshio. "Great Exhibitions Before 1851." *History Workshop* 9 (1980).

Luckhurst, Kenneth. *The Story of Exhibitions.* New York: The Studio Publications, 1951.

Lukes, Stephen. "Political Ritual and Social Integration." In *Essays in Social Theory.* New York: Columbia University Press, 1977.

Kumar, Deepak. "Patterns of Colonial Science in India." *Indian Journal of History of Science* 15 (1980).

———. *Science and the Raj, 1857–1905.* New York: Oxford University Press, 1995.

MacKenzie, John M. *Propaganda and Empire: The Manipulation of British Public Opinion, 1880 –1960.* Dover, NH: Manchester University Press, 1985.

———, ed. *Imperialism and Popular Culture.* Dover, NH: Manchester University Press, 1986.

Macleod, Roy. "On Visiting the 'Moving Metropolis': Reflections on the Architecture of Imperial Science." *Historical Records of Australian Science* 5 (1982).

———, ed. *Government and Expertise: Specialists, Administrators, and Professionals, 1860 –1919.* New York: Cambridge University Press, 1988.

McArthur, Colin. "The Dialectic of National Identity: The Glasgow Empire Exhibition of 1938." In Tony Bennett, Colin Mercer, and Janet Woollacott, eds., *Popular Culture and Social Relations*. Milton Keynes, England: Open University Press, 1986.

McKeough, Carmel, and Norman Etherington. "Jubilee 50." *Journal of the Historical Society of South Australia* 12 (1984).

Metcalf, Thomas. *The Aftermath of Revolt: India, 1857–1870*. New Delhi: Manohar Publications, 1990.

———. *An Imperial Vision: Indian Architecture and Britain's Raj*. Berkeley, CA: University of California Press, 1989.

———. *Ideologies of the Raj*. New York: Cambridge University Press, 1997.

Minihan, Janet. *The Nationalization of Culture: The Development of State Subsidies to the Arts in Great Britain*. New York: New York University Press, 1977.

Mitchell, Timothy. *Colonising Egypt*. New York: Cambridge University Press, 1988.

———. "The World as Exhibition." *Comparative Studies in Society and History* 31 (1989).

Mitter, Partha. *Much Maligned Monsters: A History of European Reactions to Indian Art*. Chicago: University of Chicago Press, 1992.

———. *Art and Nationalism in Colonial India, 1850–1922: Occidental Orientations*. New York: Cambridge University Press, 1994.

Mumford, Lewis. "Authoritarian and Democratic Technics." *Technology and Culture* 5 (1964).

Nadel, George. *Australia's Colonial Culture: Ideas, Men, and Institutions in Mid-Nineteenth Century Eastern Australia*. Melbourne, Victoria: F. W. Cheshire, 1957.

Niquette, Manon, and William J. Buxton. "Meet Me at the Fair: Sociability and Reflexivity in Nineteenth-Century World Expositions." *Canadian Journal of Communications* 22 (1997).

Parris, John, and A. G. L. Shaw. "The Melbourne International Exhibition, 1880–1881." *Victorian Historical Journal* 51 (1980).

Parsons, T. G. "Technological Change in the Melbourne Flour-Milling and Brewing Industries, 1870–1890." *Australian Economic History Review* 11 (1971).

Perkin, Harold. *The Rise of Professional Society: England Since 1880*. New York: Routledge, 1990.

Pinney, Christopher. "Classification and Fantasy in the Photographic Construction of Caste and Tribe." *Visual Anthropology* 3 (1990).

Quartermaine, Peter. "International Exhibitions and Emigration: The Photographic Enterprise of Richard Daintree, Agent-General for Queensland." *Journal of Australian Studies* 13 (1973).

Reingold, Nathan, and Marc Rothenberg, eds. *Scientific Colonialism: A Cross-Cultural Comparison. Papers from a Conference at Melbourne, Australia, 25–30 May 1981*. Washington, DC: Smithsonian Institution Press, 1987.

Richards, Thomas. *The Commodity Culture of Victorian Britain: Advertising and Spectacle, 1851–1914*. Stanford, CA: Stanford University Press, 1990.
————. *The Imperial Archive: Knowledge and the Fantasy of Empire*. New York: Verso, 1993.
Roe, Michael. *Quest for Authority in Eastern Australia, 1835–1851*. New York: Cambridge University Press, 1965.
Rosaldo, Renato. "Imperialist Nostalgia." *Representations* 26 (1989).
Rothenberg, Marc, and Peter H. Hoffenberg. "Australia at the 1876 Exhibition in Philadelphia." *Historical Records of Australian Science* 8 (1990).
Ryan, Peter. *Redmond Barry, A Colonial Life, 1813–1880*. Melbourne, Victoria: Melbourne University Press, 1980.
Rydell, Robert. *All the World's a Fair: Visions of Empire at American International Exhibitions, 1876–1916*. Chicago: University of Chicago Press, 1987.
————. *World of Fairs: The Century-of-Progress Expositions*. Chicago: University of Chicago Press, 1993.
Said, Edward. *Orientalism*. New York: Vintage Books, 1979.
————. *Culture and Imperialism*. New York: Alfred A. Knopf, 1993.
Samuel, Raphael. "The Workshop of the World: Steam Power and Hand Technology in Mid-Victorian Britain." *History Workshop* 3 (1977).
Sheets-Pyenson, Susan. *Cathedrals of Science: The Development of Colonial Natural History Museums during the Late Nineteenth Century*. Montreal: McGill-Queen's University Press, 1988.
Sherman, Daniel. "Art Museums, Inspections, and the Limits to Cultural Policy." *Historical Reflections / Reflexions Historiques* 15 (1988).
————. *Worthy Monuments: Art Museums and the Politics of Culture in Nineteenth-Century France*. Cambridge, MA: Harvard University Press, 1989.
Short, Audrey. "Workers Under Glass." *Victorian Studies* 10 (1966).
Silverman, Debora. "The 1889 Exhibition: The Crisis in Bourgeois Individualism." *Oppositions* 8 (1977).
Sinclair, Bruce. "Technology on Its Toes: Late Victorian Ballets, Pageants, and Industrial Exhibitions." In Stephen H. Cutliffe and Robert C. Post, eds., *In Context: History and the History of Technology. Essays in Honor of Melvin Kranzberg*. Research in Technology Series, vol. 1. Bethlehem, PA: Lehigh University Press, 1989.
Sontag, Susan. *On Photography*. New York: Viking Penguin, 1986.
Specker, Konrad. "Madras Handlooms in the Nineteenth Century." *Indian Economic and Social History Review* 26 (1989).
Stocking, Jr., George W. *Victorian Anthropology*. New York: The Free Press, 1987.
Suleiman, Susan R., and Inge Crosman, eds. *The Reader in the Text: Essay on Audience and Interpretations*. Princeton, NJ: Princeton University Press, 1980.
Walton, John R. "Mechanization in Agriculture: A Study of the Adoption Pro-

cess." In S. A. Fox and R. A. Butlin, eds., *Change in the Countryside: Essays on Rural England, 1500–1900*. London: Institute of British Geographers, 1979.

White, Richard. *Inventing Australia: Images and Identity, 1688–1980*. Boston, MA: George Allen and Unwin, 1981.

Winner, Langdon. "Do Artifacts Have Politics?" *Daedalus* 109 (1980).

Wolpert, Stanley. *A New History of India*. 6th ed. New York: Oxford University Press, 2000.

Wolff, Janet, and John Seed, eds. *The Culture of Capital: Art, Power and the Nineteenth-Century Middle Class*. Manchester: University of Manchester Press, 1988.

Young, Linda. *Let Them See How Much Like England We Can Be: An Account of the Sydney International Exhibition, 1879*. M.A. thesis, University of Sydney, June 1983.

Index